GUIDEBOOK
of the
SAN LUIS BASIN,
COLORADO

H. L. JAMES
Editor

NEW MEXICO GEOLOGICAL SOCIETY

TWENTY-SECOND FIELD CONFERENCE—September 30-October 1-2, 1971

CONTENTS

PRESIDENT'S MESSAGE iv
A MESSAGE FROM THE EDITOR v
WELCOME LETTERS vi
COMMITTEES viii
PUBLICATIONS OF THE NEW MEXICO GEOLOGICAL SOCIETY x
CONFERENCE MAP xi
SCHEDULE OF CONFERENCE xii

ROAD LOGS

FIRST DAY: Alamosa to the Eastern San Juan Mountains, via Alamosa River, Jasper, Summitville, South Fork and Return 1

SECOND DAY: Alamosa to the Great Sand Dunes National Monument, Poncha Pass, Salida, Howard and Return via Saguache and Monte Vista 15

THIRD DAY: Rail Log from Antonito, Colorado, to Chama, New Mexico 43

SUPPLEMENTAL LOGS

LOG NO. 1: Villa Grove to Bonanza 70
LOG NO. 2: Del Norte to Summer Coon Volcanic Area and Return 73
LOG NO. 3: Fort Garland to Romeo, via San Luis, San Acacio and Manassa 78
LOG NO. 4: Chama, New Mexico, to Antonito, Colorado 82

ARTICLES

The Crest of the Continent .... Ernest Ingersoll 88
Lexicon of Stratigraphic Names .... Christina Lochman-Balk and James E. Bruning 101
Physiographic Subdivisions of the San Luis Valley, Southern Colorado .... J. E. Upson 113
The Great Sand Dunes of Southern Colorado .... Ross B. Johnson 123
Water Resources of the San Luis Valley, Colorado .... Phillip A. Emery 129
Flora of the San Luis Valley .... Hobart N. Dixon 133
Fauna of the San Luis Valley .... Veryl F. Keen 137
Pennsylvanian and Permian Stratigraphy, Tectonism and History, Northern Sangre de Cristo Range, Colorado .... Richard H. De Voto, Frederick A. Peel and Walter H. Pierce 141

Glaciation in the Sangre de Cristo Range, Colorado .... Richard C. Peterson 165

Allochthonous Paleozoic Blocks in the Tertiary San Luis-Upper Arkansas Graben,
  Colorado .... Ralph E. Van Alstine 169

Results of Preliminary Studies of the Air Pollution Meteorology of Limited Areas in the
  San Luis Valley .... Theodore A. Mueller 179

Stratigraphic Relations Between Bonanza Center and Adjacent Parts of the San Juan Volcanic Field,
  South-Central Colorado .... Dennis L. Bruns, Rudy C. Epis, Robert J. Weimer and Thomas A. Steven 183

The Rio Grande Rift, Part I: Modifications and Additions .... Charles E. Chapin 191

"They Came to Hunt." Early Man in the San Luis Valley .... Dorothy D. Wilson 203

Cenozoic Geology of the Arkansas Hills Region of the Southern Mosquito Range,
  Central Colorado .... Gary R. Lowell 209

Preliminary Paleopalynological Analysis of Alamosa Formation Sediments .... Charles R. Price 219

Reconnaissance Geology and Economic Significance of the Platoro Caldera,
  Southeastern San Juan Mountains, Colorado .... Peter W. Lipman and Thomas A. Steven 221

Minerals of the San Luis Valley and Adjacent Areas of Colorado .... Charles F. Bauer 231

Some Petrologic and Alteration Aspects of the Alum Creek Area, San Juan Volcanic Field,
  Colorado .... William S. Calkin 235

The San Luis Valley—A Land of Paradox .... Robert H. Buchanan 243

Creede Shale Fossils .... J. Robert Thompson, Jr. 247

Geological Development of the Bonanza-San Luis Valley-Sangre de Cristo Range Area,
  South-Central Colorado .... Daniel H. Knepper, Jr. and Ronald W. Marrs 249

The Summer Coon Volcano, Eastern San Juan Mountains, Colorado .... Stanley A. Mertzman, Jr. 265

A Study of Recent Sedimentation in the San Luis Hills .... Robert P. Fling 273

Geology of the San Luis Hills, South-Central Colorado .... Richard L. Burroughs 277

Tertiary Volcanic Stratigraphy of the Eastern Tusas Mountains, Southwest of the San Luis Valley,
  Colorado-New Mexico .... Arthur P. Butler, Jr. 289

Historical Sketch of Fort Garland .... William Hoagland 301

Narrow Gauge over Cumbres .... Gordon Chappell 305

History, Location and Development of the Johns-Manville Perlite Deposits,
  No Agua, New Mexico .... M. B. Mickelsen 321

ABSTRACTS

ABSTRACTS OF TECHNICAL PAPERS, NEW MEXICO GEOLOGICAL SOCIETY, 25th ANNUAL
  MEETING, ROSWELL, NEW MEXICO, MAY 14, 1971 323

BACK POCKET PLATES

De Voto, Peel, Pierce (1), Knepper-Marrs (1), Lowell (1), Mertzman (2)

PRESIDENT'S MESSAGE

This year's New Mexico Geological Society Field Conference—our twenty-second—is the brainchild of Harold James. He proposed the rail trip early in the year, even before there was any assurance that the railroad would be in operation, and saw the whole project of trip planning and guidebook preparation through to a most successful result. The conference promises to be a memorable one because of the exposure to a great variety of intriguing geology and because the rail trip will be something new and exciting for all of us.

It is especially appropriate for the Society to be among the first groups to travel the newly resurrected rail line and take advantage of its almost unique geologic appeal; the first and second day trips into the eastern San Juans and the western flank of the Sangre de Cristos provide what would be, under ordinary circumstances, a first-rate conference in themselves. Adams State College has made every effort to see that our Alamosa headquarters is all that a conference group such as this could hope for.

The Society itself is well into its third decade of success, still demonstrating the wisdom of the founders who saw a genuine need and structured an organization to fulfill it. It has for twenty-two years managed to provide a focus for the interest of New Mexico geologists and sustained a uniformly strong series of publications on a self-supporting basis; several years ago our finances seem to have stabilized in a healthy cycle and continued success seems assured. Though the Society is self-supporting in the sense that no outside financial support is necessary to keep its activities, publications in particular, progressing from year to year, it is vital that members continue to be interested enough to provide lavish support in time and effort. That was the original design and will continue to be the key.

The "loosely knit" nature of the organization, as Bill King put it in his presidential message in 1968, really is the reason that it has functioned so well for so long. That has allowed people and policy to change to suit the interests of our membership and our conference guests. In some organizations, the desire for "progress," more polish, bigger programs, continuity, more diversity in goals, and so forth, has led to a trend toward paid management, various mergers and affiliations, and pursuit of outside money, and moved the whole affair further from the members. I'm for staying with the proven formula.

To return to the subject for which this book was prepared, I would welcome everyone to the conference and thank the people responsible for it—particularly Harold James of the New Mexico State Highway Commission, Dick Burroughs and Dick Peterson of Adams State, Roy Foster and Chuck Chapin of the New Mexico Bureau of Mines, and the committee members, trip leaders, and authors.

John W. Shomaker

A MESSAGE FROM THE EDITOR...

The 22nd annual field conference embraces the San Luis Basin and its highland environs. Most people refer to this agricultural gem as "San Luis Valley," but geologically it is one of the truly great intermontane structural basins of the Rocky Mountain-Southwest; bounded on the east by the uplifted Sangre de Cristo Range and hinged on the west by the volcanic heights of the San Juans. Its width is 50 miles; its length a surprising 150 miles, stretching from Poncha Pass on the north and inclusive of the Taos Plateau south into New Mexico. It is a beautiful expanse that is dotted with volcanos, fertile farms and lush ranchlands. It is ribboned by a great river of history and set in the midst of Swiss-like mountains. Indeed, an in-interesting field for study.

Many people are responsible for the building of this book. First, to all of the authors of articles contained herein—a job well done. All of the manuscripts were received on or before the assigned deadline and all were in excellent editorial condition. The SOCIETY appreciates very much your time and effort in submitting such excellent articles to the conference. A special word of thanks to Chuck Chapin, Dick Burroughs, and Fred Trauger for help in the gathering of papers. To Art Butler and Pete Lipman for their indispensable contributions to the road logs. To Roy Foster for handling the logging chores and last but not least to Bob Price for an excellent piece of drafting on the conference map. The pen sketches used throughout the book are the courtesy of the New Mexico State Bureau of Mines and Mineral Resources. The cartoon drawings used in the rail log are the talents of George Swain. I would also like to take this opportunity to direct the reader to the Professional Directory in the back of the book. If a need arises, please consult the services they represent.

Traditionally the SOCIETY has reflected a diversity of papers in its guidebooks; to produce a scope of presentations that will encompass all of the interesting facets of the study area, both geologic and non-geologic. Thirty-five authors are represented in this guidebook spanning nearly every major subject on the geology of the area. This number includes contributions by experts in the fields of physics, biology, archaeology and history.

On behalf of the NEW MEXICO GEOLOGICAL SOCIETY I welcome you to these pages on the San Luis Basin. I sincerely hope that the contents will be as stimulating as its compilation and that the publication will be regarded as an authoritative reference for years to come.

H. L. James

"Shades of Hayden." Rail loggers at field base camp at Sublette, early spring (and d — — — cold!).

September 30, 1971

A SINCERE WELCOME
TO THE
NEW MEXICO GEOLOGICAL SURVEY

We are deeply pleased you have chosen Alamosa and the San Luis Valley as your convention site for 1971. You will, we are sure, find this a most interesting geological area offering a variety of fascinating features most deserving of your attention.

In addition you will enjoy comfortable accommodations and facilities complimented by pleasing personalities whose every desire will be to make yours a truly relaxing stay.

We look forward to visiting with each of you and repaying the compliment you have afforded us. We will do our rock bottom best to be your most gracious hosts.

Most sincerely,

John T. O'Leary
Secretary-Manager

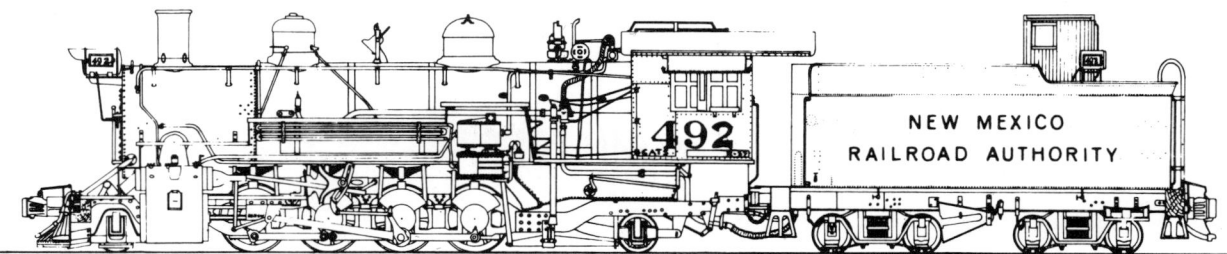

po box b santa fe new mexico 87501

chairman: gov. bruce king
vice-chairman: terence w ross
james dillard
franklin jones
markley mcmahon
robert mead
steve reynolds
eddie vigil

September 30, 1971

New Mexico Geological Society
Alamosa, Colorado

Hello!

Thirty air miles, yet sixty-four tortuous train miles, taking over one year of original back-breaking construction time; this is all that remains of a once vast narrow gauge railroad empire. Saturday you will have the opportunity to experience what the 1880 traveler found tucked magnificently away in the remote southern rocky mountains.

It has not been without your organization's assistance that this adventure awaits you. Mr. Harold James and your Board were the only individuals who stayed steadfast through the everyday political traumas that for four years continuously buffeted the dream of preserving the last main line narrow gauge railroad in the United States.

It is therefore a great pleasure for the Colorado and New Mexico Railroad Authorities to welcome you to the Cumbres And Toltec Scenic railroad as you cross our friendly state border eleven times on your trip from Antonito to Chama.

Sincerely,

Terence W. Ross, Chairman
Joint Executive Committee
Colorado and New Mexico Railroad Authorities
1111 Barcelona Lane
Santa Fe, NM 87501

TWR/sb

COMMITTEES:

Executive:

John W. Shomaker, *President*	New Mexico Bureau of Mines and Mineral Resources
William J. LeMay, *Vice President*	Consulting Geologist
William W. Baltosser, *Secretary*	Kennecott Copper Corporation
William L. Hiss, *Treasurer*	U.S. Geological Survey
Edward E. Kinney, *Past President*	Consulting Geologist

Field Conference:

Richard L. Burroughs, *General Chairman*	Adams State College

Guidebook:

H. L. James, *Editor*	New Mexico State Highway Commission

Advertising:

A. E. Saucier	Continental Oil Company

Registration:

Robin C. Lease	New Mexico Bureau of Mines and Mineral Resources

Caravan:

Richard C. Peterson, *Chairman*	Adams State College
Assisted By:	
Robert Fling	Adams State College
Alexander Hill	Adams State College
Nadine Lutes	Adams State College
Steve Reyher	Adams State College
Hayward Risser	Adams State College
Gary Roberts	Adams State College

Publicity and Photography:

H. L. James	New Mexico State Highway Commission

Publications:

Fred Trauger	U.S. Geological Survey

Road Logging:

Roy W. Foster, *Chairman*	New Mexico Bureau of Mines and Mineral Resources
Assisted By:	
Dennis L. Bruns	Colorado School of Mines
Richard L. Burroughs	Adams State College
Arthur P. Butler	U.S. Geological Survey
William S. Calkin	University of Denver
Charles E. Chapin	New Mexico Bureau of Mines and Mineral Resources
Lee C. Gerhard	Southern Colorado State College
H. L. James	New Mexico State Highway Commission
Dan H. Knepper	Colorado School of Mines
Peter W. Lipman	U.S. Geological Survey
Ron W. Marrs	Colorado School of Mines
Fred Peel	Consulting Geologist
Richard C. Peterson	Adams State College
Ralph E. Van Alstine	U.S. Geological Survey

PUBLICATIONS OF THE NEW MEXICO GEOLOGICAL SOCIETY

FIELD CONFERENCE GUIDEBOOKS
* Out of Print

1. San Juan Basin [covering north and east sides], New Mexico and Colorado, 1950, Vincent C. Kelley, ed., 152 p., 40 illus. Second printing, 1971 ....$5.00

2. San Juan Basin [covering south and west sides], New Mexico and Arizona, 1951, Clay T. Smith and Caswell Silver, eds., 163 p., 71 illus. Second printing, 1971. $5.00

*3. Rio Grande country, central New Mexico, 1952, Ross B. Johnson and Charles B. Read, eds., 126 p., 50 illus.

4. Southwestern New Mexico, 1953, Frank E. Kottlowski, ed., 153 p., 70 illus. $5.00

5. Southeastern New Mexico, 1954, T. F. Stipp, ed., 209 p., 76 illus. $5.00

*6. South-central New Mexico, 1955, J. Paul Fitzsimmons, 193 p., 66 illus. Prepared with the cooperation of the Roswell Geological Society.

7. Southeastern Sangre de Cristo Mountains, New Mexico, 1956, A. Rosenzweig, ed., 151 p., 61 illus. ...$7.00

8. Southwestern San Juan Mountains, Colorado, 1957, Frank E. Kottlowski and Brewster Baldwin, eds., 258 p., 110 illus. $7.00

9. Black Mesa Basin [northeastern Arizona], 1958, Roger Y. Anderson and John W. Harshbarger, eds., 205 p., 106 illus. Prepared in cooperation with the Arizona Geological Society. $8.50

10. West-central New Mexico, 1959, James E. Weir, Jr., and Elmer H. Baltz, eds., 162 p., 91 illus. $8.50

11. Rio Chama country [New Mexico and Colorado] 1960, Edward C. Beaumont and Charles B. Read, eds., 129 p., 35 illus. $8.50

12. Albuquerque country [New Mexico], 1961, Stuart A. Northrop, ed., 199 p., 83 illus. $9.50

13. Mogollon Rim region [east-central Arizona], 1962, Robert H. Weber and H. Wesley Peirce, eds., 175 p., 77 illus. Prepared in cooperation with the Arizona Geological Society. $9.50

14. Socorro region [New Mexico], 1963, Frederick J. Kuellmer, ed., 240 p., 90 illus. $9.00

15. Ruidoso country [New Mexico], 1964, Sidney R. Ash and Leon V. Davis, eds., 195 p., 64 illus. $9.00

16. Southwestern New Mexico II, 1965, J. Paul Fitzsimmons and Christina Lochman Balk, eds., 244 p., 73 illus. $9.50

17. Taos–Raton–Spanish Peaks country [New Mexico and Colorado], 1966, Stuart A. Northrop and Charles B. Read, eds., 128 p., 40 illus. $7.50

18. Defiance–Zuni–Mt. Taylor region [Arizona and New Mexico], 1967, Fred Trauger, ed, 228 p., 98 illus. $9.00

19. San Juan–San Miguel–La Plata Region [New Mexico and Colorado], 1968, John Shomaker, ed., 212 p., 95 illus. $9.00

20. The Border Region [Chihuahua and the United States], 1969, Córdoba, Wengerd Shomaker, eds., 228 p., 159 illus. $13.50

21. Tyrone–Big Hatchet Mountains–Florida Mountains Region [New Mexico], 1970, Woodward, ed., 176 p., 84 illus. $12.50

22. San Luis Basin (Colorado), 1971, H. L. James, ed., 340 p., 226 illus. $15.00

SPECIAL PUBLICATIONS

1. Bibliography and index of the New Mexico Geological Society Guidebooks, 1950-63; compiled by Sidney R. Ash. $0.75

2. A history of the New Mexico Geological Society; by Stuart A. Northrop.

3. The San Andres Limestone: a reservoir for oil, gas and water ... [a symposium]; F. E. Kottlowski and W. K. Summers, eds. $3.00

MAPS

a. Geologic highway map of New Mexico, in color, 23x29 in.; compiled by Frank E. Kottlowski and others. ....$1.00 folded; $1.25 rolled

b. Geologic map of the Sierra County Region, compiled by Vincent C. Kelley; in Guidebook 6. ....$0.50

c. Geologic map of the Rio Chama country; compiled by Clay T. Smith and William R. Muehlberger, in Guidebook 11. ....$0.50

d. Geologic map of the Albuquerque country; compiled by Stuart A. Northrop and Arlette Hill; in Guidebook 12. ....$0.50

e. Tectonic map of the Ruidoso–Carrizozo region compiled by V. C. Kelley and Tommy B. Thompson; in Guidebook 15. ....$0.75

f. Tectonic map of the Defiance–Zuni–Mt. Taylor region; compiled by V. C. Kelley; in Guidebook 18 ....$1.50

All publications are available by mail (please add 25 cents for postage and handling each guidebook) from, or over the counter, at the New Mexico Bureau of Mines and Mineral Resources, Socorro, New Mexico. Guidebooks, and the geologic highway maps are available over the counter at the Dept. of Geology, Univ. of N. Mex., Albuquerque; Holmans, Albuquerque; Roswell Map Service, Roswell; and the Museum of Northern Arizona, Flagstaff, Arizona.

Checks should be made payable to the New Mexico Geological Society.

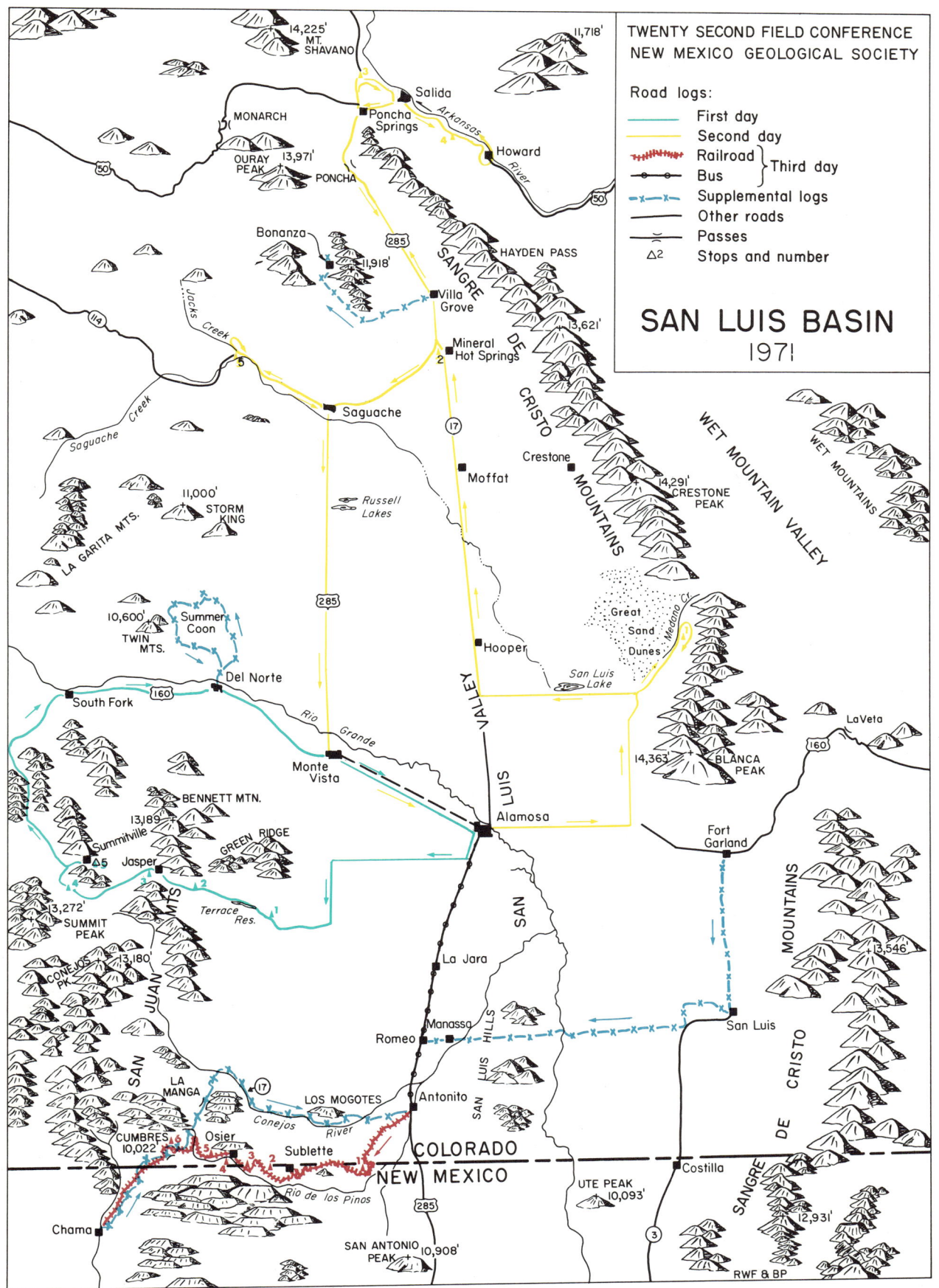

FIELD CONFERENCE MAP

1971
FIELD CONFERENCE SCHEDULE

Wednesday, September 29th   *REGISTRATION DAY*

1:00 P.M.-10:00 P.M.   Registration in lobby of Student Center Building on the campus of Adams State College, Alamosa, Colorado.

Thursday, September 30th   *FIRST DAY FIELD TRIP*

7:00 A.M.-7:30 A.M.   Auto-caravan will assemble at the Alamosa Auction Barn on U.S. 285 at the south city limits of Alamosa.

Trip will include a circuitous route through the eastern San Juan Mountains, via the Alamosa River, Jasper (*lunch stop*), Summitville, and South Fork.

7:00 P.M.-9:00 P.M.   "ICE-BREAKER" PARTY at the Alamosa Inn.

Friday, October 1st   *SECOND DAY FIELD TRIP*

7:00 A.M.-7:30 A.M.   Auto-caravan will assemble on U.S. 160 at the east city limits of Alamosa (east of junction of State Highway 17 near D&RG Railroad siding).

Trip will include a visit to the Great Sand Dunes National Monument. The geologic character of the San Luis Basin and the east flanking Sangre de Cristo Mountains will be studied on today's trip. The caravan will extend as far north as the Arkansas River, via Poncha Pass and Salida (*lunch and gas stop*) before retracing the route back on U.S. 285 to view volcanic outcrops to the west near Saguache.

8:00 P.M.-10:00 P.M.   *ANNUAL FALL BANQUET* to be held in the dining hall at the Student Center Building on the Campus of Adams State College. A welcome address will be delivered by Dr. James F. Craft, Chairman of the Division of Science and Mathematics at Adams State College. The principal speaker will be Mr. Terance W. Ross, Vice Chairman of the New Mexico Railroad Authority, Santa Fe, New Mexico. Mr. Ross will speak and narrate slides on his title, "Save The Narrow Gauge."

Saturday, October 2nd   *THIRD DAY FIELD TRIP*

7:00 A.M.-7:30 A.M.   Conferees will board chartered busses at the east football field parking lot (opposite Student Center Building at Adams State College). Personal cars may be left in lot until return. Busses will depart *promptly* at 7:30 A.M. for Antonito, Colorado, for boarding on the Cumbres and Toltec Scenic Railroad. (Note: If you miss your bus you can drive to the boarding site at the south city limits of Antonito near the junction of U.S. 285 and State Highway 17). Rail excursion will depart *promptly* at 8:30 A.M. for Chama, New Mexico. Box lunches and soft drinks will be provided enroute. (*PLEASE! NO ALCOHOLIC BEVERAGES.* State law prohibits its use on Colorado/New Mexico property). Lunch stop scheduled at ghost town of Osier.

The Third Day promises to be a full 16 hours of wild activity coupled with magnificent scenery and interesting geology. Schedules and the best laid plans will probably run amuck, but on a grand excursion such as this—who cares! Dress warmly as elevations exceed 10,000 feet in the Cumbres Pass section. Watch your step at the Toltec Gorge Stop; the first step is 3 feet, the second one—600'. Oh yes, one other thing—registration fee does not include toilet paper.

6:00 P.M.-6:30 P.M.   Tentative arrival in Chama, New Mexico. Reboard chartered busses for 25-mile trip to Elk Creek Campground.

7:00 P.M.-9:00 P.M.   *BARBECUE PICNIC* at Elk Creek Campground (Conejos River Valley).

9:00 P.M.   Reboard chartered busses for return to Alamosa.

END OF CONFERENCE!

IT WAS A PLEASURE TO HAVE YOU AS OUR GUESTS.

SEE YOU NEXT YEAR?

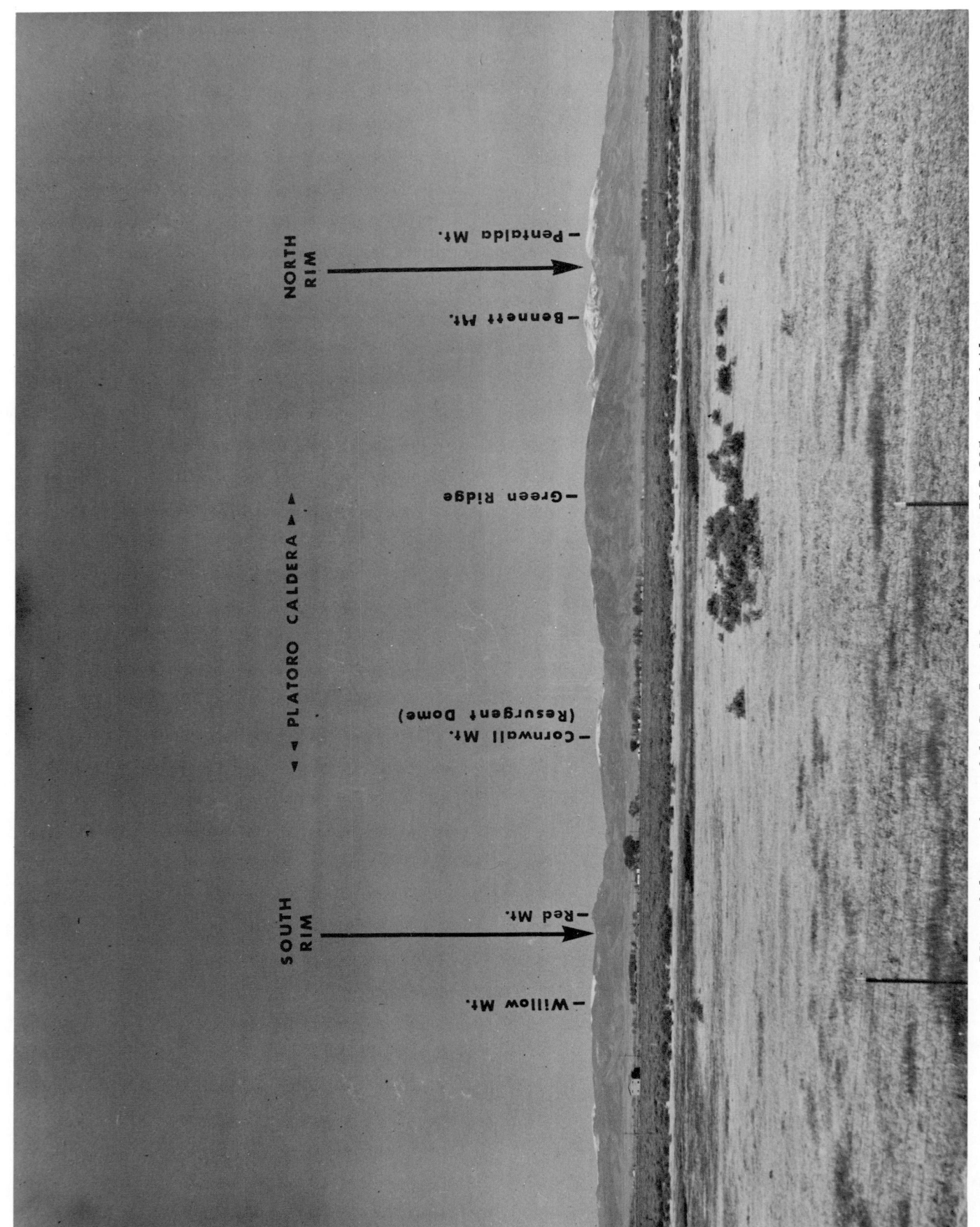

View of the east front of the San Juan Mountains from U.S. 285 south of Alamosa.

FIRST DAY

ROAD LOG FROM ALAMOSA TO THE EASTERN SAN JUAN MOUNTAINS, VIA ALAMOSA RIVER, JASPER, SUMMITVILLE, SOUTH FORK, AND RETURN

September 30, 1971

ASSEMBLY: Alamosa Auction Barn on U.S. 285, South of City Limits of Alamosa.
TIME: 7:00-7:30 A.M.
DISTANCE: 140.4 miles.
TRIP LEADERS: William S. Calkin, Robert Kendall, Peter W. Lipman.

PREFACE:

The Platoro caldera is a composite collapse structure about 20 km in diameter that formed as a result of ash-flow eruption of the Upper Oligocene Treasure Mountain Tuff. Three major ash-flow sheets of the Treasure Mountain Tuff—the La Jara Canyon, Ojito Creek, and Ra Jadero Members in ascending order—are approximately coextensive and cover about 5,000 km² in the southeastern San Juan Mountains. Major collapse of the Platoro caldera occurred during eruption of quartz latitic ash-flows that form the La Jara Canyon Member; late ash-flows of this member accumulated within the collapsing caldera to a thickness of more than 800 m. The core of the collapsed block was resurgently domed, and the marginal moat was then filled to overflowing by more than 700 m of andesitic lavas. Renewed ash-flow eruption of the quartz latitic Ojito Creek and Ra Jadero Members resulted in further collapse in the northern part of the main caldera. No resurgence seems to be associated with this late caldera, but it was also filled to overflowing by a thick accumulation of andesitic lavas. Genetically related quartz latitic dikes and granitic stocks, with associated porphyritic rhyodacitic to quartz latitic lavas, were emplaced repeatedly around the margins of the late caldera. Associated hydrothermal alteration and local ore deposition took place in the Summitville and Platoro mining districts, as well as other nearby mineralized areas at Stunner, Gilmore, Jasper, Crater Creek and Cat Creek (see Lipman and Steven, this guidebook).

The field trip approaches the caldera from the southeast side, where the stratigraphically and structurally simple regional volcanic sequence is well displayed dipping gently toward the San Luis Valley. The trip then follows the Alamosa River Canyon, which permits a spectacularly exposed east-west cross section through the complex interior of the caldera. Leaving the caldera at its northwest rim, the trip passes by the recently reopened (1970) copper-gold mine at Summitville; then descends along tributaries of the Rio Grande, where outcrops are mainly of younger ash-flow sheets from calderas farther northwest in the central San Juan Mountains.

0.0 Alamosa Auction Barn parking area. Proceed south on U.S. 285.
    2.6

2.6 Junction Colorado 370. TURN RIGHT. After turn, Green Ridge (straight ahead) is the northeast flank of the eroded Cat Creek stratovolcano (28 m.y. old) located on the east side of Platoro caldera. Green Ridge consists of rhyodacite and quartz latite lava flows capped by Hinsdale Basalt. Cornwall Mountain, to the left of Green Ridge, is a structurally uplifted resurgent dome of densely welded ash-flow (La Jara Canyon Member, Treasure Mountain Tuff) within Platoro caldera. Bennett Mountain (13,189′) to the right of Green Ridge consists of post-caldera andesite lavas and quartz latite welded tuffs, also within the caldera.
    6.5

9.1 Waverly. La Garita Mountains at 1:30 are the resurgent core of a caldera, 30 miles in diameter, in the central San Juan Mountains; south end of Sawatch Range at 2:30. San Antonio Mountain at 9:00 is a Pliocene stratovolcano of hypersthene quartz latite. The eroded shield volcano of Los Mogotes at 10:00 consists of Hinsdale Basalt. The basalt has been dated at 5 m.y.
    2.0

11.1 Enter Rio Grande County.
    0.1

11.2 Bridge over canal. In this area the valley is underlain by thick Miocene and younger volcanic rocks and associated clastic sediments from the San Juan volcanic field. The San Luis Basin is a northerly extension of the Rio Grande depression, and is strikingly similar to structures of the Basin-Range province. The major bounding fault system is on the east side, against the Sangre de Cristo Mountains; the western boundary is a dip slope of eastward-tilted volcanic rocks of the San Juan Mountains. This dip slope is cut by numerous small north-trending antithetic normal faults, dropped down to the west, in opposition to the structural effect of the dip of the rocks. A 50-70 milligal gravity anomaly at the base of Blanca Peak on the east side of the basin suggests a maximum of 30,000 feet of Late Cenozoic basin-fill sediments within the lowland.

1.9

13.1 Junction Colorado 368; CONTINUE STRAIGHT AHEAD.

2.2

15.3 Canal.

2.0

17.3 Junction Colorado 15. TURN LEFT. On right, cliffs half way up Green Mountain are porphyritic quartz latite flows dated at 28.5 m.y. Talus slopes above are Hinsdale Basalt and basaltic andesite. To the south, mesas underlain by Treasure Mountain Tuff from the Platoro caldera dip gently into the San Luis Valley. Compare this simple topography of the regional volcanic sequence with the complex topography of the caldera area.

2.0

19.3 Entering Conejos County. Road on right to Platoro. CONTINUE STRAIGHT AHEAD.

0.6

19.9 Cornwall Mountain at 3:00. Leaving San Luis Valley; ascending Alamosa River fan.

3.6

23.5 Alamosa River Road. TURN RIGHT. After turn Chiquito Peak (9,635') at 12:30 consists of lavas and breccias of intermediate composition on the southeast flank of Cat Creek volcano: Green Ridge is the northeast flank. This volcano post-dates the welded tuffs of Platoro caldera but predates most of the younger ash-flow sheets from the central San Juan calderas such as La Garita and Creede.

The higher mountains in the distance between Green Ridge and Chiquito Peak are mostly rhyodacite lavas within the Platoro caldera.

1.5

25.0 Narrow bridge over irrigation ditch.

2.2

27.2 Crest of rise; begin descent into Alamosa River Canyon. Road is on coarse mud flow breccias of the Los Pinos Formation. Cat Creek volcano is the main source for these breccias. Along the road poor outcrops can be seen of the underlying slabby-weathering pyroxene-plagioclase rhyodacite flows. At 9:00 across the canyon a lava flow overlies conglomerates, sandstones, and tuffs of the Los Pinos Formation.

0.9

28.1 Descending steep hill from Pleistocene outwash terrace toward Alamosa River. Massive cliffs are Masonic Park Tuff, a regional ash-flow sheet 28.2 m.y.) erupted from Mt. Hope caldera near Wolf Creek Pass. The tuff is a quartz latite 65-67% SiO_2) containing 30-50 percent phenocrysts of plagioclase, biotite, and augite. It underlies lava flows from Cat Creek volcano. Larson and Cross (1956) included this tuff in their Treasure Mountain Rhyolite, but it is now considered a separate formation because it is believed to have been erupted from a different caldera than the rest of the Treasure Mountain. The Masonic Park has been traced into New Mexico and will be seen on the third day along the narrow gauge railroad.

0.3

28.4 Bridge over Alamosa River.

0.3

28.7 Glacial outwash gravel on left.

0.5

29.2 Junction. TURN RIGHT toward Terrace Reservoir.

0.6

29.8 Descending from terrace of outwash gravels. Ra Jadero Member of Treasure Mountain Tuff on left above terrace. Jacobs Hill on left is capped by Los Pinos conglomerates (detritus from the Cat Creek volcano) underlain by cliff-forming

Alamosa River at milepost 28.4. North bordering cliffs are tuffs of the Masonic Park.

Masonic Park Tuff. On the right, across Alamosa River (Chiquito Peak), are good exposures of lavas and flow breccias of Cat Creek volcano overlying Masonic Park Tuff and the Ra Jadero and Ojito Creek Members of the Treasure Mountain Tuff. These Treasure Mountain tuffs (29 m.y. old) are quartz latite to low-silica rhyolite (67-70% SiO_2), believed to have erupted during late collapse of the composite Platoro caldera. The Ra Jadero Member has reversed magnetic polarity; the Ojito Creek, normal magnetic polarity.

0.7

30.5 Rio Grande National Forest.

0.2

30.7 Bridge over Alamosa River.

0.3

31.0 At 10:00 bedded white and pink ash-fall tuffs below Ojito Creek Member. This is part of the informal middle member of the Treasure Mountain Tuff.

0.4

31.4 STOP 1 at road cut on right. Pull off to the right as far as possible. There will be a discussion of the volcanic sequence in this area and an opportunity to examine several of these units. Please follow directions in climbing and be careful not to dislodge rocks on the cars and people below.

Cuts are in ash-fall and ash-flow tuffs of the Middle Member of the Treasure Mountain Tuff. Above the terrace are the Ojito Creek and Rajadero members. Note the difference in sorting and bedding between ash-fall and ash-flow deposits of the Middle Member, and the texture, welding and crystallization features of the three ash-flow sheets.

0.4

31.8 La Jara Canyon Member, lowest and largest ash-flow sheet of the Treasure Mountain Tuff, exposed along Alamosa River on the left. Road continues in glacial outwash.

Tuff of the Treasure Mountain at Stop 1.

0.6
32.4 Cliffs of La Jara Canyon Member on both sides of Alamosa River. The La Jara Canyon (29.8 m.y.) is a quartz latite tuff (65-69% SiO_2) with 20-35 percent phenocrysts of plagioclase, biotite, and clinopyroxene. It contains more phenocrysts, smaller amounts of pumice, and fewer xenolithic fragments than the upper members of the Treasure Mountain Tuff. It was erupted from the Platoro caldera and caused the collapse of the caldera. Like the Ra Jadero Member, it has reversed magentic polarity.
0.2
32.6 Terrace Reservoir spillway. The dam is constructed around a Wisconsin terminal moraine.
0.3
32.9 Quartz latite porphyry dike, striking nearly parallel to road, forms cliffs on right. Dike is radial from Cat Creek volcanic center. Terminal moraine on left.
0.8
33.7 Junction; CONTINUE STRAIGHT AHEAD. Slabby, jointed upper part of La Jara Canyon ash-flow tuff.
0.1
33.8 Terrace Reservoir.
0.4
34.2 Prospect pit on right in altered nonwelded base of La Jara Canyon Member.
0.2
34.4 Dark gray nonporphyritic Conejos andesitic lavas, underlying the Treasure Mountain Tuff.
0.5
34.9 Curve to left. After curve, a quartz latite porphyry intrusive (64% SiO_2) at 12:00. Terrace laccolith at 11:30 on north side of Alamosa River. Beneath the cliff are mud flow breccias of the Conejos Formation.
1.4
36.3 Cabin on left. Cliffs across Alamosa River are Conejos andesite lavas and breccias, capped at top of hill by Terrace laccolith. On right, cliffs of Terrace laccolith. Straight up road a 1200-foot thick sequence of mud-flow breccias (lower two-thirds) and lavas (upper one-third) of Conejos Formation.
0.3
36.6 Steep contact between laccolith and volcanics follows drainage on right.
0.2
36.8 Phillips University Science Camp.
0.2
37.0 Alamosa Campground. Exposures along road in Conejos mudflows of andesitic composition.
1.8
38.8 Entrance to cabins on left. Crudely stratified outcrops of Conejos mudflows. Cornwall Mountain at 11:00 is structurally uplifted resurgent dome of thick La Jara Canyon Member of Treasure Mountain Tuff inside Platoro caldera.
0.5
39.3 Road to Silver Lakes on left.
0.4
39.7 Ranger Creek Forest Service Guard Station.
0.3
40.0 STOP 2. Pull off road to right as far as possible. Assemble near east edge of series of road cuts.
Now inside Platoro caldera near the east wall. Exposures are dark, nonporphyritic andesite lavas and interlayered tuffaceous sandstones, overlain up the hill by the Ojito Creek ash-flow sheet. These lap out to the east against a steep west-dipping surface of Conejos flows and breccias. High on the contact are well bedded ash-fall tuffs that were welded and agglutinated because of deposition while they were still hot. These must have erupted nearby to permit sorting, yet deposition before cooling. Angular blocks of lava as much as five feet across occur in the sedimentary intervals within the caldera. These may be ejected blocks or may have slid off the caldera wall. For the next several miles similar caldera-fill rocks crop out along the road.
0.2
40.2 Intracaldera andesite flows on right. Large landslide across Alamosa River.
1.1
41.3 Cattleguard. Intracaldera andesite.
1.3
42.6 Silver Creek. On right bedded tuffaceous sand-

Terrace laccolith.

Andesite lavas and interlayered tuffaceous sandstones at Stop 2.

stone interlayered with andesitic lava flows similar to that at Stop 2. Across river at 10:00 the large mountain mass (Cornwall Mountain) is mainly La Jara Canyon Tuff in the structurally uplifted central part of the caldera.

1.0

43.6 Small outcrops along the road of reddish-brown, propylitized, densely welded, intracaldera La Jara Canyon Member. These are overlain by intracaldara flows that dip to the east away from the resurgent core of the caldera. The intracaldera tuffs are much higher south of the river, continuing to top of Cornwall Mountain, because of uplift along fault near base of mountain.

1.0

44.6 Fern Creek. Cliffs above road on right just before creek are stratified tuffaceous sandstones between the La Jara Canyon Member of the Treasure Mountain Tuff and overlying intracaldera andesitic lava flows.

0.5

45.1 Jasper. Town was founded and mining began about 1874-1875. The largest workings were

Close-up of angular lava block occurring within the tuffaceous sediments.

mainly along the south side of the Alamosa River, along structures and alteration related to the southeast rim of the late collapse structure of the composite Platoro caldera. Small amounts of rich gold-silver ore were produced from quartz-pyrite veins, with associated sphalerite and galena (Patton, 1917). Production, (mostly or entirely before the area was studied by Patton in 1913), was apparently small and complicated by acidic mine waters.

    0.4
45.5 Blowout Pass Road on right.
    0.4
45.9 Burnt Creek.
    0.1
46.0 STOP 3. Forest Service Road. LUNCH STOP. Leave cars on road, pulling off to right as far as possible, and walk across bridge to dumps of Miser Mine for lunch and discussion of geology.

The Cornwall fault defines the south structural boundary of a younger caldera within the northwest part of the main Platoro caldera. This younger caldera is the source for the Ojito Creek and Ra Jadero Members of the Treasure Mountain Tuff. The small adit to the east is in a monzonite porphyry intruded along the Cornwall fault zone. Propylitized La Jara Canyon Member underlies Cornwall Mountain to the top. The base is not exposed but a minimum thickness of 3,000 feet for this member at this locality is indicated. This is typical of intracaldera tuff units. The alteration north of Jasper is related to fault intersections along the east boundary of the young caldera, along which monzonitic and porphyritic intrusions were emplaced.

View is north overlooking the Miser mill site at Jasper. Note hydrothermally altered zones on center horizon.

The Miser Mine was opened and most of the development work done in the 1880's. Patton (1917) reports that specimens assaying as much as $52,000 per ton were found. The main tunnel extends about 700 feet directly into the mountain side, and apparently intersected the Cornwall fault, along which the richest ore was found—vein quartz with gold stringers.
    0.5
46.5 Site of Fassetts General Store (1900-1905).
    0.6
47.1 Along road and on Cornwall's Nose across river (12:00 high) are massive, cliff-forming exposures of andesite flows and breccias within younger caldera.
    0.4
47.5 Cattleguard.
    1.2
48.7 Along road and low on south side of Alamosa River are andesite lavas inside younger caldera. Upper slopes are intracaldera tuffs of La Jara Canyon Member on upthrown side of Cornwall fault.
    0.7
49.4 Wrightman Fork. Thick intracaldera flows and breccias of dark nonporphyritic andesite.
    1.1
50.5 Lookout Mountain (12,448). Caprock is unaltered 22 m.y. old siliceous quartz latite (71% SiO_2). These rocks unconformably overlie solfatarically altered rock of the younger caldera.
    0.7
51.2 Cut on right in iron-stained Alamosa River stock; a 28 m.y. monzonite (57-62% SiO_2).
    0.2
51.4 Bridge over Bitter Creek. Kaolinite and quartz-sericite alteration of Alamosa River stock along road.
    0.8
52.2 Eastern Star Mine.
    0.4
52.6 Bridge over Alum Creek. Junction Platoro-Elwood Pass Road. BEAR RIGHT. Hydrothermally altered area to north in Alum Creek porphyry, a younger, more silicic phase (64% SiO_2) of the Alamosa River stock (see Calkin, this guidebook).
    0.4
53.0 Stunner Campground Road on left.
    0.6
53.6 Cattleguard. Hydrothermally altered Alamosa River stock.
    0.5
54.1 Sanidine, quartz latite dike intruding Alamosa River stock. This stock also underlies Klondike Mountain to the south.
    0.7
54.8 Southeast side of Lookout Mountain.
    0.7
55.5 Iron Creek. Leaving Alamosa River stock.
    0.2
55.7 Altered andesitic lava flows within younger caldera.
    0.7
56.4 Porphyritic quartz latite dike, typical of numerous dikes that radiate outward from the Alamosa River stock.
    0.3
56.7 Lake DeNolda.
    0.3
57.0 STOP 4. West end of Lake DeNolda. View east (across lake) to Lookout Mountain (12,448') with 22 m.y. capping quartz latitic lava flow overlying altered rocks within younger caldera. View north at south face of Prospect Mountain (12,245') displaying features of east rim of main Platoro caldera. West side of Prospect Mountain is capped by welded ash-flow tuff of the La Jara Canyon Member, which overlies andesitic lavas and breccias of the Conejos Formation of caldera rim. East side of Prospect Mountain consists of altered andesitic lavas and tuffaceous sediments within the caldera.

High on the south face of Prospect Mountain, on the central rib between the two gullies, welded tuff of the La Jara Canyon Member is plastered against steep caldera wall with compaction dips as steep as 60°.

Upon leaving Stop 4 TAKE RIGHT FORK (Elwood Pass Road). Exposures ahead are lavas, breccias, and tuffaceous sediments of Conejos Formation.
    1.3
58.3 Porphyritic quartz latite dike containing large ovoid sanidine phenocrysts, mantled by plagioclase rims (rapakivi texture).
    0.7
59.0 Road cuts of crudely bedded welded quartz latitic tuff—agglutinated ash-fall—that occurs locally beneath the La Jara Canyon Member near the caldera rim.
    0.6
59.6 Post-caldera andesitic lavas above the La Jara Canyon Member just outside caldera, where they overflowed the rim.
    1.0
60.6 Porphyritic quartz latite dike (ahead at curve) contains large mantled sanidine phenocrysts.

Lookout Mountain as seen from Lake DeNolda.

1.2
61.8 Cabin on right, Elwood Pass Trail on left. Just beyond trail, post-caldera andesite lavas are overlain by rhyodacite-quartz latite lavas—parts of late lava domes around north rim of caldera. Road cuts for next 3 miles are in these lavas.
1.2
63.0 Pass at head of Park Creek, a tributary of the South Fork of the Rio Grande.
2.1
65.1 Junction. Park Creek and Summitville roads. TURN RIGHT. Porphyritic quartz latite lava flows are part of the ring dome complex along the northwest rim of Platoro caldera.
0.8
65.9 Summitville Pass. Wightman Fork drainage to the east empties into Alamosa River west of Jasper. North Mountain (12,727′) at 12:00 and South Mountain at 3:30 are porphyritic quartz latite lava domes. Crossing Summitville fault with porphyritic quartz latite down on west against intracaldera andesitic lavas to the east.
1.9
67.8 STOP 5. Summitville. Park as directed. Discovery of gold in the Summitville area in 1870 and in the Silverton area in the same year were the first successful mining discoveries in the San Juan Mountains. The gold-silver-copper ore at Summitville occurs in a shallow volcanic environment within the South Mountain volcanic dome of coarsely porphyritic quartz latite, lo-

South face of Prospect Mountain seen at Stop 4. Welded ash-flow tuffs (La Jara Canyon Member) overlying andesitic lavas of the Conejos Formation display the east rim of the Platoro caldera.

Elwood Pass area.

cated approximately on the northwest rim of Platoro caldera. The ore occurs in intensely altered pipes and irregular tabular masses of quartz-alunite rocks that replaced the quartz latite along northwest-trending fracture zones. Metallic minerals, chiefly pyrite and enargite, fill irregular vugs that formed by local intense leaching of the quartz-alunite rock. The quartz-alunite masses are surrounded successively by soft argillically altered envelopes (illite-kaolinite zone) and by pervasively propylitized rocks (montmorillonite-chlorite zone). The alteration is interpreted to have resulted from shallow solfataric activity. An intense exploration program over the past several years has resulted in reopening of the mines, which went into production again in the spring of 1971 after having been shut down since 1949. Total past production of about $7,500,000 was mostly from gold; however, in the new operation the main value will be from copper. (Steven and Ratté, 1960; Lipman and Steven 1970. After Stop 5 retrace route to Park Creek Road.

0.8

68.6 High peaks ahead to the west on Continental

Summitville Mine operations at the base of South Mountain.

Divide are Summit (13,272') on left and Montezuma (13,150') on right. These peaks consist of andesitic lavas overlying La Jara Canyon Member of the Treasure Mountain Tuff. The andesites correlate with intracaldera andesites that filled Platoro caldera and overflowed to the west.
1.8

70.4 Junction Park Creek Road; CONTINUE STRAIGHT AHEAD.
0.2

70.6 Road cut in late lavas of porphyritic quartz latite on northwest rim of Platoro caldera. At 10:00 the light green cliffs are a vent-cone complex, and the source for some of the late rim lavas. At 12:00 on the horizon, Sawtooth Mountain is within Mt. Hope caldera, the source of the Masonic Park Tuff. Continue through porphyritic quartz latite, moraine, and landslide for next 5 miles. The rim on this side of Platoro caldera is mostly covered by post-collapse lavas.
2.9

73.5 Cliffs across Park Creek are post-collapse porphyritic quartz latite intrusive into ash-flow sheets of the Treasure Mountain Tuff.
1.0

74.5 Handerchief Mesa ahead is capped by Hinsdale basalt flows underlain by Fish Canyon and Carpenter Ridge ash-flow tuffs from the La Garita and Bachelor calderas respectively. These calderas are located to the northwest (see Lipman and Steven, this guidebook).
1.1

75.6 Road cut on right in Masonic Park Tuff.
0.2

75.8 Road cut on right in pinkish altered tuff at contact between nonwelded to partly welded Masonic Park and overlying partly welded basal Fish Canyon Tuff. The Fish Canyon (27.8 m.y.) is a phyenocryst-rich quartz-latite tuff (66-68% SiO_2) superficially similar to the Masonic Park Tuff. The two are distinguished on phenocrysts, magnetic polarity, and amount of xenoliths. Both contain plagioclase and biotite phenocrysts but the Fish Canyon has sparse hornblende, quartz, sanidine, and sphene while the Masonic Park has fairly abundant clinopyroxene. The Fish Canyon Tuff has normal magnetic polarity; Masonic Park, reversed. Xenoliths are more abundant in the Masonic Park Tuff.

Fox Mountain, at 11:00 across Park Creek, is a structurally simple sequence of northeast dipping thin ash-flows including Masonic Park, Fish Canyon, Carpenter Ridge and younger sheets, all from centers to the northwest, and capped by Hinsdale Basalt.
1.0

76.8 Road cuts on right in Carpenter Ridge Tuff, a phenocryst-poor rhyolite (73% SiO_2) with phenocrysts of sanidine, plagioclase, and biotite.
0.2

77.0 Porphyritic plagioclase andesite flows and breccias (Huerto Formation of Larson and Cross, 1956) between Carpenter Ridge and Fish Canyon Tuffs.
0.9

77.9 Trail Park on left.
0.2

78.1 Junction with Lost Mine Creek Road; CONTINUE STRAIGHT AHEAD. Outcrops ahead of Fish Canyon Tuff and glacial outwash.
0.5

78.6 Cattleguard. Cliffs of Fish Canyon Tuff across river.
0.4

79.0 Road cut on left in Masonic Park Tuff underlying Fish Canyon Tuff. The wall of Mt. Hope caldera is west of these outcrops, but is buried beneath thick Fish Canyon Tuff.
0.9

79.9 Road cut on right in Masonic Park Tuff.
0.2

80.1 Kelly Park.
0.7

80.8 Coal Mine Park.
0.4

81.2 Road cut on right in Fish Canyon Tuff. In this area the road is near or just inside the east rim of Mt. Hope caldera. This caldera was the source for the Masonic Park Tuff and later was almost entirely filled and buried by Fish Canyon Tuff from the La Garita caldera.
1.0

82.2 Corral Park.
0.4

82.6 Corral Park Road on left.
0.7

83.3 Bridge over Park Creek.
1.8

85.1 Cattleguard. Fish Canyon Tuff.
0.1

85.2 Bridge over Park Creek.
0.7

85.9 Bridge over South Fork of Rio Grande and junction with U.S. 160. TURN RIGHT. Continue through exposures of thick Fish Canyon Tuff. To the west along U.S. 160 exposures to

Fish Canyon Tuff exposed along canyon walls in lower Park Creek.

the summit of Wolf Creek Pass are almost entirely Fish Canyon Tuff.

1.3

87.2 Moon Valley Store on left. All cliffs are Fish Canyon Tuff.

0.3

87.5 Enter Rio Grande County; leave Mineral County.

0.7

88.2 Leaving South Fork flood plain through road cuts in Fish Canyon Tuff.

1.1

89.3 Highway Spring Campground on right. Masonic Park Tuff exposed along road on left below higher cliffs of Fish Canyon Tuff. Numerous northwest trending faults between here and South Fork define a complex graben system.

1.3

90.6 South Fork Campground. Cliffs of Fish Canyon Tuff on left.

0.5

91.1 Curve to right, then left. Masonic Park Tuff below cliffs of Fish Canyon.

0.8

91.9 Curve to left. Contact in cut on left at base of Fish Canyon ash-flow sheet underlain by local ash-fall deposits and tuffaceous sediments.

0.3

92.2 Beaver Creek Road on right.

1.0

93.2 Entering South Fork, Colorado. To the west at 3:00 (up Rio Grande Valley) note palisades of Masonic Park and Fish Canyon ash-flow tuffs. In this area the Rio Grande follows the graben system previously mentioned. Fish Canyon beds on the south side of the river are dropped down against Masonic Park tuffs on the north. On the right across South Fork the low cliffs are Conejos breccias overlain by Masonic Park Tuff. The Treasure Mountain Tuff that occurs between these two units to the south and east is not present this far northwest.

0.2

93.4 Junction Colorado 149 to Creede; BEAR RIGHT on U.S. 160 (see Thompson, this guidebook). The type locality of the Masonic Park Tuff is named for the hamlet of Masonic Park 5 miles west of the junction.

0.4

93.8 Bridge over South Fork.

1.6

95.4 Bridge over Willow Creek. Low cliffs ahead of Conejos andesite flows and breccias. High mesa to north (Agua Ramon Mountain) is composed of Fish Canyon Tuff.

1.6

97.0 Twin Peaks at 10:00 are rhyolite lava flows in Conejos Formation. Twin Peaks are on the southeast flank of the Baughman Creek volcanic center, the intrusive focus of which is in the basin at 9:00 to the west of the peaks.

1.9

98.9 Rest area on left.

2.0

100.9 Del Norte Peak (12,378′) at 4:00 is capped by Hinsdale Basalt. Lower timbered slopes are landslide covering young units of the ash-flow sequence and the long timbered ridge to the east at 3:00 is capped by La Jara Canyon Member of the Treasure Mountain Tuff. At 2:00 in far distance are Bennett (right) and Pentalda peaks. The northeast wall of Platoro caldera is in the saddle between the peaks. Sangre de

Cristo Mountains at 12:00 across San Luis Valley.

4.8

105.7 Exposures in hills of Conejos age hornblende andesite and rhyodacite probably erupted from Summer Coon volcano to the north.

1.1

106.8 Bridge over West Branch of Pinos Creek.

0.8

107.6 Bridge over East Branch, Pinos Creek. Hills on right, south of Del Norte, are andesitic lavas of the Conejos Formation with thin capping of La Jara Canyon Member of the Treasure Mountain Tuff. The Treasure Mountain tuffs do not extend north of U.S. 160.

1.9

109.5 Pinos Creek Road on right along cliff of Conejos hornblende rhyodacite lava flow with spectacular exposure of basal flow breccia. Entering Del Norte, Colorado.

0.5

110.0 Junction Colorado 112. Supplemental Log No. 2 for the Summer Coon volcanic center begins at this point and continues north on Colorado 112. CONTINUE STRAIGHT AHEAD.

4.1

114.1 Lower cliffs just above irrigation ditch in hill to right are Carpenter Ridge Tuff. Top of ridge is Hinsdale Basalt. A small fault in gully drops Hinsdale on right down against Carpenter Ridge. Teepee-shaped hills to the right are underlain from top by Carpenter Ridge, Fish Canyon, Masonic Park and Treasure Mountain ash-flow tuffs.

0.2

114.3 Leaving Rio Grande flood plain. At road cut ahead rising up an extensive terrace level controlled by the Carpenter Ridge Tuff.

1.6

115.9 Great Sand Dunes National Monument at 9:30; Blanca Peak at 10:00.

7.5

123.4 Entering Monte Vista, Colorado.

3.7

127.1 Entering Alamosa County. Principal crops grown in the San Luis Valley are lettuce, alfalfa, and the world famous "Red McClure" potato. Barley is another major item. The Coors Brewing Company of Golden, Colorado, utilizes much of the barley holdings in the valley, including maintaining experiment labs, test plots, storage areas, and shipping facilities. "Let's all have 3 cheers for the barley farmer!"

13.3

140.4 City limits of Alamosa. END OF LOG.

Localized fault zone at milepost 114.1 dropping the Hinsdale Basalt (Th) against the Carpenter Ridge Tuff (Tcr).

SECOND DAY

ROAD LOG FROM ALAMOSA TO THE GREAT SAND DUNES NATIONAL MONUMENT, PONCHA PASS, SALIDA, HOWARD, AND RETURN VIA SAGUACHE, AND MONTE VISTA

October 1, 1971

ASSEMBLY: D&RG Railroad Siding on U.S. 160, East City Limits of Alamosa.

TIME: 7:00-7:30 A.M.

DISTANCE: 284.8 miles.

TRIP LEADERS: Dennis Bruns, James Carrico, Charles E. Chapin, Richard H. De Voto, Rudy C. Epis, Lee C. Gerhard, Dan H. Knepper, Gary R. Lowell, Ron Marrs, Fred Peel, Ralph E. Van Alstine.

PREFACE:

The trip heads east from Alamosa down the broad alluvial fan of the Rio Grande, which forms a barrier that makes the northern half of the San Luis Valley a closed basin. At the foot of Sierra Blanca (14,363 ft.), whose Precambrian rocks tower 6,500 feet above the valley floor, the route turns north along the base of the Sangre de Cristo Mountains to the Great Sand Dunes National Monument. Here, sand picked up by southwesterly winds blowing across the Rio Grande flood plain has been piled against the base of the Sangre de Cristo Mountains to form transverse dunes as high as 700 feet.

We then journey northward up the center of the San Luis Valley to Mineral Hot Springs for a discussion of the structural development of this part of the Rio Grande rift zone. Transverse faults have broken the San Luis graben into a series of blocks which are progressively lower to the south. The deepest part of the basin is along the foot of the Sangre de Cristo Range northwest of the sand dunes. Gravity data suggest that in this area basement rocks have been displaced about 36,000 feet between the floor of the graben and the crest of the range. Thus, the San Luis graben appears to be hinged on the west with the greatest relief along the east side.

From Mineral Hot Springs we proceed northwestward over Poncha Pass where recent investigations have revealed that the rift zone is structurally continuous with the upper Arkansas graben to the north. Our lunch stop is on the Arkansas River north of Poncha Springs where the upper Arkansas segment of the rift zone will be discussed. Here, we will see graben-fill sediments of the Miocene-Pliocene Dry Union Formation which are equivalent to parts of the Santa Fe Group in New Mexico. Oligocene volcanic rocks in east-trending paleovalleys are visible along the east side of the rift zone and again along the valley floor where north-trending step faults have lowered them about 2,900 feet. When 2,000 feet of alluvial fill is added to this figure, the maximum displacement is about 5,000 feet relative to the east rim. Maximum displacement relative to the west rim appears to be somewhat greater, or about 7,000 feet.

From the Poncha Springs-Salida area, the caravan exits from the rift zone and follows the sinuous gorge of the Arkansas River to the vicinity of Howard for a discussion of Permo-Pennsylvanian stratigraphy and tectonics. The canyon provides an impressive cross-section of several thousand feet of Paleozoic sedimentary rocks on the east flank of the Sawatch anticline. The Paleozoic section begins with the Manitou Dolomite of Ordovician age and extends upward through the Harding, Fremont, Chaffee, and Leadville Formations and into a very thick Permo-Pennsylvanian section of the Kerber, Madera, and Sangre de Cristo Formations. Intra-formational unconformities with several thousand feet of relief have been documented by the work of De Voto, Peel, and Pierce.

The route then doubles back over Poncha Pass to the Saguache area at the northwest corner of the San Luis Valley for a discussion of the stratigraphic relationships between volcanic rocks of the San Juan field and the Bonanza center. The last stop of the day will be made along side an eroded and breached volcano in the Rawley Andesite of Oligocene age. Ash-flows from both the San Juan field and Bonanza center flowed around and into the breached volcano. Stratigraphically higher units are topographically lower because of relief on the post-Rawley surface. The Rawley Andesite of the Bonanza area has been correlated with the lower Conejos Formation of the San Juan field and the Bonanza Tuff is observed underlying the Fish Canyon Tuff which was erupted from a center near Creede. For a discussion of these relationships see Bruns, Epis, Steven, and Weimer, this guidebook.

The starved and weary riders of the rift zone then head (stampede?) south from Saguache past bubbling artesian wells to Alamosa and the "big feed" (and to carbonated springs which bubble late into the night).

- 0.0 Denver and Rio Grande Railroad siding east of Alamosa on U.S. 160. This narrow gauge remnant ran up the San Luis Valley to Salida before it was abandoned in 1959. It joined the Pueblo mainline here at Alamosa for points east, via La Veta Pass.
  0.9
- 0.9 Sand dunes at 10:00. Sierra Blanca (14,363 ft.) at 11:00. La Veta Pass (9,382 ft.) at 12:00. Topographers of the Hayden Survey thought that Sierra Blanca was the highest peak in the southern Rockies. Actually, it is 68 feet lower than Mt. Elbert in the Sawatch Range.
  0.7
- 1.6 Harmony Road
  1.0
- 2.6 Junction with road to Alamosa National Wildlife Refuge on right. Bare and gullied slopes on large alluvial fans at 11:00 are the results of a program of the Bureau of Land Management to improve grazing! Ute Mountain at 3:00 and San Antonio Mountain at 3:30 are Late Tertiary stratovolcanoes near the New Mexico-Colorado line. The San Luis Hills in the middle distance on both sides of Ute Mountain are fault blocks of Oligocene volcanic rocks which project more than 1,000 feet above the alluvial fill of the San Luis Valley (see Burroughs, this guidebook). The Rio Grande flows southward through a break in these hills to the right of Ute Mountain. From 12:00 to 2:30 the backbone of the Sangre de Cristo ("blood of Christ") Range extends southward into New Mexico.

  Zebulon Pike built a stockade at the north end of the San Luis Hills early in 1807. This area was Spanish territory at the time and he was captured by military authorities from Santa Fe.
  1.9
- 4.5 Crossing flood plain of Rio Grande. The sand which built the Great Sand Dunes was picked up by prevailing southwesterly winds crossing the flood plain and then deposited against the mountain front.
  0.5
- 5.0 Entering stabilized dune area.
  1.0
- 6.0 Highway rises slightly onto Hansen Bluff. About 6 miles to the south along the bluff is the type section of the Alamosa Formation (Siebenthal, 1910) which is composed of Pleistocene river deposits of the ancestral Rio Grande (see Price, this guidebook).

Sierra Blanca.

2.1
8.1 Fort Garland questa at 1:00 capped by Late Tertiary basalt flow interbedded with the Santa Fe Formation. Fort Garland was a frontier cavalry post from 1858 to 1883 (see Hoagland, this guidebook). Garland City nearby became an important railhead in 1877 while the D&RG construction was temporarily halted there for lack of funds. The D&RG was stymied in its quest for a route to Santa Fe and El Paso (via Raton Pass) by the AT&SF, whose construction crew occupied Raton Pass 30 minutes before the D&RG crew arrived. From 1876 to 1878, the D&RG built westward over La Veta Pass to Alamosa and by 1880 had extended their narrow gauge line as far south as Espanola, New Mexico, before abandoning their southward expansion at the conference table in settling their feud with the Santa Fe Railroad.

5.8
13.9 Junction with graded road. TURN LEFT and proceed north to Great Sand Dunes National Monument. For geological coverage of the southeastern portion of the basin consult Supplemental Log No. 3.

Glacial valleys at 2:00 on Sierra Blanca. Note how streams draining the cirques turn and follow the south edge of the alluvial fans. Cause? A terminal moraine is present in the center valley at timberline. The jeep road at 2:00 leads up into the glacial valley and Sierra Blanca may be climbed from there—the view is spectacular! Note fault scarp at 3:00 cutting the top of an alluvial fan. Other recent scarps, which testify to continued mountain building, will be visible as we proceed north along the mountain front.

The San Luis Valley is about 105 miles long and at this latitude about 50 miles wide. The elevation of the valley floor ranges from 7,400 feet where the Rio Grande crosses the state line to a remarkably consistent 8,000 feet along the bases of the flanking mountain ranges. Geophysical surveys by Gaca and Karig (1966) and by Kelinkopf, Peterson, and Johnson (1970) reveal a 30 mgal gravity low along the east side of the San Luis Valley with the center of the anomaly about 10 miles northwest of Great Sand Dunes National Monument. These authors suggest that the anomaly is caused by a maximum of 30,000 feet of sediment along the east side of the San Luis graben. Precambrian rocks form the crest of the Sangre de Cristo Range immediately east of the anomaly and 6,000 feet above the valley floor. If the geophysical interpretations are correct, there may be as much as 36,000 feet (7 miles) of relief on the Precambrian rocks in about 10 miles laterally! Recent fault scarps cutting alluvial fans indicate that the mountains are still rising!

3.2
17.1 Cattleguard.
0.2
17.3 Gate on right. Road leads to Lake Como in glacial valley on Sierra Blanca.
1.3
18.6 Note environmental impact of BLM project.
1.1
19.7 Cattleguard.
2.5
22.2 Cattleguard.
1.2
23.4 Junction with dirt road on right.
0.4
22.8 Cattleguard.
1.1
24.9 Ascend hill onto alluvial fan.
1.2
26.1 Cattleguard. Road on right leads to Zapata Falls. Note sharp notch at 2:00.
1.0
27.1 Zapata Ranch on left.
0.2
27.3 Sand dunes at 12:00. Crestone Needles at 11:00. Medano Peak at 12:00.
0.7
28.0 Junction with Colorado 150. TURN RIGHT.
0.4
28.4 Curve to left. Cattleguard.
0.8
29.2 Curve to left. Note recent scarp crossing head of small alluvial fan at 3:00.
0.3
29.5 The Dunes Outpost on left.
1.4
30.9 Cattleguard. Entering Great Sand Dunes National Monument. Barchan dunes at 8:30 along fence line, stabilized longitudinal dunes in foreground at 12:00 (see Johnson, this guidebook).
1.3
32.2 Road on right. A recent fault scarp marked by vegetation change and springs crosses the heads of the alluvial fans on right.
0.8
33.0 Photo turnout.
0.7
33.7 Check station for Great Sand Dunes National Monument.

Great Sand Dunes National Monument.

    0.4
- 34.1 At 10:00 the sand dunes have encroached on the vegetation.
    0.3
- 34.4 Entrance to Visitors Center on left. CONTINUE STRAIGHT AHEAD.
    0.3
- 34.7 Junction with road to picnic grounds on left. CONTINUE STRAIGHT AHEAD.
    0.4
- 35.1 Medano Creek extends along the edge of the sand dunes. The creek flows with a curious pulsing action that is presently being studied.
    0.2
- 35.3 Amphitheater. CONTINUE STRAIGHT AHEAD for turn around and parking.
    0.1
- 35.4 Loop #1 road on left. CONTINUE STRAIGHT AHEAD.
    0.1
- 35.5 Loop #2 road on left. CONTINUE STRAIGHT AHEAD. Loop #3 ahead. TURN RIGHT. Drive carefully through camping area.
    0.3
- 35.8 TURN RIGHT and rejoin main road.
    0.2
- 36.0 STOP 1. Amphitheater. Park as directed, then walk up to amphitheater for discussion of the sand dunes by National Park Service staff. *Please do not leave the caravan; we will be here only a short time.*

Prevailing southwesterly winds blow sand out of the floodplain of the Rio Grande and, being unable to carry it over the Sangre de Cristo Mountains, deposit the sand at the base of the range. The dunes have formed as the result of a favorable combination of factors; these are: (1) the abundant supply of sand on the Rio Grande floodplain, (2) strong and frequent southwesterly winds, (3) the semi-arid climate and sparse vegetation, and (4) the magnificent barrier of the Sangre de Cristo Mountains. The largest dunes are transverse dunes which rise nearly 700 feet above Medano Creek. Parabolic, longitudinal, barchan, and climbing dunes are also present. The transverse dunes are probably increasing in volume but do not appear to be migrating northeasterly.
    0.6
- 36.6 Junction with road to picnic area. CONTINUE STRAIGHT AHEAD.
    0.3
- 36.9 Visitors Center on right.
    0.7
- 37.6 Check station.
    1.1
- 38.7 Note vegetation change where recent fault scarp crosses alluvial fan at 10:30.

Telephoto view mashes dunes against Medano Peak. Line of vegetation along toe of dunes marks the course of Medano Creek.

1.7

40.4 Cattleguard. Leaving Great Sand Dunes National Monument.

2.9

43.3 Junction with road south to U.S. 160. CONTINUE STRAIGHT AHEAD on Colorado 150.

4.6

47.9 Road on right leads to San Luis Lake. This is the sump for the north half of the San Luis Valley. The broad, low, alluvial fan of the Rio Grande extends eastward from Del Norte across three fourths of San Luis Valley to form a natural barrier to surface drainage from the north. This barrier, and the tendency for runoff to sink into the unconsolidated sediments which floor the valley, have produced the sink. San Luis Lake has no outlet; the major inlet is San Luis Creek which heads on Poncha Pass at the north end of the valley. Considering the Pleistocene glacial runoff and the winter snowpack and thunderstorm precipitation on the adjacent mountains, it is not hard to visualize the San Luis graben as an enormous ground-water reservoir. This is an over-simplification, of course, as permeability within the alluvial fill is quite variable, but artesian wells and springs are numerous.

8.7

56.6 Junction with road 112. CONTINUE STRAIGHT AHEAD.

2.1

58.7 Junction with road 110. CONTINUE STRAIGHT AHEAD.

0.9

59.6 Junction with Colorado 17. TURN RIGHT and proceed northward up the San Luis Valley.

5.5

65.1 Entering Hooper.

0.4

65.5 Junction with Colorado 112. CONTINUE STRAIGHT AHEAD. Entering Saguache County. La Garita Mountains at 9:30.

1.7

67.2 San Juan volcanic field and the Bonanza volcanic field at 11:00. Crestone Needles (14,191 ft.) at 2:00. These jagged spires are composed of the Crestone Conglomerate Member of the Sangre de Cristo Formation of Pennsylvanian and Permian age.

"Any 'hangovers' from last night's party? Now's your chance for a quick nap!"

15.6

82.8 Junction with road to Crestone on right. CONTINUE STRAIGHT AHEAD.

Crestone is an old gold camp at the foot of the Sangre de Cristo Range. The veins follow shear zones in Precambrian rocks and contain free gold and considerable pyrite. Minor amounts of chalcopyrite, sphalerite, and galena also are present. Considerable mining was done before 1900 but, with one or two exceptions, the ore bodies were small. A D&RG spur line to the camp was abandoned in 1929. A standing joke in Leadville, Colorado, was that if a farmer had a wagon load of pumpkins for sale on the opposite side of Mosquito Pass, General Palmer (President and founder of the D&RG) would build a branch line across the mountains to reach him. The history of the Denver and Rio Grande Western Railroad, with its constant battles to raise money and to span the mountains before other railroads could preempt the territory, is fascinating reading (see Rebel of the Rockies by R. G. Athearn, Yale Univ. Press, 1962).

0.2

83.0 Entering Moffat. We are paralleling the D&RG narrow gauge from Alamosa to Salida and some of the small towns along the route are named for prominent D&RG officials. David H. Moffat, a wealthy mine-owner and financier, was president of the D&RG from 1887 to 1891. He later lost his personal fortune and his health trying to build a more direct railroad route west from Denver to Salt Lake City. His dream of a tunnel beneath the continental divide later became a reality and was named for him. The town of Hooper, a few miles back, was named for Major Shadrach K. Hooper who built up the D&RG tourist trade in the 1890's by publishing a number of illustrated booklets about the Colorado Rockies. One was entitled "A Honeymoon Letter From a Bride to her Chum Describing the Beauties of Colorado."

6.5

89.5 Roadside table. Coalescing alluvial fans form a prominent bajada along the base of the Sangre de Cristo Mountains. Note the alignment of triangular facets on the ridge spurs above the bajada. A major fault zone parallels the base of the range and is responsible for the facets; recurrent movement along subsidiary faults has formed numerous small fault scarps which cut the alluvial fans.

3.1

92.6 Gravel pit on left.

2.6

95.2 Junction. TURN SHARP LEFT onto dirt road. Mineral Hot Springs ahead on right.

0.4

95.6 STOP 2. Park as directed along both sides of road for discussion of the northern San Luis Valley, the Sangre de Cristo Mountains, and the Bonanza Remote Sensing Project.

The Rio Grande rift zone at the north end of the San Luis Valley is fragmented by transverse faults into a series of blocks which are progressively lower to the south. (Knepper, 1970; see Knepper and Marrs, this guidebook). To the north of Mineral Hot Springs, Precambrian basement rocks lie at very shallow depths. (0-300 feet) below the valley floor which is covered by thin pediment gravels or alluvial fan deposits and occasionally by Tertiary volcanic rocks. Southward from Mineral Hot Springs, the San Luis Valley becomes a progressively deeper structural and sedimentary basin.

A Laramide thrust zone which is present in the Sangre de Cristo Range near Valley View Hot Springs appears to cross beneath the alluvial fill near Mineral Hot Springs and emerge to the northwest along Kerber Creek. This zone may have been reactivated by Late Tertiary block faulting to form one of the transverse faults of the rift zone. Immediately south of this fault, Precambrian rocks are 1,800 to 2,200 feet below the valley floor. Depth to basement increases southward to about 8,000 feet near Center, Colorado, and to nearly 30,000 feet (as interpreted from gravity data) along the east side of the trough northwest of Sierra Blanca.

Faceted spurs along the west flank of the Sangre de Cristo Range are evidence of a major fault zone along the east side of the rift zone. However, as is common all along the rift zone, it is not a single fault but a series of longitudinal faults progressively downthrown towards the valley axis. Small fault scarps cutting Pleistocene alluvial fans indicate that development of the rift zone is continuing into the present time. Scott (1970) reports scarps in Pleistocene gravel that are as much as 25 feet high and which extend from Crestone to north of Villa Grove. These faults cut both Bull Lake and Pinedale outwash fans, but not Upper Holocene deposits. The time of the last displacement can thus be established as less than 10,000 years ago. Scott warns that because of the thousands of feet of pre-Quaternary movement and the lateness of the last movement, this fault zone probably has the greatest likelihood of future harmful earthquakes in east-central Colorado. Groundwater is frequently impounded on the uphill side of faults with resultant development of sag-ponds, springs, and changes in vegetation. The variation in soil moisture on opposite sides of these faults is readily apparent on aerial photographs, thermal infrared imagery, and radar imagery.

At Mineral Hot Springs there are several active and dormant springs, some with sinter mounds. Temperatures range between 90° and 131° F. Valley View Hot Springs are located about 6 miles east-northeast at the mountain front. Water temperatures here are about 97° F. and flows as much as 200 gpm have been recorded. Hot springs are a common feature of the Rio Grande rift zone, as are Late Tertiary epithermal fluorspar deposits which were probably formed in a hot spring environment (see Chapin, this guidebook).

The iron-stained outcroppings about 1½ miles north of Valley View Hot Spring are at the Orient Iron Mine. Production began in 1881 with the construction of a D&RG spur (General Palmer founded both the D&RG and the Colorado Fuel and Iron Corp., whose captive business was a great asset to the railroad) and continued for over 50 years, although total production was only about 2,000,000 tons. The ore bodies consist of irregular lenses and pipes of limonite within the lower part of the Leadville Limestone of Mississippian age. Ore was developed over a vertical range of 1,000 feet and some pipes had horizontal sections of 80 by 200 feet. Stone (1934) theorized that the iron was introduced by ascending solutions to form siderite and that oxidation of the primary ore to limonite was accomplished by descending meteoric waters. Oxidation is remarkably deep, perhaps because of channelways along faults bounding the rift zone.

0.6

96.2 Junction with U.S. 285. TURN RIGHT and proceed north up the valley.

0.2

96.4 Precambrian rocks exposed in low hills at 9:00.

1.1

97.5 Junction with Colorado 17. CONTINUE STRAIGHT AHEAD. The high peak at 3:00 is Cottonwood Peak (13,573 ft.), a Tertiary stock intruded into the Sangre de Cristo Formation.

2.4

99.9 Complexly folded and faulted Paleozoic rocks in hills on left. Hayden Pass (10,700 ft.) Road at 2:00.

The caravan route will make a large V from this point to Salida at the apex and then down the Arkansas River to Howard in order to circumvent the northwest-trending Sangre de Cristo Range. From here to the Arkansas River across Hayden Pass is only about 15 miles "as the crow flies," whereas, via the present highway system it is 48 miles. Hayden Pass is under consideration as a possible highway route. At Hayden Pass the east-dipping Paleozoic formations cross the range diagonally. Northwest of Hayden Pass the top of the range is made of Precambrian rocks; southeast of the pass the crest is composed of generally clastic rocks of Pennsylvanian and Permian age as far south as the Precambrian massif of Sierra Blanca.

1.8

101.7 Entering Villa Grove.

0.3

102.0 Junction with Hayden Pass Road on right. CONTINUE STRAIGHT AHEAD on U.S. 285.

0.2

102.2 Junction with road to Bonanza on left (see Supplemental Log No. 1). CONTINUE STRAIGHT AHEAD on U.S. 285. The lead and silver deposits of the Bonanza (Kerber Creek) district were located early in the history of the San Juan country and the town was bustling by 1880. Total production to 1946 was about $9,000,000, most of which came from the Rawley vein which was tapped by a 6,200 foot drainage tunnel in 1912. Most of this ore was mined between 1923 and 1930; other operations in the district have been small. The deposits are complex base metal ores, although a few veins containing tellurides of silver and gold were found in the northern part of the district. The mineralization is associated with the Bonanza center which was the source of a widespread ash-flow tuff sheet, which will be discussed at Stop 5.

Note development of pediment surfaces on the left (west) side of the valley and the large alluvial fan of Spring Creek. Four levels of pedimentation have been distinguished along the west side of the San Luis Valley in this vicinity. Only one pediment, however, has been found on the east side of the valley along the front of the Sangre de Cristo Range. A similar relationship exists in the upper Arkansas segment of the rift zone.

2.1

104.3 Sawatch Range at 12:00.

0.5

104.8 Road on left leads to the Hall Mine, an intermittent turquoise producer. The value of production from 1952 to 1957 was reported to be $77,765. In 1957, 420 pounds sold for $15,600, or about $37 per pound. Turquoise ranked second in Saguache County in value produced. The turquoise occurs in veins and nodules filling cavities in a weathered felsite porphyry flow of the Bonanza volcanic pile. Precipitation from meteoric waters, which had leached the essential constituents from surficial rocks, is thought to have been the origin of the turquoise.

4.6

109.4 Spring Creek Road and Bonanza volcanic rocks on left.

2.6

112.0 Alder Creek. Note displacement of alluvial fan at 3:00. From 12:30 to 1:30 several variably-dipping surfaces developed on Precambrian rocks can be seen. These surfaces may be exhumed and faulted remnants of the erosion surface on which the Oligocene volcanic rocks were deposited. One small remnant of volcanic rocks is preserved on the southernmost surface.

0.6

112.6 Round Hill at 12:30 is composed of a fine-grained andesitic flow of the Rawley Andesite, the Conejos equivalent in the Bonanza volcanic pile. Fault in small gulch to right of hill places Precambrian rocks and andesite in juxtaposition.

0.4

113.0 Clover Creek.

1.0

114.0 Foundation of water tower on right. This was a watering stop on the D&RG narrow gauge line from Salida to Alamosa. The tower disappeared during the past winter.

0.1

114.1 Road cut on left in porphyritic latite unit of the Rawley Andesite.

2.6

116.7 Summit of Poncha Pass (elevation 9,010 ft.); divide between Rio Grande and Arkansas watersheds. Mt. Ouray (elevation 13,971 ft.) at 11:00 named for Chief Ouray (pronounced "you-ray") of the Ute Indian tribe. Note large cirque at base of summit. Monarch Pass at 12:00, Sawatch Range 12:00 to 2:00, WNW-trending shoulder of Sangre de Cristo Range from 2:00 to 4:00 is composed of Precambrian rocks and forms the main barrier between the San Luis and Arkansas valleys. This barrier is a northwest-trending horst uplifted along faults transverse to the rift zone. Methodist Mountain (11,655 ft.) at 4:00 is the northernmost high peak of the Sangre de Cristo Range.

0.3

117.0 Road cut on right in porphyritic latite in the Rawley Andesite.

0.4

117.4 Fault zone, note highly sheared Precambrian rocks in road cut on left; white outcrops and mica prospect ahead on right are sheared Precambrian muscovite quartz schist and gneiss.

0.2

117.6 Road cut to right in porphyritic latite flows of Rawley Andesite.

0.1

117.7 Entering San Isabel National Forest. Precambrian rocks in road cut ahead on right.

0.2

117.9 Entering Chaffee County. D&RG narrow gauge line on left. We are approaching Mears Junction where the line from Alamosa joined the narrow gauge mainline. The junction is named for Otto Mears, a pioneer builder of wagon toll roads and narrow gauge short lines, who became known as the "Pathfinder of the San Juan." He built the Silverton Railroad between Silverton and Ouray (1887) and the Rio Grande Southern Railroad from Ridgeway through Placerville and Rico to Durango (1891).

The original narrow gauge mainline of the Denver and Rio Grande Railroad between Denver and Salt Lake City ran up Poncha Creek and over Marshall Pass (10,586 ft.) to Gunnison. The D&RG flung the roadbed across Marshall Pass in a desperate race to beat the Denver, South Park, and Pacific Railroad into Gunnison. Between Salida and the Summit of Marshall Pass, the rails gain 3,806 feet of elevation in 25.6 miles with maximum grades of 4% and curves as sharp as 24 degrees. On the other side, the line drops 2,379 feet in 16.5 miles. The DSP&P built their line west from Buena Vista up Chalk Creek and constructed the 1,800 foot Alpine tunnel to penetrate the Sawatch Range at an elevation of nearly 12,000 feet. Both routes were formidable undertakings; the D&RG won the epic battle (partly by buying Otto Mears' toll road over Marshall Pass) and the first train rolled into Gunnison on August 8, 1881, 13 months ahead of the DSP&P. The line to Salt Lake City was completed in April 1883. A through passenger train was operated daily in each direction, running the distance in 41½ hours westbound and 39 hours eastbound, for an average speed of about 20 miles per hour.

0.3

118.2 Mine shaft at 12:00 in Precambrian rocks.

0.9

119.1 Mears Junction. Poncha Creek and Marshall Pass Road (Chaffee County 200) on left. Sheep Mountain (12,243 ft.) visible up Poncha Creek. Late Miocene-Pliocene gravels of the Dry Union Formation ahead on left. These are graben-fill sediments in a narrow trough connecting the San Luis and upper Arkansas segments of the Rio Grande rift zone. Investigations by Van Alstine (1968) have shown that the Arkansas and San Luis Valleys of south-central Colorado are connected by a structural trough containing volcanic rocks and sediments of Late Tertiary

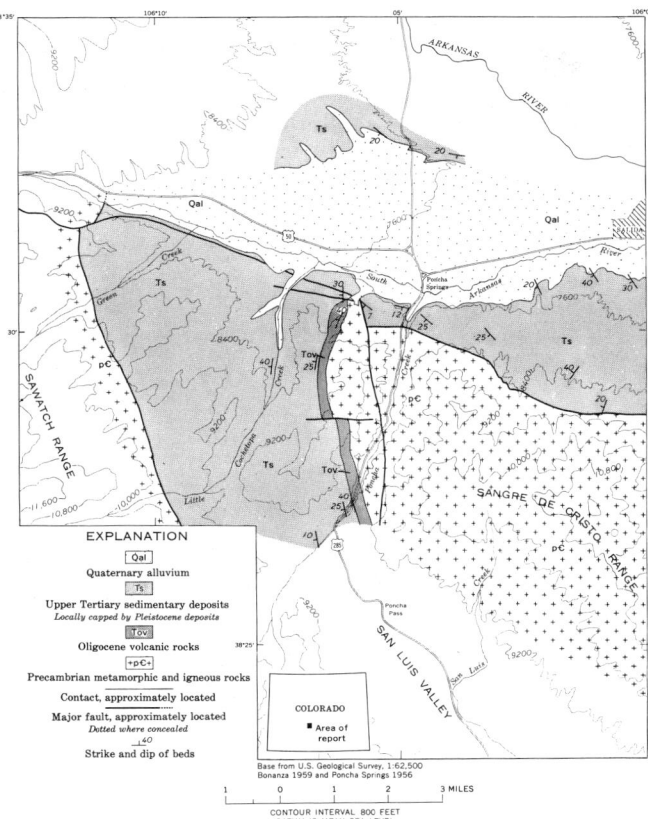

FIGURE 1.
Generalized geologic map of the area between the Arkansas and San Luis valleys, south-central Colorado.*

age, rather than being separated by a barrier of Precambrian rocks as previously believed. The existence of this trough indicates that the Rio Grande depression extends continuously northward, beyond its previously reported end at the head of the San Luis Valley, into the upper Arkansas Valley in central Colorado (see fig. 1).

0.3

119.4 Dry Union gravels dipping about 30° to SW. Slow down for important outcrop ahead.

0.2

119.6 East edge of Rio Grande trough which extends northward to the vicinity of Climax, Colorado. Dry Union Formation of Late Miocene-Pliocene age dips 25°-40° west above Oligocene lava flow of rhyodacite, dated here at about 33.5 m.y. The rhyodacite is underlain by rhyolitic Ash-Flow 1 of the Thirtynine Mile volcanic field to the NE and the trachy-andesite flow and is overlain by Ash-Flow 7 of the Thirtynine Mile field. The volcanic rocks rest on Precambrian metamorphic rocks, mainly light-colored gneiss, granofels, quartzite, and amphibolite.

0.4

120.0 Stone foundations of the Denver and Rio Grande Railroad bridge on right. Road cuts on left are still in the thick rhyodacite flow beneath the Dry Union Formation.

0.1

120.1 Stratified angular colluvium of rhyodacite in large road cut on left. At the north end of the cut, the contact between colluvium and Precambrian rocks dips very steeply towards the road and the toe of the colluvium has been undercut—slope stability problems coming up?

0.4

120.5 Cleveland Mountain visible up valley on left. The slopes are Precambrian rocks capped by Oligocene volcanic rocks which dip westward beneath Dry Union sediments of the Rio Grande rift zone. Poncha Creek has cut the gorge we are following after being superimposed onto the horst of Precambrian rocks which form the NE shoulder of the Sangre de Cristo Range; thus, the extension of the Rio Grande trough through Poncha Pass is not obvious from U.S. 285.

0.1

120.6 On the left, stratified boulder alluvium of Quaternary age occupies a channel carved in Precambrian rocks.

0.3

120.9 Crossing fault zone exposed in cut on left. Note shearing and limonite staining of Precambrian rocks.

0.3

121.2 Road cut on left in Precambrian metasedimentary rocks which consist of alternating thin beds of amphibolite and micaceous quartzites. Deformation is prominent in the micaceous beds.

0.2

121.4 Curve to left; Arkansas Valley visible ahead. Road cut ahead on left in Precambrian metasedimentary rocks injected by basic dikes metamorphosed to amphibolites. For the next 1.5 miles the slopes on both sides of the valley are Precambrian rocks. The highway cuts through several alluvial fans at the mouths of gulleys revealing cross sections of coarse boulder deposits.

1.0

122.4 Road on right leads to the open-pit fluorspar mine and mill of Reynolds Metals Co. The

---

* Reprinted from U.S. Geological Survey Prof. Paper 600-C.

Road cut in Precambrian metasedimentary rocks at milepost 121.2.

stone bed of the Denver and Rio Grande Railroad is above the highway on the left.

0.5

122.9 Reynolds fluorspar mill visible up gully at 3:00. Crudely stratified cross section of alluvial fan on left. Entering major southeast-trending fault zone which bounds the south end of the upper Arkansas Valley. The fault is upthrown on the south placing Poncha Pass and the northern San Luis Valley structurally and topographically higher than the Arkansas Valley. Note highly sheared Precambrian rocks in cut on left. Buff colored strata at 10:00 are graben-fill sediments of the Dry Union Formation of Late Miocene-Pliocene age. Here against the mountain front the beds contain much coarse gravel and cobble alluvium. At our next stop, near the center of the valley, the Dry Union beds are much finer with sands and silts predominating.

0.5

123.4 Cameron Mountain (10,993 ft) visible across Arkansas Valley at 12:30. The Whitehorn stock, a Late Cretaceous (69-70 m.y.) granodiorite pluton, intrudes Paleozoic sedimentary rocks along the Arkansas Hills which form the east side of the upper Arkansas graben. Minor gold mineralization gave rise to the mining camps of Turret, Whitehorn, and Futurity. Contact metasomatic iron deposits at the Calumet Iron Mine were exploited almost continuously by the Colorado Fuel and Iron Corporation from 1882 to 1900. Total recorded production was about 228,781 long tons which ran as high as 60% Fe during the early years but dropped to 43-45% and became uneconomical. The ore body is a contact metasomatic deposit in the Leadville Limestone and is located between two granodiorite sills along the west margin of the Whitehorn stock. The mine dumps are well-known among mineral collectors; minerals reported are: epidote, uralite, garnet, diopside, actinolite, tremolite, calcite, magnetite, hematite, pyrite, chalcopyrite, biotite, wernerite, and corundum. Several hundred workers lived

North side of Poncha Pass entering the Arkansas River Valley.

at Calumet City during the heyday of the operation.

0.1

123.5 Poncha Springs city limit. Elevation 7,500 feet.

0.2

123.7 Flood plain of the South Fork of the Arkansas River whose headwaters are in the Monarch Pass area at 9:30. Sawatch Range from 9:30 to 10:30. Entrance to Poncha Hot Springs on right. These springs only flow about 15 gallons per minute but are quite hot, about 150° F., and have about twice the mineral content of the Valley View Hot Springs near our last stop.

0.1

123.8 Bridge. South fork of Arkansas River.

0.2

124.0 Junction U.S. 285 and U.S. 50. CONTINUE STRAIGHT AHEAD on U.S. 285 and U.S. 50 west.

0.1

124.1 Junction. CONTINUE STRAIGHT AHEAD.

0.1

124.2 Yield sign, merging traffic from right. CONTINUE STRAIGHT AHEAD.

0.1

124.3 Railroad crossing for Denver and Rio Grande spur to the Monarch mining district. This district is located near the south end of the Mount Princeton quartz monzonite batholith of Tertiary age. The production was mainly lead, silver, zinc, and gold from replacement bodies in Paleozoic limestones and dolomites.

0.2

124.5 Junction U.S. 50 and U.S. 285. TURN RIGHT onto U.S. 285.

0.4

124.9 Ascend long hill that climbs from flood plain of the South Fork of the Arkansas River onto a pediment surface capped by Pleistocene outwash gravels.

0.4

125.3 Road cuts in Pleistocene gravels.

0.3

125.6 Junction with Salida airport road on right. CONTINUE STRAIGHT AHEAD. The Sawatch Range (9:00-11:00) contains the highest peaks in Colorado. U-shaped glacial valley at 9:30, Shavano Peak (14,225 ft.) at 10:00; a trail leads to mines at 13,400 ft. level on the south shoulder. Mount Antero (14,269 ft.) at 10:30, Buffalo Peaks (12,892 ft.) at 12:00 consist of mid-Tertiary volcanic rocks atop the south end of the Mosquito Range, Arkansas Hills at 12:30 to 3:00.

The rather subdued crest of the Arkansas Hills is an exhumed Late Eocene erosion surface on which remnants of Early Oligocene ash-flow tuffs have been found. These tuffs have been stepped down into the upper Arkansas graben by north-trending faults along the east side of the rift zone (see Lowell, this guidebook). The apparent displacement between tuffs at river level in the Browns Canyon area and the highest outcrops along the Arkansas Hills is about 2,900 feet. However, these tuffs disappear beneath the alluvial fill of the Arkansas Valley west of Browns Canyon and the depth of this fill must be added to the above figure to obtain the maximum depth of the rift valley. Van Alstine (1969) has estimated that 500 feet of Dry Union beds are exposed in the Salida area and Tweto (1961) reports a maximum thickness of 2,000 feet based on geophysical data. Total displacement in the upper Arkansas graben as measured from the east rim may be as much as 5,000 feet. Another ash-flow tuff caps Brittle Silver Peak at an elevation of 12,200 feet in the Sawatch Range almost due west of Browns Canyon. Total displacement along the west side of the Arkansas graben may be as great as 7,000 feet.

0.8

126.4 Curve to left, start descent of long hill. Buff-colored badlands straight ahead are Late Miocene-Pliocene sediments of the Dry Union Formation, which is equivalent in age and origin to parts of the Santa Fe Group of New Mexico. Note the similarity of these outcrops to those in the Espanola Basin. A species of fossil horse found in the Dry Union beds is characteristic of the Late Miocene Tesuque Formation of the Santa Fe Group.

A Late Tertiary pediment, largely stripped of its gravels, slopes west from the Arkansas Hills; three Early Pleistocene pediments slope east from the Sawatch Range. Multiple stages of glaciation in the Sawatch Range resulted in deposition of 9 Pleistocene outwash gravels which mantle the east-sloping pediment surfaces and much of the Dry Union Formation. Five of the gravels are Wisconsin in age and four are older. Rhyolitic volcanic ash in the third oldest gravel may be equivalent to the Pearlette Ash of the Great Plains.

The high peak at 12:00 is Mt. Princeton (14,197 ft.). The Chalk Cliffs along its east flank are hydrothermally altered rocks along the margin of the Mt. Princeton quartz monzonite batholith of Tertiary age, which comprises the bulk of the Sawatch Range from Monarch Pass north to Buena Vista. Buffalo Peaks (12,892 ft.) at 1:00 are remnants of mid-Tertiary volcanic rocks atop the south end of the Mosquito Range. They were the subject of U.S.G.S. Bulletin No. 1 published by Whitman Cross and S. F. Emmons in 1883.

1.1

127.5 Junction Chaffee County 160 on right. CONTINUE STRAIGHT AHEAD. Brown's Canyon at 12:00; here the Arkansas River has been superimposed onto a NW-trending horst of Precambrian rocks and has carved a gorge into bedrock which is about 9 miles long and more than 500 feet deep. Epithermal fluorspar deposits in the Browns Canyon area yielded about $5,000,000 worth of ore between 1929 and 1949. The main normal fault zone bounding the horst on the SW is mineralized with fluorspar almost continuously for about 3,000 feet. The veins range in thickness up to about 40 feet and the CaF_2 content ranges from 15 to 75 percent. The fluorspar deposits are Late Tertiary in age; similar deposits occur at intermittent points along the Rio Grande rift zone. The deposits formed under surface hot spring conditions from very dilute fluids. Study of fluid inclusions in the fluorite indicates that the depositing fluids were essentially fresh water and that the temperatures of deposition were in the range of 119° to 168° C (R. E. Van Alstine, 1969). Van Alstine has estimated that fluorspar resources of the Browns Canyon district are about two million short tons averaging more than 15 percent CaF_2.

0.8

128.3 Road cuts in Dry Union Formation. CAUTION! SLOW for sharp right turn onto county road at foot of hill.

0.3

128.6 Junction with Chaffee County 165. TURN RIGHT and curve to south.

0.2
128.8 Cattleguard. Arkansas River on left. Dry Union Formation at 12:00.
0.3
129.1 Ascend hill and cross narrow steel bridge. Junction with Chaffee County 163. CONTINUE STRAIGHT AHEAD.
0.1
129.2 STOP 3. Gravel Pit on right. LUNCH STOP. Discussion of the upper Arkansas rift zone.

The upper Arkansas Valley is an elongate graben which extends from Salida to north of Leadville, Colorado, a distance of about 60 miles. It is the northern-most basin of the Rio Grande rift system and while narrower and shallower than the structural depressions to the south, it shows many similarities to them. (see Chapin, this guidebook) The upper Arkansas graben truncates the east flank of the north-trending Sawatch anticline formed during Laramide uplift; consequently Paleozoic formations along the east side of the rift zone dip eastward away from the valley. Development of the rift system in this area can be bracketed between the 36 m.y. K/Ar age of ash-flow tuffs which followed east-trending paleovalleys prior to graben formation (Chapin, Epis, and Lowell, 1970) and the Late Miocene age of Dry Union graben-fill sediments as determined from vertebrate remains (Van Alstine and Lewis, 1960; Van Alstine, 1969).

The upper Arkansas graben is a complex structural feature formed by a series of semi-parallel faults which step-down older rock units into the graben. In some cases, this step-down arrangement is so subtle as to give the illusion that Oligocene ash-flow tuffs flowed into the valley and came to rest with steep primary dips. The graben is broken by many transverse blocks such as the NW-trending horst at Browns Canyon. Subsurface data indicate a relief of more than 1,000 feet for the bedrock floor of the valley (Tweto, 1961).

The Late Tertiary sedimentary fill in the valley was named the Dry Union Formation by Tweto (1961) for exposures near Leadville. This formation consists mainly of massive, brown to buff, sandy silt beds with interbedded lenses of sand and gravel and occasional volcanic ash beds. Near the edges of the valley, coarse alluvial fan deposits become prominent. The fill is thought to have originated partly by coalescing alluvial fans and partly by an ancestral Arkansas River which flowed southward from the Leadville area. Evidence for existence of a through-going stream consists of pebbles found in the Salida area of garnet-bearing rhyolite from the Nathrop volcanics near Buena Vista and pebbles of the Pando Porphyry from the Leadville area. Whether the river exited at Salida, as it does today, or flowed southward into the San Luis Valley is uncertain; it may have done both at different times during the complex structural history of the rift. About 500 feet of Dry Union beds are exposed in the Salida area but geophysical data suggests that the formation may locally be as much as 2,000 feet thick.

After Stop 3 CONTINUE SOUTH toward Salida.
0.3
129.5 Cattleguard. Reynolds fluorspar mine at 11:30, Poncha Pass at 12:30.
0.4
129.9 Junction with Chaffee County 160. TURN LEFT. After turn, Big Baldy Mountain (10,742 ft.) at the south end of the Arkansas Hills at 12:00. Oligocene ash-flows tuffs which crop out near river level in the Browns Canyon area are present on the south shoulder of Big Baldy Mountain, 2,900 feet higher in elevation. Most of Big Baldy consists of the Late Cretaceous Whitehorn stock which was exposed by erosion prior to Early Oligocene volcanism. East-dipping Paleozoic formations make up most of the lower slopes.
1.3
131.2 Junction with Chaffee County 163 on left. CONTINUE STRAIGHT AHEAD.
0.3
131.5 SHARP TURN TO RIGHT.
0.2
131.7 Junction Chaffee County 166 on left. CONTINUE STRAIGHT AHEAD.
0.1
131.8 SHARP TURN TO LEFT.
0.8
132.6 Community Hall on left. The slag dumps, foundations and chimney stack of the Ohio Smelting and Refining Co. are visible across the Arkansas River. Note the old powerhouse at river level. The smelter treated ores from Leadville, Telluride, and Monarch mining districts. In 1920, after the smelter was shut down, a wedding was held on top of the stack. "Now there is a valuable piece of information that could only be found in a New Mexico Geological Society guidebook!"

1.1

133.7 Entrance to Mt. Shavano fish hatchery and park on left. CONTINUE STRAIGHT AHEAD and ascend hill.
0.1

133.8 Junction Chaffee County 144. TURN SHARP RIGHT. Reynolds fluorspar mine at 11:00, Poncha Pass between 11:30 and 12:00, Chalk Cliffs at 3:00.
0.3

134.1 SHARP CURVE TO LEFT.
0.1

134.2 Entrance to Fairview cemetery on right.
0.3

134.5 Junction with Salida airport road. TURN LEFT towards Salida. Beyond turn, Spiral Drive on Tenderfoot Hill at 11:30. This hill is part of a sequence of basalt flows and interbedded gravels which dip 25 to 50 degrees westward into the upper Arkansas graben. These basalts have not been dated, but they appear to be interbedded with sediments of the Dry Union Formation of Late Miocene-Pliocene age.

Welded-tuff outcrops behind and to the left of Spiral Drive belong to the Ash Flow 1 unit of the Thirtynine Mile volcanic field which extends northeastward for about 50 miles. Outcrops of these tuffs in the Browns Canyon area have been dated at about 36 m.y. by Van Alstine. They predate the rift zone and have been stepped-down almost to the valley floor by a series of subparallel faults along the east side of the graben. The same tuffs outcrop near the skyline on Big Baldy Mountain.

Note the river terrace south of Spiral Drive which extends towards the Arkansas Gorge at 1:00. Salida means "exit" in Spanish and it is here that the Arkansas River leaves the rift zone to carve a sinuous gorge eastward across the north-trending structural fabric of the Rocky Mountains and emerge on the high plains at Canon City.
0.5

135.0 Poncha Springs Grange No. 117 on right. TURN RIGHT through the Grange yard.
0.1

135.1 TURN RIGHT onto Chaffee County Road. After turn; at 10:00, west-dipping Dry Union beds are exposed beneath a bench-like remnant of a pediment surface. A major southeast-trending fault south of the pediment terminates the upper Arkansas graben and bounds the north end of the Sangre de Cristo Range. The caravan crossed this fault zone at the foot of Poncha Pass when we left the Precambrian rocks and entered the Dry Union Formation. Uplift on the south side of this fault formed the horst of Precambrian rocks which we crossed at Poncha Pass and was probably responsible for diverting the ancestral Arkansas River from the rift zone at Salida.

Site of Reynolds fluorspar mine at 11:45. The mine was operated for a short time in the early 1950's by Reynolds Metals Co. The mill was dismantled in 1954 and shipped to Eagle Pass, Texas, where the company is a major processor of Mexican fluorspar. The fluorspar mineralization occurs in a NNW-trending fault zone which is over 100 feet wide and is exposed for several thousand feet along strike. The ore consists of epithermal fracture fillings of fluorite, quartz, and calcite in brecciated Precambrian rocks and is said to average 25 to 30% recoverable fluorspar. Another deposit located about one mile to the south on the same fault zone is now being explored. The deposits are of Late Tertiary age and were localized by rift-zone faulting.

Cleveland Mountain and Poncha Pass at 12:00. Oligocene volcanic rocks on Cleveland Mountain dip westward beneath gravels visible from 12:30 to 1:00. Van Alstine (see paper, this guidebook) has mapped more than 20 allochthonous Paleozoic blocks which were emplaced within the Dry Union Formation by gravitational gliding several miles eastward from the Sawatch Range. The largest of these blocks has dimensions of 400 by 800 by 150 feet. Emplacement of the blocks occurred after Early Oligocene volcanism and before deposition of overlying beds containing Late Miocene vertebrate fossils.

Monarch Pass at 1:30, Sawatch Range from 1:30 to 3:00, Chalk Cliffs at 3:00.
0.6

135.7 Dip. Valley to left carved in Dry Union Formation by the South Fork of the Arkansas River. The county road we are following is on Pleistocene outwash gravels. Methodist Mountain at 9:00 is the northern-most high peak of the Sangre de Cristo Range.
0.7

136.4 Junction with Chaffee County 125. TURN LEFT and descend hill onto flood plain of the South Fork of the Arkansas.
0.2

136.6 CAUTION! Railroad crossing.

0.2
136.8 Junction with U.S. 50. TURN LEFT towards Salida.
1.1
137.9 Spiral Drive at 10:00. A topographical feature called "The Crater" is visible to the right of Spiral Drive and near the skyline. It is actually a landslide scar in which a dark andesite flow which dips towards the valley slid down revealing white tuffs behind it. The feature was interpreted as a crater by Arthur Lakes in one of the early reports on Colorado geology.
0.2
138.1 Salida Hot Springs and Municipal Swimming Pool on left. Note the miniature locomotive and caboose at 10:00. They were used to haul ties to a Salida creosote plant from 1926 to 1953.
1.0
139.1 Reddish-brown outcrops of Oligocene welded tuffs behind Spiral Drive at 10:00. River terrace from 10:00 to 12:15.
0.3
139.4 Junction with Colorado 291 on left. CONTINUE STRAIGHT AHEAD.
0.1
139.5 Bridge over the South Fork of the Arkansas River near its junction with the main stream. Annual boat races are held down the Arkansas from this point to Cotopaxi (13 miles downstream).
0.9
140.4 Highway curves to left. Junction with Chaffee County 105 on left. Light colored Dry Union beds at 12:30 dip to the south off a knob of Precambrian granodiorite exposed at the bridge ahead.
0.2
140.6 Entrance to Rocky Mountain Livestock Market and Cleora Station of D&R.G.W. on left. Road cut in Precambrian granodiorite on right.
0.4
141.0 At 3:00 contact of granodiorite on right with Precambrian metasedimentary rocks on left. Note prospect pits. The road cuts will be in Precambrian rocks for the next 1.8 miles at which point we will enter east-dipping beds of Lower Paleozoic age.
0.2
141.2 Bridge over Silver Heel Creek.
0.6
141.8 Bridge over Bear Creek.
0.2
142.0 Curve to right. East-dipping Ordovician formations visible ahead. They are in ascending stratigraphic order: Manitou Dolomite, Harding Sandstone and Fremont Limestone.
0.7
142.7 Entering Fremont County.
0.5
143.2 Ordovician Manitou Dolomite in road cut on right. Overlying the Manitou is a reddish-gray series of sandstones and shales of the Harding Sandstone followed by massive gray dolomites of the Fremont. The red zone across the river belongs to the Harding Sandstone.
0.2
143.4 Quarry to north of Arkansas River in Fremont Limestone. Syncline at 12:00 in cliff above the highway; the Fremont Limestone is at road level and the brownish beds above are the Parting Sandstone of the Chaffee Group (Upper Devonian).
0.2
143.6 Road cut in Fremont Limestone on right.
0.2
143.8 Curve to right. Well-exposed synclinal fold across the river. A major northwest-trending fault zone passes just north of the river.
0.2
144.0 Across the river, some of the pink shales of the Harding Sandstone are involved in the faulting. The brown beds are sandstones of the Parting Sandstone.
0.9
144.9 The large travertine quarry across the river is located in a fault zone in the Leadville Limestone of Mississippian age. At the village of Calcite, about 4 miles to the southeast, travertine has been extensively quarried from the same fault zone. The travertine appears to have

Distorted beds of Harding (pink shales) and Parting (sandstone) at milepost 144.0.

Beautiful Salida nestled in the Arkansas River Valley. Sawatch Range in background. View is to the southwest from atop Tenderfoot Hill.

been deposited by ground waters flowing along faults in the cavernous Leadville Limestone.

0.3

145.2 Leadville Limestone in large road cut on right. Junction with Box Canyon road ahead on right. The canyon is in the Leadville Limestone. The Pennsylvanian Kerber Formation begins at about the base of the telephone pole on the east side of the canyon. Coal dumps nearby contain plant spores of Early Pennsylvanian age. Across the Arkansas River the Pennsylvanian beds begin east of the travertine quarry and consist of cyclical thin limestones and red shales. The limestones become less abundant upward in the section. Tertiary andesite flows cap the high ridge north of the river.

0.2

145.4 Road cut in the Kerber Formation, followed by road cut in Sharpsdale Formation of Pennsylvanian age. SLOW. Stop 4 ahead.

1.1

146.5 Entering Swissvale.

0.1

146.6 STOP 4. Pull off into borrow pit on right for discussion of Permo-Pennsylvanian stratigraphy and tectonics. Note Tertiary lava flow at 11:00 deposited on slope of paleovalley.

The thick sequence of Pennsylvanian and Permian sedimentary rocks that comprise much of the northern Sangre de Cristo Range are well exposed along the Arkansas River Valley. The exposures, combined with fairly simple structures, have facilitated the study of this sequence of rocks and they have been subdivided, primarily on the basis of color, into five mappable units; Kerber Formation, Sharpsdale Formation, Madera Formation and Upper and Lower members of the Sangre de Cristo Formation. From this vantage point the distinct color differences of the Kerber (buff), Sharpsdale (deep red) and Madera (reddish green) may be seen to the northwest.

Correlation of these units along the Sangre de Cristo Range and subsequent stratigraphic studies have led to the hypothesis that major faulting occurred throughout much of the Pennsylvanian and Permian. This faulting not only controlled the shape of the Central Colorado trough but strongly affected the sedimentation patterns. Many of these faults were reactivated during the Laramide.

0.3

146.9 Road cuts on right in Madera Limestone of Pennsylvanian age (see De Voto, Peel, and Pierce, this guidebook).

0.2

147.1 Contact between Madera Formation and Sangre de Cristo Formation of Pennsylvanian and Permian age on right.

0.3

147.4 Tertiary lava flows capping the Lower Member of the Sangre de Cristo Formation ahead. Coal dump on left across Arkansas River.

0.2

147.6 Bridge over Spring Creek.

0.2

147.8 Cross section of SE-trending paleovalley at 10:00 (opposite turnout on right) carved in the Sangre de Cristo Formation and filled with porphyritic andesite and andesitic gravel of Late Tertiary age. Ancestral Arkansas Valley? Note lava tube with concentric joint pattern in lowest part of channel.

0.8

148.6 Roadside table. Paleovalley again at 11:00.

0.6

149.2 Railroad and pipeline bridges on left. Badger Creek Valley enters from north. Unconformity between the Lower and Upper members of the Sangre de Cristo Formation at 9:00. The low hills are the Lower Member; the color change at the break in slope is the base of the Upper Member. Late Tertiary lava flow dipping towards river at 11:00.

0.5

149.7 Gray beds across the river are the tuffs of Badger Creek, an Oligocene ash-flow of the Thirtynine Mile field.

0.3

150.0 Bridge.

0.6

150.6 Jakes Beaver Pond. SLOW. Caravan leaves highway 0.2 mile ahead. Tertiary stock and Cottonwood Peak at 12:00. The stock has intruded east-dipping Pennsylvanian and Permian clastic rocks. At 2:00 the Three Sisters Peaks in the northern Sangre de Cristo Range are composed of Precambrian rock on their west sides and summits; the flatirons on their east faces are formed by Lower Paleozoic formations. Hayden Pass is at 1:00; here the east-dipping Paleozoic beds cross over the crest of the Sangre de Cristo Range and comprise the bulk of the range for many miles to the south. The Wet Mountain Valley, a Late Tertiary NNW-trending graben, which bounds the Sangre de Cristo Range on the east, is partly visible at 11:00.

Three Sisters Peaks near Howard.

0.2
150.8 Entering Howard. TURN RIGHT on dirt road about 50 feet before the Howard sign.
0.1
150.9 Curve left past A-frame. TAKE UPPER ROAD through the Holliday Hills subdivision. *Drive slowly* and watch for children.
0.2
151.1 BEAR LEFT between houses.
0.1
151.2 TURN LEFT down hill.
0.1
151.3 Note spectacular unconformity at 10:00 between the Sangre de Cristo Formation and a Late Tertiary lava flow which congealed on the side of a paleovalley.
0.1
151.4 Junction with U.S. 50. TURN LEFT towards Salida. After turn, Big Baldy Mountain at 11:30. Salida and the Rio Grande rift zone are behind it.
1.0
152.4 Bridge. Sawatch Range at 11:30.
0.7
153.1 Pipeline bridge across the Arkansas River and railroad bridge over Badger Creek on right. Badger Creek is the major drainage along the east side of the Arkansas Hills and heads along the southern edge of South Park. It has carved a very rugged and largely inaccessible gorge extending for 14 miles from here to Gribbles Park. Large springs issue from the Leadville Limestone near the head of the gorge and contribute large quantities of water to the stream. In the lower half of the gorge, Badger Creek follows the east-dipping, high-angle, Pleasant Valley thrust.
0.2
153.3 Note unconformity in Pennsylvanian-Permian beds at 12:30 (just over powerline).
0.9
154.2 River terrace and small hogback on inside of

meander bend.
1.2
155.4 Entering Swissvale.
1.6
157.0 U.S. Soil Conditioning plant at Wellsville across river. Travertine quarry behind plant.
0.6
157.6 Folded and faulted Lower Paleozoic strata at 12:30. Note unconformity at 1:00 where terrace gravels were deposited on beveled Paleozoic beds.
1.7
159.3 Entering Chaffee County.
1.5
160.8 Bridge over Silver Heel Creek. Prospect pits on left at contact between Precambrian metasedimentary rocks on the east and Precambrian granodiorite on the west. Entering upper Arkansas Valley. Note U-shaped glacial valley in the Sawatch Range at 12:00.
1.2
162.0 Chalk Cliffs and Mt. Princeton at 11:30. Note steep dip into the graben of interbedded basalt flows and gravels on Tenderfoot Hill (Spiral Drive) at 12:30.
0.4
162.4 Bridge over South Fork of Arkansas River. Junction of U.S. 50 and Colorado 291. CONTINUE LEFT on U.S. 50. *Stop at the gas station of your choice. The caravan will reassemble on U.S. 50 between Salida and Poncha Springs just west of the Roley Egg Farm Road. Numerous gas stations are available between this junction and the Salida Municipal Swimming Pool.*
0.9
163.3 Entering Salida (7,036′).
0.6
163.9 Salida Hot Springs and Municipal Swimming Pool on right. There are no gas stations between here and Poncha Springs.
0.9
164.8 Tilted Dry Union beds at 9:00, Reynolds fluorspar mine at 10:30, Cleveland Mountain and Poncha Pass at 11:00, rift zone gravels from 11:30 to 12:30, Monarch Pass at 1:00.
0.5
165.3 Junction with Chaffee County 125 (road to Roley Egg Farm) on right. *Reassemble caravan on right shoulder* west of the junction.
1.9
167.2 Entering Poncha Springs. Elevation 7,380 ft.
0.5
167.7 Three-pronged junction of U.S. 50 and U.S.

Amphibolite dikes in road cut at milepost 170.5.

285. CONTINUE STRAIGHT AHEAD on middle prong to stop sign.
0.1
167.8 Stop sign. TURN LEFT towards Poncha Pass on U.S. 285.
2.7
170.5 In road cut ahead on right, Precambrian basic dikes (amphibolites) injected into micaceous quartzites.
5.1
175.6 Summit of Poncha Pass. Elevation 9,010 ft.
5.1
180.7 Note faceted spurs of Sangre de Cristo Range at 10:00. Sierra Blanca and sand dunes at 12:00.
9.4
190.1 Junction with Bonanza Road on right. Hayden Pass at 9:00. Villa Grove ahead.
1.5
191.6 Sangre de Cristo Mountains in New Mexico at 11:00. Complexly folded and faulted Permo-Pennsylvanian rocks in low hills at 1:00.
3.1
194.7 Junction with Colorado 17 on left. CONTINUE STRAIGHT AHEAD on U.S. 285 towards Saguache. Precambrian rocks in low hills at 2:00.
1.4
196.1 Road to Mineral Hot Springs on left. CONTINUE STRAIGHT AHEAD. San Juan Mountains ahead. Knobs of Precambrian rocks at 2:30.
1.8
197.9 Rocks of the Bonanza volcanic pile dipping south from 12:00 to 2:00.
2.1
200.0 Powerline.

North-south trending Sangre de Cristo Range at the north end of the San Luis Basin. View is south from Alder Creek.

3.3
203.3 Knob of Precambrian rocks overlain by Bonanza Tuff at 3:00.
0.9
204.2 Curve to right around ridge of Bonanza volcanic rocks.
0.4
204.6 Road cut on right in laharic (mudflow) breccias and fluvial volcaniclastic sediments of the Rawley Andesite. These units are typical of much of the lower portion of the Rawley elsewhere in the area.
0.4
205.0 Road cuts in laharic breccias of the Rawley Andesite. Rattlesnake Hill on left.
3.2
208.2 Road cut on right in stratified volcaniclastic sandstone overlain by laharic breccias.
0.3
208.5 Road cuts in mudflow breccias of Rawley Andesite.
0.2
208.7 Entering Saguache, Colorado. (Elev. 7,775 ft.). Road cut on right in volcanic rocks of the Bonanza center.
0.4
209.1 Junction with Colorado 114. CONTINUE STRAIGHT AHEAD to Colorado 114.
1.8
210.9 Airport on left. Houghland Hill at 11:30 is capped by Hinsdale Basalt of Miocene or Pliocene age, the slope below the caprock is the Carpenter Ridge Tuff and the cliffs about half way down the hill are of the Fish Canyon Tuff. Both are Oligocene (26 to 28 m.y.) ash-flow tuffs erupted from calderas near Creede. The lower slope is the Oligocene Bonanza Tuff of the Bonanza volcanic center. The low hills at 1:00 are the Rawley Andesite which is an extensive blanket of intermediate lavas and breccias erupted from many centers. The Rawley Andesite is equivalent to the lower part of the Conejos Formation in the San Juan field. From 1:00 to 2:00 the Bonanza Tuff comprises the lower two-thirds of the hill and is capped by andesitic flows and breccias. The Fish Canyon Tuff is missing north of the highway. Pumice processing plant at 3:00. Rawley Andesite behind plant.

Five south-dipping cooling units of the Bonanza Tuff at 1:00 can be seen to merge northward into two units. This exposure is on the south flank of the Bonanza center which is about 12 miles to the NNE near the old mining town of Bonanza. Burbank (1937) recognized that doming and subsequent collapse had occurred in the Bonanza volcanic center. Karig (1965) demonstrated that a gravity low, about 10 miles in diameter and with at least 12 mgal closure, existed at Bonanza and approximately coincided with a circle of peaks about the district. He also pointed to the quaquaversal dips of ash-flow tuffs away from the center and to the existence of basement rocks at relatively high elevations on three sides of the Bonanza volcanic center. The district is being mapped in detail as part of the Bonanza Remote Sensing Project of the Colorado School of Mines.
1.1
212.0 Road to Findley Gulch on right.
1.8
213.8 The low hills in the valley to the left are Precambrian rocks.
0.9
214.7 More small knobs of Precambrian rocks to the left.
0.9
215.6 Bridge.
0.5
216.1 Road cuts in Precambrian rocks.
0.6
216.1 Road cuts in Precambrian rocks. lain by Rawley Andesite.
0.5
217.2 Cliffs on right are crystal-rich latitic ash flows of the Bonanza Tuff. The lower reddish hills in the background are Bonanza Tuff overlain by andesitic flows and breccias. On Houghland Hill at 9:00, the Fish Canyon Tuff forms cliffs about halfway up and is overlain by the Carpenter Ridge Tuff. Hinsdale Basalt caps the hill.
1.0
218.2 Curve to right. Fault at 9:00 cutting Bonanza Tuff. The west side is up. Note drag on east side.
1.3
219.5 Laharic breccias of the Rawley Andesite on right. These breccias are on the southeast flank of the Jacks Creek volcanic center.
0.2
219.7 Ranch road on right leads up the Middle Creek Valley formed by erosion along a pre-volcanic fault on which there was minor post-volcanic displacement. This fault continues to Marshall Pass, about 16 miles to the north, where it is exposed in Precambrian rocks.
0.3
220.0 TURN RIGHT onto Jacks Creek Road.

Jacks Creek volcano.

0.3
220.3 Road cut to right in Rawley Andesite. Bonanza Tuff on left.

0.6
220.9 Road forks. BEAR RIGHT, then loop to left around Forest Service sign and retrace route to highway for Stop 5. Note east-dipping flows and breccias on the flanks of the Jacks Creek andesitic volcano. The center of the structure is about 2 miles up the road to the left. At 9:00 the flows and breccias dip southeast away from the center.

1.0
221.9 STOP 5. Discussion of the stratigraphic relationships between rocks of the San Juan volcanic field and the Bonanza volcanic center (see Bruns, Epis, Steven and Weimer, this guidebook; also Lipman, Steven, and Mehnert, 1970).

The hill to the west is the southeast flank of the Jacks Creek volcano within the Rawley Andesite (31.1 to 34.7 m.y.). The low bench in front of the hill is the Bonanza Tuff which is younger than the Rawley. Note that here it is topographically lower but stratigraphically higher. The Jacks Creek volcano was deeply eroded and breached before eruption of the Bonanza Tuff. The cliff in the middle background to the left of the hill is the Fish Canyon Tuff (27.8 m.y.) which flowed around the flanks of the Jacks Creek volcano and into the breached center. The Fish Canyon Tuff continues upstream to the southwest and forms the cliff at the bend in the river. The low cliffs along the valley floor and beneath the Fish Canyon Tuff are the Sapinero Mesa Tuff and interbedded air-fall tuffs. The hill to the south across Sagauche Creek is capped by Fish Canyon Tuff resting on the Bonanza Tuff.

The early intermediate flows and breccias of the Bonanza area are called the Rawley Andesite (33.4, 34.2 m.y.) and are correlative in age and lithology with the lower part of the Conejos Formation (32.1 m.y. to 34.7 m.y.) of the San Juan field. After a period of erosion, the Bonanza Tuff was erupted from the Bonanza center; hydrothermal alteration and base metal deposition followed. The Bonanza Tuff has not yet been dated but it is older than the Fish Canyon Tuff (27.8 m.y.) of the San Juan field and younger than the Rawley Andesite (33.4, 34.2 m.y.).

Lipman (1970) and Lipman, Steven, and Mehnert (1970) have pointed out that most Cenozoic volcanic fields in the western United States began with copious outpourings of intermediate lavas onto eroded tectonically stable terrains. These lavas are predominantly alkalic andesites which had a remarkable tendency to brecciate; true basalts are rare. They estimate that in the San Juan field intermediate rocks covered an area of more than 25,000 km^2 and had an original volume of at least 40,000 km^3. The Rawley Andesite of the Bonanza field and the Thirtynine Mile Andesite (34 m.y.) are comparable to the Conejos Formation in age, lithology and position at the base of their respective volcanic piles. The younger caldera complexes appear to have formed by collapse resulting from voluminous ash-flow eruptions from silicic cupolas over larger batholiths of andesitic composition. In Early Miocene time, the character of volcanism changed from intermediate lavas and somewhat more silicic ash-flows to a bimodal association of alkali olivine basalt and silicic alkali rhyolite. This change coincided with development of the Rio Grande rift zone and widespread crustal extension in western North America.

TURN LEFT onto Colorado 114 and proceed back to Saguache.
1.5
223.4 Rise in road at curve. Cliff at 11:00 to 12:00 is the Bonanza Tuff overlain by andesite flows.
5.3
228.7 Culvert. Note change of dip in Conejos Formation (?) on ridge from 1:00 to 3:00.

Road cut south of Saguache in felsic lava flow at milepost 235.4.

1.2
229.9 Findley Gulch Road on left. Rawley Andesite at 12:00 dips to south away from the Bonanza center.
2.6
232.5 Entering Saguache, Colorado.
0.3
232.8 Junction with U.S. 285. TURN RIGHT and proceed towards Monte Vista, Colorado.
1.2
234.0 Bridge over Saguache Creek.
0.8
234.8 Junction with road to Moffat on left. CONTINUE STRAIGHT AHEAD. Large road cut ahead in felsic lava flow.
0.6
235.4 Large road cut with spectacular exposure of the contact between two felsic lava flows. The north half of the cut shows coarse autobrecciated rubble at top of lower flow overlain by 2 to 6 feet of volcaniclastic sediments and tuffs. The upper flow has an autobrecciated rubble zone at the base and was probably moving east as a lobate flow.
1.8
237.2 High mountains of Summitville area at 1:00.
4.6
241.8 First of several artesian wells on left. The water table nearly coincides with the ground surface in this part of the San Luis Valley—"drool you desert rats!"

1.3
243.1 Bridge. Outcrop of water table on left is known as Russell Lakes (see Emery, this guidebook).
1.2
244.3 Bridge.
6.2
250.5 Road to La Garita on right. The dipping volcanic rocks at 2:00 are on the flanks of the Summer Coon volcano (32.4 m.y.) in the Conejos Formation (see Supplemental Log No. 2, this guidebook). Sand dunes at 9:00.
5.7
256.2 Farmer's Union Canal.
0.5
256.7 Junction with Colorado 112. CONTINUE STRAIGHT AHEAD. Enter Rio Grande County.
5.0
261.7 Junction with Colorado 374. CONTINUE STRAIGHT AHEAD.
4.7
266.4 Bridge over Rio Grande. Entering Monte Vista, Colorado.
2.0
268.4 Crossing D&RG narrow gauge line to Creede; built in 1881.
0.1
268.5 Junction with Colorado 160 in Monte Vista. TURN LEFT toward Alamosa.
16.3
284.8 City limits of Alamosa. END OF LOG.

SPECIAL STEAM EXCURSION
Cumbres and Toltec Scenic Railroad
Antonito, Colorado to Chama, New Mexico   October 2, 1971

BREAKFAST

Menu

À LA CARTE

STRAWBERRIES AND CREAM, 20
FRESH FRUIT, 15   PRESERVED FIGS, 20
CRACKED WHEAT, WITH CREAM, 20   OAT MEAL, WITH CREAM, 20

COFFEE, PER CUP, 10   COFFEE, PER POT, 15
MILK, PER GLASS, 10
COFFEE, PER POT, FOR TWO, 25   CREAM, PER GLASS, 15
ENGLISH BREAKFAST OR GREEN TEA, PER POT, 15.. PER POT, FOR TWO, 25
CHOCOLATE OR COCOA, WITH WHIPPED CREAM, PER CUP, 15

CELERY, 15   CUCUMBERS, 15   SLICED TOMATOES, 15

BROILED WHITE FISH, 35   BROILED OR BOILED SALT MACKEREL, 35
MOUNTAIN TROUT IN SEASON,   CODFISH BALLS, 30

TENDERLOIN STEAK, 50   SIRLOIN STEAK, 60
EXTRA SIRLOIN STEAK, FOR TWO, 1.00
SPRING CHICKEN, WHOLE, 85; HALF, 50   LAMB CHOPS, 45
MUTTON CHOPS, 40   BACON (FULL ORDER), 35
BROILED OR FRIED HAM, 35   VEAL CUTLET, PLAIN OR BREADED, 40
HAM AND EGGS, 50   CALF'S LIVER AND BACON, 40
BACON AND EGGS, 40

WITH ABOVE ORDERS (EXTRA)
MUSHROOMS OR FRENCH PEAS, 15   TOMATO SAUCE, 10
RASHER OF BACON, 10

EGGS
BOILED, FRIED, SCRAMBLED, SHIRRED, 20   PLAIN OMELET, 20
POACHED, ON TOAST, 30   HAM, CHEESE, OR JELLY OMELET, 30
SPANISH OR MUSHROOM OMELET, 35

POTATOES
BAKED OR FRENCH FRIED, 10   LYONNAISE, 15
HASHED BROWN, 15   GERMAN FRIED, 15   AU GRATIN, 15

HOT ROLLS, 10   CORN MUFFINS, 10   DRY TOAST, 10   MILK TOAST, 15
BUTTERED TOAST, 10   CREAM TOAST, 25
WHEAT CAKES, WITH MAPLE SYRUP, 20

BREAD, BUTTER AND FRENCH FRIED OR BAKED POTATOES SERVED WITH MEAT OR FISH ORDERS WITHOUT EXTRA CHARGE.

NO ORDER TAKEN OR CHECK ISSUED FOR A LESS AMOUNT THAN 25 CENTS FOR EACH PERSON. A CHARGE OF 25 CENTS IS MADE FOR EACH EXTRA PERSON SERVED FROM A SINGLE MEAT OR FISH ORDER.

SERVICE BY WAITER OUTSIDE OF DINING CAR, 25 CENTS EXTRA FOR EACH PERSON SERVED.

THIS MENU MAY BE RETAINED AS A SOUVENIR

Reprinted from: Narrow Gauge in the Rockies by Lucius Beebe and Charles Clegg (Howell-North Books)

Wine List

		QTS.	PTS.
CHAMPAGNES	G. H. Mumm & Co., Extra Dry	4.00	2.00
	Pommery & Greno "Sec"	4.00	2.00
	Moet & Chandon White Seal	4.00	2.00
	Dry Monopole H. & Co., Extra	4.00	2.00
	Veuve Cliquot, Yellow Label	4.00	2.00
	Cook's Imperial	2.00	1.25
	Ruinart Vin Brut, half pts. only, 1.00		
WHITE WINES	Latour Blanche, Cruse Fils Freres	2.50	1.50
	Haut Sauterne, Cruse Fils Freres	2.00	1.00
CLARETS	St. Julien, Cruse Fils Freres	1.25	.75
	Pontet Canet, Cruse Fils Freres	2.00	1.00
	Chateau La Rose, Cruse Fils Freres	2.50	1.50
RHINE WINES	Rudesheimer, Carl Acker	2.00	1.00
	Niersteiner, Carl Acker	1.50	.75
CALIFORNIA WINES	Chablis (C. C. McIver)	.75	.50
	Linda Vista Zinfandel (C. C. McIver)	.75	.50
	Riesling Anslese (C. C. McIver)	.75	.50
	Sauterne (Cresta Blanca), (1-2 pts., 25)	.75	.50
	St. Julien (Cresta Blanca)	.75	.50
ALES, BEERS, ETC.	Bass & Co., D. H. & W. L.		.30
	Guinness Extra Stout		.30
	Zang's, Neff's and Coor's Denver Beers		.20
	Salt Lake, Fisher, Wagner and Margett's Salt Lake City Beers		.20
	Pabst Export		.20
	Schlitz Export		.20
	Lemp's Extra Pale		.20
	Anheuser-Busch Budweiser		.20
	Club Soda, C. & C.		.25
	Imported Ginger Ale, C. & C.		.25
	Manitou Ginger Champagne		.25

		1-4 PT.	GLASS.
LIQUORS, ETC.	Old Sherry, 1-2 Pint, 50		
	Walker's Canadian Club, 1-2 pt., 50	.40	.20
	Bourbon Whiskey	.40	.20
	Rye Whiskey	.40	.20
	Scotch Whiskey		.25
	Brandy	.50	.30
	Plymouth or Holland Gin	.40	.20
	Club Cocktails, Whiskey, Gin, Etc.		.20
	Creme de Menthe		.20
	Lemonade		.15

			PTS.
WATERS, ETC.	Manitou Water		.25
	Apollinaris Water		.25
	Hathorn Water		.25
	Hunyadi, Glass, 15; Bottle, 35.		
	Bromo Soda, Glass, 10; Bottle, 35.		
CIGARS	Havana, Key West and Domestic, 10 each; 2 for 25; 15 each; 3 for 50; 25 each Cigarettes, Domestic, 15 and 20 per package; Imported, 45 per pkg. Playing Cards, 50 per pack.		

Reprinted from: *Narrow Gauge in the Rockies* by Lucius Beebe and Charles Clegg (Howell-North Books)

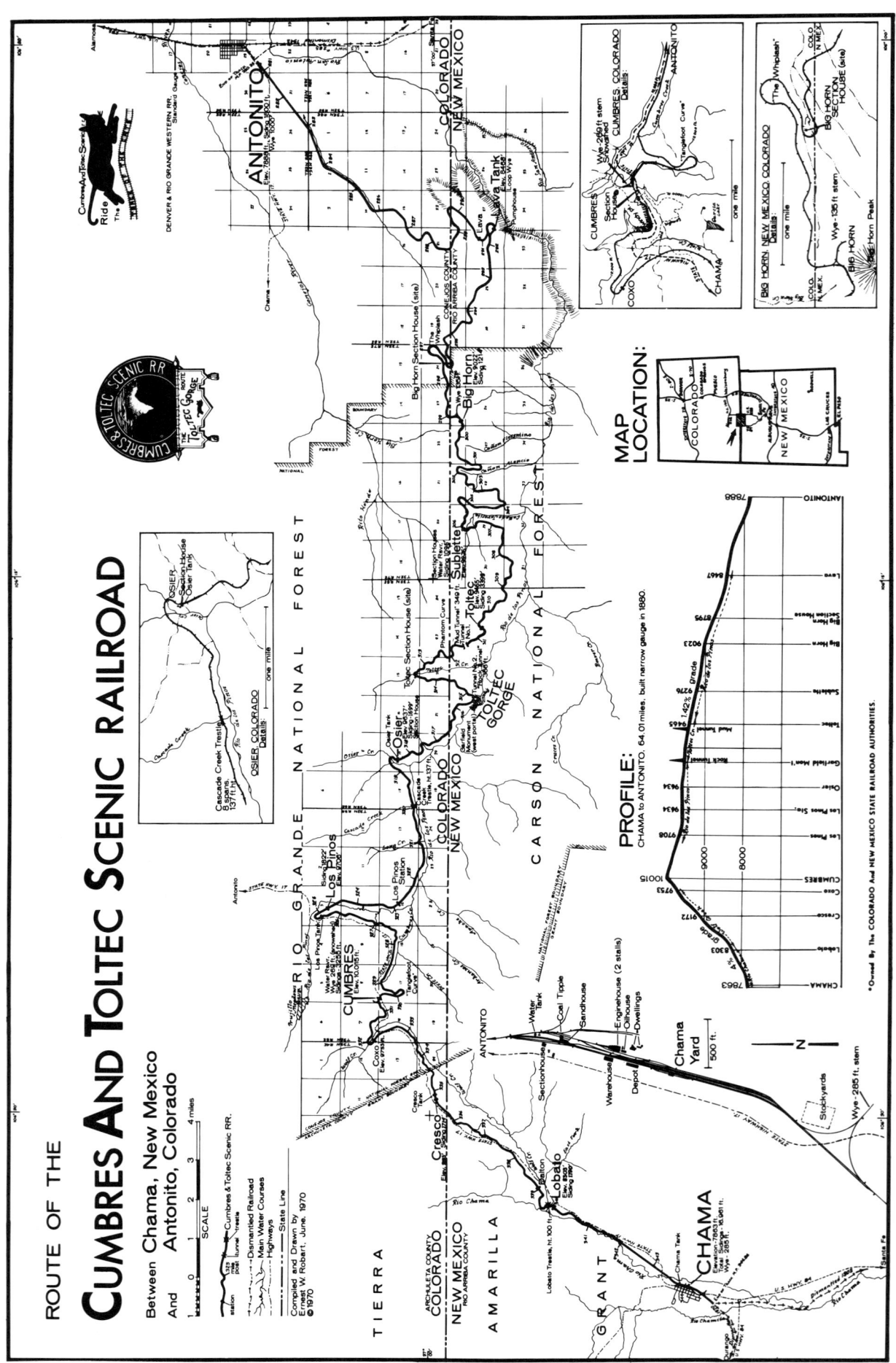

THIRD DAY

RAIL LOG

ANTONITO, COLORADO TO CHAMA, NEW MEXICO

October 2, 1971

ASSEMBLY: Board busses at east football field parking lot at Adams State College for charter to Antonito.
TIME: 7:00-7:30 A.M. (Busses). 8:30-9:00 A.M. (Train)
DISTANCE: 64 miles.
TRIP LEADERS: Richard L. Burroughs, Arthur P. Butler.

PREFACE:

Today we ride the Track of The CATS—The Cumbres And Toltec Scenic Railroad. A resurrected bit of Americana saved by far-sighted individuals with a keen sense of history and a love of national heritage; to be preserved and enjoyed for decades to come. In marked contrast to the country's number one railroad newsmaker, AMTRAK, the Cumbres And Toltec will sell its passengers on ancient equipment and leisurely train speeds through scenic mountain country along the southern shoulders of the San Juan Mountains.

Today we step back in history—a nostalgic step into an era of the mournful wail of a steam engine, the aroma of coal, a trail of ashes above your head, and an occasional cinder in the eye. As we head west from Antonito and slowly leave the San Luis Valley and begin the ascent of the bordering hills, let your imagination go—indeed it could easily be the 19th century again.

In 1880, lured by $3 a day salaries, gangs of gutty French-Canadians wrestled with a mountain to carve a railroad in southern Colorado and northern New Mexico. It took over a year of sweat and shivers to lay a winding track of 64 miles from Antonito, Colorado, to Chama, New Mexico; to move 35 miles "as the crow flies." At the "Whiplash," 17 miles west of Antonito, the rail bed had to double back twice on itself (making three parallel tracks) to gain the altitude of Big Horn Mesa. The Durango, Colorado HERALD quipped, "that section hands who worked the 'whiplash' were generally pretty well acquainted with passengers before the train actually passed."

The line, then known as the Denver And Rio Grande Western, originated in Denver. Its overall scheme was to push through to the rich mining fields at Durango and Silverton. It turned out to be one of the wildest and most remote ventures to be found anywhere. The Antonito-Chama section of the line has been described as "one of the most awesomely spectacular examples of mountain railroading in North America. The 64-mile trek features fantastic geologic displays as tracks negotiate the infamous "Phantom Curve" and "Calico Cut" and tunnels the brim of 1,100-foot Toltec Gorge. Magnificent "high country" scenery develops along the Rio de Los Pinos (River of the Pines) and "over-the-top" at 10,015-foot aspen-colored Cumbres Pass, billed as the highest railroad pass in the United States. Enroute are the rail ghost towns of Sublette and Osier, both dating back to the construction of the line.

Scheduled passenger service on the line, the *San Juan Express*, America's last narrow gauge luxury train, made its final run on January 31, 1951. Freight hauling continued until 1968 when the D&RGW petitioned the ICC for complete abandonment. A "grass-roots" campaign, headed by conservation groups and railroad

Get it right the first time!

clubs, began shortly thereafter to save the "Little Train" and its trackage and facilities from being razed. The effort culminated in 1970 when the progressive legislatures of Colorado and New Mexico established a Joint Railroad Authority and purchased the line for $547,210. In 1971 additional operating and restoration funds were appropriated by the states and Scenic Railways Inc. of Los Altos, California, was selected to operate the railroad.

On June 27, 1971, the railroad made its inaugural run carrying legislators and members of the press of both states. The first year of operation included 16 public trips; eight originating at each terminal. On this date, October 2, 1971, the NEW MEXICO GEOLOGICAL SOCIETY is proud to be the first scheduled charter excursion aboard the "high-flying" Cumbres And Toltec Scenic Railroad.

The mileages given in the log are at mileposts along the track and represent the distance by rail from Denver. For the most part geologic discussions are keyed to these mileposts or recognizable features such as curves, bridges, cattleguards, cuts, etc. The geologic strip maps will further aid in locating specific points. The maps were taken from several sources, most at different scales, and representing various degrees of detail. For this reason the geology from one map to the next will not match exactly in every case.

280.0 Antonito, Colorado (7,888′) is the eastern terminus of the Cumbres And Toltec Scenic Rail-

New Mexico Geological Society—Twenty-Second Field Conference

road. Established in the late 1870's it is oriented principally to the servicing of area ranches and farms.

Grade crossing of U.S. 285 at western yard limit.

1.0

281.0 Grade crossing opposite Colorado Highway Department maintenance yard.

1.0

282.0 Grade crossing just beyond milepost. The tracks are crossing the alluvial fan of the Conejos (Spanish for "rabbit") River and heading west into a rather broad valley bordered by basalt-capped mesas. Los Mogotes ("horns of young animals") (9,820′) at 2:00; Blanca Peak (14,-363′) at 5:00; San Luis Hills at 6:00; Sangre de Cristo Mountains in New Mexico at 8:00; Cerro de La Olla (9,464′) at 9:00; San Antonio Mountain (10,935′) at 10:00; and Big Horn Peak (9,442′) at 12:00.

1.0

283.0 Approaching western border of the San Luis Valley. The scenery is characterized by wide sweeping vistas as the line traverses an area of high semi-arid plains. Sagebrush and chamisa being the principal ground cover. The area abounds in game, with jackrabbits and cottontails by literally the thousands, and numerous deer.

1.0

284.0 Curve to left. Cisneros Basalt (Barker, 1958) caps the mesa to the right. Los Mogotes is the probable source for this flow. Mesas on both

Recently constructed CATS station at Antonito.

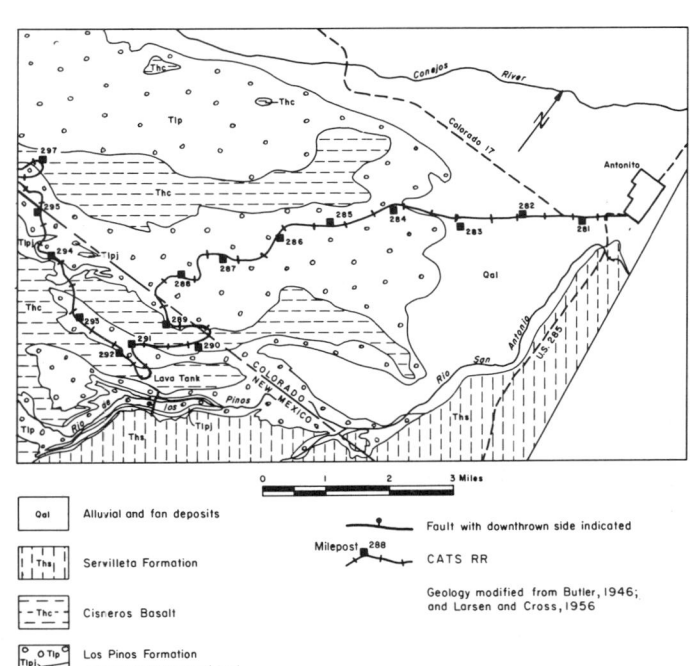

Geology between mileposts 281 and 294.

sides are underlain by gravels of the Los Pinos Formation.

1.87

285.87 Bridge.

0.13

286.0 Cuts in tuffaceous sandstones of the Los Pinos Formation.

1.0

287.0 Cattleguard and curve ahead. Cut beyond bridge in basalt flow in the Los Pinos Formation. The flow is probably equivalent to the Jarita Basalt (Barker, 1958) that will be seen at Stop 1. (see Butler, this guidebook).

1.25

288.25 Long curve to the left. At cattleguard beyond enter New Mexico; the first of eleven state line crossings. Note vegetation change along fence line separating the two states. Railroad begins ascent at Lava Tank Mesa. Cuts ahead in Jarita Basalt and sandstones of the Los Pinos Formation.

0.75

289.0 Slump blocks of Cisneros Basalt. Good view of Blanca Peak and San Luis Hills ahead and Los Mogotes to the left.

Nearing crest of Lava Tank Mesa. Reenter Colorado and abruptly return to New Mexico at curve on the summit. Cuts in Cisneros Basalt capping Lava Tank Mesa.

1.0

290.0 Lava Station ahead on right ("don't blink, its a small lobby type"). Exposures of sandstones and conglomerates of the Cordito Member of the Los Pinos Formation.

1.0

291.0 STOP 1. Lava Tank (8,468'). Approximately half way between mileposts 291 and 292. Walk south to escarpment of the Rio de Los Pinos for discussion of Tertiary stratigraphy.

The lower basalt in the canyon wall is the Jarita Member of the Los Pinos Formation. The Jarita Basalt pinches out to the southwest

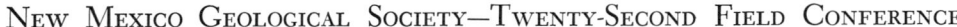

Lava Tank backdropped by rotundus San Antonio Mountain.

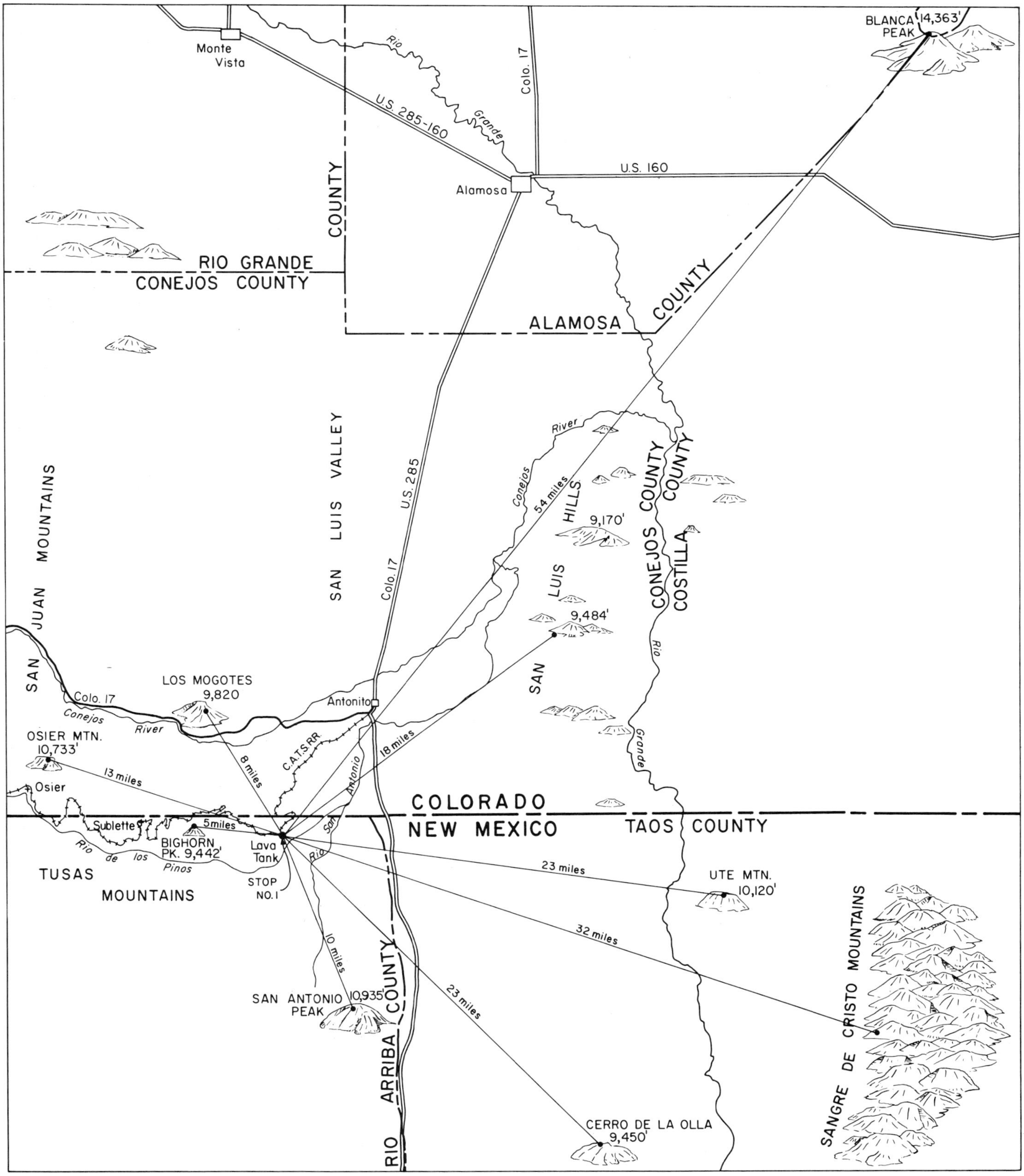

New Mexico Geological Society—Twenty-Second Field Conference

PANORAMIC INDEX FROM STOP 1

about a mile upstream but reappears as the cap-rock on the wooded mesa about 4 miles to the southwest. At the overlook we are standing on Cisneros Basalt, the lowermost flow unit of the Hinsdale volcanic series in this area. The rimrock on the other side of the canyon is Servilleta Basalt, the youngest member of the Hinsdale. The Servilleta overlies an erosion surface that truncates the upper part of the Los Pinos Formation and the Jarita Basalt Member. Servilleta basalts and interbedded conglomerates underlie the Taos Plateau to the south.

The basalt interpreted as belonging to the Jarita Basalt Member of Barker (1958) in the vicinity of the Rio de Los Pinos is represented by two slightly different types of rock. A more abundant variety is moderately fine-grained, sparsely prophyritic, and has some intergranular pore space. It carries small rusty-appearing phenocrysts of altered olivine and sparse phenocrysts of plagioclase gradational in size to those of the groundmass. Locally, it contains amygdules and veinlets of chalcedony. A less abundant variety contains sparse phenocrysts of pyroxene as well as those of plagioclase and olivine and lacks intergranular pores. The olivine is yellowish brown and only partly altered.

Flows of the Lower Basalt Member of the Hinsdale Formation, Cisneros Basalt of Barker (1958), the surface rock at this stop, consists mostly of inconspicuously porphyritic rock characterized by scattered phenocrysts of olivine and of sparse plagioclase, Elsewhere, some flows are conspicuously porphyritic and contain abundant plagioclase. Olivine in both is mostly fresh or only slightly altered. The groundmass of both varieties is very fine-grained to aphanitic. Small, smooth-walled, symmetrical vesicles are common in some flows, but they are rarely amygdaloidal.

The fine-grained to aphanitic, non-porous groundmass of the sparsely porphyritic variety aids in distinguishing it from basalt of the older Jarita Member and from that of the younger Servilleta Formation. The sharp contrast between plagioclase phenocrysts and groundmass is distinctive of the porphyritic variety.

Basalt of the Servilleta is generally coarse-grained, non-porphyritic to sub-porphyritic, and intergranular pore space is abundant. Plagioclase and olivine, mostly fresh, are generally distinguishable megascopically.

Los Mogotes, a vent west of Antonito, Colorado, and a hill about 6 miles southeast of San Antonio Mountain with gentle slopes and a summit crater, were sources for some flows of Cisneros Basalt. The sources for the Jarita Basalt Member of the Los Pinos Formation and for basalt of the Servilleta Formation have not been identified.

The rocks viewed at this stop accummulated during an interval of the Tertiary that extends possibly from Late Oligocene to the latter half of the Pliocene. The Los Pinos Formation rests on tuff of the Masonic Park, which has a radiometric age of 28.2 m.y. Basalt on the north rim of Los Mogotes, which overlies other flows that rest on the Los Pinos Formation, and a dike within the crater have a mean age of 5.0 m.y. A flow of Cisneros Basalt south of San Antonio Mountain overlies gravel that contains fragments of obsidian from No Agua Mountain, and obsidian from that mountain has a fission track-age of 4.8 m.y. As the flow at this stop and other flows of Cisneros Basalt farther south in New Mexico rest with a slight unconformity on the Los Pinos Formation, the main period of deposition of the Los Pinos Formation must have ended some time before basalt of those ages was erupted.

Volcanic activity in this general area ended with the eruption of basalt of the Servilleta Formation that caps the opposite (southeast) rim of the canyon of the Rio de Los Pinos. This was in the latter half of the Pliocene as indicated by ages (3.6 to 4.5 m.y.) of basalt flows in the Rio Grande Gorge west of Taos, New Mexico, including several of Servilleta type.

The San Luis Hills to the east are a fault block range of volcanics that are correlated with the Conejos Formation and are older than any of the volcanics seen thus far.

After leaving Lava Tank the railroad traverses a long cut in Cisneros Basalt.

    2.0

293.0 Track speed marker, 15 mph. The tracks in the valley below are about 5 rail miles away. Cuts ahead are in lower flow of the Cisneros Basalt, conglomerates and sandstones of the underlying Cordito Member of the Los Pinos Formation, and the Jarita Basalt.

The line now begins to gain in elevation. The shrubs of the lower elevations have begun to give way to the firs, spruce, Ponderosa pines, junipers, mountain mahogany, and aspen of the higher transition zones. Deer, and occasionally elk, along with a few bear characterize the big

Stop. 1. Canyon of the Rio de Los Pinos.

game of this area. Hunting is reportedly good. "Texas already knows that, though."

1.0
294.0 Rail cut in Jarita Basalt just beyond milepost.
1.0
295.0 Reenter Colorado. Los Pinos Formation in cut. Cisneros Basalt caps mesa across canyon to north. East dips of the Jarita Basalt are greater than the Cisneros Basalt.

The Los Pinos Formation consists largely of clastic rocks. In part, these were spread as an apron around centers of active volcanism, and in part were derived from erosion of older volcanic rocks. The part of the formation near the rail route consists of sandstone, tuffaceous sandstone, conglomerate, some air-fall tuff, and various mixtures of these lithologies.

Tuff is more common near the bottom of the formation than near the top. It is mostly felsic, buff, light gray, creamy white and composed of angular mineral grains distributed through a matrix of glass shards. Some of it contains angular pebbles.

Although beds of conglomerate, generally less than 10 feet thick, form only a small portion of the formation, cobbles and boulders litter most slopes underlain by it. The clasts are mostly less than 4 inches in diameter, but some are as much as 4 feet in diameter. They are mainly of volcanic rocks. Dark-colored andesite-like rocks are

distributed throughout but are particularly abundant near the base. Other conspicuous clasts are gray to maroon, coarsely porphyritic felsite in which phenocrysts of feldspar are as much as 1.5 cm long. Many other less distinctive types of rock are also present. The thickness of the Los Pinos Formation is about 600 feet in the valley of the Rio de Los Pinos directly south of here.

Reenter New Mexico before milepost 296.
1.0
296.0 Big Horn Curve. Reenter Colorado.
0.08
296.08 Bridge. Site of Big Horn section house (8,790') in small valley to the right. During earlier days of the line a hotel was operated here. It was a regular stop on passenger runs, specializing in excellent meals (see Ingersoll, this guidebook).

Entering the "Whiplash." Tracks just a little over 100 feet above us are almost two rail miles away. Good exposures of boulder gravels in the Los Pinos Formation ahead. Nearing top of Big Horn Mesa. Rail cuts in Cisneros Basalt.
0.92
297.0 Excellent view of Conejos River Valley and Los Mogotes to the north. Cuts ahead in Los Pinos Formation overlain by Cisneros Basalt.
1.0
298.0 Cisneros Basalt on right. Big Horn Peak ahead on the left.

1.0
299.0 A short distance beyond milepost reenter New Mexico.

Big Horn Wye. This "turn-around" marks the eastern tour limit of the CATS regular excursions departing from Chama.

Big Horn Peak is capped by the Jarita Basalt Member of the Los Pinos Formation. Beyond wye cuts are in conglomerates and sandstones of the Los Pinos Formation. Route continues in this formation to beyond milepost 303.
2.0
301.0 After curve (beyond milepost) railroad begins the first of several long loops around the heads of south-flowing tributaries to the Rio de Los Pinos. This tributary is called Canon Florentino.
1.0
302.0 Curve at head of Canon Atencio. Heading south toward the Rio de Los Pinos.
2.0
304.0 Deep cut with tuff of Masonic Park, a welded ash-flow at the top underlain by nonwelded tuff, underlain in turn in the lower portions of

Geology between mileposts 294 and 314.

"Perils of rail logging." Scene is west of Big Horn on first expedition in April.

the cut by tuffaceous sandstones and conglomerates of the Treasure Mountain Tuff.

The main welded part of the tuff is a gray to purple-gray, and locally pinkish rock that weathers to characteristic platy tablets. It is fine-grained fragmental to aphanitic and generally porphyritic. Plagioclase and biotite are the common phenocrysts; green pyroxene is generally sparsely present. It is from 50 to 100 feet thick on this side of the Rio de Los Pinos. As noted in the Platoro caldera road log, it was erupted from the Mount Hope caldera about 50 miles northwest from here.

Beyond cut a beautiful view opens up on the Rio de Los Pinos, one of the finest stretches of trout water in New Mexico.

Cliffs below are in Conejos andesite breccias.

Tracks curve northward up Canada Jarosita. Buildings to the northwest (at head of canyon) are at Sublette.
1.0

305.0 Just before milepost track crosses top of slabby-weathering tuff of Masonic Park. Low hills ahead and to the right are underlain by the Los Pinos Formation. Yard limit east of Sublette in tuff of Masonic Park underlain by the Treasure Mountain.
1.0

306.0 Sublette. Water stop, 5 minutes: DO NOT DETRAIN. Yard cuts in the Treasure Mountain Tuff. This formation was named by Larsen and Cross (1956). Along the route of the CATS it varies from 60 to 300 feet in thickness and unconformably overlies the Conejos Formation on a surface with a relief up to 300 feet. The basal unit in this vicinity is a welded ash-flow consisting of two parts, a generally lower part of black porphyritic vitrophyre and an upper more persistent part of dull brown, aphanitic and porphyritic rock. Overlying beds consist of ash-fall tuff, tuff breccia, tuffaceous sandstone, conglomerate and mudstone. The tuff of Masonic Park was formerly considered to be the top unit of the Treasure Mountain Formation and was informally named the Osier Mountain Welded Tuff by Trice, 1957. The tracing of the unit from Mount Hope caldera resulted in the separation of the unit from the Treasure Mountain and establishing of a type section at Masonic Park northwest of South Fork, Colorado.
1.0

307.0 Cuts ahead in Treasure Mountain Tuff. Cliffs of the Conejos Formation below.
1.0

308.0 Large cuts ahead in Conejos quartz latite and andesite breccia, flow breccia, mudflows, and basaltic andesite. The Conejos Formation ranges from over 1,000 feet thick to zero where it wedges out against hills of Precambrian rock and is overlapped by the Treasure Mountain Tuff. The considerable relief on the Precambrian surface in this part of New Mexico is strikingly demonstrated at Toltec Gorge.
1.0

309.0 Continue through cuts and past massive cliffs of Conejos breccias. Beaver Creek confluences with the Rio de Los Pinos across canyon to the southwest.

Ghost town of Sublette.

Milepost 304.0. Cut in Masonic Park welded ash-flow, underlain by tuffaceous sandstone and conglomerates of the Treasure Mountain Tuff.

        1.0
310.0 Toltec siding (9,465') about half way to milepost 311.
        1.0
311.0 Beautiful view to the west up canyon to mouth of Toltec Gorge. Route is to the north up Toltec Creek. Mud Tunnel ("comforting name!") ahead. The tunnel is 349' long and penetrates a mud flow breccia of the Conejos Formation.
        1.0
312.0 STOP 2. Phantom Curve. This will be a "walking stop." In the cuts ahead we will be afforded to view and examine close hand a magnificent display of chaotic breccias in the Conejos Formation and the many pedestal rocks left by erosion of the alternating soft and hard breccias, flows, and conglomerates (see Butler, this guidebook). As we walk the Phantom Curve the state line is crossed again for the eighth time. We will reboard train beyond curve. Have your cameras at the ready for a spectacular shot as the train negotiates the curve to rejoin us. PLEASE STAND CLEAR OF TRACKS.
        1.0
313.0 Calico Cut on the right. The altered Conejos breccia was probably contemporaneous with the volcanism that formed the deposits. This is one of the major annual slide problem areas of the railroad. Here, on February 11, 1948, a snow-

Massive cliffs of Conejos breccia between mileposts 308 and 309.

slide derailed two units of a passenger train, carrying the cars 300 feet into Toltec Creek below. Miraculously, only a few were injured (see Chappell, this guidebook).

Curve ahead crosses Toltec Creek. Site of Toltec section house. Good view of the entirety of Calico Cut to the left and rear.

    1.0

314.0 Conejos Formation in rail cuts on right. Basal part of the Treasure Mountain Tuff in float above cuts.

Reenter New Mexico half way between mileposts 314 and 315.

    1.0

315.0 Cliffs on the south side of the Rio de Los Pinos are Precambrian. Rock Tunnel (366' long) in Precambrian just ahead.

STOP 3. Toltec Gorge. CAUTION: PLEASE BE CAREFUL. Here at the west portal we are at an altitude of 9,631 feet. The bottom of the gorge is plotted at 9,030 feet. So keep in mind that 600' is a long OOPS! The south face of the gorge represents an additional 500 feet. Thus the total depth of the canyon cut by the Rio de Los Pinos is on the order of 1,100 feet. Precambrian rocks in the area consist of gneiss, quartz-biotite schist, and amphibolite intruded by granite and aplite and pegmatite dikes. As indicated previously, the relief on the Precambrian surface (not in the gorge) is the result of pre-Conejos erosion, not faulting. The bulk of the Conejos Formation wedges out against this formerly buried mountain mass.

Garfield Monument at west portal reads: "In Memoriam: James Abram Garfield, President of the United States. Died September 19, 1881. Mourned by all the people. Erected by members of the national association of general passenger and ticket agents, who held memorial services on this spot September 26, 1881."

A short distance past the west portal the railroad passes back into the Conejos Formation.

    1.0

316.0 Good view to the left of Precambrian, aspen-covered landslide, and canyon of the Rio de Los Pinos. Reenter Colorado half way between mileposts 316 and 317.

    1.0

317.0 Cuts ahead in flows and breccias of the Conejos Formation.

Mud Tunnel.

East view of Toltec Gorge from milepost 311. Faint scars on mountainside (extreme upper right corner) are rail cuts in the vicinity of milepost 315 prior to entering Rock Tunnel.

1.5
318.5 STOP 4. Osier.* LUNCH STOP. At Osier (halfway point on the run) the country opens up as the line passes through an area which was burned over in 1879. Osier Mountain (10,746') to the north is capped by basalt of Hinsdale.

Beyond Osier the tracks curve and cross Osier Creek and then on a more or less level grade follows the meadows of the Rio de Los Pinos. The geology is relatively simple from here to Cumbres Pass, a distance of about 12 miles. We will continue to traverse the Conejos Formation which is overlain on the higher mesas by the Treasure Mountain Tuff. In this area the Conejos contains a larger proportion of flow rock than to the east. There are numerous cuts and exposures in quartz latite flows for the next several miles.

1.0
319.5 Good view up the meadows of the Rio de Los Pinos. Note excellent examples of exfoliation along cooling joints in the Conejos flows; also numerous rock glaciers.

0.5
320.0 STOP 5. PHOTO STOP. Cascade Creek Trestle (137' high) is the highest structure on the run. We will detrain on the west side. The train will back up beyond the east approach and with a couple of "toots" will come roaring across. "You can't hear the engine for the clicks of the camera shutters."

* Now a ghost town, Osier was once a hell-raising, rip-snorting tent city during construction of the line. One of the more recent functions of the deserted buildings was to host God-fearing, blizzard-stranded geologists compiling this rail log.

Phantom Curve.

Columns of Conejos breccia at Phantom Curve.

Calico Cut.

View of east portal of Rock Tunnel.

View inside Rock Tunnel.

Ghost town of Osier. "High, cold, windy, and lonesome."

West portal of Rock Tunnel at Toltec Gorge.   B. J. Rodgers

Beyond trestle exposures of Conejos breccia in flanking valley walls. Note terraces along south side of Rio de Los Pinos.

1.0

321.0 Long Creek coming in from the north. With the exception of that portion of the rails west of Antonito, the "meadow section" of the run represents the most level expanse of rail grade (less than 1%). "Old Timers" will tell you that lost time can be made-up on the meadows.

NEW MEXICO GEOLOGICAL SOCIETY—TWENTY-SECOND FIELD CONFERENCE

Cascade Creek Trestle. B. J. Rodgers

"Hang on to your hat." . . . we don't know if we have an "Old Timer" at the throttle, or not. It's been reported though, that daring and carefree engineers have attained the dizzy speeds of 30 mph in this area. WOW!

1.0
322.0 Confluence of Apache Creek to the south. Excellent fly-fishing reported along these waters of the Rio de Los Pinos.
1.0
323.0 Tracks curve north up the Rio de Los Pinos Valley. Cumbres Creek confluence across valley to the southwest.
1.75
324.75 Bridge across Rio de Los Pinos. North Fork of the Rio de Los Pinos joins the master stream a short distance upstream.

Los Pinos Loop. "Fast freight to Antonito," circa. 1962.

0.25
325.0 Los Pinos Loop. As tracks curve to the south to begin a 1.42% climb toward Cumbres Pass we say farewell to the Rio de Los Pinos, our beautiful guideline since Lava Tank.

Los Pinos water tank on right. Route now parallels Colorado Highway 17.

1.0
326.0 Unnamed lake on left.

2.0
328.0 Grade crossing just before milepost. Tracks now head west up Cumbres Creek.

1.0
329.0 High fill crossing of Cumbres Creek. Beginning Tanglefoot Curve switchback.

1.0
330.0 Route is north. Neff Mountain (10,880') ahead is capped by Masonic Park Tuff.

0.5
330.5 Grade crossing of Colorado 17. Cumbres Pass station ahead. STOP 6. PHOTO STOP. Renowned Cumbres Pass (10,015') is the divide between the Rio de Los Pinos and the Rio Chama. Cumbres (Spanish for "summit") is the highest railroad pass in the United States. Heavy snows are a formidable obstacle during the winter months. A chilling memory occurred when 3 trains and 40 crewmen were stranded on the pass during a January, 1957 storm. It took Army half-tracks a week to break through 35-foot drifts to rescue.

0.5
331.0 Curve ahead around Windy Point. Excellent exposures of altered Conejos breccias. Beautiful view of glaciated Wolf Creek Valley below. We now commence the "downhill run" to Chama (4.0% in 14 miles).

The west side of Cumbres Pass is a region of lush beautiful scenery and steep, steep railroad grades. The country is characterized by dense groves of aspen and pines interspersed with open meadows which in the summer are a riot of colorful wildflowers. In the fall, the contrast between the golden aspen, the red of the oak-

NEW MEXICO GEOLOGICAL SOCIETY—TWENTY-SECOND FIELD CONFERENCE

Tanglefoot curve

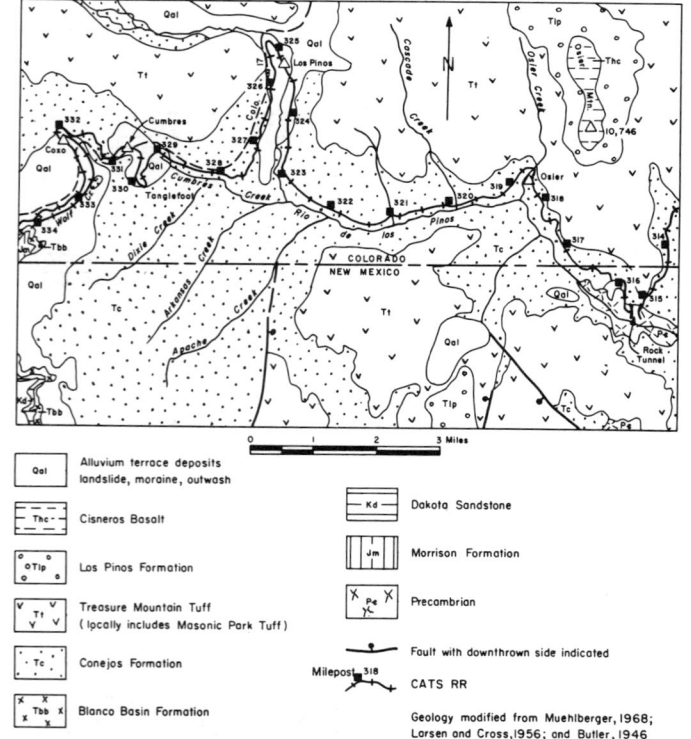

Geology between mileposts 314 and 334.

Cumbres Pass.

brush, the green of the pines, and the deep blue skies, makes this area a photographer's Valhalla. The surrounding countryside abounds with all sorts of wild game. Deer are numerous; elk are frequently seen, and the normally scarce grouse seem to be relatively abundant. The fishing in Wolf Creek and the Rio Chama is good.

Shed-covered wye at Cumbres.

1.0
332.0 Curve. Culvert over Wolf Creek. Site of Coxo section house. Entering glaciated Wolf Creek Valley.
0.5
332.5 Grade crossing of Colorado 17. Dramatic view of the fortress of Windy Point to the left.
1.5
334.0 Shallow cuts ahead in moraine with landslide covers. Rock cuts beyond (right) are in the Tertiary Blanco Basin Formation. WATCH ON LEFT on opposite ravine wall for red and green shales and sandstones of the Jurassic Morrison Formation dipping west and unconformably overlain by the Blanco Basin.

Rail cuts continue in the Morrison. A sudden color change to red marks where the Cretaceous Dakota Sandstone is faulted down to the south against the Morrison.

Rail cuts in Dakota; return shortly to moraine.
1.0
335.0 Cresco Tank ahead. Note destruction of the aspen forest in the Cresco area. The trees are being feasted upon by a caterpillar called the "Tented Killer," that breed their larvae in web-like nests suspended on the branches. At times the rails become so saturated with worms that they lubricate the tracks, causing traction problems. Sanding is sometimes required after east-bound water stops at Cresco. Reenter New Mexico a short distance south of Cresco Tank; the 11th and final state line crossing.
1.0
336.0 Note red-colored outcrops of Blanco Basin Formation above the highway on the right. The formation was named by Larsen and Cross (1956) and consists of white, red, and pink arkosic sandstones, conglomerates and red

Southerly view of glaciated Wolf Creek Valley from Windy Point.

Angular unconformity between the Blanco Basin (Tbb) and the Morrison Formation (Jm) between mileposts 334 and 335.

Glacial erratic.

shales. It is non-volcanic and is approximately 600 feet thick in this area, much of it commonly covered by slide debris. It unconformably overlies Mesozoic rocks and is overlain, apparently conformably, by the Conejos Formation. Larsen and Cross considered the Blanco Basin to be of Oligocene (?) age. Cuts at track level are in Upper Cretaceous Niobrara and Carlile Shales. Rail bed on lateral moraine.

1.0

337.0 Grade crossing of New Mexico 17. Large highway cut on right in lateral moraine. Numerous glacial erratics of Conejos breccia dot the surrounding landscape. Note poorly preserved recessional moraines forming low, dissected ridges across valley. Slopes on east side of Wolf Creek Valley are mostly landslide with a few exposures of Blanco Basin and Dakota Sandstone.

Lobato Trestle.

1.5
338.5 Grade crossing of Forest Service Road to Chama River. Erratic zone ahead.
0.5
339.0 Grade crossing to Lobo Lodge cabins on right. Cuts in medial moraine between Chama and Wolf Creek glacier lobes.
0.78
339.78 Lobato trestle (100' high) over Wolf Creek. The confluence of Wolf Creek with the Rio Chama is a short distance downstream. High canyon walls to the west are composed of the Dakota Sandstone overlain by the Blanco Basin Formation; in turn, blanketed with landslide covers.

0.22
340.0 Lobato siding. Water tower and station are a part of a permanent movie set called "Weed City." Two Westerns, "The Good Guys And The Bad Guys" (1968) with Robert Mitchum, and "Shoot Out" (1970) staring Gregory Peck, were filmed here.
0.5
340.5 Railroad enters the "narrows" section of the Rio Chama. Views are generally blocked by trees and brush. Large highway cuts above (left) are in the Morrison Formation overlain by slide debris. Trackage in the "narrows" was severely damaged by the widening improvement of State Highway 17 during the summer

Weed City (?) at Lobato siding.

NEW MEXICO GEOLOGICAL SOCIETY—TWENTY-SECOND FIELD CONFERENCE

Track condition in the "narrows" during construction of New Mexico 17. Summer, 1970.

of 1970. The confinement of the location caused highway fill sections to spill-over onto the rail bed; in some areas the rails were completely obliterated. After the purchase of the line by the Joint Railroad Authority, volunteer labor spent many hours in the "narrows" repairing this portion of the line.

    1.0

341.0 Bluffs of Dakota Sandstone across river. Just ahead a small fault has displaced the Dakota Sandstone down to the north (see photograph, Supplemental Log. No. 4).

    1.0

342.0 Leaving the "narrows." Rail bed on glacial outwash terrace gravels. Note size and rounding of boulders.

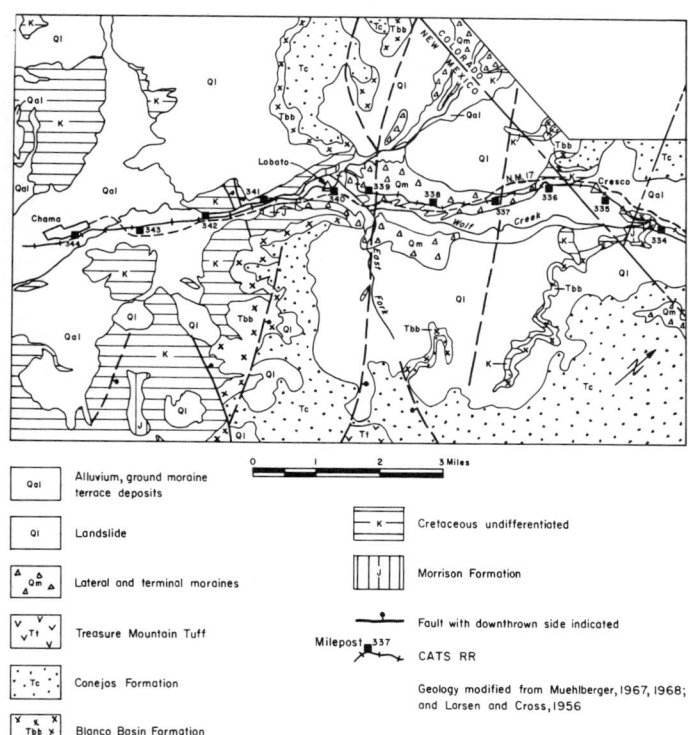

Geology between mileposts 334 and 344.

Railyard at Chama.

1.0
343.0 Grade crossing of New Mexico 17. Cuts beyond in glacial outwash gravels.
1.0
344.0 Bridge over Rio Chama.
1.0
345.0 Chama, New Mexico, (7,863') is the headquarters and western terminus of the Cumbres And Toltec Scenic Railroad.

Chama is situated along the trout meadows of the Rio Chama. Its hundred-year-old history has revolved around ranching, lumbering, and the narrow gauge railroad. The town was a division point on the Rio Grande System between Alamosa and Durango and the railroad maintained elaborate facilities here to accomodate the numerous amount of motive power needed to boost freight tonnage up the 4% grade to Cumbres Pass. The large railyard is complete with engine service facilities, storage wyes, and includes one of the few remaining coal tipples in the United States. Every effort is being made to maintain the historic authenticity of the railyard.

END OF RAIL LOG. Board busses for return to Alamosa. For geological coverage on return trip, consult Supplemental Log No. 4.

"Old rail loggers never die, they just . . . ."

SUPPLEMENTAL

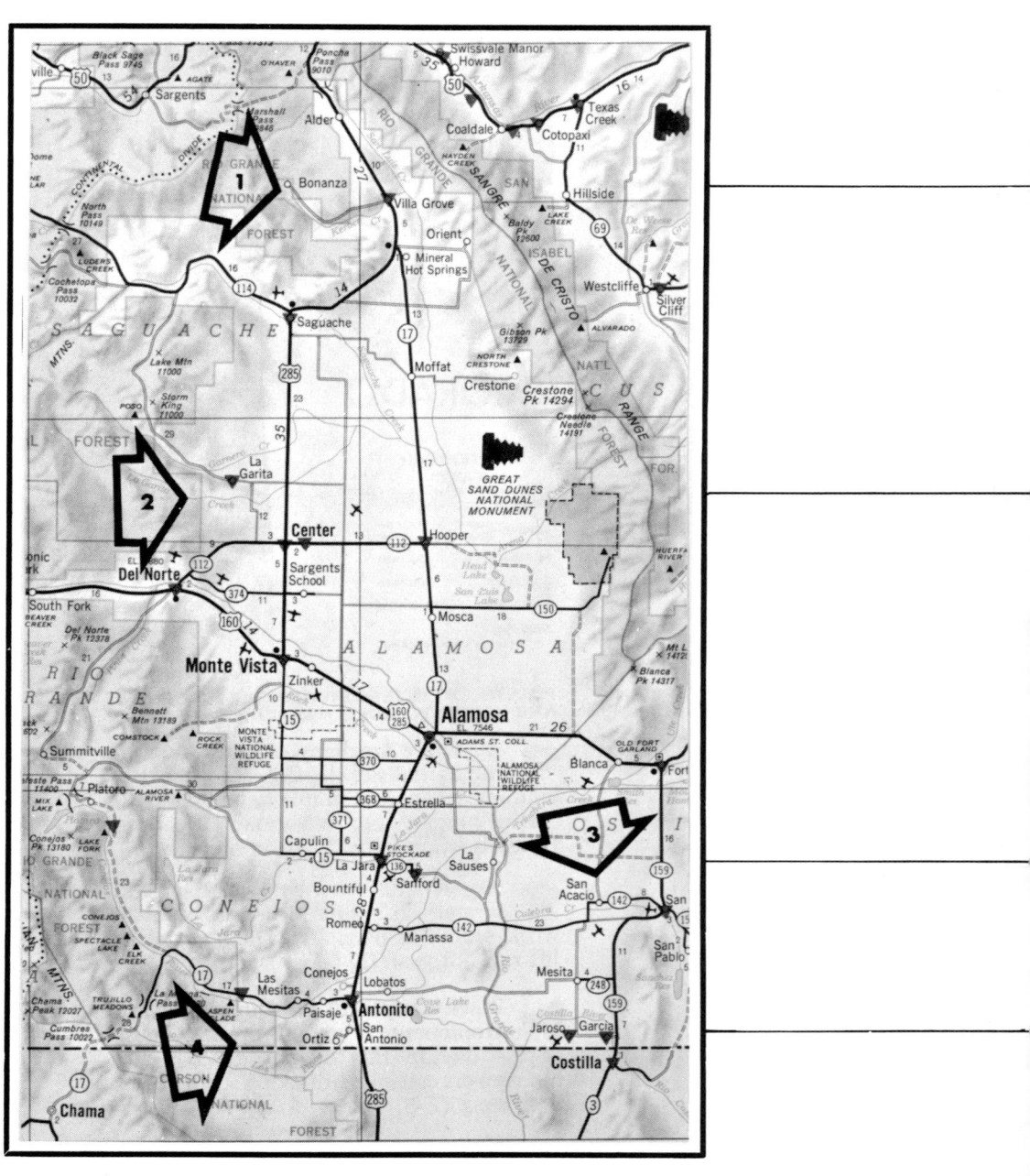

ROAD LOGS

—Log No. 1–Villa Grove to Bonanza

—Log No. 2.–Del Norte to Summer Coon Volcanic Area and Return

—Log No. 3–Fort Garland to Romeo, Via San Luis, San Acacio and Manassa

—Log No. 4–Chama, New Mexico to Antonito, Colorado

SUPPLEMENTAL ROAD LOG NO. 1

VILLA GROVE TO BONANZA

DISTANCE: 17.0 miles.

0.0 Junction of U.S. 285 and Saguache County 16 north of Villa Grove, Colorado. PROCEED WEST towards Bonanza. Road climbs onto second oldest pediment surface.
2.5

2.5 Cattleguard. We are entering an area of complexly folded and faulted Lower and Middle Paleozoic rocks. The first structure traversed is the Eastern anticline of Burbank (1932); the axis of this fold trends northwest from Clayton Cone (the small hill on the south side of Kerber Creek) to a low ridge of Precambrian rocks which projects above the surficial deposits on the north (right) side of the road.
1.6

4.1 Road cut on right in Lower Pennsylvanian sandstones and shales.
0.8

4.9 Cattleguard.
0.2

5.1 Road cut on right in faulted and fractured Leadville Limestone on the eastern flank of the Central anticline (Burbank, 1932).
0.1

5.2 Fault up gulley to right places Leadville Limestone against Precambrian rocks on the west. We are entering the core of the northwest-trending Central anticline which disappears beneath the Rawley Andesite of Oligocene age age about 1.5 miles to the northwest. The structure plunges to the southeast so that the Precambrian core disappears beneath Lower Paleozoic rocks about half way up the hill at 9:00 across Kerber Creek.
1.3

6.5 End of pavement.
0.3

6.8 Across Kerber Creek at 9:00, southwest-dipping Lower Paleozoic rocks mark the west flank of the Central anticline. The complete Paleozoic section is observed here. One discrepancy exists in the section in what Burbank (1932) called the Tomichi Formation. This rests on Precambrian rocks and is overlain by Devonian (?). The lithology consists of a lower cherty carbonate, a middle quartzose sand and shale, and an upper carbonate. The Tomichi of Burbank is obviously a composite section of Manitou Dolomite (Canadian), Harding Sandstone (Champlainian) and Fremont Limestone (Cinncinattian); names which are now used through the former area of the Tomichi from Monarch Pass to Crested Butte, as well as in the original area of central Colorado. Correlation aids are fish plates in the Harding and chert beds in the Manitou. This section of rocks along Kerber Creek is now being studied to determine the influence of the southeastern part of the Uncompahgre arch upon Ordovician sedimentation.
0.4

7.2 Road cut on right in Kerber Formation of Early Pennsylvanian age. The Kerber consists of a series of coarse-grained sandstones and carbonaceous shales which unconformably overlie the Leadville Limestone and extend upward to the base of the lowest red micaceous sediment or sandy shales of the Sharpsdale Formation. Brill (1952) assigned a Morrowan or Early Atokan age to the Kerber; he believed the Kerber to be the nonmarine facies of the Belden Formation which is a dominantly marine unit in the northern part of the Central Colorado geosyncline. The Kerber is about 200 feet thick in the type area.
0.4

7.6 Road cut on right in Rawley Andesite.
0.5

8.1 Junction with Little Kerber Creek Road on left. CONTINUE STRAIGHT AHEAD. Note outcrops on right of fault breccia composed of Precambrian and Paleozoic rocks. Across Kerber Creek, the small hill at 3:00 is also composed of tectonic breccia. At this point, the breccia is composed almost exclusively of boulders of Precambrian rocks in a matrix of crushed granite and gneiss. The breccias formed during the second stage of folding and thrusting along the sole of a northward-directed thrust plate during Laramide orogeny. This is believed to be the same thrust zone that crosses beneath the alluvial fill of the San Luis Valley at Mineral Hot

Springs. Precambrian rocks have been thrust over Paleozoic sedimentary rocks which had previously been folded into northwest-trending anticlines and synclines during the first stage of Laramide deformation. The location of the thrust may be seen at the change in slope about 0.5 mile south of Kerber Creek at 7:00 to 9:00.

0.2

8.3 Outcrops of Rawley Andesite and later intrusives along both sides of Kerber Creek. The Rawley Andesite is a basal unit of intermediate flows and breccias which underlies the more silicic pyroclastic rocks and flows of the Bonanza pile. The Rawley is equivalent in age and lithology to the lower Conejos Formation of the San Juan Field. Antero Peak (13,266 ft.) at 12:00 is the highest summit in the area.

0.4

8.7 Old tailings pond on left.

0.8

9.5 Abandoned mill at 9:00. Continue up Kerber Creek through highly faulted flows and breccias of the Rawley Andesite.

0.9

10.4 Kerber Creek substation on right.

1.3

11.7 Hayden Peak (12,135 ft.) is visible at 3:00 at the head of Greenback Gulch. This peak is visible as a prominent pyramid from the San Luis Valley and was used as a triangulation station during the Geological and Geographical Surveys of the Territories conducted under the leadership of F. V. Hayden; more popularly known as the Hayden Survey.

0.7

12.4 Old tailings pond on left.

1.7

14.1 Bridge on left. Little Bonanza Mill across Kerber Creek.

0.1

14.2 Bridge over Kerber Creek at junction with Brewery Creek coming in from left. Site of old town of Sedgwick on aspen-covered slopes to right.

0.2

14.4 Road on left leads up Brewery and Slaughterhouse Creeks to nearly 11,000 feet on the slopes of Antero Peak.

0.2

14.6 Elkhorn Gulch and Elkhorn Peak (12,030 ft.) on right. Kerber City was located at the mouth of Elkhorn Gulch. Rawley Andesite in roadcuts ahead on left.

0.5

15.1 Entering Bonanza (Elev. 9,465 ft.). Copper Gulch and Whale Hill (12,142 ft.) on right. The original discovery in the district was reportedly made in 1880 by Tom Cooke of Salida who came over the range looking for horses and found some rich "float" in Copper Gulch (Patton, 1915). The town of Bonanza mushroomed to a population of between 1000 and 1500 people within two years. According to Patton, the population in those days was estimated by counting the number of saloons and dance halls. Ferreting out the prospectors and miners in the hills would certainly have been a formidable task for a census taker, but of course they all came to "water." Bonanza possessed no less than 36 saloons and 7 dance halls during its heyday!

The town declined nearly as fast as it began. By 1882, only two years after the initial discovery, miners became discouraged by the apparent lack of high-grade ores necessary for profitable mining and the camp rapidly dwindled. One testimony to its rapid decline is the fact that it is one of the few mining camps in Colorado to which General Palmer did not build a narrow gauge line.

1.0

16.1 St. Joe Mine on right.

0.2

16.3 Bridge.

0.6

16.9 Road forks. Rawley Gulch road on right. CONTINUE STRAIGHT AHEAD.

0.1

17.0 Kerber Creek-Squirrel Creek road straight ahead. TURN AROUND and return to U.S. 285.

The town of Bonanza. "Kinda quiet now."

0.4

17.4 St. Joe Mine on left. The St. Joe Mine produced lead, zinc, silver, and gold ores from two sets of cross-cutting fissures trending northeast and northwest in the Rawley Andesite. A few veins in the northern part of the district were mined for gold and silver tellurides. Sporadic exploration has continued to the present, but the future of the district depends upon discovery of new orebodies with sufficient tonnage to overcome the economic disadvantages that the small operations have faced.

The Bonanza volcanic center is located between the San Juan volcanic field to the southwest and the Thirtynine Mile volcanic field to the northeast. These fields were part of a very large composite field which developed during the Oligocene and covered much of central and southern Colorado and northern New Mexico (Steven and Epis, 1968). Late Tertiary faulting and ensuing erosion have dissected this field into the segments we know today. Volcanism began with the emplacement of a widespread blanket of intermediate lavas and breccias which includes the Thirtynine Mile Andesite (34 m.y.), the Rawley Andesite of the Bonanza center (33.4, 34.2 m.y.), and the Conejos Formation (31.1 to 34.7 m.y.) (see Bruns, Epis, Steven, and Weimer, this guidebook).

Widespread ash-flow sheets were then emplaced on top of the andesitic rocks and numerous caldera complexes developed by subsidence over shallow magma chambers which were being rapidly drained by ash-flow eruptions.

Mineralization at Bonanza is associated with faults bounding innumerable small blocks formed during collapse of a dome. The structure map of the area is so complex as to resemble a shattered windshield (see Burbank, 1947). The extreme fracturing tended to disperse the mineralizing solutions into many small fissures and ore shoots that frequently terminated against cross faults which may or may not be mineralized. Consequently, most operations in the district have been small and the larger operations have generally failed to return the principal and interest on capital invested.

In 1911 and 1912, a 6,200 foot drainage tunnel was driven eastward from Squirrel Creek to tap the Rawley vein. A substantial quantity of lead, silver and copper ore was developed above the tunnel level and was mined and milled between 1923 and 1930 (the equivalent of 5000 tons of zinc was not recovered during milling). The total production of the district to 1946 was about $9,000,000, most of which came from the Rawley Mine.

END OF LOG.

SUPPLEMENTAL ROAD LOG NO. 2

DEL NORTE TO SUMMER COON VOLCANIC AREA AND RETURN

DISTANCE: 30.6 miles.

PREFACE:

The Summer Coon volcanic area is a dissected strato-volcano located a few miles north of Del Norte, Colorado. It consists of 32-33 m.y. old intrusive and extrusive rocks that range from basalt to rhyolite. The core of the Summer Coon volcano is a nearly circular mosaic of small altered stocks ranging from diorite to quartz monzonite porphyry. Radiating from this core are hundreds of basaltic to rhyolitic dikes. Mafic dikes are the most numrous and the smallest; the more silicic dikes are sparser but larger, locally being as much as 3 miles long and 200 feet wide. The radial pattern is so ideal that no dike intersections that would indicate relative ages were observed. Sequence of dike injection and other aspects of the eruptive history can be inferred, however, from the sequence of outward-dipping lava flows and breccias that flank the core and that are petrographically similar to the radial dikes (Lipman, 1968). Thick basal olivine basalt and andesite (SiO_2, 51-56 percent) are overlain by local phenocryst-poor rhyolite (SiO_2, 71 percent) and finally by varied phenocryst-rich rhyodacite and quartz latite (SiO_2, 57-64 percent). Dike relations are in accord with this sequence: mafic dikes intrude only mafic breccias and flows; a rhyolite dike is overlain unconformably by intermediate flows, and intermediate dikes intrude flows of all ages. (see Mertzman, this guidebook).

The log proceeds counter-clockwise around the Summer Coon volcanic area. Beginning in younger Oligocene ash-flow sheets that were deposited around the flanks of the eroded volcano, the road approaches the oldest rocks of the volcano (mainly basaltic andesite breccias) from the east, and gradually climbs westward through the volcanic sequence. On the west side after passing a few small outcrops of rhyolitic lavas of the intermediate eruptive stage, the road heads south away from the volcano through heterogeneous rhyodacite-quartz latite lavas that represent the late eruptive stage.

0.0 Junction U.S. 160 and Colorado 112. Del Norte, Colorado. PROCEED NORTH on Colorado 112.
   0.4

0.4 Denver and Rio Grande Western railroad crossing.
   0.1

0.5 Bridge over Rio Grande. Junction just beyond on left with County Road 15. KEEP RIGHT.
   0.9

1.4 Junction Colorado 374. CONTINUE STRAIGHT AHEAD on Colorado 112.
   0.4

1.8 Rio Grande canal. Low, east dipping cuesta at 10:00 is Masonic Park Tuff, a 28-29 m.y. ash-flow sheet (Lipman and others, 1970) that was deposited around the eroded flanks of the Summer Coon center.
   1.5

3.3 Junction. TURN LEFT. Outcrops of Fish Canyon Tuff that have weathered to distinctive bouldery outcrops. Fish Canyon Tuff is another ash-flow sheet (age 27.8 m.y.) that conformably overlies the Masonic Park Tuff.

Bouldery outcrops of Fish Canyon Tuff.

    0.5
3.8 Canal.
    0.2
4.0 Pavement ends.
    1.1
5.1 Curve to left. Cuestas from 12 to 2:00 capped by thin Carpenter Ridge Tuff, a yet younger ash-flow sheet (27.8 m.y. > age > 26.5 m.y.). Fish Canyon Tuff on left.
    2.8
7.9 Road curves left. High hills ahead are quartz latite to andesite lavas and breccias from Beidell volcanic center (34 m.y.). Discovery locality of beidellite, one of the montmorillonites of hydrous aluminum silicates with varying amounts of calicum and sodium.
    1.6
9.5 Junction. TURN LEFT on Natural Arch Road. Hills at 12:00 are olivine-bearing basaltic andesite from Summer Coon volcano.
    0.6
10.1 Fish Canyon Tuff on left. Ash-flow sheets lapped around edges, but probably never covered Summer Coon.
    0.3
10.4 On right basaltic andesite lava flow dipping east, away from center. Below lava flow are explosion breccias of basaltic andesite cone.
    0.6
11.0 Entering Rio Grande National Forest.
    0.4
11.4 Crudely stratified rocks on high hills at 12:00 are basaltic andesite explosion breccias dipping gently north on north flank of Summer Coon volcano. All outcrops on right are explosion breccias. Explosion breccias form cliffs where deposited as hot agglutinate.
    1.4
12.8 Numerous thin dikes of basaltic andesite exposed on slopes below massive cliffs of explosion breccia. Large rhyolite dike at 3:00.
    0.2
13.0 Low hills from 9:00 to 10:00 are central intrusive complex at core of Summer Coon volcano.

Cliffs of explosion breccias of basaltic andesite near milepost 11.4.

Rocks range in composition from porphyritic diorite to porphyritic quartz monzonite and intrusive rhyolite tuff breccia. At 8:00 in front of Bennett Peak are late rhyodacite-quartz latite lavas, dipping south on south flank of volcano. East-striking porphyritic quartz latite dike forms serrated ridge at 7:00. Similar dike in medium distance at 2:00.
0.6

13.6 Junction. TURN RIGHT on road to Natural Arch.
0.2

13.8 Dike ahead of porphyritic quartz latite.
1.1

14.9 On right in gully, small olivine andesite dike intruding agglutinated explosion breccia.
0.4

15.3 La Ventana Natural Arch is erosion cavity in large dike of porphyritic quartz latite. RETRACE ROUTE to main road.
1.6

16.9 Rejoin main road. TURN RIGHT.
0.5

17.4 At 9:00 north end of central intrusive complex. At 2:00 crudely stratified explosion breccia on north flank of volcano.
3.0

20.4 First hill across valley is olivine andesite breccia capped by a late porphyritic quartz latite lava flow. Twin Peaks in far distance are rhyolite lava flows on southeast flank of next volcano to west; the Baughman Creek area.
0.4

20.8 Old Woman Creek. KEEP LEFT.
0.4

21.2 Leaving Rio Grande National Forest. At 11:00 small plug-shaped intrusion of porphyritic quartz latite.
0.8

22.0 Large rhyodacite dike on left.
0.4

22.4 At 9:00 light yellowish brown patch of rhyolite lava across creek. High hill in medium distance is rhyolite vent dome complex overlain on this side by late rhyodacite lava flows.
1.0

23.4 Rhyolite lava flow on left capped by rhyodacite lava.
1.3

24.7 Old Woman Creek.
0.3

25.0 Junction on right. CONTINUE STRAIGHT AHEAD. Low hills to left and ahead are late porphyritic (hornblende phenocrysts) lava flows of intermediate composition.
1.8

26.8 Junction. Pavement begins.
1.0

27.8 At 8:00 Indian Head Peak consists of a stubby dike-like body of porphyritic rhyodacite. It may be the volcanic neck feeder for petrographically similar rhyodacite lavas in nearby hills.
2.0

29.8 Junction County 15. TURN RIGHT across canal.
0.8

30.6 Junction Colorado 112. Cross Rio Grande to Del Norte, Colorado. END OF LOG.

Dike of porphyritic quartz latite west of milepost 14.9.

La Ventana Natural Arch. Erosion cavity in large dike of porphyritic quartz latite.

SUPPLEMENTAL ROAD LOG
NO. 3

FORT GARLAND TO ROMEO, VIA SAN LUIS, SAN ACACIO AND MANASSA

DISTANCE: 51.2 miles.

0.0 Junction U.S. 160 and Colorado 159, Fort Garland. PROCEED SOUTH on Colorado 159.

Sierra Blanca massif (5:00-6:00), including Blanca Peak, elevation 14,363 ft. and Mt. Lindsay, elevation 14,125 ft. The massif is predominately composed of Precambrian granites and gneiss with the pyramid-shaped Mt. Lindsay at 6:00 being composed of Precambrian rocks thrust over sedimentary beds of the Pennsylvanian-Permian Sangre de Cristo Formation. The thrust plane extends nearly horizontally around Mt. Lindsay and occurs at a break in the slope on the peak just above timberline. Gently dipping Sangre de Cristo beds occur in the zone of dark timber lying unconformably on the Precambrian rocks below, in the aspen zone. Note triangular facets along treeless slopes at the foot of the mountains and the pediment surface south of the facets. Tertiary volcanics lie on the pediment surface, in which underlying rocks are Precambrian. Along north side of town note old terrace levels.

Cross railroad tracks.

0.2

0.2 Old Fort Garland on right (see Hoagland, this guidebook). The fort was built in 1858, replacing Fort Massachusetts, six miles to the north, which had been built in 1852. Fort Massachusetts was abandoned because it was found vulnerable to Indian attack, being so situated that hostiles could fire from the hills down into the fort.

Fort Garland was named after the commander of the Department of New Mexico, Colonel Brevet Brigadier General John Garland. It served as a garrison for troops protecting settlers for 25 years. Kit Carson commanded the fort from 1866-67 as an officer in the New Mexico volunteers. The fort was abandoned in 1883.

0.9

1.1 Cross Sangre de Cristo Creek. At 2:00 in middle distance are the San Luis Hills. At 10:00 is Garland questa capped by Servilleta basalts overlying sediments of the Santa Fe Formation. Low mesa extending from 12:00-2:00 is the Basaltic Hills made up of Servilleta olivine basalts. These basalts represent a northward extension of lava capping San Pedro Mesa which extends south from San Luis, Colorado, to the state line.

3.9

5.0 Latir Peaks at 12:00. High peak at 10:00 is Culebra Peak (14,000+ ft.), followed in order (southward) by Red Mountain, Vermejo Peak and Purgatoire Peak. Basaltic Hills from 12:00 to 3:00.

5.0

10.0 Eastern San Luis Hills at 3:00. Large flat-top mesas in background are part of western San Luis Hills. South-flowing Rio Grande is dividing line between eastern and western parts of San Luis Hills.

3.6

13.6 Servilleta basalt on right. Low hills at 9:00 composed of sediments of the Santa Fe Formation.

1.2

14.8 Sangre de Cristo Comprehensive Health Center on left.

0.9

15.7 Enter San Luis, Colorado, elevation 7,965 ft. Billed as the oldest town in Colorado, established 1851, by Spanish settlers from Taos, New Mexico. A small ditch under the date of 1852 is the Number One water right priority of the state of Colorado.

0.5

16.2 Cross Rito Seco, Junction Colorado 142. TURN RIGHT, proceed west toward San Acacio.

0.3

16.5 Good exposures of Santa Fe Formation capped with Servilleta basalts for next half mile in cuts along north (right) side of road. At 9:00 north end of San Pedro Mesa across valley of Culebra Creek. Caprock of Servilleta basalts above Santa Fe sediments. Mesa is faulted along west side with displacements being about zero in this area and gradually increasing to about 2,100

"Kit Carson slept here." Old Fort Garland.

feet near the Colorado-New Mexico state line. From this area southward to the state line both sides of mesa have been subjected to pronounced recent slumping.

1.5

18.0 Crossing Costilla Plains (see Upson, this guidebook). Note river terraces on south side of Culebra Creek at 9:00.

1.6

19.6 Crest of hill—panoramic view of San Luis Hills at 12:00. Ute Mountain stratovolcano at 10:00. San Antonio Mountain stratovolcano at 11:00.

0.4

20.0 Driving on terrace of Culebra Creek.

1.0

21.0 From 1:00 to 2:00 low hills are composed of basaltic-appearing rhyodacite flows of Lower Manassa Member of Conejos Formation.

2.0

23.0 Flat-topped Mesa de La Sauses at 12:00 is west of Rio Grande; capped by basaltic-appearing, olivine rhyodacite flows of Upper Manassa Member overlying explosion breccia of Lower Manassa Member.

1.3

24.3 Enter San Acacio. Former railroad and large potato shipping center. Established in 1901 in conjunction with a lottery for small tracts of farm land.

0.8

25.1 Curve.

0.4

25.5 Ute Mountain at 1:00.

0.5

26.0 Dropping off terrace to lower level of Culebra Creek. Note two terrace levels straight ahead.

1.3

27.3 Road turns right on lower terrace level.

0.2

27.5 Dropping off lower terrace. Upson (1936) has mapped four major erosion surfaces in the area of the Culebra reentrant and Costilla Plains.

1.5

29.0 Piñon Hills at 12:00 consist of basaltic-appear-

Looking west across Costilla Plains toward the San Luis Hills. View is on Colorado 142 at milepost 19.6.

ing rhyodacite flows of Manassa Member. Stocks present along south, east, and north sides of hills.

3.5

32.5 Note southeast dip of flows (Manassa Member) making up hills in foreground at 3:00. Although a flowing stream at San Luis, Culebra Creek rarely flows to the Rio Grande even during maximum runoff. Water sinks into the loosely consolidated gravel of the Santa Fe Formation several miles upstream.

1.2

33.7 Road curves. Low hill at 11:00 is Volcano de La Culebra composed of Mesita Member of the Servilleta Formation. Type area of the Mesita Member is small volcano at Mesita, Colorado, about 7 miles southeast of here.

0.8

34.5 Above terrace at 10:00 are the South Piñon Hills. Stock dated at 27.4 ± 0.6 and 27.9 ± 0.6 m.y. (Upper Oligocene).

1.0

35.5 Contorted-appearing strata in hills at 3:00 composed of crystal tuffs and tuff breccia in the La Sauses Member of the Conejos Formation. Minor folding of beds; some small faults. Flows within section also moved over local irregular surfaces. Volcanics intruded by several north-south trending dikes.

0.5

36.0 Curve.

0.2

36.2 Bridge across Rio Grande. Enter Conejos County. Gorge at 3:00 cut in La Sauses volcanics. Several large north-south trending dikes 2 miles north of here parallel and cross gorge. Dikes follow weak planes produced by major north-south fault zone which parallels Rio Grande. Eastern San Luis Hills faulted up relative to the western San Luis Hills. Note that western hills are topographically higher. Rio Grande superposed across hills at this point. Terraces north of gorge correlate with terrace levels east of Volcano de La Culebra (see Burroughs, this guidebook).

Ghost town of San Acacio stands silent; guarded by mighty Sierra Blanca (background).

Colorado 142 crossing of the Rio Grande. Surrounding terrain composed of La Sauses volcanics.

0.9
37.1 Junction with road to La Sauses. CONTINUE STRAIGHT AHEAD.
0.5
37.6 Low hill at 11:00 is the site of King Turquoise Mine. Turquoise from this area was worked by early Indians. The area is probably the general vicinity of the center for volcanic eruptions making up most, if not all, of the San Luis Hills.
1.5
39.1 Piñon Hills stock intruding flows of Manassa Member at 10:00.

East-west trending Manassa dike (right) and lava flows of the Conejos (left) north of milepost 40.6. Note dip of lower unit.

0.5
39.6 At 3:00 lower slopes of Mesa de La Sauses made up of explosive breccia (scoria) capped by rhyodacite flows of Manassa Member.
0.5
40.1 East-west trending Manassa Dike at 3:00. The dike contains fresh green hornblende crystals up to 5 mm. in size.
0.5
40.6 At 3:00 note tilt of lower lava flows at base of cliffs in contrast to horizontal flows at top. Flows of Manassa Member lapping up against buried hill of La Sauses Member exposed along southwest edge of cliff.
1.3
41.9 Descending alluvial fan. San Juan Mountains ahead on skyline. Eight miles to the north, at the north end of the San Luis Hills, is Pike's Stockade built early in 1807 in Spanish territory. Pike was later captured here by Spanish military authorities from Santa Fe. The stockade was built on the north bank of the Conejos River near its confluence with the Rio Grande.
2.6
44.5 Crossing Rio San Antonio.
0.1
44.6 Road cut on left in flows and breccia of Manassa Member of Conejos Formation.
1.4
46.0 Crossing north-flowing Conejos River.
1.8
47.8 Entering Morman settlement of Manassa, elevation 7,700 ft. (*Birth place of Jack Dempsey, the Manassa Mauler.*)
0.4
48.2 Dempsey Park and museum on left.
1.8
50.0 San Antonio Mountain stratovolcano at 9:00. At 10:00 Los Mogotes volcano of Upper Hinsdale age is dated at 4.7 m.y.
0.8
50.8 Enter Romeo, Colorado. Romeo was founded in 1892 and was first called Romero for a prominent citizen. The U.S. Post Office complained there were other towns by that name so the citizens decided to drop an "r" from Romero; hence the place name.
0.4
51.2 Junction U.S. 285. END OF LOG.

SUPPLEMENTAL ROAD LOG NO. 4

CHAMA, NEW MEXICO TO ANTONITO, COLORADO, VIA NEW MEXICO AND COLORADO 17

PREFACE:

The route parallels the narrow gauge railroad to the bridge over the Rio de Los Pinos. After crossing La Manga Pass the road follows the Conejos River to Antonito. Except for the few exposures of pre-Tertiary rocks seen north of Chama the geology will be almost exclusively Tertiary volcanics and sediments and Quaternary alluvium, fan and glacial deposits.

0.0 Chama, New Mexico. Log begins on New Mexico 17 at railroad station. Road cut on left after leaving Chama is in a Wisconsin-age terrace.

0.8
0.8 Bridge over Rio Chama. Railroad crossing ahead. The railroad tracks to the north are in a glacial outwash channel. Note channel rims and coarse gravels on both sides. After curve, just beyond railroad crossing, the higher parts of the mountains to the right are capped by the Conejos Formation. The underlying red sandstones and conglomerates are part of the Blanco Basin Formation. Both of these units dip gently to the east. The tree-covered lower slopes are underlain by the Dakota Sandstone dipping west toward the road. The mesa to the northwest also is underlain by the Conejos and Blan-

Faulted Dakota Sandstone across Rio Chama west of milepost 2.9.

co Basin with lower slopes consisting of landslide material. Chama Peak (12,027') to the left beyond in Colorado.
0.9

1.7 Curve to left. Low gravel ridge on right is a glacial outwash (possibly kame) terrace of Durango age.
0.7

2.4 Beginning series of road cuts in terrace gravels underlain by Dakota Sandstone. Entering "narrows" of the Rio Chama.
0.3

2.7 Landslide in cuts on right; rock glacier above.
0.2

2.9 Faults across river drop Dakota Sandstone down to the north. In this area the Dakota consists of an upper sandstone, middle shale, and lower double sandstone cliff. The covered slopes above are underlain by Graneros and Carlile Shales.
0.3

3.2 Road cut in red shale and sandstone of the Morrison Formation.
0.6

3.8 Exposures of Blanco Basin and Conejos Formations capping mesa to left.
0.4

4.2 Lobato siding. Road continues up Wolf Creek.
0.1

4.3 Curve to right. Low hills ahead on the left are a medial moraine between the Chama and Wolf Creek lobes.
0.4

4.7 Cuts in lateral moraine of Wolf Creek on right. Ground moraine below to the left.
0.3

5.0 Culvert over Wolf Creek. East Fork of Wolf

Road cut in recessional moraine north of Wolf Creek crossing.

Road cut in glacial erratic at milepost 6.2.

Creek on right. Cross recessional moraine just beyond culvert.
0.5

5.5 Road on left to Lobo Lodge. Road continues on ground moraine with lateral moraines on both sides of valley. Several remnants of recessional moraines are crossed just ahead. Large glacial erratics of Conejos breccias dot the surface of the moraines.
0.7

6.2 Road cut in large glacial erratic.
0.5

6.7 Cross tracks of CATS Railroad. Large cut on left in lateral moraine.
0.1

6.8 Road curves right. Slide Rock Point at 4:00 is capped by Masonic Park ash-flow.
0.3

7.1 Good exposures ahead of Blanco Basin overlain by Conejos. Larsen and Cross (1956) measured 575 feet of Blanco Basin at this locality.
1.0

8.1 Road cut in Niobrara Shale.
0.1

8.2 Cuts ahead on left in landslide consisting of material from the Blanco Basin and Niobrara.
0.3

8.5 Enter Colorado. Archuleta County.
0.2

8.7 Road cut in Niobrara Shale.
1.1

9.8 Conejos County. Entering Rio Grande National Forest.
0.2

10.0 Across Wolf Creek the Morrison Formation is unconformably overlain by arkosic conglomerates of the Blanco Basin Formation. Breccias in the Conejos Formation ahead.

Windy Point (left center) composed of craggy-weathered Conejos breccia.

0.8
10.8 Windy Point. Railroad at base of craggy-weathering Conejos breccias. Tuff of Masonic Park caps the high flat area beyond and is underlain by Treasure Mountain Tuff.
0.6
11.4 Cross railroad tracks.
0.3
11.7 Culvert over Wolf Creek.
0.3
12.0 Road cuts in altered breccias of the Conejos Formation.
0.7
12.7 Cumbres Pass (10,022′). Railroad station and snow shed. Divide between Chama River and Rio de Los Pinos drainage.
0.1
12.8 Cross railroad tracks. Neff Mountain at 12:00 is capped by tuff of Masonic Park, underlain by Treasure Mountain Tuff. Slopes above highway underlain by Conejos Formation.
0.3
13.1 Cumbres Creek. Cuts ahead in landslides debris from Conejos Formation.
1.2
14.3 Cuts on left in Conejos Formation.
0.1
14.4 Dixie Creek at 3:00. Hills of Conejos on all sides.
0.6
15.0 Pinorealosa Mountain at 2:00. Lower slopes at south end underlain by Conejos; above are beds of the Treasure Mountain Formation.

1.6
16.6 At 11:00 from valley to cliff is Treasure Mountain Formation. Cliff is tuff of Masonic Park and slopes above are Los Pinos Formation. Los Pinos railroad loop and water tower on right.
0.5
17.1 Cross Rio de Los Pinos. Road cut in lower part of Treasure Mountain Tuff; includes dark colored vitrophyre.
0.8
17.9 North Fork of Rio de Los Pinos. North Fork follows a fault with the west side down. Displacement is about 800 feet.
0.5
18.4 Treasure Mountain Formation underlies Pinorealosa Mountain at 3:00. Forest Service sign on right. "Pinorealosa Mountain 10,902′. The high ridge beyond this sign was named Pinorealosa 'land of many spruces' by Spanish settlers. The name remained even after the Ozier burn of 1879 razed the trees. Reforestation now underway will soon make this a Pinorealosa again." "After all it's only been a little over 90 years."
1.1
19.5 Culvert crossing of Grouse Creek.
0.2
19.7 Red Lake Trail on left.
0.1
19.8 Hill at 12:00 on skyline is capped by tuff of Masonic Park. Road cuts on left in Los Pinos Formation.

Glaciated Conejos River Valley. View is northwest from La Manga Pass.

0.5
20.3 La Manga Pass (10,230′) Conejos-Rio de Los Pinos divide. Road cut on left in Los Pinos Formation.
1.5
21.8 La Manga Creek on left. Descending through landslides debris toward Conejos River Valley.
1.1
22.9 Looking up Conejos River Valley at 12:00. Lower slopes of canyon on right are Conejos Formation. Cliffs are in the Treasure Mountain Tuff and tuff of Masonic Park caps the Mountain.
1.3
24.2 Cross La Manga Creek.
0.6
24.8 Good exposures of Treasure Mountain and Conejos in cliffs across Conejos River.
0.9
25.7 Fault at 11:00. Down on west side.
0.2
25.9 Elk Creek Campground to left.
0.1
26.0 Bridge over Conejos River. A short distance up the river there are small exposures of Precambrian granites underlying the Conejos Formation.
0.2
26.2 Platoro turnoff.
0.7
26.9 At 3:00 the upper smooth cliffs are Treasure Mountain Tuff. Lower cliffs are breccias in the Conejos Formation.
2.4
29.3 Menkhaven. At 12:00 toe of major landslide. Cliff of Conejos on left.
0.7
30.0 Crossing slide.
0.4
30.4 At 12:00 lower slopes are Conejos. Grass-covered slopes above are underlain by Treasure Mountain Tuff.
0.2
30.6 Note terraces along Conejos River.
0.9
31.5 Forest Service sign. "The Tented Killers: The slate-colored aspen trees on the slopes across the Conejos River are dead—victims of the tent caterpillars."
0.4
31.9 Conejos Formation in road cut.
0.3
32.2 Bear Creek at 3:00.

0.6
32.8 At 3:00 across river at terrace level are outcrops of Precambrian granite.
0.7
33.5 Cattleguard.
0.4
33.9 River Springs Ranger Station.
0.9
34.8 Los Mogotes volcano on skyline at 12:00.
0.7
35.5 Treasure Mountain Tuff at road level on left.
0.4
35.9 Leaving Rio Grande National Forest. Los Mogotes at 12:00 is an uppermost Hinsdale vent that has been dated at 5.0 m.y. Continue through outcrops of Treasure Mountain Tuff.
2.4
38.3 Road cuts in slump blocks of basalt from Los Mogotes.
0.3
38.6 Road cut on left in Los Pinos Formation.
0.6
39.2 On the right across Conejos River. Los Pinos Formation capped by Hinsdale Basalt from Los Mogotes.
2.7
41.9 San Luis Hills in center of San Luis Valley at 12:00.
1.3
43.2 Enter Mesitas. Road on alluvial fan of Conejos River.
1.0
44.2 Cross Conejos River.
0.2
44.4 Enter Mogotes. Leaving San Juan Mountains and entering San Luis Valley.
1.5
45.9 Blanca Peak at 10:00; San Luis Hills from 10:30 to 1:00; Ute Mountain at 1:00; San Antonio Mountain at 2:30.
3.1
49.0 Junction U.S. 285. END OF LOG.

REFERENCES

Larsen, E. S., Jr., and Cross, W., 1956, Geology and petrology of the San Juan region, southwestern Colorado: U.S. Geol. Survey Prof. Paper 258, 303 p.

Lipman, P. W., 1968, Geology of Summer Coon volcanic center, eastern San Juan Mountains, Colorado, Epis, R. C., Ed., Cenozoic volcanism in the southern Rocky Mountains: Colo. School Mines Quart., v. 63, no. 3, p. 211-236.

Lipman, P. W., Steven, T. A., and Mehnert, H. H., 1970, Volcanic history of the San Juan Mountains, Colorado, as indicated by potassium-argon dating: Geol. Soc. America Bull., v. 81, p. 2329-2352.

Lipman, P. W., and Steven, T. A., 1970, Reconnaissance geology and economic significance of the Platoro caldera, southeastern San Juan Mountains, Colorado: U.S. Geol. Survey Prof. Paper 700-C, p. C19-C29.

Patton, H. B., 1917, Geology and ore deposits of the Platoro-Summitville mining district, Colorado: Colorado Geol. Survey Bull. 13, 122 p.

Steven, T. A., and Ratté, J. C., 1960, Geology and ore deposits of the Summitville district, San Juan Mountains, Colorado: U.S. Geol. Survey Prof. Paper 343, 70 p.

Conejos River.

"We climbed the rock-built breasts of earth!
We saw the snowy mountains rolled
Like mighty billows; saw the birth
Of sudden dawn; beheld the gold
Of awful sunsets; saw the face
Of God, and named it boundless space."

EDITOR'S NOTE: The New Mexico Geological Society is grateful to Mr. Robert B. McCoy, President of Rio Grande Press, Inc., for permission to use a portion of Ernest Ingersoll's classic, The Crest Of The Continent. For those who like railroads, this story is an unsurpassed treasure. A thoroughly entertaining little gem of Americana; vividly warm with its view and perspectives directed toward another time—and in effect, another place.

Arriving in Denver in the summer of 1883, the author was captivated by the Rocky Mountains. He wrote, "I confess (I should be ashamed not to), that my first view of the Rocky Mountains had no way of expressing itself save in tears. To see what they looked, and to know what they were, was like a sudden revelation of the truth that the spiritual is the only real and substantial; that the eternal things of the universe are they which, afar off, seem dim and faint." The realization of his dream was in the form of a chartered train on the Denver and Rio Grande Western Railroad. During the autumn months that followed, Ingersoll, his wife, and several friends enjoyed a grand ramble through the Rocky Mountains of Colorado, New Mexico, and Utah. They "rocked-along" as far south as Santa Fe, and to the northwest to Salt Lake City and Ogden. During the course of his fleeting love affair with the mountains, Ingersoll diligently recorded recollections, descriptions, and memories of his adventure. Upon returning to the east he published, The Crest Of The Continent, in 1885. The book was widely popular from the beginning. It went through 42 editions, at least, and one can speculate that as many as 75,000 to 100,000 copies reached the market between 1885 and the year it went out of print (1901).

Ernest Ingersoll was born at Monroe, Michigan, on March 13, 1852. He attended the public schools of his native town, and early displayed an inquiring mind into subjects of natural history. In 1867 he entered Oberlin College, where after 2 years, his scientific aptitudes led him to the curatorship of the college museum. He went on to Harvard, and subsequently became affiliated with the Smithsonian Institute. He entered the United States Geological Survey, and served for a period as a naturalist under Hayden. He was a correspondent of the New York Tribune during 1874, being the first to publish the discovery of the cliff-dweller ruins along the San Juan River. Mr. Ingersoll contributed popular freelance articles and stories to Scribner's, Harper's and other prominent magazines of the late 19th century. He traveled widely and was much in demand as a speaker on natural history. He was the author of several books. Besides Crest Of The Continent, probably his most popular work was Knocking 'Round The Rockies (1882). In his later years he lived in Montreal and supervised the publication office of the Canadian Pacific Railroad. He moved to New Haven, Connecticut, and in 1888 to New York City. He died in Battleboro, Vermont, on November 13, 1946, bringing to a close 94 varied and fruitful years as a distinguished naturalist, scientist, and lecturer.

—H.L.J.

AN Luis Park, exceeding in size the State of Connecticut, is identified with the earliest and most romantic history of Colorado. It was here that brave old pioneer, Colonel Zebulon Pike, established his winter quarters almost a century ago, and was captured by the Mexican forces, for at that time all this region was Spanish territory. It was here the northernmost habitations of the Mexican people, the ranches at Conejos, Del Norte, and all along between, were placed, and so became the first farms in what now is Colorado. Here were pastured the first herds and flocks of the early settlers, and the great Maxwell grant, whose ownership has been the subject of so much litigation, included a large portion of this park. To this region, long ago Governor Gilpin directed the attention of immigrants, and lauded it as the "garden of the world." Gardening is practicable here, without doubt; but colonists have found other parts of the State so much more favorable, that, in spite of its superior advertising, the park has kept nearly its pristine innocence of agriculture outside of the old Mexican estates along the principal streams.

> *The plain was grassy, wild and bare,*
> *Wide, wild, and open to the air.*
> —TENNYSON.

That Colorado can ever produce cereals enough for the sustenance of a large population is doubtful. The great rarity and dryness of the atmosphere; the light rainfall, and almost instant disappearance of moisture; the large proportion of alkaline constituents in the earth, and the climate caused by great altitude, seem to handicap this region when compared with the Mississippi valley or the Pacific coast. By irrigation only, can agriculture thrive in this State; and the amount of arable land that can be cultivated without enormous expenditure for irrigating canals can hardly be considered wide enough to long supply the local population, which increases faster than the acreage under the plow is extended. The nature of the soil, and the effect of the short, hot seasons, under careful regularity of watering, combine, however, to make the product of Colorado farms extremely heavy to the acre, and of the finest quality in every article grown.

"The San Luis valley," says a recent report to the Government, "bears witness to the wealth of the produce returned by the soil under proper cultivation. In following up the Rio Grande, the Mexicans ascended divers tributary waters, and upon these and along the main river can their apologies for farms be seen. Generally content with simple existence, but little variety in the products of their land is observed. The turning of the earth with oxen and a sharpened stick, the threshing by flail and trampling under foot, and the crushing of the grain between stones, can be so frequently seen, that the charm of novelty is lacking and one's curiosity is soon satiated. Progress is not their hope or desire, and, content to eke out a bare subsistence, their ambition does not extend beyond a *baile*, or the tripping of the 'light fantastic,' with surroundings that are here, as a rule, far from enchanting.

"Their cultivation of the ground tells of eastern origin and traditions, and is by irrigation from *acequias* or canals. Smaller ditches at intervals lead out from the main, and furrows of earth of varying height, connected thereto, are raised at stated points parallel to one another, cutting up the entire area into many patches nearly square and of small extent. With the planting of the seed and the main ditch filled, all the smaller outlets and various sections being simultaneously overflowed, the entire area is carefully submerged, the little furrows confining the water in each section. To the inexperienced farmer, the first successful irrigation of his land is a matter of considerable labor and pains. Besides the thorough moistening of the earth, obtained by the gradual settling of the waters, a fertilizing process is at the same time ensured. These streams carry in solution much rich and valuable material from the denudation of sections drained in their passage, which is left in deposit like a substratum of manure. The latter is never used, the farmer depending on irrigation for the supply of those constituents extracted from the soil in the growth of produce.

"The Rio Grande descends from seven thousand seven hundred and fifty feet at Del Norte, to seven thousand four hundred on leaving the State for New Mexico. Upon its western side numbers of locations are along the Piedra Pintada, which sinks a few miles from the Rio Grande, the Alamosa and La Jara, but chiefly along the Conejos, the most thickly settled of all its tributaries; upon the eastern side are the Trinchera, Culebra, Costilla, the Culebra above San Luis being on this side the seat of largest habitation. In the upper part of San Luis valley is situated the finest land of the section, with the mountain range encircling it upon the east, north and west. Exposed only upon the south, whence do not come the heavy snow storms and coldest winds, it contains the best lands for cereal and other productions. Drained by the San Luis creek, and the Saguache, its tributary, the ranchmen who have located along the streams have been rewarded for their labor by very abundant crops of all kinds. Throughout the valley large herds of cattle find ample sustenance, the property mainly of Americans, while numerous flocks of sheep of Mexican ownership, are driven to and fro. The valley of the Conejos, with its affluents, San Antonio and Los Pinos creeks, is a most fertile region. Several miles east of Conejos, during the highest stages of the rivers, in June, water from the San Antonio finds its way into the former river above the latter's mouth, forming an island. This section is especially rich, and there exists almost a natural irrigation, the Mexican ranchmen raising large crops of all kinds at the cost of but little labor therefor.

"The Alamosa and La Jara, during the lower parts of their courses upon the plains, run side by side. At the foothills they diverge, the head of the Alamosa being in the northwest, its course throughout in a generally narrow and very deep cañon, while the upper waters of the La Jara are due west. All the portions of the former that are available for agriculture, are its banks on the plain and a short part of its cañon-valley within the foothills, upon which the Mexican ranches are found. Upon the La Jara are a few more Americans than upon the former, the ranch-owners being mainly, however, of Mexican descent. A tributary is called by the geographer North Fork, but is locally known as Aguas Calientes, or Hot Springs Creek, and where its land is represented as suitable for grazing only, it is found in reality to be adapted to the agriculture of the Mexicans, ranches at intervals being passed along its banks.

"The entire course of the La Jara may be likened in its direction to a huge frying-pan in outline, the long handle upon the plain extending to the Rio Grande, the basin within the foothills to its source. Before reaching the plains the stream flows to the south, east, and north, the latter part in a steep, precipitous cañon, strewed with basaltic, which the road avoids. This road, built by the county over a natural route, is in good order, and affords the residents of the lower river easy access to its upper part, which, as we ascend and pass over the intervening rolling foothills, we find within a lovely valley, called by the Mexicans *El Valle*, to which they resort for hay. The volcanic rocks strewn along the foothills, well timbered with piñon, we leave behind us as we descend into the valley, a basin eroded from the general plateau by the waters of the stream, which has cut for itself, in its lower and more rapid descent, a small but impassable cañon. This valley, several miles long and of a varying width of from three-fourths to one and a half miles, is a beautiful spot, and has been located upon by several persons for cattle ranches. The grazing is very fine, and so nearly level is the land, that the stream, here small and at its headwaters, pursues a most tortuous course. Trout are found more abundantly than at any other point."

While we can scarcely compliment the syntax of the report above quoted, the facts are trustworthy.

Fairly out into the valley, where Ute creek, Sangre de Cristo, and one or two other streamlets unite to form the Trinchera, stands an old military post, Fort Garland. In one of the cañons near by was a still older one, Fort Massachusetts, now abandoned or used only as a cavalry cantonment when a larger body of troops is assembled here than there are barracks for. In 1852 and 1856, the dates when the two forts respectively were founded, the Indians—Utes, Apaches, Comanches, and Navajoes—were all troublesome, and the men were kept very busy in scouting, if not in resisting attacks. Now the crumbling buildings of adobe shelter only a score or so of men, and serve merely as a depot of supplies, a large amount of government stores being guarded here. Fort Garland is a pretty place, and from it will be likely to make his start anybody who wishes to ascend old Sierra Blanca, the loftiest peak in Colorado, whose triple head stands grandly opposite and near the railway; the United States Geological Survey is his sole predecessor.

The railway down San Luis Park is straight as a surveyor's line, and trains often run at a high rate of speed

Sierra Blanca.

with perfect safety. At Alamosa it halted in construction for a long time. The town then became the forwarding point for all southern Colorado and New Mexico. Very large commission houses were placed there, enormous trains of wagons and pack mules were coming and going, stages left daily for Lake City and Gunnison, Saguache and Pitkin, Tierra Amarilla and the lower San Juan, Taos and Santa Fe, and the vim and excitement of an outfitting station prevailed. But presently the railway moved southward and westward, and Alamosa settled down into a quiet yet prosperous place, with a local agricultural population to back it, and the headquarters of the second division of the railway which extends to—to—well *towards* Mexico.

Twenty-nine miles south of Alamosa is Antonito, where the line branches off to the San Juan country. The town is supported by the money the railway and the passengers spend, and is quite uninteresting; but over to the westward is the larger and older village of Conejos, which is better, though "distance lends enchantment." Conejos means *hares*: probably the Mexican pioneers found a superfluity of jack-rabbits there. The place has been a farming and grazing center of supplies for many years. Along Conejos creek are numerous small Mexican ranches, good enough types of their sort (we shall find far better ahead), but the town itself has been Americanized until its claim to being a Mexican plaza is about lost; nor have the innovations added to its interest in any degree. In a real Mexican town, for example, the church is always an entertaining place to visit, because it is ruinously ancient and strange; but here the large, well-conditioned structure has been roofed, painted and modernized until it is not worth a glance except from the point of comfort and security from decay. Annexed to it is an academy for boys, and another for girls, both under the charge of priests and nuns of the Roman Catholic Church. These schools have no counterparts among the Mexicans nearer than Santa Fe, and have a wide reputation.

Lacking interest for the tourist, the practical man will learn that Conejos is a very fair business place in certain lines. It is the headquarters of the sheep and cattle men of the San Luis Park. In sheep, I learn that although about two hundred and fifty thousand are sold out of the park annually, fully five hundred thousand are left. The large majority of these are of the inferior sort called Mexican sheep, which are worth from one dollar to one dollar and twenty-five cents a head. The better minority sell at one dollar and fifty cents and two dollars a head, and this minority is increasing through a constant effort to improve the breed by introducing highly-bred Merino and Cotswold rams. The average yield is two and a half pounds of wool annually, and the product is shipped almost entirely to Philadelphia, for use in making carpets. Cattle is less an industry here, because the sheep are so numerous as to consume most of the pasturage. Something like ten thousand head, however, are able to exist in the park and adjacent foothills, and are sold to great advantage.

Nearly midway between Alamosa and Antonito, and easterly, but within sight of the railway, the Mormon settlements of Manassa and Ephraim have been founded, and have now a population of about six hundred. These people do not practice polygamy, and are frugal, industrious and prosperous. They are under the jurisdiction of the church in Utah, which also maintains similar colonies in the corners of Arizona and New Mexico adjacent to the Utah and Colorado line.

> *I'll look no more;*
> *Lest my brain turn, and the deficient sight*
> *Topple down headlong.*
> —KING LEAR.

A long line of telegraph poles stretches out from Antonito into a true vanishing point across the park, and the train follows it San Juanward. The noble Sangre de Cristo looms up higher and higher behind us as we proceed, a mirage lifting the line of cottonwoods along the Rio Grande into impossibly tall and spindling caricatures of trees; while the Jemez mountains away to the south are not yet lost to view, and the striking landmark of Mount San Antonio, smooth and round, is close at hand. A few miles beyond it the arid level of the lake-spread plain breaks into white, stony eminences, reared in a bold front. To surmount these the track is arranged in long, ingenious loops, in one place, known as the "Whiplash," extending into three parallel lines, scarcely a stone's throw apart, but disposed terrace-like on the hillside. On top of the mesa the sage-brush disappears, grass, piñons and yellow pines taking its place, and we begin to wind among the long, straight lava ridges at the foot of the divide between the Los Pinos and the Chama, whence the backward view is remarkably fine. The road here is like a goat's path in its vagaries, and wagers are made as to the point of the compass to be aimed at five minutes in advance, or whether the track on the opposite side of the crevasse is the one we have just come over, or are now about to pursue.

Describing a number of large curves around constantly deepening depressions, we reached the breast of a mountain, whence we obtained our first glimpse into Los Pinos valley; and it came like a sudden revelation of beauty and grandeur. The approach had been picturesque and gentle in character. Now we found our train clinging to a narrow pathway carved out far up the mountain's side, while great masses of a volcanic conglomerate towered overhead, and the face of the opposing heights broke off into bristling crags. The river sank deeper and deeper into the narrowing vale, and the space beneath us to its banks was excitingly precipitous. We crowded upon the platform, the outer step of which sometimes hung over an abyss that made us shudder, till some friendly bank placed itself between us and the almost unbroken descent. But we learned to enjoy the imminent edge, along which the train crept so cautiously, and begrudged every instant that the landscape was shut out by intervening objects.

To say that the vision here is grand, awe-inspiring, painfully impressive or memorable, falls short of the truth in each case. It is too much to take in at once, and we were glad to pause again for a little brain-rest at a telegraph station, hung almost like a bird's nest among the rocks,— to grow used by degrees to the stupendous picture spread before us. We were so high that not only the bottom of the valley, where the silver ribbon of the Los Pinos trailed in and out among the trees, and underneath the headlands, but even the wooded tops of the further rounded hills were below us, and we could count the dim, distant peaks in New Mexico.

Six miles ahead lay the cañon of which we had heard so much,—the Toltec Gorge, whose praises could not be overdrawn. Evidently his majesty had entrenched himself in glories beside which any ordinary monarch would lose his magnificence. Was this king of cañons really so great he could afford to risk all rivalry? Here, on the left, what noble martello-tower of native lava is that which stands undizzied on the very brink of the precipice? I should like to roll it off and watch it cut a swath through that puny forest down there, and dam up the whole stream with its huge breadth. How these passages of spongy rock resound as our engine drags the long train we have again mounted through their lofty portals! How narrow apparently are these curved and smooth embankments that carry us across the ravines, and how spidery look the firmly-braced bridges that span the torrents! All the way the road-bed is heaped up or dug out artifically. It is merely a shelf near the summit. It hugs the wall like a chamois-stalker, creeping stealthily out to the end of and around each projecting spur; its explores every in-bending gulch, boldly strides across the water channels, and walks undismayed upon the utmost verge, where rough cliffs overhang it, and the gulf sinks away hundreds of feet beneath.

In the most secluded nook of the mountains we come upon Phantom Curve, with its company of isolated rocks, made of stuff so hard as to have stood upright, tall, grotesque, and sunburned, beside the pigmy firs and cowering boulders with which they are surrounded. Miles away you can trace these black pinnacles, like sentinels, mid-way up the slopes; but here at hand they fill the eye, and in their fantastic resemblance to human shapes and things we know in miniature, seem to us crumbled images of the days when there were giants, and men of Titanic mold set up mementoes of their brawny heroes,—

> *the height, the space, the gloom, the glory.*
> *A mount of marble, a hundred spires!*
> —TENNYSON.

Phantoms, they are called, and the statuesque shadows they cast, moving mysteriously along the white bluffs, as the sun declines, are uncanny and ghost-like, perhaps; but the brown, rough, grandly grouping monoliths of lava themselves, are no more phantoms than are the pyramids of Sahara, and beside them the Theban monuments of the mighty Rameses would sink into insignificance.

Winding along the slender track, among these solemn forms, we approach the gorge, the vastly seamed and wrinkled face of whose opposite wall confronts us under

Phantom Curve.

Phantom Rocks.

the frown of an intense shade,—unused to the light from all eternity; but on this, the sunny side, a rosy pile, lifts its massive head proudly far above us, its square, fearless forehead,—

> "Fronting heaven's splendor,
> Strong and full and clear."

How should we pass it? On the right stood the solid palisade of the sierra, rising unbroken to the ultimate heights; on the left the gulf, its sides more and more nearly vertical, more and more terrible in their armature of splintered ledges and pike-pointed tree-tops,—more often breaking away into perpendicular cliffs, whence we could hurl a pebble, or ourselves, into the mad torrent easily seen but too far below to be heard; and as we draw nearer, the rosy crags rise higher and more distinct across our path. We turn a curve in the track, the cars leaning toward the inside, as if they, too, retreated from the look down into that "vasty deep," and lo! a gateway tunneled through,—the barrier is conquered!

The blank of the tunnel gives one time to think. Pictures of the beetling, ebony-pillared cliffs linger in the retina suddenly deprived of the reality, and reproduce the seamed and jagged rocks in fiery similitude upon the darkness. In a twinkling the impression fades, and at the same instant you catch a gleam of advancing light, and dash out into the sunshine,—into the sunshine only? Oh, no, out into the air,—an awful leap abroad into invisibly bounded space; and you catch your breath, startled beyond self-control!

Then it is all over, and you are still on your feet, listening to the familiar ring of the brown walls as they fly past.

What was it you saw that made your breathing cease, and the blood chill in your heart with swift terror? It is hard to remember; but there remains a feeling of an instant's suspension over an irregular chasm that seemed cut to the very center of the earth, and, to your dilated eye, gleamed brightly at the bottom, as though it penetrated even the realms of Pluto. You knew it opened outwardly into the gorge, for there in front stood the mighty wall, bracing the mountain far overhead, and below flashed the foaming river. This is the sum of your recollection, photographed upon your brain by a mental process more instantaneous than any application of art, and never to be erased. Gradually you conclude that the train ran directly out upon a short trestle, one end of which rests in the mouth of the tunnel, and the other in the jaws of a rock cutting. This is the fact; but the traveler reasons it out, for he cannot see the support beneath his car, which, to all intents, takes a flying bound across a cleft in the granite eleven hundred measured feet in depth.

Our train having halted, the Artist sought a favorable position for obtaining the sketch of Toltec Gorge which adorns these pages, the Photographer became similarly absorbed, and the remaining members of the expedition zealously examined a spot whose counterpart in rugged and inspiring sublimity probably does not exist elsewhere in America. A few rods up the cañon a thin and ragged pinnacle rises abruptly from the very bottom to a level with the railway track. This point has been christened Eva Cliff, and when we had gained its crest by dint of much laborious and hazardous climbing over a narrow gangway of rocks, by which it is barely connected with the neighboring bank, our exertions were well repaid by the splendid view of the gorge it afforded.

Just west of the tunnel, and close beside the track, the rocks have been broken and leveled into a small smooth space, and here, on the 26th of September, 1881, that gloomiest day in the decade for our people, were celebrated as impressive memorial services for GARFIELD, the noble man and beloved president, then lying dead on his stately catafalque in Cleveland, as were anywhere seen. The weather itself, in these remote and lonely mountains, seemed in unison with the sadness of the nation, for heavy black clouds swept overhead, and the wind made solemn moanings in the shaken trees. It was under circumstances so fittingly mournful that an excursion party, gathered from nearly every state in the Union, paused to express the universal sorrow, and to conceive the foundation of the massive monument which catches the traveler's eye on the brink of the gorge, and upon whose polished tablet are engraved these words:

> There in the gorges that widen, descending
> From cloud and from cold into summer eternal,
> Gather the threads of the ice-gendered fountains,—
> Gather to riotous torrents of crystal,
> And giving each shelvy recess where they dally
> The blooms of the north and its evergreen turfage.
>
> —BAYARD TAYLOR.

Garfield Memorial.

Though the climax of the pass to the sight-seer is Toltec Gorge, the actual crest of the Pinos-Chama divide is at Cumbres, some fifteen miles westward, and several hundred feet higher. After leaving Toltec, the brink of the cliff is skirted for some time, and many grand and exciting views are presented; but the stream is broken into cascades, and rapidly rises to the plane of the track. Passing a number of snow-sheds, the train is soon twisting around shallow side ravines, and at last, after making a great circle of nearly a mile, there comes a stoppage of that dragging sensation which the wheels impart on an upward grade, and the cars halt on the little level space at the summit. From Antonito to Cumbres the maximum ascent to the mile is only seventy-five feet, while on the western slope the descent per mile reaches two hundred and eleven feet. This intrepid railway crosses the main ranges of the Rocky Mountains over seven or eight distinct passes; and in every instance the locating engineers have followed one watercourse upward to its head, and another downward to the valley, finding invariably the sources of these oppositely-flowing brooks to be in springs only a few feet or rods apart at the top. In the present case so slight is the separa-

Toltec Gorge.

Pinos-Chama Divide at Cumbres.

tion that we seem to stop beside the Los Pinos, and to start beside Wolf Creek. Although at an altitude of about 9,500 feet, the neat station buildings at Cumbres are located in a depressed indentation, whence the surrounding hills shut off all outlook.

Our train is scarcely in motion again, however, ere a deep gully opens at our feet, and we commence to crawl cautiously around the protruding face of Cumbres Mountain, with its curiously-piled top of red and gray sandstone, and its precipitous front, in which is hewn midway a shelf for the track. Beyond this we pass a great curve, and then overlook a beautiful valley, which leads down into the broad basin through which the Rio Chama pursues its way southeasterly to its junction with the Rio Grande at Chamita. The view here is picturesque, and well worthy the reproduction our artist has seen fit to give it. There are glimpses of far-off, white-edged mesa-lands, with spaces of shadowy cobalt between. The brook sinks deeper, and its grassy banks are full of yellow and purple asters, in brightest bloom, glorifying the whole hillside up to where, a short distance from its bed, begins the solid spruce and aspen forest. Near Lobato, the track crosses from one tawny ridge to another, on a lofty iron bridge, and we note that Wolf Creek is here a lovely stream, with many cozy nooks in which the sportsman may pitch his tent, and are informed that the water is full of trout, while the wooded mountain slopes abound in large and small game. Once down in the valley, the way is through smooth lawns and pleasant groves until Chama is reached, and here we pause to ask questions about sheep.

Our cars were set aside in the very woods, far from the noisy station; a Y runs southward there, the germ perhaps of a railway down the river to Chamita, where it may join the southern line. All about us are the never-silent pines, and the breezes that whisper among their rugged branches blow laden with balsamic odors. Close by is the Rio Chama, hidden between dense and continuous thickets, through which the cattle can tell you of winding and mysterious paths. Everything in the landscape is soft and peaceful. The grass lies green and tender; the rounded clusters of willows, blending with the glowing masses of poplar behind them, bright in their new autumn colors, make no sharp line against the pine copse, nor this against the swelling, gaily-clothed background of the hills above.

Long ere this we had become domesticated in our cars, and now I may digress sufficiently to jot down a little description of them. As a have said, there were three, and we spoke of them as our "train." The first was a parlor-car. It usually ran in the rear, and gave us the advantage of a lookout behind, something worth having among the mountains. This car was not homelike enough to suit us, however, so we rarely occupied it, when we were stationary, except as a bed-room for our masculine guests. But when running, this car was our resort. Into it we would hustle the Madame's sewing-basket and fancy work, a lot of books and papers, spy-glasses, wraps, and luncheon, and have the gayest of times as we sped along, unconfined by limited space, unsolicitous about baggage or appearances, unannoyed by other passengers, and above all, thank heaven! safe from the peanut-boy. If we were to run at night we converted it into a sleeper. Curtains were hung up at intervals, making staterooms; easy chairs were faced, a stool placed between them, then a mattress spread across, forming a capital bed; or else we simply cleared a place on the floor, spread our mattresses down, and camped. Usually both methods were followed by different occupants. It was snug, there was good ventilation, and we slept such slumbers as seemed to prove us in the poet's category of the "just." Where a long stay was made, cots were set up, and the car became a bed-room exclusively. I doubt whether our porter enjoyed it, though, as much as we. He rarely rode upon its easy springs, and he had a constant fight with circumstances to keep it neat.

The other two sections of our train were box-cars, fresh from the shops, and of the most improved pattern. All through the trip, I may say in advance, they rode splendidly, though often attached to express trains which rattled them along at twice the speed the maker ever intended. Each of these cars had a door cut in one end, and these door-way ends were placed in juxtaposition and remained so always. At first two elaborate platforms were hinged to one of the cars, bridging the space between them; but they were smashed on almost the first curve, after which we laid a series of boards down from one bufferhead to the other and took them up whenever we moved—that is, if the porter didn't forget it, or get left. Here comes in the chronicle of our steps, the portable stairway by which we ascended and descended to and from our elevated house; *sed revocare gradus*,—"but to recall those steps" in their entirety would, I fear, be a hopeless task. The first set we had fell under the wheels and immediately became of no further interest to us. Then our invaluable forager found this second set, and thereby saddled himself with a responsibility he never could shake off. The whole Denver and Rio Grande railway corporation seemed to be bent on their destruction. Time fails me to tell of the numberless occasions when they were apparently crushed by some jar of the cars, as they stood in position at a station, and of the wrenchings that required a new hammering and more spikes to correct. But watched jealously by the porter, and lashed securely on the end of the car when we moved, they survived it all, and gave us *facilis decensus* from first to last.

One of these box-cars became kitchen and commissary office. A partition was thrown across one-third of the distance from the end, forming a room for our porter and also a place of storage for our supplies. There was everything in there, from a pepper-box to a mattress, and from a lamp-chimney to a Winchester rifle. It had a table which might have been let down, two windows, and sundry racks and clothes-hooks. The remaining two-thirds of the car was devoted to the kitchen. One corner contained a monstrous ice-chest, and opposite it stood a huge wood-and-coal box, which it was the constant ambition of our boy to keep piled with kindling stuff almost to the ceiling; the result being, that frequently his improvised racks would come to pieces with the jarring of some rapid run, and the fuel be heaped up "mighty promiscuous" on the floor. The other corners of the kitchen held a fair-sized cooking-stove, securely bolted, and, lastly, an iron water-tank, as large as a barrel and mounted on a stand. With this water-tank we had a long contest. The face of our first colored cook, never much more cheerful than the big end of a coffin, took on a doubly rueful aspect at the conclusion of our first day out. The tank had been well filled before starting, but the cover fitted so loosely that half a barrel or so of the liquid splashed out, and the floor of the car was like a little sea. The Photographer generously sacrificed a blanket to spread across underneath the cover, and we were careful afterward not to fill the tank quite to the top; but it always shot jets and sprays down the back of your neck when you least expected, if you went near it when in motion. Then one day the faucet burst, and deluged the place with a stream like that from a hose-pipe. Next it fell to leaking, and so to the end of the trip we had that persistently mischievous tank to contend with. Beside the stove stood a narrow cupboard, the top of which was intended to be the kitchen-table; but we found water leaking through into the flour, etc., underneath, and so built another table, hinging it to the opposite side of the car, between the tank and the fuel box. There were plenty of shelves and racks; and, the two side-doors having been fastened shut, the walls of the car were soon garnished with all sorts of wares that could be hung up. After a week it was learned how to stow everything so well that almost no breakage occurred.

The dining-car was exactly similar in size, twenty-four feet long by seven feet wide. It had four windows, and we used to slide back the great doors on one or both sides when the weather was warm and pleasant. If cool or stormy we locked them, wedged them tight and caulked the cracks, yet could never quite keep out the gales. The wind, I found, bloweth not only where "*it* listeth," but also where *I* listed. We thought it a very cheerful place, as we entered this snug home—for it was the "living-room" of the train—after a hard tramp, or gathered about the dinner table in the strong rays of mail lamps, and the softer light from railway candles. The gayly striped *portiére* shutting off the Madame's little nook of a bed-room at the rear end of the car; the bright oilcloth that covered the floor; the rich oak-brown of the paint on the door-frames, wainscoting, and stanchions that at frequent intervals supported the roof; the ruddy glow of the Turkey-red cloth filling all the panels, and the pictures, books, Indian pottery, burnished firearms and bits of decoration here and there, made a picture that never lost its cheer and air of comfort. Here were my friendly books and writing-desk, with all the little literary applicances, and pigeon-holes full of manuscript, memoranda and correspondence. Here was the easy chair behind the spindle-shaped, upright stove. Here was the Madame's rocking-chair and her work-stand, while the parted curtains let us peep into a diminutive but carefully convenient boudoir just behind her. Here stood her wardrobe—a trunk which lost its identity under the warm zigzags of a Navajo blanket; and here our hospitable dining-table, around which, perched on camp-stools, we ate good food with royal appetites, drank red wine with keen delight, and summoned all the imps of fun to laugh with us over quips and quirks to which, no doubt, the mad spirit of the day lent more wit than the brains of their makers. Shakespeare says,—

> "A jest's prosperity lies in the ear
> Of him that hears it, never in the tongue
> Of him that makes it."

Here work was done, too. Have I not seen the Madame busily sewing, and quiet? Did not the Artist often paint, I know not how long, without speaking?—I know not how long because I was so intent upon shaping this chronicle you read. If our trip had been all picnic and void of serious purpose, we should not have enjoyed it half so well. Charles Lamb asked pettishly,—

> "Who first invented work, and bound the free
> And holiday-rejoicing spirit down?"

But surely our holiday was fraught with a deeper zest, because our not too onerous duties now and then encroached upon our pleasures, and so made us value merry times the higher.

Well, now you may understand how and where we lived, and moved, and had our work and play. It was a warm, snug, handsome home and office, bed-chamber and kitchen on wheels. There were little hardships and annoyances, no doubt, but why remember them? *Le diable est mort!*

LEXICON OF STRATIGRAPHIC NAMES USED IN SOUTH-CENTRAL COLORADO AND NORTHERN NEW MEXICO, SAN LUIS BASIN

by

CHRISTINA LOCHMAN-BALK AND JAMES E. BRUNING

New Mexico Institute of Mining and Technology
Socorro, New Mexico

This lexicon is an alphabetical listing of the stratigraphic names used in the Guidebook of The New Mexico Geological Society—22nd Field Conference. Unit names (formation or group) system or period. Names printed in boldface are currently accepted by the U.S. Geological Survey. Many of the names printed in caps and lower case are those that the Survey has had no occasion to consider for use.

1) Areal distribution given in original description.
2) Reference in which unit was first defined or mentioned.
3) Type locality.
4) Short lithologic description (and thickness) at the type locality or in the type area.
5) Age to stage; contacts; emending or refining descriptions of note; additional areal distribution; additional information on thickness, lithology, and character of the beds in the area of the 22nd Field Conference (1971).

The following glossary of abbreviations contains those used in the list of names that are not widely used and known. Most abbreviations used herein for lithologic description are well known to all geologist, and are not included in the glossary.

alt. . . . . . . alternating
ascend. . . . . . . ascending, in ascending order
btw. . . . . . . between
calc. . . . . . . calcareous
calcar. . . . . . . calcarenites
char. . . . . . . characterized
conf. . . . . . . conformable or conformably. Used also with prefixial "un" and "dis."
cont. . . . . . . continental
correl. . . . . . . correlative or correlated
depos. . . . . . . deposited
descend. . . . . . . descending, in descending order
desig. . . . . . . designated
equiv. . . . . . . equivalent
fang. . . . . . . fanglomerate
fluv. . . . . . . fluviatile
gradat. . . . . . . gradational
gr. . . . . . . grain(ed)
gran. . . . . . . granular
grav. . . . . . . gravel
interb. . . . . . . interbedded

L. . . . . . . lower
lent. . . . . . . lenticular
lithog. . . . . . . lithographic
mass. . . . . . . massive
min. . . . . . . minimum
occas. . . . . . . occasional
perst. . . . . . . persistent
por. . . . . . . porous
pred. . . . . . . predominantly
sdy. . . . . . . sandy
slit. . . . . . . slightly
transit. . . . . . . transitional
U. . . . . . . upper
undif. . . . . . . undifferentiated

ALBOROTO RHYOLITE—U. Oligocene
1) SW Colorado.
2) E. S. Larsen, 1917, Colo. G. Survey Bull. 13, p. 20, 36; Larsen and Cross, 1956, U.S.G.S. Prof. Pap. 258, p. 132-143.
3) Alboroto Peak, San Cristobal Quadr., Hinsdale Co., Colo.
4) Low. part (1/5) of tridymite rhy.-thin flows and assoc. tuffs (0-500′) Up. part (4/5) of biotite hornblende latite and rhyolite (0-3,000′).
5) Disconf. on Sheep Mtn. Qtz. Latite; overlain conf. by Huerto Qtz. Latite; covers over 100 mi. in San Juan Mtns., max. thick. in Creede Quad.; Low. pt. incl. (Campbell Mtn. rhy., Willow Creek rhy.).,= Bachelor Mtn. Rhyolite, Outlet Tunnel qtz. latite; Up. pt. incl. Equity and Phoenix Park qtz. latites;= Fish Canyon Tuff-La Garita Qtz. Latite and Andesite of Saguache Cr. (27.8 m.y.).
L. membs. = Blue Mesa Tuff, Dillon Mesa Tuff. Sapinero Mesa. Tuff. U. memb. = Fish Canyon Tuff (Olson, Hedlund and Hansen, 1968).

Antero Formation—Oligocene
1) Cent. Colorado.
2) J. T. Stark et al., 1949, Geol. Soc. Am. Mem. 33, p. 63.
3) In Ts. 12-15 S., Rs. 75-76 W., south and west of Hartsel, Park Co., Colo.
4) Lake seds.—3 mems., ascend.—thin algal lss. at base, tuff, sss., cgls., minor shs., basal cgls. lentic., poor. sort. tuff interb. with shs., up to 100′ thick; mid memb. fine gr. pumice, tuffs (50′) at base, overlain

by lent. dense shs. and fossil. algal lss.; up memb. cgls. with ss. interb. (600'-2,000').
5) White River age; vert. fossils, fresh water gastro., ostracods, algae, wood: Disconf. on Blafour Fm., unconf. overlain by Wagontongue Fm., deposits of Lake Antero.

Abiquiu Tuff—Miocene
1) N. Cent. New Mexico.
2) H. T. U. Smith, 1938, Jour. Geol. v. 46, p. 944.
3) Along the Chama Valley west of Abiquiu, Rio Arriba Co., New Mexico.
4) Wh., lt. gry. to orange, fin. lamin. to mass. bed. tuff and volc. cgl., stream laid, few interb. lava flows; forms steep cliffs (1,000'-1,250').
5) Disconf. on El Rito Fm., unconf. on Precamb. granite; overlain conf. and gradat. by Santa Fe Fm.; E. of El Rito Cr. cgls. and sss. pred. interb. with tuff. layers in up. pt. = up. pt. of Los Pinos Fm. and low. pt. of Santa Fe Fm.; Consid. memb. of Santa Fe Fm. by Budding, Pitrat and Smith (1960).

ALAMOSA FORMATION—Pliocene-Pleistocene
1) S. Cent. Colorado.
2) C. E. Siebenthal, 1910, U.S.G.S. Wat. Sup. Pap. 240, p. 40.
3) Hansen Bluff, E. bank Rio Grande Riv., SE. of Alamosa, and logs of test wells, T. 39 N., T. 40 N., R. 11 E., (W. J. Powell, 1958), Alamosa Co., Colo.
4) Buff-red uncon. grav., sss., silt, clay; qtz. pebb.; br. to blu-gry. clay in up. pt; all lithol. rapid lat. and vert. changes (0-2,000').
5) Siebenthal put top below first perst. fine ss. or clay; Powell includes all Recent ss. and grav.; deepest: grav. at 72'; below blu. clay alter. with fine ss.; great. thick near depo. center of San Luis Valley; fresh water snails and vert. frags. age Late Plio. and/or Early Pleisto.

BACHELOR MOUNTAIN RHYOLITE—U. Oligocene
1) SW Colorado.
2) T. A. Steven and J. C. Ratté, 1965, U.S.G.S. Prof. Pap. 475-D, p. D57.
3) Bachelor Mtn. NW of Creede, Mineral Co., Colo.
4) Lt. gry. dens. weld. rhy. tuff at base grad. up to compact weld. tuff in mid., to por. nonweld. tuff at top (4,000'+).
5) Btw. 26.7 and 27.8 m.y.; intracaldera equiv. of Carpenter Ridge Tuff; 3 membs. ascend.:—Willow Cr. Memb., Campbell Mtn. Memb., Windy Gulch Memb.

Badger Creek Tuff (see Informal Names List)

Beidell Quartz Latite (see Conejos Formation)

BELDEN SHALE or FORMATION—Pennsylvanian
1) NW Colorado.
2) K. G. Brill Jr., 1942, AAPG Bull. 26, p. 1384-1387
3) N. side of Rock Cr. along U.S. Hwy. 24 (1938) 0.2 m. N. of Gilman, Eagle Co., Colo.
4) Interb. drk. gry. argill. lss. and lam. carbonac. shs., thin sss., and a few imp. coals (25'-200') increase to S. to 1,100' in Chaffee and Gunnison Cos., (Dings and Robison 1957).
5) Desmoinesian; raised to Fm. by Brill (1944), replaces Weber Sh. for basal Penn. in Colo.; unconf. on Leadville Ls., overlain conf. and gradat. by Minturn Fm.; Dings and Robinson recogn. 3 membs., ascend.-drk. sh.; interb. lss. and shs.; shs. with qtzite.

Big Baldy Andesite (see Informal Names List)

Biscara Member (of Los Pinos Formation)—Miocene? or Pliocene?
Biscara—Esquibel member; Biscara intrusive andesite
1) N. Cent. N. Mex.
2) Fred Barker, 1958, N. Mex. Bur. Min. and Miner. Res. Bull. 45, p. 44.
3) In Biscara Canyon 1.5 mi. from mouth, Las Tablas Quad., Rio Arriba Co., N. Mex.
4) Interb. tuffac. sss., tuff, cgls. and volc. flow brecc.; low. unit of gry. rhy. tuff, water-laid tuffac. cgls.; up. unit of poor. sort. cgls. of qtzite, pegmat. in ark. matrix (650'-700').
5) Unconf. on Precamb. rocks; overlain disconf. by Jarita Memb. and Cordito Memb. overlap from S. to N.; grades N. into Biscara-Esquibel Memb.

Biscara-Esquibel Memb.—(of Los Pinos Formation)—Miocene? or Pliocene?
Undif. sss., tuff, cgls., and volc. flow brecc. of low. Los Pinos Fm. below Jarita Bas.; mapp. as single unit by Fred Barker, 1958.

BLANCO BASIN FORMATION—Oligocene?
1) SW Colorado.
2) E. S. Larsen, 1935, U.S.G.S. Bull. 843, p. 48.
3) E. side of Chama Riv., near S. edge of Summitville Quad., Archuleta Co., Colo.
4) Ark. sss., cgls., shs., no volc. mater.; 3 memb., ascend.; brit. red, soft, mdy., sss. and shs.; brok. cliff of interb. wh. sss. and red shs.; cliff of wh. sss. (500'-600').
5) Unconf. on Cret. fms. and Animas Fm., overlain conform. by Conejos Fm.; F. B. Houton (1957)—Blanco Basin and equiv. Telluride Fm. are ark. fang. (bord. facies) of U. Paleocene—L. Eocene San Jose Fm. = Wasatch Fm.

BLUE MESA TUFF—U. Oligocene
1) SW Colorado.
2) J. C. Olson, D. C. Hedlund, and W. R. Hansen, 1968, U.S.G.S. Bull. 1251-C p. 15.
3) Rim of Blue Mesa, S. side of Black Canyon above Blue Mesa Dam, Gunnison Co. Colo.
4) Red br. to wh.-purp. wh. dens. weld. devitr. qtz. latite tuff, up. 40' strati. grades into few ft. of thin por. non-weld tuff (0-240'+).
5) Disc f. on old erod. surface, overlain conf. by ash-

fall? and water-laid tuffs.; onsid. equiv. of Treasure Mtn. Rhyolite and Andesite of Ford Creek, (Bruns, Epis, Weimer, and Steven, this guidebook).

BONANZA LATITE, TUFF—U. Oligocene
1) S. Colorado.
2) H. B. Patton, 1916, Col. G. Sur. Bull. 9, p. 29; W. S. Burbank, 1932, U.S.G.S. Prof. Pap. 169, p. 21.
3) Along Kerber Cr. S. of Bonanza, Saguache Co., Colo.
4) Two membs., ascend:-drk. red. br. to bl.-gry, mass. qtz. latite weld. tuff and brecc.; gry.: wh., pink-gry. soft poor weld. qtz. latite tuffs, few breccs. (300′ to 1,000′).
5) Bonanza Latite of Patton applied only to Low Memb.; unconf. on the Rawley Andesite, unconf. overlain by Squirrel Gulch Latite; replac. to S. by Hayden Peak Latite; Bonanza Latite is an ash-flow tuff, overlies Rawley Andesite, (Bruns, Epis, Weimer and Steven, this guidebook).

BREWER CREEK LATITE—U. Oligocene
1) S. Colorado.
2) W. S. Burbank, 1932, U.S.G.S. Prof. Pap. 169, p. 29
3) Along Brewer Cr. 2-3 mi. W. of Bonanza, Saguache Co., Colo.
4) Purp.-gry. to br.-gry, or brick red porphy. qtz.-mica latite mass. flows, up. pt. por. with tridymite (500′)
5) Conf. on Squirrel Gulch latite in S., and overlies unconf. Porphy. Peak Rhyolite to N.; overlain disconf. by upper andesite flows maybe equiv. to water laid and air-fall tuffs of Saguache Cr., (Bruns, Epis, Weimer and Steven, this guidebook).

CARLILE SHALE (in Colorado Group)—U. Cretaceous
1) E. Colorado, NW Iowa, W. Kansas, SE Montana, W. Nebraska, South Dakota, E. Wyoming, NE New Mexico.
2) G. K. Gilbert, 1896, U.S.G.S. 17th Ann. Rept. pt. 2, p. 565.
3) Carlile Spring and Carlile Station 21 miles W. of Pueblo, Pueblo Co., Colo.
4) Drk.-gry. to blk. argill. shs. with thin lss. beds, fossil. lss. nods, and large septarian concret.; calc. sss. and sdy. shs. (180′-700′).
5) M.-U. Turonian: Conf. on Greenhorn Ls., overlain conf. or discf. by Fort Hays Ls. (of Niobrara Fm. in N. Cent. and NE New Mex.); Kauffman (1967) recogn. 4 units ascend.—Fairport Chalky Sh. Memb. (br.- buff, speck., cal. shs. and thin, slab. calcars., abund. ls. conc., 6 bent. beds, very fossil., 220′); Blue Hill Sh. Memb. (low. unit of interb. drk.-blu.-gry. to br. noncal. clay sh. slitly slty., large septarian and ls. concret.: up. unit of drk. gry. to br. slty. and sdy. interb. at top with br. sss., sdy. shs. and sltst., 220′, septarian concret.); gradat. into Codell Ss. Memb. (mass. to slby., tan-buff, fine to med. gr., sss. carbonac. sss. and sdy. shs., rapid facies changes—in N. Mex. from a drk. slty. sh. to lent. thin sss., sltst. to mass. ss., 0-50′); Juana Lopez Memb. (br. to br.-gry. slby. to mass. calcars. local. upto 60% mature qtz. grs., Inoceramus prisms, oyster and fish debris, 1′-4′ in E., expands to 200′ in San Juan Bas. and pred. cal. clay sh. interb. with calcars., very fossil): Unnamed Sh. Memb. (drk. gry. to drk. br. lam. clay sh., calcars. bents. and lss. concret. in up. pt.) pre-Niobrara erosion may cut out top two membs and part of Codell Ss.

CAMPBELL MTN. RYH. (see Bachelor Mtn. Rhy.)

Carpenter Ridge Tuff—U. Oligocene
1) SW Colorado.
2) J. C. Olson, D. C. Hedlund and W. R. Hansen, 1968, U.S.G.S. Bull. 1251-C, p. 23.
3) S. end of Carpenter Ridge, cent. Cebolla Quad., Gunnison Co., Colo.
4) Two ash-flows of br. red.-lt. gry., devitri. qtz. latite weld tuff, wh. to lt. buff nonweld. pumic. tuff at base, tuffac. brecc. at top (0-300′).
5) Btw. 26.7 and 27.8 m.y.: Disconf. on Fish Canyon Tuff and older rocks; erupt. from Bachelor caldera and equiv. of Bachelor Mtn. Rhyolite.

CHAFFEE FORMATION—U. Devonian
1) Cent. Colorado.
2) E. Kirk, 1931, Amer. Jour. Sci. 5th, v. 22, p. 229.
3) On S. side of Arkansas Riv. 5 mi. SE. of Salida, Chaffee Co., Colo.
4) Two membs. ascend. Parting Qtzite Memb., lt. gry. to wh. buff, coarse-med. gr., sss., qtzite, cgls., xbed., Dyer Memb. gry.-buff, thin to med. bed. fossil. lss., dolo. (70′-250′).
5) Famennian: Paraconf. on Manitou Dol., Harding Ss. or Fremont Dol.; overlain disconf. by Leadville Dol., equiv. of Elbert of SW Colorado.

Cisneros Basalt (in Hinsdale Series)—Pliocene
1) N. Cent. New Mexico.
2) Fred Barker, 1958, New Mex. Bur. Min. and Miner. Res. Bull. 45, p. 51.
3) Cisneros Park in NW¼ T. 29 N., R. 8 E., Rio Arriba Co., New Mex.
4) Drk. gry. slit. vesicul., porphy. olivine basalt (10′-30′).
5) Unconf. on Cordito Memb. of Los Pinos Fm., up. surface erod.

CONEJOS FORMATION (in Potosi Volcanic Group)—M. Oligocene
Conejos Andesite, Conejos Quartz Latite
1) SW Colorado and N. New Mexico.
2) E. S. Larsen, 1917, Colo. G. Sur. Bull. 13, p. 38; Larsen and Cross, 1956, U.S.G.S. Prof. Pap. 258, p. 96-102.
3) Along Conejos Riv. for 3 mi. downstream from Platoro, Conejos Co., Colo.
4) Interb. lavas and breccs. of andesit.-qtz. latite, drk.

rhyodacite, fine-gr. bed. drk. gr. tuffs and tuffac. sss., (1,000′-4,000′).
5) Btw. 31.1 and 34.7 m.y.: center in Summitville, Conejo and Del Norte Quads. 130 mi. N-S, 50 mil. wide; extends 40 mi. into N. Mex. is thin and pred. ss. and grav. of volc. frags.: Disconf. on Blanco Basin Fm. overlain unconf. by Treasure Mtn. Rhyolite and Fisher Qtz. Latite; age equiv. of Lake Fork Fm., West Elk Breccia and San Juan Fm., Beidel and Tracey Qtz. Latites, and Rawley Andesite (Lipman, Steven and Mehnert, 1970).

Cordito Member (of Los Pinos Formation)—Pliocene
1) N. Cent. New Mexico.
2) Fred Barker, 1958, New Mex. Bur. Min. and Miner. Res. Bull. 45, p. 48.
3) In Canyon de Cordito, 4 mi. S. of Tres Piedras, Taos Co., New Mex.
4) Lt. gry-gry. gr.-buff interb. rhy. cgls., tuffs, tuffac. sss. and slst. a few ash-flows (250′-1,000′).
5) Disconf. on Jarita, Esquibel and Biscara Membs. and Precam. rocks: Unconf. overlain by Cisneros and Dorado Basalts; along S. bord. of Las Tablas Quad. is equiv. to Abiquiu Tuff of H. T. U. Smith (Budding, Pitrat, Smith, 1960).

CREEDE FORMATION—U. Oligocene
1) SW Colorado.
2) W. H. Emmons and E. S. Larsen, 1923, U.S.G.S. Bull. 718, p. 61: Larsen and Cross, 1956, U.S.G.S. Prof. Pap. 258, p. 167-172.
3) Valley of Willow Creek at Creede, Mineral Co., Colo.
4) Volc. clastics, water-laid; two membs. ascend.-wh. lam. shy. tuff, lent. sss., breccs., cgls., interb. with travertine (lake beds with plants and insects); mod. sort. coarse rhy. cgls. interb. with thin lava flows, shy. beds and lens. (0-2,000′).
5) Older than 26.8 m.y., cut and overlain by Fisher Qtz. Latite.: Disconf. on Potosi Gp. rocks.

Crestone Conglomerate Member (of Sangre de Cristo Formation)—Permian
1) S. Cent. Colorado.
2) F. A. Melton, 1925, Jour. Geol. v. 33, p. 812.
3) Crestone Peak, near Crestone, Saguache Co., Colo.
4) Drk. red, mass. bedd. bould. and cobble cgls. with some thin interb. ark. sss. (500′-5,500′).
5) Wolfcampian: Disconf. on Low. Memb. of Sangre de Cristo Fm., overlain conf. in subsurf. by Yeso Fm. (Shaw, 1956), in surface unconf. by Entrada Ss.

DAKOTA SANDSTONE, FORMATION or GROUP—L. and U. Cretaceous
1) E. Colorado, Nebraska, Kansas, Minnesota, SE. Montana, E. Wyoming, N. Dakota, W. Oklahoma, NE New Mexico.
2) F. B. Meek and F. V. Hayden, 1862, Phila. Acad. Nat. Sci. Proc. v. 13, 419.
3) In Missouri Riv. bluffs, NE¼ Sec. 13, T. 27 N., R. 4 E., 1 miles SE of Homer, Dakota Co., Nebraska.
4) Buff, red, wh., fine-coarse gr. sss. or qtzite, locally 2 or 3 mass. bed. sss. separ. by thin gry., blk. or varig. clay shs., plant fossil, thin lignit. cliff-form. (100′-400′).
5) Albian Cenomanian: Disconf. on Morrison Fm. or conf. Purgatoire Fm., overlain conf. by Mowry and Graneros Shs., in Mora Co., N. Mex. 180′ thick.

DILLON MESA TUFF—U. Oligocene
1) SW Colorado.
2) J. C. Olson, D. C. Hedlund, and W. R. Hansen, 1968, U.S.G.S. Bull. 1251-C p. 17.
3) On Dillon Mesa, N. side of Gunnison Riv.; 4 miles above Blue Mesa Dam, Gunnison Co. Colo.
4) Lt. br., slit. porphy. weld qtz. latite tuff, up to 55′ basal cgl.; up. unit nonweld tuff and tuffac. brecc. (0-180″).
5) 28.2 m.y.: disconf. on Blue Mesa Tuff, overlain disconf. by Sapinero Mesa Tuff; equiv. to tuff of Masonic Park. (Bruns, Epis, Weimer, and Steven, this guidebook).

Dorado Basalt (in Hinsdale Series)—Pliocene
1) N. Cent. New Mexico.
2) Fred Barker, 1958, New Mex. Bur. Min. and Miner. Res. Bull. 45, p. 53.
3) In Dorado Canyon, NE of Petaca, Rio Arriba Co., New Mex.
4) Drk. fine-gr. olivine basalt, basalt and qtz. basalt (40′-100′).
5) Unconf. on Cordito Memb. of Los Pinos Fm., up. surface eroded.

Dry Union Formation—U. Miocene-Pliocene
1) Cent. Colorado.
2) Ogden Tweto, 1961, U.S.G.S. Prof. Pap. 424-B p. B133.
3) Dry Union Gulch, Sec. 23, T. 10 S., R. 80 W., 5 miles S. of Leadville, Lake Co., Colo.
4) Mass. br. sdy. sltst. interb. sss. and grav. minor volc. ash; poor. sort. (800′-2,000′).
5) Unconf. on Mesozoic and Paleogene rocks; lake beds in earlier repts. (Emmons, Irving and Loughlin, 1927); underlies Arkansas Valley from Leadville to Salida; age deter. by vert. fossils (Van Alstine and Lewis, 1960; Van Alstine, 1970); Tenderfoot Hill volcanic sequence (Lowell, 1969) or Tenderfoot Hill facies (Lowell, 1971, this guidebook)—basic lava flows interb. with uncons. gravs. (0-450′).

DYER DOLOMITE MEMBER (of Chaffee Formation)—U. Devonian
1) Cent. Colorado.
2) C. H. Behre, Jr., 1932, Colo. Sci. Soc. Proc. v. 13, p. 60.
3) On West Dyer and Dyer Mtns. 5 miles E. of Leadville, Lake Co., Colo.

ls. (Thatcher Ls.) in low. mid. of fm. in SE. Colo. and San Juan Bas., New Mex. and a mass to shy. gry. to tan ss. (20'-50') lens (cf. Tres Hermanos Ss.) in up. pt. in N. New Mex.

HARDING SANDSTONE, QUARTZITE—
Mid. Ordovician
1) Cent. Colorado.
2) C. D. Walcott, 1892, Geol. Soc. Am. Bull. 3, p. 155.
3) Harding Quarry, 1 mi. NW of Canyon City, Fremont Co., Colo.
4) Tan, pink, wh. gry., br., blu.-blk., fine-med. gr. sss. or qtzites, fish debris common (120'-200').
5) Paraconf. on Manitou Dolo. or unconf. on Precamb.; overlain disconf. by Fremont Dol.

HAYDEN PEAK LATITE—M. Oligocene
1) S. Colorado.
2) H. B. Patton, 1916, Colo. Geol. Sur. Bull. 9, p. 21
3) On Haydens Peak, 2.5 mi. SE of Bonanza, Saguache Co., Colo.
4) Br.-gry., fine-gr. porphy. qtz. latite flows, tuffs and breccs. (1,000'-2,000').
5) 33.2 m.y.: Overlies Rawley Andesite, overlain unconf. by Bonanza Tuff; age equiv. of flows in Conejos Fm.

HINSDALE FORMATION—M. Miocene—
M. Pliocene
Hinsdale Basalt
1) SW Colorado, NW New Mexico.
2) W. Cross, 1911, U.S.G.S. Bull. 478, p. 22: Larsen and Cross, 1956, U.S.G.S. Prof. Pap. 258, p. 192-207.
3) Divide btw. Lake Fork and Cebolla Creeks, E. of Lake City, Hinsdale Co., Colo.
4) Two membs., ascend.:—wh. high sili., alk. rhy. weld. tuffs, breccs., intrusives, volc. cones and thin basalt flows (0-2,000'); flows and volc. cones of alk. olivine basalt (0-1,500').
5) Low. memb. 23-21 m.y., up. memb. 17-4 m.y.; Unconf. on Fisher Qtz. Latite and Los Pinos Grav.

HUERTO QUARTZ LATITE, FORMATION (in Potosi Volcanic Group)—U. Oligocene
1) SW Colorado.
2) E. S. Larsen, 1917, Colo. Geol. Sur. Bull. 13, p. 20: Larsen and Cross, U.S.G.S. Prof. Pap. 258, p. 143.
3) Huerto Peak, 10 mi. SE of Rio Grande Resv., San Cristobal Quad., Hinsdale Co., Colo.
4) Drk., fine-gr., pyrox. qtz. latite, dacite, lt. gry. hornbl. qtz. latite, flows, tuffs and breccs. interb. (0-2,500')
5) 26.7 m.y.: breccs. and lavas of Huerto underlie Mammoth Mt. Rhyolite (which is later than Farmers Creek Rhyolite), and underlie and overlie Wason Park Rhyolite (Steven and Ratté, 1964)—all units pt. of Lower Memb. of Piedra Rhyolite.

JACQUE MOUNTAIN LIMESTONE MEMBER (of Minturn Formation)—Pennsylvanian
1) W. Cent. Colorado.
2) S. F. Emmons, 1898, U.S.G.S. Atlas Folio 48, p. 2 "Tenmile District."
3) On lower slopes of Jacque Mtn. near Kokomo, Summit Co., Colo.
4) Lt. gry. to drk. blu. fine-gr. lss., some beds ooli. or brecc., cephal. and gastro., (15'-30').
5) Virgilian: Top unit of Minturn Fm., good horizon marker, conf. on top brit. red and shy. ss. approx. 900' above White Quail Ls. Memb., overlain conf. by brit. red ark. cgls. of basal Maroon Fm.

Jarita Basalt Member (of Los Pinos Formation)—U. Oligocene to M. Miocene
1) N. Cent. New Mexico.
2) Fred Barker, 1958, New Mex. Bur. Min. and Miner. Res. Bull. 45, p. 46.
3) West rim of La Jarita Mesa, NE of Vallecitos, Rio Arriba Co., New Mex.
4) Drk. gry., br. fine-med. gr. flows of olivine basalt (0-50').
5) Conf. on Esquibel Memb., overlain disconf. by Cordito Memb.; vesicles aligned in S.40°W, Barker believes source to NE.

KERBER FORMATION—Pennsylvanian
1) S. Colorado.
2) W. S. Burbank, 1932, U.S.G.S. Prof. Pap. 169, p. 13.
3) Along Kerber Creek, 6 mi. SE. of Bonanza, Saguache Co., Colo.
4) Interb. wh., gry., buff coarse-med. gr. qtz. sss., xbedd., and blk. carbonac. shs. and imp. coal (200'-300').
5) Morrowan: Paraconf. on Leadville Ls., overlain disconf. by Minturn Fm.

LA GARITA QUARTZ—U. Oligocene
1) SW Colorado.
2) T. A. Steven and J. C. Ratté, 1964, U.S.G.S. Prof. Pap. 475-D, p. D57: Prof. Pap. 487, p. 15-18.
3) La Garita Mts., 7 mi. NE of Creede, Mineral Co., Colo.
4) Drk. br., drk. gray. cryst. rich, dens. weld. ash-flow tuffs and breccs. (0-2,500+').
5) 27.8 m.y.: Two membs, ascend.—Outlet Tunnel Memb. (pre-La Garita Cauldron Subsidence); Phoenix Park Memb. equiv. of low. membs. of Bachelor Mtn. Rhyolite: Formerly in Alboroto Rhyolite.

LA JARA CANYON MEMBER (of Treasure Mountain Rhyolite, Tuff)—U. Oligocene
1) Cent. Colorado.
2) P. W. Lipman and T. A. Steven, 1970, U.S.G.S. Prof. Pap. 700-C, p. C21.
3) La Jara Canyon, 17.5 mi. SE of Platoro, Conejos Co., Colo.
4) Dens. cryst. rich weld. qtz. latite ash-flows and tuffs (300'-2,500').
5) 29.8 m.y.: Conf. on lower air-fall and ash-flow tuff, overlain by middle tuff; max. thick within Platoro caldera.

4) Lt. gry., drk. gry.-buff, thin-med. bed., sugary dolo. lss. and dolos. (60'-85').
5) Famennian: Conf. on Parting Ss. Memb., overlain disconf. by Gilman Ss. Memb. of Leadville Dol.

Eagle Nest Formation—Pliocene?
1) N. Cent. New Mexico.
2) L. L. Ray and J. F. Smith, Jr., 1941, Geol. Soc. Am. Bull. 52, p. 190.
3) Along U.S. Hgwy. 24, N. of Eagle Nest Lake, Colfax Co., New Mex.
4) Unconsol. red clay, wh. tuff interb. with coarse wh. to buff ss. and grav. (1,000'+).
5) Top and base of fm. not seen; is fang. fill of Moreno Valley after faulting.

ENTRADA SANDSTONE (in San Rafael Group)— U. Jurassic
1) S. and E. Utah, NE Arizona, W. Cent., SE Colorado, NW New Mexico.
2) J. Gilluly and J. B. Reeside, Jr., 1926, U.S.G.S. Press Bull. 6064: 1928, U.S.G.S. Prof. Pap. 150-D, p. 76.
3) Entrada Point, north San Rafael Swell, Emery Co., Utah.
4) Drk. br., red br., buff to gry., thin to mass. bedd. sss., earthy to clean, well sort., xbed., interb. with a few thin bed. gry.-grn. lam. sdy. chs., cliffs, (200'-850').
5) Conf. on Carmel or disconf. Navajo Ss., overlain disconf. by Curtis Fm. or Summerville Fm.; in N. New Mex. overlies paraconf. Chinle Fm.

Esquibel Member (of Los Pinos Formation)— Miocene? or Pliocene?
1) N. Cent. New Mexico.
2) Fred Barker, 1958, New Mex. Bur. Min. and Miner. Res. Bull. 45, p. 45.
3) Esquibel Canyon, Las Tablas Quad., Rio Arriba Co., New Mex.
4) Gry. interb. fels. tuff., tuffac. sss. and cgls., buff ark. sss. and cgls., sltsts. (600').
5) Conf. and gradat. on Biscara Memb., overlain unconf. by Jarita Basalt Memb. or Cordito Memb.

FARMERS CREEK RHYOLITE (See Huerto Fm.)

FISH CANYON TUFF—U. Oligocene
1) SW Colorado.
2) J. C. Olson, D. C. Hedlund and W. R. Hansen, 1968, U.S.G.S. Bull. 1251-C, p. 20.
3) In Fish Canyon near south border of Rudolph Hill Quad., Gunnison Co., Colo.
4) Lt.-gry., buff to wh., med.-gr., cryst. rich qtz. latite weld. tuff, grad. upward and lateral. into nonweld. tuff, grad. upward and lateral. into nonweld. tuff, large angul. frags. of Precamb. and Mesozoic rocks near base (0-1,280').
5) 27.8 m.y.; large air-fall and ash-flow sheet from S. source; traced S. into Rio Grande drainage basin; correl. with Alboroto Rhyolite erupt. from La Garita caldera, equiv. of La Garita Quartz Latite. (Bruns, Epis, Weimer and Steven, this guidebook).

FISHER QUARTZ LATITE—U. Oligocene
Fisher Latite-Andesite
1) SW Colorado.
2) E. S. Larsen, 1917, Colo. Geol. Sur. Bull. 13, p. 23: Larsen and Cross, 1956, U.S.G.S. Prof. Pap. 258, p. 172-185.
3) Fisher Mountain, 12 mi. S. of Creede, Mineral Co., Colo.
4) Wh. tuff and tuff brecc. thin lava flows at base, overlain by thick flow of coars. porphy. qtz. latite, gry.-purp. pumice. flow brecc. and pink porphy. vesicu. latite flow (0-2,000+') (Steven and Ratté, 1965).
5) 26.4 m.y.: Disconf. on Snowshoe Mountain ash-flow, local. Overlain disconf. by Hinsdale Fm.; age equiv. of Creede Fm.

FREMONT LIMESTONE, DOLOMITE— U. Ordovician
Fremont Formation
1) E. and Cent. Colorado.
2) C. D. Walcott, 1892, Geol. Soc. Am. Bull. 3, p. 156
3) Harding Quarry, 1 mi. NW of Canyon City, Fremont Co., Colo.
4) Two membs. ascend., blu.-gry. to gry. mass. pure dolo. with zone of blk. chert and coral bed near base; thin-bed, shy. to sdy. dolo. (Priest Canyon Memb.) (200'-400').
5) Eden-Richmond: Disconf. on Harding Ss., overlain paraconf. by Parting Qtzite.

GILA CONGLOMERATE—Miocene-Pleistocene
1) SE Arizona, SW New Mexico.
2) G. K. Gilbert, 1875, U.S. Geog. & Geol. Sur. 100th Mer., v. 3, p. 540.
3) Gorges of upper Gila Riv., Greenlee Co. Ariz., Hidalgo and Grant Cos. New Mex.
4) Buff to br. fangs. of interb. cgls., sss. sltst. and clay (200'-500').
5) Base 21 m.y.: Disconf. on Oligo. volc.; 3 membs. recogn. in Safford Valley, Ariz. (P. A. Wood, 1959).

GRANEROS SHALE (in Colorado Group)— U. Cretaceous
1) NW Iowa, W. Kansas, E. Colorado, SE Montana, Nebraska, South Dakota, E. Wyoming, NE New Mexico.
2) G. K. Gilbert, 1896, U.S.G.S. 17th Ann. Rept., pt. 2, p. 564.
3) Graneros Creek, Walsenburg Quad., Pueblo Co., Colo.
4) Blk., drk. gry, oliv., gry.-br. noncal. to silt. cal., lam. clay shs., many perst. bent. beds, argill. ls. concret., cone-in-cone ls. and thin calcar. in mid. and up. pt., local. thin br. sss. near top (30'-250').
5) Cenomanian: Conf. and gradat. on Dakota Ss., overlain conf. by Greenhorn Ls.; perst. mass. argill. fossil.

**LAKE FORK QUARTZ LATITE FORMATION—
M. Oligocene**
1) W. Cent. Colorado.
2) W. Cross and E. S. Larsen, 1923, U.S.G.S. Prof. Pap. 131, tab. opp. p. 184: Larsen and Cross, 1956, U.S.G.S. Prof. Pap. 258, p. 64-68.
3) Valley of Lake Fork of Gunnison Riv. 5-15 mi. N. of Lake City, Hinsdale Co., Colo.
4) Lt. gry. rhyodacite, drk. br.-blk. dens. andesite, interb. flows, breccs. and tuffs, air-fall tuffs, cgls. (0-4,000′).
5) 31.1-34.7 m.y.: Unconf. on M. Cret. fms., overlain disconf. by Blue Mesa and younger ash-flow tuffs; 3 units, ascend., 600′ grav., volc. cgls., tuff, andesite flows and breccs; 900′-3,000′+ volc. breccs., cgls. depos. as lahars., interb. tuff and thin rhyodacite flows, 900′ hornbl. rhyodacite flows and autobreccs., age equiv. of Conejos Fm., San Juan Fm. (Olson, et al., 1968).

**LA SAUSES MEMBER (of Conejos Formation)—
M. Oligocene**
1) S. Cent. Colorado.
2) R. L. Burroughs, 1971, this guidebook.
3) Cliffs along Wildhorse Ridge, 1-7 mi. E. of La Sauses, Conejos Co., Colo.
4) Gry.-pink, red br., lt.-drk. gry. interb. tuff breccs., pumice. tuffs, lahars, dens. cryst. tuffs, latite flows, tuffac. sss. and gravs. (50′-800′).
5) Conf. on Wildhorse Memb., overlain disconf. by Manassa Memb.

**LEADVILLE LIMESTONE, DOLOMITE—
Mississippian**
1) Colorado.
2) G. H. Eldridge in S. F. Emmons, et al., 1894, U.S.G.S. Atlas Folio 9, p. 6.
3) Expos. at Leadville, Lake Co., Colo.
4) Yel. calc. ss., sdy. chrty. ls. and dol. at base, overlain by drk. gry., thick-bed to mass. chrty. lss. ooli., and chrty.-dolos. (75′-300′).
5) Kinderhook-Meramac: Disconf. on Chaffee, overlain paraconf. by Belden Fm. with basal Molas Memb.

LOS PINOS GRAVEL, FORMATION—Miocene
1) S. Cent. Colorado, N. New Mexico.
2) W. W. Atwood and K. F. Mather, 1932, U.S.G.S. Prof. Pap. 166, p. 92-100.
3) Los Pinos Canyon, near San Miguel, Rio Arriba Co., New Mex.
4) Fangs. of sss., gravs. tuffs, thin olivine basalt flows (0-2,000+′).
5) 25.9 m.y.: Unconf. on older volc. and Precamb. rocks on San Juan peneplane, overlain disconf. by basalts and fangs. of Hinsdale Fm.: 4 membs. ascend.-Biscara, Esquibel, Jarita Basalt, Cordito.

MADERA LIMESTONE, FORMATION (in Magdalena Group)—Pennslvanian
1) S. Colorado, N. and Cent. New Mexico.
2) C. R. Keyes, 1903, Ores and Metals, v. 12, p. 48.
3) E. slope of Sandia Mtns., Bernalillo Co., New Mex.
4) Two membs., ascend., interb. gry., blu.-gry., chrty. lss. and calc. shs.; br. ark. sss., ark. lss. and lt. gry. lss. (0-3,000′).
5) Desmoinesian-Virgilian: Conf. and grad. on Sandia Fm., overlain conf. or disconf. by Sangre de Cristo Fm., grad. later. N. into Sangre de Cristo or Minturn Fms.

**Manassa Member (of Conejos Formation)—
M. Oligocene**
1) S. Cent. Colorado.
2) R. L. Burroughs, 1971, this guidebook.
3) In Western San Luis Hills, E. of Manassa, Conejos Co., Colo.
4) Drk. br., blk. andesite flows, drk. red scoria with fine tuffac. matrix, flow breccs., explosive breccs. (0-1,500′).
5) Disconf. on La Sauses Memb., overlain unconf. by Santa Fe Fm.

**MAMMOTH MOUNTAIN RHYOLITE—
U. Oligocene**
1) SW Colorado.
2) W. S. Emmons and E. S. Larsen, 1923, U.S.G.S. Bull. 718, p. 40; redefin. T. A. Steven and J. C. Ratté, 1964, U.S.G.S. Prof. Pap. 475-D, p. D. 59
3) Mammoth Mountain, 2-3 mi. NE. of Creede, Mineral Co., Colo.
4) Rhy. to qtz. latite, cryst. poor to cryst. rich, red-br. weld. and some non-weld. ash-flow tuffs (0-2,000′).
5) 26.7 m.y.: Disconf. on Farmers Creek Rhyolite, overlain disconf. by Wasson Park Rhyolite; former. low. memb. of Piedra Rhyolite (Larsen and Cross, 1956).

MANITOU LIMESTONE, DOLOMITE, FORMATION—Ordovician
1) E. Colorado.
2) W. Cross, 1894, U.S.G.S. Geol. Atlas Folio 7, p. 2.
3) E. side of canyon, above Narrows of William Canyon, SW ¼, sec. 32, T. 13 S., R. 67 W., El Paso Co., Colo.
4) Gry. to blu.-gry., local red, thin bedd.-mass. lss., dolo. lss., dolos. (100′-370′).
5) Canadian: paraconf. on Peerless Fm., Sawatch Qtzite., or unconf. on Precamb. rocks, overlain paraconf. by Harding ss. or Parting Qtzite. of Chaffee Fm.

Mesita Member (of Servillita Formation)—Pliocene
1) S. Cent. Colorado.
2) R. L. Burroughs, 1971, this guidebook.
3) Mesita Crater, near Mesita, Conejos Co., Colo.

4) Drk. red trachyandesite scoria and scoriac flows.
5) Youngest unit of Servilleta Fm., forms small hills on plateau basalts.

OJITO CREEK MEMBER (of Treasure Mountain Rhyolite, Tuff)—U. Oligocene
1) SW Colorado.
2) P. W. Lipman and T. A. Steven, 1970, U.S.G.S. Prof. Pap. 700-C, p. C21.
3) At the head of Ojito Creek, 13.5 mi. E. of Platoro, Conejos Co., Colo.
4) Drk. br., dens. weld. qtz. latite ash-flow tuff (30'-60').
5) About 29 m.y.: Conf. on middle air-fall tuff and ash-flows, overlain conf. by Ra Jadero Memb.

Outlet Tunnel Member (see La Garita Quartz Latite).

PARTING QUARTZITE MEMBER (of Chaffee Formation)—U. Devonian
1) Cent. Colorado.
2) S. F. Emmons, 1882, U.S.G.S. 2nd Ann. Rept. p. 215.
3) On Parting Spur extend. NW from Dyer Mtn., Lake Co., Colo.
4) Wh. coarse-gr. mass. qtzite and qtzite cgls. (35'-115').
5) Famennian: Paraconf. on Harding Ss. or Manitou Dol., conf. overlain by Dyer Memb.

PHOENIX PARK MEMBER (see La Garita Quartz Latite)

PICURIS TUFF—Miocene?
1) N. New Mexico.
2) E. C. Cabot, 1938, Jour. Geol. v. 46, p. 91.
3) Expos. btw. Badito and Placitas, Taos Co., New Mex.
4) Buff tuffac. sss. and tuff, interb. cons. gravs., pink sdy. clay, coarse cgls. (1,250'-1,750').
5) Paraconf. on Magdalena Gp.; overlain? unconf. by Santa Fe Fm.

PIEDRA RHYOLITE (in Potosi Volcanic Group)
1) SW Colorado.
2) E. S. Larsen, 1917, Colo. Geol. Sur. Bull. 13, p. 36: Larsen and Cross, 1956, U.S.G.S. Prof. Pap. 258, p. 144-156.
3) Piedra Peak, 21 mi. SW of Creede, Hinsdale Co., Colo.
4) Name not used by Steven and Ratté, 1964; four membs. of Larsen and Cross, 1956 =ascend.-Low Rhy. = Farmers Creek Rhy., Mammoth Mtn. Rhy., Shallow Creek Qtz. Latite, Windy Gulch Memb. of Bachelor Mtn. Rhy. (0-2,000'); Tridymite Latite Memb. = Wason Park Rhy., (0-700'); Tuff Memb. = Rat Creek Qtz. Latite, (0-1,000'); Rhyolit. latite Memb. = Nelson Mtn. Qtz. Latite (0-4,000').
5) 27.8-26.5 m.y.: Unconf. on Campbell Mtn. Memb. of Bachelor Mtn. Rhy., disconf. overlain by Fisher Qtz. Latite and Creede Fm.

POPOTOSA FORMATION—U. Miocene
1) Cent. New Mexico.
2) C. S. Denny, 1940, Jour. Geol. v. 48, p. 77.
3) Valley of Silver Creek, T. 1 N., R. 2 W., Socorro Co., Colo.
4) Red to gry. br., buff xbedd. tuffac. sss., grav. lens., tuff, sdy. silt xbedd. sss., volc. clasts. pred. (0-5,000').
5) 16 m.y.: Disconf. and conf. on Miocene? volcs., overlain disconf. of Santa Fe Fm.

PORPHYRY PEAK RHYOLITE—U. Oligocene
1) S. Cent. Colorado.
2) W. S. Burbank, 1932, U.S.G.S. Prof. Pap. 169, p. 26
3) Porphyry Peak, 4.5 mi. N. of Bonanza, Saguache Co., Colo.
4) Wh., lt. gry. to br. gry. mod. cryst. rich ash-flow tuffs, some air-fall tuffs and breccs., qtz. latite to rhyolite (0-1,000').
5) Disconf. on Brewer Cr. Latite or Squirrel Gulch Latite.

POTOSI VOLCANIC GROUP—U. Oligocene
1) SW Colorado.
2) W. Cross, 1899, U.S.G.S. Geol. Atlas Folio 57. Larsen and Cross, 1956, U.S.G.S. Prof. Pap. 258, p. 90-166: R. G. Luedke, W. S. Burbank, 1963, U.S.G.S. Prof. Pap. 475-C, p. C43, redefin. and name restrict to type area.
3) Potosi Peak, 5 mi. SW of Ouray, Ouray Co., Colo.
4) Two memb., ascend., Gilpin Peak Tuff, 6 mod. cryst. rich weld. ash-flow tuffs and 1 rework. air-fall fossil. Tuff. pred. qtz. latite, range rhyodacite to rhyolite (0-3,500'); Sunshine Peak Rhyolite, mod. cryst. rich weld. ash-flow tuff, qtz. latite to rhyolite (0-300').
5) Btw. 28.4 m.y. and 27.8 m.y.: Unconf. on Silverton Volcanic Gp., overlain disconf. by Fish Canyon Tuff (Lipman et al., 1970).

RA JADERO MEMBER (of Treasure Mountain Rhyolite, Tuff)—U. Oligocene
1) SW Cent. Colorado.
2) P. W. Lipman and T. A. Steven, 1970, U.S.G.S. Prof. Pap. 700-C, p. C21.
3) In Ra Jadero Canyon, 17 mi. SE of Platoro, Conejos Co., Colo.
4) Drk. br., dens. weld. qtz. latite, abund. sanidine, ash-flow tuff (30'-60').
5) About 28.9 m.y.: Conf. on Ojito Creek Memb., overlain conf. by the upper air-fall tuff and ash-flows, or disconf. by the tuff of Masonic Park (28.2 m.y.).

RAWLEY ANDESITE—M. Oligocene
1) S. Cent. Colorado.
2) W. S. Burbank, 1932, U.S.G.S. Prof. Pap. 169, p. 16-21.
3) Rawley Gulch, and in Rawley Mine, 2.5 mi. NE of Bonanza, Saguache Co., Colo.
4) Dr. gry., red br., grn. gry. interb. andesite flows, breccs., air-fall tuffs and cgls. (0-2,000')

5) 31.3-34.7 m.y.: Unconf. on Precam. rocks, grads. lateral into Hayden Peak Latite, overlain disconf. by Bonanza Tuff.

Ritito Conglomerate—Miocene
1) N. Cent. New Mexico.
2) Fred Barker, 1958, New Mex. Bur. Min. and Miner. Res. Bull. 45, p. 42.
3) Ritito Canyon, secs. 11 and 14, T. 27 N., R. 7 E., Rio Arriba Co., New Mex.
4) Gry. cgl. of Precam. bould. and grav., friab. (0-400′).
5) Unconf. on Precamb. rocks, overlain disconf. by Cordito Memb. of Los Pinos Fm.

SANGRE DE CRISTO FORMATION—Pennsylvanian and Permian
1) S. Colorado and N. New Mexico.
2) R. C. Hills, 1899, U.S.G.S. Geol. Atlas Folio 58, p. 1.
3) E. of Crestone on W. flank of anticline btw. Crestone Needle and Eureka Mtn., Saguache Co., Colo.
4) Red, piedmont cycloth., ark. cgl., sltst. and sss., shs., thin, nodul. non-ark. lss. (500′-9,500′).
5) Missourian-Wolfcampian: Conf. on Whiskey Cr. Ls. Memb. or later. gradat. into Madera Fm. in New Mex. or disconf. on Minturn Fm.; overlain conf. and gradat. by Yeso Fm. in New Mex. and Maroon Fm. in Colo.: Crestone Cgl. upper cgl. memb. in type area.

SAN JUAN BRECCIA, FORMATION—
M. Oligocene
San Juan Tuff
1) SW Colorado.
2) W. Cross, 1896, Colo. Sci. Soc. Proc. v. 5, p. 225-228: Larsen and Cross, 1956, U.S.G.S. Prof. Pap. 258, p. 69-75: R. G. Luedke and W. S. Burbank, 1963 U.S.G.S. Prof. Pap. 475-C, p. C39.
3) Vicinity of Telluride, San Miguel Co., Colo.
4) Drk. gry. to gry. br. rhyodacite tuff brecc., volc. cgls., air-fall tuffs; rhyobasaltic-rhyodacitic lava flows, flow breccs., rhyodactic-qtz. latite weld. ash-flow tuffs (0-3,000′).
5) 31.1-34.2 m.y.: Conf. on Telluride Fm. or unconf. on Paleoz. fms., overlain disconf. by Silverton Volcanic Group.

SANTA FE FORMATION or GROUP—
M. Miocene—Pleistocene
1) N. New Mexico and S. Cent. Colorado.
2) V. F. Hayden, 1869, U.S. Geol. and Geog. Sur. Terr. 3rd Ann. Rept. p. 66.
3) Btw. Sangre de Cristo and Jemez Mtns., N. of Santa Fe, Santa Fe and Sandoval Cos., New Mex.
4) Varigat. fangs. of mod. coarse grav. lenss., coarse-fine sss. sdy. silt., slty. clays, tuffac. sss. and local drk. interb. basalt flows (500-6,000+′).
5) Unconf. on Miocene and older volcanics, Cret. fms. and Precamb. rocks; in Chama Basin grad. with Abiquiu Tuff and equiv. to up. pt. of Los Pinos Fm. (Budding, Pitrat and Smith, 1960); Nambe Tuff, 18 m.y. (Kottlowski, Weber, and Willard, 1969), vert. fossils (Galusha and Blick, 1971).

Sapinero Mesa Tuff—U. Oligocene
1) SW Colorado.
2) J. C. Olson, D. C. Hedlund and W. R. Hansen, 1968, U.S.G.S. Bull. 1251-C p. 19.
3) Tenmile Springs at southern Sapinero Mesa, south central Cebolla Quad., Gunnison Co., Colo.
4) Thin lt. gry. poor. weld. base grading up into red.-br. devitri. qtz. latite weld. tuff with lt. gry. nonweld. tuffs at top (0-200′).
5) 28.0 m.y.: Unconf. or disconf. on Precm. rocks, Blue Mesa Tuff, Dillon Mesa Tuff, andesite of Ford Cr. and local gravs. at its base, overlain disconf. by Fish Canyon Tuff.

Servilleta Formation—U. Pliocene—L. Pleistocene
1) N. Cent. New Mexico.
2) A. Montgomery, 1953, New Mex. Bur. Min. and Miner. Res. Bull. 30, p. 53.
3) Along NE and N. Cent. edge of Picuris Range, Taos Co., New Mex.
4) Buff, gry. clays, sss., grav. interb. with olivine tholeiite basalt flows (0-1,500′).
5) 3.6-4.5 m.y.: Unconf. on Hinsdale Fm. and Picuris Tuff, discounf. on Santa Fe Fm.; flows aver. 50′ thick, are undeform. and underlie the Taos Plateau of Upson (1939).

Sharpsdale Formation—Pennsylvanian
1) SW Colorado.
2) D. W. Williamson and L. Burgin, 1960 Colo. Sch. Min. Miner. Indust. Bull. 3, p. 11.
3) No type desig.; somewhere in Fremont Co., Colo.
4) Red-gry. interb. sss., sltst., cgls. and a few fossil. lss. (400′).
5) Conf. on Kerber Fm., overlain conf. and grad. by Madera Fm.: prob. tongue of Sangre de Cristo Fm.

SHEEP MOUNTAIN QUARTZ LATITE (in Potosi Volcanic Group)
1) SW Colorado.
2) E. S. Larsen, 1917, Colo. Geol. Surv. Bull. 13, p. 36: Larsen and Cross, 1956, U.S.G.S. Prof. Pap. 258, p. 124-132: not recogn. Lipman and Steven, 1970.
3) Sheep Mountain, 4 mi. N. of Jasper, Rio Grande Co., Colo. (error original designation by Larsen and Cross, 1956).
4) Drk. br. qtz. latite flows and breccs.
5) Errors in naming and designating type loc. require name be aband. type area map. as andesite and rhyodacite lava flows assoc. with up. pt. of Treasure Mtn. Tuff (Lipman and Steven, 1970).

SNOWSHOE MOUNTAIN QUARTZ LATITE— U. Oligocene
1) SW Colorado.
2) T. A. Steven and J. C. Ratté, 1964, U.S.G.S. Prof. Pap. 475-D, p. D61.
3) Snowshoe Mtn., 7 mi. S. of Creede, Mineral Co., Colo.
4) Drb., cryst. rich. dens. weld. qtz. latite ash-flows with local talus breccs. (0-6,000′).
5) Btw. 26.7 and 26.4 m.y.: forms core of Creede Caldera; young. than Nelson Mtn. Qtz. Latite, older. than Fisher Qtz. Latite.

SQUIRREL GULCH LATITE—U. Oligocene
1) S. Colorado.
2) W. S. Burbank, 1932, U.S.G.S. Prof. Pap. 169, p. 25.
3) Along head of Squirrel Gulch, 3 mi. N. of Bonanza, Saguache Co., Colo.
4) Drk. gry. dens. weld. ash-flow of hornbl. latite (300′-500′).
5) Disconf. on Bonanza Tuff, overlain disconf. by Brewer Creek Latite Tenderfoot Hill facies, Tenderfoot Hill volcanic sequence (see Dry Union Formation).

TESUQUE FORMATION (in Santa Fe Group)— U. Miocene to L. Pliocene
1) N. Cent. New Mexico.
2) F. E. Kottlowski, 1953, New Mex. Geol. Soc. Gdbk. 4th Fld. Conf. p. 148.
3) In Sangre de Cristo Mtns., 10 mi. N. of Santa Fe, Santa Fe Co., New Mex.
4) Ledges of soft, pink-tan sss. (0-10,000′).
5) Unconf. on old. Mioc. volcanics; unconf. overlain by Puye Grav., Ancha Fm. or Tuerto Grav. of Santa Fe Gp.

Thurman Formation—Oligocene—NOT VALID
1) SW New Mexico..
2) V. C. Kelley and Caswell Silver, 1952, New Mex. Univ. Publ. in Geol. 4, p. 121.
3) Along rd. to Palm Park Barite mine, secs. 35 and 36, T. 18 S., R. 3 W. Dona Ana Co., New Mex.
4) Wh., tan, buff, at base dens. rhy. tuff-brecc., above interb. pink sdy. clay, cryst. tuff, tuffac. sss. with local. drk. amygdal. basalt. (0-2,100′).
5) 31.1 m.y.: Conf. on Palm Park Fm., unconf. overlain by Santa Fe Fm.

Tracey Quartz Latite (See Conejos Formation)

TREASURE MOUNTAIN QUARTZ LATITE, RHYOLITE, TUFF—U. Oligocene
1) S. Cent. Colorado.
2) H. B. Patton, 1917, Colo. Geol. Surv. Bull. 13, p. 33-35: Larsen and Cross, 1956, U.S.G.S. Prof. Pap. 258, p. 117-124: redefin. by P. W. Lipman and T. A. Steven, 1970, U.S.G.S. Prof. Pap. 700-C, p. C21.
3) Treasure Mtn., 13 mi. W. of Summitville, Mineral Co., Colo.
4) Gry. cryst rich qtz. latite weld. tuffs and air-fall tuff, Ojito Cr. ash-flow, Ra Jadero ash-flow, up. tuff (0-3,000′).
5) 29.8-28.8 m.y.: Unconf. on Conejos Fm., overlain disconf. by tuff of Masonic Peak; relat. largely to Platoro Caldera.

Trump Conglomerate—U. Miocene–Pliocene?
1) Cent. Colorado.
2) J. T. Stark, et al., 1949, Geol. Soc. Am. Mem. 33, p. 70.
3) On pediments below Coffman Ridge, T. 14 S., R. 76 W., 10 mi. S. of Antero Reservoir, Park Co., Colo.
4) Poor. strat. to bedd. fang. with qtz. ss. matrix (0-500′).
5) Unconf. on Antero Fm. and older fms.; lateral equiv. Wagontongue Fm. (DeVoto, 1964).

Wagontongue Formation—U. Miocene–Pliocene
1) Cent. Colorado.
2) J. H. Johnson, 1937, Colo. Univ. Stud. v. 25, p. 77: J. T. Stark, et al., 1949, Geol. Soc. Am. Mem. 33, p. 68-69.
3) Along Wagontongue Cr. in NE ¼, sec. 6, T. 15 S., R. 75 W., Park Co., Colo.
4) Poor. cons. interb. buff ark. sss. xbedd., yell.-br. calc. sdy. clays, tuffac. and pumic. sss., lens. of cgls. (110′-500′).
5) Unconf. on Antero Fm., lateral equiv. of Trump Fm. (DeVoto, 1964); vert. bones and teeth, perfect jaw of equid. dates fm., ilic. wood.

WASON PARK RHYOLITE—U. Oligocene
1) SW Colorado.
2) T. A. Steven and J. C. Ratté, 1964, U.S.G.S. Prof. Pap. 475-D, p. D-59.
3) Wason Park on S. flank of La Garita Mtn., 5 mi. NE of Creede, Mineral Co., Colo.
4) Drk. to lt. gry. cryst. rich dens. weld. ash-flow tuff, rhyolitic with char. tridymitic streaks (0-700′).
5) Btw. 26.7 and 26.4 m.y.; tong. of Huerto Fm. separ. Mammoth Mtn. Rhy. from Wason Park Rhy. S. of Bristol Head, overlain unconf. by Fisher Qtz. Latite and Creede Fm.

WEST ELK BRECCIA—M. Oligocene
1) W. Cent. Colorado.
2) W. Cross, in S. F. Emmons, et al., 1894, U.S.G.S. Atlas Folio 9, col. sect.
3) West Elk Montains, 9 mi. S. of Crested Butte, Gunnison Co., Colo.
4) Lt. gry.-purp. gry. coarse to fine gr. volc. brecc. and cgl. beds, depos. as lahars, interb. local. with air-fall and weld. ash-flow tuff and thin rhyodacite flows (0-2,000′).
5) 31.1-34.7 m.y.: Age equiv. of mid. unit of Lake Fork

Fm.: Unconf. on Up. Cret. fms., overlain disconf. by Blue Mesa Tuff (Olsen, et al., 1968).

Whiskey Creek Pass Limestone Member (of Madera Formation)—Pennsylvanian
1) S. Cent. Colorado and N. Cent. New Mexico.
2) K. G. Brill, Jr., 1952, Geol. Soc. Am. Bull. 63, p. 819
3) At 13,000' on the N. side of the N. Fork of Whiskey Cr., Las Animas Co., Colo.
4) Perst. horiz. of interb. gry. sdy. lss., cal. sss. and ooli. lss. (150'-200').
5) Desmoinesian: Conf. on Arkos. Memb. of Madera Fm., overlain conf. by Up. Madera or disconf. by Maroon Fm.

Wildhorse Member (of Conejos Formation)— M. Oligocene
1) S. Cent. Colorado.
2) R. L. Burroughs, 1971, this guidebook.
3) N. end of Wildhorse Ridge, 1.7 mi. E. of Las Sauses, Conejos Co., Colo.
4) Dr. br. porphy. andesite flows, lahars and flow breccs., autobrecc., interb. sort. bedd. tufface sss. and grav. (650+').
5) Base not expos., overlain conf. by La Sauses Memb.

Willow Creek Rhyolite (See Bachelor Mountain Rhyolite)

Windy Gulch Rhyolite (See Bachelor Mountain Rhyolite)

INFORMAL NAMES USED IN THIS GUIDEBOOK

Andesite of Ford Creek—Bruns, Epis, Weimer and Steven.
Andesite of Saguache Creek—Bruns, Epis, Weimer and Steven.
Andesite of Trickle Mountain, Bruns, Epis, Weimer and Steven.
Ash Flow 7—Thirtynine Mile volcanic field, Bruns, Epis, Weimer and Steven.
Badger Creek Tuff—G. Lowell.
Big Baldy Andesite—G. Lowell.
Rhyolite of No Agua Mtn. (4.8 m.y.), A. P. Butler, Jr.
Summer Coon volcanic center—Mertzman.
Tuff of Masonic Park, Bruns, Epis, Weimer and Steven.
Water laid and air-fall tuffs of Saguache Creek—Bruns, Epis, Weimer and Steven.
Waugh Mountain Latite—G. Lowell.

PHYSIOGRAPHIC SUBDIVISIONS OF THE SAN LUIS VALLEY, SOUTHERN COLORADO*

by

J. E. UPSON†

University of Idaho
Moscow, Idaho

EDITOR'S NOTE: *The New Mexico Geological Society is grateful to the Journal of Geology for permission to reprint this classic article. After 32 years the work still remains the most quoted reference in its field on the basin. The photographs were retaken under Mr. Upson's direction and duplicate the originals as closely as possible, with the exception of Figure 5, which was taken a short distance "north" of the mouth of the Rio Costilla. Slight editorial changes in punctuation and capitalization were made on the article to conform to present day usage.*

INTRODUCTION

The San Luis Valley, forming the upper end of the great valley of the Rio Grande, is one of the most impressive topographic features of southern Colorado. As originally outlined by Siebenthal,[1] it is a great lowland about 150 miles long and 50 miles in maximum width, flanked on the east by the linear Sangre de Cristo Range and on the west by the eastern portion of the more extensive San Juan Mountains. It is, in a sense, part of the chain of intermontane basins, or parks,[2] lying west of the Southern Rocky Mountain front ranges, but is unlike the others in having no southern mountain border. The meeting of the Sangre de Cristo Range and the San Juan Mountains about 135 miles north of the Colorado-New Mexico state boundary forms a natural northern limit to the valley. The southern limit is indistinct and was arbitrarily placed by Siebenthal about 15 miles south of the Colorado border (see index map, fig. 1).

During the course of geological field work conducted during the summers of 1935, 1936 and part of 1937 in the southeastern part of the San Luis Valley, it became apparent that the valley is not a unit either geographically or geologically. To the south it actually merges with the great structural depression of the Rio Grande[3] in New Mexico and within its own boundaries consists of five distinct subdivisions. Each of these smaller units, having

---
* Reprinted from the Journal of Geology, vol. XLVII, no. 7, 1939.
† Presently U.S. Geological Survey, Water Resources Division, Washington, D.C.
[1] C. E. Siebenthal, "Geology and Water Resources of the San Luis Valley, Colorado," *U.S. Geol. Survey Water-Supply Paper 240* (1910), p. 9.
[2] N. M. Fenneman, *Physiography of Western United States* (New York and London: McGraw-Hill Book Co., 1931), pp. 125-32.
[3] Kirk Bryan, "Outline of the Geology and Ground-Water Conditions of the Rio Grande depression in Colorado and New Mexico" (mimeographed report, Rio Grande Joint Investigation, National Resources Committee, 1936).

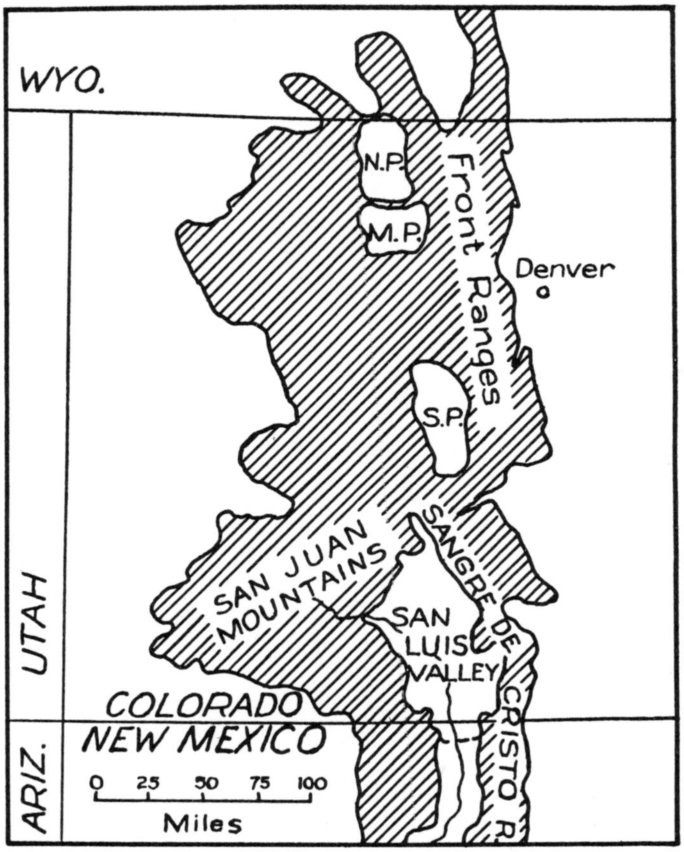

FIGURE 1.

Index map showing the position of the San Luis Valley in the Southern Rocky Mountains (shaded) and its relation to the intermontane parks: N.P., North Park; M.P., Middle Park; S.P., South Park. Boundaries from Fenneman, slightly modified.

had a somewhat different geologic history, now possesses distinctive geologic and topographic characteristics and is therefore considered as a distinct physiographic subprovince. In the following pages is presented a description of these subprovinces and a brief account of their geologic backgrounds. The subdivisions described are named and located as follows: the Alamosa Basin, the main northern part of the San Luis Valley; the San Luis Hills, forming most of the southeastern border of the basin; the Taos Plateau, extending southward from the San Luis Hills; the Costilla Plains, constituting an alluvium-mantled strip

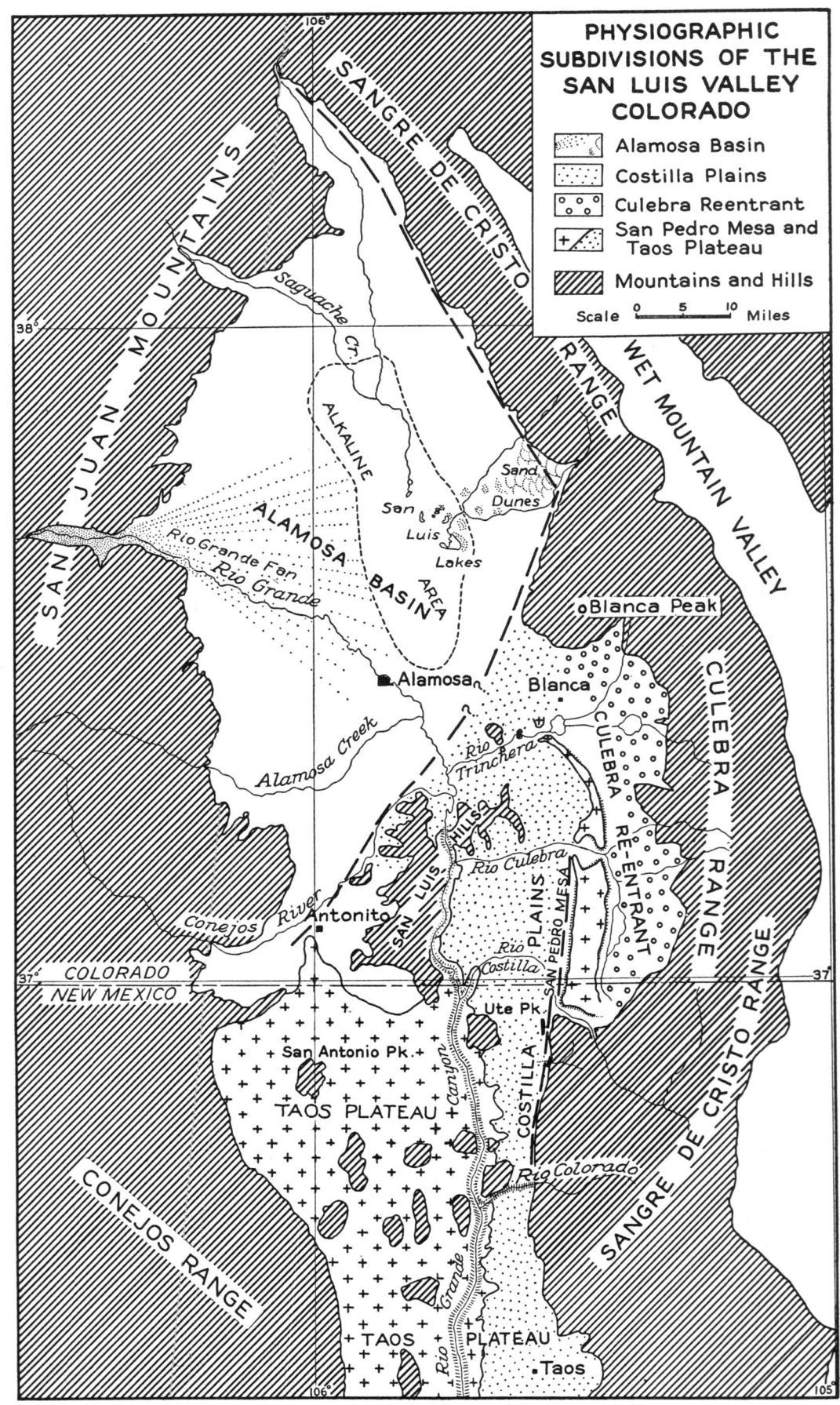

FIGURE 2.

Physiographic subdivisions. Approximate location of the principal late faults shown by heavy, dashed lines. Two recent scarplets east and southeast of Ute Peak indicated by short, heavy lines.

FIGURE 3.

Sierra Blanca from the southwest showing the glaciated valleys and the bordering alluvial fans. The level plain in the fore- and middle-ground is that in which the Alamosa Basin merges with the Costilla Plains and the Culebra reentrant.

along the east side of the Taos Plateau; and finally, the Culebra reentrant, that part of the San Luis Valley lying east of the previously named areas (fig. 2). Many of the geomorphologic interpretations herein presented are the result of fairly detailed structural and stratigraphic work. The writer intends to discuss those studies directly in later papers. They will be little more than mentioned here.

Dominating the San Luis Valley region is the high and rugged Sangre de Cristo Range along the east side. The range consists of two parts: the northern part extending in a general southeasterly direction for 50 miles and the southern part pursuing a southerly or slightly southwesterly course for an additional 18 miles. From north to south the range crest gradually increases in elevation, culminating east of Alamosa in a mass of rugged peaks separated from each other by cirques and glaciated valleys. Highest of these is Blanca Peak, 14,390 feet above sea-level (Appendix, note 1). The entire group of peaks may be designated by the Spanish term, "Sierra Blanca" (fig. 3).

From Sierra Blanca northward to Poncha Pass, at the junction of the Sangre de Cristo Range with the San Juans, the range possesses a bold, linear west front undoubtedly indicative of relatively recent uplift along normal faults. Not even the accumulation of considerable debris in the form of alluvial fans can modify the sharp topographic break between the abrupt mountain slope and the relatively flat valley floor (Appendix, note 2). South of Sierra Blanca, however, the main part of the range is sharply offset to the east about 15 miles, and the steep and abrupt character of the mountain front is conspicuously absent. The front here is subdued and highly irregular, consisting of long mountain spurs which merge westward with an extensive belt of foothills.

The offset portion of the range is about 40 miles long and extends in a southerly direction to a little beyond the Colorado-New Mexico border. Near that boundary the Sangre de Cristo Range is offset westward and exhibits the abrupt, straight, and steep western front like that of the range farther north and similarly indicative of considerable displacement on one or more faults. Thus immediately west of the eastwardly offset part of the range is a sort of indentation, or reentrant. The offset part of the range bears the local name, "Culebra Range," and the reentrant is herein named the "Culebra reentrant." It is geologically the most significant of the physiographic subdivisions to be subsequently described, as in it may be seen rock bodies and structural relationships which do not seem to be visible elsewhere in the area. The subdivisions of the valley will be defined and described in the order in which they were previously listed.

ALAMOSA BASIN

Siebenthal's work in the San Luis Valley was largely restricted to the main northern part of the area lying north of the San Luis Hills. He appears to have considered the other portion of the valley peripheral and of little importance. From the standpoint of water supply this view is justified, but in a physiographic consideration of the San Luis Valley as a whole, the area emphasized by Siebenthal plays a more subordinate role. It is therefore proposed to make that area a physiographic subdivision of the valley as herein defined and to name it the "Alamosa Basin" after the principal town, Alamosa.

The Alamosa Basin is a roughly triangular-shaped area bordered on the west by the San Juan Mountains and on the northeast by the Sangre de Cristo Range. The southeast side is incompletely marked, partly by the Sangre de Cristo Range and partly by the San Luis Hills. Between these hills and the southwest end of the Sangre de Cristo Range is a low, nearly flat area (fig. 3) across which the Alamosa Basin merges imperceptibly with two of the other physiographic subdivisions of the area—the Costilla Plains and the Culebra reentrant.

The principal characteristics of the Alamosa Basin are its nearly featureless floor, the recency of the deposits in the basin and the remarkable course of the Rio Grande directly across the area from the west to the southeast sides. Actually, most of the valley floor slopes inward on all sides toward the lowest portion near the eastern margin. On the east side are numerous alluvial fans whose heads lie at the mouths of short, precipitous canyons in the Sangre de Cristo Range. Streams entering the basin from the west are much longer, have more extensive drainage basins in the San Juan Mountains and have developed much broader and more gently sloping alluvial fans. At a few miles north of Alamosa an observer appears to be surrounded by a level plain. This seeming plain is actually the surface of the Rio Grande fan; the slope so gentle as to be perceptible only on a topographic map. Thus, underlain directly by modern alluvial fan deposits, the Alamosa Basin is essentially an area of deposition. Only at the north where San Luis Creek flows out of Poncha Pass and at the south where the Rio Grande leaves the area through the San Luis Hills is there any dissection of the alluvial surface.

The visible deposits in the Alamosa Basin constitute the upper layers of the Alamosa Formation which was originally named by Siebenthal[4] and held by him to be of Pleistocene age. Beds of the formation are known only from well-logs and from a few scanty exposures near the south end of the basin where the Rio Grande has cut a shallow trench. The sediments appear to be nearly flat-lying but possess sufficient centripetal inclination to make a good artesian basin, from which most of the water supply of the northern part of the San Luis Valley is derived (Appendix, note 3). As indicated by well-logs, the deposits are at least 4,000 feet thick below the lowest part of the basin (Appendix, note 4). Deposition was apparently accompanied by downward tilting of the valley block along great faults bordering the Sangre de Cristo Range and the northwest side of the San Luis Hills (fig. 2). Evidence for the faulting is mainly topographic and was recognized by Siebenthal,[5] Atwood and Mather,[6] Cross and Larsen,[7] and others.

Partly because of the location of the faults, and partly because of the huge size of the western alluvial fans, the lowest part of the basin is near the eastern margin. Here are shallow lakes which have become somewhat alkaline through evaporation (fig. 2). In fact the central part of the basin is known as the "Alkaline Area" because of the alkalinity of the water. Wind-blown sand has accumulated around the lakes and, in times of relative aridity, seems to be subject to deflation by the prevailing southwesterly winds. As a result, considerable sand has been piled up at the mountain front near by. This body of sand has recently been set aside by the government as the Great Sand Dunes National Monument (fig. 4). The writer, jointly with Professor H. T. U. Smith of the University of Kansas, has begun a more detailed study of these dunes (Appendix, note 5).

SAN LUIS HILLS

The Alamosa Basin is nearly completely separated from the rest of the San Luis Valley to the south by the San Luis Hills. They constitute a fairly rugged mass of hills and tilted mesas 500 to 1,000 feet high, extending from near the town of Antonito, Colorado, across the Rio Grande to near the town of Blanca, Colorado. Beginning at a broad pass near Antonito they rise to their full height above the surrounding plain. Toward the northeast they gradually decrease in altitude to pass beneath alluvium a few miles south of Blanca. The continuity of the hills as a single mass is broken only by the canyon of the Rio Grande, beginning a few miles south of Alamosa.

The San Luis Hills were apparently carved out of dominantly andesitic volcanic rocks correlated with portions of the mid-Tertiary volcanic series of the San Juan Mountains after the development of the San Juan peneplain of Atwood and Mather. The dissection of the hills resulted from post-peneplain uplifts on normal faults situated along their northwest flank.[8] The present writer believes that the faults are probably the southward continuation of those bordering the west flank of the Sangre de Cristo Range.

---

[4] *Op. cit.*, p. 40.

[5] *Ibid.*, pp. 38-39 and 51.

[6] W. W. Atwood and K. F. Mather, "Physiography and Quaternary Geology of the San Juan Mountains, Colorado," *U.S. Geol. Surv. Prof. Paper* 166 (1932), pp. 23, 25, and 99.

[7] Whitman Cross and E. S. Larsen, Jr., "A Brief Review of the Geology of the San Juan Region of Southwestern Colorado," *U.S. Geol. Surv. Bull.* 843 (1935), p. 113.

[8] Atwood and Mather, *op. cit.*, p. 23.

FIGURE 4.
Sand dunes of the Great Sand Dunes National Mounment.

Recurrent movements accompanied the development of the Alamosa Basin and at the same time served to maintain the hills as a prominent topographic feature.

After dissection had proceeded to the development of a mature topography, the San Luis Hills were surrounded by basalt flows belonging to the Hinsdale Series.[9] (Appendix, note 6). The basalt extended over large areas in the San Juan Mountains and for many miles down the Rio Grande Valley to the south. At one time the hills rose fairly abruptly from the surrounding flood of lava—a feature at present preserved only along their southern side. On the northwest side of the hills the lava is buried by beds of the Alamosa Formation, which rests with fault contact against the older mid-Tertiary volcanics.

Because of the island-like relationship of the San Luis Hills to the lavas, they might be considered as part of the Taos Plateau—the next subdivision to be discussed. There hills of older rocks rise above the Hinsdale flows as do the San Luis Hills, and many of them appear to be composed of volcanics of the same general series. However, the San Luis Hills are not isolated from each other as are those farther south but form a nearly continuous group both topographically and apparently also lithologically. In addition the Hinsdale has been downfaulted along the northwest side of the hills. They are therefore considered as a distinct physiographic subdivision but are not, however, distinguished from other mountains and hills in Figure 2.

TAOS PLATEAU

The Taos Plateau is an extensive plateau-like area which lies south of the San Luis Hills and extends about 60 miles southward into New Mexico. Its distinguishing features are a broadly undulating character, the presence of rounded hills rising above the general level and the deep entrenchment of the Rio Grande and other streams. The name was suggested by Kirk Bryan from the clear development of its broad, undulating character near and west of Taos, New Mexico. The plateau is largely underlain by basalt belonging to the Hinsdale Series. The hills rising above the rolling surface of the lava are composed of older Tertiary and Precambrian rocks, against which, in several

---
[9] Cross and Larsen, op. cit., pp. 94-100; Atwood and Mather, op. cit., p. 21.

FIGURE 5.
Rio Grande Canyon about ½ mile south of mouth of Rio Costilla. Canyon walls, developed in Hinsdale Basalt underlying the Taos Plateau, exhibit evidence of two stages of erosion (Appendix, note 6).

places, the basalt may be seen to rest unconformably.[10]

The Taos Plateau is trenched near its eastern side by the Rio Grande Canyon which, only about 50 feet deep at the mouth of the Rio Culebra in Colorado, becomes progressively deeper to the south. At the mouth of the Rio Costilla the river is approximately 200 feet below the surface of the lava (fig. 5). At its southern end, near Embudo, New Mexico, the canyon is about 1,000 feet deep. There the plateau-like character of the physiographic subdivision is most apparent.

On the west side of the Rio Grande Canyon the basalt essentially forms the surface of the plateau except for the projecting hills of older rocks. As the basalt is slightly deformed, so also is the plateau surface. The lava is known to be broken by normal faults near the western margin of the northern portion of the plateau;[11] and in the vicinity of Dunn's Bridge, across the Rio Grande northwest of Taos, the basalt is believed by Kirk Bryan[12] to be slightly deformed. Because of the regional eastward tilt of the lava the surface of the plateau is somewhat higher west of the Rio Grande than east of it.

East of the Rio Grande the plateau exhibits different features in that the basalt has been buried beneath a considerable accumulation of alluvium derived from the Sangre de Cristo Range. However, from the Rio Colorado southward the area is deeply trenched by large canyons made by the Rio Colorado itself, by the Rio Hondo, and by other streams issuing from the Sangre de Cristo Range. This dissection emphasizes the plateau-like character of the region sufficiently to warrant its inclusion as part of the Taos Plateau in spite of the alluvial cover on the basalt.

The upper layers of the alluvium, as exposed in canyon walls near the Rio Grande west of Taos, clearly overlie the basalt. Farther up the tributary streams, however, the lava is either missing or not exposed, and the precise relationships of the alluvium there are unknown. It may contain parts of more than one formation.

---

[10] Bryan, "Geology of the Rio Grande Canyon," in preliminary report of the New Mexico state engineer (1928-30).

[11] A. P. Butler, Jr., Doctor's thesis (Harvard University) in preparation.

[12] Personal communication.

North of the Rio Colorado the surface of the alluvium is very little dissected and the area is considered as a separate physiographic subdivision.

COSTILLA PLAINS

The area flanking the Sangre de Cristo Range north of the Rio Colorado, lying east of the Rio Grande, and extending northward to a little beyond the Rio Trinchera in Colorado, is called the Costilla Plains. The term is derived from the town of Costilla, New Mexico, situated where the Rio Costilla crosses the Colorado-New Mexico boundary near the mountain front. In this subdivision the alluvial deposits blanketing the eastward extension of the Hinsdale Basalt are practically undissected except at the very mouths of the streams tributary to the Rio Grande. But for the slight westward slope of the surface of the alluvial fans heading in the canyons of the Sangre de Cristo Range, the area is nearly featureless. North of the Colorado-New Mexico boundary it is nearly a level surface.

The Costilla Plains are only about 4 miles wide near their southern end but are considerably wider in Colorado where they reach a maximum of about 15 miles a few miles north of the New Mexico border. Their western limit is strictly the edge of the alluvium, but that is very near the Rio Grande Canyon, so that natural barrier is made the western border of the Costilla Plains in Figure 2. On the east the plains abut against the southern portion of the Sangre de Cristo Range and against the San Pedro Mesa (fig. 2). Corresponding as it does with the western front of the mountain range, the east border of the plains is nearly a straight line and probably marks or closely parallels the trace of the normal fault along the edge of the mountains. The alinement of the west side of the San Pedro Mesa with this mountain scarp to the south suggests that the concealed fault continues to or beyond the north end of the mesa.

More definite evidence of the existence of the fault is furnished by two small scarplets in the alluvium. One of these is about 70 feet high and crosses the upper portion of the alluvial fan of La Jara Creek approximately at the mountain front. La Jara Creek is the small, unnamed stream southeast of Ute Peak, shown in Figure 2. The other scarplet is somewhat longer and lower, being about 30 feet high and extending for about a mile across the lower portion of the fan of Cedros Creek—the next stream north of La Jara Creek. It is not shown in Figure 2, although the location of the scarplets is indicated. The longer scarplet approximately parallels the mountain front and can be readily seen a few hundred yards east of the road to Taos and 3 or 4 miles south of the Colorado state line (fig. 6).

Whereas most of the surface of the Costilla Plains is untrenched by streams, Rio Trinchera, Rio Culebra, and Rio Costilla in Colorado have formed floodplains about 100 feet below the general surface. That surface therefore constitutes a terrace. There are also remnants of a lower terrace about 55 feet above present stream grades. The generally fine, sandy, unconsolidated deposits visible in a few places in the sides of the terraces are tentatively correlated with the Alamosa Formation of Siebenthal in the Alamosa Basin.

Topographically the Costilla Plains are very similar to the Alamosa Basin but are believed to be different in that at least the Colorado portion of their surface is mainly erosional, whereas the surface of the Alamosa Basin is largely depositional. Additional cause for separating the Costilla Plains from the Alamosa Basin lies in the fact that they are almost entirely cut off from the basin by the San Luis Hills. However, the Costilla Plains, the Culebra reentrant, and the Alamosa Basin actually merge together in the small area west of the town of Blanca. For that reason physiographic boundaries are not drawn in that area on Figure 2.

CULEBRA REENTRANT

The Culebra reentrant differs markedly from the other physiographic subdivisions of the San Luis Valley. The topography is considerably diversified and exhibits a mature stage of dissection. In contrast to the San Luis Hills, which also possess a mature topography, the hills of the reentrant have not been surrounded or buried by basalt flows.

Although the Culebra reentrant is somewhat isolated and appears to be insignificant in comparison with the topographically conspicuous and economically important Alamosa Basin, it is geologically very important. In the reentrant are exposed formations of which only one, or at most two, crop out in any one of the other subdivisions. The formations of the other areas, however, do occur in the reentrant with the exception of the Alamosa Formation, which is represented only by local alluvium. Consequently, only in the reentrant can the structural relations of all the rock bodies of the region be satisfactorily determined.

The Precambrian rocks of the Culebra Range have been uplifted on a series of normal faults separating the range from the area to the west, which is underlain by deformed Tertiary volcanic rocks and fluvial deposits (Appendix, note 7). The topographic border of the mountains follows the fault boundary fairly closely, but in the southern part is very complicated. It is generalized in Figure 2. The term "Culebra reentrant" is restricted to the area lying west of the faults. In that area three formations are exposed: (1) the Early Tertiary Vallejo Formation,[13] hitherto undescribed; (2) an overlying body of flows and tuffs; and (3) a still younger, thick body of alluvial-fan sand and gravel interbedded with the basalt that elsewhere surrounds the San Luis Hills (Appendix, note 8). These rocks and their structural relationships are significant here mainly because as a body the rocks were deformed and subject to erosion considerably before the fault movements along the east side of the Alamosa Basin and the Costilla Plains had ceased. Indeed, as previously indicated, movement on these faults has been very recent, and the deformation may be thought of as continuing into the present. Because movement on the faults of the Culebra reentrant ceased relatively early, that area became one of dissection, while de-

---

[13] J. E. Upson, "The Vallejo Formation—New Early Tertiary Red-Beds in Southern Colorado" (in preparation).

FIGURE 6.

Slightly dissected Recent fault scarp across alluvial fan and nearly parallel to the west front of the Sangre de Cristo Range near Costilla, New Mexico. View looking northeast.

position continued in the Alamosa Basin and Costilla Plains. The comparatively great length of time since the erosion of the reentrant rocks began is the reason for the mature topography of that area in contrast to the nearly featureless Alamosa Basin and Costilla Plains and the youthfully trenched Taos Plateau. The mature topography of the San Luis Hills may be considered as a fossil topography preserved by the flood of younger basalt. When the dissection of the Taos Plateau began is not known and is an inviting field for further study.

The Culebra reentrant is herein considered as a single physiographic subdivision because it seems to have had the same geologic history in all parts. It is, however, a topographically diversified area. Differences are largely the result of the details of the Late Tertiary normal faulting acting on the volcanics and fluvial deposits. The major trend of the normal faults is north-south and movement on the faults was such as to divide the area into three parts: (1) a relatively elevated belt of foothills near the mountains; (2) a central graben, subsequently eroded so as to preserve the original topographic depression; and (3) a prominent horst—the San Pedro Mesa (Appendix, note 9).

The eastern border of the belt of foothills is not conspicuous, as those hills merge with the long spurs and ridges cut out of the Precambrian rocks of the Culebra Range proper without prominent topographic break. The latest movement on the faults separating the range from the foothills was probably not younger than Early Pleistocene, and subsequently erosion has greatly modified the fault scarps that must once have existed. As a result the western front of the Culebra Range is noticeably less abrupt and imposing than the corresponding fronts of the Sangre de Cristo Range, both north and south of the reentrant. The range crest itself, however, is in some respects more rugged than those to the north and south.

The foothills are widest in the northern part of the reentrant where their western edge is 8 to 10 miles from the mountain border on the east. In the southern part of the area their width decreases from about 6 miles near the Rio Culebra to nearly zero at the Rio Costilla. The main feature of the foothill belt is the preservation of remnants of at least four erosion surfaces cut across the deformed Tertiary rocks. In the north very few residuals rise above the highest erosion remnants, which lie at 450 to 500 feet above the present stream grades.

Remnants of apparently the same erosion surfaces are recognizable, but less extensively preserved, in the southern part of the reentrant. There numerous foothill summits, rising as much as 10,000 feet above sea-level, are residual above the highest erosion remnants.

Extensive development of comparable erosion surfaces is not known in the other subdivisions of the San Luis Valley. In a few localities, however, there are small remnants of terraces, possibly erosional, which may be the correlatives of the surfaces in the reentrant. Accurate information regarding such possible correlatives is not now at hand.

As a sort of outlier of the northern part of the foothill belt in the Culebra reentrant are two prominent basalt-capped mesas called the Garland Mesas, situated immediately southeast of the town of Fort Garland, 5 miles east of Blanca. The southern of the two mesas rises over 500 feet above the surrounding lowlands. The rocks of these mesas have been uplifted on a normal fault of considerable magnitude, first recognized by Atwood and Mather.[14]

Extending northward from the southwest corner of the reentrant is the similarly basalt-capped mesa, the San Pedro Mesa. It is 1,000 feet high at the south end and forms a prominent table-land, particularly when viewed from the west, extending northward for about 15 miles from the Rio Costilla to the Rio Culebra. Near the Rio Culebra the mesa decreases in elevation and the capping basalt assumes a gentle westerly dip. The basalt outcrop crosses the Rio Culebra and, maintaining the westerly dip, forms a narrow, cuesta-like ridge, extending for about 10 miles north of Rio Culebra and presenting a low but fairly steep escarpment toward the east. This ridge is the northward continuation of the San Pedro Mesa and is called the San Pedro Cuesta in this paper. It dies out a short distance north of the Rio Trinchera.

The San Pedro Mesa is apparently bordered by faults on both the east and west sides. As the upthrow sides of each of these faults is on the mesa side, it is structurally a horst. The fault on the east side continues north along the foot of the San Pedro Cuesta.

There are also a few small normal faults along the western margin of the foothills with downthrow on the west. The region between the San Pedro Mesa and the foothills is therefore structurally a graben. The fault movements are believed to have carried the basalt of the mesas down so as to render the graben easily eroded. At present the feature is topographically fairly conspicuous and was designated by Stephenson,[15] the "Culebra Park." The writer sees no reason to change this name. The Culebra Park extends in a northerly direction from near the Rio Costilla, where it is very shallow but where its floor is about 500 feet above the level of that stream. This relationship suggests that at some previous time the upper Rio Costilla flowed northward through the Culebra Park but was diverted by the present Costilla cutting headward across the south end of the San Pedro Mesa from the west. North of Rito Seco the park is broader and deeper, assumes a northwesterly trend, and extends past the town of Blanca to merge with the surface of the Alamosa Basin in the northwest part of the reentrant.

North of the Rio Costilla the surface of the Culebra Park is about at the level of the present stream grades except in the region between Rito Seco and Rio Trinchera. There the floor of the park is 20 to 100 feet above the level of the streams, and on the flanks of the divide thus formed low terraces may once have been developed. They are at present so mantled by later alluvium as to be unrecognizable.

ACKNOWLEDGMENTS

Acknowledgments are due principally to Professor Kirk Bryan of Harvard University, who, long familiar with the region, first suggested the possibility of subdividing the San Luis Valley. Professor Bryan criticized the manuscript many times in its formative stages, aided much in the drafting of Figure 2, and is the originator of some of the subdivision names. Mr. Edward Schmitz also contributed to the preparation of Figure 2. The writer is indebted to many inhabitants of the Culebra reentrant for assistance and hospitality during the field work there—notably, Mr. and Mrs. S. H. Shannon and family of the Trinchera Ranch, Fort Garland. During the field work the writer was ably assisted at different times by H. G. Peacock, A. P. Butler, Jr., W. S. Brandhorst, R. W. Day, and the writer's brother, D. R. Upson.

APPENDIX

Note: To this reprinted paper, published nearly 32 years ago, there are added certain explanatory comments and references to later papers which may serve to bring the paper more nearly up to date. There is still room for further work.

J. E. Upson

1. Altitude given as 14,345 feet on Blanca Peak quadrangle, 1:24,000, 1967. Presently accepted elevation is 14,363—Ed.
2. Scarps in the alluvium at and north of Valley View Hot Springs have been mapped by Glenn R. Scott, 1970.
3. Wells drilled in 1959 indicate depth to Precambrian rocks in excess of 10,000 feet. Much of this interval may be in unconsolidated deposits, and the thickness perhaps substantially more than 4,000 feet. (Unpublished information from P. A. Emery.)
4. A gravity survey in the Alamosa Basin done at various times from 1961-64 indicates that the basement structure is more complex than a single east-tilted block; and that thickness of valley fill at the deepest place is probably at least 16,000 feet and perhaps as much as 30,000 feet depending on density contrasts assumed. See Gaca and Karig, 1965.
5. The writer and H. T. U. Smith have done little further work. An excellent study, with clear differentiation of dune types, was made by Johnson (1967) in the sixties.
6. Now considered part of the Servilleta formation of Butler, this formation is younger than the Hinsdale Basalt of older workers. See Lipman, 1969. Editor's Note: Photo taken ½ mile north of mouth of Rio Costilla.
7. More recent reconnaissance mapping by Johnson (1969) shows

---

[14] *Op. cit.*, p. 100.
[15] J. J. Stephenson, "Report on the Geology of a Portion of Colorado Examined in 1873," *U.S. Geog. Surv. West of the 100th Meridian*, Vol. III (Supplement Geology, 1881), p. 363.

the complex boundary between the Precambrian rocks and the Tertiary volcanics and other deposits, but it is interpreted with fewer faults.

8. See References, Upson.
9. San Pedro Mesa may not be faulted on the east side.

REFERENCES

Butler, A. P., Jr., 1946, Tertiary and Quaternary geology of the Tusas-Tres Piedras area, N. Mex.; Harvard Univ., Cambridge, Mass., Ph.D. dissert. 188 p.

Gaca, J. Robert, and Karig, Daniel E., 1965, Gravity Survey in the San Luis area, Colorado: U.S. Geol. Survey, open-file report, 21 p., plus gravity data, maps, and sections.

Johnson, Ross B., 1967, The Great Sand Dunes of Southern Colorado: U.S. Geol. Survey Prof. Paper 575-C, p. C177-C183.

Johnson, Ross B., 1969, Geologic map of the Trinidad quadrangle south-central Colorado: U.S. Geol. Survey, Miscellaneous Geologic Investigations, Map I-558.

Lipman, Peter W., 1969, Alkalic and tholeiitic basaltic volcanism related to the Rio Grande Depression, southern Colorado and northern New Mexico: Geol. Soc. America Bull. V. 80, p. 1347 ff.

Powell, Wm. J., 1958, Ground-water resources of the San Luis Valley, Colorado: U.S. Geol. Survey Water Supply Paper 1379, 284 p.

Scott, Glenn R., 1970, Quaternary faulting and potential earthquakes in east-central Colorado: U.S. Geol. Survey, Prof. Paper 700-C, p. C16-C17.

Upson, Joseph E., 1941, The Vallejo Formation: New Early Tertiary red-beds in Southern Colorado: Am. Jour. Sci., Vol. 239, p. 577-589.

THE GREAT SAND DUNES OF SOUTHERN COLORADO*

by

Ross B. Johnson

U.S. Geological Survey
Denver, Colorado

Prevailing southwesterly winds that have blown for centuries across the flat expanse of the San Luis Valley of south-central Colorado have deposited a great mass of loose sand near the western flank of the Sangre de Cristo Mountains (fig. 1). This mass of sand is made up of several types of dunes whose structure depends upon the amount of sand available for transport, wind speed, and the amount of vegetation. The most spectacular dunes are high transverse dunes that are almost barren of vegetation; a tract of land has been set aside as Great Sand Dunes National Monument (fig. 2) to preserve these dunes.

Although the transverse dunes are among the highest in the United States, they cover only about a fourth of the 150-square-mile area of dunes in the San Luis Valley. The rest of the dunes are less spectacular types, but they, too, contribute to the interesting story of the origin and formation of the dunes in and near Great Sand Dunes National Monument.

GEOGRAPHIC SETTING

The sand dunes are located in the San Luis Valley northeast of Alamosa, Colorado, and the greatest accumulation of sand is in a small reentrant in the Sangre de Cristo Mountains north of Sierra Blanca where Medano Creek emerges from the mountains (fig. 3). Medano Pass is a low pass (about 10,150 feet) in this high rugged range, which in this part of Colorado has many peaks more than 14,000 feet high. Medano Creek flows from the pass to the dunes through a steep canyon that strikes northeast and forms a natural outlet for the high-velocity, southwesterly winds blowing over the dunes from the valley.

The San Luis Valley lies between the Sangre de Cristo Mountains to the east and the San Juan Mountains to the west. The valley is 105 miles long and 40 miles wide at the latitude of the dunes. The valley terminates northward at Poncha Pass, which separates the Rio Grande drainage from that of the Arkansas. Southward the valley extends a short distance into New Mexico (Baltz, 1965, p. 2068) where it merges with the Taos Plateau (Upson, 1939, p. 722).

The valley is exceedingly flat over most of its extent, except for the San Luis Hills southeast of Alamosa (fig. 1). The altitude of the valley floor ranges from 7,400 feet near the Rio Grande at the Colorado-New Mexico boundary to a remarkably consistent 8,000 feet around the periphery of the valley along the bases of the mountain ranges. However, the flat summits of the San Luis Hills are above 9,100

*Reprinted from U.S. Geol. Survey Prof. Paper 575-C, Pages C177-C183.

feet and are more than 1,000 feet higher than the highest part of this vast intermontane valley in which they lie.

The principal stream is the Rio Grande, which drains that part of the San Juan Mountains lying east of the Continental Divide. The Rio Grande flows generally eastward in the mountains until it emerges on the San Luis Valley at Del Norte (fig. 1). It meanders slowly in a southeasterly direction past Alamosa across a broad, flat flood plain to the north end of the San Luis Hills. The gradient increases as it flows south through the San Luis Hills into New Mexico.

North of Alamosa is a large area of interior drainage, in which the streams flowing from the mountains sink into the unconsolidated sediments that floor the valley. The area of interior drainage appears to center in the vicinity of San Luis Lake (fig. 2). San Luis Creek flowing from Poncha Pass and Sand Creek flowing from a cirque in the Sangre de Cristo Mountains terminate in San Luis Lake, which has no outlet. South of Alamosa and east of the Rio Grande, although not in an area of interior drainage, the water of many of the streams sinks beneath the valley floor before reaching the Rio Grande.

The climate of the San Luis Valley is semiarid. The total normal annual precipitation amounts to 6.56 inches at Alamosa and 9.69 inches at Great Sand Dunes National Monument. Showers are most prevalent in April, and thunderstorms are frequent in July and August. Even during the rainiest months, there are few available hours during which the sun does not shine, and evaporation and transpiration are high. Strong dry winds blow throughout the year from the southwest and dry out the soil and vegetation. During winter storms, high-velocity cold winds blow from the northeast for short periods of time. The strongest winds occur in the spring and early summer when dust storms are fairly common. Occasionally, the winds are so strong that clouds of dust are lifted across the Sangre de Cristo Mountains.

GENERAL GEOLOGY

The geologic structure and rock types of the San Luis Valley, the Sangre de Cristo Mountains, and the San Juan Mountains have largely controlled the formation and composition of the sand dunes. The San Luis Valley is a large north-trending structural depression that lies between the two mountain ranges. This depression is filled with 5,000-7,000 feet of alluvial fan gravel, volcanic debris, and interbedded basaltic flows which are here all included in the Pliocene and Pleistocene undifferentiated Santa Fe and Alamosa formations. Quaternary stream deposits, pedi-

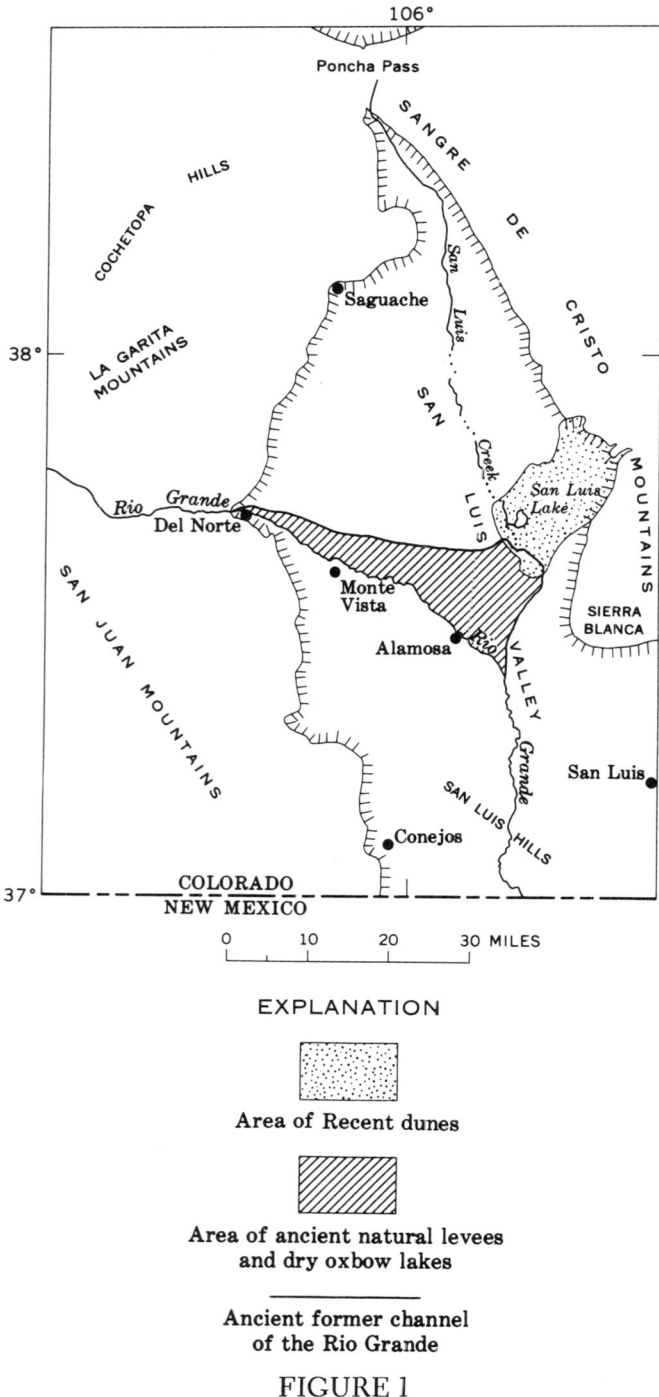

FIGURE 1
Location map of sand dunes in southern Colorado.

mostly Precambrian gneiss, granite, and granodiorite; almost all the debris being eroded from the Sangre de Cristo Mountains into San Luis Valley is derived from these Precambrian rocks. Alluvial fan material, an extension of that filling the San Luis Valley, covers many of the rocks and structural features on the west-facing slopes south of Sierra Blanca (fig. 1).

The San Juan Mountains that border the San Luis Valley on the west are composed mainly of volcanic rocks of Middle Tertiary age (A. Steven, oral commun., 1966). The principal rocks are flows, tuffs, and breccias that range in type from quartz latite to rhyolite (Larsen and Cross, 1956, p. 157).

DESCRIPTION OF THE DUNES

The sand dunes in and adjacent to Great Sand Dunes National Monument were mapped according to the classification of Hack (1941, p. 240-245) as transverse, parabolic, and longitudinal dunes (fig. 2). Parabolic dunes are divided into parabolic dunes of deflation and parabolic dunes of accumulation (Hack, 1941, p. 242-243). The parabolic dunes of accumulation are further subdivided into fixed and active. Special dune features such as barchans, climbing dunes, and large blowouts are also present (fig. 2). Locally, there is mixing of several types of dunes, and precise delineation is not always possible.

The parabolic dunes of deflation cover a large area southwest, or windward, of all the other dune types (fig. 2), and leeward of an area of ancient oxbow lakes and natural levees (fig. 1) abandoned by the Rio Grande during its lateral migration to the southwest. The parabolic dunes of deflation consist largely of low mounds of loose sand that are covered by grass and shrubs in most places. Blowouts form on the windward side of the dunes and are the sources of sand being supplied to the actively forming dunes downwind. The blowouts range in size from a few feet to several thousand feet across. Large lakes and barren playas are characteristic of this area of dunes. In fact, the lakes and playas may have originated as blowouts and reached their present size by wind deflation.

Both the longitudinal dunes and the fixed parabolic dunes of accumulation form downwind from the parabolic dunes of deflation. The longitudinal dunes lie in a long, low, and slightly arcuate area south and east of the parabolic and transverse dunes (fig. 2). The longitudinal dunes are lower than the parabolic dunes of deflation, and are only slightly higher than the duneless valley floor to the south. These dunes are long, low mounds containing a little loose sand at the surface and are covered with grass and a few scattered small shrubs. Although formed here under maximum wind velocities, the longitudinal dunes are stable south and east of Medano Creek. Grains of sand mainly from the parabolic dunes of deflation are piled up by strong winds to form two groups of barchans in the upper and lower reaches of the longitudinal dunes (fig. 2). The upper barchans are now slowly covering a grove of ponderosa pine. Sand and silt are also winnowed from coalescing alluvial fans nearby to add material to these dunes.

The main area of parabolic dunes of accumulation is lee-

ment gravels, and alluvial fan materials mantle most of the valley floor, and a smaller part of the floor is overlain by dune deposits which are younger than most of the alluvium.

The Sangre de Cristo Mountains are composed of a wide variety of igneous and metamorphic rocks of Precambrian age, sedimentary rocks of Paleozoic and Mesozoic age, and igneous intrusive and volcanic rocks of Tertiary age. The bedrock on the western slope of the mountains is

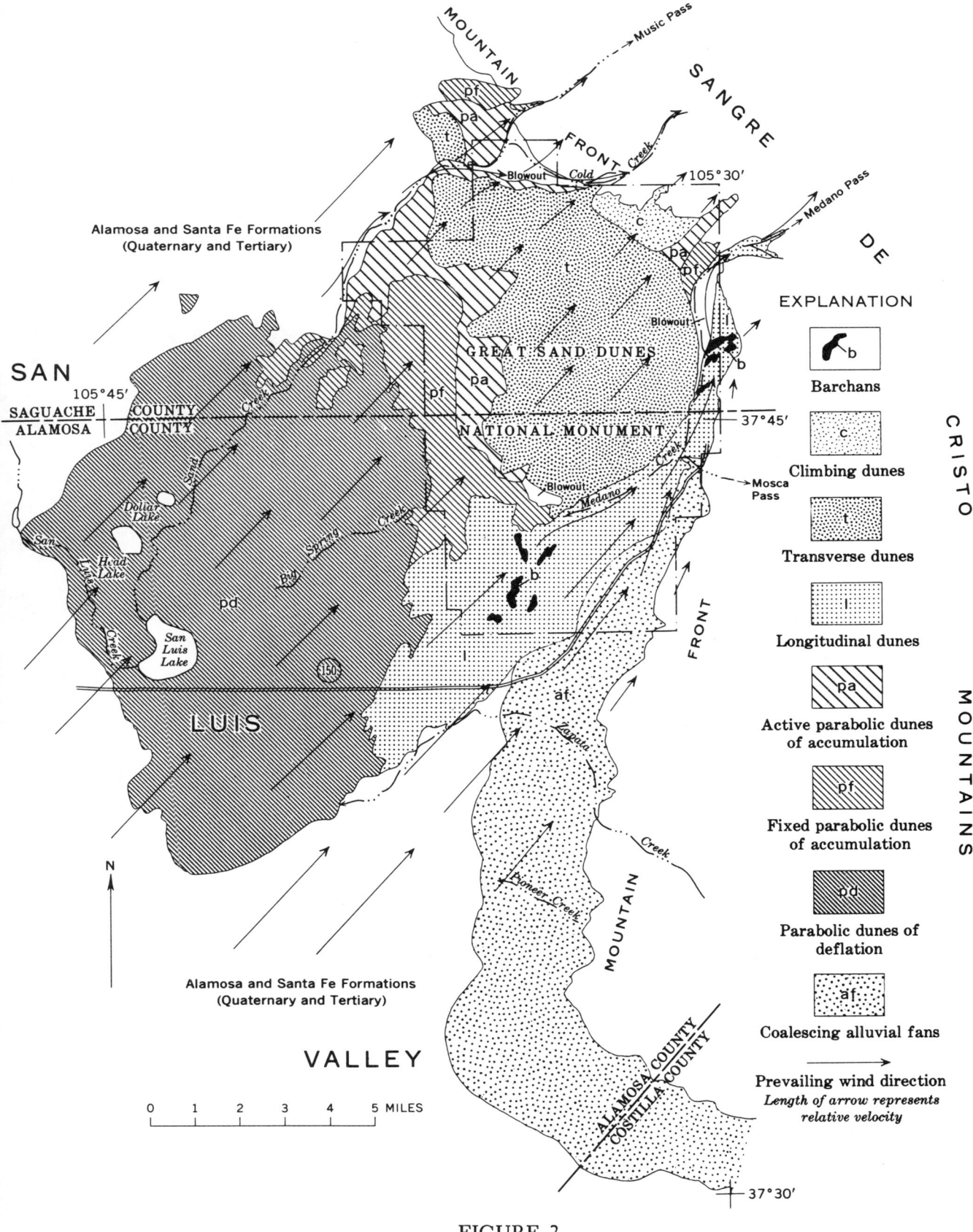

FIGURE 2

Map showing types of sand dunes in Great Sand Dunes National Monument, Colorado, and vicinity, July 1965.

FIGURE 3

Southeast margin of transverse dunes. Medano Creek in foreground is clogged by eolian sand. View is north toward Sangre de Cristo Mountains.

W. H. Hill, National Park Service

ward of the parabolic dunes of deflation and north of the longitudinal dunes. The fixed parabolic dunes of accumulation are upwind from the active dunes of accumulation. The area of fixed dunes stands generally only a few feet higher than the parabolic dunes of deflation and longitudinal dunes, whereas the active dunes rise for 100-200 feet on a rather steep slope from the fixed dunes to the transverse dunes. Smaller isolated patches of parabolic dunes of accumulation occur near the mouth of the canyons of Medano Creek and Sand Creek (fig. 2). The fixed parabolic dunes are sparsely covered with grass and low shrubs, and the active dunes are even more sparsely covered. The fixed dunes seem to be almost inactive at the present time; only small amounts of sand are collecting on the leeward side of some plants. Most of the sand derived from blowouts in the area of parabolic dunes of deflation seems to be blown across this area to the active parabolic dunes of accumulation.

The transverse dunes from which the Great Sand Dunes National Monument draws its fame (figs. 3, 4) stand 500-600 feet above the parabolic dunes of accumulation to the west and nearly 700 feet above the logitudinal dunes along Medano Creek. The transverse dunes are downwind from the main bulk of the active parabolic dunes of accumulation, which appear to be the immediate source of sand for the transverse dunes. North of Sand Creek (fig. 2) a small patch of transverse dunes is upwind from parabolic dunes. This apparent anomaly may be due to wind eddies. Occasionally strong winds of short duration, especially during the winter (R. L. Burroughs, oral commun., 1966), blow from the northeast and east (Merk, 1960, p. 128) and every winter reverse the crests of the transverse dunes (fig. 4).

The transverse dunes are relatively stable and do not appear to be migrating northeasterly (Merk, 1960, p. 129). Sand blown up from the active parabolic dunes of accumulation appears to be adding mainly to the bulk of the transverse dunes; a small amount of sand blows beyond to form dunes of other types. These great transverse dunes are almost barren of vegetation; the small amount that is present grows in the interdune hollows where the sand is damp.

FIGURE 4

Transverse dunes showing reversal of crests by strong northeasterly winds of short duration. The eastward-facing slopes are steeper than westward-facing slopes and indicate that predominant winds are from the west. Lag gravels cover floor of blowout in foreground. View is north toward Sangre de Cristo Mountains.

W. H. Hill, National Park Service

Blowouts occur at three places adjacent to the transverse dunes (fig. 2) and are the result of eddying. The blowouts north and east of the transverse dunes appear to be created by strong eddies resulting from sharp changes in wind direction as the prevailing winds funnel into the steep mountain canyons. No reason has been determined for the origin of the eddies that have formed the blowout at the south end of the transverse dunes. Sand is being actively removed from the blowout and moved to the east.

Where Medano Creek emerges from the mountains, strong winds blowing northerly here must turn nearly at right angles to blow easterly up the canyon through Medano Pass. The entire area of the longitudinal dunes is in effect a wind tunnel, and strong eddies are formed where the wind must turn easterly up the canyon. Here these eddies have created a blowout opposite the mouth of the canyon, and have piled up high parabolic dunes north of the canyon mouth, and have carried some sand up the canyon to form barren longitudinal dunes with much loose sand. The longitudinal dunes are unstable in the canyon and could be easily converted to other dune types by seasonal variations in wind velocity and sand supply.

Climbing dunes (Hack, 1941, p. 241) are northeast, or leeward, of the transverse dunes between Medano and Cold creeks (fig. 2). These dunes are piled up against the steep western flank of the Sangre de Cristo Mountains opposite the highest part of the transverse dunes from which the climbing dunes are derived. They rise from about 8,800 feet to 9,500 feet in about a mile. The climbing dunes have no regular dunelike surface features but seem to consist of irregular mounds and swales on a steeply rising slope. They are practically devoid of vegetation, and appear to be accumulating rather rapidly at the present time as the result of the prevailing winds not being able to carry their load of sand over the mountains at this point. However, the turbulence of the eddies that form the large blowouts on either side of the climbing dunes (fig. 2) may have an important influence in containing the dunes laterally.

HISTORY OF THE DUNES AND SOURCES OF THE SAND

Eolian sand, which makes up the dunes, is derived from alluvium deposited by the Rio Grande in the San Luis Valley. During Late Pleistocene time the Rio Grande flowed directly eastward from the San Juan Mountains across the San Luis Valley to the vicinity of San Luis Lake where the river made a 90° bend and flowed directly south through the San Luis Hills (fig. 1). Since that time the Rio Grande has gradually moved southwestward away from this sharp bend until it now occupies a gently curved channel between the east flank of the San Juans and the north end of the San Luis Hills (fig. 1). The area between the oldest and youngest channels now consists of shallow crescent-shaped swales that are abandoned oxbow lakes and low serpentine-shaped mounds of loose sand and silt that are ancient natural levees of the Rio Grande.

The original source area of most of the grains of sand that make up the dunes is the volcanic terrane in that part of the San Juan Mountains drained by the upper reaches of the Rio Grande and the western tributaries of San Luis Creek. Much smaller amounts of sand were derived from streams flowing into the San Luis Valley from the crystalline and sedimentary rocks of the Sangre de Cristo Mountains north of Sierra Blanca. Alluvial material from these two mountainous terranes was deposited by the Rio Grande and San Luis Creek in the area of ancient natural levees and dry oxbow lakes (fig. 1). This area of loose sand and silt was the ready, immediate source of abundant material for the prevailing southwesterlies to build parabolic dunes to the northeast.

The remnants of these earliest dunes are the parabolic dunes of deflation (fig. 2). The structure of the dunes of deflation appears to have been parabolic when deposited and gives no indication of a history of longitudinal or transverse structures. An increase in vegetation due to an increase in rainfall or relatively low wind velocity has tended to stabilize or fix these early parabolic dunes.

Strong southwesterly winds continued to blow sand out of the Rio Grande flood plain and across the early parabolic dunes. Newly formed parabolic dunes migrated downwind until they reached nearly to the mountain front. There, wind turbulence and eddying were so violent that the sand began to pile up, but a wind-swept valley was kept open along the face of the mountains to the south. As the wind continued to bring in more sand, this sand was piled higher in a transverse pattern, and the interface between the transverse and parabolic dunes gradually moved westward as the large pile of sand stopped the migration of parabolic dunes. A steady and continuous supply of sand accumulated on top of this large pile of transverse dunes and formed climbing dunes against the high barrier formed by the Sangre de Cristo Mountains.

Today, sand is still being derived from the area of natural levees and oxbow lakes and the area of the parabolic dunes of deflation. It is blown across the fixed parabolic dunes to the active parabolic dunes of accumulation to collect in small amounts; however, most of the sand accumulates in the area of transverse dunes. Excess sand from the transverse dunes forms the climbing dunes. Small amounts of sand blow across the long expanse of longitudinal dunes to collect only temporarily on the barchans, but eventually sand is blown up Medano Pass or piled upon the south side of the climbing dunes as parabolic dunes.

REFERENCES

Baltz, E. H., 1965, Stratigraphy and history of Raton basin and notes on San Luis basin, Colorado-New Mexico: Am. Assoc. Petroleum Geologists Bull., v. 49, no. 11, p. 2041-2075.

Hack, J. T., 1941, Dunes of the western Navajo country: Geog. Rev., v. 31, p. 240-263.

Larsen, E. S., Jr., and Cross, Whitman, 1956, Geology and petrology of the San Juan region, southwestern Colorado: U.S. Geol. Survey Prof. Paper 258, 303 p.

Merk, G. P., 1960, Great sand dunes of Colorado, in Rocky Mtn. Assoc. Geologists Guide to the geology of Colorado: Denver, p. 127-129.

Upson, J. E., 1939, Physiographic subdivisions of the San Luis Valley, southern Colorado: Jour. Geology, v. 47, p. 721-736.

WATER RESOURCES OF THE SAN LUIS VALLEY, COLORADO*

by

Philip A. Emery

U.S. Geological Survey
Pueblo, Colorado

INTRODUCTION

An investigation of the water resources of the San Luis Valley, Colorado, was begun in 1966 by the U.S. Geological Survey in cooperation with the Colorado Water Conservation Board and the Colorado Division of Water Resources. Preliminary results of the investigations are being published as U.S. Geological Survey Hydrologic Investigations Atlas HA-381 (Emery and others, 1971). This paper is adapted from the atlas, but includes data collected since the atlas was compiled.

The San Luis Valley of Colorado (fig. 1) extends about 100 miles from Poncha Pass to the Colorado-New Mexico State line—an area of about 3,200 square miles. The valley floor, which has an average altitude of about 7,700 feet, is nearly flat except for the San Luis Hills and a few other small areas. Bounding the valley on the west are the San Juan Mountains, and on the east, the Sangre de Cristo Mountains. Most of the valley floor is bordered by alluvial fans, the most extensive being the Rio Grande fan (fig. 1). The Rio Grande fan extends about 30 miles along the west side of the valley and about 20 miles eastward into the valley, and has an average gradient of about 12 feet per mile.

Most of the streamflow is derived from snowmelt from about 4,700 square miles of watershed in the surrounding mountains. The northern part of the valley is internally drained and is referred to as a closed basin. The lowest part of this area is known locally as the "sump." The southern part of the valley is drained by the Rio Grande and its tributaries.

The climate of the San Luis Valley is arid and is characterized by cold winters, moderate summers, and much sunshine. The average annual precipitation on the valley floor ranges from 7 to 10 inches and as much as 50 inches occur in the neighboring highlands. More than one-half of the precipitation occurs from July to September. Owing to the short growing season (90-120 days), crops are restricted mainly to barley, oats, potatoes, and other vegetables. A successful agricultural economy would be impossible without irrigation.

HYDROGEOLOGY

The San Luis Valley is a large north-trending structural depression that is downfaulted on the eastern border and hinged on the western side. The valley contains as much as 30,000 feet (Gaca and Karig, 1966, p. 1) of alluvium, volcanic debris, and interbedded volcanic flows and tuffs of Oligocene to Holocene age. Although Siebenthal (1910, p. 39) subdivided the deposits into the Santa Fe and Alamosa Formations, later information indicates that it is impossible to differentiate the formations except locally. In this paper, all deposits above the Precambrian crystalline rocks are referred to as valley fill (table 1).

The Sangre de Cristo Mountains are composed of igneous, metamorphic, and sedimentary rocks, whereas the San Juan Mountains are composed mainly of volcanic flows, tuffs, and breccias (Larsen and Cross, 1956). Many of the lava flows and tuffs from the San Juans dip generally eastward under the valley floor, and in the southwestern part of the valley they restrict the vertical movement of ground water. Geophysical and drillers' logs indicate that a "clay series," 10 to 80 feet thick, occurs throughout much of the central and northern parts of the valley at depths ranging from 20 to 120 feet below land surface. The "clay series" restricts the vertical movement of ground water.

The total annual water supply to the San Luis Valley averages about 2,500,000 acre-feet. About 1,500,000 acre-feet is streamflow derived chiefly from snowmelt in the surrounding mountains and 1,000,000 acre-feet is from precipitation on the valley floor. Discharge of water from the valley averages about 2,000,000 acre-feet per year by evapotranspiration and about 500,000 acre-feet per year as stream flow and ground-water underflow across the state line. The annual streamflow at the state line averages 445,000 acre-feet and ground-water underflow accounts for the remainder, currently estimated at 55,000 acre-feet. About one-half of the evapotranspiration is nonbeneficial; that is, it does not contribute to the growth of plants having economic value. Much of the nonbeneficial consumption is by phreatophytes, mostly greasewood (Sarcobatus), rabbitbrush (Chrysothamnus), and saltgrass (Distichlis), in areas where the depth to water is less than 12 feet.

Ground water in the San Luis Valley is obtained from unconfined and confined aquifers. These aquifers contain at least 2 billion acre-feet of water in storage in the upper 6,000 feet. They are separated by a confining "clay series" or by confining layers of volcanic rocks. These confining beds are discontinuous and lenticular so it is difficult to differentiate between unconfined and confined aquifers except locally. This discontinuity in the "clay series" creates varying degrees of hydraulic connection between the aquifers.

Shallow unconfined ground water occurs almost everywhere in the valley and extends 50 to 200 feet beneath the land surface. The depth to water in about one-half of the valley is less than 12 feet (fig. 1).

Recharge to the unconfined aquifer is mainly by infiltration of applied irrigation water and leakage from canals and ditches. Water infiltrating from the many streams en-

---

* Publication authorized by the Director, U.S. Geological Survey.

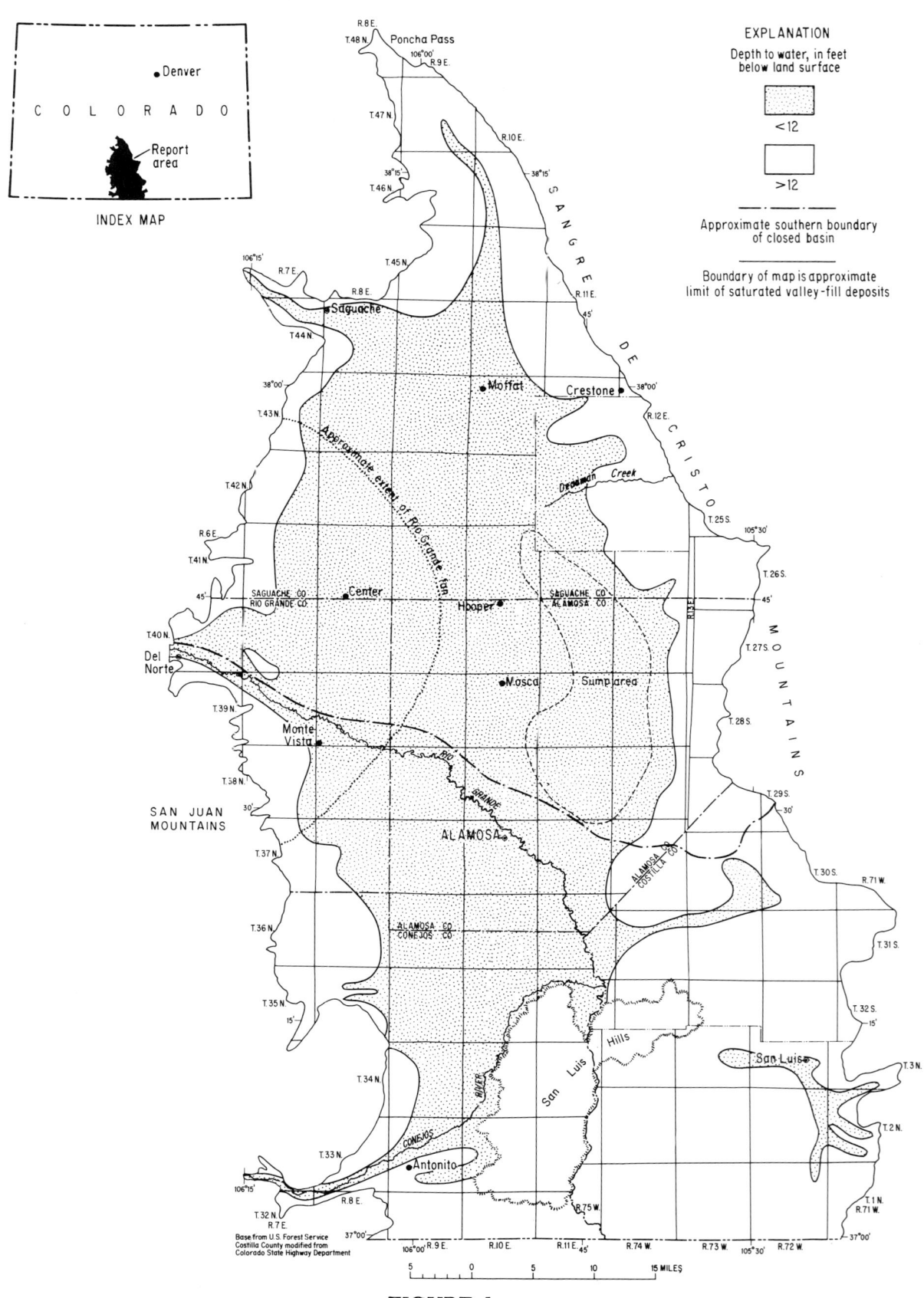

FIGURE 1.

Map of San Luis Valley showing depth to water, December 1969, and major physiographic features.

TABLE 1.
Summary of the hydrologic character of the geologic units, San Luis Valley, Colorado.

SYSTEM OR SERIES	GEOLOGIC UNIT	HYDROLOGIC UNIT	THICKNESS (FEET)	PHYSICAL CHARACTER	HYDROLOGIC CHARACTER	WATER SUPPLY
Holocene to Oligocene	Valley fill	Unconfined aquifer	0–200	Unconsolidated clay, silt, sand, and gravel.	Transmissivity ranges from 1,000 to 250,000 gallons per day per foot (134-33,500 square feet per day). Specific yield is estimated to be 0.20.	Yields as much as 3,000 gallons per minute to wells.
		Confined aquifer	50–30,000	Unconsolidated clay, silt, sand, and gravel interbedded with volcanic flows and tuffs.	Transmissivity ranges from 1,500 to 1,500,000 gallons per day per foot (201-201,000 square feet per day) in zones tapped by existing wells. Storage coefficient is estimated to be 0.008. Water is under pressure.	Yields as much as 4,000 gallons per minute to wells.
Precambrian	Crystalline rocks			Granite, gneiss, and schist.	Not tapped by wells. Probably not water bearing.	None.

tering the valley and precipitation on the valley floor provide recharge to the unconfined aquifer. Upward leakage from the confined aquifer is also a source of recharge. Discharge from this aquifer is by wells, evapotranspiration, and seepage to streams.

The principal source of recharge to the confined aquifer is seepage from mountain streams that flow across the alluvial fans flanking the valley floor. The "clay series" is absent at the edge of the valley, permitting recharge to beds that constitute the confined aquifer in the main part of the valley. The mountain streams show significant losses as they cross the porous surface of the fans. For example, seepage measurements made July 6, 1967, on Deadman Creek south of Crestone (northeast part of valley) showed that the 7 cfs (cubic feet per second) measured at the canyon mouth was completely dissipated within about 8 miles; all but 1 cfs was lost in the first 3.7 miles. The confined aquifer underlies most of the valley and the water has sufficient head to flow at the land surface in an area of approximately 1,400 square miles. The major discharge from the confined aquifer is by wells, springs, and upward leakage through the confining beds into the unconfined aquifer. A small amount may discharge as underflow into New Mexico.

The quality of water in the confined aquifer generally is better than that in the unconfined aquifer according to Powell (1958). The concentration of dissolved solids in 41 samples from the confined aquifer ranged from 70 to 437 mg/l (milligrams per liter) and, in 271 samples from the unconfined aquifer, ranged from 52 to 13,800 mg/l. The least mineralized water in the unconfined aquifer occurs on the west side of the valley. The mineral concentration increases toward the sump area of the closed basin probably because of solution of aquifer materials and by evaporative concentration in areas of a shallow water table.

DEVELOPMENT OF WATER SUPPLIES

The principal source of water for irrigation in the San Luis Valley between 1880 and 1950 was surface water. A large network of canals was built in 1880-90 to irrigate lands in the eastern and central parts of the closed basin. By 1915 most of the area around Mosca and Hooper (central part of valley) became waterlogged because of this irrigation. Drainage systems constructed between 1911 and 1921 to reclaim waterlogged lands alleviated some of the problems but created waterlogging in areas downgradient. Other areas are intentionally waterlogged in the process of subirrigation. The subirrigation practice continues because locally it is considered to be essential to successful growth of crops.

The number of large-capacity wells (yield more than 300 gallons per minute) in the San Luis Valley has more than quadrupled during the last 20 years. By the end of 1969 there were about 2,920 large-capacity irrigation wells in the valley. Of this total, about 2,270 tap the unconfined aquifer and about 650 tap the confined aquifer. Of the 650 large-capacity irrigation wells tapping the confined aquifer, 94 range in depth from 1,000 to 2,000 feet, and 19 are over 2,000 feet deep. Most of these deep wells flow, some exceeding 3,000 gallons per minute. In addition to the large-capacity wells, there are more than 7,000 small-capacity wells, most of which provide water for domestic and stock use.

Ground-water withdrawal for recent years averaged about 750,000 acre-feet per year. Withdrawal by large-capacity irrigation wells was about 450,000 acre-feet per year and withdrawal by small-capacity wells was an estimated 300,000 acre-feet per year. In 1970 the unconfined aquifer accounted for 78 percent of the ground water withdrawn from large-capacity wells. Many of the small capacity wells are uncontrolled and flow continuously. Perhaps 150,000 acre-feet per year from these wells might be considered waste. It does not contribute to crop production but causes additional waterlogging.

The annual water use of the valley is substantial. Despite the abundant supply, water-use practices over the past 100 years have created water problems. Surface-water use has resulted in the waterlogging of large areas of the valley. The valley-fill deposits in the northern part of the valley are recharged with water yielded from watersheds tributary to the closed basin and from diverted Rio Grande water. Crop productions are good in part of the area, but generally it results in high nonbeneficial water usage. Furthermore, the soils in the waterlogged areas have become alkaline, and the ground water has become highly mineralized because of evaporative concentration of salts. A major part of the valley south and west of Alamosa, likewise, is waterlogged.

Deliveries of water under the Rio Grande Compact with New Mexico and Texas have been deficient, accruing a deficit of 944,000 acre-feet by the end of 1967. Colorado has managed to improve the situation by making the required deliveries in recent years and has reduced the deficit to approximately 830,000 acre-feet by the end of 1970.

The U.S. Geological Survey, as part of its present study of the San Luis Valley, has constructed a multiaquifer electric analog model, simulating the upper 3,120 feet of valley fill. A single aquifer version of the model (Emery, 1970) has been utilized to evaluate a water-salvage plan proposed by the U.S. Bureau of Reclamation (U.S. Bureau of Reclamation, 1963). When testing of the model is complete, it will be used for more complex analyses related to water management.

REFERENCES

Emery, P. A., 1970, Electric analog model evaluation of a water-salvage plan, San Luis Valley, south-central Colorado: Colorado Water Conserv. Board Circ. 14, 11 p.

Emery, P. A., Boettcher, A. J., Snipes, R. J., and McIntyre, H. J., Jr., 1971, Hydrology of the San Luis Valley, south-central Colorado: U.S. Geol. Survey Hydrol. Inv. Atlas HA-381. [In press.]

Gaca J. R., and Karig, D. E., 1966, Gravity survey in the San Luis Valley area, Colorado: U.S. Geol. Survey open-file report, 21 p.

Johnson, R. B., 1967, The great sand dunes of southern Colorado: Art. in U.S. Geol. Survey Prof. Paper 575-C, C177-C183.

Larsen, E. S., Jr., and Cross, Whitman, 1956, Geology and petrology of the San Juan region, southwestern Colorado: U.S. Geol. Survey Prof. Paper 258, 303 p.

McConaghy, J. A., and Colburn, G. W., 1964, Records of wells in Colorado: Colorado Water Conserv. Board Basic-Data Release 17, 384 p.

Powell, W. J., 1958, Ground-water resources of the San Luis Valley, Colorado: U.S. Geol. Survey Water-Supply Paper 1379, 284 p.

Robinson, T. W., Jr., and Waite, H. A., 1938, Ground water in the San Luis Valley, Colorado, in Regional Plan., pt. 6, Upper Rio Grande: Washington, U.S. Govt. Printing Office, U.S. Natl. Resources Planning Comm., p. 226-267.

Siebenthal, C. E., 1910, Geology and water resources of the San Luis Valley, Colorado: U.S. Geol. Survey Water-Supply Paper 240, 128 p.

Upson, J. E., 1939, Physiographic subdivisions of the San Luis Valley, southern Colorado: Jour. Geology, v. 47, no. 7, p. 721-736.

U.S. Bureau of Reclamation, 1963, Plan for development of Closed Basin Division, San Luis Valley project, Colorado: Amarillo, Tex., U.S. Bur. Reclamation, Region 5, Project Plan. Rept., 87 p.

Winograd, I. J., 1959, Ground-water conditions and geology of Sunshine Valley and western Taos County, New Mexico: New Mexico State Engineer Office Tech. Rept., no. 12, 70 p.

FLORA OF THE SAN LUIS VALLEY

by

Hobart N. Dixon

Biology Department
Adams State College
Alamosa, Colorado

The Rocky Mountains in southern Colorado present a broad spectrum of vegetation types ranging from dry grasslands to moist spruce-fir forests. Where the different types of vegetation are found depends upon the environment and how it effects the plants by satisfying requirements or by exceeding the tolerances of the plants.

All species of plants have distinctive ranges of distribution which coincide with and which are controlled by patterns of the environment. The ranges of plants overlap in various combinations, usually in fairly constant associations which are called plant communities. These plant communities, composed of reasonably constant plant associations, are named for the dominant species in each community. Dominant species are the most obvious and abundant plants in the community. For example, ponderosa pine forests are dominated by ponderosa pines, but in this community type there are dozens of other plants which are overlooked due to small size or lack of abundance. In this paper we will consider the distribution of plant communities in the San Luis Valley as they relate to environment and as they can be identified by the dominant species. (Appendix 1 is a taxonomic key for the identification of the specific plants listed below.)

The distribution, or zonation, of plant communities is most obviously related to altitude, especially where the gradient is steep as in the Sangre de Cristo Mountains. (NOTE: There have been other, perhaps more familiar, schemes proposed for the naming of vegetation. Some of these different schemes are compared in Table 1). Of many environmental factors which change with altitude, two might be singled out as more important than others: (1) Temperatures decrease with altitude. (2) At higher altitudes there is more water available because of increased precipitation (annual precipitation at Alamosa is seven inches, while that at Wolf Creek Pass is over forty inches), and a decrease in the evaporative power of the air because of increasing relative humidities.

GREASEWOOD: Commonly called "chico" in the San Luis Valley, greasewood (*Sarcobatus vermiculatus*) is a low shrub which is adapted to areas where drainage is poor and where high concentrations of salt in the soil are common.

RABBITBRUSH: Several varieties of *Chrysothamnus nauseousus* are found on the valley floor. The distribution of the varieties is related to elevation and depth to water-table. Toward the lower parts of the valley, this small, greenish shrub is found intermingled with the greasewood in communities where the two plants are dominant, but away from the center of the valley the rabbitbrush becomes dominant.

GRASSLAND-SHRUB STEPPE: The grassland which originally occupied the region between the rabbitbrush type and the piñon-juniper woodland has been severely overgrazed. As a consequence, the original grasses have been replaced by several types of low-growing woody plants which include several types of rabbitbrush and other shrubs.

SAGEBRUSH: Probably because of slightly greater amounts of snow in the eastern parts of the valley, sage-

TABLE 1.

A comparison of some different classifications of vegetation zones in the Rocky Mountains.

COMMUNITY TYPE USED IN THIS PAPER	ALTITUDIAL DISTRIBUTION (ft. above sea level X 1000)	CLASSIFICATION OF VEGETATION ZONE ACCORDING TO:		
		Bailey (1913)	Ramaley (1942)	Marr (1964)
Tundra	11.5–14	Arctic-alpine	Not mentioned	Alpine tundra
Spruce-fir	10.5–12.5	Hudsonian	Coniferous forest	Subalpine
Lodgepole pine	9.5–11	Transition	Coniferous forest	Subalpine
Mixed Conifer	8–11	Transition	Coniferous forest	Upper montane
Douglas fir	8–10.5	Transition	Coniferous forest	Upper montane
Ponderosa pine	8.5–10	Transition	Coniferous forest	Lower montane
Piñon-juniper	8–9.5	Upper Sonoran	Piñon-cedar	Lower montane
Sagebrush	8–9	Transition	Oak-scrubland	Plains grassland
Scrub-oak	8–9	Upper Sonoran	Oak-chaparral	Plains grassland
Grassland-shrub-steppe	7.7–8.5	Upper Sonoran	Grassland	Plains grassland
Rabbitbrush	7.5–9	Upper Sonoran	Greasewood scrub	Plains grassland
Greasewood	7.5–8	Lower Sonoran	Greasewood scrub	Plains grassland
Aspen	8–11.5	Canadian	Aspen groves	Subalpine
Limber-Bristle-cone pine	8–12.5	Canadian	Coniferous forest	Upper montane
Willow-cottonwood	7.5–11	Upper Sonoran	Stream-valley	Lower montane

Piñon Needles

brush (Artemisia tridentata) replaces the dried shrub-steppe vegetation. South of Mount Blanca, sagebrush forms extensive stands below the piñon-juniper woodland. Soils in the sagebrush type are deep and fine textured and are very productive when cultivated.

SCRUB OAK: In the northern end of the valley, Quercus gambellii, a shrub 6 to 12 feet high, is found just below the piñon-juniper woodland. Dense stands of scrub oak are associated with rich soils and are frequently mixed with sagebrush.

Juniper   Piñon

Shooting Star

menziesii) in the southern Rocky Mountains are small (rarely over 2 feet in diameter or 70 feet in height). In the San Luis Valley these trees are found in pure stands above the ponderosa pine type and on north-facing slopes from 8,000 to 11,000 feet altitude.

MIXED-CONIFER: The mixed-conifer vegetation type is frequently found in a narrow, ill-defined band just above ponderosa pine, and in the ponderosa pine type along water courses on cool, shaded hillsides along the canyons. This type is composed of several trees which include aspen (Populus tremuloides), white fir (Abies concolor), Douglas fir, and Colorado Blue Spruce (Picea pungens).

SUBALPINE SPRUCE-FIR: The subalpine spruce (Picea engelmannii) and subalpine fir (Abies lasiocarpa) form the highest forest type in the Rockies. These trees, reaching heights of 100 feet, are shaped like tall pyramids and gradually become more and more stunted toward timberline. The spruce makes good lumber and most of the logging in the San Luis Valley is in this high altitude forest type.

PIÑON-JUNIPER: The woodland vegetation type is dominated by the piñon (Pinus edulis) and by either Rocky Mountain Juniper (Juniperus scopulorum) or one-seed juniper (Juniperus monosperma). All are small shrub-like trees seldom exceeding 20 feet in height. Soils in this vegetation type are rocky and well drained and support little except the piñon and juniper. Along water courses and on north-facing hillsides occasional stands of ponderosa pine and Douglas fir occur.

PONDEROSA PINE: Lying above and intermingled with the piñon-juniper type is the ponderosa pine vegetation type (Pinus ponderosa). These tall (up to 100 feet), open-spaced pines are found throughout the Southwest and are often logged. In topographic situations which allow for greater amounts of soil moisture, the Douglas fir or mixed-conifer type of vegetation will replace the ponderosa pine.

DOUGLAS FIR: When compared with the same species in the Pacific Northwest, Douglas firs (Pseudotsuga

TUNDRA: The alpine tundra is found above timberline where all vegetation is characteristically long-growing. Dwarf willows and other shrubs dominate parts of the tundra while grasses, sedges, and other herbaceous plants dominate others. Soils in the tundra are unstable because they contain abundant water and because of frequent freeze-thaw cycles. Consequently only those plants adapted to moving soil are successful in many areas. Also, constant strong winds in the tundra dry and kill the foilage of exposed plants, they carry snow and other materials which abrade the plants, and they move the snow about so that plants on windswept ridges receive little moisture

Bluebells

from snow while plants on leeward slopes receive a great deal.

ASPEN: Aspen groves, found throughout the Rocky Mountains, are the first trees to become established following forest fires and logging. When aspen trees are shaded by invading conifers they are unable to compete and tend to be replaced by the conifers; however, stands of aspen are frequently permanent on sites where there is sufficient moisture. Aspens range altitudinally from below 8,000 feet to timberline. These trees are generally not large and trunks with a diameter of 1 foot or heights of over 50 feet are considered large.

LODGEPOLE PINE: Lodgepole pine (*Pinus contorta*) is another tree which is successional following fires. Found on La Veta Pass and in the northwest part of the basin, these trees are characterized by having trunks with little taper. (Plains Indians used saplings of this species for their lodgepoles, hence the name). Cones, which remain closed on the trees for many years, release millions of seeds when the heat of fires softens the resins which stick the cone scales together. At lower elevations the lodgepole pine is replaced by ponderosa pine, Douglas fir, or mixed-conifer and at higher altitudes it is replaced by spruce-fir.

LIMBER PINE, BRISTLECONE PINE: Scattered throughout the mountains on rocky, wind-swept ridges are many local stands of limber pine (*Pinus flexilis*) at low altitudes and bristlecone pine (*Pinus aristata*) at high altitudes. These trees are small (seldom over 30 feet high), and much-branched. They are not successful except on ridgetops.

COTTONWOOD-WILLOW: At elevations below 11,000 feet, the banks of streams are characteristically occupied by cottonwood (*Populus* spp.) and willows (*Salix* spp.). These plants require much water and are restricted to situations where there is ample, shallow water.

COMMON JUNIPER: Although not a dominant in any vegetation type, *Juniperus communis* is frequently encountered in all types above piñon-juniper and deserves some mention. This dense, low shrub is common to all mountainous regions and is a distinctive part of many communities.

APPENDIX 1.

Key to some dominant native trees and shrubs of the San Luis Valley

1. Plants evergreen, leaves needle-like, scale-like, or awl-like .... 2 (conifers)
1. Plants not evergreen, leaves otherwise .... 14 (flowering plants)
2. Leaves needle-like, more than ½ inch long 3
2. Leaves awl or scale-like, less than ½ inch long .... 12 (junipers)
3. Needles fascicled (in groups surrounded by papery sheaths) .... 4 (pines)
3. Needles not fascicled, single 8
4. Needles in groups of 5 (sometimes 4) .... 5 (white pines)
4. Needles in groups of 3 (sometimes 2) .... 6 (yellow pines)
5. Mature cones long, without bristles .... Pinus flexilis (limber pine)
5. Mature cones short, with bristles .... Pinus aristata (bristlecone pine)
6. Mature cones closed, top-shaped, less than 2 inches long, remain on tree many years .... Pinus contorta (lodgepole pine)
6. Mature cones open, ovoid, more than 2 inches long, fall soon after maturity 7
7. Needles more than 3 inches long .... Pinus ponderosa (ponderosa pine)
7. Needles less than 3 inches long .... Pinus edulis (piñon pine)
8. Needles square or diamond-shaped in cross section, sharp-pointed .... 9 (spruce)
8. Needles flat in cross section, not sharp-pointed 10
9. Tree growing at high altitude, cone sless than 2 inches long .... Picea engelmannii (Engelmann spruce)
9. Tree growing at low altitude, cones more than 2 inches long .... Picea pungens (Colo. Blue Spruce)
10. Buds pointed; cones dry, pendant, with 3-lobed bracts, falling entire .... Pseudotsuga menziesii (Douglas fir)
10. Buds round; cones fleshy, upright, falling apart on tree .... 11 (true firs)
11. Needles more than 1½ inches long; usually found below 11,000 feet .... Abies concolor (white fir)
11. Needles less than 1 inch long; found above 11,000 feet .... Abies lasiocarpa (subalpine fir)
12. Leaves awl-like; plant low growing, shrubby .... Juniperus communis (common juniper)
12. Leaves scale-like; plant tree-like 13
13. Fruits usually with more than 1 seed; branches in flat sprays .... Juniperus scopulorum (Rky. Mt. juniper)
13. Fruits with 1 seed; branches not in flat sprays .... Juniperus monosperma (one-seed juniper)
14. Trees, with single trunks generally over 6 inches in diameter 15
14. Shrubs, with many small, woody stems 19
15. Leaves 4 to 6 times longer than wide 16
15. Leaves about as long as wide 17
16. Buds sticky with resin .... Populus angustifolia (narrowleaf cottonwood)
16. Buds without resin .... Salix spp. (willows)
17. Bark white, powdery to base of tree .... Populus tremuloides (aspen)
17. Bark not white at base 18
18. Leaves deeply lobed; plants of dry hillsides .... Quercus gambellii (scrub oak)
18. Leaves shallowly toothed; streamside plants .... Populus spp. (cottonwoods)
19. Leaves cyclindrical, succulent; brittle thorns present .... Sarcobatus vermiculatus (greasewood)
19. Leaves flat, not succulent; thorns absent 20
20. Leaves grey, small, 3-lobed, aromatic .... Artemisia tridentata (sagebrush)
20. Leaves green, large, not aromatic 21
21. Leaves deeply lobed, about twice as long as broad .... Quercus gambellii (scrub oak)
21. Leaves not deeply lobed, more than 3 times as long as broad 22
22. Shrubs of streamsides .... Salix spp. (willows)
22. Shrubs of dry areas .... Chrysothamnus nauseosus (rabbitbrush)

FAUNA OF THE SAN LUIS VALLEY

by

Veryl F. Keen

Biology Department
Adams State College
Alamosa, Colorado

INTRODUCTION

This paper is a brief resume of the animals commonly found in the San Luis Valley of Colorado. For the convenience of both the writer and reader the animals are listed under three major groups: (1) the herpetofauna, (2) the birds, and (3) the mammals. The reader should understand that this is not a complete list. It does not include many species which might be considered as only occasional visitors.

HERPETOFAUNA

The herpetofauna of the San Luis Valley is rather limited. This is due for the most part to the comparatively severe environmental conditions in the Valley. Therefore, only a few of the more hardy anura, sauria, caudata, and serpentes are to be found. There are no testudines in the Valley.

ANURA

Bufo cognatus Say (Great Plains Toad)
Bufo woodhousei woodhousei Girard (Rocky Mountain Toad)
Pseudacris triseriata maculata (Agassiz) (Boreal Chorus Frog)
Rana catesbiana Shaw (Bullfrog)
Rana pipiens brachycephala Cope (Leopard Frog)
Spea bombifrons (Cope) (Plains Spadefoot Toad)

CAUDATA

Ambystoma tigrinium mavortium Baird (Barred Tiger Salamander)
Ambystoma tigrinium utahense Lowe

SAURIA

Eumeces multivirgatus gaigeae Taylor (Skink)
Phyrnosoma douglassi ornatissimum Girard (Horned Lizard)
Sceloporus undulatus erythrocheilus Maslin (Fence Lizard)

SERPENTES

Crotalus viridis viridis (Rafinesque) (Prairie Rattlesnake)
Pituophis melanoleucus sayi (Schelegel) (Bullsnake)
Thamnophis elegans vagrans (Baird and Girard) (Mountain Garter Snake)
Thamnophis sirtalis ornatus (Baird) (Garter Snake)

MAMMALS

The mammals of the San Luis Valley appear to show overlapping into the valley of some species normally found to the north and to the south of the valley. Examples of this include the wolverine which has been reported at least twice near Mt. Blanca by reliable observers, and the ringtail cat from the southern limits of the valley. There are several small mammals which are very numerous. These include the Least Chipmunk (*Eutamias minimus caryi*), the Ord Kangaroo Rat (*Dipodomys ordi*), and *Lepus* sp. along with *Sylvilagus auduboni* (Desert Cottontail).

Eutamias minimus caryi is considered as being endemic to the San Luis Valley of Colorado. It is quite abundant in the chico and rabbitbrush of the valley floor, and is also found sharing the same habitats with the Colorado Chipmunk at higher elevations.

Antilocapra americana (Pronghorn)
Aplodontia rufa (Mountain Beaver)
Canis latrans (Coyote)
Cervus canadensis (American Elk)
Chiroptera (Bats)
Citellus lateralis (Golden-Mantled Ground Squirrel)
Citellus lateralis (Golden-Mantled Ground Squirrel)
Cleithronomys gapperi (Red-backed Vole)
Cynomys ludovicianus (Blacktail Prairie Dog)
Dama hemionus (Mule Deer)
Dipodomys ordi (Ord Kangaroo Rat)
Erithizon dorsatum (Porcupine)
Euarctos americana (Black bear)
Eutamias minimus (Least Chipmunk)
Eutamias quadrivittatus (Colorado Chipmunk)
Felis concolor (Mountain Lion)
Insectivora (Shrews)
Lepus sp. (Jackrabbit)
Lynx rufus (Bobcat)
Marmota flaviventris (Marmot)
Mephitus mephitus (Striped Skunk)
Microtus montanus (Mountain Vole)
Mustella frenata (Long-tailed Weasel)
Neotoma cinera (Bushy-tailed Woodrat)
Ochotona princeps (Pika)
Ondatra zibethica (Muskrat)
Onychomys leucogaster (Northern Grasshopper Mouse)
Peromyscus maniculatus rufinus (Deer Mouse)
Reithrodontomys sp. (Harvest Mouse)
Sylvilagus sp. (Cottontail Rabbit)
Tamiasciurus hudsonicus (Pine Squirrel)
Thomomys talpoides (Northern Pocket Gopher)

Grizzly Bear

Elk

make this area a home for many diverse species. Marsh species are quite abundant and include such species as ducks, rails, wrens, blackbirds, yellowthroat, snowy egrets, black-crowned night herons, black terns, avocets, marsh hawks, and short-eared owls.

There are two large national wildlife refuges in the valley (at Monte Vista and Alamosa), which provide high-quality nesting and feeding habitat for mallard and other waterfowl. The Monte Vista National Wildlife Refuge bird list contains 172 species ranging from abundant to rare. Some of the abundant species include the mallard, teal, and ring-necked pheasant. The rare species include

BIRDS

The San Luis Valley affords some of the best bird-study areas to be found in the Rocky Mountain region. The chico and rabbitbrush of the valley floor, the rushes and cattails, the cottonwoods and willows along stream banks, the conifers at higher elevations, and the water all combine to

Beaver and Beaver Dam

the white-fronted, snow, and blue geese; also the peregrine falcon, caspian tern, belted kingfisher, and poor-will to name a few.

The following list includes those species which an observer might normally expect to find during the late spring and summer months.

Mule Deer

American Avocet	Common Grackle
American Bittern	Common Nighthawk
American Coot	Common Raven
American Goldfinch	Cooper's Hawk
Bald Eagle	Crow
Band-tailed Pigeon	Downy Woodpecker
Bank Swallow	Eastern Kingbird
Barn Owl	Evening Grosbeak
Barn Swallow	Gadwall
Black-billed Magpie	Golden Eagle
Black-crowned Night Heron	Gray-headed Junco
Black-headed Grosbeak	Great Blue Heron
Black Tern	Great Horned Owl
Blue Grosbeak	Green-tailed Towhee
Blue Grouse	Green-winged Teal
Blue-winged Teal	Gray Jay
Brewer's Blackbird	Hairy Woodpecker
Broad-tailed Hummingbird	Horned Lark
Brown-headed Cowbird	House Finch
Brown Towhee	House Sparrow
Burrowing Owl	House Wren
Canada Goose	Hummingbird
Canvasback	Killdeer
Cassin's Finch	Lark Bunting
Cassin's Sparrow	Lesser Yellow Legs
Cinnamon Teal	Lewis' Woodpecker
Clark's Nutcracker	Loggerhead Shrike
Cliff Swallows	Long-billed Curlew

Long-billed Dowitcher
Long-billed Marsh Wren
Mallard
Mountain Bluebird
Mourning Dove
Pied-billed Grebe
Pine Grosbeak
Pine Siskin
Piñon Jay
Pintail Duck
Redhead Duck
Red-shafted Flicker
Red-tailed Hawk
Red-winged Blackbird
Ring-neck Pheasant
Robin
Rock Dove
Ruddy Duck

Rufus Hummingbird
Sage Thrasher
Sandhill Crane
Say's Phoebe
Short-eared Owl
Shoveler Duck
Snowy Egret
Sparrow Hawk
Spotted Sandpiper
Starling
Steller's Jay
Swainson's Hawk
Townsend's Solitaire
Turkey Vulture
Vesper Sparrow
Western Grebe
Western Kingbird
Western Meadowlark

Western Tanager
White-crowned Sparrow
White-faced Ibis
Williamson's Sapsucker

Wilson's Phalarope
Wilson's Warbler
Yellow-headed Blackbird
Yellow Warbler

REFERENCES

Burt, William H., and Richard P. Grossenheider, 1964, A Field Guide to the Mammals. 2nd ed. Cambridge: The Riverside Press.

Conat, Roger, 1958, A Field Guide to Reptiles and Amphibians. Cambridge: The Riverside Press.

Palmer, Ralph S., 1954, The Mammal Guide. Garden City: Doubleday and Company, Inc.

Smith, Hobart M., Maslin, T. Paul., and Brown, Robert L., 1965, Summary of the Distribution of the Herpetofauna of Colorado. University of Colorado Studies. No. 15.

Tomberlin, Donald R., 1967, Population Ecology of Two Chipmunk Populations in South Central Colorado. Masters Thesis. 76 p.

PENNSYLVANIAN AND PERMIAN STRATIGRAPHY, TECTONISM, AND HISTORY, NORTHERN SANGRE DE CRISTO RANGE, COLORADO

by

Richard H. De Voto

and

Frederick A. Peel

Colorado School of Mines
Golden, Colorado

and

Walter H. Pierce

Ball State University
Muncie, Indiana

INTRODUCTION

In portions of the northern Sangre de Cristo Range the Pennsylvanian and Permian sedimentary rocks are at least 18,000 feet thick (figs. 1 and 2). Folding and faulting have disrupted the rocks so that complete stratigraphic sections are almost nonexistent. The structural complexity and the abrupt facies changes that occur within this stratigraphic sequence have led to major difficulties in subdividing the section into distinct mappable units. This paper presents the results of detailed mapping of lithologic units within the thick Pennsylvanian and Permian sequence in the Arkansas River Valley (Pierce, 1969) (fig. 2) and the same lithologic units throughout the northern Sangre de Cristo Range by means of field work, and the use of high-altitude color and color infrared air photographs (Peel, 1971) (see plate 1, back pocket). The stratigraphic mapping and sedimentologic observations have permitted significant conclusions concerning sedimentation patterns and tectonism in this area during the Pennsylvanian and Permian.

STRATIGRAPHY

Pierce (1969) subdivided the Pennsylvanian and Permian sedimentary rocks that are exposed along the Arkansas River Valley southwest of Salida into seven major mappable units which he labeled, from oldest to youngest, Unit I through Unit VII. Based primarily on color, these divisions make excellent bases for subdividing and mapping the Pennsylvanian and Permian sedimentary rocks throughout the northern Sangre de Cristo Range as shown in Figure 3. The units, with only minor changes, may also be adjusted to the existing nomenclature as follows:

Pierce (1969)	This paper
Units VI & VII	—Upper Member—Sangre de Cristo Formation (including Crestone Conglomerate)
Units IV & V	—Lower Member—Sangre de Cristo Formation
Unit III	—Madera Formation
Unit II	—Sharpsdale Formation
Unit I	—Kerber Formation

Table 1 shows the historical development of the stratigraphic nomenclature of the Pennsylvanian and Permian rocks in the area. Table 2 graphically depicts the relationship of these formations from one locality to the next throughout the northern Sangre de Cristo Range.

KERBER FORMATION

Type Locality

The Kerber Formation contains the oldest Pennsylvanian sedimentary rocks in south-central Colorado. It was first described and named by Burbank (1933, p. 13) in the vicinity of Kerber Creek (T. 46 N., R. 9 E.) a few miles west of the hamlet of Villa Grove (see fig. 2). Burbank described the formation as a 200-foot sequence of carbonaceous shales, coarse-grained sandstones and "grits," occasionally interbedded with thin coals. At the type section, the Kerber formation rests unconformably on the Leadville Limestone (Mississippian) and conformably beneath the Sharpsdale Formation.

Lithology

Throughout south-central Colorado the sandstones of the Kerber Formation are typically quartzose, light gray, and tan to buff; the quartz grains tend to be subrounded to rounded. White kaolinite in many cases is a common matrix constituent. The kaolinite matrix, the quartzose mineralogy, and light gray to buff colors distinguish the Kerber Formation from the overlying red feldspathic rocks of the Sharpsdale Formation. Sandstones of the Kerber are, in some localities, conglomeratic, with pebbles averaging between ¼ to ½ inch in diameter. The shales are buff

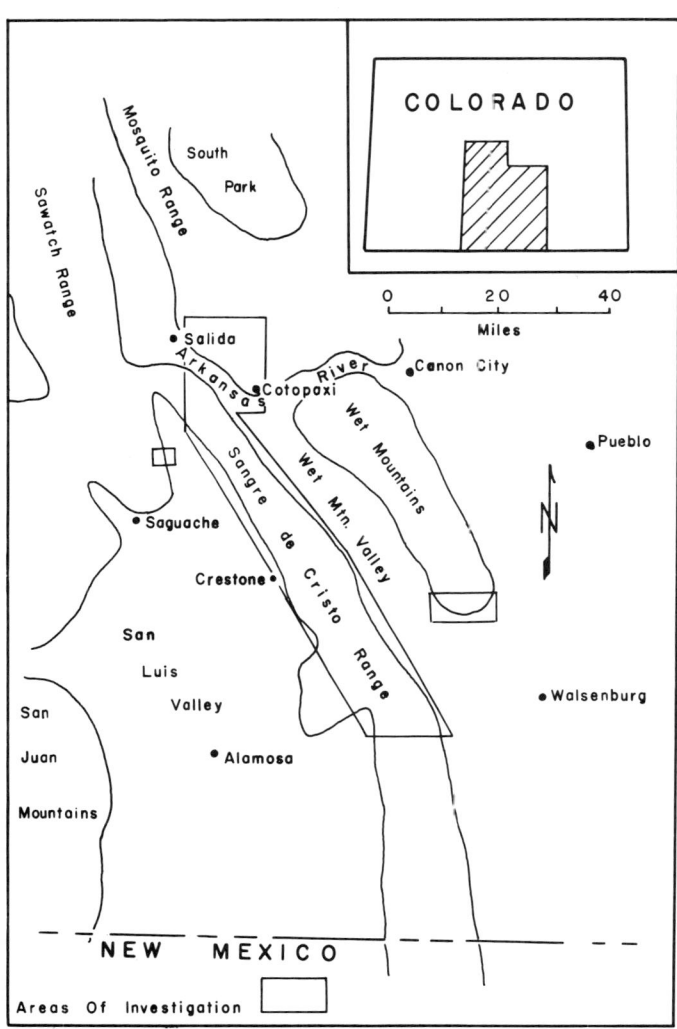

FIGURE 1.
Index map.

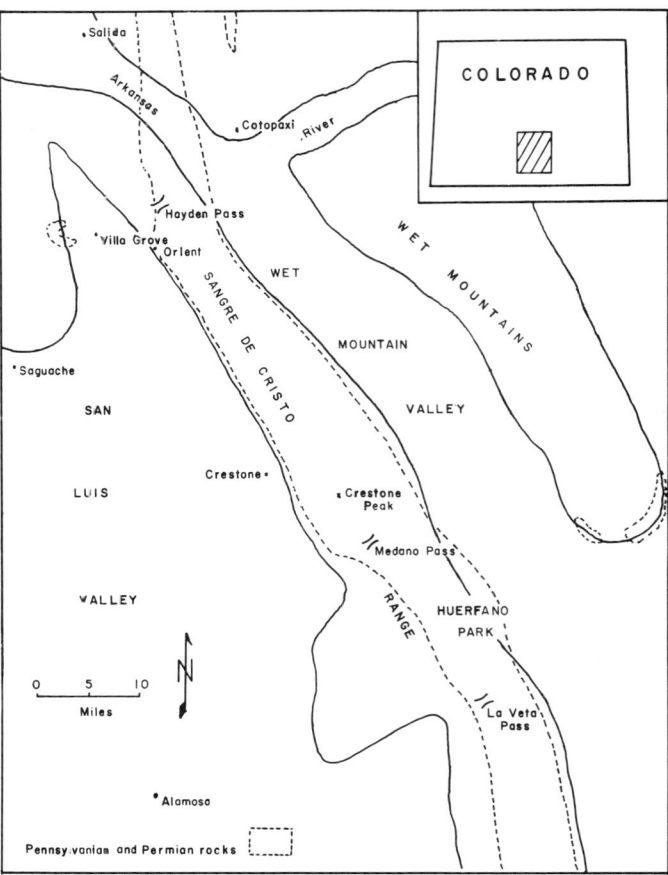

FIGURE 2.
Map of Pennsylvanian and Permian outcrops, south-central Colorado.

to dark brownish gray and are thinly laminated with an abundance of carbonaceous plant debris. Thin, fossiliferous, marine limestones and coal beds are present at a few localities within the formation.

The Kerber Formation is relatively nonresistant to weathering and, as a result, outcrops are sparse and poorly exposed. The formation is poorly stratified and sandstones pinch out laterally within short distances (500 to 800 feet). Some outcrops exhibit crude cyclic and graded bedding with coarse-grained, conglomeratic sandstones grading upward into siltstones and shales at the top of each cycle. The more coarse-grained sandstone beds exhibit some cross stratification or horizontal bedding. In some exposure cut-and-fill structures or scour features are present at the base of some of the sandstones and some of these contain lithoclasts of the underlying siltstones and shales.

The gray to buff quartzose sandstones, shales, and a few thin coal and limestone beds of the Kerber Formation occur ubiquitously at the depositional contact of the Pennsylvanian rocks with the underlying Paleozoic rocks and in some places with Precambrian rocks throughout south-central Colorado (figs. 4, 5, and 6). Along the Arkansas River Valley the Kerber Formation contains 300 to 400 feet of gray to buff, medium- to coarse-grained, quartzose sandstones and buff to tan, siltstones interbedded with a few thin, black carbonaceous shales. At least 3 brachiopod-bearing limestones are interbedded with the shales near the top of the formation.

At the north end of the Cotopaxi inlier, 8 miles north of the town of Cotopaxi, approximately 90 feet of gray to light gray, kaolinitic, quartzose sandstones interbedded with slightly carbonaceous shales are present at the base of the Pennsylvanian section. These beds, previously mapped as part of the Minturn Formation (Vargus, 1961) have the typical lithologic characteristics of the Kerber Formation and should be mapped as such (see plate 1, back pocket).

Kerber lithologies can be traced from known outcrops, with the aid of high-altitude color and color-infrared air photographs, south from the Arkansas River Valley over Hayden Pass along the western flank of the Sangre de Cristo Range to Major Creek (see Plate 1, back pocket). South of Major Creek the Kerber Formation is complexly faulted and the more continuous outcrop pattern that is found to the north ceases to exist. Despite the complex structure, Kerber lithologies are present in the North

FIGURE 3. High altitude air photograph of the Arkansas River Valley showing subdivisions of Pennsylvanian and Permian strata. Kerber (P_k), Sharpsdale (P_s), Madera (P_m), Sangre de Cristo Fm., Lower Member (P_{sl}), Upper Member (P_{su}).

TABLE 1. History of the Pennsylvanian and Permian nomenclature, south-central Colorado.

BURBANK & GODDARD 1937	BRILL 1952 Arkansas River	BRILL 1952 Huerfano Park	BOLYARD 1959 Northern Sangre de Cristo Range	PIERCE 1969 Howard Area	THIS PAPER Northern Sangre de Cristo Range
Sangre de Cristo Formation: Crestone Congl. Phase	Sangre de Cristo Formation	Sangre de Cristo Formation: Badito Formation	Sangre de Cristo Formation: Crestone Congl. Member	Unit VII	Sangre de Cristo Formation: upper member
Congl. Red Beds		Crestone Phase		Unit VI	Crestone Congl. Member
	Jacque Mtn. Ls.		Lower Member	Unit V	lower member
Rico Fm.	Minturn Formation	Whiskey Cr. Pass Ls. (Madera Formation)	Whiskey Cr. Pass Ls. (Madera Formation)	Unit IV	Whiskey Cr. Pass Ls. (Madera Formation)
Hermosa Formation		Arkosic Member / Gray Ls. Member (Madera Formation)	Deer Creek Formation	Unit III	Sharpsdale Formation
		Sandia Formation		Unit II	
Kerber Formation	Kerber Formation	Kerber Formation	Kerber Formation	Unit I	Kerber Formation

TABLE 2.

Correlation chart of Pennsylvanian and Permian rocks in south-central Colorado. For locations see Figure 2.

		Arkansas River	Orient	Crestone	Huerfano Park	
JURASSIC					Entrada Ss.	
PERMIAN		Upper mem.	Upper mem.	Upper mem. / Crestone Conglomerate	Upper mem.	Sangre de Cristo Fm.
		lower mem.	lower mem.	lower mem.	lower mem.	
PENN	Des Moinesian	Whiskey Cr. Pass Ls.	Whiskey Cr. Pass Ls.	Whiskey Cr. Pass Ls.	Whiskey Cr. Pass Ls.	
		Madera Fm.	Madera Fm.	Madera Fm.	Madera Fm.	
	Atokan	Sharpsdale Fm.	Sharpsdale Fm.	Sharpsdale Fm.	Sharpsdale Fm.	
	Morrowan	Kerber Fm.	Kerber Fm.	Kerber Fm.	Kerber Fm.	
PRE-PENN		Leadville Ls.	Leadville Ls.	Leadville Ls.	Precambrian	

Crestone Creek area (T. 44 N., R. 12 E.) along Burnt Gulch (T. 44 N., R. 12 E.) and along Deer Creek (T. 27 S., R. 72 W.) at the type section of the Sharpsdale Formation.

Although Burbank and Goddard (1937) recognized and described Kerber lithologies at Grayback Mountain, west of Huerfano Park, recent investigators have tended to ignore this and have placed these beds within the Sharpsdale Formation. Along Deer Creek (T. 27 S., R. 72 W.), at the type section of the Sharpsdale Formation, Bolyard (1959, p. 1908) described 104 feet of light gray to grayish yellow, quartzose sandstones and conglomerates resting unconformably on Precambrian crystalline rocks. Upon examination of this section the authors believe that these rocks, because of their lithology and stratigraphic position beneath the Sharpsdale Formation, should be mapped as the Kerber Formation (fig. 7). Because the lithologic changes are gradational, the Kerber-Sharpsdale contact is arbitrarily placed at the position in the section where the lithologies change vertically to predominently arkosic sandstones and overall deep red color. This places the top of the Kerber between Bolyard's intervals 11 and 12 of the type measured section of the Sharpsdale.

Contrary to Bolyard's belief (1961, p. 22) that sporadic occurrence of the Kerber Formation suggests erosion of much of the formation in south-central Colorado, the authors found Kerber lithologies everywhere the Sharpsdale occurs, except where they have been faulted out. Although the Kerber thins to the south of Crestone, it was probably deposited over the whole of the area. The gradational contact with the overlying Sharpsdale indicates that no post-Kerber, pre-Sharpsdale erosion has taken place in the northern Sangre de Cristo Range.

The rocks in the upper one-third of the Kerber are finer-grained and the percentage of limestones, shales, and siltstones increases with respect to the rocks of the lower part of the Kerber, except at Kerber Creek and Deer Creek. At Kerber Creek and Deer Creek, however, sandstones and conglomerates predominate and are evenly distributed throughout the section.

FORMATION BOUNDARIES

Throughout south-central Colorado the Kerber Formation generally rests disconformably on the Leadville Limestone (Mississippian) (fig. 4). A longer period of pre-Kerber erosion occurred near the margins of the Central Colorado trough, a narrow north-northwest-trending Pennsylvanian and Permian basin which existed between the Uncompahgre Highland on the southwest and the Wet Mountain (Apishapa) Highland on the east (fig. 5). The

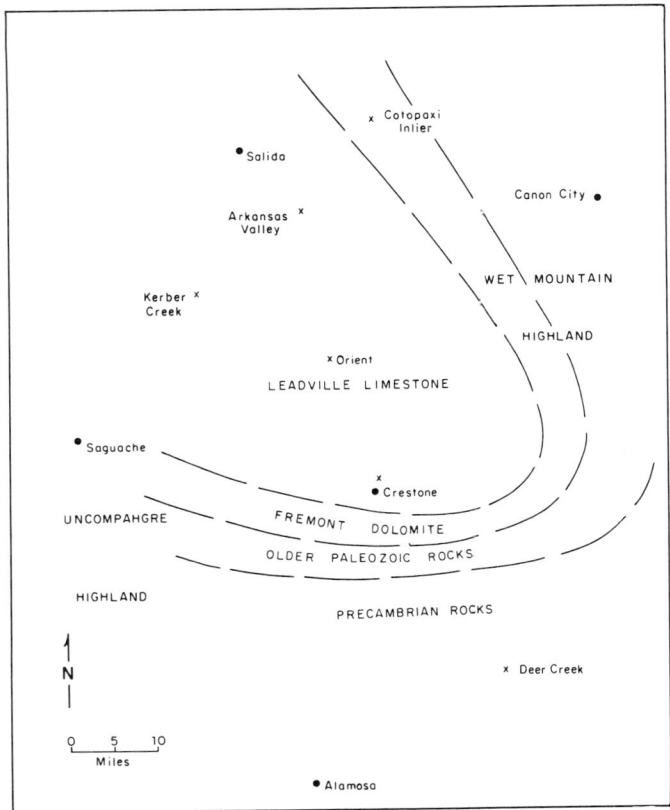

FIGURE 4.

Restored paleogeologic map of the rocks subcropping beneath the Kerber Formation.

incipient basin development and greater erosion in the areas of the adjacent highlands caused the Kerber to overlap the Middle and Lower Paleozoic rocks onto Precambrian rocks, as shown on Figure 4. Hence, the Kerber rests on the Fremont Dolomite (Late Ordovician) in the Cotopasic inlier (T. 49 N., R. 12 E.). A gradual thinning of the Leadville Limestone, the unit directly beneath the Kerber, occurs along the western flank of the Sangre de Cristo Range between Major Creek (T. 45 N., R. 11 E.) and Willow Creek (T. 43 N., R. 12 E.), so that further south Kerber lithologies lie directly on Precambrian crystalline rocks at Deer Creek (Sec. 23, T. 27 S., R. 72 W.) in Huerfano Park (fig. 4).

Although Bolyard (1961, p. 22) postulated an erosional contact at the top of the Kerber Formation, the authors have found Kerber lithologies to grade upward into Sharpsdale lithologies. Burbank (1933, p. 14) originally placed the top of the Kerber Formation at the base of the lowest stratigraphic position of micaceous shale occurring in the Pennsylvanian section. This criterion can only be used in the area of the type section. Therefore in this study the contact is arbitrarily placed at the stratigraphic position where the gray, light gray, and buff, quartzose sandstones of the Kerber change to the overlying arkosic, deep-red, Sharpsdale lithologies. This basis for mapping the contact between the Kerber and Sharpsdale can be used effectively throughout south-central Colorado.

DEPOSITIONAL ENVIRONMENT AND AGE

The abundant plant material, coal beds, and lenticular channel sandstones in the Kerber indicate that most of the Kerber section was deposited in nonmarine coastal plain and low-lying swamps and mudflat environments. The lithofacies and isopach map of the Kerber (fig. 4) reflects deposition in a narrow north-northwest-trending trough, the center of which roughly parallels the eastern edge of the present Sangre de Cristo Range. The Kerber thins and becomes more coarse grained toward the edges of the trough. The rough coincidence of the coarse-grained facies in the Kerber (fig. 4) with the deep pre-Kerber erosion into the Paleozoic and Precambrian section (fig. 3) suggests that incipient uplift of the adjacent highland areas occurred prior to the deposition of the Kerber and that a longer period of pre-Pennsylvanian erosion prevailed along the edge of the depositional trough, followed by eventual onlap of the Kerber Formation. The coarse-grained rocks along the edge of the trough were deposited in fluvial, coastal-plain environments, while the finer-grained facies with coals and carbonaceous shales were accumulating in the center of the basin.

Regional correlations show that the Kerber lithologies change facies to marine black shales and limestones of the Beldon Formation to the north of the Arkansas River Valley (Brill, 1952, p. 814; De Voto, 1965). An increase in the number of limestones in the upper part of the Kerber Formation at the Arkansas River Valley suggests that this area was influenced by more marine conditions toward the later stages of deposition.

No diagnostic fossils have been found in the Kerber. Fossils found in the overlying Sharpsdale Formation and the facies relationships of the Kerber with the fossiliferous Beldon suggest that the Kerber was deposited during the Morrowan and possibly Early Atokan.

SHARPSDALE FORMATION

TYPE LOCALITY

Bolyard (1956, p. 116-125) described a section of interbedded, deep-red arkosic sandstones, siltstones and shales lying unconformably on Precambrian crystalline rocks along Deer Creek (Sec. 23 and 24, T. 27 S., R. 72 W.) which he named the Deer Creek Formation. Chronic (1958, p. 61) later stated that the term Deer Creek had been pre-empted and consequently substituted the term "Sharpsdale" after the nearest settlement, the only one in the township. Bolyard (1961, p. 123) rejected the Sharpsdale name because it was derived from a "one-room log schoolhouse" no longer standing. Workers from Michigan State University (Rhodes, 1964, p. 18; Volkman, 1965, p. 33 and others) have introduced the term "Red Wing Formation" for the same sequence of rocks.

The authors propose that the term "Sharpsdale" be accepted for the typically deep-red, arkosic sandstones and shales which occur stratigraphically above the Kerber Formation and below the Madera Formation and that all others be dropped. The Code of Stratigraphic Nomenclature (1961, p. 652) clearly states that "Names derived

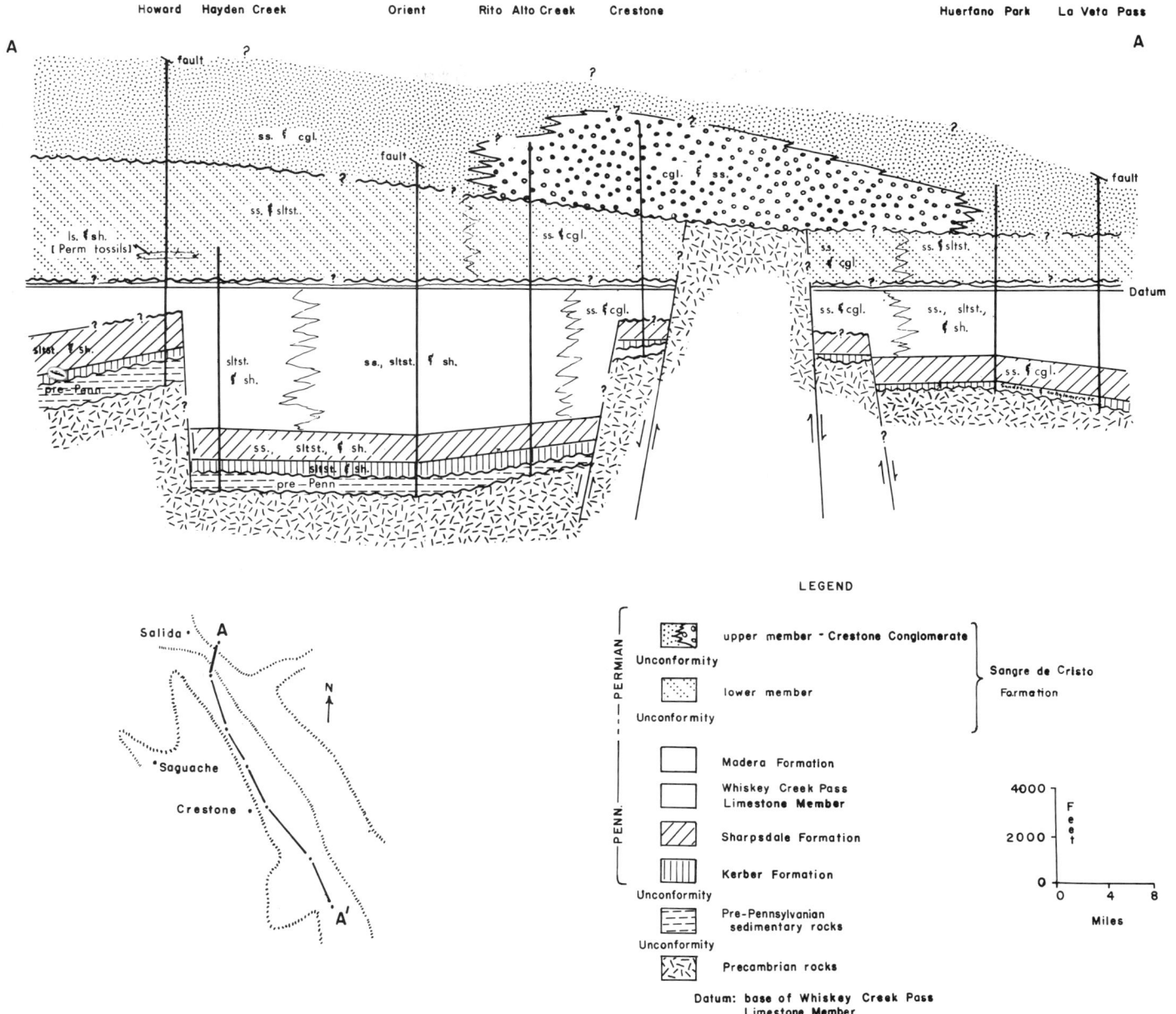

FIGURE 5.
Restored north-south stratigraphic section.

from changeable sources as the names of farms or ranches, churches, schools, and small communities are not entirely satisfactory but are acceptable if no others are available." Since the term "Deer Creek" has been pre-empted and the term "Red Wing" has not formally appeared in the literature, the term "Sharpsdale" is, in this case, the most satisfactory.

The basal 104 feet of Bolyard's type section of the Sharpsdale Formation at Deer Creek contains Kerber Lithologies. The lower boundary of the Sharpsdale Formation at the type section is, therefore, placed between intervals 11 and 12 of Bolyard's measured section. By redefinition of its lower boundary, the Sharpsdale Formation is restricted to the predominantly reddish-brown arkosic sandstones and deep-red shales, making the formation a more easily recognizable and mappable unit.

LITHOLOGY

The Sharpsdale Formation consists predominantly of red to deep red, fine- to coarse-grained, angular to subangular, micaceous, feldspathic to arkosic sandstones interbedded with deep-red shales and siltstones. Conglomeratic sandstones and conglomerates are not uncommon, and several beds of thin gray limestones, ranging to as much as 30 feet thick, are present throughout the section.

The conglomerates contain quartz, granite and gneiss pebbles and boulders as large as 8 inches in diameter. The matrix is generally fine-grained, argillaceous, feldspathic, sandstone. Most beds are lenticular, poorly sorted and extremely variable in thickness.

The limestones contain brachiopods and ostrocodes, but many contain as much as 40 percent clay, siltstone and/or sandstone. They commonly grade both laterally and vertically into sandstones and shales.

The sandstones, siltstones and shales generally are poorly sorted, containing varying amounts of clay, sand, and silt. Cross bedding and cut-and-fill stratification are common. Clasts of deep-red shale are common near the base of the sandstones that exhibit the cut-and-fill stratification. Although red and deep-red beds predominate, a few greenish-red and gray beds are present; dark gray to black beds are almost nonexistent.

Contrary to Bolyard's (1956) belief that the Huerfano River marked the northern extent of the Sharpsdale Formation, Karig (1964, p. 25) recognized 1,000 feet of the Sharpsdale along North Crestone Creek and Peel (1971) has traced the Sharpsdale north along the west flank of the Sangre de Cristo Range into the Arkansas River Valley (see plate 1, back pocket). Here the formation is 1,800 feet thick and corresponds exceptionally well with Pierce's Unit II (1969). The Sharpsdale is also present within the Cotopaxi inlier (see plate 1, back pocket) and at Kerber Creek.

Along the Arkansas River Valley the lower 400 feet is predominantly deep-red, micaceous siltstones and shales with thin brachiopod-bearing limestones. The upper 1,400 feet contains no limestones and is comprised of deep-red shales and siltstones interbedded with lenticular, red, arkosic sandstones. Although sandstones, siltstones and shales are equally distributed throughout the Sharpsdale at Kerber Creek, the brachiopod-bearing limestones are concentrated in the lower portion of the section.

As in the Arkansas River Valley section, gray shales and siltstones predominate the lower 300 to 400 feet of the Sharpsdale at Orient and North Crestone Creek. Thin arkosic sandstones are interbedded with the shales and siltstones but no limestones are present. The upper 500 to 600 feet at these localities are predominantly arkosic sandstones.

Sandstones comprise the major portion of the Sharpsdale at Deer Creek. Shales, siltstones and limestones are evenly distributed throughout. In this section the limestones are thicker and more common than elsewhere in the northern Sangre de Cristo Range.

FORMATION BOUNDARIES

The contact between the Sharpsdale and Kerber Formations is gradational and the base of the Sharpsdale is placed at the change from predominantly gray to buff, quartzose sandstones of the Kerber to the red, arkosic sandstones and deep red shales of the Sharpsdale. In many outcrops throughout Huerfano Park, as well as farther south, the Sharpsdale is in fault contact with Precambrian rocks. As much as 600 feet of the lower portion of the formation may be missing as a result of faulting. An excellent example of this relationship can be observed at La Veta Pass, 1.1 miles east of the Russell Post Office, where the fault contact is well exposed in an old prospect pit.

Throughout much of south-central Colorado, at Kerber Creek, Hayden Creek, Orient, Rito Alto Creek, Huerfano Park, and La Veta Pass (figs. 5 and 6), the upper contact of the Sharpsdale is gradational with the overlying Madera Formation and the red sandstones of the Sharpsdale intertongue with the gray-green sandstones and black shales of the overlying Madera Formation. In the Arkansas River Valley, however, this contact is relatively sharp and no intertonguing occurs. The regional stratigraphic relationships, as displayed in Figures 5 and 6, suggest that erosion or nondeposition occurred at the contact between the Sharpsdale and Madera Formations at Howard and Cotopaxi, north of the Arkansas River (fig. 6), and in the area between Crestone and Huerfano Park (fig. 5) on upthrown fault blocks.

DEPOSITIONAL ENVIRONMENTS AND AGE

As suggested by the isopach and lithofacies map (fig. 8) the Sharpsdale Formation was deposited in the same narrow north-northwest-trending basin as was the Kerber Formation. The coincidence of occurrence of red colors, angular pebbles of Precambrian rocks, abundant feldspar grains in the sandstones in the Sharpsdale beds in striking contrast with the gray to buff colors of the quartzose sandstones and shales of the Kerber suggests that the environment of deposition of the Sharpsdale was markedly different from that of the Kerber. The red colors of the Sharpsdale beds indicate that the interstitial ground waters soon after deposition were oxidizing and alkaline, probably fresh ground water in an arid, nonmarine environment. The red colors are due to hematite which is derived from iron-bearing minerals in these conditions. Hence, the change from coals, carbonaceous shales, and gray colors of the Kerber to the red colors and absence of preserved plant debris of the Sharpsdale indicates that the climate became more arid, producing the Sharpsdale lithologies.

The presence of abundant iron-bearing minerals, feldspar, and granite pebbles in the Sharpsdale beds indicates that the Paleozoic rocks had been stripped from the erosional areas in the adjacent highlands and that detritus from Precambrian rocks was being transported into the basin during the deposition of the Sharpsdale. Block faulting at the margins of the basin and highlands could have produced a climate change to an arid climate and erosion of Precambrian detritus in the highland areas. The block faults interpreted from the restored sections (figs. 5 and 6) to have been active subsequent to the deposition of the Sharpsdale and prior to the deposition of the Madera may have also been active in the creation of uplift blocks during the time of Sharpsdale deposition.

The coarse-grained facies and the current transport directions obtained by cross-strata measurements of the Sharpsdale, shown on fig. 8, suggest that streams flowed off the uplift blocks, depositing the coarsest material close to the source areas. Thus, the conglomerates and sandstones in the Sharpsdale in the Deer Creek and La Veta Pass areas were derived by southward transport from an uplift block to the north (figs. 5 and 8). The conglomerates and sandstones of the Cotopaxi inlier probably were derived

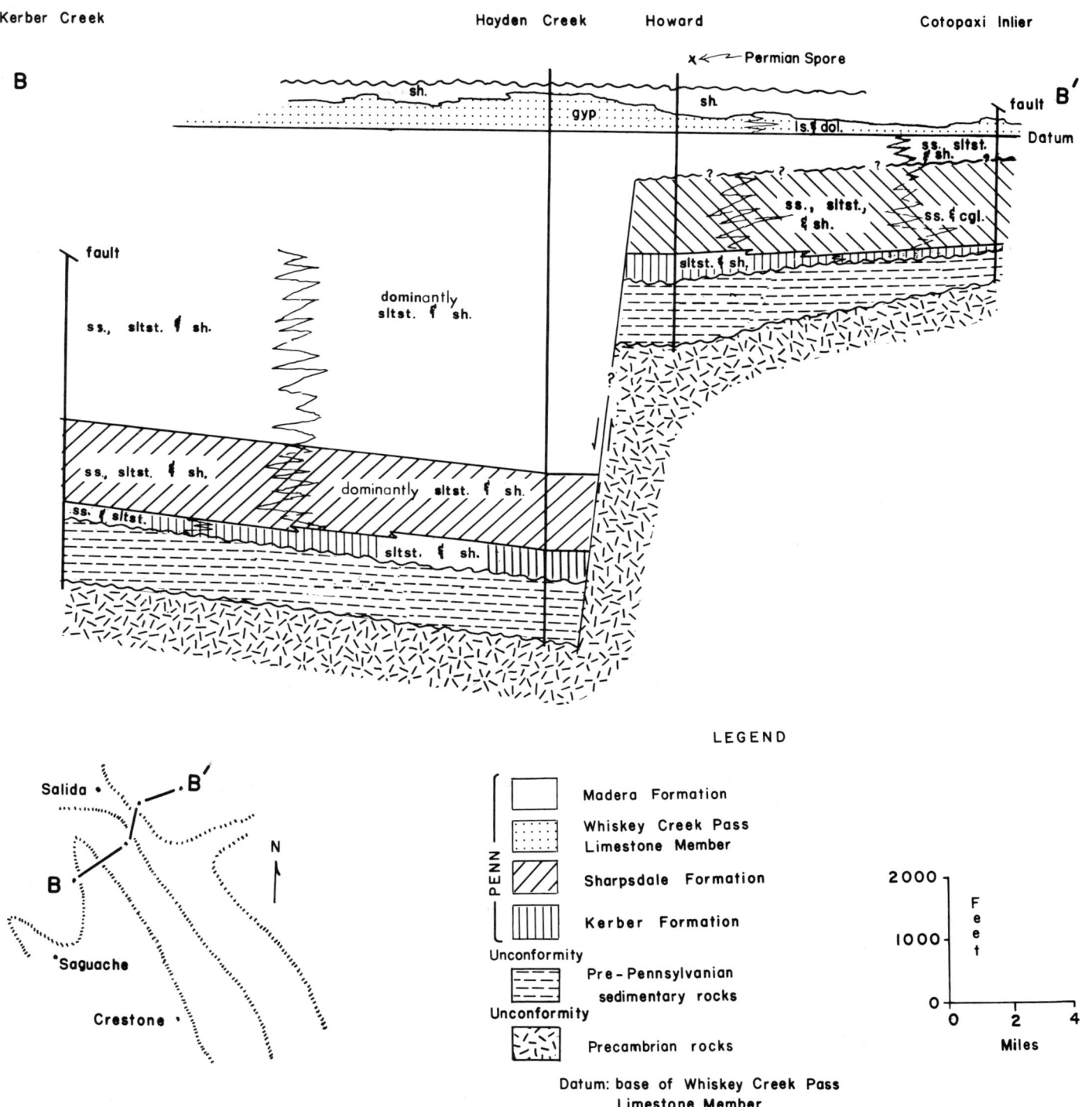

FIGURE 6.
Restored east-west stratigraphic section.

from an uplift block to the south (fig. 8) or immediately to the west. The Sharpsdale at Kerber Creek and the Arkansas Valley sections are comprised of finer detritus derived by northeast transport from the Uncompahgre Highland to the southwest.

These facies patterns and the presence of marine limestones within the Sharpsdale indicate that the structural activity was sporadic and recurrent during the deposition of the Sharpsdale. The presence of marine carbonates in the Sharpsdale at the Arkansas River Valley section and at Deer Creek and their absence in the northern Sangre de Cristo Range suggest that marine waters invaded the Central Colorado trough along its axis both from the north and south, probably due to structural movements of the

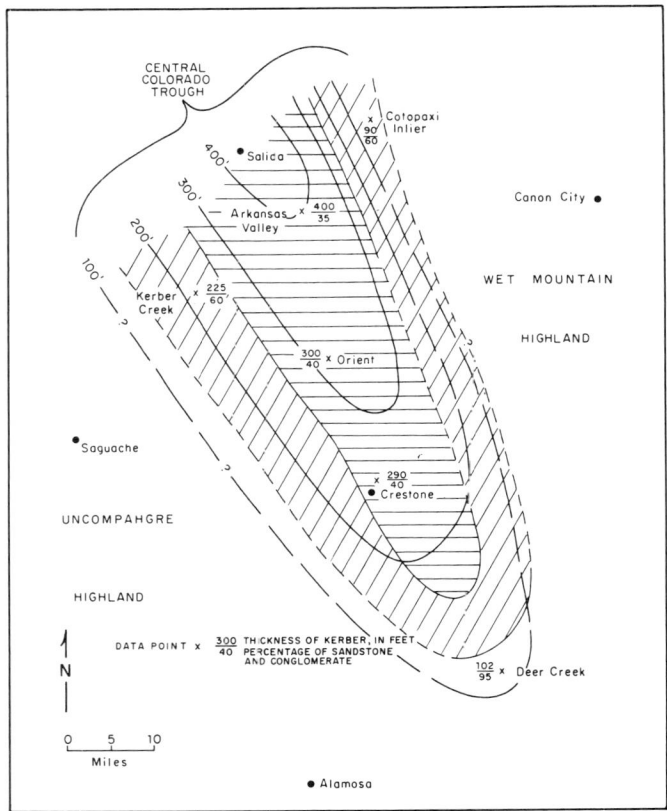

FIGURE 7.

Isopach and lithofacies map of the Kerber Formation in the Sangre de Cristo Range, Colorado.

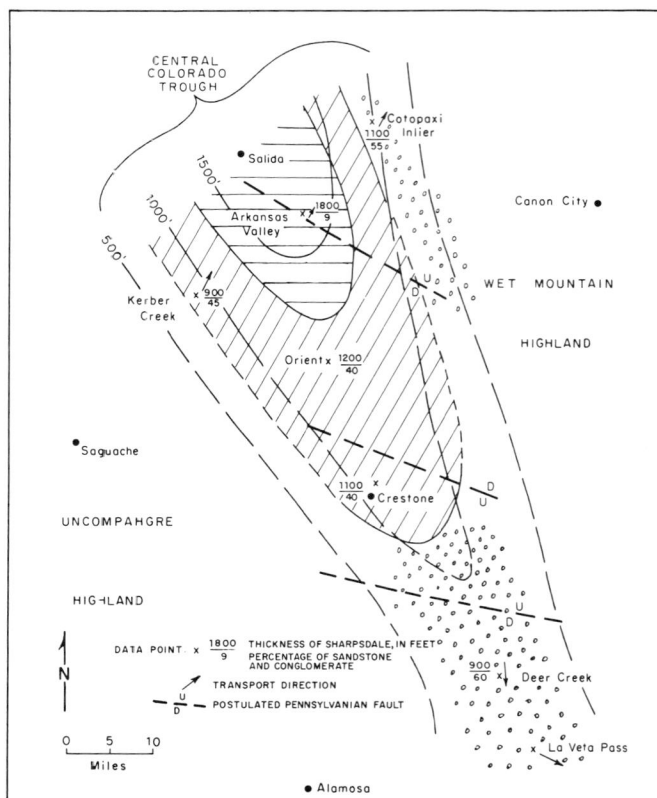

FIGURE 8.

Isopach and lithofacies map of the Sharpsdale Formation in the Sangre de Cristo Range, Colorado.

area. The uplift block between Crestone and Huerfano Park may have acted as a barrier to marine transgression during the times of the invasion of marine waters into the trough.

Thus, the Sharpsdale strata were deposited on alluvial fans and alluvial plains adjacent to actively rising uplift blocks in an arid climate. Marine transgressions occurred occasionally along the basin axis from the north and south.

Fossils found in the Sharpsdale (*Fusulinella devexa* in Huerfano Park and ostracodes in the Arkansas River section) (Brill, 1952, p. 830) and regional stratigraphic relationships (De Voto, 1965) indicate that the Sharpsdale was deposited in the Atokan and possibly the Early Desmoinesian.

MADERA FORMATION

Lithology

Brill (1952, p. 818) traced the Madera Formation into the south-central Colorado from its type locality in New Mexico and correlated it with the Minturn Formation of central Colorado. The formation grades laterally from a predominantly carbonate type section in New Mexico to a predominantly clastic section in south-central Colorado.

White to light-gray and greenish-gray sandstones and conglomerates, micaceous siltstones, and black shales comprise the bulk of the Madera Formation. The formation, deposited in the Desmoinesian, rests stratigraphically on the red sandstones and siltstones of the Sharpsdale and underlies the red sandstones and conglomerates of the Lower Member of the Sangre de Cristo Formation.

The Madera Formation is present throughout the northern Sangre de Cristo Range (see plate 1, back pocket) but complete sections are uncommon due to faulting and erosion. The formation reaches a maximum thickness of 5,500 feet near Orient, but thins markedly to the north and to the south (fig. 5), so that it is about 1,200 feet thick north of the Arkansas River and 1,000 feet thick near Crestone. South of Medano Pass (T. 24 S., R. 72 W.) the formation thickens more gradually. Along the Arkansas River Valley the Madera consists of green, pale gray-green, and brown, feldspathic sandstones and interbedded dark-gray to black shale. The sandstones are poorly sorted, but may exhibit trough cross stratification and scour features. Black micaceous shale, thin dolomite, lime-

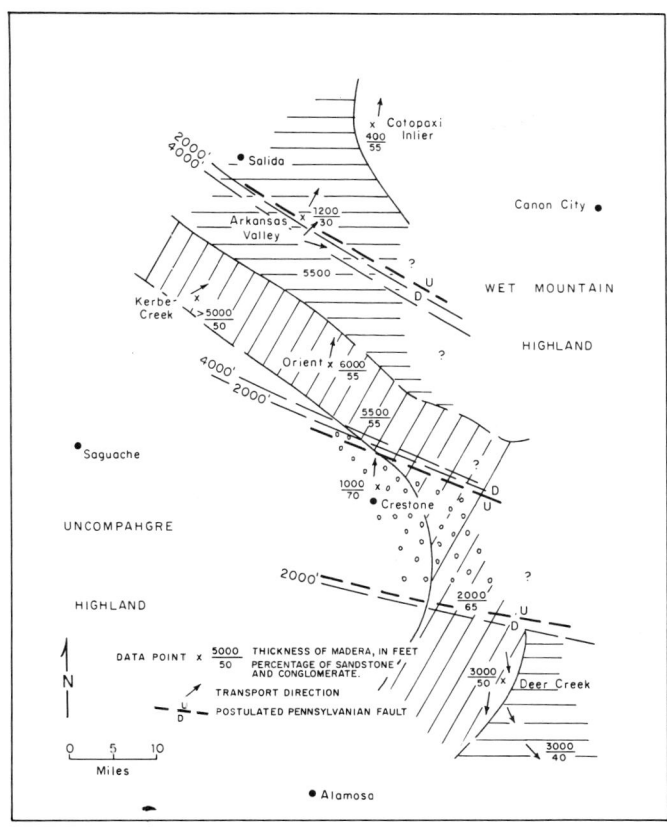

FIGURE 9.
Isopach and lithofacies map of the Madera Formation (excluding the Whiskey Creek Pass Limestone Member) Sangre de Cristo Range, Colorado.

stone and gypsum beds dominate the upper 150 feet of the section. In this upper zone sandstones are lighter hued and more mineralogically mature than those stratigraphically lower in the Madera.

A similar thickness and lithology were noted in the Cotopaxi inlier. Sandstones, however, are thicker, more coarse-grained and more prominent throughout the section than at the Arkansas Valley section (fig. 9). Gypsum beds are not present at the top of the formation, but two bioherms (fig. 10), which occupy approximately the same stratigraphic horizon as the gypsum beds at the Arkansas Valley section, develop to the maximum thickness of 200 feet and length of 2,000 feet. Their bases grade laterally into sandstone and siltstone; the upper half grades into black marine shale (fig. 10).

South of Orient the Madera Formation gradually becomes coarser-grained and includes a greater percentage of sandstones and conglomerates (fig. 9). In the vicinity of North Crestone Creek the conglomeratic material ranges from a few inches to three feet in diameter. Pebbles and boulders are chiefly comprised of quartz, feldspar, and granite, although some mica schist and gneiss pebbles are present. The most coarsely grained material is present between Rito Alto Creek (T. 45 N., R. 11 E.) and Arena Creek (T. 27 S., R. 22 W.) (see plate 1, back pocket). Along Middle Taylor Creek (T. 45 N., R. 12 E.) the conglomerate clasts increase in size stratigraphically upward to a position 2,500 feet below the top of the formation. Above this horizon the rocks are composed chiefly of pebbles and coarse-grained sandstone. Dark gray and black shales and siltstones are interstratified throughout the section with the sandstones and conglomerates but comprise only a small percentage of the total thickness. These shales and siltstones are thin but usually can be traced in the outcrop for several thousands of feet.

South of Arena Creek the formation again grades laterally into fine-grained lithologies, and limestones are present throughout the section. At La Veta Pass the sedimentation has been cyclic, with fine-grained sandstones grading upward into siltstones, shales and limestones.

The Whiskey Creek Pass Limestone Member, at the top of the Madera Formation, consists of 150 to 300 feet of interbedded gray limestone, black shale and siltstone, and greenish-gray sandstone. Limestones are more abundant near the base of the member and thin and thicken from locality to locality. At La Veta Pass the Whiskey Creek Pass Limestone Member is 160 feet thick (Brill, 1952, p. 829) and contains thin-bedded to massive gray oolitic limestones. Most limestones in this area contain a high percentage of sand and silt particles. Brill (1952, p. 818) reported gastropods and pectinoid pelecypods within the limestones.

Although a continuous outcrop does not exist, Bolyard (1959, p. 1915) has indicated that the Whiskey Creek Pass Limestone Member correlates with a similar zone at Marble Mountain (T. 24 S., R. 73 W.) and at South Colony Creek (T. 24 S., R. 73 W.). Two thick biohermal mounds are developed at Marble Mountain and have been described in detail by Berg (1967). Bolyard was able to trace this zone from South Colony Creek north to Rito Alto Creek and Munger (1959) was able to trace it, in almost continuous outcrop, to the Cotton Creek area (T. 45 N., R. 12 E.) where, he states, it appears to be Litsey's (1958) "D" zone. This zone can then be traced in outcrop to Big Cottonwood Creek (T. 47 N., R. 11 E.).

The authors believe that these zones are stratigraphic equivalents and may be correlated with the Whiskey Creek Pass Limestone Member because: (1) they are all stratigraphically located at the top of the Madera Formation and directly beneath the red, coarse-grained, arkosic lithologies distinctive of the overlying Sangre de Cristo Formation, and (2) although the zone varies in thickness throughout the northern Sangre de Cristo Range, the black shales, siltstones and gray fossiliferous limestones are everywhere similar. Fossil assemblages collected from this zone from different localities vary considerably, but crinoid columnals, gastropods, and pelecypods are common almost everywhere. With the exception of fossils dated as Late Cherokeean by Berg (1967, p. 10) most fossils from this zone have long ranges and can only be dated as Desmoinesian.

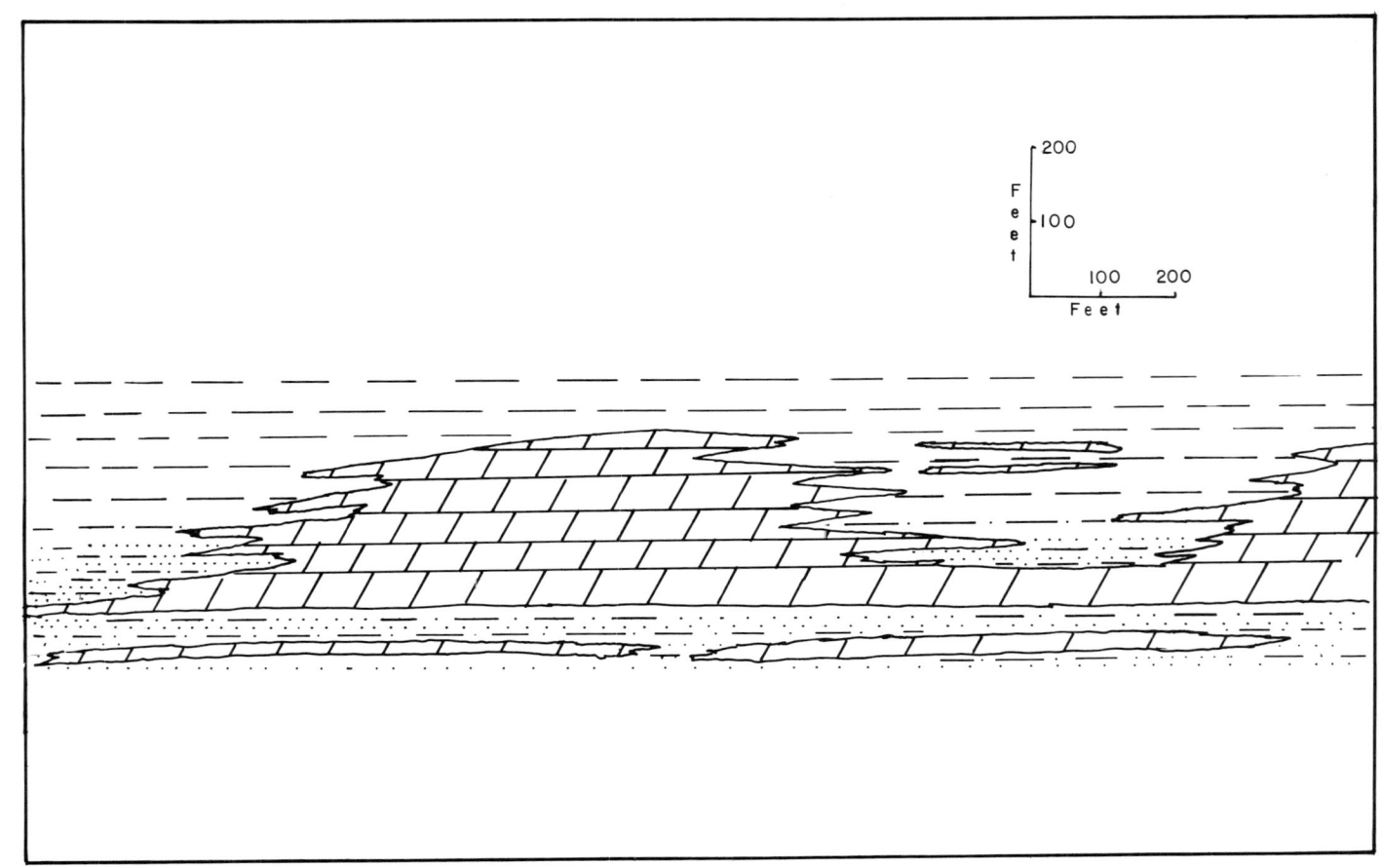

FIGURE 10.
Field sketch of bioherm in the Madera Formation at Cotopaxi inlier (Sec. 7, T. 49 N., R. 11 E.) showing lateral facies relationships.

FORMATION BOUNDARIES

As previously discussed, the contact between the Sharpsdale and Madera Formation is in places gradational and marked by the intervening of different lithologies. When intertonging occurs, the contact is placed at the change from predominantly red arkosic Sharpsdale lithologies to the green, feldspathic Madera strata. As interpreted, in other places the contact between the Madera and Sharpsdale is sharp and erosional (figs. 5 and 6).

The top of the Madera Formation is placed at the first occurrence of red arkosic sandstones, siltstones and shales characteristic of the Sangre de Cristo Formation. Throughout the northern Sangre de Cristo Range this change to redbeds is closely parallelled by the Whiskey Creek Pass Limestone Member, a 150- to 300-foot zone of gray marine limestones, black shales and siltstones, which occur directly beneath the contact in the uppermost part of the Madera.

In the Arkansas River Valley Brill (1952, p. 832) chose to place the top of the Madera Formation at the top of the highest marine limestone in the Pennsylvanian and Permian section. This falls at the top of a 200-foot sequence of gypsum, limestone, dolomite, and black shale. He believed that this sequence was correlative with the Whiskey Creek Pass Limestone Member of the Madera Formation and the Jacque Mountain Limestone Member of the Minturn Formation of north-central Colorado. However, below this sequence of limestone and shale is 1,850 feet of red, arkosic sandstones typical of the Sangre de Cristo Formation (figs. 5 and 6). Paleontologic data of Scott (1967) and White (1912) suggest that this uppermost marine sequence is of Permian rather than Desmoinesian age. White (1912) collected a number of fossil plants from this sequence where it crops out at the D & R G railroad tunnel in Sec. 28, T. 49 N., R. 10 E., which he considered as definitely Permian. Scott (1967) identified *Bisaccate gymnospermous* pollen collected along U.S. Highway 50, SE¼ SE¼ Sec. 18, T. 48 N., R. 11 E., which suggests a Permian age. The pollen was collected from beds near the base of what the authors consider typical Sangre de Cristo lithologies, stratigraphically below the uppermost marine limestones. If these sedimentary rocks are Permian, as indicated by fossil data, the uppermost marine limestones and shales cannot correlate with the Whiskey Creek Pass Limestone or Jacque Mountain Limestone as believed by Brill. Therefore, the sequence of limestone, gypsum, siltstone and shale previously mentioned to occur at the top of the gray-green feldspathic sandstones and siltstones more logically correlates with the

Whiskey Creek Pass Limestone and subsequently the top of the Madera should be placed at the top of this sequence (figs. 5 and 6).

Brill (1952, p. 811) assumed that the absence of datable Missourian and Virgilian beds was evidence of an unconformity at the base of the Sangre de Cristo Formation. Pierce (1963, p. 29) also suggests the possibility of an unconformity between his Unit III and Unit IV. The age of the Whiskey Creek Pass Limestone, on the basis of fossil data, is Desmoinesian and pollen found in the lower beds of the Sangre de Cristo Formation, approximately is dated as Permian. This indicates a break in the record with Missourian and Virgilian strata missing between the Madera and Sangre de Cristo Formation. The contact between these two formations in Big Cottonwood Creek when viewed from Nipple Mountain (T. 46 N., R. 11 E.) displays a slight angular discordance (fig. 11). Thus, the contact between the Madera and Sangre de Cristo Formations is probably unconformable throughout the northern Sangre de Cristo Range.

FIGURE 11.

Angular unconformity between the Madera Formation (P_m) and Lower Member of the Sangre de Cristo Formation (P_{sl}) at the head of Big Cottonwood Creek (Sec. 11, T. 47 N., R. 11 E.). Looking southeast from Nipple Mountain.

DEPOSITIONAL ENVIRONMENT

The distinct color change from the redbeds of the Sharpsdale to the green, gray, and black beds of Madera suggest that the Madera deposits accumulated in environments with different ground-water chemistry, i.e., in coastal plains and mudflats and/or marine conditions where the ground water table was shallow, allowing the preservation of organic debris and a reducing environment. The Whiskey Creek Pass Limestone Member accumulated in marine water with a diminished supply of terrigenous sediment. Bedded gypsum developed locally due to restricted bodies of marine water.

The configuration of the basin during the deposition of the Madera was markedly different from its configuration earlier in the Pennsylvanian. Block faulting that influenced the Sharpsdale deposition and the locally developed erosion surface on the top of the Sharpsdale significantly affected the facies patterns, thickness variations, and transport directions of the Madera beds (fig. 9). The highland uplift block between Crestone and Huerfano Park shed coarse-grained detritus to the north and south. Cross-stratification, current-transport directions (fig. 9) suggest that this east-southeast-trending horst block is probably an eastward extension of the Uncompahgre Highland. Finer-grained sediment shed from the Uncompahgre was transported to the northeast to the area of the Arkansas River Valley. On the downthrown side of the postulated fault in the Arkansas River Valley, two dominant transport directions were obtained from the Madera strata: (1) S. 50 E. from the lower 4,500 feet and (2) N. 55 E. from the upper 1,200 feet. This data suggests that the fault in the Arkansas River Valley may have diverted the drainage to the southeast during the deposition of the lower Madera beds and that the fault may have been overlapped by the upper beds of the Madera with renewed north and northeast transport (figs. 5, 6, and 9). The coarser grained sediment of the Cotopaxi inlier may have been derived from a northern projection of the Wet Mountain Highland.

Environmental conditions varied periodically throughout the deposition of the Madera, as both marine and nonmarine rocks occur in most sections. The area north of Orient was dominated by marine, coastal mudflat and deltaic conditions, with minor periods of alluvial deposition. Poorly sorted sandstones, some exhibiting ripple marks along bedding planes, intertongue with black marine shales and are probably marine and transitional in origin. Other coarser grained, trough, cross-bedded sandstones, which show cut-and-fill features, were probably deposited in fluvial environments.

In the Cotopaxi inlier, at Deer Creek and Kerber Creek fluvial sandstones comprise a greater percentage of the strata. Fine-grained littoral sandstones and a few black marine shales are present but in less abundance. At these localities the environment was probably a coastal plain with alternating periods of emergence and submergence.

On the horst block at Crestone the sandstones are coarse-grained and conglomerates are not uncommon. Some near-shore marine strata are interbedded with cross-bedded fluvial sandstones, suggesting that this area was dominantly alluvial plain subject to occasional periods of submergence.

The strata of the Whiskey Creek Pass Limestone Member are predominantly marine and the cross-bedded fluvial sandstones are confined to the lower ⅓ to ½ of the section. Gypsum beds in the Arkansas River Valley section within this stratigraphic horizon indicate periods when portions of the trough were restricted, probably by carbonate reef developments.

SANGRE DE CRISTO FORMATION

The name "Sangre de Cristo Conglomerate" was first used by Hills (1899, 1900, 1901) and later by Melton (1925a, 1925b) for the entire Pennsylvanian and Permian sequence of strata in the Sangre de Cristo Range. Brill (1952, p. 821) redefined the Sangre de Cristo Formation to include only those beds above the Madera Formation.

Bolyard (1959, p. 1923) subdivided the Sangre de Cristo Formation into the Lower Member and the overlying Crestone Conglomerate Member in the Crestone area. Inasmuch as no type area had been chosen for the Sangre de Cristo Formation, he proposed the area between Crestone Needle (T. 24 S., R. 73 W.) and Eureka Mountain (T. 44 N., R. 12 E.) as the type locality for the formation. Although both members are present and well exposed in this area, a continuous section could not be designated because of complex faulting, rugged topography, and inaccessibility.

In the Arkansas River Valley Pierce (1969) recognized and mapped four Permian units above the Madera Formation. He termed these subdivisions, Unit IV through Unit VII. Although his individual units can not be mapped throughout the northern Sangre de Cristo Range, Units IV and V, when combined, are equivalent to Bolyard's Lower Member, and Units VI and VII are a lateral facies of the Crestone Conglomerate (table 1, fig. 5).

Pierce discovered and mapped an angular unconformity between Unit V and Unit VI. This unconformity represents a major period of tectonism and erosion during the Permian in the Arkansas River Valley area (Pierce, 1969).

The authors prefer to retain the established Sangre de Cristo nomenclature with the addition of the term "Upper Member" of the Sangre de Cristo Formation. The "Upper Member" is herein defined as the finer grained, lateral equivalent of the Crestone Conglomerate and includes all Permian strata above the unconformity which forms the contact between it and the underlying Lower Member. Table 2 graphically depicts this interpretation.

LOWER MEMBER

Lithology—The type section near Eureka Mountain consists mainly of red, grayish-red, maroon and grayish-green, arkosic sandstone and conglomerate, interbedded with red siltstone, light gray mudstone, and limestone. The section is comprised of cyclic deposits each cycle grading upward from conglomerates and conglomeratic sandstone to highly indurated, fine-grained sandstones, siltstones and shales. Limestone is present in several localities near the top of some of the cyclic units. Figure 12 is a photograph and field sketch, looking south from the head of Cloverdale Basin (T. 46 N., R. 11 E.), which shows the cyclic nature of the bedding. The coarser rocks at the base of each cycle tend to be less resistant to weathering than the finer grained material at the top. Each cycle averages between 500 and 700 feet in thickness. Large-scale inclined strata within several cycles suggest alluvial fan deposition from the west (fig. 12).

UPPER MEMBER

Lithology—The most complete section of the Upper Member is present in the Arkansas River Valley and has been measured and described in detail by Brill (1952, p. 865). The Upper Member is included in his intervals 331

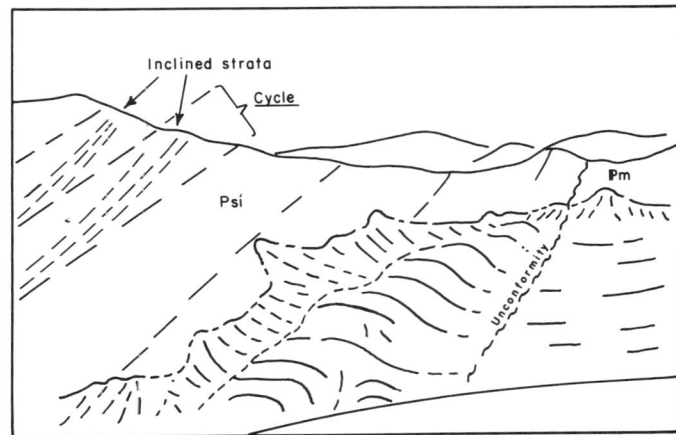

FIGURE 12.

Cycles within the Lower Member of the Sangre de Cristo Formation (P_{sl}). Looking southeast at the head of Cloverdale Basin, Sec. 24, T. 46 N., R. 11 E. Large scale inclined strata within several cycles suggest alluvial-fan deposition from the west to the east.

through 471. The section consists of red to brown, coarse-grained, arkosic sandstones interbedded with red, micaceous shales and siltstones.

The coarse-grained, arkosic sandstones are commonly thick bedded and poorly sorted but grade upward into medium-grained sandstones. Trough cross bedding and scour features are common. In some localities cobbles, as much as 3 feet in diameter, are present in the coarser grained sandstones and generally are composed of granite and gneiss.

The red, micaceous siltstones and shales are thin bedded to finely laminated and exhibit ripple marks and mud cracks. These shales in places are carbonaceous and black.

One of the most striking characteristics of the Upper Member is the occurrence of cobble conglomerates comprised of flat limestone cobbles in a coarse-grained, arkosic matrix.

The Upper Member exhibits a cyclic nature similar to the Lower Member except that the cycles are thinner. Each cycle is coarser grained at the base and grades upward into finer grained sandstones, siltstones and shales.

The member as a whole shows a general upward gradation to finer grained rocks.

The Upper Member crops out north of the Arkansas River, in the Rito Alto Creek to Medano Pass area (see plate 1, back pocket) at Huerfano Park and possibly La Veta Pass, but faulting and erosion have removed much of the section and a complete section is nonexistent. The most complete section of the Upper Member of the Sangre de Cristo Formation occurs in the Arkansas River Valley where Pierce (1969) measured 8,500 feet to 9,000 feet.

Bolyard (1959) described a thick section of coarse-grained, boulder conglomerates with some thin beds of arkosic sandstone in the area of Crestone Peak. He designated this unit, which lies above the Lower Member, as the Crestone Conglomerate Member of the Sangre de Cristo Formation. On a regional scale, the Crestone Conglomerate is a lens (or lentil) within the Upper Member and it disappears through facies changes both north and south of the type area (fig. 5).

The Crestone Conglomerate consists of sub-rounded boulders, as large as 20 feet in diameter, of granite and gneiss, with some mica schist and other rock types. These are generally found in a matrix of fine- to coarse-grained, arkosic sandstone and siltstone. Although the boulder beds appear to be massive, when viewed at a distance under proper lighting conditions they do exhibit a faint horizontal stratification. Sandstones and siltstones are poorly sorted and show some trough cross stratification.

Exposures of the Crestone Conglomerate are confined to the area between Rito Alto Creek and Medano Pass (see plate 1, back pocket). A short distance to the north of Rito Alto Creek and south of Medano Pass the conglomerates decrease in coarseness and the sandstones increase in number and thickness (fig. 5).

Peel (1971) has recognized a subtle angular discordance between the Lower Member and the Crestone Conglomerate on high-altitude color air photographs in the vicinity of San Isabell Lake and Groundhog Basin in T. 44 N., R. 12 E. (see plate 1, back pocket). The unconformity reported by Pierce in the Arkansas River Valley and the one in the San Isabell—Groundhog Basin area occur at approximately the same stratigraphic position.

The Lower Member is distinguished from the overlying sedimentary rocks by its finer grain size and higher percentage of red shales and siltstones. The red color of the Upper Member is also more drab than that of the Lower Member.

Depositional Environment—Trough cross-bedding, scour features, very poor sorting and large-scale inclined bedding in the sandstones and conglomerates and desiccation cracks in the siltstones and mudstones indicate that the Lower Member was deposited on an aggrading alluvial plain under predominantly fluvial conditions. The abundant cycles in the section suggest recurrent structural activity or climatic cycles in or adjacent to the depositional basin. The overall gradual upward coarsening of grain size in the section suggests progressive uplift of the adjacent highland blocks. The isopach and lithofacies map (fig. 13) indicates

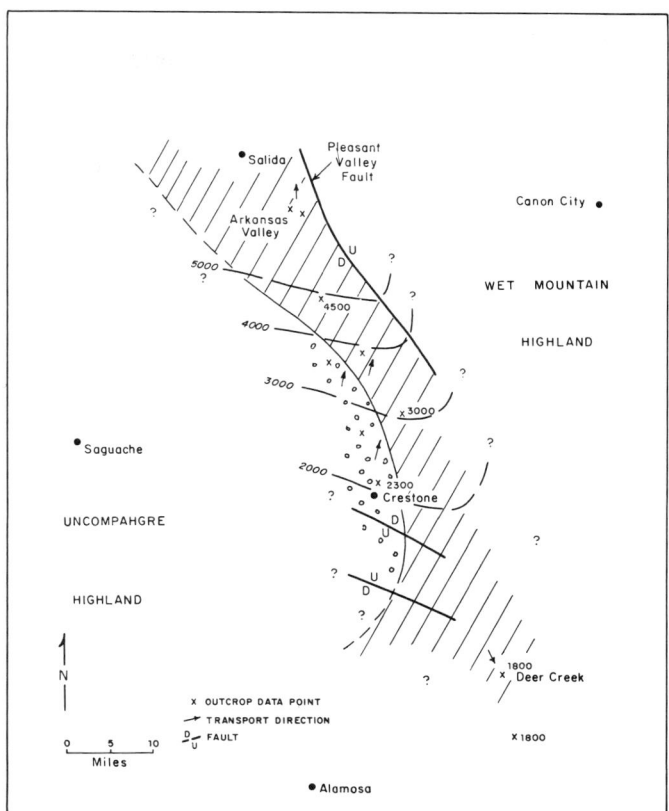

FIGURE 13.

Isopach and lithofacies map of the Lower Member, Sangre de Cristo Formation, south-central Colorado.

that the detritus was probably dominantly shed from an eastward projection of the Uncompahgre Highland, which may have been recurrent movement on the horst block in the Crestone area previously discussed (fig. 9). The occurrence of marine limestone interbedded with sandstones and siltstones suggests that parts of the trough were submergent for short periods of time.

The conglomerates and conglomeratic sandstones are composed of well rounded pebbles, cobbles, and, in some localities, boulders which reach a diameter of 1 foot. The stream-rounded pebbles and cobbles consist of granite, gneiss, and mica schist, with some sandstone and siltstone derived from the Lower Member itself. Arkosic sandstone generally composes the matrix of the conglomerates.

The arkosic sandstones are poorly sorted, fine- to coarse-grained and commonly are very micaceous and argillaceous. They are thin to thick bedded and contain trough cross stratification and cut-and-fill features throughout.

Although no fossils have been found, the thin gray limestones which are rarely more than 3 feet thick, are considered marine in origin. Some of the limestones exhibit stromatolitic banding and are cherty. Black shales occur only sparsely throughout the Lower Member.

The Lower Member gradually thickens from 2,300 feet

at Crestone Peak to 4,500 feet at Orient and 6,000 feet in the Arkansas River Valley.

Figure 13, a lithofacies map of the Lower Member, shows the lateral facies changes within this member throughout the northern Sangre de Cristo Range. Fine-grained sandstones and siltstones dominate the section on the Arkansas River Valley and along the eastern flank of the Sangre de Cristo Range in Huerfano Park and La Veta Pass. These sedimentary rocks grade laterally to dominantly medium- to coarse-grained sandstones and conglomerates at Orient, Crestone and the northern end of Huerfano Park. Most sections show a gradual coarsening of the conglomerates toward the top of the member.

Member Boundaries—The contact between the Lower Member of the Sangre de Cristo Formation and the underlying Madera Formation is probably an unconformity, as discussed previously. The contact is easily recognized by a change from gray-green, feldspathic sandstones, siltstones and black shales of the Madera Formation to the predominantly maroon to red arkosic sandstones and red shales of the Lower Member.

The contact between the Lower Member and the overlying Upper Member is unconformable in many places also. Pierce (1969) discovered an angular discordance between his Units V and VI which is the contact between the Lower Member and the Upper Member in the Arkansas River Valley (table 1). Erosion at the unconformity truncates 6,000 feet of underlying Pennsylvanian and Permian strata in a distance of 3 miles as the Pleasant Valley fault is approached (figs. 14 and 15). Anticlinal and synclinal folding developed in the beds underlying the unconformity before the overlying beds were deposited.

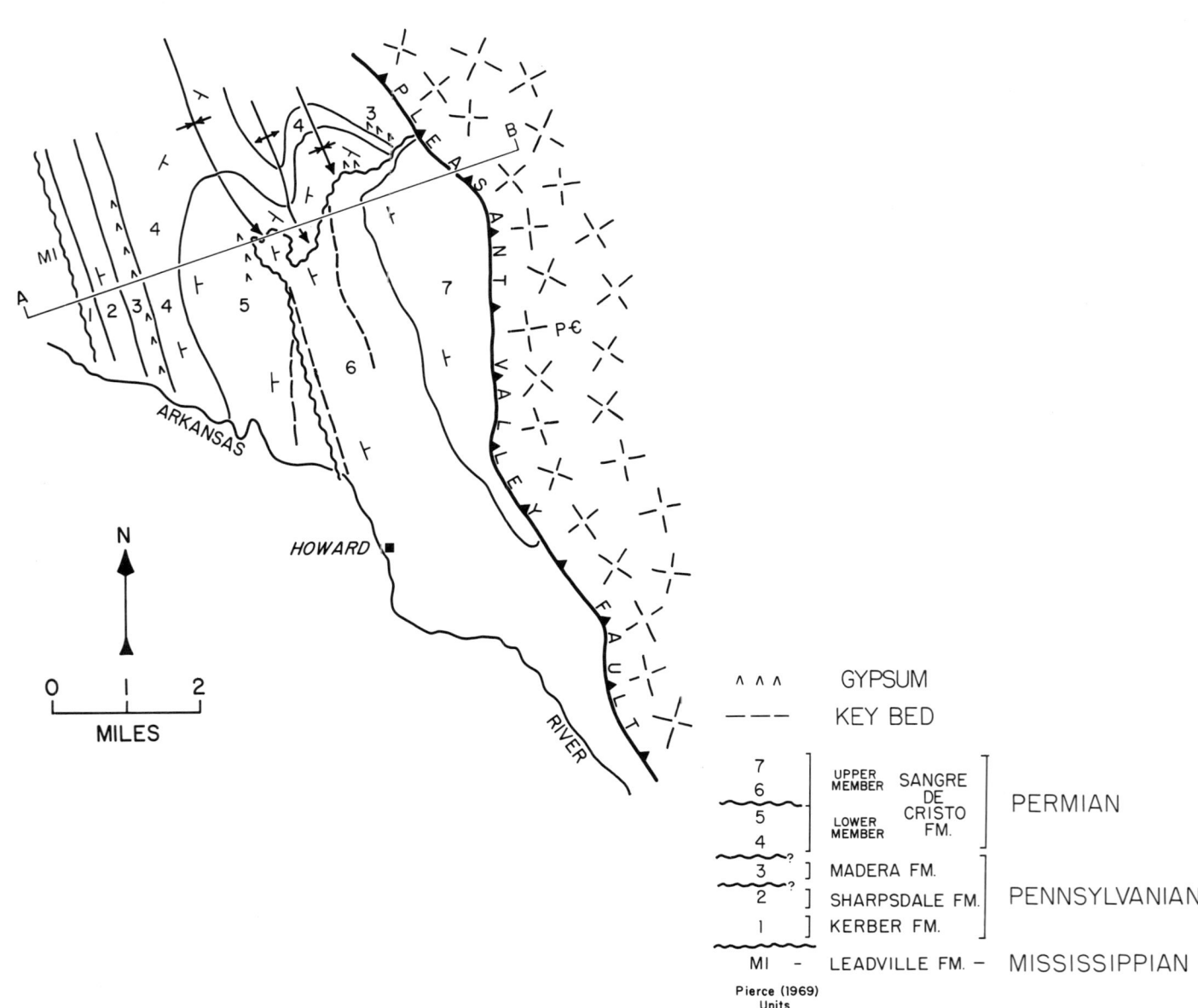

FIGURE 14.
Pennsylvanian and Permian mappable units, Arkansas River Valley, Colorado.

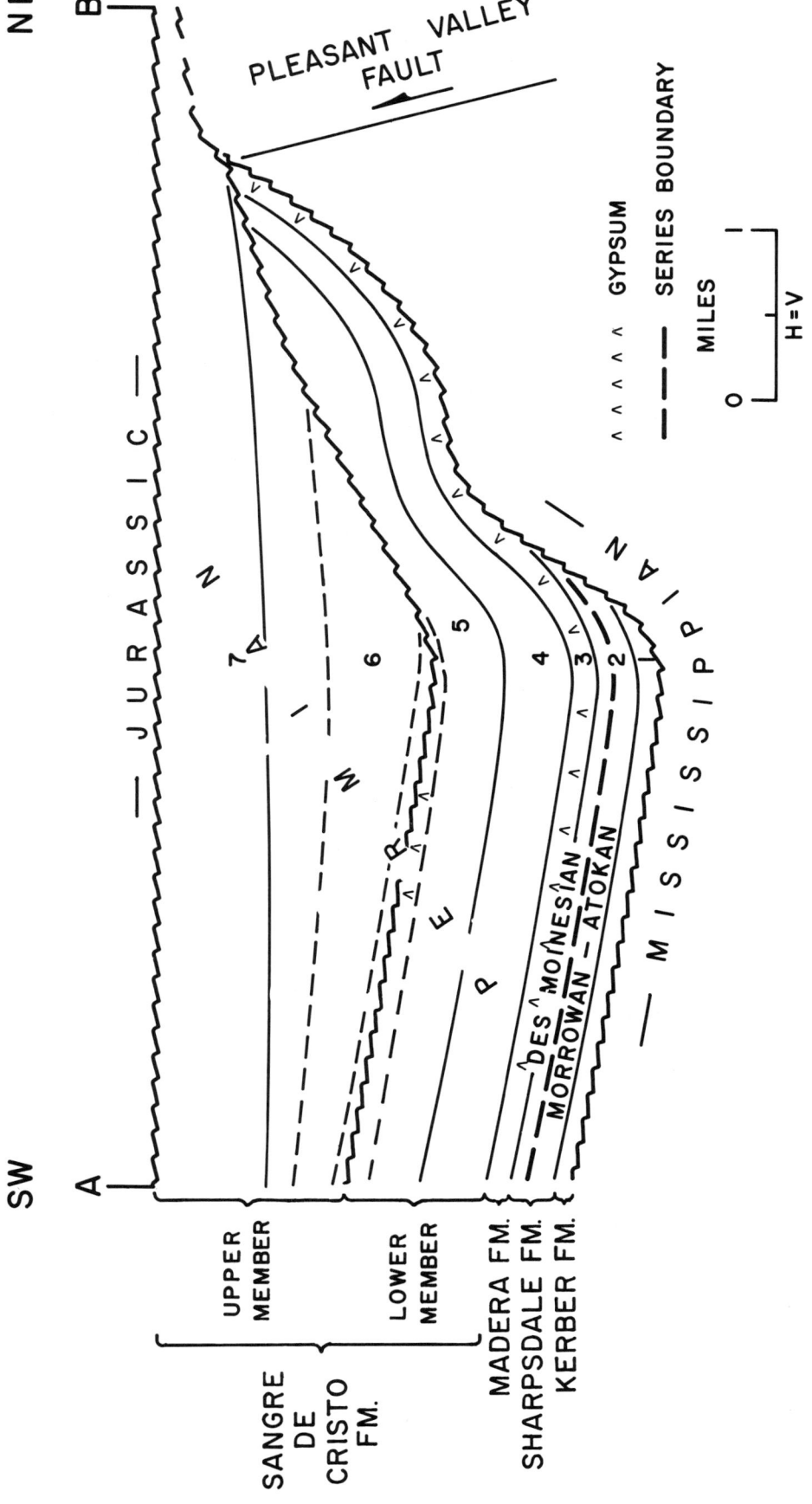

FIGURE 15. Restored section, Pennsylvanian and Permian rocks, Arkansas River Valley, Colorado (after Pierce, 1969). Line of section shown on Figure 14.

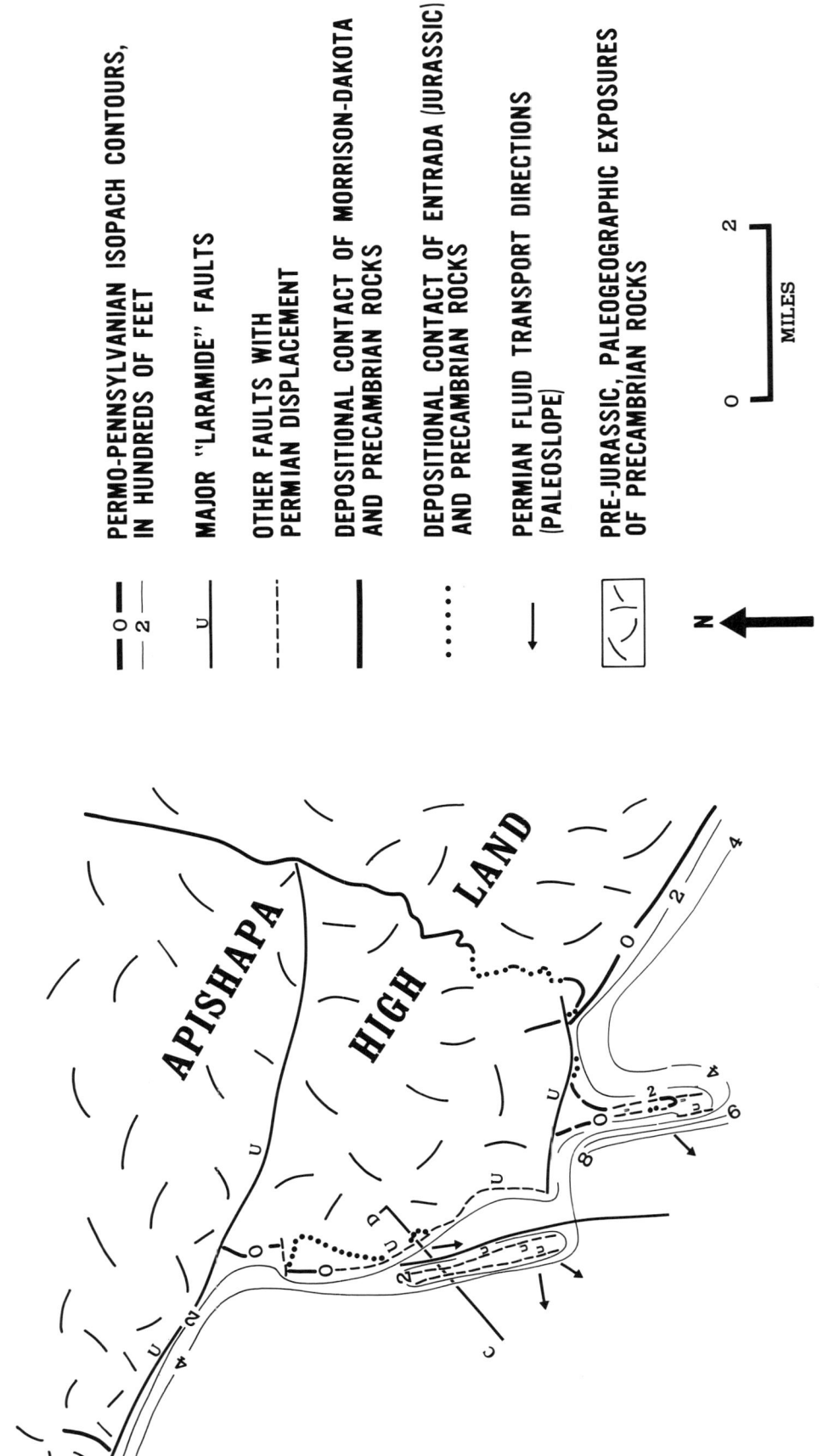

FIGURE 16. Restored geographic and isopach map showing Permian faulting, southern Wet Mountains, Colorado.

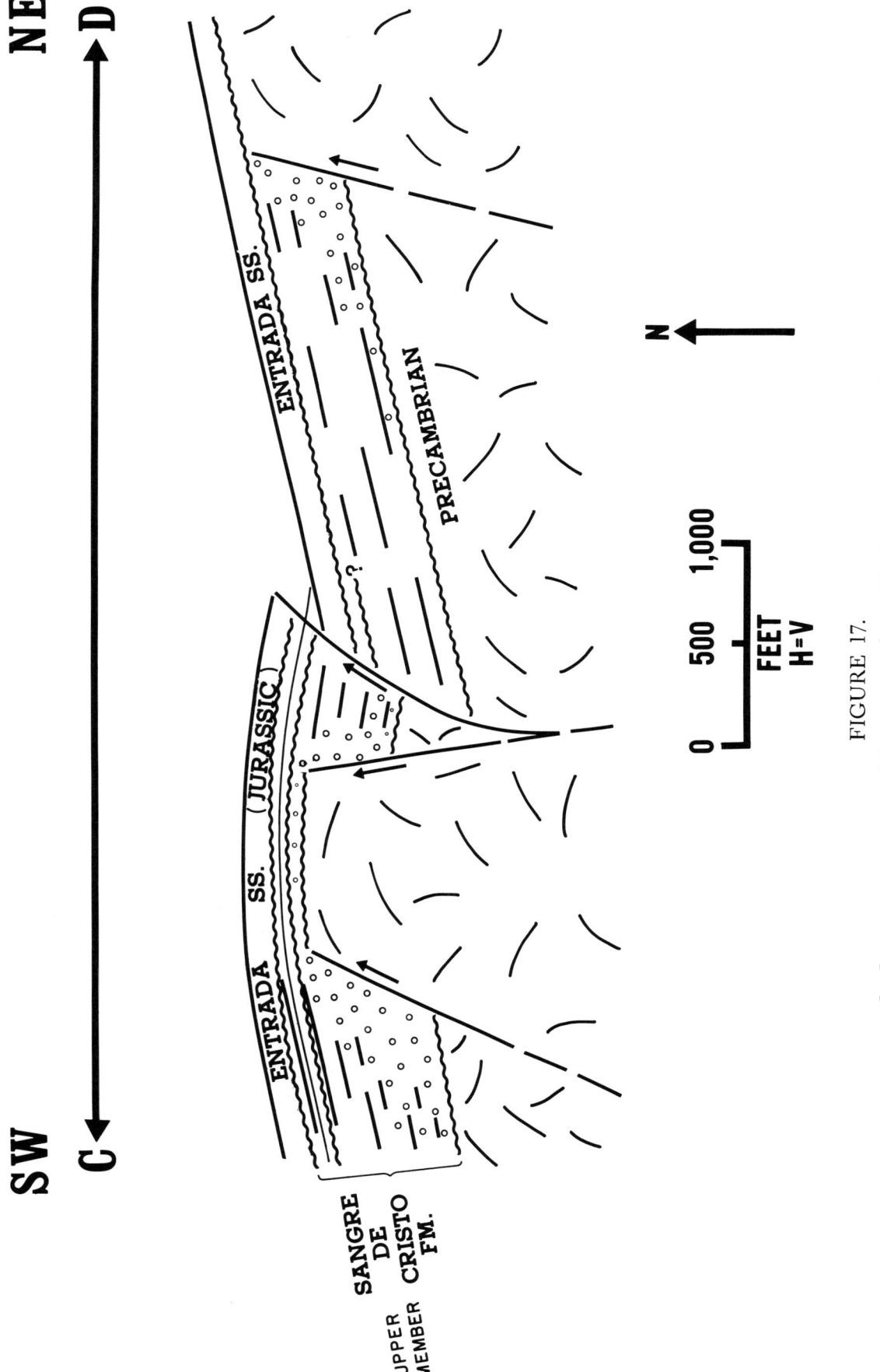

FIGURE 17. Geologic cross section, Red Canyon, southern Wet Mountains, Colorado.

More than 5,000 feet of the Upper Member of the Sangre de Cristo Formation onlap the unconformity in the Arkansas River Valley area. The amount of truncation of underlying strata, the angular discordance at the unconformity and the onlapping relationships increase as the Pleasant Valley fault is approached. Thus, the unconformity between the Upper and Lower Members of the Sangre de Cristo Formation in the Arkansas River Valley area is related to Permian structural movements on the Pleasant Valley fault. The section is not complete, but Bolyard (1959) has estimated the Crestone Conglomerate to be 6,000 feet thick in the Crestone Peak area.

Member Boundaries—The Upper Member of the Sangre de Cristo Formation generally lies unconformably on the Lower Member. However, in the Medano Creek area (see plate 1, back pocket) and at the southern end of the Wet Mountains (figs. 16 and 17) it overlaps the Lower Member and rests unconformably on Precambrian rocks. The contact of the Upper Member of the Sangre de Cristo Formation with the overlying Jurassic Entrada Sandstone is unconformable.

Depositional Environment—Continental, primarily fluvial, deposits comprise the bulk of the Upper Member. The great thickness, extreme coarseness, poor sorting, poor bedding and interbeds of thin sandstone and siltstone suggest a sequence of coalescing alluvial fans formed at the base of a rising highland. South of Music Mountain near Medano Pass (see plate 1, back pocket) the Crestone Conglomerate lies directly on Precambrian rocks suggesting that some of the faults in this area were active well into Permian time. The facies change, north and south of the Crestone area, to finer-grained conglomerates and sandstones (fig. 18) suggests that these areas were farther from the source area and that there was a decrease in stream gradient, with stream-transport directions of the uplift block in the Crestone area to the north and south.

The pronounced angular unconformity between the Upper and Lower Members, the increased grain size of the detritus in the Upper Member, the onlapping relationships of the beds of the Upper Member onto the uplift block, and the discordance of structures beneath and above the unconformity indicate that the Pleasant Valley fault was active during the Permian and significantly influenced sedimentation. Doubtlessly detritus was shed from the up-

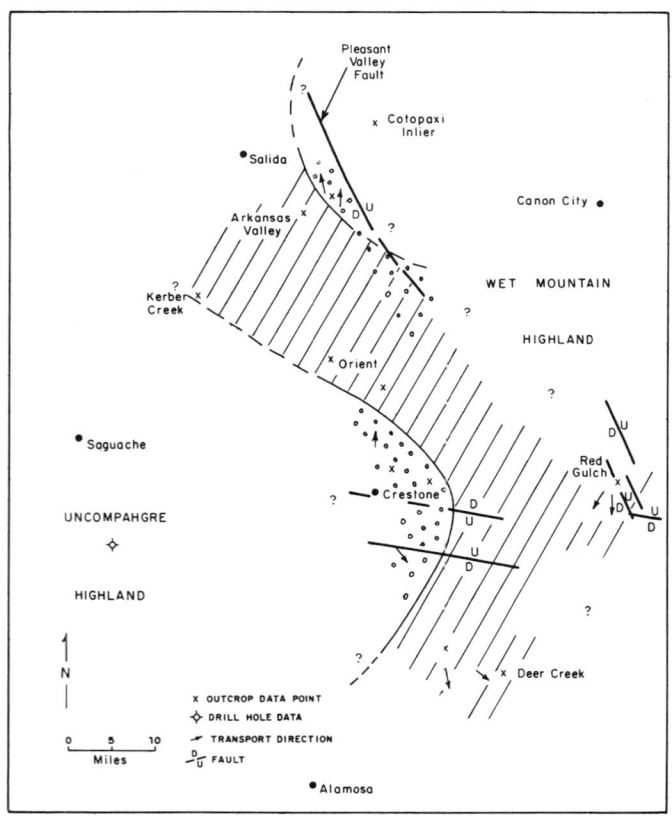

FIGURE 18.

Lithofacies map of the Upper Member, Sangre de Cristo Formation, south-central Colorado.

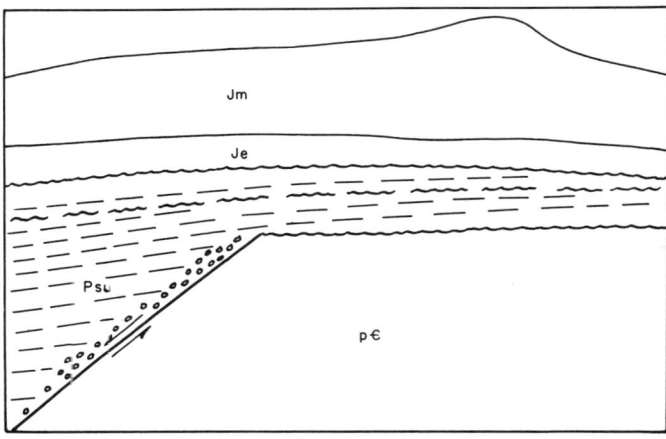

FIGURE 19.

Permian fault contact between Permian sedimentary rocks (P_{su}) and Precambrian crystalline rocks (Pϵ). Photograph looking toward the north wall of Red Canyon located at the southern end of the Wet Mountains in sec. 7, T. 26 S., R. 68 W. The Entrada (Je) and Morrison (Jm) formations overlie the Permian strata.

lift block into the asymmetric basin, the axis of which developed close to the downdropped west side of the fault.

Field studies along the southern end of the Wet Mountains indicate Permian fault relationships between Permian sedimentary rocks and Precambrian crystalline rocks (figs. 16 and 17). Figure 19 is a photograph and field sketch of one such outcrop in Red Canyon in Sec. 7, T. 26 S., R. 68 W. (fig. 17) which illustrates the following observed relationships:

1. Bedding trends into and is truncated at or near the contact between the Upper Member of the Sangre de Cristo Formation and Precambrian rocks.
2. The Permian rocks are unbedded near the contact.
3. For a distance of 5 to 20 feet from the contact the Permian rocks are conglomeritic and very poorly sorted.
4. The Permian rocks decrease in grain size away from the contact.
5. The uppermost Permian sedimentary rock beds of the Upper Member of the Sangre de Cristo Formation overlap the fault and are folded slightly with the fold axis positioned directly over the fault.
6. An angular unconformity is present within the upper part of the Upper Member of the Sangre de Cristo Formation.

The above evidence indicates that a Permian normal fault was active during the deposition of the beds of the Upper Member of the Sangre de Cristo Formation. At least several hundred feet of relief resulted from the faulting. Near the end of Permian deposition, the fault became inactive and was then overlapped by the upper beds. Later, slight reactivation of the fault caused minor folding or draping of the overlapping sediments, without rupture. Similar fault relationships were observed in Secs. 6, 21, and 28, T. 26 S., R. 68 W. (see fig. 16). At these locations the Permian rocks end abruptly at the fault contacts with Precambrian rocks but the faults are overlapped by the Jurassic Entrada Formation. On the downthrown block the Entrada lies unconformably above the Permian strata, while on the upthrown block it rests unconformably on Precambrian rocks. Thus, several east-west and north-northwest-trending faults at the south end of the Wet Mountains suffered recurrent displacements during the deposition of the Upper Member of the Sangre de Cristo Formation. Detritus was shed from the uplift blocks to the south and southwest (figs. 16, 17, and 18).

AGE

Due to the lack of marine fossils, the age of the Sangre de Cristo Formation is uncertain. Brill (1952) suggested two possibilities: (1) the Lower Member of the Sangre de Cristo Formation in southern Colorado is the nonmarine equivalent of the Upper Pennsylvanian marine rocks found in New Mexico, or; (2) Wolfcampian erosion truncated Upper Pennsylvanian strata and, therefore, they wedge out in northern New Mexico. Scott (1967) identified *Bisaccate gymnospermous* pollen, collected from beds the authors have interpreted as being the lower part of the Lower Member (SE¼ SE¼, Sec. 18, T. 48 N., R. 11 E.), and suggested a Permian age. White (1912) collected the following fossils, near the south portal of the Denver and Rio Grande Tunnel (Sec. 28, T. 49 N., R. 10 E.) from strata believed to be approximately 1,300 feet above the base of the lower member:

Callipteris sp.
Psygmophyllum cf. *cuneifolium*
Odontopteris subcrenulata Rost?
Macrostachya? sp.
Sigillariostrobus nastatus
Walchia cf. *piniformis*
Walchia cf. *imbricata*
Rhabdocarpos dyadicus Geinitz?

White believed those with the asterisk to be definitely Permian. *Calamities* sp. are common throughout the Upper Member. On the basis of the above fossil data, the authors tentatively conclude that Missourian and Virgilian probably are not present in the northern Sangre de Cristo Range. Vaughn (1969, p. 26), however, on the basis of preliminary studies of vertebrate fossils (diadectes) he collected from Brill's measured inverval 300 (Lower Member), believes that they are actually Upper Pennsylvanian *Desmatodon* remains.

PENNSYLVANIAN AND PERMIAN HISTORY

Prior to deposition in the Morrowan, portions of south-central Colorado were uplifted to cause erosion of the widespread marine rocks that had been deposited earlier in the Paleozoic. Thus an east-west trending structural element became active south of Crestone, causing erosion of the Middle and Lower Paleozoic rocks (fig. 4). Similarly a north-south structural element developed to the east of the Arkansas River Valley section in the Late Mississippian and early in the Pennsylvanian.

Subsequent to and possibly during the erosion of the Lower and Middle Paleozoic rocks from the adjacent highland areas, the marine shales and limestones of the Beldon Formation were deposited to the north while the quartzose sandstones, shales, and coal beds of the Kerber Formation accumulated to the south in nonmarine coastal-plain and low-lying swamp and mudflat environments in the incipient Central Colorado trough (fig. 7). The sea invaded further into the trough from the north as the Morrowan progressed, as evinced by the fossilferous marine limestones in the upper part of the Kerber. The facies relations and isopach data of the Kerber beds indicate that the adjacent highland areas shed sediment into the narrow subsiding, north-northwest-trending trough.

Block faulting at the basin margins during the Atokon probably produced the changes in climatic conditions and depth of erosion which resulted in the deposition of the red, hematite-stained, arkosic sandstones, siltstones, and shales of the Sharpsdale Formation. This block faulting probably created the topographic relief and stream gradients which caused coarse-grained sediments to be deposited in the Cotopaxi inlier and Deer Creek areas. Recurrent movements along these same faults could have produced the erosional unconformity at the top of the Sharpsdale locally in south-central Colorado (figs. 5, 6, and 8). The facies patterns and the presence of marine limestones within the Sharpsdale indicate that the structural activity was sporadic and recurrent during the deposition of the Sharpsdale. The uplift block between Crestone and Huerfano Park may have acted as a barrier to marine transgression during the times of invasion of marine waters into the trough from the north and south.

The Sharpsdale was deposited dominantly on alluvial fans and alluvial plains adjacent to actively rising uplift blocks in an arid climate. Marine transgressions occurred occasionally during this Atokan deposition.

A thick sequence of greenish-gray sandstones, siltstones, and black shales, with an upper zone of limestones and marine shales, accumulated in the Central Colorado trough during the Desmoinesian and comprise the Madera Formation. The distinct color-changes from the redbeds of the Sharpsdale to the green, gray, and black beds of Madera suggests that the Madera accumulated on low-lying coastal plains and mudflats and/or conditions where the ground-water table was shallow.

The facies patterns abrupt thickness variations, and current transport directions in the Madera indicate that the basin configuration was markedly different during Madera deposition (figs. 5, 6, and 9). The northwest-trending block uplift between Crestone and Huerfano Park shed coarse-grained detritus to the north and south. The coarser grained beds of the Cotopaxi inlier probably were shed northward from the Wet Mountain Highland. The abrupt thickness variations indicate onlap of the Madera onto the upthrown side of the fault blocks, as shown on figs. 5 and 6.

Environmental conditions varied throughout the deposition of the Madera from marine to coastal mudflat and deltaic conditions. The limestone beds of the upper Whiskey Creek Pass Limestone Member connote occasional widespread marine inundation of the Central Colorado trough.

The apparent absence of Missourian and Virgilian strata in the Central Colorado trough suggests that erosion occurred subsequent to Madera deposition and prior to deposition of the Sangre de Cristo beds in the Permian.

Red arkosic sandstones, conglomerates, siltstones and mudstones of the Lower Member of the Sangre de Cristo Formation were deposited in the Permian on an aggrading alluvial plain under predominantly fluvial conditions. Abundant cycles of grain-size variations (fig. 12) suggest recurrent structural activity. The lithofacies map (fig. 13) indicates that the detritus was probably dominantly shed from the eastward projection of the Uncompahgre Highland.

Subsequent to the deposition of the Lower Member of the Sangre de Cristo Formation in the Permian, major tectonic activity occurred throughout south-central Colorado, in many cases along faults which were also active later in the Laramide. In the Arkansas River Valley area, the Pleasant Valley fault suffered more than 11,000 feet of Permian displacement and the nearby Pennsylvanian and Permian rocks were complexly folded as well (see figs. 14 and 15). A major uplift block in the Medano Creek area caused the beds of the Upper Member of the Sangre de Cristo Formation to be very coarsely conglomeratic (fig. 18) and to lap onto Precambrian rocks (see plate 1, back pocket). Several east-west and north-northwest-trending faults at the south end of the Wet Mountains suffered recurrent displacements during the deposition of the Upper Member of the Sangre de Cristo Formation (and later in the Laramide) and detritus was shed off these uplift blocks to the southwest (see figs. 16, 17 and 18). Thus, angular discordance at the base of the Upper Member and coarse-grained facies lapping onto the unconformity at several localities indicate that the Permian tectonic activity along east-west and north-northwest-trending structures significantly affected sedimentation patterns.

The coarse-grained redbeds of the Upper Member and its Crestone Conglomerate facies of the Sangre de Cristo were shed from the uplift blocks onto alluvial fans and plains in the block-fault basins. The basins filled with detritus so that the deposits encroached upon the adjacent uplift areas, onlapping them and reducing the topographic relief of the terrain in the Permian.

REFERENCES

American Commission on Stratigraphic Nomenclature, 1961, Code of stratigraphic nomenclature: Am. Assoc. Petroleum Geologists Bull., v. 45, no. 5, p. 645-665.

Berg, T. M., 1967, Pennsylvanian Biohermal limestones of Marble Mountain, south-central Colorado: Unpublished M.Sc. thesis, Univ. of Colorado.

Bolyard, D. W., 1956, Permo-Pennsylvanian section at La Veta Pass, Colorado, in Guidebook to the Geology of the Raton Basin, Colorado: Rocky Mountain Assoc. Geolgists, p. 52-55.

——————, 1959, Pennsylvanian and Permian stratigraphy in the Sangre de Cristo Mountains between La Veta Pass and Westcliff, Colorado: Am. Assoc. Petroleum Geologists Bull., v. 43, no. 8, p. 1896-1939.

——————, 1960, Perm-Pennsylvanian stratigraphy in the Sangre de Cristo Mountains, Colorado, in Guide to the Geology of Colorado: Geol. Soc. America, p. 121-126.

Boyer, R. E., 1962, Petrology and structure of the southern Wet Mountains, Colorado: Geol. Soc. America Bull., v. 73, p. 1047-1070.

Brill, K. G., Jr., 1952, Stratigraphy in the Permo-Pennsylvanian zeugogeosyncline of Colorado and northern New Mexico: Geol. Soc. America Bull., v. 63, no. 8, p. 809-880.

Burbank, W. S., 1932, Geology and ore deposits of the Bonanza Mining District, Colorado: U.S. Geol. Survey Prof. Paper 169, 166 p.

Burbank, W. S., and Goddard, E. N., 1937, Thrusting in Huerfano Park, Colorado, and related problems of orogeny in the Sangre de Cristo Mountains: Geol. Soc. America Bull., v. 48, p. 931-976.

Burford, A. E., 1960, Geology of the Medano Peak area, Sangre de Cristo Mountains, Colorado: Unpublished Ph.D. dissertation Univ. Michigan, Ann Arbor.

Chronic, John, 1958, Pennsylvanian rocks in central Colorado: in Symposium on Pennsylvanian rocks of Colorado and adjacent areas, Rocky Mountain Assoc. Geologists, p. 59-63.

De Vota, R. H., 1965, Pennsylvanian and Permian stratigraphy of central Colorado: The Mountain Geologist, v. 2, p. 209-228.

Hills, R. C., 1899, Description of the Elmoro Quadrangle, Colorado: U.S. Geol. Survey Geol. Atlas Folio 58.

——————, 1900, Description of the Walsenburg Quadrangle, Colorado: ibid., folio 68.

——————, 1901, Description of the Spanish Peaks Quadrangle, Colorado: ibid., folio 71.
Karig, D. E., 1964, Structural analysis of the Sangre de Cristo Range, Venable Peak to Crestone Peak, Custer and Saguache Co., Colorado: Unpublished M.Sc. thesis, Colorado School of Mines.
Koch, R. W., 1963, Geology of the Venable Peak area, Sangre de Cristo Mountains, Colorado: Unpublished M.Sc. thesis, Colorado School of Mines.
Litsey, L. R., 1958, Stratigraphy and structure of the northern Sangre de Cristo Mountains: Geol. Soc. America Bull., v. 69, p. 1143-1178.
Melton, F. A., 1925a, The Ancestral Rocky Mountains of Colorado and New Mexico: Jour. Geol., v. 33, p. 84-89.
——————, 1925b, Correlation of Permo-Carbonaceous red beds in southern Colorado and northern New Mexico: ibid., v. 33, p. 807-815.
Munger, R. D., 1959, Geology of the Spread Eagle Peak area, Sangre de Cristo Mountains, Colorado: Unpublished M.Sc. thesis, University of Colorado.
Nicolaysen, G. G., 1971, Geology of the Coaldale area, Fremont County, Colorado: Unpublished M.Sc. thesis, Colorado School of Mines, in progress.
Nolting, R., 1970, Permo-Pennsylvanian stratigraphy and structural geology of the Orient-Cotton Creek area, Colorado: Unpublished M.Sc. thesis, Colorado School of Mines.

Peel, F. A., 1971, New Interpretations of Pennsylvanian and Permian stratigraphy and structural history, northern Sangre de Cristo Range, Colorado: Unpublished M.Sc. thesis, Colorado School of Mines.
Pierce, W. H., 1969, Geology and Pennsylvanian-Permian Stratigraphy of the Howard area, Fremont County, Colorado: Unpublished M.Sc. thesis, Colorado School of Mines.
Rhodes, J. A., 1964, Stratigraphy and origin of the Pennsylvanian-Permian rocks of the Huerfano Park quadrangle, Colorado: Unpublished Ph.D. dissertation, Univ. of Michigan.
Tischler, Herbert, 1960, The Pennsylvanian and Permian Stratigraphy of the Huerfano Park area, Colorado: Unpublished Ph.D. dissertation, Univ. of Michigan.
Tweto, Ogden, 1949, Stratigraphy of the Pando area, Eagle County, Colorado: Color Sci. Soc. Proc., v. 15, p. 149-235.
Vargus, F. H., 1961, Geology of the Cotopaxi inlier on the northern trend of the Sangre de Cristo Range, Fremont County, Colorado: Unpublished M.Sc. thesis, Colorado School of Mines.
Vaughn, P. P., 1969, Upper Pennsylvanian vertibrates from the Sangre de Cristo Formation of Central Colorado: Contributions in Science, Los Angeles County Museum no. 164, p. 1-28.
Volckman, R. P., 1965, Geology of the Crestone Peak area, Sangre de Cristo Range, Colorado: Unpublished Ph.D. dissertation, Univ. of Michigan.

GLACIATION IN THE SANGRE DE CRISTO RANGE, COLORADO

by

Richard C. Peterson

Department of Geology
Adams State College
Alamosa, Colorado

Glaciated summits of the Sangre de Cristos.

Looking eastward from any vantage point within the San Luis Valley one may observe some of natures most spectacular sculpture. The rugged Sangre de Cristo Range, with towering Blanca Peak, elevation 14,363 feet, attest to the relentless work of the glaciers during that period that was the Pleistocene.

Although the results of the glaciation may be readily observed, surprisingly little has been written concerning this phase in the development of the range. Endlich (1875) made perhaps the earliest mention of glacial action in the range. Stevenson (1881) remarked about the evidence of the existence of glaciers above 10,000 feet in the Culebra and Taos ranges and in the east side of the Sangre de Cristos of the Wet Mountain Valley area. He stated (p. 434), "the eastern slope of the Sangre de Cristo Mountains is literally gashed to the central line by universal glacial gorges which are closed by enormous moraines extending hundreds of feet into the valley." Siebenthal (1907 and 1910) has made the most extensive report on the glacial aspects of the west side of the range. Upson (1938) included a short note on the glaciation in his study of the physiography of the Culebra reentrant. Ray (1939 and 1940) discussed, in detail, selected areas within the east side of the range. Authors of several theses written on the mountains have very briefly commented on the glacial history. In all, no one has made a study of the physiography and Quaternary geology of the Sangre de Cristo Range as complete and as thorough as Atwood and Mather (1932) did in the San Juan Mountains.

What follows here is a brief summary of the current knowledge regarding the glacial history of the Sangre de Cristo Range.

The east side of the mountains had perhaps the longest period of glaciation or perhaps the record of the glacial epoch is better preserved on this side. At least five substages of the Wisconsin Glacial Stage have been recognized in such areas as the Huerfano River Valley, West Spanish Peak, and Trinchera Peak in the Culebra Range (Ray, 1940).

Substage I is recognized by terminal moraines at elevations ranging from 8,800 feet in the Huerfano River Valley, 9,000 feet in Wahatoya Canyon on West Spanish Peak, to 9,900 feet on the east side of Trinchera Peak between Cuchara Camps and Blue Lake.

Substage II is usually marked by smaller moraines which in the case of the Culebra Range are plastered against the sides of the higher and larger substage I moraine. Wisconsin II moraines are located at 8,800 feet in the valleys northeast of Blanca Peak, at 9,800 feet on West Spanish Peak, and at approximately 9,900 feet at Bear Lakes in the Culebras where the lakes are impounded by the moraine. The second glacial advance of the Wisconsin had as great an extent as did the first in the main part of the range. However, on West Spanish Peak the second substage fell 800 feet short of the first glaciation. Ray (1940) admits that the evidence for the substages in Wahatoya Canyon is not complete. Perhaps the second substage glaciers did extend farther down the canyon, only additional field work will tell.

Ray (1940, p. 1885) also notes that in the valleys of the

Huerfano River there is evidence of uplift and stream incision in the interstadial interval between Wisconsin I and Wisconsin II. He also noted the similarity to the incision of streams in the San Juan Mountains and commented, "this is the only area in the Southern Rocky Mountains where this marked canyon cutting during the Wisconsin stage was seen."

Substage III is marked by terminal moraines found farther up in the canyons. The Huerfano River Valley again witnessed the lowest glacial advance where moraines are found at 9,100 feet. On West Spanish Peak the Wisconsin III moraine is at 10,500 feet. In the Culebras, "below the lip of the three cirques north of Trinchera Peak are large masses of hummocky moraine material interpreted as deposition during Wisconsin III when glaciers evidently only moved a short distance," (Ray, 1940, p. 1887).

Substage III obviously had a lesser extent than did I and II, and substage IV was of even lesser span reaching only as low as 10,200 feet on Blanca Peak and 11,500 feet in Wahatoya Canyon. In the Culebra Range, most of the Wisconsin IV moraines occupy areas at the lip of the cirques.

Protalus ramparts of varying sizes developed in all areas after the final disappearance of the glaciers. In the Blanca Peak region, the protalus ramparts, if formed during Wisconsin V, "have been obliterated by rock glaciers which either buried or swept them away," (Ray, 1940, p. 1884). Ray also states (1940, p. 1885), "A rock glacier was probably initiated during the rigorous climate of the fifth Wisconsin substage. The present climate is such that additions to the talus are sufficient to keep the rock glaciers in motion." There seems to be a question as to whether protalus ramparts ever existed in the Blanca Peak area.

In contrast to the rather well documented five substages of the Wisconsin on the east side of the Sangre de Cristo Range, there are only isolated and incomplete reports of glacial activity on the west side. Upson (p. 197) reports a glacier that extended down the North Fork of Rio Culebra to a locality near the contact between the Precambrian and softer basin sediment deposits. "Here, two high ridges, whose crests are about 400 feet above the present stream bed and flanking the valley on each side, extend downstream from higher hills." These are lateral portions of terminal moraines which Ray (1940) correlates with the second Wisconsin substage. However, since both the first and second substages extend to the same elevation on the opposite side of the range, and since the first glaciation built larger moraines, it would seem that perhaps the moraine described by Upson is in reality representative of the first substage rather than the second.

Siebenthal (1910, p. 37-38) summarizes the glaciation of the west side of the Sangre de Cristo Range from Blanca Peak northward as follows:

"The various stream valleys heading against the crest of the Sangre de Cristo Range all held Pleistocene glaciers, the morainic remains of which fall into two systems showing the existence of two periods of glaciation. The moraines ordinarily reach down to about 9,500 to 9,000 feet above sea level and crown the summits of the great alluvial cones that spread out from the mouths of the stream canyons. The moraines of both systems are comparatively fresh looking, and the outer, older ones are not noticeably more eroded than or different topographically from the inner, later ones.

Black Canyon, just east of Orient, has lateral moraines on either side of the valley, 100 to 200 feet high and reaching to the alluvial slope at the mouth of the canyon. A prominent moraine juts out from the Willow Creek canyon, east of Crestone. Behind the moraine is the park or meadow, the bed of an extinct glacial lake. Two existing glacial lakes are found in the U-shaped valley above the park, as well as striae, roches moutonnees, and other evidences of ice occupation. South Zapata Creek Valley, heading in the Blanca massif, exhibits the same evidences of ice occupation, together with a double crescentic moraine crowning a great alluvial fan at the height of 1,500 feet above the level of the valley. The inner moraine formerly inclosed a small lake, the outlet of which cut through the moraine where it adjoined the canyon wall on the north side and, once incised in the rock, has continued to cut back a narrow winding cleft, through which water pours, forming the picturesque Zapata Falls. Middle, Bear, Little Bear, Blanca, and Ute creeks, the circle of radiating streams flowing down the west and south sides of Blanca Peak, each held a glacier which came down to and terminated upon the apex of its alluvial fan."

The author speculates that the terminal moraines that are found at the 9,000 foot elevation are probably related to the first or second Wisconsin substage and those at the 9,500 foot level correlatable with the third substage. The only reason for this speculation is the similarity in elevations of morainal material on opposite sides of the range.

Furthermore, the author theorizes that the large well-displayed alluvial fans at the base of the west side of the range are underlain by extensive outwash plains. What would be more natural than to have outwash associated with terminal moraines? The present fans are merely a present day modification of the Pleistocene outwash.

Within the Sangre de Cristo Mountains of southern Colorado there are two relics of the Pleistocene that are worthy of mention in this paper.

At the head of the Huerfano River, on the northeast side of Blanca Peak, two small glaciers exist today. The width of the larger glacier is about 800 feet, its greatest length is about 1,000 feet, and its vertical thickness over 80 feet (Siebenthal, 1907, p. 20). The size and shape naturally vary with annual snowfall and temperature. As Siebenthal (1907, p. 22) says, "The Blanca Glaciers possess an added interest in being the southernmost existing glaciers yet reported in the Rocky Mountains, and, so far as known to the writer, the southernmost in the United States."

On Mount Mestas, 8½ miles east of Blanca Peak, are excellently displayed rock glaciers or rock streams. The two most spectacular streams are on the west slope at elevations between 8,500 and 10,000 feet (Johnson, p. D217). Ice which forms the matrix of the rock stream was encountered at depths ranging from 10 to 30 feet. The interstitial ice appears blue on the outcrop but is crystal clear in the hand. Below the troughs the ice is locally granular as if structurally crushed during movement. Rock fragments incorporated into the streams range in size from rock flour to blocks more than five feet in maximum dimension. According to Johnson (p. D220), the fronts of the rock streams have moved forward only a few feet in 25 years. Movement may be due largely to the deformation of the interstitial ice, but some movement may be initiated by the seasonal freezing and thawing of this ice. Because of the absence of cirques on Mount Mestas and the low latitude and elevation of the Mount Mestas rock streams, probably the original source of the ice was not a true valley glacier. The ice more likely was derived from the freezing at depth of downward moving rainwater and melted snow. These interesting features may be seen when traveling eastward along old U.S. Highway 160 on La Veta Pass.

In summary, it is apparent that at least five substages of the Wisconsin Glacial Stage are observable in the Sangre de Cristo Range. These substages are correlatable from valley to valley on the east side (Ray, 1940), but due to the lack of data on the west side nothing conclusive may be said regarding substages or correlation with the east side. This interesting facet of the history of the range is certainly worthy of investigation. Perhaps in the future some inspired geologist will undertake a study of the physiography and Quaternary geology of the Sangre de Cristo Range.

REFERENCES

Atwood, W. W. and Mather, K. F., 1932, Physiography and Quaternary Geology of the San Juan Mountains, Colorado: U.S. Geol. Survey Prof. Paper 166, 176 p.

Endlich, F. M., 1875, U.S. Geological and Geographical Survey of the Territories, Annual Report, p. 220.

Johnson, Ross B., 1967, Rock Streams on Mount Mestas, Sangre de Cristo Mountains, Southern Colorado: U.S. Geol. Survey Prof. Paper 575D, p. D217-D220.

Ray, Louis L., 1939, Subdivision of the last glacial stage in the Southern Rocky Mountains: Geol. Soc. America Bull., v. 50, p. 2006-2007.

——— 1940, Glacial Chronology of the Southern Rocky Mountains: Geol. Soc. America Bull., v. 51, p. 1851-1918.

Siebenthal, C. E., 1907, Notes on Glaciation in the Sangre de Cristo Range, Colorado: Jour. Geology, v. 15, p. 15-22.

——— 1910, Geology and Water Resources of the San Luis Valley, Colorado: U.S. Geol. Survey Water-Supply Paper 240, 128 p.

Stevenson, J. J., 1881, Report upon geological examinations in Southern Colorado and northern New Mexico during the years 1878 and 1879 in Wheeler, G. M., U.S. Geographical Surveys West of the 100th Meridian, v. III, p. 434-435.

Upson, J. E., 1938, Tertiary geology and geomorphology of the Culebra Reentrant, Southern Colorado: unpublished Ph.D. dissertation, Harvard University.

ALLOCHTHONOUS PALEOZOIC BLOCKS IN THE TERTIARY SAN LUIS–UPPER ARKANSAS GRABEN, COLORADO*

by

Ralph E. Van Alstine

U.S. Geological Survey
Washington, D.C.

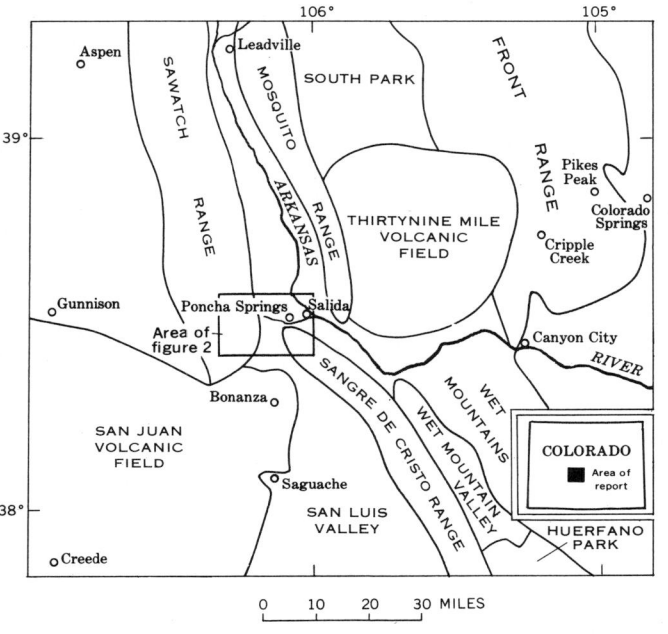

FIGURE 1.

Index map of south-central Colorado.

Geologic investigations, made in cooperation with the Colorado State Mining Industrial Development Board, southwest of Salida in the Southern Rocky Mountains of south-central Colorado (fig. 1), revealed more than 20 detached Paleozoic blocks within and adjacent to a Late Tertiary trough (Van Alstine, 1968). This narrow trough between the Sawatch and Sangre de Cristo ranges is part of the San Luis-Upper Arkansas graben (Tweto, 1968, p. 566, 582) and is the northward continuation of the Rio Grande depression (Bryan and McCann, 1938, p. 2-3; Kelley, 1956), a fault structure typical of the Basin and Range province. The detached blocks (fig. 2), composed mainly of brecciated carbonate rocks, are too large to have been transported by water. They were emplaced at several stratigraphic levels in the Dry Union Formation of Miocene and Pliocene age that fills the trough, evidently by gravitational sliding eastward from a structural high, the Sawatch Range (fig. 3). The trough deposits were derived largely from the same source area that shed the detached

---

* Reprinted from U.S. Geol. Survey Prof. Paper 700-B, Pages B43-B51.

blocks. The Paleozoic blocks are now being exposed as the adjacent basin fill is removed by erosion.

Other interpretations have been given to several of the Paleozoic remnants. For example, from the presence of some of the brecciated Paleozoic masses, Russell (1950, pl. 1 and p. 17-18) inferred two steep fault zones and concluded that Paleozoic sedimentary rocks underlie the trough fill here.

DRY UNION FORMATION

The Dry Union Formation, named and defined by Tweto (1961) in the Leadville area about 45 miles north of Poncha Springs, records various geologic events that occurred in this area in Late Tertiary time. The formation is chiefly composed of unconsolidated gravel, sand, silt, clay, volcanic ash, and limestone deposited in alluvial-fan, mudflow, and pond environments, and it contains the detached Paleozoic blocks (fig. 4). The basal part is largely mudflow material consisting of unstratified gravel containing abundant clasts of vesicular basalt, andesite, and latite derived from Lower Oligocene lava flows at the eastern and southwestern edges of the trough. Especially conspicuous at many weathered outcrops are agates and blue-gray angular jasperoid fragments of intensely silicified volcanic rocks transported from the Bonanza volcanic center to the southwest (Burbank, 1932, p. 71-77; Cook, 1961, p. 289).

Within the Tertiary sediments above the basal volcanic gravel, clasts of Paleozoic rocks are common among the debris. They have lithologies and ages similar to those of the adjacent detached Paleozoic blocks found at several stratigraphic horizons. On the ridge crest east of Little Cochetopa Creek, blocks of limestone (some fetid and containing black chert) and dolomite (without chert) probably are from the Leadville Limestone of Mississippian age; fossils in similar limestone clasts in the adjacent debris were identified as (1) fragments of *Ovtia* cf. *O. laevicosta* (White), known to occur in the Leadville Limestone, (2) echinoderm debris, and (3) fragments of a syringoporoid coral (J. T. Dutro, Jr., written commun., Feb. 7, 1969). Precambrian debris containing gneiss, granite, and pegmatite boulders as much as 12 feet in diameter is predominant in the upper part of the trough fill. Thus, the stratigraphy of the Dry Union Formation locally reflects, in reverse, the sequence of rocks in the adjoining source areas; debris, first from Tertiary volcanic rocks and then from progressively older Paleozoic and Precambrian formations, was stripped, carried into the trough, and deposited.

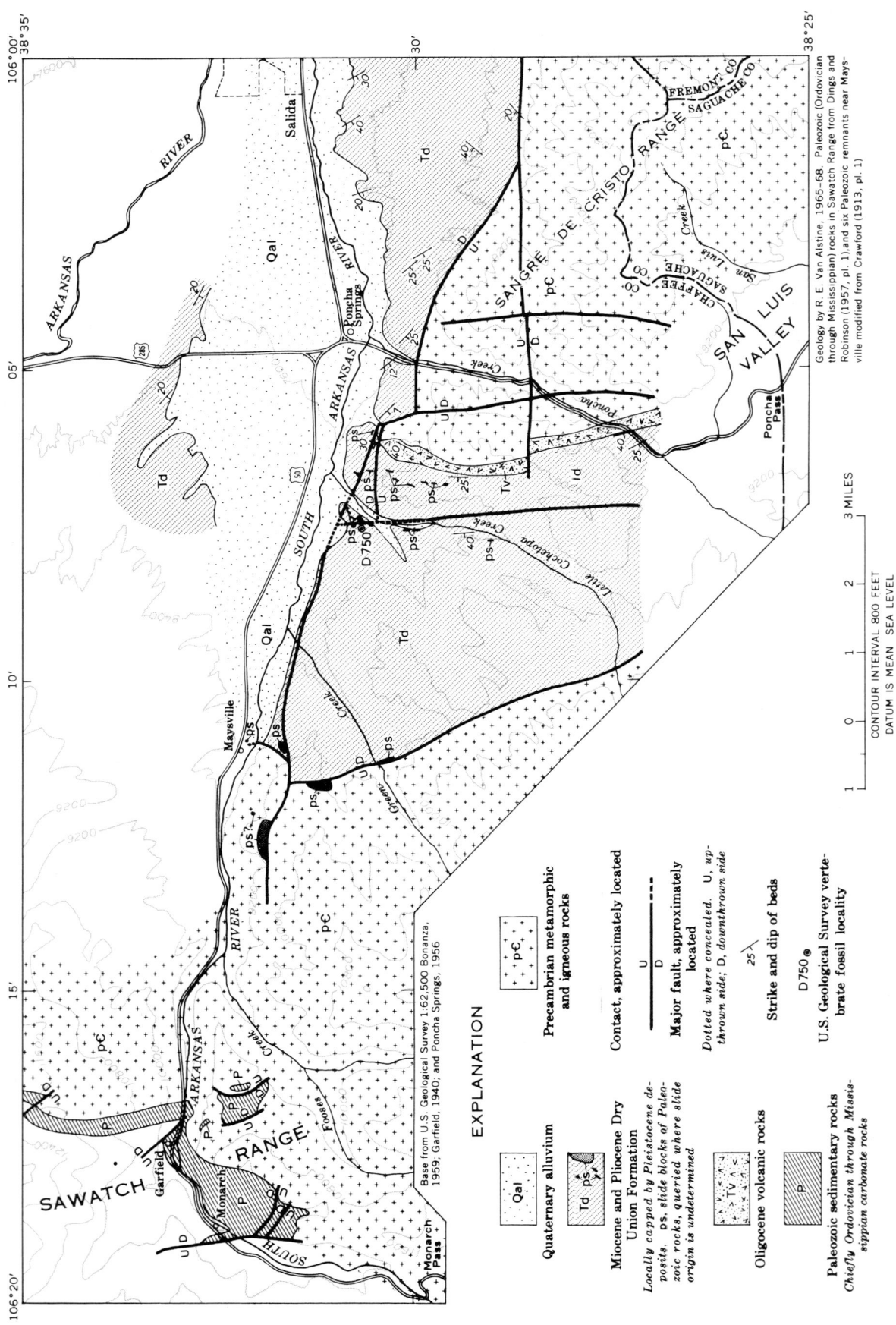

FIGURE 2. Generalized geologic map of area between the Sawatch and Sangre de Cristo ranges, Chaffee County, Colo.

FIGURE 3.
View west across Late Tertiary trough to source area of slide blocks in the Sawatch Range, showing Dry Union sediments (Td) faulted against Precambrian gneisses (P€).

Mesozoic rock fragments from the Morrison Formation, Dakota Sandstone and Mancos Shale were not observed among the clasts in the Dry Union Formation and evidently were not shed eastward into this trough. These three formations are exposed on the west edge of the Sawatch Range. Dings and Robinson (1957, p. 9, 18-19) suggested that possibly several thousand feet of Mesozoic sedimentary rock was removed from the range by erosion. The apparent lack of Mesozoic debris in the Tertiary trough deposits indicates that the three Mesozoic units may not have covered the base- and precious-metal district near Monarch and Garfield in Tertiary time when the mineralization occurred.

In the area near Little Cochetopa Creek, the Dry Union Formation may be more than 10,000 feet thick, if the moderate westward dip persists to the fault at the west edge of the trough. The westward tilting possibly is related to Late Pliocene uplift of the Sangre de Cristo Range to the east.

The Pliocene age of some of the trough deposits now assigned to the Dry Union Formation was determined from fossil horse teeth and camel bones found to the east and north in the Arkansas Valley (Powers, 1935, p. 189; Van Alstine and Lewis, 1960). The age, however, is now extended to Late Miocene, for at vertebrate fossil locality D750 (fig. 2) several identifiable horse teeth were collected from locally gypsiferous greenish clays and silts. G. E. Lewis (written commun., Dec. 17, 1968) reported the fossils to be cheek teeth of *Merychippus* cf. *M. calamarius* (Cope) and stated that this species is characteristic of the Upper Miocene part of the middle (?) Miocene to lower Pliocene Tesuque Formation of the Santa Fe Group of New Mexico in the southern part of the same structural trough (Spiegel and others, 1963, p. 39-43, 62-63). Possibly, older Miocene fossils could be found in the trough fill below the beds at fossil locality D750 or to the east, nearer the contact of the deposits with the Lower Oligocene volcanic rocks. Fossil charophytes, ostracodes, gastropods, and pelecypods were collected from the pond sediments immediately beneath the strata at the vertebrate fossil locality. Specimens of the genus *Chara* probably are late Tertiary in age (R. E. Peck, written commun., June 6, 1967). Some of the ostracodes were identified as *Candona* spp. and *Darwinula?* sp., smooth, fresh-water types common in Tertiary sediments (I. G. Sohn, written communs., May 10, 1967, and Mar. 5, 1968). The other invertebrate fossils have not yet been studied.

ALLOCHTHONOUS PALEOZOIC BLOCKS

Seventeen detached Paleozoic blocks of various sizes are exposed within the Dry Union Formation east and west of Little Cochetopa Creek; similar blocks, mostly larger, are found in Precambrian terrane and trough fill at higher altitudes about 4 miles farther west (fig. 2). The blocks near Little Cochetopa Creek crop out at altitudes between

FIGURE 4.

View south along Little Cochetopa Creek, showing faulted Miocene and Pliocene sediments (Dry Union Formation, Td) containing blocks of Paleozoic rocks (ps); underlying Oligocene volcanic rocks (Tv) rest on Precambrian gneiss (p€) of Sangre de Cristo Range.

7,830 and 8,880 feet. In outcrop they commonly are longer north-south, are arranged mainly in two north-trending belts, and are oriented approximately parallel to the attitude of the enclosing sediments at several stratigraphic horizons, calculated at 700 to 2,600 feet above the base of the Dry Union Formation. One of the belts of Paleozoic blocks sustains a prominent ridge east of Little Cochetopa Creek.

The Paleozoic formations found in the detached blocks are the Manitou Dolomite, Harding Quartzite, and Fremont Dolomite of Early, Middle, and Late Ordovician ages, respectively; the Chaffee Formation of Late Devonian age; and the Leadville Limestone of Mississippian age. Especially distinctive among the predominantly carbonate rocks are the Harding Quartzite containing conspicuous fossil fish plates, the fossiliferous Fremont Dolomite, and the basal argillaceous part of the Chaffee Formation. Criteria for the recognition of the various Paleozoic formations, as found at higher altitudes in the Sawatch Range to the west, were given by Johnson (1944) and by Dings and Robinson (1957, p. 11-18). Litsey (1958, p. 1150-1161) has also described these units at a locality a few miles to the east at lower altitudes on the northeast flank of the Sangre de Cristo Range.

Although most detached blocks are composed of one or two of the Paleozoic formation, some contain as many as four. Near the west edge of Little Cochetopa Creek Valley just below an altitude of 8,000 feet, the largest and most accessible allochthonous block here is exposed in an area of about 400 by 800 feet and for a height of about 150 feet (fig. 5). Remnants of the Manitou, Harding, and Fremont Formations appear along the cliffed east face,

FIGURE 5.

Allochthonous Paleozoic block in the Dry Union Formation near the west edge of Little Cochetopa Creek Valley. View north.

and the crest and west slope are occupied by the Chaffee Formation. These brecciated Paleozoic units make up about 300 feet of strata in the exposure; the four units total approximately 540-700 feet in thickness where they are completely exposed in the Sawatch Range about 8 miles to the west (Dings and Robinson, 1957, p. 11-15) and in the Sangre de Cristo Range at a locality about 9½ miles to the east (Litsey, 1958, p. 1149). The bedding, still recognizable locally in this detached block, dips 25°-50° W., approximately parallel to the dip of the enclosing Tertiary beds; the steeper dips are near Late Tertiary faults.

The Paleozoic blocks are made up predominantly of crackled and brecciated dolomite and limestone. Much of the material, especially that near the base, consists of breccia fragments less than 2 inches in diameter. Sharply angular fragments and others rounded by abrasion are set in a highly indurated matrix of crushed carbonate rock cemented by calcite, generally fine grained but locally coarsely crystalline. Bedding is no longer evident in this type of breccia but is discernible in less brecciated parts of blocks. Irregularities of adjacent breccia fragments generally do not correspond in shape, which further suggests relative movement following brecciation. Brecciation occurred before the Paleozoic blocks came to rest within the Tertiary sediments, for fragments of brecciated Paleozoic rocks commonly occur in the immediately overlying and surrounding beds. Miocene ostracodal limestone beds of the Dry Union Formation above the largest Paleozoic block immediately west of Little Cochetopa Creek Valley contain small angular and rounded clasts of brecciated Paleozoic rocks (fig. 6).

Three and one-half to 5 miles west of Little Cochetopa Creek (fig. 2), Crawford (1913, pl. 2) mapped six patches of Paleozoic carbonate rocks, ranging in age from Ordovician to Mississippian. Some of these remnants of Paleozoic rock were shown in areas underlain by Precambrian gneiss; others were in areas underlain by unconsolidated fill. The remnants are at altitudes of 8,200 to 9,600 feet, about 3½ miles east of a large faulted synclinal mass composed of the same formations (fig. 2), which is exposed

FIGURE 6.

Angular and rounded clasts of brecciated Paleozoic limestone, dolomite, and chert in Miocene ostracodal limestone of the Dry Union Formation.

2-4 miles east of the Continental Divide and at altitudes of 10,500 to 12,000 feet (Dings and Robinson, 1957, pl. 1). Recent examination of the four Paleozoic remnants along the west edge of the Tertiary trough suggests that they are detached blocks; they are composed of thoroughly brecciated and calcite-cemented material typical of the other slide blocks farther east. Crawford (1913, p. 88, 101, and pl. 3, sec. E-E') regarded two of the six Paleozoic remnants as synclines. Gabelman (1952, p. 1594) similarly interpreted the patches of east-dipping to nearly horizontal Paleozoic rocks as evidence for a synclinal area between the uplifted Sawatch and Sangre de Cristo ranges. Evidence for the east limb of this proposed syncline, however, is even less convincing, because on the west flank of the Sangre de Cristo Range, at its north end, the rocks that underlie the fill in the trough and overlie the Precambrian basement are not Paleozoic sedimentary rocks but volcanic rocks of Oligocene age (fig. 2).

TERTIARY FAULTING RELATED TO DETACHED BLOCKS

In this region near the junction of the San Luis and Arkansas valleys, Tertiary faulting probably occurred before, during, and after emplacement of the detached Paleozoic blocks in the Tertiary sediments. The continuity of the faults in many places is evident on aerial photographs but is not obvious in the field; this is especially true of the faults in the unconsolidated Dry Union Formation. The dip of the fault and the amount and direction of displacement commonly are not determinable.

LARAMIDE FAULTS

Possibly Early Tertiary faulting and associated folding initiated the conditions favorable for detachment and transport of the allochthonous Paleozoic blocks in later Tertiary time. In the adjoining quadrangle west of the area of detached breccia blocks, Dings and Robinson (1957, p. 36-40) described various types of Laramide faults, some mineralized with base metals. Their Tincup-Morning Glim fault (1957, p. 36), the mineralized Chester fault of the Marshall Pass uranium district about 10 miles south of Garfield (Wright and Everhart, 1960, p. 357-359), and the Eocene faults in the Bonanza mining district (Burbank, 1932, p. 38-41) about 15 miles south-southwest of Poncha Springs are all reported as thrust faults that displaced Precambrian rocks chiefly northward or westward over Paleozoic rocks. To the north near Aspen, Colo., the Elk Range thrust sheet may have formed in Early Tertiary time by gravity sliding of a thick section of Upper Paleozoic and Mesozoic sedimentary rocks off the steep western flank of the Sawatch Range uplift (Bryant, 1966).

MIOCENE NORTH-TRENDING BORDER FAULTS

The north end of the San Luis Valley, structurally part of the Rio Grande depression, is bordered on the east by a steep fault that formed chiefly from Late Oligocene to the end of Tertiary time, according to Burbank and Goddard (1937, p. 965). More recently, others have reported that downfaulting of this depression began in Miocene time (Gabelman, 1952, p. 1606; Kelley, 1956; Lipman and Mehnert, 1968; Steven and Epis, 1968, p. 248-249). Recent fieldwork in the Poncha Springs and Bonanza quadrangles similarly shows that faults bordering the trough formed at some time between the eruption of Oligocene volcanic rocks and the deposition of sediments of Late Miocene age. As suggested below, recurrent movement of the fault at the west border of the trough (fig. 2) may have helped the eastward transfer of the detached Paleozoic blocks along their underlying slide surfaces and over the Tertiary sediments.

POST-PLIOCENE FAULTS

Steep north-trending and east-trending faults cut some of the detached Paleozoic blocks and the adjacent Dry Union sediments of Miocene age near Little Cochetopa Creek (fig. 2), as well as the fossiliferous Pliocene part of the Dry Union Formation farther north and east. West of the creek, a north-trending fault zone dips about 70° W.; argillaceous beds near the base of the Chaffee Formation of Late Devonian age that are normally pink are locally green and sheared along this fault zone. The east-trending fault cutting the Dry Union Formation south of the South Arkansas River (fig. 2) dips steeply north and offsets the linear belts of detached Paleozoic blocks near Little Cochetopa Creek. Along the fault, the north side has been displaced downward and to the east. The Arkansas Valley is about 1,000 feet lower than the San Luis Valley as a result of downfaulting along the east-trending and north-trending Late Tertiary structures and also because of more active erosion in the Arkansas drainage during Pleistocene and Holocene time (Van Alstine, 1970). About 3 miles east of Salida, Rold (1961, p. 116 and fig. 4) also reported right-lateral movement on a probably related east-trending fault zone on the northeast flank of the Sangre de Cristo Range.

EMPLACEMENT OF THE DETACHED BLOCKS

Detachment of the Paleozoic blocks evidently resulted from recurrent gravitational sliding off the flank of the Sawatch anticline and off the upthrown side of the fault at the margin of the Late Tertiary trough. Emplacement of the blocks within the Dry Union Formation near Little Cochetopa Creek is dated fairly closely, for it occurred after Oligocene volcanism, during Dry Union sedimentation, and before deposition of the beds containing the vertebrate fossils of Late Miocene age. At this time the Paleozoic rocks to the west were being very actively eroded, as shown by the abundant clasts from Lower, Middle, and Upper Paleozoic carbonate rocks, Lower Paleozoic quartzite, and Upper Paleozoic arkosic sandstones found within the Tertiary sediments immediately above and below the blocks. Mudflows associated with the blocks in the Dry Union Formation further indicate that landslides were very active at this time.

The blocks are not overturned, suggesting that the sliding was not accompanied by toppling that occurs during rockfall or flow; the normal stratigraphic section of Paleozoic rocks can be recognized in less brecciated parts of some blocks, as previously described. The brittle carbonate rocks and quartzite were broken into many detached blocks that moved independently and were emplaced without markedly disturbing the underlying Tertiary sediments. Near the northeast crest of the ridge east of Little Cochetopa Creek, the lower surfaces of two blocks strike about N. 20° E. and dip about 20° W.; this attitude is approximately parallel to that of the enclosing Tertiary sediments, as shown locally by stratification and by the orientation of boulders and cobbles in the underlying mudflow. The material immediately beneath these Paleozoic blocks is made up of unbrecciated clasts consisting largely of Tertiary volcanic and Paleozoic carbonate rocks in a clayey gouge. The contacts between the underlying sediments and the bases of the breccia blocks obviously were the surfaces along which the blocks slid.

Intrusion of a batholith and stocks northwest of the area and local differential movement may have increased the gravitational potential for sliding. Doming probably accompanied emplacement of the Mount Princeton batholith and other intrusive bodies (Dings and Robinson, 1957, p. 25-27, 31-32); these Tertiary intrusives have not yet been precisely dated. Differential movement caused by uplift of the Sawatch Range or lowering of the Rio Grande trough in Miocene time probably triggered the eastward transfer of Paleozoic blocks over the Precambrian terrane and down the flank of the Sawatch anticline, the major Laramide structure. Some detached blocks came to rest on Precambrian gneiss and on trough fill near the fault at the west edge of the Tertiary depression. Other blocks slid farther east over the well-lubricated mudflows and other unconsolidated sediments of Late Tertiary age.

Although a highland source area for the detached blocks is available to the west in the Sawatch Range, the actual bedrock structure or structures that furnished the slide blocks are not definitely known. The downfolded and downfaulted masses of Lower and Middle Paleozoic bedrock near Monarch and Garfield (fig. 2) are the most probable sources now remaining in this extensively eroded, largely Precambrian terrane. These masses in the Monarch district were locally mineralized with base-metal sulfide minerals in Early Tertiary time (Crawford, 1913, p. 195-283; Dings and Robinson, 1957, p. 81-95), but sulfide minerals were not seen in the detached breccia blocks in the trough.

The magnitude of slope of the surface of transport is not definitely known. If the blocks now at an altitude of about 8,800 feet near the fault along the west border of the Tertiary trough slid eastward about 3½ miles from the nearest large synclinal mass, which is at an altitude of about 10,500 feet (fig. 2), the inclined slide surface would slope east at about 5°; such a slope is well within the range in which mudflows respond to gravity and twice the slope angle of the Wyoming Heart Mountain detachment fault along which Paleozoic masses slid (Pierce, 1963, p. 1234). One cannot estimate the slope angle of the similar inclined surface of transport from the possible source area in the Sawatch Range eastward for 9½ miles to the Paleozoic blocks beyond Little Cochetopa Creek; this surface would cross the border fault of the Tertiary trough, which probably was active during and has been active since the time of gravitational sliding. A further complication is the fact that the Paleozoic blocks and enclosing Tertiary beds have been tilted westward since emplacement.

Furthermore, no estimate can be made of the attenuation that occurred in individual blocks during gravity sliding, because examination of the detached blocks fails to show precisely when brecciation and thinning of the stratigraphic section took place; an unknown amount perhaps occurred before the masses were freed from the bedrock to slide as isolated blocks. In the probable source area to the west, all Paleozoic formations are separated by erosional unconformities, and reduced thicknesses of the Lower Paleozoic rocks also resulted from Laramide faulting and squeezing of the beds (Dings and Robinson, 1957, p. 9, 11).

OTHER EXAMPLES OF GRAVITATIONAL SLIDES IN THE WESTERN UNITED STATES

Other areas of the Western United States contain excellent, well-documented examples of localities where gravitational sliding is the suggested mechanism for the formation of detached and brecciated blocks. About 50 miles east of the area under investigation, in the Milsap Creek area of Fremont County, Colorado, blocks of Lower Paleozoic carbonate and Precambrian rocks slid westward, probably in Late Cenozoic time, down the flank of the Cripple Creek arch and onto Upper Paleozoic rocks in a graben (Gerhard and Wahlstedt, 1965). Along the Front Range west of Fort Collins, Colorado, blocks of sandstone of the Dakota Group slid down the dip slopes of hogbacks in Pleistocene time and overrode younger Cretaceous strata (Braddock and Eicher, 1962). South of the Owl Creek Range, Wyoming, brecciated Paleozoic blocks moved during Early Tertiary time by gravity sliding across a frontal fault zone and onto Triassic redbeds in the Wind River Basin (Wise, 1963).

Even more analogous to the detached blocks southwest of Salida, Colorado, are various structures formed when gravity sliding occurred during deposition within Tertiary basins and when the blocks became incorporated within the sediments. Pierce (1957, 1960, 1963) has given detailed accounts of detachment faults on the west side of the Bighorn Basin, Wyoming, along which allochthonous blocks of brecciated Paleozoic rocks moved 5 to 30 miles basinward; some finally came to rest within Eocene sediments (Pierce and Nelson, 1968).

The Basin and Range province of the southwest similarly contains many gravity slide blocks formed in Cenozoic time. In the Shadow Mountains area, San Bernardino County, California, beds or large lenses of brecciated carbonate rocks of Early Paleozoic age occur at several horizons in sediments of Middle Tertiary age; detached blocks moved laterally and evidently were emplaced under the influence of gravity (Hewett, 1956, p. 88-90, 96, 99). About

100 miles southwest of there, large blocks of brecciated Paleozoic limestone slid northward, possibly on a cushion of trapped air (Shreve, 1968), for several miles beyond the San Bernardino Mountains and onto Upper Tertiary sediments of the Mojave Desert (Woodford and Harriss, 1928, p. 279-283, 287-290). Gravity sliding attenuated the stratigraphic section to one-fourth the normal thickness in allochthonous Paleozoic masses in Miocene-Pliocene sediments in the Horse Range of east-central Nevada (Moores, 1968, p. 94-96; Moores and others, 1968, p. 1716, 1719). In the San Manuel area, Pinal County, Arizona, a large lens about 500 feet thick and 4,500 feet long, composed chiefly of blocks of Paleozoic limestone and Precambrian diabase, slid laterally about 8 miles from the probable source area to the resting place within Upper Tertiary sediments of the basin (Creasey, 1965, p. 20-22). Sheets of Upper Cretaceous sandstone in the Jicarilla Mountains of central New Mexico moved under the influence of gravity from an area domed by intrusion; the blocks rest on the eroded surface of Triassic and Permian rocks and are partly covered by the Ogallala Formation of Pliocene age (Budding, 1963).

Gravity slide blocks may also occur near the east edge of the Rio Grande trough in the Santa Fe area, New Mexico. Large detached blocks of Pennsylvanian (?) quartzite are arranged in a linear belt parallel to the strike of adjacent strata in the Tesuque Formation (Miocene and Pliocene) of the Santa Fe Group (Spiegel and others, 1963, p. 63, 76-78). The authors suggested that the blocks may represent ancient talus from basement rocks raised to the surface along a fault not yet recognized; the possible origin of the blocks by gravity sliding from reported exposures at greater altitudes several miles to the east seems worthy of further consideration.

REFERENCES

Braddock, W. A., and Eicher, D. L., 1962, Block-glide landslides in the Dakota Group of the Front Range foothills, Colorado: Geol. Soc. America Bull., v. 73, no. 3, p. 317-323.

Bryan, Kirk, and McCann, F. T., 1937-38, The Ceja del Rio Puerco, a border feature of the Basin and Range province in New Mexico: Jour. Geology, v. 45, no. 8, p. 801-828; v. 46, no. 1, p. 1-16.

Bryant, Bruce, 1966, Possible window in the Elk Range thrust sheet near Aspen, Colorado, in Geological Survey Research 1966; U.S. Geol. Survey Prof. Paper 550-D, p. D1-D8.

Budding, A. J., 1963, Origin and age of superficial structures, Jicarilla Mountains, central New Mexico: Geol. Soc. America Bull., v. 74, no. 2, p. 203-208.

Burbank, W. S., and Goddard, E. N., 1937, Thrusting in Huerfano mining district, Colorado: U.S. Geol. Survey Prof. Paper 169, 166 p.

Burbank, W. S., and Goddard, E. N., 1937, Thrusting in Tuerfano Park, Colorado, and related problems of orogeny in the Sangre de Cristo Mountains: Geol. Soc. America Bull., v. 48, no. 7, p. 931-976.

Cook, D. R., 1961, Bonanza project, Bear Creek Mining Company: Am. Inst. Mining, Metall. and Petroleum Engineers Trans. 1960, v. 217, p. 285-295.

Crawford, R. D., 1913, Geology and ore deposits of the Monarch and Tomichi districts, Colorado: Colorado Geol. Survey Bull. 4, 317 p.

Creasey, S. C., 1965, Geology of the San Manuel area, Pinal County, Arizona: U.S. Geol. Survey Prof. Paper 471, 64 p.

Dings, M. G., and Robinson, C. S., 1957, Geology and ore deposits of the Garfield quadrangle, Colorado: U.S. Geol. Survey Prof. Paper 289, 110 p.

Gabelman, J. W., 1952, Structure and origin of northern Sangre de Cristo Range, Colorado: Am. Assoc. Petroleum Geologists Bull., v. 36, no. 8, p. 1574-1612.

Gerhard, L. C., and Wahlstedt, W. J., 1965, Milsap Creek fault block, a gravitational structure: Mtn. Geologist, v. 2, no. 4, p. 203-208.

Hewett, D. F., 1956, Geology and mineral resources of the Ivanpah quadrangle, California and Nevada: U.S. Geol. Survey Prof. Paper 275, 172 p.

Johnson, J. H., 1944, Paleozoic stratigraphy of the Sawatch Range, Colorado: Geol. Soc. America Bull., v. 55, no. 3, p. 303-378.

Kelley, V. C., 1956, The Rio Grande depression from Taos to Santa Fe, in New Mexico Geol. Soc., Guidebook of southeastern Sangre de Cristo Mountains, New Mexico, 7th field conference, Oct. 19-21, 1956: p. 109-114.

Lipman, P. W., and Mehnert, H. H., 1968, Structural history of the eastern San Juan Mountains and the San Luis Valley, Colorado [abs.]: Geol. Soc. America, Cordilleran Sec., 64th Ann. Mtg., Tucson, Ariz., 1968, Program, p. 76-77.

Litsey, L. R., 1958, Stratigraphy and structure of the northern Sangre de Cristo Mountains, Colorado: Geol. Soc. America Bull., v. 69, no. 9, p. 1143-1178.

Moores, E. M., 1968, Mio-Pliocene sediments, gravity slides, and their tectonic significance, east-central Nevada: Jour. Geology, v. 76, no. 1, p. 88-98.

Moores, E. M., Scott, R. B., and Lumsden, W. W., 1968, Tertiary tectonics of the White Pine-Grant Range region, east-central Nevada, and some regional implications: Geol. Soc. America Bull., v. 79, no. 12, p. 1703-1726.

Pierce, W. G., 1957, Heart Mountain and South Fork detachment thrusts of Wyoming: Am. Assoc. Petroleum Geologists Bull., v. 41, no. 4, p. 591-626.

——— 1960, The "break-away" point of the Heart Mountain detachment fault in northwestern Wyoming: Art. 106 in U.S. Geol. Survey Prof. Paper 400-B, p. B236-B237.

——— 1963, Reef Creek detachment fault, northwestern Wyoming: Geol. Soc. America Bull., v. 74, no. 10, p. 1225-1236.

Pierce, W. G., and Nelson, W. H., 1968, Geologic map of the Pat O'Hara Mountain quadrangle, Park County, Wyoming: U.S. Geol. Survey Geol. Quad. Map GQ-755, scale 1:62,500.

Powers, W. E., 1935, Physiographic history of the upper Arkansas River valley and the Royal Gorge, Colorado: Jour. Geology, v. 43, no. 2, p. 184-199.

Rold, J. W., 1961, The structure and lower and middle Paleozoic stratigraphy of the Wellsville area, Colorado, in Symposium on lower and middle Paleozoic rocks of Colorado, 12th field conference: Denver, Colo., Rocky Mountain Assoc. Geologists, p. 107-117.

Russell, R. T., 1950, The geology of the Poncha fluorspar district, Chaffee County, Colorado: Cincinnati, Ohio, Univ. Cincinnati, unpub. Ph.D. thesis, 70 p.

Shreve, R. L., 1968, The Blackhawk landslide: Geol. Soc. America Spec. Paper 108, 47 p.

Spiegel, Zane, Baldwin, Brewster, Kottlowski, F. E., Barrows, E. L., and Winkler, H. A., 1963, Geology and water resources of the Santa Fe area, New Mexico: U.S. Geol. Survey Water-Supply Paper 1525, 258 p.

Steven, T. A., and Epis, R. C., 1968, Oligocene volcanism in south-central Colorado, in Cenozoic volcanism in the Southern Rocky Mountains: Colorado School Mines Quart., v. 63, no. 3, p. 241-258.

Tweto, Ogden, 1961, Late Cenozoic events of the Leadville district and upper Arkansas Valley, Colorado: Art. 56 in U.S. Geol. Survey Prof. Paper 424-B, p. B133-B135.

——— 1968, Geologic setting and interrelationships of mineral deposits in the mountain province of Colorado and south-central Wyoming, in Ridge, J. D., ed., Ore deposits of the United States, 1933-1967 (Graton-Sales volume): New York, Am. Inst. Mining, Metall., and Petroleum Engineers, v. 1, p. 551-588.

Van Alstine, R. E., 1968, Tertiary trough between the Arkansas and

San Luis Valleys, Colorado, *in* Geological Survey Research 1968: U.S. Geol. Survey Prof. Paper 600-C, p. C158-C160.

————— 1970, Geology and mineral deposits of the Poncha Springs NE quadrangle, Chaffee County, Colorado: U.S. Geol. Survey Prof. Paper 626, 52 p. [1970]

Van Alstine, R. E., and Lewis, G. E., 1960, Pliocene sediments near Salida, Chaffee County, Colorado: Art. 111 *in* U.S. Geol. Survey Prof. Paper 400-B, p. B245.

Wise, D. U., 1963, Keystone faulting and gravity sliding driven by basement uplift of Owl Creek Mountains, Wyoming: Am. Assoc. Petroleum Geologists Bull., v. 47, no. 4, p. 586-598.

Woodford, A. O., and Harriss, T. F., 1928, Geology of Blackhawk Canyon, San Bernardino Mountains, California: California Univ., Dept. Geol. Sci. Bull., v. 17, no. 8, p. 265-304.

Wright, R. J., and Everhart, D. L., 1960, Uranium, chap. 5 *in* Del Rio, S. M., comp., and others, Mineral resources of Colorado, 1st sequel: Denver, Colorado Mineral Resources Board, p. 327-365.

RESULTS OF PRELIMINARY STUDIES OF THE AIR POLLUTION METEOROLOGY OF LIMITED AREAS IN THE SAN LUIS VALLEY

by

THEODORE A. MUELLER

Physics Department
Adams State College
Alamosa, Colorado

BLANCA

A wind recording station was established at Blanca by the Colorado Air Pollution Control Division during the winter and spring of 1969-1970. The wind patterns measured by that station showed the usual night-day reversal with high day and low night wind speeds typical of valleys. However, the directions were not those observed in Alamosa.

During the winter, the predominant wind directions were day NW and night E and S; while in the spring and summer they were day NW and night varying between S and W. It is tempting to speculate that Blanca sits not in the San Luis Valley but in a sub valley showing distinct air movement properties. From the point of view of air pollution meteorology, a valley can be considered to have sides as low as 100 ft. (Weedfall, 1967). Such a rise in elevation can be found to the south of Blanca on the south side of Trinchera Creek. It is possible to visualize three valleys; one running W-E, another NW-SE, as well as a N-S valley to the west and south of Blanca. (fig. 1). It is usual to talk about a down-valley flow of air at night, and an up-valley flow of air during the day. If the three possible valleys to the east and south of Blanca assume different importance with various seasons and meteorological conditions, it is easy to see a possible explanation to the observed wind patterns.

These are not academic speculations for it was at one time proposed to put a paper pulp mill just west of Blanca. It has been calculated that the vapors from this plant would have affected Alamosa due to the patterns of wind direction and speed.*

GREAT SAND DUNES NATIONAL MONUMENT

The state maintains a particulate matter sampler at the Sand Dunes. This station showed an annual average of 24 ug/M^3 with a maximum of 112 ug/M^3 and a minimum of 2 ug/M^3. These are the lowest figures in all categories out of the 50 stations reporting in the state. The new state standards allow 55 ug/M^3 particulate matter. Thus you are breathing some of the purest air in the state, provided you do not run into a sandstorm. Of the 24 ug/M^3 only 1.2 ug represents benzene solubles. In all likelihood, these would be primarily hydrocarbons.

If the valley is viewed from the dunes, the cities of Alamosa and Monte Vista can be easily identified by the plume of material rising into the air above them. Also easily seen, if burning, are the teepee burners at the various sawmills in the valley. When the wind conditions are right, there will be a haze layer extending from the south, along the west side of the valley and thinning out just beyond Del Norte. This layer is not entirely natural, having man made components in it. Pollutants will not rise through it, but will rise to join this layer and add to it. Usually the layer will have a sharp cut off on top indicating that the upper limit is not diffusion controlled. In general, the layer is thicker to the south. This is for two reasons:

(1) The viewing angle produces greater layer depth to the south.
(2) The pollution sources to the south, including a contribution from New Mexico, (most likely originating

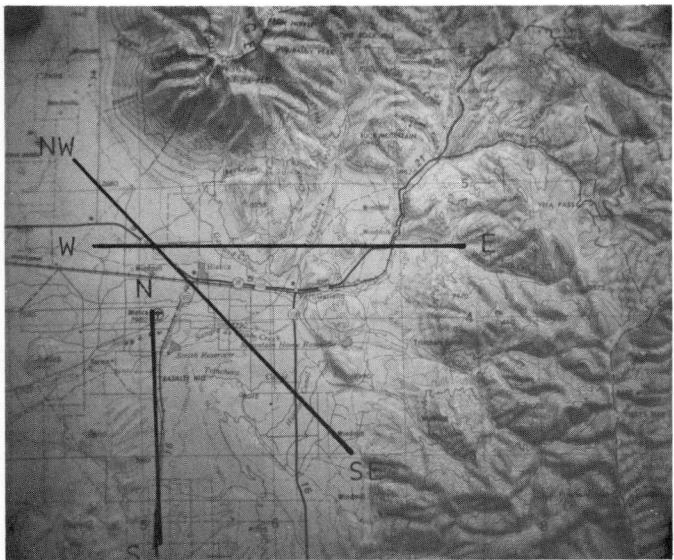

FIGURE 1.
Photograph of plastic relief map, Fort Garland-Blanca area prepared by the U.S. Army Corps of Engineers.

---

* Calculations done by the Colorado Air Pollution Control Division of the Colorado Department of Health.

on the Taos Plateau), produce materials carried into the valley by southerly winds.

Scientists at Los Alamos have reported on particulate matter haze in the Rio Grande Valley opposite Los Alamos (Liebenbert & Schulte, 1970). It was proposed the haze was due to the power plants in the Four Corners. I would like to suggest that at least part of the haze is due to sources on the Taos Plateau, being the same ones contributing to the haze seen here.

Major particulate sources in the San Luis Valley would be agricultural burning of ditches and fields in the spring and late fall. Yearly sources are teepee burners of lumber mills and various county and city dumps. In addition there is the contribution of the cities in the valley.

All monthly averages shown are based on data taken during 1970, although conclusions were drawn from total data available to date. Numerical data were taken from the Colorado Air Pollution Control Division reports. On occasions, Alamosa particulate matter levels equal those of Denver. (Table I). However, the benzene solubles

TABLE I
COMPARISON OF ALAMOSA AND DENVER IN PARTICULATE MATTER POLLUTION FOR 1970
MEASURED PARTICULATE MATER IN ug/M³

	ALAMOSA	MIN.-MAX. RANGE IN GREATER DENVER AREA	
		CASTLE ROCK	GATES
Annual Average	73	61	132
Maximum	345	127	404
Minimum	24	24	54

Benzene soluble in ug/M³			
	ALAMOSA	CHERRY CR. DR.	GATES
Annual Average	3.7	2.5	9.6
Maximum	11.0	8.6	36.9
Minimum	0.9	0.7	2.8

TABLE II
MONTHLY AVERAGES OF POLLUTION INDICES IN ALAMOSA FOR 1970

	PARTICULATE MATTER ug/M³	BENZENE SOLUBLES ug/M³	SULFATION SO₃-Mg/100cm³/day
Jan	72	6.5	0.01
Feb.	71	6.4	0.03
Mar	73	2.6	0.02
Apr	70	3.3	0.03
May	78	3.1	0.03
June	69	2.7	0.00
July	60	2.5	0.07
Aug	55	2.6	0.04
Sept	59	3.7	0.02
Oct	78	3.1	—
Nov	121	3.7	0.02
*Dec	82	4.7	0.03

* Storm fronts established strong winds for greater than ½ of this month.

would indicate that we are at no time nearly as high as Denver in hydrocarbon concentration, (Table II), or, from other data, in oxide pollutants, (NO, NO₂, SO₃, CO, etc.). (figs. 2 & 3). The Gelman data shows a bimodal pattern in the particulate matter pollution, with both peaks occurring at night. (fig. 4). The predominant pollution episode is at night due to the very common occurrence of inversions over the city. These are at a very low altitude, less than 100 ft. for those which have been measured. Particulate matter values are obtained from 24 hour averages. Since our pollution occurs mainly at night, the values during the episode would be approximately 1½ the average shown.

The data can be explained under the following assumptions, although what follows does not constitute a proof.

(1) The major source of pollution in Alamosa, at present, is home heating.
(2) Inversion or stagnant air conditions occur almost nightly during the winter.
(3) There is a small ventilation* factor (horizontal), which is not capable of clearing the air under the maximum pollution rate.
(4) There are two temperature drops of large proportions; one at sunset and one at sunrise.

At sunset the temperature drops suddenly; all home furnaces come on to keep up with this, as well as the added load of cooled air introduced into the homes due to the many entrances and exists from many homes at this time. Also occurring is the onset of the inversion to trap this increased output of pollution. The horizontal ventilation cannot keep up and there is an increase in pollution concentration. After 8:00 p.m. the furnaces catch up and activity slows down, resulting in a decreased pollution output rate. The ventilation then starts to reduce the level of pollution under the inversion, but it decreases towards morning as the wind speed decreases. This results in a slight pollution buildup during the night after an initial drop. With sunrise there is another drop in temperature and an increase in activity resulting in another peak of pollution output. With sunrise there also occurs the breaking of the inversion and both horizontal and vertical ventilation increases significantly, clearing the air for the Chamber of Commerce's "pure, clean San Luis Valley air."

The small peak at midnight is not accounted for by this explanation. What would be needed to explain it would be some localized source with an output just after midnight.

MONTE VISTA

Monte Vista has problems similar to Alamosa (and possibly worse), but documentation is not available.

ANTONITO

The Mobile Air Quality Laboratory was stationed in Antonito from April 13-21, 1971. During this time it measured CO, NO, NO₂, TO$_x$ concentrations. All of these quantities were what would be considered background range (fig. 5). However, the particulate matter count averaged 224 ug/M³ for the three 24 hour samples taken during this period. No confirmation of the source of this pollution was made and this needs further checking.

* Ventilation-air movement resulting in removal of dilution of pollutants.

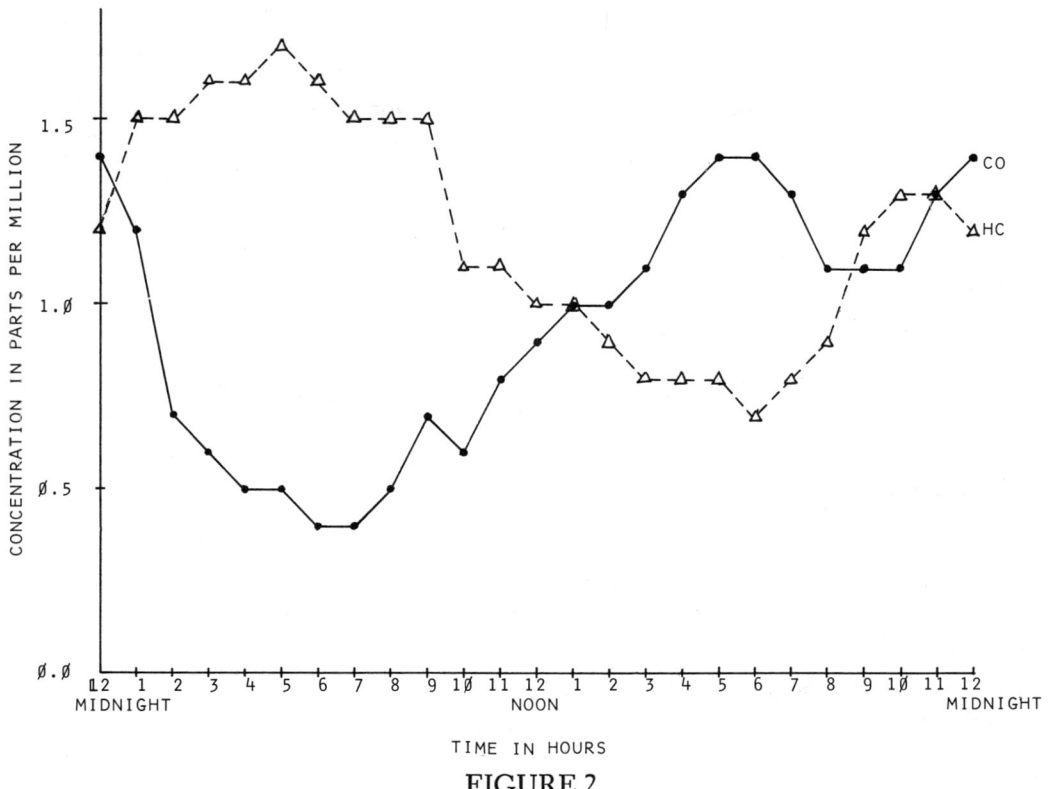

FIGURE 2.

Daily pattern of carbon monoxide (CO) and total hydrocarbons (HC) in Alamosa averaged over a three week period during March, 1971. Data taken by the Colorado Mobile Air Quality Lab.

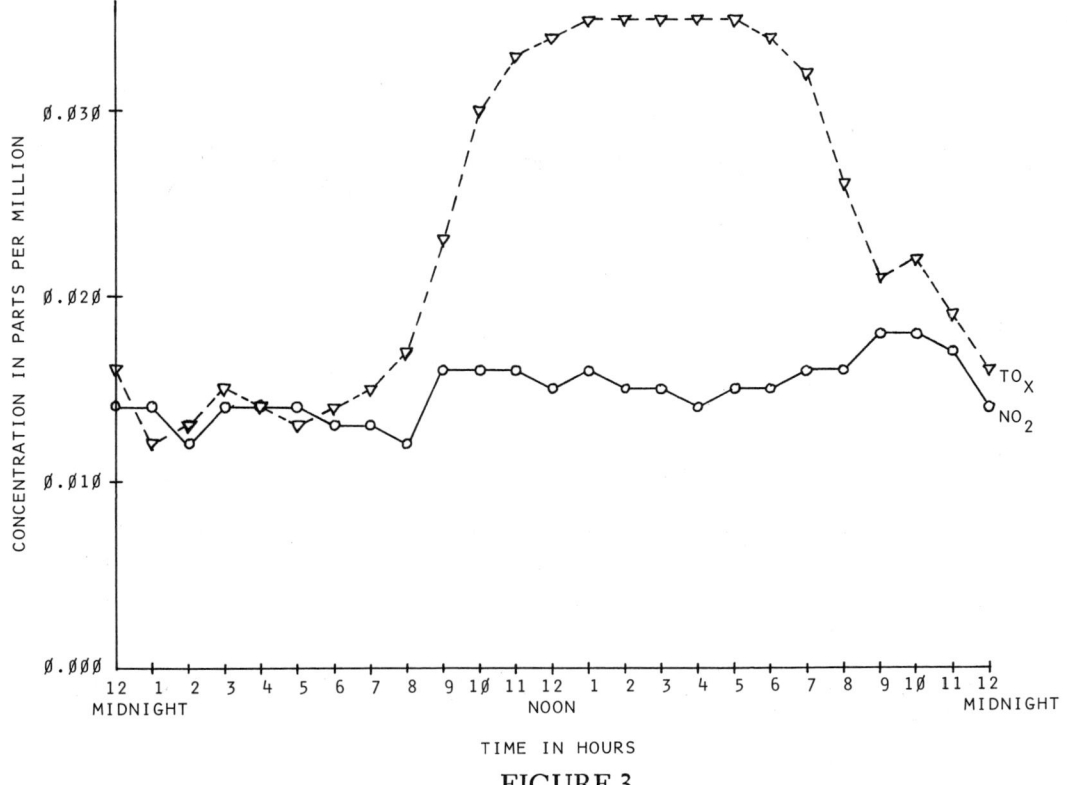

FIGURE 3.

Daily pattern of total oxidant (TO_x) and nitrogen dioxide (NO_2) levels in Alamosa over a three week period during March, 1971. Data taken by the Colorado Mobile Air Quality Lab.

REFERENCES

Weedfall, Robert O., 1967, A Mesoclimatological Classification System for Air Pollution Engineers. M.S. Dissertation, West Virginia University.

D. H. Liebenbert, and H. F. Schulte, 1970, Recent Volz Sunphotometer and Correlated Ground Level Particulate Measurement in Los Alamos. Paper given at the April meeting of the Southwestern and Rocky Mountain Division American Association for the Advancement of Science.

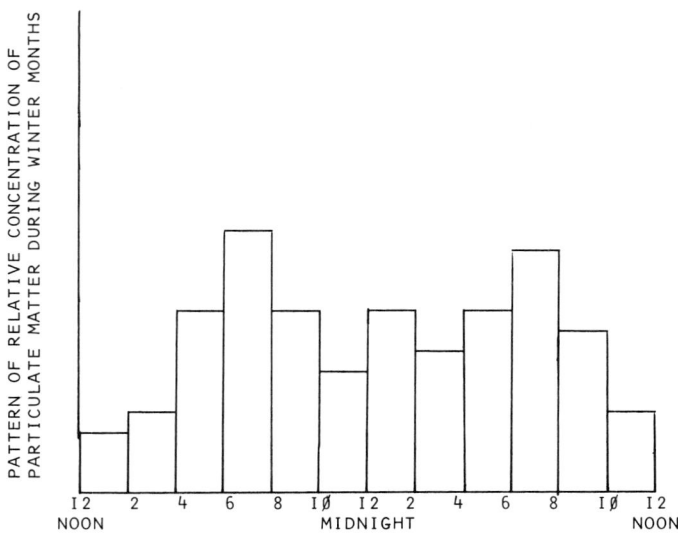

FIGURE 4.

Daily particulate matter pollution time pattern for Alamosa during the winter months 1970-71.

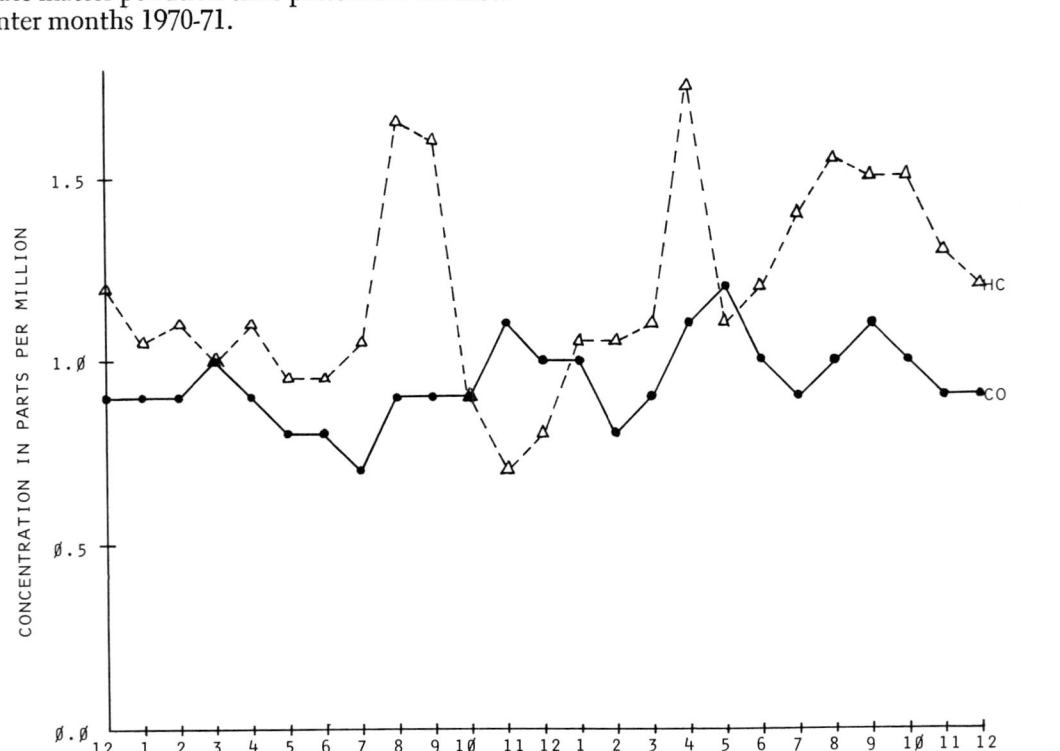

FIGURE 5.

Daily pattern of carbon monoxide (CO) and total hydrocarbons (HC) in Antonito averaged over a 9-day period in April, 1971. Data taken by the Colorado Mobile Air Quality Lab.

STRATIGRAPHIC RELATIONS BETWEEN BONANZA CENTER AND ADJACENT PARTS OF THE SAN JUAN VOLCANIC FIELD, SOUTH-CENTRAL COLORADO

by

Dennis L. Bruns[1], Rudy C. Epis[1],
Robert J. Weimer[1] and Thomas A. Steven[2]

INTRODUCTION

Stratigraphic relations of units derived from the Bonanza volcanic center in the northeastern part of the San Juan volcanic field and units from sources in the central and western parts of the field are well exposed in the Trickle Mountain and Lake Mountain NE quadrangles, 8-16 miles northwest of Saguache, Colorado (figs. 1 and 2), where Saguache Creek and its tributaries East Pass, Sheep, Jacks, Cross, Middle and Ford Creeks have cut numerous valleys into the Cenozoic volcanic rocks. These exposures show that many of the rocks from the Bonanza center are generally equivalent in age to the early intermediate rocks in the rest of the San Juan volcanic field, and are older

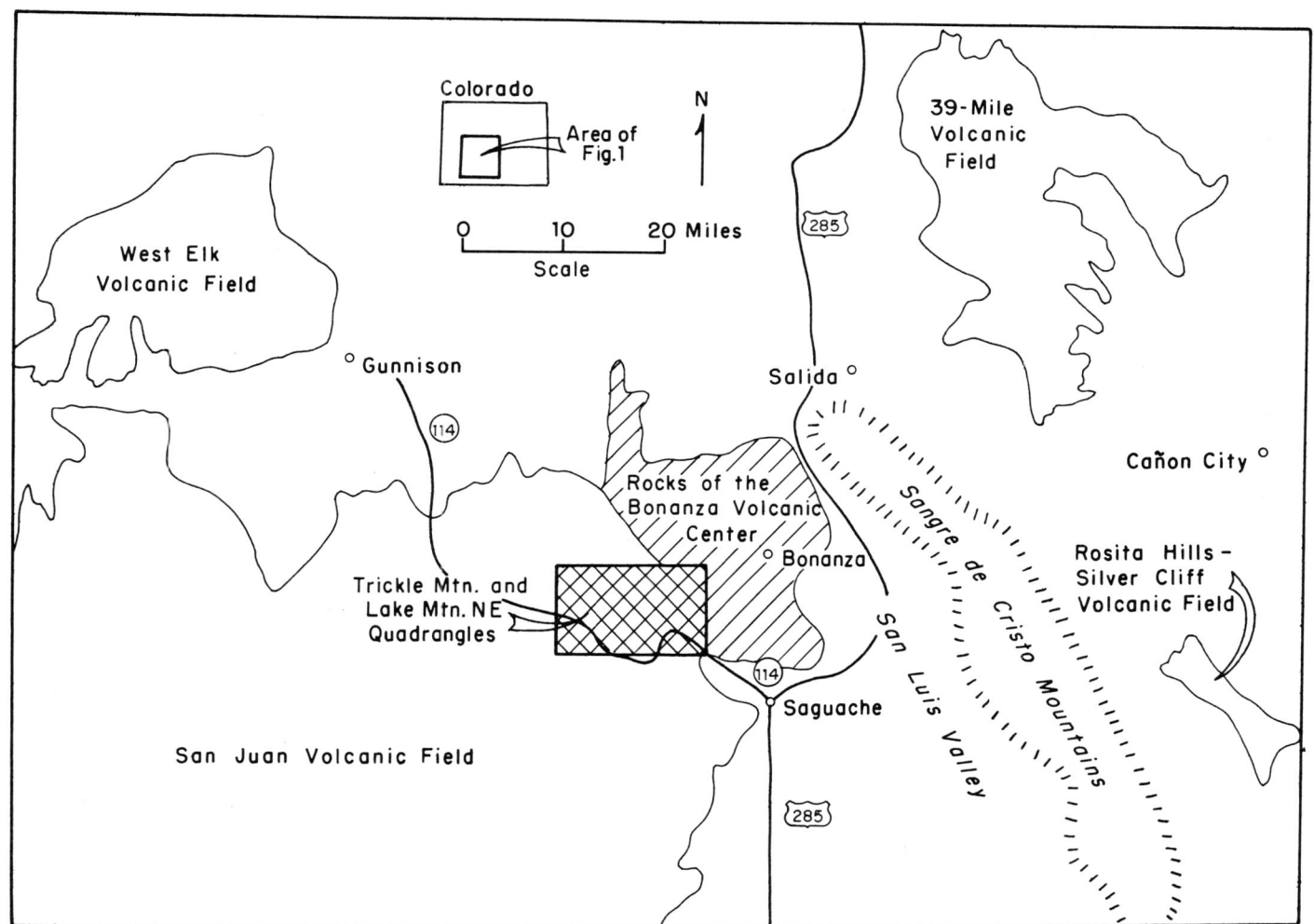

FIGURE 1.
Location of the Trickle Mountain and Lake Mountain NE quadrangles in the San Juan volcanic field, Colorado.

[1] Colorado School of Mines, Golden, Colorado
[2] U.S. Geological Survey, Denver, Colorado

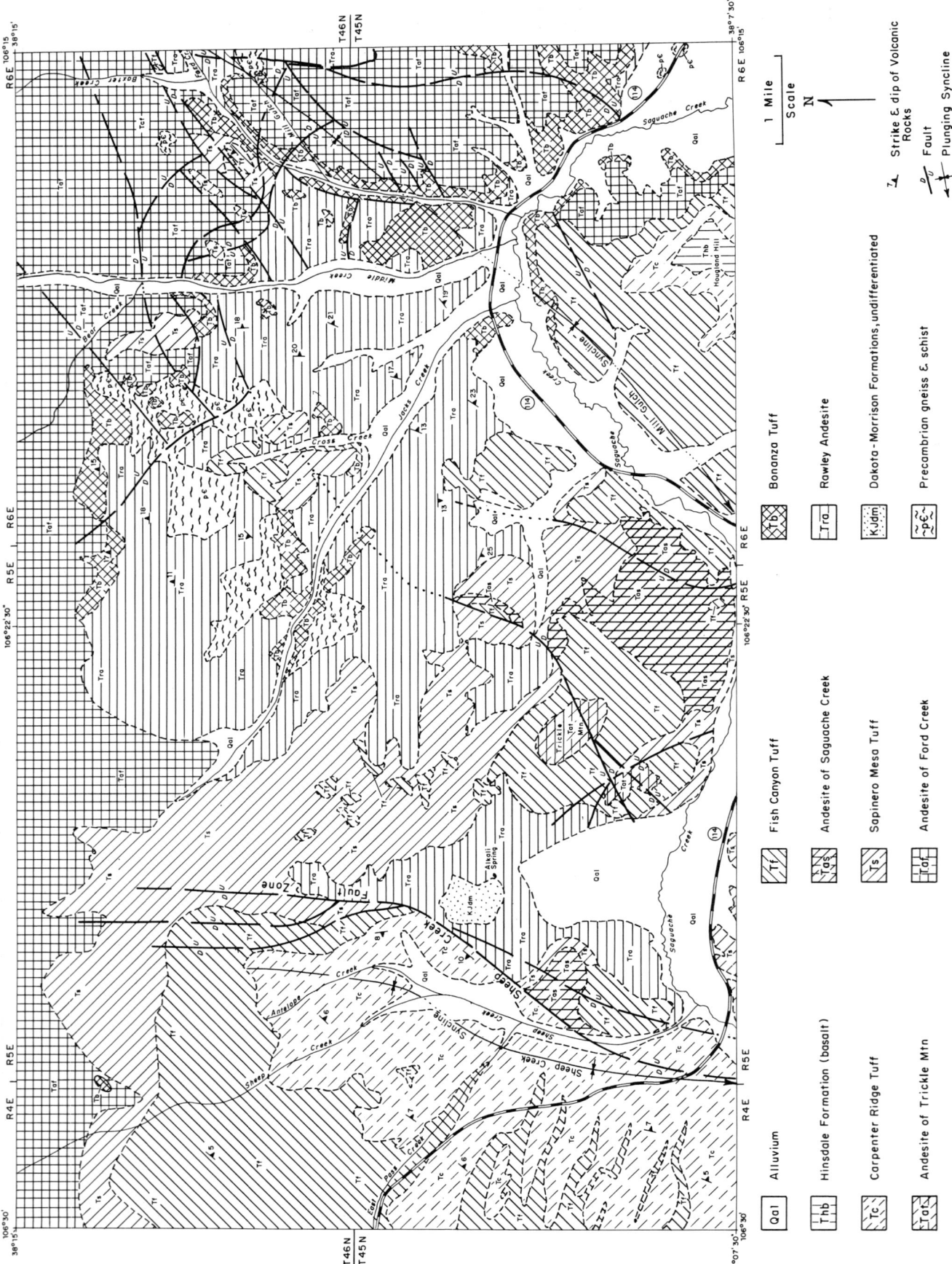

FIGURE 2. Geologic map of Trickle Mountain and Lake Mountain NE quadrangles, San Juan volcanic field, Colorado.

than most of the ash-flow tuffs derived from caldera source areas in the central and western parts of the field.

PREVIOUS WORK

The San Juan volcanic field has been studied by many geologists in the past 100 years. Much of the earlier work was summarized by Larsen and Cross (1956), who included the volcanic rocks in and adjacent to the southern and western parts of the area described here in the Conejos Quartz Latite, Treasure Mountain Rhyolite, Sheep Mountain Quartz Latite, Alboroto Rhyolite, and Piedra Rhyolite of the Potosi Volcanic Series (fig. 3).

Later work in the western San Juan Mountains by Luedke and Burbank (1963) led to redefinition of the Potosi Volcanic Series to Potosi Volcanic Group, and to include a specific assemblage of ash-flow units there.

Steven and Ratté (1965, p. 13) abandoned use of the Potosi in the Creede area in the central part of the San Juan volcanic field. Olson, Hedlund, and Hansen (1968) re-studied ash-flow tuffs in the Powderhorn-Gunnison River region where they defined the Blue Mesa, Dillon Mesa, Sapinero Mesa, Fish Canyon, and Carpenter Ridge Tuffs. These units were formerly mapped by Larsen and Cross as the Alboroto and Piedra Rhyolites. Olson, Hedlund, and Hansen (1968) retained the name Conejos Quartz Latite where previously used and included it, together with the Lake Fork Formation and the West Elk Breccia, as part of an assemblage of "older volcanic rocks of Tertiary age" (fig. 3).

Recently, Lipman, Steven, and Mehnert (1970) interpreted the volcanic history of the San Juan field on the basis of potassium-argon dating. They presented a major three-fold petrologic subdivision of the volcanic rocks: early intermediate lavas and breccias (generally 35-30 m.y. old), followed closely in time by more silicic ash-flow tuffs and related lavas (30-26.5 m.y.), and ending with a bimodal association of basalt and rhyolite (23.5-5 m.y.). They used the term Conejos Formation for the early intermediate rocks in the central and eastern parts of the San Juan volcanic field, and on the basis of radiometric ages, suggested that the Bonanza volcanic pile was correlative (fig. 3).

The volcanic rocks of the Bonanza center were first described by Patton (1916), and were treated in more detail in a comprehensive report by Burbank (1932). A summary of local stratigraphic terminology as proposed by Burbank is shown in figure 3.

Recent graduate thesis research by students from the Colorado School of Mines (Mayhew, 1969, Bruns, 1971, Perry, 1971, and Marrs, in progress), has expanded the knowledge of the Bonanza pile outward from the central mineralized area studied by Patton and Burbank. Burbank (1932) considered the Hayden Peak Latite to be younger than the Rawley Andesite, but additional work by Mayhew (1969) indicates that in large part the two units intertongue. Patton (1916) originally named the Bonanza Latite, and this usage was followed by Burbank (1932). Mayhew (1969) identified the Bonanza Latite as an ash-flow tuff and emphasized its stratigraphic and structural importance. The ash-flow sheet has since been traced from the northeastern and central parts of the Bonanza volcanic pile southwestward into the Trickle Mountain and Lake Mountain NE quadrangles by work of Marrs and Bruns, and students of the Geology Summer Field

Modified after Larsen and Cross (1956)	Olson, Hedlund, and Hansen (1968)	Modified after Lipman, Steven, and Mehnert (1970)	This Report	Burbank (1932)
Hinsdale Formation Basalt and Rhyolite	Hinsdale Formation	Hinsdale Formation Basalt (4.7-23.4 m.y.) and Rhyolite (4.8-22.4 m.y.) ASH-FLOW TUFFS AND RELATED ROCKS	Hinsdale Formation	
Piedra Rhyolite	Carpenter Ridge Tuff	Carpenter Ridge Tuff-Bachelor Mtn. Rhyolite	Carpenter Ridge Tuff	
Alboroto Rhyolite	Fish Canyon Tuff	Fish Canyon Tuff-La Garita Qtz. Latite (27.8 m.y.)	Fish Canyon Tuff	
Sheep Mtn. Quartz Latite			Andesite of Saguache Creek Water-laid and air-fall tuffs of Saguache Creek	Porphyry Peak Rhyolite Brewer Creek Latite
Treasure Mtn. Rhyolite	Sapinero Mesa Tuff Dillon Mesa Tuff Blue Mesa Tuff	Tuff of Masonic Park (28.2 m.y.) Treasure Mtn. Rhyolite (29.8 m.y.) EARLY INTERMEDIATE LAVAS AND BRECCIAS	Sapinero Mesa Tuff Andesite of Ford Creek Bonanza Tuff	Squirrel Gulch Latite Bonanza Latite
Conejos Quartz Latite Bonanza volcanic pile	"OLDER VOLCANICS" Conejos Quartz Latite, Lake Fork Formation, and West Elk Breccia	Conejos Formation (31.1-34.7 m.y.), Lake Fork Formation, West Elk Breccia and San Juan Fm. (Included Bonanza volcanic pile)	Rawley Andesite	Hayden Peak Latite and Rawley Andesite

FIGURE 3.

Summary and Correlation of Stratigraphic Terminology of the San Juan volcanic field and the Bonanza center. Established correlations are shown by horizonal dotted lines.

Course (1965-71) of the Colorado School of Mines under the direction of R. C. Epis and R. J. Weimer.

The area south and southwest of the Trickle Mountain and Lake Mountain NE quadrangles has been mapped by T. A. Steven of the U. S. Geological Survey, who extended his studies to Houghland Hill in the Lake Mountain NE quadrangle to establish a stratigraphic tie of his units with those derived from the Bonanza center.

STRATIGRAPHY OF THE TRICKLE MOUNTAIN AND LAKE MOUNTAIN NE QUADRANGLES

All major units discussed in this report that have been named by previous workers have been used in the form already established, except that Bonanza Tuff is proposed instead of Bonanza Latite, so as to describe the unit more clearly and to bring the terminology into conformity with that used for most other major ash-flow tuff units in the San Juan volcanic field. Informal designations have been used for all units not previously named formally.

PRE-VOLCANIC ROCKS

Pre-volcanic rocks crop out in several erosional windows where streams have cut through the volcanic rocks to expose some of the higher parts of the pre-volcanic topography. The older rocks consist largely of Precambrian crystalline rocks, but sedimentary rocks of the Morrison Formation and Dakota Sandstone are exposed in one window. Precambrian rocks are mainly medium- to coarse-grained quartz-biotite-microcline schist and gneiss with smaller quantities of fine- to medium-grained granite and granitic pegmatite. The largest and most numerous outcrops of Precambrian rocks are in the northwestern part of the Lake Mountain NE quadrangle between Jacks Creek and Middle Creek. Smaller outcrops are scattered about elsewhere, as for example, the three exposures along Colorado State Highway 114 near the southeastern corner of the Lake Mountain NE quadrangle. The Morrison Formation and Dakota Sandstone are exposed near the center of the Trickle Mountain quadrangle, immediately northwest of Alkali Spring. Here the Morrison is in depositional contact with the Precambrian and consists of about 30-50 feet of red, green, and tan mudstones, siltstones, and shales. The Morrison is overlain by about 50-70 feet of fine- to medium-grained, ferruginous orthoquartzite of the Dakota Sandstone. Conglomerate layers with pebbles of chert and quartzite up to one-half inch in diameter are found in the lower part of the Dakota.

In the area described, the pre-volcanic (pre-Early Oligocene) topography must have had moderate relief inasmuch as the present maximum difference in elevation on the top of the underlying Precambrian rocks is 1,370 feet. Some of this difference can be accounted for by post-volcanic faulting, but a topographically high area of pre-volcanic rocks trending northeastward between Jacks Creek and Middle Creek, and measuring about 2 by 4 miles, does appear to have existed. Whether this high area resulted from pre-volcanic structural disruption cannot be determined locally because of the extensive cover of Tertiary volcanic rocks.

TERTIARY VOLCANIC ROCKS

Conejos Formation

The Conejos Formation, as used by Larsen and Cross (1956, pl. 1) and more recently in extensive reconnaissance and detailed studies in the San Juan Mountains by T. A. Steven and P. W. Lipman of the U. S. Geological Survey (oral communication, 1971), is an accumulation of lavas and breccias, largely of intermediate composition, that was erupted from a number of local volcanoes throughout the eastern and central parts of the San Juan volcanic field. Considering the broad and rather loose definition of the Conejos that has grown by usage, the more general term "early intermediate rocks" used by Lipman, Steven, and Mehnert (1970) is perhaps preferable. Equivalent rocks in local areas such as the western San Juan Mountains and around Bonanza, have been subdivided into smaller mappable units, many of which warrant formational rank.

Each of the early intermediate (Conejos Formation) centers had its own local volcanic history, and commonly it is difficult to establish specific equivalencies between local units derived from nearby centers. It is especially difficult to do so between units from distant centers. Broad equivalencies have been indicated by potassium-argon dating (Lipman, Steven, and Mehnert, 1970), and by marginal intertonguing of locally derived rocks from adjacent centers. Most of the early intermediate rocks (Conejos Formation) appear to have been erupted between 35 and 30 m.y. ago.

In the type locality of the Conejos Formation along the Conejos River in the southeastern San Juan Mountains, the formation is overlain by the La Jara Canyon Member of the Treasure Mountain Tuff (age 29.8 m.y. according to Lipman, Steven, and Mehnert, 1970). This relationship has been traced northward to within a few miles of the Rio Grande west of Del Norte, Colorado, where the Treasure Mountain overlies rocks along the south flanks of the Summer Coon, Twin Peaks, and Baughman Creek volcanoes within the Conejos Formation.

Rawley Andesite

The oldest volcanic rocks in the Trickle Mountain and Lake Mountain NE quadrangles are a heterogeneous assemblage of andesite flows, breccias, and agglomerates that underlie the distinctive Bonanza Tuff. These rocks probably are largely locally derived, but they correlate in a broad sense with the lithologically similar Rawley Andesite and Hayden Peak Latite which underlie the Bonanza Tuff near the center of the Bonanza pile. Marrs, (in progress; see also Knepper and Marrs, this quidebook), has traced the Rawley Andesite and overlying Bonanza Tuff into the eastern part of the Lake Mountain NE quadrangle. Lipman, Steven, and Mehnert (1970) report ages of 33.4 and 34.2 m.y. for the Rawley, which are within the range (35-30 m.y.) they suggest for the more general Conejos Formation.

FIGURE 4.

Photograph looking southwest at Houghland Hill from above Ford Creek. Outcrops in the foreground (Taf) are part of the andesite of Ford Creek. The lower (Tbl) and upper (Tbu) cooling units of the Bonanza Tuff present in the area can be seen overlain in part by the andesite of Ford Creek (Taf) and the later Fish Canyon Tuff (Tf), Carpenter Ridge Tuff (Tc), and Hinsdale Basalt (Thb). The Bonanza Tuff has been displaced 60 to 80 feet by a fault and erosion has removed the andesite of Ford Creek from the upthrown side of the fault prior to deposition of the Fish Canyon Tuff.

Bonanza Tuff

The Bonanza Tuff is the most distinctive stratigraphic unit derived from the Bonanza center (Mayhew, 1969). The unit is a widespread ash-flow sheet that separates lithologically similar assemblages of intermediate volcanic rocks in the older Rawley Andesite and Hayden Peak Latite and the younger Squirrel Gulch and Brewer Creek Latites. As shown in figures 2 and 3, the Bonanza Tuff and associated intermediate volcanic formations derived from the Bonanza center are overlain by major ash-flow sheets (Sapinero Mesa, Fish Canyon, and Carpenter Ridge Tuffs), derived from caldera sources in the central and western parts of the San Juan volcanic field. These relations are clearly revealed in outcrops in the central and southern Lake Mountain NE quadrangle, particularly along the valley of Saguache Creek and the slopes of Houghland Hill (fig. 4).

The maximum thickness of the Bonanza Tuff in the Trickle Mountain and Lake Mountain NE quadrangles is about 450 feet, although it generally is thinner, and locally is absent where it wedges out against the higher parts of pre-existing topography. Locally the Bonanza Tuff consists of 2 cooling units. The lower unit forms prominent dark reddish brown outcrops. It is a moderately to densely welded rock that contains phenocrysts of sanidine, andesine, and biotite, as well as characteristic purplish-gray lithic lapilli. The upper unit is lighter in color, less welded, and generally does not form good outcrops. The upper unit also contains fewer andesine and biotite phenocrysts and lithic lapilli. A few miles northeast of the Lake Mountain NE quadrangle, along Findley Gulch, the Bonanza Tuff is considerably thicker and displays at least 5 separate cooling units. Good exposures of the Bonanza Tuff occur along Colorado State Highway 114 northeast of Houghland Hill.

Mapping is incomplete in and around the Bonanza volcanic field, and the source and lateral distribution of the Bonanza Tuff are unknown. The unit is suspected to have originated from the Bonanza volcanic center as suggested by Burbank (1932) and Mayhew (1969), and it may be equivalent to Ash-Flow 7 of the Thirtynine Mile volcanic field (Epis and Chapin, 1968) northeast of Salida, Colorado. These relationships are as yet unconfirmed and a more complete evaluation must wait further field and petrographic work.

Andesite of Ford Creek

A series of interbedded andesitic and latitic flows and flow breccias intervene between the Bonanza and Sapinero Mesa Tuffs in the northern and eastern parts of the area of figure 1. The flows are well exposed along the valleys of Ford Creek and Bear Creek, and the informal name is taken from the former locality. The rocks thicken to the northwest and northeast, and appear to have been derived from separate centers in these respective directions; the maximum thickness exposed in the Trickle Mountain and Lake Mountain NE quadrangles is about 1,100 feet. The andesites along Ford Creek may represent southwestern extensions of the Squirrel Gulch and Brewer Creek Latites which overlie the Bonanza Tuff near the center of the Bonanza pile (figs. 3 and 4).

On the southeast side of Houghland Hill just south of

the area of fig. 2, the andesite of Ford Creek intertongues with thick intermediate flows forming part of an assemblage that extends southward at the top of the section of early intermediate rocks to the vicinity of Carnero Creek, 12 miles north of Del Norte, Colorado. This assemblage overlies rocks from Conejos-age volcanoes at Tracey Creek, Beidel, Summer Coon, and Baughman Creek, and was mapped separately by Larsen and Cross (1956, pl. 1) as Sheep Mountain Quartz Latite. Regional studies by T. A. Steven and P. W. Lipman (oral commun., 1971) have cast doubt on the correlation of these flows with the type Sheep Mountain west of Wolf Creek Pass, but the problem of age still exists. For convenience, Steven and Lipman have included these thick flows in the early intermediate assemblage (Conejos Formation) in reconnaissance mapping of the Durango 1° x 2° quadrangle, but recognize that this assignment is arbitrary. Geologically, the flows are bracketed by dated rocks in the Conejos volcanoes at Beidel and Summer Coon (34-32 m.y.) and the Sapinero Mesa Tuff (older than 28 m.y.); (Lipman, Steven and Mehnert, 1970), and conceivably could be equivalent to some of the lavas intertongued elsewhere with the ash-flow sequence. Additional data, especially radiometric ages for the Bonanza Tuff, are badly needed before precise correlations can be made.

SAPINERO MESA TUFF

The Sapinero Mesa Tuff (Olson, Hedlund and Hansen, 1968) is the oldest of the major ash-flow sheets derived from the central or western parts of the San Juan volcanic field that is present in the area of this report (fig. 3). It underlies most of the northwestern and central parts of the area, and in the northeastern part, it rests directly on the andesite of Ford Creek. The Sapinero Mesa Tuff consists of a single cooling unit with a thin, light gray, poorly welded base grading upward into a thick, cliff-forming, densely welded, reddish-brown devitrified interior, and finally into a thin, light-colored nonwelded upper zone. Locally, the densely welded zone develops lenticular vugs up to 4 inches in diameter that represent lithophysae and weathered-out devitrification spherulites.

The Sapinero Mesa is a crystal-poor quartz latite tuff with 5-10 per cent phenocrysts of andesine, sanidine, biotite, quartz and minor hornblende. Flattened pumice lapilli are common. It attains a maximum thickness of 200 feet in the area. Locally it is underlain by light-colored air-fall and water-laid tuffs and tuffaceous sedimentary rocks, but outcrops of these units are too thin and small to show in figure 2. The Sapinero Mesa Tuff extends more than 80 miles from its pinchout in the Houghland Hill area westward toward its probable source in the caldera areas in the western part of the San Juan volcanic field.

WATER-LAID AND AIR-FALL TUFFS OF SAGUACHE CREEK

The Sapinero Mesa Tuff is overlain by as much as 200 feet of light gray water-laid and air-fall tuffs. These are best exposed on both sides of Saguache Creek between Trickle Mountain and Houghland Hill. The tuffs are predominantly of air-fall origin, but there are many interbedded zones showing reworking, channeling and cross-stratification. Several of the reworked layers contain volcanic gravels mainly of andesitic composition.

ANDESITE OF SAGUACHE CREEK

A local accumulation of gray andesitic lavas as much as 200 feet thick occurs between the Sapinero Mesa Tuff and the Fish Canyon Tuff just north of Saguache Creek along the south-central margin of the map area where they overlie the water-laid and air-fall tuffs described above. The andesitic lavas form prominent cliffs, and lithologically resemble the andesite of Ford Creek. This younger accumulation of andesite within the ash-flow sequence is similar to the intermediate lavas interbedded and associated with the major ash-flow sheets of the San Juan volcanic field as described by Lipman, Steven and Mehnert (1970).

FISH CANYON TUFF

The Fish Canyon Tuff is a distinctive ash-flow tuff that characteristically forms light salmon-colored vertical cliffs and rounded, pedestal and beehive forms on the mesas above these cliffs. Many of the surface characteristics result from weathering of a moderately welded crystal-rich tuff cut by crude columnar joints. Extensive outcrops are found along the western portion of the map area and on the slopes of Trickle Mountain and Houghland Hill (fig. 4). A local maximum thickness is about 550 feet.

The Fish Canyon is a crystal-rich quartz latite tuff, commonly containing more than 50 percent phenocrysts. The phenocrysts are mainly andesine, sanidine, and biotite, with lesser quartz and hornblende. Pumice lapilli are also common. Lipman, Steven and Mehnert (1970) indicate that it was erupted from the La Garita caldera, some 30-40 miles southwest of the area about 28 m.y. ago. The La Garita Quartz Latite represents the intercaldera equivalent (fig. 3). They estimate the area covered by the Fish Canyon Tuff to have been 15,000 sq. km. with a volume in excess of 3,000 cu. km.

ANDESITE OF TRICKLE MOUNTAIN

Gray, vesicular, and platy andesite comprises the upper one-third of Trickle Mountain and rests on the Fish Canyon Tuff. The rock is similar to that of the andesite of Saguache Creek but of younger stratigraphic position. Its relation to the Carpenter Ridge Tuff is unknown. The andesite of Trickle Mountain is temporally coincident with the intermediate lavas associated with the major ash-flow sheets in the San Juan field.

CARPENTER RIDGE TUFF

The youngest of the San Juan ash-flow sheets present in the Trickle Mountain and Lake Mountain NE quadrangles is the Carpenter Ridge Tuff (Olson, Hedlund and Hansen, 1968). Lipman, Steven and Mehnert (1970) show that the tuff was erupted from the Bachelor caldera along the western side of the La Garita caldera, and that its intercaldera equivalent is the Bachelor Mountain Rhyolite.

The Carpenter Ridge Tuff forms extensive grass-covered

dip slopes between Sheep Creek and the western edge of the map area. Canyons that cut these slopes are flanked by prominent cliffs formed by both the Carpenter Ridge and the Fish Canyon Tuffs; these are well displayed above Colorado State Highway 114 where it follows East Pass Creek. Other excellent outcrops of the Carpenter Ridge occur on the upper slopes of Houghland Hill where it attains a maximum thickness of about 400 feet (fig. 4).

The Carpenter Ridge Tuff generally consists of a compound cooling unit in which two densely welded zones are separated by a few feet of partially welded ash. The upper and lower densely welded zones consist of black vitrophyre which commonly contains reddish brown lithophysae and aphanitic spherulites that appear nearly identical to the densely welded, devitrified rocks in the Sapinero Mesa Tuff. The thin, light gray unwelded base of the ash-flow sheet is generally covered by talus from the overlying cliffs, but it is well exposed in the highway cuts along East Pass Creek.

The Carpenter Ridge Tuff is a crystal-poor quartz latite with 5-10 per cent phenocrysts. The phenocrysts are mainly andesine, sanidine, biotite, with lesser quartz, and hornblende. Flattened pumice lapilli are also common. The Sapinero Mesa and Carpenter Ridge Tuffs are closely similar in megascopic appearance, and the formations can easily be misidentified where the intervening, distinctive Fish Canyon Tuff is absent.

Hinsdale Formation (basalt)

Houghland Hill, in the southeastern part of the Lake Mountain NE quadrangle, is capped by about 120 feet of gray to black, vesicular basalt flows of the Hinsdale Formation (Larsen and Cross, 1956). Basalt and associated rhyolite of the Hinsdale Formation are the youngest volcanic rocks in most of the San Juan volcanic field and occur in numerous scattered and isolated outcrops. They have been shown to range in age from about 5 to 23.5 m.y. (fig. 3) by Lipman, Steven and Mehnert (1970).

Post-volcanic Deposits

The only post-volcanic units in the area include a variety of Holocene surficial deposits. These include modern stream gravels and sands, older stream terrace deposits, small alluvial fans and cones, and several small landslide blocks. They are not differentiated in the accompanying geologic map (fig. 2) and are shown collectively as Quaternary alluvium (Qal).

STRUCTURE OF THE TRICKLE MOUNTAIN AND LAKE MOUNTAIN NE QUADRANGLES

Because the main purpose of this report is a description of the stratigraphy, only a brief account of the structural geology of the quadrangles is included. The mid-Tertiary volcanic rocks have been involved in both folding and faulting. Examples of larger tectonic folds include the north-northeast-trending Sheep Creek syncline on the west and the Mill Gulch syncline on the east. Small compactional folds are common in all of the ash-flow sheets and clearly reflect topographic patterns underlying them. The most significant block-faulting is displayed along the Sheep Creek fault zone where several hundred feet of displacement can be observed. This fault zone is known to continue south of the Trickle Mountain quadrangle for more than 7 miles. A number of small northeast-trending faults in the Lake Mountain NE quadrangle may be related to a broad system of radial faults associated with the Bonanza volcanic center to the northeast (Bruns, 1971; Knepper and Marrs, this guidebook). All of the rocks in the area older than the Hinsdale basalt are involved in folding and faulting. This history probably reflects the regional period of Middle to Late Cenozoic block faulting and attendant erosion which affected large segments of south-central Colorado as outlined by Steven and Epis (1968).

SUMMARY

The Trickle Mountain and Lake Mountan NE quadrangles provide physical stratigraphic correlations between units derived from the Bonanza center and units that comprise the rest of the San Juan volcanic field. The Bonanza units are equivalent to the early intermediate rocks in the field (35-30 m.y. old), and underlie the great ash-flow sheets derived from caldera-source areas in the central and western parts of the field. The Bonanza Tuff intertongues with rocks believed to be equivalent to the upper part of the Conejos Formation as that unit has been mapped to the south. Basalt of the Hinsdale Formation caps both the units derived from the Bonanza center and the ash-flow tuffs from the west and southwest; this basalt probably was erupted some time during the Miocene or Pliocene as similar basalts have been dated as ranging between 23.5 and 5 m.y. in age. Post-Oliogocene folding and block faulting have deformed the volcanic and older rocks.

REFERENCES

Bruns, D. L., 1971, Geology of the Lake Mountain Northeast Quadrangle, Saguache County, Colorado: Unpub. M.Sc. thesis, Colorado School of Mines, 79 p.

Burbank, W. S., 1932, Geology and ore deposits of the Bonanza Mining District, Colorado: U.S. Geol. Survey Prof. paper no. 169, 166 p.

Epis, R. C., and Chapin, C. E., 1968, Geologic History of the Thirtynine Mile Volcanic Field, Central Colorado, in Epis, R. C., editor, Quart. Colo. School of Mines, v. 63, no. 3, p. 51-85.

Knepper, D. H., and Marrs, R. W., 1971, Geologic development of the northern San Luis Valley and Bonanza volcanic center: this volume.

Larsen,, E. S., and Cross, W., 1956, Geology and petrology of the San Juan region, southwestern Colorado: U.S. Geol. Survey Prof. Paper no. 285, 303 p.

Lipman, P. W., 1968, Geology of Summer Coon volcanic center, eastern San Juan Mountains, Colorado, in Epis, R. C., editor, Cenozoic volcanism in the southern Rocky Mountains, Quart., Colo. School of Mines, v. 63, no. 3, p. 211-236.

Lipman, P. W., Steven, T. A., and Mehnert, H. H., 1970, volcanic history of the San Juan Mountains, Colorado, as indicated by potassium-argon dating: Geol. Soc. of Amer. Bull., v. 81, p. 2329-2352.

Luedke, R. G., and Burbank, W. S., 1963, Tertiary volcanic stratigraphy in the western San Juan Mountains, Colorado, in Short papers in geology and hydrology: U.S. Geol. Survey Prof. Paper 475-C, p. C39-C44.

Marrs, R. W., in progress, Geology of the southwestern part of the Bonanza volcanic center, Saguache County, Colorado: Ph.D. dissertation, Colorado School of Mines.

Mayhew, J. D., 1969, Geology of the eastern part of the Bonanza volcanic field, Saguache County, Colorado: Unpub. M.Sc. thesis, Colorado School of Mines, 94 p.

Olson, J. C., Hedlund, D. C., and Hansen, W. R., 1968, Tertiary region, Gunnison and Montrose counties, Colorado. U.S. Geol. Survey Bull. 1251-C, 29 p.

Patton, H. B., 1916, Geology and ore deposits of the Bonanza District, Saguache County, Colorado: Colorado State Geol. Survey Bull. no. 9, 136 p.

Perry, H. A., 1971, Geology of the northern part of the Bonanza volcanic field, Saguache County, Colorado: Unpub. M.Sc. thesis, Colorado School of Mines, 96 p.

Steven, T. A., and Ratté, J. C., 1965, Geology and structural control of ore deposition in the Creede district, San Juan Mountains, Colorado: U.S. Geol. Survey Prof. Paper 487, 90 p.

Steven, T. A., and Epis, R. C., 1968, Oligocene volcanism in south-central Colorado, in Epis, R. C., editor, Cenozoic volcanism in the southern Rocky Mountains: Quart. Colo. School of Mines, v. 63, no. 3., p. 241-258.

THE RIO GRANDE RIFT, PART I: MODIFICATIONS AND ADDITIONS

by

Charles E. Chapin

New Mexico Bureau of Mines and Mineral Resources
Socorro, New Mexico

INTRODUCTION

The Rio Grande rift cleaves New Mexico in two and splits Colorado halfway up the middle. For about 600 miles, it provides the highest mountains and deepest intermontane basins of the territory it traverses. It is somewhat like a plowed furrow with raised shoulders and half full of soil (see fig. 1). Topographic relief ranges up to 8,000 feet and averages about 5,000 feet along the main basins. Bedrock relief varies from several hundred feet in some of the smaller basins to a staggering 36,000 feet in the San Luis Basin. Thickness of alluvial fill ranges from 400 feet in the embryonic Estancia Basin to an estimated 30,000 feet in the San Luis Basin and probably averages at least 5,000 feet. Three-fourths of the population of New Mexico, plus the inhabitants of a number of communities in Colorado, Texas, and Chihuahua, live along this gigantic scar and derive much of their irrigable land and water supply from it.

Bryan (1938, p. 197, fig. 45; p. 198) coined the term "Rio Grande depression" to describe the series of basins followed by the Rio Grande from the San Luis Valley of Colorado through New Mexico to El Paso, Texas. Within this length, he outlined 8 structural basins (San Luis, Espanola, Santo Domingo, Albuquerque-Belen, Socorro, Engle, Rincon, or Las Palomas and Mesilla) separated from each other by canyons or constrictions and likened the Rio Grande to: ". . . a stream flowing from one sand-filled tub to another through narrow troughs" (op. cit., p. 198). Kelley (1952, 1954, 1956) described many structural details of the depression and discussed their regional tectonic setting. Much of our understanding of the rift has developed over a period of many years from stratigraphic, paleontologic and hydrologic investigations of the alluvial fill, from geomorphic studies of erosion surfaces and from geophysical profiles of the rift structure. So many researchers are involved that space does not permit a systematic review of their contributions; some of the more important papers are cited in the text.

The purpose of this paper is to examine the extent and boundaries of the rift and to propose modifications where necessary. The central portion of the rift is relatively distinct geomorphically, but the ends need some discussion and modification. In the following sections, evidence will be presented for adding the upper Arkansas graben at the north end, for including a number of small downwarps along the inflection line of the uplifted eastern border, for widening the rift south of the Albuquerque Basin into a series of parallel basins separated by intrarift horsts, for bifurcation of the rift along a weakly-developed, southwest-trending limb through the San Augustin Basin and for a possible extension of the rift into the Los Muertos Basin of northern Chihuahua. Figure 2 shows the extent of the rift as visualized by the author and some of the features to be discussed later.

It was originally intended to center the paper around a series of observations about the rift and a model synthesized from them. However, in the process of writing the paper, it was realized: (1) that the characteristics of an object are somewhat dependent upon where the boundaries are placed and (2) that data from geological field work over the past decade suggests that a number of modifications should be made to the boundaries of the Rio Grande rift from those originally set forth by Bryan (1938) and Kelley (1952). To both modify the boundaries and derive the model would make this paper overly long, hence the project has been divided into two parts with the observations and the model to be published in a later paper. A brief abstract of Part II is included here to provide perspective for the boundary problems (and controversy for the field trip).

ABSTRACT OF PART II

Rifting began at least 18 million years ago as evidenced by the Middle and Late Miocene fossils in basal alluvial fill and by K-Ar dates on interbedded volcanic rocks. Concurrent volcanism has occurred mainly along the medial axis and west side of the rift; present hot spring activity (Summers, 1965) shows a similar distribution. Compared to other rift valleys, the alluvial fill in the Rio Grande depression was relatively free of interbedded volcanic rocks until about 5 million years ago when volcanism became more prominent. A histogram of published K-Ar dates, supplemented by archaeological dates and geomorphic estimates on very young flows, suggest that the rate of volcanism may be increasing. Lipman (1969) has recently demonstrated that primitive tholeiitic flood basalts were erupted in the Rio Grande rift near Taos while alkalic, crustally contaminated basalts were being erupted to either side. He suggested that high heat flow and an upward protrusion of the mantle beneath the rift may have allowed fractionation of basalt to take place at an unusually shallow depth. Renault (1970) has shown that basalts within the rift near Las Cruces and west of the rift near Grants are relatively undifferentiated compared to basalts east of the rift.

South of the upper Arkansas Valley, structural relief is greater along the east side of the rift. Precambrian and Paleozoic rocks generally comprise the uplifts to the east, whereas thick sections of Tertiary volcanic and sedimentary rocks form much of the western boundary. The

FIGURE 1.

Apollo 9 photograph looking NNW up the Rio Grande rift from an altitude of about 130 miles. To the north, the camera is looking directly up the narrow cleft of the upper Arkansas graben with the snow-covered Colorado Parks to the right. The Rio Grande rift bends to the SSW near Alamosa and trends diagonally to the left, leaving the field of view near the south end of the Albuquerque Basin. Note the Pleistocene Valles caldera on the west margin of the rift north of Albuquerque and the Estancia Basin east of Albuquerque. Sierra Blanca and the Tularosa Basin are just off the lower left corner. The Wasatch trench, which is part of a rift system bounding the west side of the Colorado Plateau in Utah and Arizona, is visible in the upper left corner. Photo courtesy of the National Aeronautics and Space Administration and the Bonanza Remote Sensing Project of the Colorado School of Mines and the Martin-Marietta Corporation.

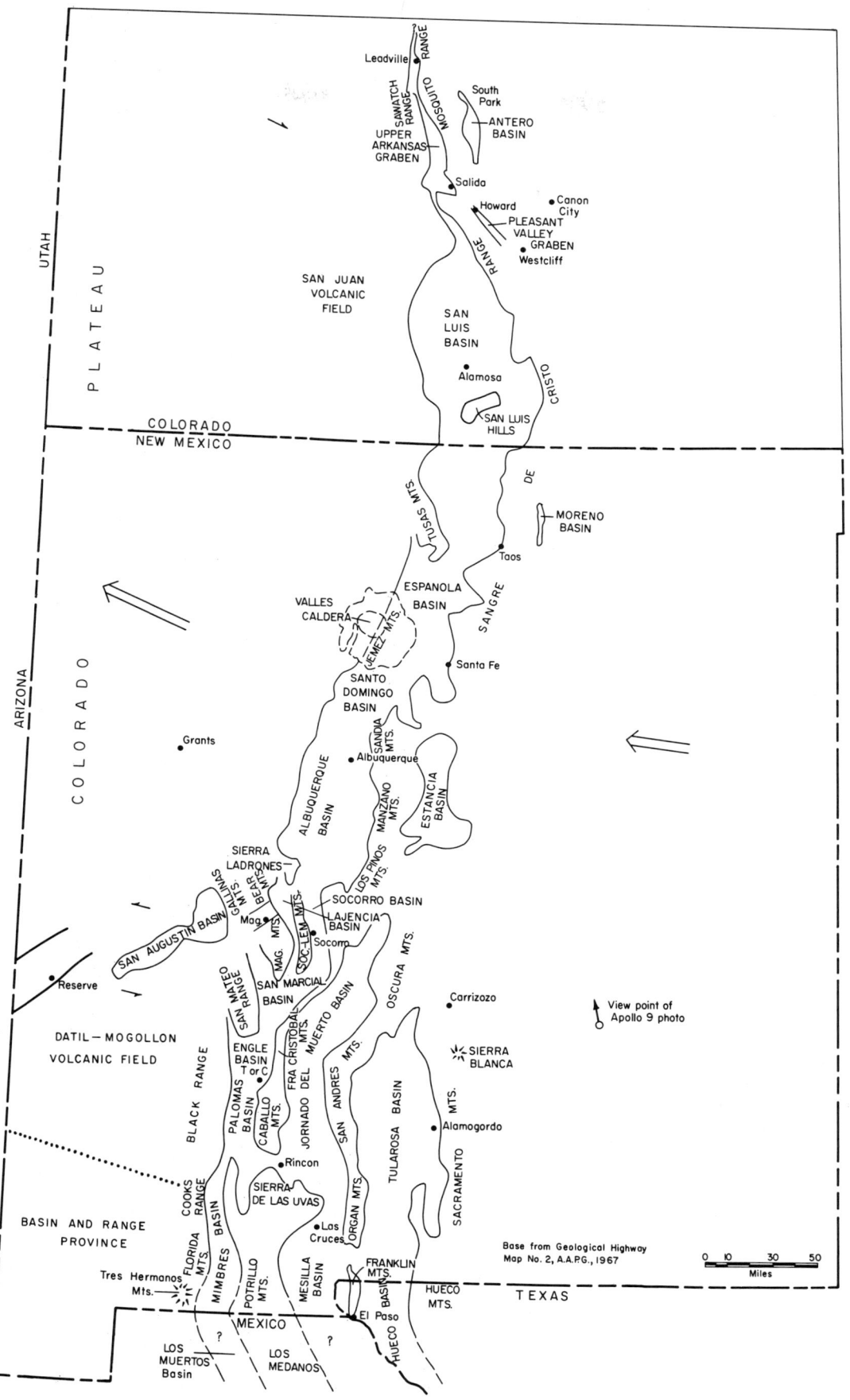

FIGURE 2.
Generalized map of the Rio Grande Rift.

southern Rocky Mountains were beveled by an erosion surface of moderately low relief in the Late Eocene; thus the disappearance of great thicknesses of Oligocene volcanic rocks across the rift must be ascribed to Late Tertiary uplift and erosion rather than to nondeposition. Assuming an average elevation of 2,000 feet for the erosion surface in Late Eocene time, minimum uplift was approximately 5,000 to 12,000 feet during Late Tertiary time for ranges east of the rift and minimum subsidence was 4,000 to 24,000 feet within the rift. Numerous fault scarps cut-

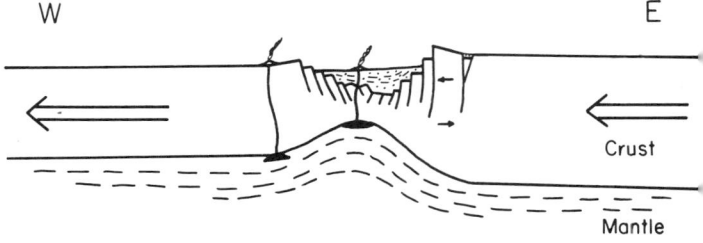

FIGURE 4.

Hypothetical cross-section of the Rio Grande rift. The large arrows indicate direction and relative rate of drift of continental plates. The small arrows indicate a force couple acting on the east shoulder of the rift. Freund (1965, p. 340) has experimentally produced a similar, but symmetric, model of the rifting and "necking" of sand above a convection current in a heavy fluid substratum.

ting alluvial fans and Pleistocene surfaces indicate that differential movement is continuing.

Synthesis of the above observations suggests the following model (see figs. 3 and 4): (1) the continental plate west of the rift is drifting faster than the continental interior (mantle convection may be pulling it over the East Pacific Rise in a "conveyor belt" manner similar to that suggested by Cook, 1962); resultant crustal attenuation formed the Basin and Range province and is splitting the Colorado Plateau block away from the interior; (2) the east side of the rift developed greater structural relief due to riding up of thicker crust onto an upward bulge of mantle material beneath the rift; (3) the west side of the rift is relatively subdued due to crustal stretching accompanied by abundant normal faulting and a tendency to pull the crust away from the mantle bulge beneath the rift; (4) stretching and normal faulting along the west side relieves subcrustal pressure and provides avenues for ascent of magmas and hydrothermal solutions; (5) longitudinal faults along the east side are relatively tight and unconducive to magmatism; westward drift of the interior block against the mantle bulge tends to rotate the fault planes to a near vertical position and may change the sense of movement from normal to reverse; (6) northwestward drift of the Colorado Plateau as suggested by Eardley (1962) causes a slight clockwise rotation against the north end of the rift which tends to keep it tight and relatively free of volcanism; this may also explain the unusually high upthrusting of the Sangre de Cristo horst along the east side of the San Luis Valley; (7) continued widening of the Rio Grande rift in New Mexico appears to be accelerating volcanism and may cause the rift to evolve into a lava-filled trough similar to the Snake River rift.

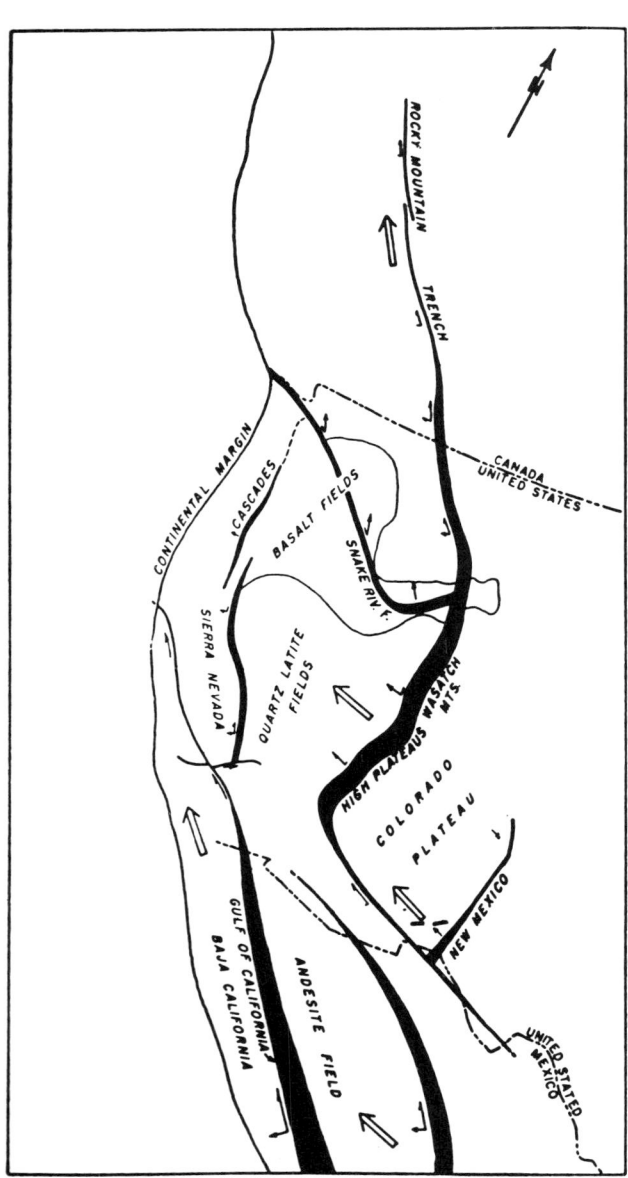

FIGURE 3.

Diagrammatic map exploring the concept of extension and drift affecting western North America. Black lines represent amount of expansion as if localized along a few separations. Small arrows represent apparent vectors of movement; large arrows the apparent resultant direction of the movement. From Eardley (1962, p. 510) with slight modifications along the Rio Grande rift.

THE UPPER ARKANSAS GRABEN AND PROBLEMS OF THE NORTH END

North of the San Luis Basin of Colorado, a narrow, north-tapering, sharply defined trough extends for at least 60 miles to the continental divide north of Leadville (fig. 2). That this basin is a graben with a tectonic style similar to the Basin and Range province has been recognized by workers in the Leadville area for many years. Emmons, Irving, and Loughlin (1927, p. 97) recognized that Lower Paleozoic strata in the Mosquito Range had undergone at least 8,000 feet of post-ore uplift relative to the same strata in the upper Arkansas Valley at Leadville. They discussed the relative merits of subsidence versus uplift and spoke of the similarity of this faulting to that in the Great Basin. Their cross-sections (pl. 12) show the same progressive stepping down of strata towards the valley axis by numerous longitudinal faults as is characteristic all along the rift. Tweto (1948, pl. 7) showed this structure very well on a cross-section of the upper Arkansas Valley at Leadville and labeled the valley a graben. Both sets of cross-sections show a progressive steepening of the fault planes towards the east boundary of the graben, which culminates in upthrusting of the crest of the Mosquito Range along reverse faults.

Gableman (1952, p. 1608-1609), in a very perceptive discussion based largely on geomorphology, projected the graben structure of the San Luis Valley northward up the Arkansas Valley to Leadville. In 1960, Van Alstine and Lewis (p. B245) described Early Pliocene fossils from a 500-foot section of alluvial fill exposed near Salida. The following year, Tweto (1961, p. B133) named the alluvial fill of the upper Arkansas Valley the Dry Union Formation for exposures near Leadville and showed their continuous distribution along the valley. He also presented evidence for recurrent faulting of unconsolidated sediments continuing into Holocene time; this phenomenon is a nearly universal characteristic of the Rio Grande rift. Chapin and Epis (1964, p. 158) presented evidence for downfaulting of Oligocene ash-flows by as much as 2,100 feet in the Browns Canyon area north of Salida. But the real breakthrough came in 1968 when R. E. Van Alstine (p. C158) demonstrated that the Arkansas and San Luis Valleys are connected by a structural trough containing Late Tertiary sediments. The trough crosses Poncha Pass west of U.S. Highway 285 and is not obvious from that route. In a later paper Van Alstine (1970, p. B46) extended the age of the Dry Union Formation to Late Miocene on the basis of vertebrate fossils identified by G. E. Lewis. On the basis of similarities in structural style, age of alluvial fill, alignment, and physical continuity, the upper Arkansas graben is clearly part of the Rio Grande rift.

How far the Rio Grande rift extends beyond Leadville is uncertain. Geomorphically, it appears to end at about the Continental Divide; however, as Tweto (1968, p. 566) has recently pointed out, scattered *en echelon* north-trending faults extend northward to near the Wyoming line and may be related to the rift. Kelley (1956, 1970) has postulated that the Rio Grande depression, the Colorado Parks, and the Laramie Basin are linked in a right-lateral *en echelon* system of intermontane troughs. However, the intermontane parks of Colorado are Laramide basins distinct in structural style and age of sedimentary deposits from the post-Laramide grabens of the rift (see summary by Tweto, 1968, p. 563, 566, 567). The contrast is especially sharp between South Park and the adjacent upper Arkansas Valley. South Park is a Laramide basin which received at least 1,000 feet of andesitic extrusives of Paleocene age (57 m.y.) and 8,000 feet of arkosic conglomerates prior to folding and thrusting in the Late Paleocene or Early Eocene (Sawatzky, 1964, 1968). During the Late Eocene, South Park was beveled by a surface of low relief onto which Oligocene eruptive rocks and volcanic detritus from the adjacent Thirtynine Mile field (Epis and Chapin, 1968, p. 56) were emplaced. The only Late Tertiary sediments of appreciable thickness occur in the Antero syncline in the extreme southwest corner of the park. This small basin developed synchronously with the Rio Grande rift as a small subsidiary downwarp along the inflection line of its uplifted eastern shoulder and will be discussed in the following section. In contrast, the area now occupied by the upper Arkansas Basin was situated high on the flanks of the Sawatch anticline until the Miocene when subsidence accompanying regional uplift split the anticline to form a narrow, highly-elongate graben. Streams flowed eastward off the Sawatch anticline in the Late Eocene and were filled with ash-flow tuffs in the Oligocene; these paleovalleys and their volcanic rocks have been tilted to the west and downfaulted over 2,000 feet into the upper Arkansas graben (Chapin, Epis, and Lowell, 1970; Lowell, 1969, and this guidebook). The upper Arkansas Valley then received 500 to 2,000 feet of Late Tertiary sediments which are very similar to those of the Santa Fe Group in New Mexico. Thus, the upper Arkansas graben is the northward extension of the Rio Grande rift, not the Colorado Parks.

INFLECTION BASINS

The sharply uplifted and outward-tilted shoulders of the rift are generally 10 to 30 miles in width beyond which the structural slope is more gentle. The change in slope is rather sharp and marked by an inflection line along which numerous faults, small folds, and local downwarps occur. These smaller structures parallel the rift and were formed contemporaneously with it. They appear to be more abundant east of the rift, probably because of the greater uplift and tilting on that side. Four local downwarps, whose development can be demonstrated to be synchronous with the rift, are the Antero, Pleasant Valley, Moreno, and Estancia basins; others probably exist.

The Antero Basin

The Antero Basin of southwestern South Park is a north-to-northwest-trending syncline, which parallels the upper Arkansas graben about 10 miles east of its rim. Oligocene ash-flow tuffs and volcaniclastic sedimentary rocks of the Thirtynine Mile field have been folded as much as 28 degrees about the synclinal axis (De Voto, 1964, p. 124). Alluvial fan deposits of the Late Tertiary Trump and Wagontongue formations are as much as 700 feet thick in the southern part of the syncline; these beds dip 5 degrees or less (op. cit.). Vertebrate fossils from the Wagontongue Formation have been identified by C. L. Gazin (in Stark and others, 1949, p. 69) and by G. E. Lewis (in De Voto, 1961, p. 168) as species of Late Miocene or Early Pliocene age. Thus, formation of the Antero Basin was approximately synchronous with development of the upper Arkansas graben. No Late Tertiary folding or sedimentation has been found east of the Antero Basin in the area occupied by South Park and the Thirtynine Mile volcanic field.

The Pleasant Valley Graben

The Pleasant Valley graben parallels the east side of the Sangre de Cristo Range from the vicinity of Westcliff in the Wet Mountain Valley northwestward to Howard in the canyon of the Arkansas River. It is about 3 miles wide and at least 25 miles long; the southern extent is difficult to determine because of cover by alluvial fans extending eastward off the Sangre de Cristo Range. Near Hillside, Oligocene ash-flow tuffs of the Thirtynine Mile field dip 10 to 20 degrees southwestward into the graben; at Goat Creek on the Sangre de Cristo side of the graben the same tuffs dip 20 to 40 degrees northeastward (Karig, 1963; Chapin and Epis, 1964, p. 158). Downfaulted blocks of these ash-flows are exposed at Oak Creek and near Howard and are overlain by alluvium which Tweto (1961, p. B133) tentatively correlated with the Dry Union Formation of the upper Arkansas Valley. The ash-flow tuffs at Oak Creek are about 1,400 feet lower in elevation than outcrops of the same units along the north rim of the Arkansas Canyon and at Goat Creek on the east flank of the Sangre de Cristo Mountains. Glenn Scott and R. B. Taylor of the U.S. Geological Survey are currently studying this area and a more complete picture is forthcoming.

The Moreno Basin

The Moreno Basin is a north-trending topographic and structural depression about 16 miles long and 3 to 4 miles wide located between the Sangre de Cristo and Cimarron Ranges in northern New Mexico. It is parallel to, and about 15 miles east of, the Rio Grande rift in the Taos area. According to Ray and Smith (1941, p. 208), the Moreno Valley is genetically similar to the Rio Grande depression and was formed approximately contemporaneously with it. The valley is a northward-plunging syncline bounded on both sides by longitudinal faults. The faulting and folding occurred after the development of a mid-Tertiary surface of low relief upon which the Picuris Formation of pre-Santa Fe age (Cabot, 1938; Galusha and Blick, 1971, p. 370) was deposited. Coalescing alluvial fans deposited an estimated 1,000 feet (Ray and Smith, p. 191) of debris within the downwarp; remnants of this alluvium, as much as 440 feet thick (Clark, 1966, p. 62), underlie the present valley and are known as the Eagle Nest Formation (Ray and Smith, p. 190).

The Estancia Basin

The Estancia Basin parallels the Albuquerque Basin about 20 miles east of its rim. With dimensions of about 55 by 35 miles, the Estancia Basin is the largest of the inflection basins considered here. It is also the youngest and contains only 300 to 400 feet of alluvial fill of Late Pliocene to Pleistocene age overlain by 100 feet of lacustrine sediments (Smith, 1957, p. 38-39; Titus, 1969, p. 40-42).

Smith correlated the alluvial fill with the upper beds of the Santa Fe Group north of Galisteo Creek; he considered the alluvium to have been "deposited in a structural basin which formed as a result of mild downwarping related to late stages of the development of the adjacent Rio Grande trough" (op. cit., p. 38). An additional 400 feet of subsidence has occurred in Late Pleistocene time (Titus, p. 153). The Estancia Basin occurs on a line connecting the Santa Fe embayment with the north end of the Tularosa Basin. Considering the youthfulness of the Estancia Basin, its recent downwarping, and the eruption of very young basalts at the north end of the Tularosa Basin (the Carrizozo flows estimated by R. H. Weber, 1971, oral communication, to be in the vicinity of 1,500 to 2,000 years old), it seems possible that the Rio Grande rift may be in the process of straightening its course between Santa Fe and the Tularosa Basin. If so, Chupadera Mesa and the Los Pinos-Manzano-Sandia uplift may become intrarift horsts as the Estancia downwarp develops into a major basin. Eardley (1962, p. 399) has also included the Estancia Basin as part of the rift belt.

PARALLEL BASINS AND INTRARIFT HORSTS

South of the Albuquerque Basin, the Rio Grande rift broadens into a series of parallel basins separated by intrarift horsts. This widens the depression from an average of about 30 miles in the northern two-thirds to about 100 miles in the southern one-third. Kelley (1952) restricted the southern portion of the rift to the narrow depression along the eastern edge of the Mogollon Plateau formed by the Socorro, San Marcial, Engle, and Palomas basins and their interspersed constrictions. Elston (1970, fig. 2) has recently shown the Rio Grande rift bifurcating to the southwest to include a number of small grabens within and around the edges of the Mogollon Plateau. Since our views differ appreciably, I will attempt in the following paragraphs to justify widening the rift to include the La Jencia, eastern Mimbres, Jornado del Muerto, Tularosa and Hueco basins. The criteria will again be similarities in alignment, age, sedimentation, and tectonic style. In this case, one additional criteria will be used: that of comparison with other rift systems which show that the maximum uplift occurs along the raised shoulders which dip away from the depression (Freund, 1965; Illies, 1969; Saggerson and Baker, 1965).

The most obvious subdivision of a basin by intrarift horsting occurs in the Socorro-La Jencia Basin. Here, the Socorro-Lemitar Mountains form a north-northwest-trending horst which splits the basin into two semiparallel halves. Uplift of this horst and accompanying volcanism began during deposition of the Popotosa Formation, a basal unit of the Santa Fe Group, and has continued to the present (Bryan, 1938; Denny, 1940; Burton, 1971). Several thousand feet of Popotosa beds have been uplifted and exposed by erosion between Polvadera Mountain and the Sierra Ladrones to yield a rare glimpse of the early sedimentary record of the Rio Grande rift. Volcanic conglomerates and playa deposits of the Popotosa Formation presently crop out as high as 2,000 feet above Socorro on the east face of Socorro Peak. Basaltic andesites, interbedded in the lower part of the Popotosa Formation and exposed along Silver Creek, have been dated at 16 million years (Weber, 1971, p. 34). They are overlain by playa deposits which have been intruded in the Socorro Peak volcanic center by rhyolitic domes and dikes. The Socorro Peak volcanism is Early Pliocene in age as indicated by K-Ar dates of 10.7 m.y. on a trachyandesite capping the peak (Weber, 1971, p. 41) and 11.7 m.y. on an intermediate dike in the adjacent Luis Lopez Manganese District (Willard, 1971). The Socorro Peak volcanism appears to have taken place largely, if not entirely, during the time span of the Popotosa Formation. Some domes were onlapped and buried by volcanic conglomerates which were later tilted and intruded by adjacent domes; flows interbedded with Popotosa beds have also been observed (Burton, 1971). Younger alluvium of the Santa Fe Group overlies the Popotosa Formation with angular unconformity; however, another period of relative uplift in the Late Pliocene or Early Pleistocene deformed the younger Santa Fe beds (Denny, 1940, p. 105; 1941, p. 259). High seismicity in the Socorro area (Sanford, 1963) and the presence of numerous Pleistocene and Holocene fault scarps (Budding and Toppozada, 1970) indicate that movement is continuing.

The Socorro-Magdalena area is a complex junction between the main south-trending stem of the rift and a weakly developed southwest-trending limb along the San Augustin Plains. The Socorro constriction of Kelley (1952, p. 97) is due to intrarift horsting which produces an illusion that the rift has narrowed. The basin in which the Popotosa Formation accumulated was at least 25 to 30 miles wide prior to horsting. Outcrops of volcanic conglomerates and mudflow breccias, very similar to beds in the Popotosa Formation on the Socorro-Lemitar uplift, occur to the east in the Joyita Hills and to the west on the summit and both flanks of the Magdalena Range. As previously noted, the Socorro-Lemitar mountains now occupy the axis of the basin as evidenced by the uplifted playa deposits. The Magdalena Range is also an intrarift horst with about 3,000 to 5,000 feet of Late Tertiary uplift relative to other Popotosa outcrops. To the west of the Magdalena Range, the San Mateo uplift appears to have been formed by block faulting along the east side of the Rio Grande rift. The extensive block faulting of the San Mateo-Magdalena area may be related to the fact that this wedge-shaped area is bounded on both the north and south by rift structures.

The Tularosa-Hueco Basin

South of Socorro, the Rio Grande rift is made up of three parallel north-trending basins separated by intrarift horsts. On the west, the San Marcial, Engle, Palomas, and eastern Mimbres basins form a narrow trough along the edge of the Mogollon Plateau. A central basin formed by the Jornado del Muerto and Mesilla basins is separated from the San Marcial-Mimbres trough by an intrarift horst made up of the Caballo, Fra Cristobal, Sierra de Las Uvas, and Potrillo mountains. An eastern basin, formed by the Tularosa and Hueco basins, is separated from the central basin by another intrarift horst formed by the Oscura, San Andres, Organ, and Franklin mountains. The Tularosa-Hueco Basin is bounded on the east by Sierra Blanca and the Sacramento and Hueco mountains which form the raised and outward-dipping eastern shoulder of the rift. Evidence to support inclusion of the above basins and horsts within the Rio Grande rift has become available largely in the last three or four years as a result of work published in the Border Stratigraphy Symposium (1969, Kottlowski and LeMone, eds.); the New Mexico Geological Society Guidebook of The Border Region (1969, Wengerd, ed.), and several reports on the ground-water resources of the area.

Each of these basins contains a substantial thickness of Late Cenozoic alluvial fill. The greatest known thickness occurs in the Tularosa-Hueco Basin where Mattick (1967, p. D85) estimated 9,000 feet of alluvium (gravity and seismic data) east of the Franklin Mountains; McLean (1970, p. 17) reported 6,015 feet of alluvium in a well drilled east of the Organ Mountains. The Tularosa-Hueco Basin is more than 160 miles long and 20 to 35 miles wide. It deepens to the south and is markedly asymmetric; the thickest fill is along the west side, the center is elevated several thousand feet as a suballuvial horst and shallower troughs occur along the east side (McLean, 1970, fig. 5). On the east side of the basin, in the vicinity of Alamogordo, seismic and gravity data indicate more than 3,000 feet of alluvium (op. cit., p. 17); the western escarpment of the Sacramento Mountains rises abruptly from this trough with about 8,600 feet of bedrock relief for 12 miles. The western border of this basin is equally abrupt and with even greater bedrock relief. The basin post-dates the uplifted and deeply dissected Sierra Blanca volcanic field (Sierra Blanca syenites, 27-34 m.y., Kottlowski, Weber, and Willard, 1969) and contains Pleistocene lacustrine sediments of Lake Cabeza de Vaca (Strain, 1966) in the upper part of the alluvial fill. The Tularosa-Hueco Basin is undoubtedly one of the major fault troughs of the southwest and is similar in age, alignment, and sedimentation to other basins of the Rio Grande rift. Eardley (1962, p. 399) has previously suggested thaat the Tularosa Basin is associated tectonically with the Rio Grande depression and is part of the general rift belt. Further evidence may be seen in a topographic profile across the rift at this latitude. The maximum elevations occur on Sierra Blanca (12,003 feet) and the Sacramento Mountains (9,686 feet) on the east and in the Black Range (10,130 feet) on the west. The intrarift horsts are generally 1,000 to 3,000 feet lower. Elevations along the other rift systems are generally greatest on the raised rims.

The Jornado Del Muerto-Mesilla Basin

The Jornado del Muerto-Mesilla Basin is about 160 miles in length above the Mexican border; averages 20 miles in width and deepens to the south. The central part of the Jornado del Muerto Basin is apparently quite shallow compared to either end (King and others, 1971, p. 17) and is different in one aspect from other basins of the rift: it is a broad syncline formed by east-dipping Paleozoic and Mesozoic strata along the Caballo-Fra Cristobal uplift and west-dipping Paleozoic strata in the San Andres Mountains. However, this structure is inherited from its location between two Laramide uplifts (Eardley, 1962, p. 399) and is not part of the Late Tertiary structural style. A gravity survey by Sanford (1968, p. 4, fig. 5) has revealed a deep depression in the northern end of the Jornado del Muerto which appears to be bounded by a sharp fault along its western margin and is estimated to contain about 3,000 feet of alluvial fill (op. cit., fig. 9). The south end of the Jornado del Muerto merges imperceptibly with the Mesilla Basin which is unquestionably a graben. An oil test in the north-central part of the Mesilla basin encountered 3,790 feet of alluvial fill (King and others, 1971, p. 22).

Uplift and erosion on the Caballo-Sierra de Las Uvas horst has exposed a thick section of lower and middle Santa Fe sediments in the Rincon-San Diego Mountain area at the southwest edge of the Jornado del Muerto. This area is similar to the Socorro-Lemitar uplift in providing an unusual opportunity to observe the basal Santa Fe sediments. Only by intrarift horsting or sharp tilting along the edge of a graben, as in the Espanola and upper Arkansas basins, is such an opportunity afforded. Hawley and others (1969, p. 68) and Seager and others (in press) measured 3,567 feet of Santa Fe Group alluvium in the Rincon-San Diego Mountain area. These sediments overlie mid-Tertiary volcanic rocks (Thurman Rhyolite Tuff, 33 m.y.; Uvas Basalt, 31 m.y.; Kottlowski, Weber, and Willard, 1969) and contain a basalt flow near the middle of the section which has been dated at 13 m.y. (Selden Basalt, op. cit.). Pleistocene deposits of Lake Cabeza de Vaca (Strain, 1966) and widespread alluvial deposits comprise the upper part of the Santa Fe Group in the Mesilla Basin. The Jornado del Muerto-Mesilla Basin is similar in age, alignment, and sedimentation to other basins of the Rio Grande rift in spite of having an inherited Laramide syncline in its central portion.

The San Marcial-Engle-Palomas-Eastern Mimbres Basin

The San Marcial, Engle, Palomas and eastern Mimbres basins form the narrowest of the three major parallel basins discussed in this section. Inclusion of the eastern Mimbres Basin is the main point to be considered here, since the other basins have already been included in the Rio Grande rift by Bryan and Kelley. Kottlowski (1958, p. 51) suggested that the Rio Grande rift terminates against the Sierra de Las Uvas at the south end of the Palomas Basin, while Bryan (1938) and Kelley (1954) considered it to extend southward to the Mexican border. Reeves (1969, p. 153), from a study of Pleistocene lake deposits and basin fill, has suggested that the Rio Grande depression might extend into the Los Muertos Basin of northern Chihuahua. As previously noted, there is an adequate thickness of Santa Fe sediments in the Mesilla Basin to justify extending the rift southward along the east side of the Sierra de Las Uvas and East Potrillo Mountains. Considering the general north-northeast trend of the rift, it seems inconsistent for the rift to abruptly jog eastward around the Sierra de Las Uvas in order to follow the Mesilla Basin. In the author's opinion, it is more likely that the Sierra de Las Uvas and Potrillo Mountains are an extension of the Caballo-Fra Cristobal intrarift horst and that the west edge of the Rio Grande trough extends southward along the east side of the Cooks and Florida mountains. Evidence to support such an extension may be found in (1) the northerly trend of Cooks Range and the Florida Mountains, as opposed to the strong northwesterly trend of ranges to the south and west; (2) the great depth of alluvial fill between the Tres Hermanos and Potrillo Mountains; (3) the presence of fault scarps along both sides of the Potrillo Mountain block which suggests that it is a horst bounded on both sides by grabens (see Reeves, 1960, figs. 1 and 8); and (4) Late Tertiary structural doming of the Sierra de Las Uvas and uplift of basal Santa Fe sediments along the Sierra de Las Uvas-Caballo axis which again suggests an intrabasin horst. Data on depth of alluvial fill in the eastern Mimbres Basin is very sparse. The Skelley No. 1A oil test between the Tres Hermanos and West Potrillo mountains encountered 4,650 feet of Santa Fe-Gila Conglomerate alluvium (Kottlowski, Foster, and Wengerd, 1969, p. 194). A short distance to the east, on the Potrillo horst, the Sunray No. 1 test penetrated only 520 feet of fill (op. cit., p. 193). Between these two drill holes is a north-northeast trending fault scarp which may mark the boundary of the eastern Mimbres Basin and the Potrillo Mountains horst. The same fault scarp turns southeastward at the Mexican border and extends over 70 miles into northern Chihuahua along the east side of the Los Muertos Basin (see Reeves, 1969, figs. 1 and 9).

THE PLEISTOCENE SUMP AND PROBLEMS OF THE SOUTH END

The basins and uplifts of the Rio Grande rift are predominantly north-trending structures in contrast to the northwesterly trends of the adjoining Mexican Highlands section of the Basin and Range province. The Hueco, Franklin, and Florida mountains are the southernmost ranges along the rift which have northerly trends; south of these ranges, the structural fabric is dominated by northwest trends. Using this criteria, the Rio Grande rift might be terminated along a line passing through El Paso and trending northwesterly along the south end of the Hueco, Franklin, and Florida mountains. Thus defined, the rift would end approximately at the Mexican border.

Using the criteria of sedimentation related to the rift, a case can be made for extending the rift at least 70 miles into northwestern Chihuahua. After through drainage was established along the Rio Grande rift in Early to Middle Pleistocene time (Kottlowski, 1958) large lakes developed in southern New Mexico, in the Hueco Basin of Texas, and in northern Chihuahua. These lakes were the "sump" for the ancestral Rio Grande, which lacked a passage to the sea until its capture at El Paso in mid-Pleistocene time (Late Kansan-Early Illinoian; Kottlowski, 1958; Strain, 1959, p. 377; 1969, p. 122). The lake basins received enormous quantities of sediment and must have subsided rapidly to accommodate the filling. Lake Cabeza de Vaca (Strain, 1966) covered part of the Tularosa Basin, most of the Hueco and Mesilla basins, and extended southward for at least 100 miles into Chihuahua during Early to mid-

Pleistocene time. About 600 feet of lacustrine deposits are exposed along the Rio Grande Valley southeast of El Paso and these have been dated as early to mid-Pleistocene by vertebrate remains (Strain, 1966). The maximum thickness of Lake Cabeza de Vaca sediments is unknown; several thousand feet of alluvial fill underlies the area, but how much of this is Late Tertiary bolson deposits rather than Pleistocene lacustrine sediments is uncertain.

Following capture of the ancestral Rio Grande and entrenchment of its valley, about 3,000 square miles in the Los Muertos Basin of northwestern Chihuahua and the eastern Mimbres Basin of New Mexico was inundated by pluvial Lake Palomas (Reeves, 1969). The lake appears to have been controlled in part by uplift of the Potrillo Mountains-Los Medanos block, thus forming a barrier between the Mimbres and Rio Cases Grandes drainages to the west and the Rio Grande drainage to the east. The Camel Mountain escarpment which bounds the west side of the Potrillo Mountains in New Mexico bends to the southeast at the international border and extends for at least 70 miles into Chihuahua. The escarpment is in part due to Pleistocene faulting (Reeves, 1969, p. 150) and figures 1, 3, and 8 of Reeves (op. cit.) show that the eastern boundary of Lake Palomas approximately coincides with this scarp. Gravity surveys across the southern part of the Los Muertos Basin indicate 3,500 to 13,000 feet of alluvial fill which Reeves (1969, p. 153) suggested might be another indication of the extent of the Rio Grande depression.

Thus, the question of the southern extent of the rift seems largely one of the nature of its junction with the Basin and Range province and of whether or not to include the Pleistocene "sump." It can be argued that a rift is a structural feature and that the sump could have formed in low areas of the adjacent Basin and Range province. Also, if the Rio Grande rift is forming by the splitting away of the Colorado Plateau block from the continental interior, it may not be reasonable to extend the rift beyond the southern edge of the plateau, especially since its southern boundary is probably a major zone of strike slip movement (Eardley, 1962, p. 311). Also involved are questions as to whether an upwelling of mantle material is causing the rift, or whether the pulling away of the Colorado Plateau is causing an upwelling of mantle material; or, as Atwater (1970) and Stewart (1971) have recently suggested, the Late Tertiary structure of the Basin and Range province may be due to tensional crustal fragmentation subsidiary to right-lateral movement between the Pacific and North American plates. These questions cannot be answered here and the nature of the southern terminus of the Rio Grande rift is not critical to the derivation of a model.

BIFURCATION ALONG THE SAN AUGUSTIN LINEAMENT

A northeast-trending lineament transects the Datil-Mogollon volcanic field and intersects the Rio Grande rift near Magdalena, New Mexico. The lineament is marked by a series of en echelon northeast-trending fault zones and grabens, the largest of which forms the San Augustin Basin. Near the southwest end of this basin, 2,000 feet of unconsolidated sediments were cored by a research group from Oberlin College (Foreman, Clisby, and Sears, 1959) without encountering volcanic rocks; two older wells are reported to have penetrated 1,000 feet of fill (Stearns, 1962, p. 31). The San Augustin Basin was the site of a Pleistocene lake which at its highest level in Wisconsinian time was 34 miles long, 11 miles wide, and 165 feet deep (op. cit., p. 29). While not conclusive evidence, a marked lithologic change at a depth of 950 feet in the Oberlin hole and the presence of a relict Tertiary flora below this depth suggests that the hole penetrated sediments as old as Pliocene (Foreman, Clisby, and Sears, 1959, p. 120). The Sun No. 1 San Augustin oil test, drilled in 1966 on a structural saddle between the southwestern and northeastern segments of the basin, penetrated only 230 feet of alluvial fill followed by 2,530 feet of the Hells Mesa Formation (31-32 m.y., Weber, 1971) and 1,860 feet of the Spears Formation 37 m.y., op. cit.) before encountering pre-Oligocene rocks (R. W. Foster, 1971, written communication). These thicknesses indicate that a nearly complete section of the Datil Group has been downfaulted and underlies the San Augustin graben. The Spears-Hells Mesa contact occurs at elevations of about 8,000 feet along the northwest side of the graben versus about 4,300 feet in the Sun No. 1 hole. The structural relief in this shallow part of the basin is about 3,700 feet; it may be twice as great in deeper portions of the basin.

Southwest of the San Augustin Basin, the town of Reserve is located in a narrow valley which follows a prominent zone of northeast-trending faults (Weber and Willard, 1959). The faults are progressively downthrown towards the valley axis to form a shallow graben which contains an unknown thickness of Gila Conglomerate. Ratté and others (1969, p. E21) have recently mapped a belt of northeast-trending faults which form a graben 15 to 30 miles wide in the Blue Range Primitive Area southwest of Reserve. This fault zone crosses the regional northwesterly structural trend and is an extension to the faulting at Reserve (op. cit., fig. 12). Faults of similar trend occur to the southwest near Morenci, Arizona. A rhyolitic ash-flow sheet dated at 25 m.y. (op. cit., p. E19) has been downfaulted 2,200 feet into the Blue River graben and is covered by at least 800 feet of Gila Conglomerate (op. cit., p. E17, E28).

Northeast of the San Augustin Basin, the lineament is marked by an alignment of low saddles between the San Mateo and Gallinas mountains and between the Magdalena and Bear mountains. Mapping in the southern Bear Mountains and Magdalena area by the author and D. M. Brown has revealed a number of northeast-trending faults which are probably related to the lineament. A major fault along U.S. Highway 60 appears to have offset the north end of the Anchor Canyon stock (28 m.y., Weber, 1971, p. 37) by left-lateral oblique slip motion; the block north of the fault has apparently been shifted 0.8 mile to the west and dropped about 2,000 feet in elevation. Along Bear Springs Draw in the southern Bear Mountains, another northeast-trending oblique-slip fault appears to have 1.0 to 1.5 miles of left-lateral movement and about 1,000 feet of uplift on the north side of the fault. Thus, the San Augustin lineament in the Magdalena area appears to be a 6-mile-wide belt of left-lateral movement which has created a zone of tension within which the crust is depressed by 1,000 to 2,000 feet relative to either side. The picture is complicated, however, by superimposed north-trending normal faults which have offset the northeast-trending faults. Such a zone of tension and left-lateral movement should be expected if the Colorado Plateau block in moving to the northwest were to partially break away from its southeastern corner (see fig. 3). Other faults along this lineament should be examined for possible left-lateral motion.

In summary, the San Augustine lineament transects rocks as young as Early Miocene and is marked by a series of *en echelon* grabens which have several hundred to several thousand feet of structural relief and which contain sediments of Late Tertiary to Pleistocene age. It is thus similar in style and age to the Rio Grande rift. As noted by Ratté and others (1969, p. E21), it crosses the northwesterly regional trend of Basin and Range structures and requires a different explanation. Elston (1970a; 1970b, fig. 2) has previously interpreted the San Augustin graben as a subsidiary structure to the Rio Grande trough. I believe that this zone represents a weakly developed southwest-trending limb of the Rio Grande rift which may have developed in an abortive attempt of the Colorado Plateau block to break away from its southeast corner. The apparent lack of fault scarplets along the San Augustin graben indicates that the zone has been quiescent in post-Wisconsin time (Stearns, 1962, p. 29). This is corroborated by a lack of recent seismicity (Sanford, 1971, oral communication).

SUMMARY

To the Rio Grande depression of Bryan (1938) and Kelley (1952), the author recommends the following modifications and additions:

(1) Extend the north end to include the upper Arkansas graben.
(2) Widen the rift south of the Albuquerque Basin to include a series of 3 major parallel basins separated by intrarift horsts. The basins are: (a) the Socorro-San Marcial-Engle-Palomas-eastern Mimbres Basin, (b) the Jornado del Muerto-Mesilla Basin, and (c) the Tularosa-Hueco Basin.
(3) Include the San Augustin lineament as a southwest-trending bifurcation.
(4) Include a number of subsidiary basins along the inflection line of the raised shoulders. Four such basins are the Antero, Pleasant Valley, Moreno, and Estancia basins; others probably exist.
(5) Consider a possible extension of the rift into northern Chihuahua along the Los Muertos Basin. This decision must await further research on the nature of the junction of the Rio Grande rift with the Basin and Range province.

REFERENCES

Atwater, T., 1970, Implications of plate tectonics for the Cenozoic tectonic evolution of western North America: Geol. Soc. America Bull., v. 81, p. 3513-3536.

Budding, A. J., and Toppozada, T. R., 1970, Late Cenozoic faulting in the Rio Grande rift valley near Socorro, New Mexico, in New Mexico Geol. Soc. Guidebook, 21st Field Conf., Oct., 1970: p. 161.

Burton, Craig, 1971, Geology of the Socorro Peak area: Socorro, N. Mex. Inst. Min. and Tech., unpub. report, 37p.

Bryan, Kirk, 1938, Geology and ground-water conditions of the Rio Grande depression in Colorado and New Mexico, p. 197-225 in Regional planning, Pt. 6, Upper Rio Grande: Washington, Natl. Resources Comm., v. 1, pt. 2, sec. 1.

Cabot, E. C., 1938, Fault border of the Sangre de Cristo Mountains north of Santa Fe, New Mexico: Jour. Geol., v. 46, p. 88-105.

Chapin, C. E., and Epis, R. C., 1964, Some stratigraphic and structural features of the Thirtynine Mile volcanic field, central Colorado: Mtn. Geologist, v. 1, p. 145-160.

Chapin, C. E., Epis R. C., and Lowell, G. R., 1970, Late Eocene paleovalleys and Oligocene volcanic rocks along the upper Arkansas Valley segment of the Rio Grande rift zone in Colorado, (abs.) in New Mexico Geol. Soc. Guidebook, 21st Field Conf., Oct., 1970: p. 159-160.

Clark, K. F., 1966, Geology of the Sangre de Cristo Mountains and adjacent areas, between Taos and Raton, New Mexico, in New Mexico Geol. Soc. Guidebook, 17th Field Conf., Oct., 1966: p. 75-65.

Cook, K. L., 1962, The problem of the mantle-crust mix: lateral inhomogeneity in the uppermost part of the earth's mantle, in Landsberg, H. E. (ed.), Advances in geophysics: New York, Academic Press, v. 9, p. 295-360.

Dane, C. H., and Bachman, G. O., 1965, Geologic map of New Mexico U.S. Geol. Survey, New Mexico Bur. Mines and Mineral Res., and Univ. of New Mexico Geology Dept.

Denny, C. S., 1940, Tertiary geology of the San Acacia area, New Mexico: Jour. Geol., v. 48, p. 73-106.

——— 1941, Quaternary geology of the San Acacia Area, New Mexico: Jour. Geol., v. 49, p. 225-260.

DeVoto, R. H., 1961, Geology of Southwestern South Park, Park and Chaffee Counties, Colorado: unpub. D.Sc. thesis, Colorado School Mines, 323p.

DeVoto, R. H., 1964, Stratigraphy and structure of Tertiary rocks in southwestern South Park: Mtn. Geologist, v. 1, no. 3, p. 117-126.

Elston, W. E., 1970, Volcano-tectonic control of ore deposits, southeastern New Mexico, in New Mexico Geol. Soc. Guidebook 21st Field Conf., Oct., 1970: p. 147-153.

Elston, W. E., Coney, P. J., and Rhodes, R. C., 1970, Progress report on the Mogollon Plateau volcanic province, Southwestern New Mexico: No. 2, in New Mexico Geol. Soc. Guidebook, 21st Field Conf., Oct., 1970: p. 75-86.

Emmons, S. F., Irving, J. D., and Loughlin, G. F., 1927, Geology and ore deposits of the Leadville mining district, Colorado: U.S. Geol. Survey Prof. Paper 148, 368p.

Epis, R. C. and Chapin, C. E., 1968, Geologic history of the Thirtynine Mile volcanic field, central Colorado, in Epis, R. C., ed., Cenozoic volcanism in the southern Rocky Mountains: Colorado Sch. Mines Quart., v. 63, no. 3, p. 51-85.

Foreman, F., Clisby, K. H., Sears, P. B., and Stearns, C. E., 1959, Plio-Pleistocene sediments and climates of the San Augustin -Plains, New Mexico, in New Mexico Geol. Soc. Guidebook, 10th Field Conf., Oct., 1959: p. 117-120.

Freund, R., 1965, Rift valleys, in Irvine, T. N., ed., The world rift system: Canada Geol. Survey, paper 66-14, p. 330-344.

Gableman, J. W., 1952, Structure and origin of northern Sangre de Cristo Range, Colorado: Am. Assoc. Petroleum Geologists Bull., v. 36, no. 8, p. 1574-1612.

Galusha, T., and Blick, J. C., 1971, Stratigraphy of the Santa Fe Group, New Mexico: Am. Mus. Nat. Hist. Bull., v. 144, art. 1.

Hawley, J. W., Kottlowski, F. E., Strain, W. S., Seager, W. R., King, W. E., and LeMone, D. V. 1969, The Santa Fe Group in the south-central New Mexico border region *in* Kottlowski, F. E., and LeMone, D. V., ed., Border Stratigraphy Symposium: New Mexico Bur. Mines and Mineral Res., Circ. 104, p. 52-76.

Illies, J. H., 1969, An intercontinental belt of the world rift system: Tectonophys., v. 8, p. 5-29.

Karig, D. E., 1963, Structural analysis of the Sangre de Cristo Range, Venable Peak to Crestone Peak, Custer and Saguache County, Colorado: Unpub. M.S. thesis, Colorado School Mines, 143p.

Kelley, V. C., 1952, Tectonics of the Rio Grande depression of central New Mexico, *in* New Mexico Geol. Soc. Guidebook, 3rd Field Conf., Oct., 1952: p. 93-105.

——— 1954, Tectonic map of a part of the Rio Grande area, New Mexico: U.S. Geol. Survey Oil and Gas Inv. Map OM-157.

——— 1956, The Rio Grande depression from Taos to Santa Fe, *in* New Mexico Geol. Soc. Guidebook, 7th Field Conf., Oct., 1956: p. 109-114.

——— 1970, Highlights of the Rio Grande depression (abs.), *in* New Mexico Geol. Soc. Guidebook, 21st Field Conf., Oct., 1970, p. 157.

King, W. E., Hawley, J. W., Taylor, A. M., and Wilson, R. P., 1971, Geology and ground-water resources of central and western Dona Ana County, New Mexico: New Mexico Bur. Mines and Mineral Res., Hydrologic Rpt. 1, 64p.

Kottlowski, F. E., 1958, Geologic history of the Rio Grande near El Paso, *in* Guidebook of Franklin and Hueco Mountains, Texas: West Texas Geol. Soc. Guidebook, Field Trip, p. 46-54.

——— Foster, R. W., and Wengerd, S. A., 1969, Key oil tests and stratigraphic sections in southwestern New Mexico, *in* New Mexico Geol. Soc. Guidebook, 20th Field Conf., Oct., 1969, p. 186-196.

——— and LeMone, D. V., editors, 1969, Border stratigraphy symposium: New Mexico Bur. Mines and Mineral Res., Circ. 104, 123 p.

——— Weber, R. H., and Willard, M. E., 1969, Tertiary intrusive-volcanic-mineralization episodes in the New Mexico region (abs.): Geol. Soc. America, Abstracts with Programs for 1969, v. 1, no. 7, p. 278-280.

Lipman, P. W., 1969, Alkalic and tholeiitic basaltic volcanism related to the Rio Grande depression, southern Colorado and northern New Mexico: Geol. Soc. America Bull., v. 80, p. 1341-1354.

Lowell, G. R., 1969, Geologic relationships of the Salida area to the Thirtynine Mile volcanic field of central Colorado: Unpub. Ph.D. dissertation, N. Mex. Inst. Min. and Tech., 113 p.

Mattick, R. E., 1967, A seismic and gravity profile across the Hueco Bolson, Texas: U.S. Geol. Survey Prof. Paper 575-D, p. D85-D91.

McLean, J. S., 1970, Saline ground-water resources of the Tularosa Basin, New Mexico: U.S. Geol. Survey OSW Report no. 14-01-0001-2091, 128p.

Oetking, P., Feray, D. E., and Renfro, H. B., 1967, Geological highway map of the southern Rocky Mountain Region: Am. Assoc. Petroleum Geol. and U.S. Geol. Survey, United States Geological Highway Map no. 2.

Ratté, J. C., Landis, E. R., Gaskill, D. L., and Raabe, R. G., 1969, Mineral resources of the Blue Range primitive area Greenlee County, Arizona, and Catron County, New Mexico, with a section on aeromagnetic interpretations by G. P. Eaton: U.S. Geol. Survey Bull. 1261-E., 91p.

Ray, L. L., and Smith, J. F., Jr., 1941, Geology of the Moreno Valley, New Mexico: Geol. Soc. America Bull., v. 52, p. 177-210.

Reeves, C. C., 1969, Pluvial Lake Palomas Northwestern Chihuahua, Mexico, *in* New Mexico Geol. Soc. Guidebook, 12th Field Conf., Oct., 1969, p. 143-154.

Renault, J., 1970, Major-element variations in the Potrillo, Carrizozo, and McCartys basalt fields, New Mexico: New Mexico Bur. Mines and Mineral Res., Circ. 113, 22p .

Saggerson, E. P., and Baker, B. H., 1965, post-Jurassic erosion surfaces in eastern Kenya and their deformation in relation to rift structure: Geol. Soc. London, Quart. Jour., v. 121, p. 51-72.

Sanford, A. R., 1963, Seismic activity near Socorro, New Mexico, *in* New Mexico Geol. Soc. Guidebook, 14th Field Conf., Oct., 1963, p. 144-151.

——— 1968, Gravity survey in central Socorro County, New Mexico: New Mexico Bur. Mines and Mineral Res., Circ. 91, 14p.

Sawatzky, D. L., 1964, Structural geology of southeastern South Park, Park County, Colorado: Mtn. Geologist, v. 1, p. 133-139.

——— 1969, The meaning of "Laramide Orogeny" in central Colorado, *in* Abstracts for 1968: Geol. Soc. America Spec. Paper 121, p. 633-634.

Seager, W. R., Hawley, J. W., and Clemons, R. E., in press, Geology of the San Diego Mountain area, Dona Ana County, New Mexico: New Mexico Bur. Mines and Mineral Res., Bull 97.

Smith, R. E., 1957, Geology and ground-water resources of Torrance County, New Mexico: New Mexico Bur. Mines and Mineral Res., Ground-water Report 5, 186p.

Stark J. T., Johnson, J. H., Behre, C. H., Jr., Powers, W. E., Howland, A. L., Gould, D. B., and others, 1949, Geology and origin of South Park Colorado: Geol. Soc. America Mem. 33, 177p.

Stearns, C. E., 1962, Geology of the north half of the Pelona Quadrangle, Catron County, New Mexico: New Mexico Bur. Mines and Mineral Res., Bull. 78, 46p.

Stewart, J. H., 1971, Basin and Range structure: a system of horsts and grabens produced by deep-seated extension: Geol. Soc. America Bull., v. 82, p. 1019-1044.

Strain, W. S., 1959, Blancan mammalian fauna from Rio Grande Valley, Hudspeth County, Texas: Geol. Soc. America Bull., v. 70, p. 375-378.

——— 1966, Blancan mammalian fauna and Pleistocene formations, Hudspeth County, Texas: Texas Mem. Mus., Bull. 10.

——— 1969, Late Cenozoic Strata of the El Paso area *in* Kottlowski, F. E., and LeMone, D. V., eds., Border Stratigraphy Symposium: New Mexico Bur. Mines and Mineral Res., Circ. 104, p. 122-123.

Summers, W. K., 1965, A preliminary report on New Mexico's geothermal energy resources: New Mexico Bur. Mines and Mineral Res., Circ. 80, 41 p.

Titus, F. B., 1969, Late Tertiary and Quaternary hydrogeology of Estancia Basin, central New Mexico: Unpub. Ph.D. dissertation, Univ. N. Mex., 179p.

Tweto, Ogden, 1948, Generalized geologic section from the Sawatch to the Mosquito Range, through Leadville *in* Guide to the geology of central Colorado: Colorado Sch. Mines Quart., v. 43, no. 2, plate 7, opposite page 98.

——— 1961, Late Cenozoic events of the Leadville district and upper Arkansas Valley, Colorado, *in* Short papers in the geologic and hydrologic sciences: U.S. Geol. Survey Prof. Paper 525-A, 376p.

——— 1968, Leadville district, Colorado, *in* Ridge, J. D., ed., Ore deposits in the United States 1933/1967: Am. Inst. Min. Met. Petrol. Engr., Graton-Sales Volume, v. 1, p. 681-705.

Van Alstine, R. E., 1968, Tertiary trough between the Arkansas and San Luis valleys, Colorado: U.S. Geol. Survey Prof. Paper 600-C, p. C158-C160.

——— 1970, Allochthonous Paleozoic blocks in the Tertiary San Luis-Upper Arkansas Graben, Colorado: U.S. Geol. Survey Prof. Paper 700-B, p. B43-B51.

——— and Lewis, G. E., 1960, Pliocene sediments near Salida, Chaffee County, Colorado, *in* Short papers in the geological sciences: U.S. Geol. Survey Prof. Paper 400-B, p. 245.

Weber, R. H., 1971, K-Ar ages of Tertiary igneous rocks in central and western New Mexico: Isochron/West, no. 71-1, p. 33-45.

——— and Willard, M. E., 1959, Reconnaissance geologic map of Reserve thirty-minute quadrangle: New Mexico Bur. Mines and Mineral Res., Geol. Map 12.

Willard, M. E., 1971, K-Ar ages of the volcanic rocks in the Luis Lopez manganese district, Socorro Co., New Mexico: Isochron/West 71-2, July 1971.

"THEY CAME TO HUNT"
Early Man In the San Luis Valley

by

Dorothy D. Wilson

Anthropology Museum
Adams State College
Alamosa, Colorado

The men who first came to the North American continent over 20,000 years ago were following big game animals over the Bering Strait when a land bridge existed there. His continued quest for game led him to all parts of the continent, and although it is questionable exactly how many thousands of years ago he first entered the San Luis Valley, he was undoubtedly following the big game trail. It seems he first came here after he had been on the continent for a considerable time because climatic conditions of the Wisconsin Glacial Period persisted longer in the valley than on the plains and conditions would not have been favorable for man or animals. But we do know he was here since we find nonperishable artifacts made of stone. It is only in the 20th Century that archaeologists have been able to establish any kind of definite dates for these artifacts when they have been found at sites connected with animal bones which could be dated. The oldest projectile point of the Paleo-Indians is the Sandia, dated at about 15,000 B.C. and associated with mastodon and mammoth bones. This was followed by the Clovis dated around 12,000 B.C. and associated with mammoth bones. A small number of each of these points have been found in the valley but not in connection with established sites.

Of Folsom man, dated at about 8,000 B.C., we have more evidence. Two sites, the Linger and the Zapata sites, located in the sand dunes area of the foot of the Sangre de Cristo Range, have been excavated, yielding bones attributed to a "Bison taylori," and Folsom points and scrapers. In 1941, C. T. Hurst with Gene Sutherland and Al Pearsall dug the Linger site and took from it 22 Folsom stone artifacts. Animal bones in a badly disintegrated condition were found with the artifacts and were identified as bison, which were in all probability an extinct species called "Bison taylori" (Hurst-1941). About a mile distant from the Linger site F. V. C. Worman investigated similar finds at the Zapata site. Six artifacts were found there in association with bones identified as bison. Folsom points found in other areas indicate men of this age hunted in most of the valley.

Following Folsom on the time scale is the Yuma, later more specifically called Eden, and Scottsbluff included in the Cody Complex. A number of these points have been found here. Points identified as Agate Basin, Meserve, Midland, and Plainview have also been found in small numbers, none however with identifiable sites. It would seem likely that as time progressed the lithic industry changed; and while we speak of Sandia, Clovis, Folsom and Yuma, we speak of an industry rather than a separate and distinctly different type of human being. Each point, in all probability, overlapped and then evolved. As an example the flaking on Clovis, Folsom and Yuma are of a similar, very fine type of workmanship. E. B. Renaud (1945) believes that Folsom man did not just disappear, but rather that his lithic industry underwent a change and evolved into another type of weapon which replaced the classical Folsom. After detailed study he feels that Folsom and Yuma (Cody Complex) are related.

Over these thousands of years—20,000 to 5,000 B.C., the big game hunters must have been influenced by the weather and came into the San Luis Valley only on brief sojourns, in small numbers, to hunt during the late spring, summer and early fall, retiring to warmer climates when winter approached. No evidence of human skeletons has been found in the valley so we have no evidence of their physical makeup. As to the clothing they wore, it must have been made from the skins of the animals they killed. In excavating kill sites it has been found that the tail bones are often missing indicating that the animals were skinned and the tail left intact on the hide.

There seems to be a span of time after 5,000 B.C. when occupancy of the valley, even briefly, died out. This could be accounted for by a look at the physiographic evidence. Starting about 8,000 B.C., the region became warmer and drier than at present and was not conducive to animal migration into the area (Ives, 1941). At this time the big game would have gone further north following the climate that produced food for their livelihood, and man would have followed them. When conditions again became favorable for animal forage, the bison, antelope, deer and elk began to frequent the area. With the influx of this new type of game we find a new type of artifact. Prior to 1942 E. B. Renaud became acquainted with points in the San Luis Valley indicating a different culture which he felt were distinct enough to warrant placing in a category of their own—the Rio Grande Points. These points were made in almost all cases from basalt, with a few from obsidian, and were found mostly along the Rio Grande in the San Luis Valley and north to the sand dunes area. Also, in a few sites in the vicinity of San Antonio Mountain in New Mexico, and west of the Rio Grande in northern New Mexico. The artifacts, Renaud states, were generally of simple form and non-specialized shapes and were made by the percussion method. Some were fairly large, but most were of medium dimensions and very few were small and fine. Many were not retouched (Renaud, 1942). A. L. Pearsall and Gene Sutherland excavated a rock shelter site in the southern part of the valley, east of the Rio Grande, in 1942 and there found a number of these artifacts below later Pueblo occupancy. While dating has not been definite, evidence indicates these people were moving up and down the Rio Grande for some time before the birth of Christ and left extensive artifacts, indicating larger groups and longer periods of occupancy. However, there is still no evidence to indicate a permanent type occupancy but only migrations in the more temperate weather. Bones found in excavating were those of deer, antelope, bison and smaller animals.

As horticulture extended northward into the southwest area of Colorado in the San Juan Basin, the nomadic Indians became semi-sedentary. Corn was the first cultivated crop, followed by squash and beans. These people in the San Juan area have been named Basket Makers and their development divided into three periods. Basket Maker I was the period during which these people first entered the area, but about whom little evidence exists. James D. Jennings (1968) states that the widespread desert culture has been accepted as accounting for them, forming the base with the requisite traits upon which pottery, horticulture, etc. were grafted. Basket Maker II (1 A.D. to 400 A.D.) was a period when the people lived in caves, alcoves or overhangs. Perishable artifacts and bodies were preserved in their living quarters because of the dry, arid conditions. During this period pit houses came into existence, and horticulture expanded. Tabeguache Cave, located in the Uncompahgre National Forest, southwest of Montrose, Colorado, revealed occupancy by Basket Maker II people when it was dug by C. T. Hurst. He felt it to be a periphial site, probably used as a summer camp, indicating people migrating northward from the culture area of the San Juan. Occupancy was apparently not continuous, but occurred during three separate intervals (Hurst, 1942).

Basket Maker III (400 A.D. to 700 A.D.) was the period when pit houses developed into a more rectangular style, still built partly into the ground, and then into surface masonry structures, while the kiva, a subterranean ceremonial structure used for ceremonies, came into existence. Weaving and basketry were more refined, and true fired, gray pottery was developed. No evidence of a pit house type structure has been found in the San Luis Valley.

It was during the Basket Maker III period and the following Pueblo I period that the bow and arrow were introduced, probably by immigrants from the north—the Athapaskans (ancestors of the Navajo and Apache), and projectile points became smaller and of a different style. Until this time projectile points were affixed to a shaft and used as a spear or as a dart propelled by the atlatl or dart thrower. The atlatl was a wooden device used to give more length to the arm of the hunter and more power to the thrust of the dart. The points were larger than later arrowheads and had notches close to the base. The Pueblo I culture developed from the third Basket Maker period and lasted from 700 A.D. to 900 A.D. At this time the rigid cradle board was first used and as a result the children's heads were permanently flattened in the back. At one time, because of the difference in cranial structure, it was thought a different people had replaced the previous dwellers. Horticulture developed to a more extensive degree—cotton was being raised and used extensively for cloth. Previously cloth had been made from feathers or rabbit fur. Yucca leaves were used to make sandals, as well as to weave baskets. This was a craft that had carried over from earlier periods. Pottery was more refined in construction and more variety of shapes was introduced.

Pueblo II, 900 A.D. to 1100 A.D., saw the advent of small one-clan masonry houses with contiguous rooms and kivas built in front of them. Corrugated pottery for cooking ware was in general use, with black-on-white decorated vessels used for containers. At about this time the mug became a popular and useful pottery piece. Pueblo III, the Golden Age of the culture, lasted from 1100 A.D. to 1300 A.D. and was characterized by the highly specialized development of pottery types and the high degree of perfection of architecture in the great multi-story communal pueblos and cliff dwellings. Great kivas were constructed, and crafts became very specialized. It was at the latter part of this period when the large pueblos and cliff dwellings at Mesa Verde, Chaco Canyon and Canyon de Chelly began to experience adverse conditions. Drouth, overcrowding, nomadic invaders, all seemed to be factors in the movement from these established settlements south to areas along the Rio Grande and to Acoma, Zuni and the Hopi pueblos.

A decline in living conditions seemed to exist until about 1600 and this period is classified as Pueblo IV. While there were changes in pottery making, and some advance in other crafts, it was after the contact with white men that many changes were made in the Indians' way of life. This period is called Pueblo V and exists to the present time.

During this entire development period, from 1 A.D. to 1600 A.D., there were evidently no attempts made to settle in the San Luis Valley, as evidence of these missing structures. They, too, apparently came as hunters from spring to fall, seeking the bountiful game and wild fowl. It is thought the birds were especially hunted for their feathers which were used in various ceremonies and dances, as well as for cloth. From evidence found at camp sites it is apparent three approaches into the valley were used by the Pueblo Indians. The one traveled most often was north from Taos, along the east side of the Rio Grande into the sand dunes area. Another route existed along the west side of the Rio Grande and extended west into the valley, but also continued north. Indians from Chama and the Pajarito Plateau came in from the San Antonio area along the Rio Tuscas, the Rio San Antonio and the Rio Vallecito. Very little pottery has been found along the last two trails. Since the horse was unknown at that time women and dogs packed the provisions. Artifacts found at the eastern sites—pottery shards, manos, metates and tools in large amounts, indicate that families traveled together and spent some time in the area. The metate and mano were used to grind wild grass seeds picked along the way, and who knows—maybe they were in the area long enough to harvest corn planted around springs and waterways. Many varieties of wild plants were plentiful and it is known they made use of yucca, cat tails (tules), piñon nuts and berries. In all probability the paleo-Indians before them also made use of the bountiful plant supply to supplement or eke out their meat diet. There is no evidence, however, of the paleo-Indians using grinding stones.

The Anasazi—a name applied to the Basket Makers and Pueblo Indians by the Navajo, meaning the "Old Ones" had no glyphic system of writing nor a calendar, but as with all people legends existing for many hundreds of years have an important place in the culture of these people. Some Pueblo Indians, whose legends tell of their ancestors emerging from the underworld through a lake to the north of New Mexico, believe the San Luis Lakes are that sacred place and also hold Sierra Blanca to be a sacred mountain (Bean, 1962).

While the remains of Basket Maker and Pueblo structures have not been found in the San Luis Valley, stone enclosures have been found south of Saguache that indicate an establishment of occupancy for short periods of time. Because of their locations on a high rocky ridge which provided a view of surrounding land for many miles, Renaud believed them to be an observation camp. The circles are made of slabs of lava rock standing on edge or leaning against one another and are enclosures rather than tepee rings. There is no evidence of mortar being used to cement the rocks in the structure. Renaud felt that the camp seemed loosely established and because of rocks, cactus and snakes would not appear attractive as permanent dwellings. Further to the south in the Rio Grande Valley and Carson National Forest, Renaud found similar sites (three in Colorado and five in New Mexico), more indicative of being dwelling places and workshops. Renaud (1941) and Huscher (1943), after examining a number of these sites and other similar ones, arrived at the conclusion that they were not early Basket Maker or Pueblo immigrants, but were rather a southward migration of Athapaskan-speaking people (probably Navajo). The stones in the enclosures were laid up without mortar and called dry-mortar construction. The Pueblean dwellings were constructed with the use of a great deal of adobe mortar, which style he was sure would have been used here if they were responsible for the construction. Hearths were also evident in the ruins of Pueblean dwellings while there were no hearths in the stone enclosures. Cooking had evidently been done outside the enclosure. While artifacts found at these sites were in some cases similar to both Pueblo and eastern tribes, he felt there was sufficient difference to classify them as belonging to a particular people migrating southward. Similar sites were found north and east of the valley, as well as south into Mexico, denoting a trail of migration. Renaud did not believe these structures could be contributed to the Utes who later occupied this area, for when the Spaniards first came into the area, the Utes they came in contact with told them the enclosures were built by the "old ones," seeming to place them at a much earlier date. In 1877 Franklin Rhoda reported a masonry ring built on the summit of Mt. Blanca and questioned its usefulness as either a lookout or hunting station. The question arises here as to whether the structure was a ceremonial ring and could be connected with the Pueblo legend.

The fact that at a number of these sites, located not only in the Rio Grande drainage but also in the drainages of the upper Colorado, the Yampa, the San Miguel, the Uncompahgre and the lower Gunnison, there were walls so located as to resemble a fort. Hurscher did not believe that they were ever used in the same way a fort would have been, but rather the walls were a type of barricade to obscure the residents. The roofs of the round stone huts would be difficult to define since no debris relative to the roof could be identified. They could have been made of brush, matting, bark or hides. Hurscher believes that these sites represent a migration over several hundreds of years and took place before and up to 1000 A.D. This would place the hogan builders in this area early enough to have influenced the Basket Maker-Pueblo culture change.

While more artifacts have been found in the eastern part of the valley and in the Saguache area, it does not mean other areas were neglected. Rock Creek, with headwaters in the San Juan Range, evidently was often the scene of hunting activities as artifacts have been found along its banks even out into the middle of the valley. Paleo-Indian points, early Pueblo pottery shards and points and Ute stone artifacts indicate that game was abundant in this area; and stone chips, tools, manos and metates in some numbers tell us the Indians camped at various sites. It is along Rock Creek that petroglyphs have been found in the area known as "picture rocks." They present pictorial evidence of the passing of people for hundreds of years and can be attributed to Basket Maker, Pueblo and Ute, even though the stories they tell cannot be clearly interpreted.

In rock shelters and caves located along the west San Juan Range, stone artifacts, corrugated Pueblo pottery, bone tools and perishable artifacts such as basketry and sandals have been found. The arid climate of the Southwest has helped to preserve many otherwise perishable artifacts and has provided archaeologists with a wider variety of evidence of occupation.

About the time that the Athapaskan-speaking Navajo and Apache were migrating from the north, another migration was taking place from the Great Basin area in the Far West. This desertic region offered little in the way of livelihood, and the Shoshonian-speaking Indians who had made this territory their home began to look for better living areas. The Piutes, Shoshone, Hopi, Ute and certain California tribes began to push eastward. Reaching Arizona and Utah they established permanent dwellings, but some of the Utes continued on east and north in their wandering and arrived in southwestern Colorado. These nomads could have been another tribe who, with the Apache and Navajo, harassed the Pueblo people and were responsible in part for the desertion of the cliff dwellings and the great pueblos.

The Southern Utes were made up of three bands—the Wiminute (Wininuche), the Mowatsi (Moache), and the Kapote (Capote). Both the Moache and Capote were in and out of the San Luis Valley, but it was the Tabeguache or Uncompahgre band who claimed the valley as their territory. They seem to have entered this area through Utah. When the Utes first came to this area they had no horses, did not practice farming and their tools and weapons were fashioned from stone. Each family unit hunted in a certain area. Provisions were carried by the women and dogs. Because of severe winters the families moved across Cochetopa Pass when cold weather came and sought more sheltered areas along the Uncompahgre and Gunnison Rivers. When spring came they would gather for the ceremonial bear dance and social activities before moving out in small family groups again for summer living. Tribes from the plains to the east of the valley visited the region to hunt, and when danger threatened from the Arapahoes, Cheyennes, Comanches, Kiowas, Sioux or Pawnees, the Ute families grouped together for defense.

These were the conditions the Spanish found when they first entered the area between 1630 and 1640. First encounters were peaceful and trading flourished. The Utes traded meat and hides for trade goods from the Spanish, but above all they bartered for the horse. Sometimes, not having sufficient meat and hides to trade, they would trade their children and the Spanish trained these children to herd sheep and cows (Rockwell, 1956).

With the added mobility provided by the horse the Utes' hunting grounds spread over the mountains to the east where they found the buffalo in plentiful numbers. Now they had a resource that provided them with tepee covers, blankets, sinew thread, bowstrings, horn glue, skin bags, moccasins and more meat than they had ever known. No longer did they have to depend on women and dogs to carry provisions. Likewise, the horse permitted them to invade and withdraw quickly from enemy territory and they became warlike and aggressive (Rockwell, 1956). Another factor that brought about the change to a more warlike nature was the influx of traders and trappers and later settlers, who were encroaching on the territory the Tabeguache had known as their own for so many years.

The Southern Utes encountered Spanish conflict sometime before the Tabeguache. The earliest known conflict came about when Governor Luis de Rosas, governor from 1637 to 1641, waged an unjust war against the Utes near the southern Colorado border. About eighty Indians were captured and forced to labor in a workshop in Santa Fe (Schroeder, 1965). Spanish and Ute conflict continued in northern New Mexico until the Pueblo Revolt in 1680 when the Spanish withdrew to the south. Then the Utes attacked the northern pueblos and by the time the Spanish returned in 1694, the strength of the Southern Utes was highly respected. Combining their efforts with the Comanches, they had open hostility with the Jicarilla Apaches and the northern Pueblos. Raiding and looting continued for a number of years, but after the Comanches gained possession of firearms in the 1720's and rose as a power in the plains, these two tribes gradually became hostile to each other and the Utes became more friendly with the Spanish. At this time they combined efforts to effect a check on the Comanche and Navajo raiding parties.

By the early 1800's the Southern Utes and Jicarilla Apaches had become friendly and were making hunting excursions across the San Luis Valley onto the eastern plains. In 1818 Jose Maria de Arze, who led a force up the Rio Grande into Colorado on a scouting expedition into Comanche country, reported Ute and Jicarilla tracks in the Alamosa area leading west toward the San Juan Mountains (Schroeder, 1965). When the Mexican people began to settle in the San Luis Valley, after the treaty following the Mexican War, the Utes were anything but friendly. In 1851 a body of soldiers were sent to establish a fort in the valley to protect the settlers. With the establishment of Ft. Massachusetts, the Utes became increasingly hostile and attacked Guadalupe and Conejos, where they were repulsed. They continued on to San Luis where the settlers had fled from their homes, so they stole horses, cows and sheep. Forces from New Mexico joined those from Ft. Massachusetts and pursued the raiders over Cochetopa Pass. Later Colonel Fauntleroy surrounded a Ute camp on the north side of Poncha Pass, killing a number of the Indians, after which the Utes asked for peace. That fall a treaty was signed with them (Bean, 1962).

Indian conflict in the valley came to an end when Chief Ouray made treaties with the United States; after which the Utes were moved onto a reservation.

Through these more than 200 years of conflict, tribes continued to traverse the San Luis Valley. The many passes in the surrounding mountains offered access to areas in all directions. To the north a favored route was from South Park across the Park Range into the upper Arkansas Valley and then across the low Poncha Pass. Utes traveling from Pagosa Springs into the valley and across the northwest foothills on their way to Bayou Salude (South Park), also made use of the easily traversed Poncha Pass. Mosca Pass was used often, as well as Medano Pass, to gain access to Wet Mountain Valley. Cochetopa Pass (Buffalo Pass) was used extensively by the Utes to reach their winter homes; and although there were never extensive herds of buffalo in the San Luis Valley, they too must have used this route for migration since the Indians named the pass for them. Migration from the southwest was accomplished by coming through the area of Wolf Creek Pass and Cumbres Pass. Southern routes skirted San Antonio Mountain in New Mexico on both sides, or followed up the Rio Grande. For thousands of years nomadic Indians have used these routes into the San Luis Valley, leaving artifacts from which we can identify them, but never staying long enough to be classified as permanent dwellers. It was only after the white men came and built houses from adobe or logs that sufficient shelter was provided to endure the winter weather. While they, too, depended on hunting for food, this was soon supplemented through the practice of horticulture and agriculture. One wonders, if the white man had not arrived when he did, would the Indians have eventually established permanent, year round dwellings here?

REFERENCES

Bean, Luther E., 1962, *Land of the Blue Sky People*. Monte Vista, Colorado: The Monte Vista Journal.

Hurst, C. T., 1941, "A Folsum Location in the San Luis Valley, Colorado," *South Western Lore*. Boulder, Colorado: University of Colorado. 1942, "Completion of Work in Tabaguache Cave," *South Western Lore*. Boulder: University of Colorado.

Huscher, Harold, 1943, "The Hogan Builders of Colorado," *South Western Lore*. Boulder: University of Colorado.

Ives, Ronald L., 1941, "A Cultural Hiatus in the Rocky Mountain Region," *South Western Lore*. Boulder: University of Colorado.

Jennings, James D., 1968, *Prehistory of North America*. New York: McGraw-Hill.

Renaud, E. B., 1945, "About the 'Disappearance' of Folsom Man and Folsom Points," *South Western Lore*. Boulder: University of Colorado. 1941, "Indian Stone Enclosures of Colorado and New Mexico," *Archaeological Series, Second Paper*. Denver: University of Denver.

Rockwell, Wilson, 1956, *Utes: a Forgotten People*. Denver: Sage.

Schroeder, Albert H., 1942, "Comments on 'Transition to History in the Pueblo Southwest'," *American Anthropologist*. 56:597-99. "A Brief History of the Southern Utes," *South Western Lore*. Boulder: University of Colorado.

CENOZOIC GEOLOGY OF THE ARKANSAS HILLS REGION OF THE SOUTHERN MOSQUITO RANGE, CENTRAL COLORADO

by

GARY R. LOWELL

Southeast Missouri State College
Cape Girardeau, Missouri

INTRODUCTION

LOCATION

The Arkansas Hills area is located northeast of Salida, Colorado, in the southernmost portion of the Mosquito Range. The study covers about 100 square miles within the southern half of the Cameron Mountain 15-minute quadrangle. Elevations range from about 6,800 feet at Salida to 10,993 feet atop Cameron Mountain. The major geologic features bounding the area include the upper Arkansas segment of the Rio Grande depression on the west, the Thirtynine Mile volcanic field on the north and east, and the canyon of the Arkansas River on the south. Adjacent communities include Salida, Wellsville, Howard, Cotopaxi, and Guffey. Accessibility is provided mainly by the Ute Trail, which connects Salida with Colorado State Highway 9, and by numerous mining and logging roads which branch from it (see figure 1).

PRE-CENOZOIC ROCKS

The pre-Cenozoic rocks in the Arkansas Hills area range in age from Precambrian to Permian and include rocks from all periods of the Paleozoic Era except Cambrian and Silurian. The Precambrian rocks consist, for the most part, of metamorphics which have been intruded by granitic and gabbroic bodies and invaded by their associated dikes and sills. Unconformably overlying the Precambrian erosion surface is a Paleozoic section which includes, from bottom to top; Manitou Dolomite (Early Ordovician), Harding Sandstone (Middle Ordovician), Fremont Dolomite (Late Ordovician), Chaffee Formation (Devonian), Leadville Limestone (Mississippian), and a very thick sequence of Permo-Pennsylvanian strata. Preservation of blocks of Paleozoic strata is largely due to down faulting during Late Paleozoic and Late Cretaceous-Early Tertiary orogenies and subsequent burial by Cenozoic sediments and volcanic rocks. Pre-Cenozoic stratigraphic and structural features are shown on the enclosed geologic map, (see back pocket).

PRE-VOLCANIC EROSION SURFACE

The Arkansas Hills are located on the western edge of an extensive pre-volcanic erosion surface described by Epis and Chapin (1968, p. 56-59). This surface covers an area of about 5,000 square miles and extends from the foot of Kenosha Pass in northeastern South Park to the northern Wet Mountains and the Wet Mountain Valley. In an east-west direction it stretches from the upper Arkansas

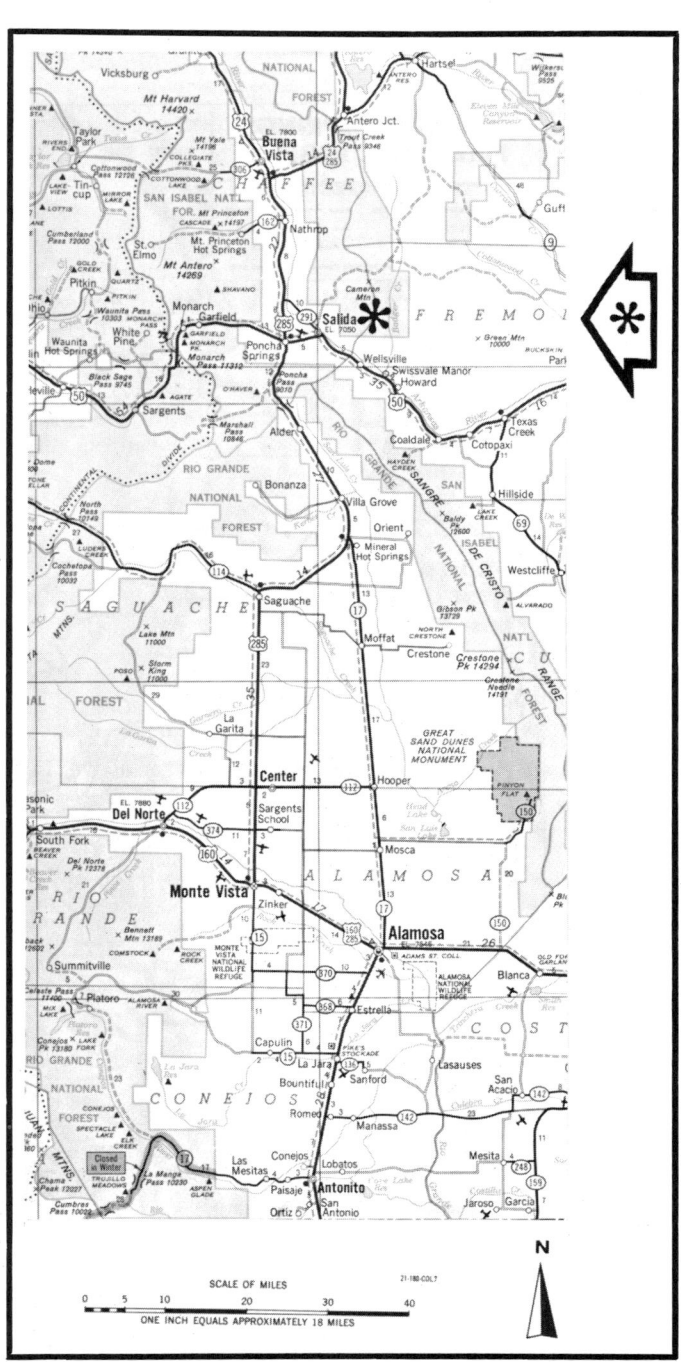

FIGURE 1.
Location map.

Valley to the Cripple Creek area, a distance of about 50 miles. According to Epis and Chapin (1968, p. 57) the pre-volcanic erosion surface was a relatively smooth plain of low relief upon which small hills, as much as 800 feet high, were present. The surface slopes southward from an elevation of about 9,500 feet in South Park to about 8,500 feet in the northern Wet Mountains. The erosion surface appears to have formed by Middle to Late Eocene time and was subsequently broken by Late Cenozoic faulting (Chapin, Epis, and Lowell, 1970).

In the area of investigation, volcanic rocks preserve an anomalous drainage pattern which trends east-west and crosses the Laramide structural grain and the present drainage at nearly a right angle. The Salida-Waugh Mountain and Gribbles Run paleovalleys are remnants of east-flowing paleodrainages incised in the pre-volcanic erosion surface and later filled by Early Oligocene volcanic rocks (see geologic map, back pocket). The Salida-Waugh Mountain paleovalley has been traced for 11 miles from near Salida eastward to Waugh Mountain. It averages 2 miles in width and has a maximum depth of about 1,000 feet (Lowell, 1969, p. 62-63; Chapin, Epis, and Lowell, 1970). The Gribbles Run paleovalley is about 4 miles long, ¼ to ½ mile wide, and about 500 feet deep. Both paleovalleys trend east-west, have westward or northwestward-forking tributaries, and are cut by steep north-trending post-volcanic faults.

CENOZOIC ROCKS

A composite table of stratigraphic units with corresponding ages and thicknesses is shown in Table 1. A brief description of the various lithologies is given together with other pertinent data.

WHITEHORN STOCK

Prior to the onset of volcanism, granodioritic magma was intruded along the axial plane of the asymmetric Pleasant Valley syncline to form the Whitehorn stock. Sills, dikes, and apophyses pierce the inclosing rocks, particularly the Permo-Pennsylvanian strata within which laterally-continuous sills are common. The nature and significance of the dikes and abundant xenoliths have been discussed by Osborn and Rainwater (1934, p. 33-35) and Bhutta (1954, p. 85). Pyrometasomatic iron-ore deposits which formed along the contacts of the stock were described by Behre, Osborn, and Rainwater (1936).

The central portion of the Whitehorn stock is characterized by knobby, bouldery outcrops, whereas towards the periphery massive, sheeted zones are common. The rock typically has a bluish "salt and pepper" appearance on fresh surfaces and a dull greenish-gray cast on weathered or altered surfaces. The rock is holocrystalline and the grain size varies from fine to coarse. Quartz and orthoclase surround and embay the earlier-formed plagioclase and ferromagnesian minerals. Accessory apatite, zircon, and sphene are prominent in hand specimens and thin sections. A detailed petrographic analysis is given by Bhutta (1954, p. 89).

The Whitehorn stock is younger than all of the Paleozoic rocks and much of their deformation is older than the last phase of Laramide tectonism. By Late Eocene time the stock had been unroofed and beveled by an erosion surface of moderate relief.

ASH FLOW 1

The basal volcanic unit in the Arkansas Hills is an extensive (chemically rhyolitic), mineralogically latitic to trachytic, ash-flow sheet which is the earliest major extrusive rock in the adjacent Thirtynine Mile volcanic field It is a multiple-flow, simple cooling unit informally designated as Ash Flow 1 by Epis and Chapin (1968). Member flows of the cooling unit are indistinguishable in the field and generally form prominent, ledgelike exposures with a striking eutaxitic fabric. The fabric is made conspicuous by the

TABLE 1.

Cenozoic stratigraphic units in the Arkansas Hills region of the southern Mosquito Range, central Colorado.

AGE	LITHOLOGIC UNIT	THICKNESS
Quaternary	Alluvium	—
	Landslides, slump blocks, and colluvial deposits	—
Late Miocene-Pliocene	Boulder gravels	—
	Dry Union Formation	—
	Tenderfoot Hill Facies of Dry Union Formation	±450'
Oligocene-Miocene	Silicic Felsite of Section 36	0-200'
	Andesite of Big Baldy	0-200' (?)
	Upper Andesite (18.9 ± 1.2 m.y.)*	300-1200'
	Latite of Waugh Mountain	200-700'
	Ash Flow 7 (34.8 ± 1.4 m.y.)*	+600'
	Latite of East Badger Creek	250-300'
	Tuff of Badger Creek	+313'
	Antero Formation	+368'
	Ash Flow 1 (40.0 ± 1.4 m.y.)*	Pre-volcanic Erosion Surface
	(37.3 ± 1.9 m.y. and 35.4 ± 1.1 m.y.)†	
Late Cretaceous-Late Eocene	Whitehorn stock	

* Epis and Chapin (1968)
† Van Alstine (1969)

presence of subparallel pumice lapilli. Where these lapilli have been removed by weathering, a distinctive "drill hole" appearance is imparted to the rock. The unit weathers to gray, buff, and dark-brown colors but when freshly exposed the rock has a reddish-brown to purplish, aphanitic matrix which contains large fractured phenocrysts of sanidine and plagioclase. The clear, unaltered, and often zoned sanidine phenocrysts range upward in size to a maximum of about 7 mm. Zoned plagioclase phenocrysts are usually smaller and are frequently altered to a dull white or yellowish color. Tiny flakes of oxidized biotite, 2 mm or less in diameter, are also present in minor amount. The matrix consists of devitrified glass shards and dust, irregular granophyric intergrowths, and patches of extremely fine-grained feldspar, tridymite, and cristobalite. Lithic inclusions are rare even in the basal member of the cooling unit. Welding ranges from moderate to dense within the cooling unit and a black vitrophyric zone about 3 feet thick is exposed in the east end of the Gribbles Run paleovalley. The maximum thickness of the cooling unit is about 100 feet.

ANTERO FORMATION

Overlying the Ash Flow 1 rocks throughout much of the project area is the Lower Tuff Member of the Antero Formation (Johnson, 1937; De Voto, 1964). Two major lithologic types of Antero tuff are recognized by the author in the Arkansas Hills. These are both andesitic in mineralogical composition and are termed the ash-flow tuff facies and the sedimentary tuff facies.

The ash-flow tuff facies forms the base of the Lower Member of the Antero Formation and has a measured thickness of 368 (Lowell, 1969, p. 27) east of Black's cabin (SE ¼, Sec. 7, R. 11 E., T. 50 N.). At this locality, the ash-flow tuff facies exhibits striking pinnacles of unwelded, pumice-rich, ash-flow tuff. These unwelded ash flows consist of phenocrysts of plagioclase, biotite, very minor sanidine, hornblende, and sphene in a whitish-gray matrix of glass shards. Lithic fragments, generally less than 3 inches in diameter, comprise about 1 percent of the rock and include Precambrian quartzite Paleozoic sandstones and carbonates, and porphyritic volcanic rocks of intermediate composition. Subrounded, uncollapsed pumice lumps which range in size from ¼ inch to 14 inches in diameter and contain abundant fresh biotite and plagioclase crystals may constitute as much as 60 percent of the rock. Two types of pumice are present, one pinkish orange in color, and the other white. The average size of the lithic inclusions and pumice lumps tends to increase upward through the section. Commonly, the pumice lumps are slightly flattened which imparts a very crude compaction foliation to the rock with which the lithic fragments roughly conform. The ash-flow tuffs of the lower facies weather to buff or light reddish-brown in color and often show a distinctive sheeting in weathered outcrop. Further petrographic and stratigraphic details have been compiled by Lowell (1969, p. 24-29).

The lower ash-flow tuff facies is overlain by, and grades into, the sedimentary tuff facies which consists of well-stratified, locally cross-bedded, pumice-rich and biotite-rich, tuffaceous sediment, The character of this facies varies from indurated, bluish sandstone containing altered biotite and rock fragments to extremely friable pumice beds which nearly lack clastic matrix. The sedimentary tuff facies is the predominant facies in the Gribbles Park area (northeast portion of geologic map, back pocket). It represents a combination of reworked, air-fall material and erosional debris derived from the colder, unwelded, Antero ash-flow tuffs.

TUFF OF BADGER CREEK

The tuff of Badger Creek is the informal name proposed for the most extensive volcanic formation in the project area (Lowell 1969, p. 25). The unit overlies the Antero Formation and Ash Flow 1 in the east-trending Salida-Waugh Mountain paleovalley (see geologic map, back pocket). A compaction foliation defined by collapsed pumice is pervasive and it occasionally contains a lineation formed by the stretching of pumice lapilli. Six, dark-gray to black, vitrophyric zones have been observed at various horizons within the unit indicating a multiple-flow origin and a compound cooling history. The vitrophyric zones grade upward into moderately and slightly welded zones where pumice is more conspicuous and thin streaks of pink, siliceous spherulites are present. Where pumice has been removed by weathering, numerous tubular cavities about 1 inch in diameter present a distinctive "Swiss cheese" appearance. The weathered rock takes on a buff to yellowish-gray color. A few Precambrian lithic fragments have been observed, but the most common inclusions are angular to subrounded volcanic rock fragments of intermediate composition which average less than 2 inches in diameter. Pumice, showing all degrees of welding, may form as much as 5 to 10 percent of the unit above the vitrophyric zones. The unwelded pumice is of two colors, pinkish-orange and white in about equal abundance, both rich in biotite and plagioclase crystals.

Mineralogically, the tuff of Badger Creek is andesitic and consists of phenocrysts of plagioclase, biotite, very minor sanidine, hornblende, and sphene combined with flattened pumice and a few lithic fragments in a matrix of cuspate glass shards. The glass shards show a wide range of welding and devitrification features. The unit has a measured thickness of 313 feet (Lowell, 1969, p. 35) north of East Badger Creek (Sec. 12, R. 11 E., T. 50 N.). The tuff of Badger Creek and the unwelded ash-flow tuffs of the Antero Formation are remarkably similar in mineralogy, lithic constituents, and pumice content. Kinship probably exists between the two units even though their respective emplacements were separated by an interval of erosion and reworking.

LATITE OF EAST BADGER CREEK

The latite of East Badger Creek is a distinctive, cliff-forming lava flow which overlies the tuff of Badger Creek along the eastern end of the Salida-Waugh Mountain paleovalley (see geologic map, back pocket). The bow is 2 to 3 miles long, about ½ mile wide, and 250 to 300 feet thick.

The rock is holocrystalline and aphanophyric, ranges in color from gray to purple, and weathers to a yellowish-brown cast. Seriate, microcrystalline feldspars comprise about 80 percent of the rock and form a pilotaxitic texture. Plagioclase phenocrysts display splotchy, irregular zoning and comprise about 10 percent of the rock. Sanidine or anorthoclase (average $2V = 49°$), forms about 8 percent of the rock and partially-oxidized biotite phenocrysts comprise the remaining 2 percent.

Ash Flow 7

A thick sequence of mineralogically trachytic to latitic ash-flow tuffs, correlated with the Ash Flow 7 cooling unit of the Thirtynine Mile volcanic field (Epis and Chapin, 1968) was mapped along the eastern margin of the Cameron Mountain quadrangle. In this region, Ash Flow 7 is a multiple-flow, compound cooling unit which forms massive cliffs along south-facing slopes.

The rock varies from dark purplish-brown to gray in color and shows a moderate to well-developed compaction foliation. Phenocrysts of sanidine, plagioclase, biotite, hornblende and sphene are contained in a glassy matrix which may variously be purple, orange, gray, or red depending upon the stratigraphic horizon (Lowell, 1969, p. 40). Pumice lumps, welded and darkened in varying degrees, are flattened into lenses averaging ¼ inch by 3 inches in cross section and may form as much as 10 percent of the rock. Angular, lithic inclusions up to 1 inch in diameter and consisting of red to black, aphanitic to porphyritic, volcanic rocks of intermediate composition are abundant. Bronzy, oxidized biotite and chatoyant sanidine phenocrysts are characteristic of the entire formation. A stratigraphic section measured north of Two Creek (Sec. 5, R. 11 E., T. 50 N.) revealed the presence of at least 4 member flows with an aggregate thickness of over 600 feet (Lowell, 1969, p. 73).

Latite of Waugh Mountain

Waugh Mountain (11,718 feet), whose western flank lies along the boundary between the Cameron Mountain and the Black Mountain quadrangles, is the dominant topographic feature in the southwestern part of the Thirtynine Mile volcanic field. A poorly exposed volcanic center near the middle of Waugh Mountain is thought to be the source of a sequence of rhyolitic to latitic flows and flow breccias 200 to 700 feet thick which occur along its western flank (Epis and Chapin, 1968, p. 73). This flow sequence, termed the latite of Waugh Mountain, overlies Ash Flow 7 and caps the ridges at the head of Two Creek along the eastern margin of the map area. The upper surface of this unit forms discontinuous patchy outcrops of resistant knobs and boulders. The formation consists of gray to pinkish-gray flows and autoclastic flow breccias which are commonly silicified. Flow bands, 1 to 4 inches thick, generally parallel the crudely-oriented breccia clasts within the framental zones.

Phenocrysts comprise 10 to 20 percent of the rock and consist of plagioclase, sanidine, and oxidized biotite in a glassy microcrystalline matrix. Trace amounts of anorthoclase, hornblende, and sphene may also be present. Lensoid axiolitic and spherulitic zones, more or less conformable with tabular and lath-shaped minerals, define the flow structure. Where brecciation has occurred, thin stringers of calcium carbonate may envelop some of the breccia clasts. Accidental lithic inclusions are rare, but types ranging from Precambrian gneiss to Tertiary volcanic rocks have been observed.

Upper Andesite

Overlying the latite of Waugh Mountain is a sequence of andesitic and basaltic flows, flow breccias, and minor laharic breccias and tuffs which have been informally named Upper Andesite by Epis and Chapin (1968, p. 76). The estimated thickness of the unit ranges from a maximum of about 1,200 feet near Waugh Mountain, the presumed source, to less than 300 feet in the southern part of the Thirtynine Mile volcanic field. Upper Andesite rocks are present along the eastern boundary of the map area (Secs. 10, 15, and 16, R. 11 E., T. 50 N.), which is a densely-wooded region, nearly barren of outcrops, where formational contacts are largely inferred from rock fragments in colluvium. A brownish-purple, aphanophyric andesite (?) which weathers to a buff color and contains a few phenocrysts of plagioclase, pyroxene, and biotite, crops out on hill "10,660 feet." These rocks display prominent but erratic sheeting. Overlying the andesite (?) is a black, vesicular olivine basalt which contains a few pinkish-white amygdules of calcite. The thickness and areal extent of these rocks could not be accurately determined from the available outcrops.

Andesite of Big Baldy

In the southwestern portion of the map area, a number of isolated patches of similar-appearing basaltic andesites are grouped under the informal designation of andesite of Big Baldy. These rocks are younger than the Antero Formation but complete stratigraphic information is lacking. Because of dissimilar petrologic characteristics and appreciable geographic separation, no direct genetic relationship to the Upper Andesite is postulated. The relative ages of these two formations are unknown. The best exposures of the andesite of Big Baldy are in the vicinity of Big Baldy Mountain (Sec. 21, R. 10 E., T. 50 N.), where andesitic lava flows, autobrecciated and silicified in part, are interstratified with minor, variegated, andesitic boulder breccias. The breccias contain red and black porphyritic andesite (?) boulders up to 4 feet in diameter and are restricted to two small outcrops west and south of the summit of Big Baldy Mountain.

The major portion of the unit consists of purplish, aphanophyric basaltic andesite which weathers brown to black. Phenocrysts of altered and zoned plagioclase containing numerous, minute apatite inclusions form 25 to 40 percent of the rock. Small amounts of altered hypersthene, basaltic hornblende, clinopyroxene, and opaque grains comprise the remaining phenocryst portion. The matrix elements are brownish glass and plagioclase microlites which vary in textural arrangement from hyalopilitic to pilotaxitic.

SILICIC FELSITE OF SECTION 36

A highly silicified lava flow which rests upon pre-volcanic rocks or upon the andesite of Big Baldy is present in the southwest portion of the map area (Sec. 36, R. 9 E., T. 50 N.). This flow, previously described by Bhutta (1954, p. 109) as pitchstone, is referred to as the Silicic Felsite of Section 36 in the present study. The massive, purplish-gray flow is locally fractured and brecciated and forms resistant cliffs along its 1 mile length. In outcrop, flow structures and phenocryst foliations are vague and extremely erratic. Fractured, white phenocrysts of zoned plagioclase comprise less than 10 percent of the rock and are usually accompanied by a few scattered phenocrysts of oxidized biotite and opaque grains. Most of the rock consists of pinkish-brown glass which in thin section displays crude banding with which the phenocrysts do not conform. A few faintly birefringent, arborescent microlites are usually visible in thin section.

MISCELLANEOUS EXTRUSIVE OR INTRUSIVE ROCKS

Three different igneous rock types of unknown stratigraphic position occur in very small isolated outcrops within the area of investigation. For convenience, these rocks appear on the geologic map (see back pocket) under the symbol Tm (Tertiary miscellaneous). Along the upper reaches of Dead Horse Gulch (NE ¼, Sec. 22, R. 9 E., T. 50 N.) a pinnacle-forming, tuffaceous body crops out. The lithic content of this body consists of: (1) extremely abundant yellow chert; (2) numerous cognate Paleozoic fragments of all shapes, sizes, and formations; and (3) angular blocks of amygdaloidal and vesicular porphyritic rock up to 1 foot in diameter which closely resembles the andesite of Big Baldy. The rock is iron stained to a bright yellow color and displays no evidence of stratification or sorting. Probably this exposure is a portion of a small, localized laharic breccia which was emplaced during, or following, the eruption of the andesite of Big Baldy.

A small body of intrusive breccia has been mapped within the Whitehorn stock (Sec. 31, R. 10 E., T. 49 N.). The breccia consists of angular fragments of gray porphyritic rock of intermediate composition and granodiorite from the Whitehorn stock in a matrix of yellowish clay. The breccia may have formed during movement along the post-Laramide Maverick fault.

Slightly less than a mile south of the intrusive breccia and on strike with the Maverick fault is an isolated body of altered felsite. The felsite has a pinkish-orange, flow-banded matrix which contains a few altered feldspar phenocrysts. Greenish-yellow hydrothermal alteration pervades the entire outcrop. The rock is extensively brecciated and incloses abundant quartz-filled vugs. The outcrop may be either a small intrusion or a flow remnant.

DRY UNION FORMATION

Northeast of Salida, Precambrian igneous and metamorphic rocks are unconformably overlain by sediments thought to be correlative with the Dry Union Formation of Tweto (1961, p. B-33). Van Alstine and Lewis (1960), and Van Alstine (1969) studied these sediments and their fossils in the Salida vicinity and concluded that they were of Late Miocene and Early Pliocene age. The formation consists of friable, poorly consolidated, tuffaceous and arkosic silts, sands, and gravels with thin, intercalated clays and calcareous zones. Pumice and biotite are present in the tuffaceous horizons and pebble to sand-size clasts of Precambrian metamorphic and Tertiary volcanic rocks are abundant.

TENDERFOOT HILL FACIES OF THE DRY UNION FORMATION

The basic volcanic rocks in the Tenderfoot Hill area, just east of Salida, have been previously described by Bhutta (1954, p. 106) as intrusive andesite porphyry. In an earlier study, the writer described these rocks under the name Tenderfoot Hill Volcanic Sequence (Lowell, 1969). The same rocks are now viewed as a volcanic facies within the Dry Union Formation.

The rocks in question are part of a steep, west-dipping, interstratified sequence of basic lava flows and unconsolidated boulder gravels of Late Tertiary age. Mapping and stratigraphic measurements indicate the presence of 6 basaltic lava flows and 5 interflow boulder gravel deposits with an aggregate thickness of at least 450 feet. Stratigraphic measurements are complicated by the presence of steep faults, landslides, and alluvium so that the true thickness, as suggested in section B-B' (see geologic map, back pocket), may be several times this value.

The lower flow members of the facies (Flows-1 and -2) are similar, black, porphyritic basalts which weather reddish brown. Approximately 25 percent of the rock is composed of phenocrysts of plagioclase, clinopyroxene, and opaque minerals. The plagioclase phenocrysts form about 20 percent of the rock and are pitted, altered, strongly zoned, and frequently contain a few tiny apatite inclusions. The clinopyroxene phenocrysts, probably augite, may reach a length of 1 inch and are often twinned and rimmed by hornblende. The matrix is pilotaxitic in texture and is composed of subequal amounts of brown glass and plagioclase microlites.

Flow-3 consists of several thin, gray to bluish gray, porphyritic flows separated by yellowish-brown soil horizons. The rock weathers to a brownish-black color and contains coarse, grayish-white, altered plagioclase phenocrysts.

Flow-4 is a thin flow of andesitic basalt whose outcrops are less resistant to weathering than other flows in the sequence. The rock varies from bluish-gray to black in color and weathers to dark brown. Conspicuous greenish and purplish altered zones pervade the outcrops. Phenocrysts of plagioclase and pyroxene (?), visible in hand specimens, are nearly always highly altered.

Flow-5 is an aphanitic, gray to black basalt which weathers to a reddish-brown color and is characterized by rubbly outcrops. The rock is strongly jointed and sheeted and exhibits numerous, small, discontinuous, red and yellow breccia zones. This flow member possesses only a few phenocrysts (less than 5 percent) of plagioclase, clinopyroxene, and opaque grains. The plagioclase crystals commonly display combined Carlsbad-albite twinning and may contain a few tiny apatite inclusions. The matrix is hyalopilitic with subequal quantities of brownish glass and plagioclase microlites. The cap of Tenderfoot Hill is probably a remnant of Flow-5.

The upper member of the sequence, Flow-6, is a reddish-brown to black, porphyritic, amygdaloidal, autobreccia of basaltic composition. The breccia clasts range in size up to 1.5 feet in diameter. Yellowish-white amygdules and thin stringers of calcium carbonate are abundant throughout the flow. Large, highly altered and zoned phenocrysts of plagioclase are very prominent.

The sediments interbedded with these flows are poorly sorted, crudely stratified, unconsolidated boulder gravels apparently of fluvial origin. Boulders of Precambrian metamorphic rocks and Tertiary volcanic rocks, ranging up to 4 feet in diameter, form as much as 60 to 70 percent of the interbeds. Some of the volcanic fragments can be recognized as belonging to the underlying member flows of the Tenderfoot Hill facies but most are of unknown derivation. The matrix is composed of greenish-gray to yellowish-gray silt and sand. The similarity of these sediments to those described by Van Alstine (1969, p. 21), and Tweto (1961) suggests that they are correlative with the Dry Union Formation.

Boulder Gravels

Subsequent to the major phases of volcanism in the Arkansas Hills region, boulder gravels were deposited in the Salida-Waugh Mountain paleovalley where they occur as isolated, erosional remnants resting upon tuff of Badger Creek, Antero Formation, or pre-volcanic rocks. The gravels consist of unstratified, angular to rounded, boulders as large as 4 feet in diameter of various rocks of Precambrian, Paleozoic, and Tertiary age. Post-depositional erosion has removed the original matrix material so that only rounded knobs of boulder-strewn debris remain.

Quaternary Deposits

For the purposes of this study, landslides, slump blocks, and colluvial deposits were mapped collectively. A number of such deposits are shown on the geologic map under the symbol Qls. The landslide associated with the feature named "The Crater" (Sec. 24, R. 9, T. 50 N.) on the Cameron Mountain 15-minute topographic quadrangle is worthy of individual mention. At this locality, the dark-purplish andesite of Big Baldy overlies the white, unwelded ash-flow tuff facies of the Antero Formation with striking color contrast. The downslope area west and southwest of "The Crater" is covered by loose andesite debris which has a decidedly hummocky and rubbly appearance. The writer views the scooped-out depression adjacent to the in situ volcanic rocks as a landslide scar rather than a volcanic crater as implied by the topographic nomenclature.

Alluvium, in this report, refers to detrital deposits of recent origin including sediments in stream beds, alluvial fans, flood plains, and valley fill. In the interest of map clarity, only a small number of such deposits are shown on the geologic map.

CENOZOIC AND LATE MESOZOIC STRUCTURES

The Arkansas Hills are a southern extension of the Mosquito Range, one of a series of north- to northwest-trending uplifts bounded by steeply dipping faults and separated by down-faulted intermontane basins or parks. Like those of other mountain ranges in central Colorado, the present structural features of this uplift are the result of three superimposed phases of Phanerozoic tectonism. The first phase occurred during Late Paleozoic and Early Mesozoic time when the ancestral Rocky Mountains were uplifted. The structural history of this orogeny is recorded in the Permo-Pennsylvanian sediments which filled the Central Colorado trough. In the faults and unconformities within these sediments, and in the stripping of Paleozoic rocks from areas to the east, and in the preservation of Paleozoic rocks in down-faulted blocks. The second phase of deformation occurred during Late Cretaceous and Early Tertiary time and consisted of uplift, folding, thrusting, and intrusion of stocks. The third phase, characterized by uplift, block faulting, and development of the Rio Grande depression, began in Middle Miocene time and is continuing today.

Pre-volcanic Folding and Thrusting

Several Laramide structures of regional importance pass through the extension of the southern Mosquito Range. These are the Pleasant Valley syncline, Pleasant Valley thrust, and Wellsville-Orient thrust (see geologic map, back pocket). The Pleasant Valley syncline is a major north-northwest-trending synclinal fold in Paleozoic strata in the southern Mosquito Range. Along Badger Creek, the eastern limb of the fold is steeply dipping to slightly overturned and is truncated by the high angle Pleasant Valley thrust. The western limb dips less steeply and is cut by the northern extension of the Wellsville-Orient thrust (Gableman, 1952, p. 1580; De Voto, 1961, p. 204). The Whitehorn stock was intruded along the eastward dipping axial plane of the syncline and obliterates most of the major structure in the map area. From the Arkansas Hills, the Pleasant Valley syncline extends northward through Bassam Park almost to Trout Creek Pass (Gableman, 1952, p. 1590), and southward into the Spread Eagle Peak area on the eastern flank of the northern Sangre de Cristo Mountains (Munger, 1965, p. 6).

The Pleasant Valley thrust is a north-trending, east-dipping, high-angle reverse fault which brings Precambrian metamorphic and igneous rocks into contact with sedimentary rocks of Permo-Pennsylvanian age along most of its length. The fault extends north from the southern boundary of the map area along Badger Creek and Willow Creek and crosses the northern boundary west of Gribbles Park. The dip varies from about 60 degrees east to vertical along this trace. Precambrian rocks are in fault contact with steeply dipping Manitou Dolomite in most of this region and the trace of the major fault is offset by numerous minor cross faults. Apparently, the fault dies out north of the map area before reaching South Park (De Voto, 1961, p.

204) rather than connecting with the London-Weston fault zone as proposed by Gableman (1952, p. 1596). Munger (1965, p. 4) shows the fault continuing south from the southern Mosquito Range across the canyon of the Arkansas River and into the northern Sangre de Cristo Mountains as far south as the Spread Eagle Peak area.

The western limb of the Pleasant Valley syncline is truncated by a steeply dipping fault that displays both normal and thrust fault characteristics. This fault is thought to be the northward continuation of the Wellsville-Orient thrust described by Gableman (1952, p. 1596). Within most of the mapped area, the fault appears to have a nearly vertical attitude. However, in some localities such as the upper reaches of Cottonwood Gulch (Sec. 28, R. 9 E., T. 49 N.), Precambrian metamorphic rocks are thrust eastward over the Manitou Dolomite along a thrust plane which dips about 15 degrees west. Similar variations in attitude have been described along the Mosquito-Weston fault north of the map area by Gableman (1952, p. 1597), and De Voto (1961, p. 206). Apparently, these variations arose when post-Laramide vertical faults, accompanied by local cross faulting and rotation, broke the former Laramide thrust plates. It is suggested here that the northward extension of the Wellsville-Orient thrust into the Arkansas Hills provides the link postulated by Burbank and Goddard (1937, p. 938) between the Wellsville-Orient fault and the Mosquito-Weston fault.

POST-VOLCANIC BLOCK FAULTING AND FORMATION OF THE UPPER ARKANSAS GRABEN

A series of parallel, north-trending, vertical faults offset the volcanic pile in the Arkansas Hills with step-down displacements toward the west. Reconstruction of the pre-volcanic drainage patterns indicates that these faults have played an important role in the formation of the upper Arkansas Valley segment of the Rio Grande rift zone (Chapin, Epis, and Lowell, 1970).

The Badger Creek fault is the easternmost of the major, north-trending, post-volcanic faults in the map area. It is a post-Laramide, vertical fault which was reactivated, in part, along the pre-existing Pleasant Valley thrust zone. At the confluence of Willow Creek and Badger Creek (Sec. 15, R. 10 E., T. 50 N.), the Badger Creek fault branches north-northeast and follows Badger Creek. The fault crosses the Gribbles Run paleovalley but appears to die out before reaching the Paleozoic strata bordering Gribbles Park. East of the fault, the pre-volcanic surface dips from 9,800 feet at the eastern boundary of the map area to 8,200 feet at Badger Creek in a distance of about 4 miles. It appears that block faulting, and perhaps doming associated with the Waugh Mountain volcanic center, has caused westward rotation of the block east of the Badger Creek fault. This rotation caused a dramatic reversal of gradient in the eastern portions of the Salida-Waugh Mountain and Gribbles Run paleovalleys which previously drained to the east (Chapin, Epis, and Lowell, 1970; Lowell, 1969, p. 73).

The Maverick fault is a vertical, north-trending fault which accounts for the presence of similar volcanic rocks differing in elevation by 600 to 1,000 feet in a distance of 1 to 2 miles. Rotation of the block west of the Maverick fault has tilted the volcanic rocks down toward the upper Arkansas Valley and produced an overall decrease in elevation of about 1,000 feet in 3 to 4 miles. The Maverick fault follows a pronounced topographic lineament along which occur intrusive breccia, altered felsite, hydrothermal alteration landslides, numerous mineral prospects, and freshwater springs.

Dead Horse fault is similar and parallel to the Maverick fault. It offsets the pre-volcanic surface at least 400 feet in a distance of ½ mile. The block west of the fault was stepped down and rotated to the west causing a gradient inversion in the western tributaries of the Salida-Waugh Mountain paleovalley (see geologic map, back pocket). The fault coincides with a prominent topographic lineament and marks the westernmost exposure of Paleozoic strata in the map area.

Dead Goat fault is a north-trending, vertical fault with minor step-down displacement on the west side. The fault is characterized by a strong topographic lineament, truncation of Tertiary rocks as young as Late Miocene-Pliocene (Dry Union Formation), severe disruption of adjacent exposures of Ash Flow 1, and landslides.

The formation of the upper Arkansas Valley appears to have been accomplished by downfaulting between the Sawatch Range on the west and the Mosquito Range on the east by recurrent movement along steep, north-trending faults such as those mapped in the Arkansas Hills. Such movements began after Oligocene volcanism and before Late Miocene time and have probably persisted intermittently into Holocene time (Chapin, Epis, and Lowell, 1970). They are thus conformable in style and timing with Basin-Range tectonism.

SUMMARY

PRE-VOLCANIC EVENTS

Late Cretaceous time marked the beginning of the Laramide Orogeny in central Colorado and early deformation produced the Pleasant Valley syncline and its bounding faults, the Pleasant Valley thrust and the Wellsville-Orient thrust in the Arkansas Hills. These early Laramide structures were partially obliterated by the subsequent emplacement of the Whitehorn stock in Early Tertiary time. The final phase of Laramide tectonism was followed by a prolonged period of erosion in central Colorado and the development of an extensive Late Eocene erosion surface. Incised in this surface were east-flowing drainages, such as the Salida-Waugh Mountain and Gribbles Run paleovalleys, which probably headed in the ancestral Sawatch Range prior to the formation of the upper Arkansas graben (Chapin, Epis, and Lowell, 1970; Lowell, 1969, p. 91).

VOLCANIC EVENTS

Volcanism in the Arkansas Hills and adjacent portions of the Thirtynine Mile volcanic field commenced in earliest Oligocene time with the deposition of Ash Flow 1 (Ash

Flow 1, 40.0 ± 1.4 m.y., Epis and Chapin, 1968, p. 52; 37.3 ± 1.9 m.y. and 35.4 ± 1.1 m.y., Van Alstine, 1969, p. 15). A thick sequence of ash-flow tuffs, lavas, and breccias were erupted from several volcanic centers. The youngest volcanic rocks dated in the adjacent Thirtynine Mile field are Middle Miocene in age (upper andesite, 18.9 ± 1.2 m.y., Epis and Chapin, 1968, p. 52), hence nearly the entire volcanic episode in the Arkansas Hills, including the time of interformational erosion, took place in about 15 to 20 million years. The bulk of this volcanic pile, however, was emplaced during 2 to 6 million years of Early Oligocene time.

The Early Oligocene eruption of Ash Flow 1 consisted of the emplacement of at least 3 member ash flows. These ash flows were probably erupted from a volcanic center in the Sawatch Range and spread eastward over the Late Eocene erosion surface at least as far as the Cripple Creek (Tobey, 1969) and Florissant areas (Niesen, 1969). The Salida-Waugh Mountain paleovalley was probably a major route by which ash flows were funneled eastward onto the erosion surface. The Gribbles Run paleovalley was probably filled by Ash Flow 1 and subsequently overrun by younger ash flows. Differential compaction and erosion led to the re-establishment of much of the pre-eruption topography following Ash Flow 1 deposition. The basal, unwelded ash flows of the Antero Formation were then erupted and these deposits filled the Salida-Waugh Mountain paleovalley and overflowed onto the adjacent erosional plateaus. Subsequent erosion of these friable, unwelded tuffs led to widespread deposition of tuffaceous sediments on the plateaus and rapid exhuming of the Salida-Waugh Mountain paleovalley.

Renewal of volcanism in the vent area of the Antero tuffs (locality uncertain but probably in the Sawatch Range), refilled the Salida-Waugh Mountain paleovalley with a sequence of at least 6 welded ash flows which comprise the tuff of Badger Creek. These welded tuffs were sufficiently resistant to erosion to preserve the Salida-Waugh paleovalley until the present time.

Initial activity at the Waugh Mountain volcanic center, east of the Arkansas Hills, began after the emplacement of the tuff of Badger Creek. With the deposition of the latite of East Badger Creek over the (then-filled), eastern end of the Salida-Waugh Mountain paleovalley. A thick sequence of ash flows correlated with the Ash Flow 7 unit of the Thirtynine Mile volcanic field, was deposited in the eastern and northeastern portion of the map area during Waugh Mountain activity. These ash flows have also been identified at Poncha Pass, Tallahassee Creek, the northern Wet Mountain Valley, and the upper Badger Creek drainage but their vent area is as yet unknown. They bear some resemblance to the Bonanza Tuff which occurs southwest of Salida and may possibly have come from the Bonanza volcanic center (see Epis, Bruns, and Weimer, this guidebook). The age of the Ash Flow 7 rocks is about 34.8 ± 1.4 m.y. (Epis and Chapin, 1968, p. 52). Continued eruptions from the Waugh Mountain volcanic center deposited the latite of Waugh Mountain above the Ash Flow 7 rocks along the eastern border of the map area. The andesitic and basaltic lavas, breccias, and tuffs of the Upper Andesite (18.9 ± 1.2 m.y.), then covered the latite of Waugh Mountain and marked the close of Waugh Mountain extrusive activity.

At approximately the same time that Waugh Mountain volcanism was occurring, the andesite of Big Baldy was deposited in the southwestern portion of the map area from an unknown eruptive source. The Silicic Felsite of Section 36 was emplaced some time after the deposition of the andesite of Big Baldy and may have been extruded from the same vent area.

The Tenderfoot Hill facies of the Dry Union Formation which is exposed along the outskirts of Salida represents the most recent phase of volcanic activity in the Arkansas Hills. The basaltic flows of the facies are interstratified with sediments which are thought to correlate with the Dry Union Formation of Late Miocene-Pliocene age. The volcanic rocks of the Tenderfoot Hill facies have been tilted steeply westward by the steep, north-trending, border faults of the upper Arkansas graben. These faults may have provided local conduits for the rise of basaltic magma during the period of crustal extension responsible for the Rio Grande rift zone.

POST-VOLCANIC EVENTS

Late Tertiary time was a period of profound structural and geomorphic modification in central Colorado. Uplift and block faulting formed the San Luis Basin and the upper Arkansas Valley segments of the Rio Grande rift zone and their bordering mountain ranges. In the Arkansas Hills, step faulting related to the formation of the upper Arkansas graben reversed stream gradients from eastward off the ancestral Sawatch Range to westward into the graben. The Salida-Waugh Mountain paleovalley was broken into 3 segments and the Gribbles Run paleovalley was broken into 2 segments. Deposition of the Dry Union Formation occurred contemporaneously with the down faulting. The basalt flows of the Tenderfoot Hill facies were emplaced within the basal portion of these sediments. The boulder gravels in the Salida-Waugh Mountain paleovalley probably represent pediment gravels deposited on a southwest-sloping, Late Tertiary, pediment surface (Van Alstine, 1969, p. 28) across which the Dry Union sediments were transported to the graben.

In Quaternary time, continued uplift and resultant erosion caused deep dissection of the Late Tertiary topography. Several periods of glaciation occurred in the Sawatch Range during the Pleistocene Epoch and extensive outwash gravels were deposited over the Dry Union Formation along the west side of the upper Arkansas Valley (Van Alstine, 1969, p. 22); however, no evidence of glaciation has been observed along the east side of the valley in the Arkansas Hills. Fault scarps cutting Late Miocene-Pliocene sediments of the Santa Fe and Dry Union Formations and Pleistocene gravels as young as Pinedale (Scott, 1970; Tweto, 1961; and Van Alstine, 1969) testify to continued tectonism along the Rio Grande rift zone.

ACKNOWLEDGMENTS

Financial support for the field work of this investigation was provided by the Geological Society of America in the form of two Penrose Bequest Research Grants of 1967 and 1968. Special thanks are expressed to Dr. C. E. Chapin who suggested and supervised the doctoral dissertation from which this paper is largely drawn. His continued support and enthusiasm are deeply appreciated. Messrs. R. E. Van Alstine and C. T. Wrucke of the U.S. Geological Survey provided the author with much valuable data. Mr. Robert Price and Miss Heidimarie Warlies greatly assisted in the task of drafting the geologic map. The author wishes to thank Dr. A. J. Budding of the New Mexico Institute of Mining and Technology, and Mr. R. E. Lewis of the U.S. Geological Survey for reading the manuscript in its early form and for offering valuable suggestions for its improvement. They are of course, not responsible for shortcomings which exist in the present form of the paper.

REFERENCES

Behre, C. H., Osborn, E. F., and Rainwater, E. H., 1936, Contact ore deposition at the Calumet Iron Mine, Colorado: Econ. Geol., v. 31, p. 781-804.

Bhutta, Muhammad, 1954, Geology of the Salida area, Chaffee and Fremont counties, Colorado: Unpublished D. Sc. thesis, Colorado School of Mines, 173 p.

Burbank, W. S., and Goddard, E. N., 1937, Thrusting in Huerfano Park, Colorado: and related problems of orogeny in the Sangre de Cristo Mountains: Geol. Soc. America Bull., v. 48, p. 931-976.

Chapin, C. E., Epis, R. C., and Lowell, G. R., 1970, Late Eocene paleovalleys and Oligocene volcanic rocks along the upper Arkansas Valley segment of the Rio Grande rift zone in Colorado (abs.): New Mexico Geological Society, program of 24th ann. mtg., p. 8.

De Vota, R. H., 1961, Geology of southwestern South Park, Park and Chaffee counties, Colorado: Unpublished D. Sc. thesis, Colorado School of Mines, 201 p.

————, 1964, Stratigraphy and structure of Tertiary rocks in southwestern South Park: Mountain Geologist, v. 1, no. 3, p. 117-126.

Epis, R. C., and Chapin, C. E., 1968, Geologic history of the Thirtynine Mile volcanic field, central Colorado: Colorado School of Mines Quart., v. 63, no. 3, p. 51-85.

Gableman, J. W., 1952, Structure and origin of northern Sangre de Cristo Range, Colorado: Am. Assoc. Petroleum Geologists Bull., v. 36, p. 1574-1612.

Johnson, J. H., 1937, The Tertiary deposits of South Park, Colorado, with a description of the Oligocene algal limestone (abs. of thesis): Colorado University Studies, v. 25, no. 1, p. 77.

Lowell, G. R., 1969, Geologic relationships of the Salida area to the Thirtynine Mile volcanic field of central Colorado: Unpublished Ph.D. dissertation, New Mexico Institute of Mining and Technology, 113 p.

Munger, R. D., 1965, Structural geology of the Spread Eagle Peak area, Sangre de Cristo Mountains, Colorado: Mountain Geologist, v. 2, no. 1, p. 3-21.

Niesen, P. L., 1969, Stratigraphic relationships of the Florissant Lake Beds to the Thirtynine Mile volcanic field of central Colorado: Unpublished M.S. thesis, New Mexico Institute of Mining and Technology, 65 p.

Osborn, E. F., and Rainwater, E. H., 1934, Geology of the Calumet, Colorado mining district: Unpublished thesis, Northwestern University, 147 p.

Scott, G. R., 1970, Quaternary faulting and potential earthquakes in east-central Colorado: U.S. Geol. Survey Research 1970, p. C11-C18.

Tobey, E. F., 1969, Geologic and petrologic relationships between the Thirtynine Mile volcanic field and the Cripple Creek volcanic center: Unpublished M.S. thesis, New Mexico Institute of Mining and Technology, 61 p.

Tweto, Ogden, 1961, Late Cenozoic events of the Leadville district and upper Arkansas Valley, Colorado, in Short papers in the geologic and hydrologic sciences, p. B133-B135.

Van Alstine, R. E., 1969, Geology and mineral deposits of the Poncha Springs NE quadrangle, Chaffee County, Colorado: U.S. Geol. Survey Prof. Paper 626, 52 p.

Van Alstine, R. E., and Lewis, G. E., 1960, Pliocene sediments near Salida, Chaffee County, Colorado: U.S. Geol. Survey Research 1960 in Short papers in the geological sciences, p. B245.

PRELIMINARY PALEOPALYNOLOGICAL ANALYSIS OF ALAMOSA FORMATION SEDIMENTS

by

CHARLES R. PRICE

Alamosa High School
Alamosa, Colorado

The gravels, sands, and clays of the San Luis Basin are divided into two groups: an older series of conglomerates with intercalated lava flows and a younger overlying series of blue clays with interstratified sand beds. The older conglomeratic series is the Santa Fe Formation, which has been shown farther south in the Rio Grande Valley to be Miocene in age (Siebenthal, 1910, p. 39). The younger, upper series of sediments of the San Luis Basin make up the Alamosa Formation (Siebenthal, 1910, p. 40).

In all places where the glaciers of the east range extended far enough, they deposited their moraines on top of the Alamosa Formation. The age of the Alamosa Formation is thus seen from its position above the Santa Fe Formation and below the glacial structures in the valley to be preglacial and post-Miocene. The evidence seems to indicate that sedimentation took place just previous to Wisconsin glaciation. The inference made is that the sediments are of Late Pliocene or Early Pleistocene age (Siebenthal, 1910, p. 46).

The sediments exposed at Hansen Bluff are in chronological order. Being thus deposited and having been mostly undisturbed, these sediments are suitable for paleopalynological analysis.

The purpose of the fossil pollen analysis project, which has been initiated this year, is to date the sediments more exactly. It is hoped that the pollen spectrograms and climatograms obtained by analysis will correlate with known changes in plant distribution or climate within the area. One such possible correlation, for example, would be the climate change and resultant ecosystem change caused by the glacial age.

The San Luis Basin is very flat and there are few natural exposures of the Alamosa Formation. Hansen Bluff, the best exposure, is located in the south-central part of the basin (E ½ sec. 10, T. 36 N., R. 11 E., Alamosa County), about six and one-half miles north of Las Sauses, Colorado. The bluff was created by the Rio Grande which has since moved its course away from the bluff. Approximately forty feet of Alamosa Formation sediments are exposed. They vary in size from fine gravel and sand to fine clay, and in color from pale red to yellowish brown.

Samples for the preliminary analysis were taken at each major change in sediment type. Nine samples were taken in the twenty-seven foot range from the upper Alamosa Formation sediment down to a hard sandy-clay layer which was chosen as a marker bed (fig. 1).

The potassium hydroxide-hydrofluoric acid-acetolysis

FIGURE 1.

Alamosa Formation exposed at Hansen Bluff.

process detailed below was used to extract the pollen from the sediment samples. The pollen is stained with saphranin "O" to make microscopic examination, identification, and counting easier. The pollen was mounted in glycerin for the preliminary analysis.

CHEMICAL TREATMENT FOR EXTRACTION OF POLLEN

1. Rub airdry sample through 1mm. mesh screen and discard all organic debris and rocks too large to pass through screen.
2. Soak sample in 10% KOH for 24 hours.
3. Strain through 1mm. mesh screen.
4. Decant back and forth to remove coarse sand.
5. Strain through 4 layers of gauze.
6. Centrifuge in polyethylene centrifuge tube at 1500 rpm for 45 seconds, decant supernatant.
7. Water wash, centrifuge and decant.
8. Hot 10% HCl, centrifuge and decant.
9. 48% HF, boiling water bath for 25 minutes, centrifuge and decant.
10. 2 hot HCl washes or more (wash until colloidal SiO_2 and silicofluorides are removed), centrifuge and decant.
11. Glacial acetic acid, transfer to glass centrifuge tube, centrifuge and decant.
12. 10cc. acetolysis mixture (9cc. acetic anhydride, 1cc. con. H_2SO_4), boiling water bath three minutes, centrifuge and decant.
13. Glacial acetic acid, centrifuge and decant.
14. 2 water washes, centrifuge and decant.
15. Strain with saphranin "O," centrifuge and decant.

16. Add glycerin mounting medium.
17. Mount slide.

Additional steps which will be used in future studies:
14. Divide sample into two equal parts, skip one part to step 18.
15. Add 5cc. glacial acetic acid, add 2 drops con. HCl, stir, add 1 drop sat. NaClO$_3$ soln., stir one minute, centrifuge and decant.
16. 2 water washes, centrifuge and decant.
17. Glacial acetic acid, centrifuge and decant.
18. 95% ethyl alcohol, centrifuge and decant.
19. Absolute ethyl alcohol, centrifuge and decant.
20. Acetone, stain part that went through 15-17 with saphranin "O," centrifuge and decant.
21. Benzene, allow to stand overnight, centrifuge and decant.
22. Silicone oil, allow to stand for two days.
23. Mount slides of each part of sample.

Many different processes use the potassium hydroxide, hydrofluoric acid, and acetolysis steps. This specific process was detailed by Dr. Hobart Dixon, Biology Department, Adams State College.

Three of the nine sediments yielded fossil pollen upon analysis. Two of these contained pollen in very low densities and the third, which also contained shells, contained a large amount of pollen. The pollen counts, however, did not include enough grains to be statistically accurate. The results, which can still be considered to indicate the fossil pollen content of the upper Alamosa Formation sediments, are shown in table 1.

Further work planned includes: complete analysis of all sediments exposed at Hansen Bluff and analysis of any subsurface samples of the Alamosa Formation which can be obtained. The same chemical processes will be used with the added bleaching and dehydration steps noted previously. The pollen will be mounted in silicone oil which should produce permanent mounts.

TABLE 1.

Pollen counts from the Alamosa Formation at Hansen Bluff. Sediment levels measured upwards from marker bed.

POLLEN TYPE	GRAINS COUNTED		
	24 FT. LEVEL	1 FT. LEVEL	MARKER BED
Chenopodiaceae		1	
Cyperaceae Carix			1
Cyperaceae Larix		1	
Gramineae		1	7
Gymnospermae (unidentifiable further)			4
Juniperus			50
Pinus	1	1	2
Conifer (unidentifiable further)			6
Plantaginaceae		3	
Taxus			5
Urticaceae		6	
Unidentified types (8 types total for simplicity)			13
Unidentified (generally because of damage to the grain)	9	4	1

REFERENCES

Siebenthal, C. E., 1910, Geology and Water Resources of the San Luis Valley, Colorado: U.S. Geol. Survey Water-Supply Paper 210, 128 p.

RECONNAISSANCE GEOLOGY AND ECONOMIC SIGNIFICANCE OF THE PLATORO CALDERA, SOUTHEASTERN SAN JUAN MOUNTAINS, COLORADO*

by

PETER W. LIPMAN AND THOMAS A. STEVEN

U.S. Geological Survey
Denver, Colorado

Recent U.S. Geological Survey investigations of volcanic rocks of the San Juan Mountains have led to recognition of numerous caldera-collapse structures (fig. 1) related to eruption of voluminous ash-flow tuffs in Oligocene time (Luedke and Burbank, 1968; Steven and Ratté, 1965; Steven and Lipman, 1968). It has also become clear that most major ore deposits of the San Juan Mountains, such as those near Creede, Silverton-Telluride-Ouray, and Lake City, are closely associated with calderas (Burbank and Luedke, 1968; Steven, 1968). An apparent exception to this association between mineralization and caldera structure seemed until recently to be the Summitville-Platoro district in the southeastern San Juan Mountains (Steven and Ratté, 1960; Steven, 1968). This paper gives a preliminary description of the newly recognized Platoro caldera and the associated mineral deposits, including those in the Summitville district.

GEOLOGIC SETTING

The San Juan volcanic field, which covers about 25,000 km² in southwestern Colorado and adjacent parts of New Mexico (fig. 1), is the largest erosional remnant of a once nearly continuous volcanic field that extended over much of the southern Rocky Mountains in Oligocene and later time (Steven and Epis, 1968). Throughout the San Juan remnant of this field, the general volcanic sequence was relatively simple: initial intermediate lavas and breccias, followed closely in time by more silicic ash-flow tuffs, and ending with a compositionally bimodal association of basalt and rhyolite (Lipman and Steven, 1969).

In the San Juan field voluminous early intermediate-composition lavas and breccias—mainly alkali andesite, rhyodacite, and mafic quartz latite—were erupted from numerous scattered central volcanoes onto an eroded tectonically stable terrane. They formed mostly during the interval 35-30 m.y. (million years) ago (Lipman and others, 1970).

About 30 m.y. ago, major volcanic activity changed to explosive ash-flow eruptions of quartz latite and low-silica rhyolite that persisted until about 26 m.y. ago. Source areas for the ash flows are marked by large calderas. Two groups of lavas and associated rocks of intermediate composition intertongue with the ash-flow sequence: (1) quartz latitic lavas that were erupted in and adjacent to caldera structures and are genetically related to the ash-flow activity, and (2) other generally more mafic lavas and related rocks that are widely distributed without evident structural relation to the ash-flow eruptive centers. The second group apparently represents a continuation of the early intermediate activity into the period of major ash-flow eruption.

In Early Miocene the character of volcanism changed notably. Whereas the Oligocene volcanics are predominantly intermediate lavas and related silicic differentiates, the younger rocks are largely a bimodal association of basalt and high-silica alkali rhyolite. Basalt and minor rhyolite were erupted intermittently through the Miocene and Pliocene, and at one time formed a widespread veneer over the older volcanic terrane.

ROCK UNITS

The stratigraphy of the Platoro caldera area is most readily summarized in terms of (1) precaldera intermediate-composition lavas and related rocks of the Conejos Formation, (2) ash-flow sheets of the Treasure Mountain Tuff erupted from the Platoro caldera, (3) lavas and intrusions related to the Platoro caldera, (4) younger ash-flow sheets from calderas farther northwest, and (5) basalt and rhyolite of the Hinsdale Formation.

CONEJOS FORMATION

All pre-caldera rocks in the Summitville-Platoro area are parts of the Conejos Formation (Larsen and Cross, 1956). This unit consists largely of lava flows and breccias that range in composition from calc-alkalic andesite to mafic quartz latite, and also contains varied volcaniclastic rocks, mainly of mudflow origin. Most rocks of the Conejos Formation were erupted in middle Oligocene time from numerous widely scattered central volcanoes, at least three of which contributed to the accumulation within the area of Figure 2. Conejos rocks in the east half of the mapped area are predominantly lavas and flow breccias, whereas the bulk of the formation southwest of the Platoro caldera consists of bedded breccias and conglomerates with minor intercalated flows.

TREASURE MOUNTAIN TUFF

The Treasure Mountain Tuff is here redefined from the Treasure Mountain Rhyolite (Larsen and Cross, 1956) to

---
* Reprinted from U.S. Geol. Survey Prof. Paper 700-C, Pages C19-C29.

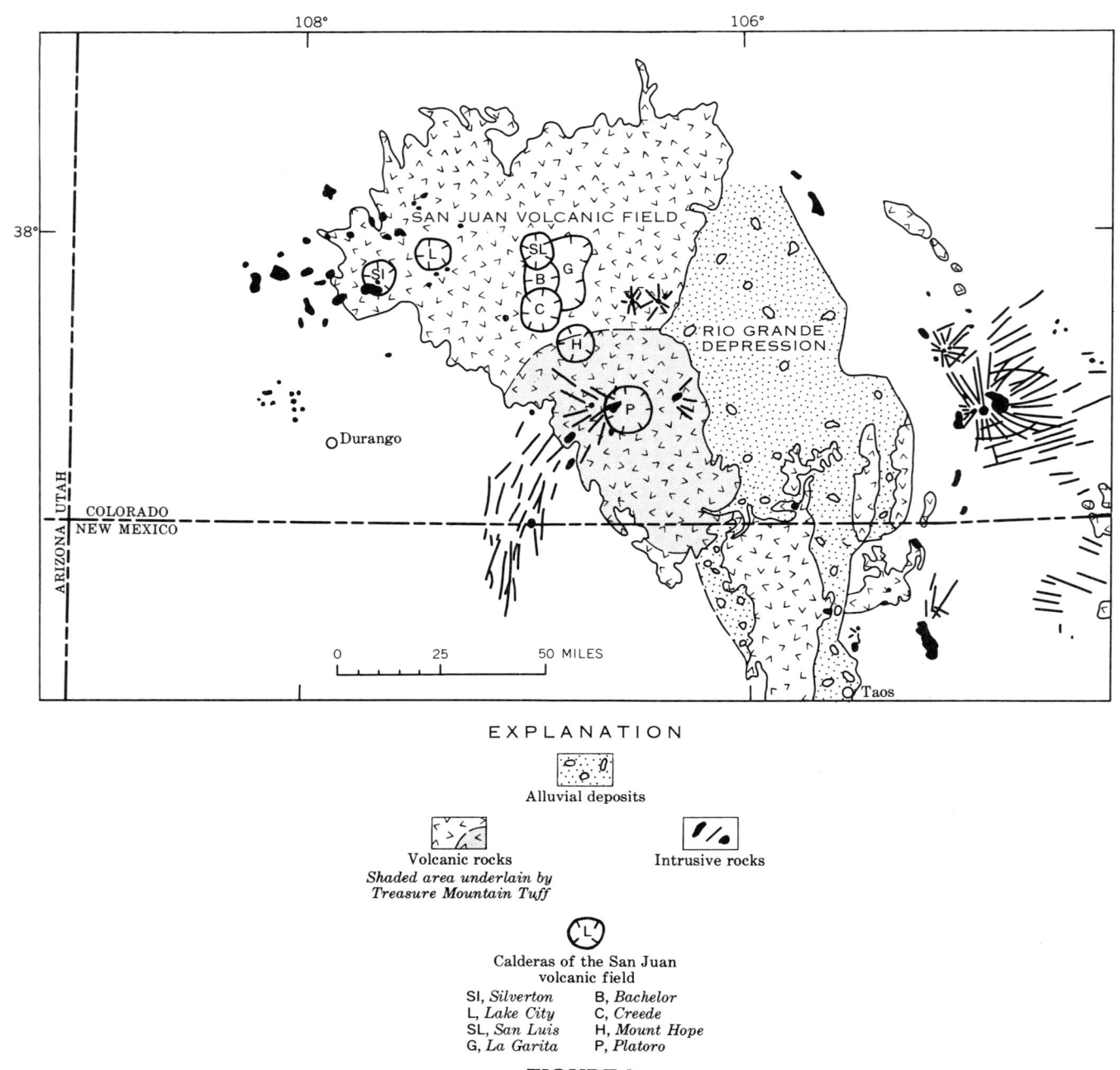

FIGURE 1.
Index map showing location of the San Juan volcanic field, calderas of the San Juan Mountains, and distribution of ash-flow tuffs erupted from the Platoro caldera. In part modified from Cohee (1961).

include only the units present at the type locality at Treasure Mountain, approximately 20 km west of Summitville, Colo., plus additional intertonguing tuffs farther to the south. Excluded from the Treasure Mountain Tuff are thick sections of other welded ash-flow tuffs that were mapped as Treasure Mountain Rhyolite in the western and central San Juan Mountains by Larsen and Cross (1956, pl. 1). The largest body of these in the western San Juan Mountains was designated the Gilpin Peak Tuff by Luedke and Burbank (1963). As redefined, the Treasure Mountain Tuff is a coextensive assemblage of ash-flow tuffs, largely or entirely related to the Platoro caldera. Three large ash-flow sheets in the Treasure Mountain Tuff that have been mapped over nearly 5,000 km² are formally designated members in this report: the La Jara Canyon, Ojito Creek, and Ra Jadero Members, in ascending order. Less widespread air-fall and ash-flow tuffs below the La Jara Canyon Member, between the La Jara Canyon and Ojito Creek Members, and above the Ra Jadero Member are informally designated the lower, middle, and upper tuffs, respectively.

The La Jara Canyon Member is a multiple-flow, compound cooling unit of phenocryst-rich quartz latite that

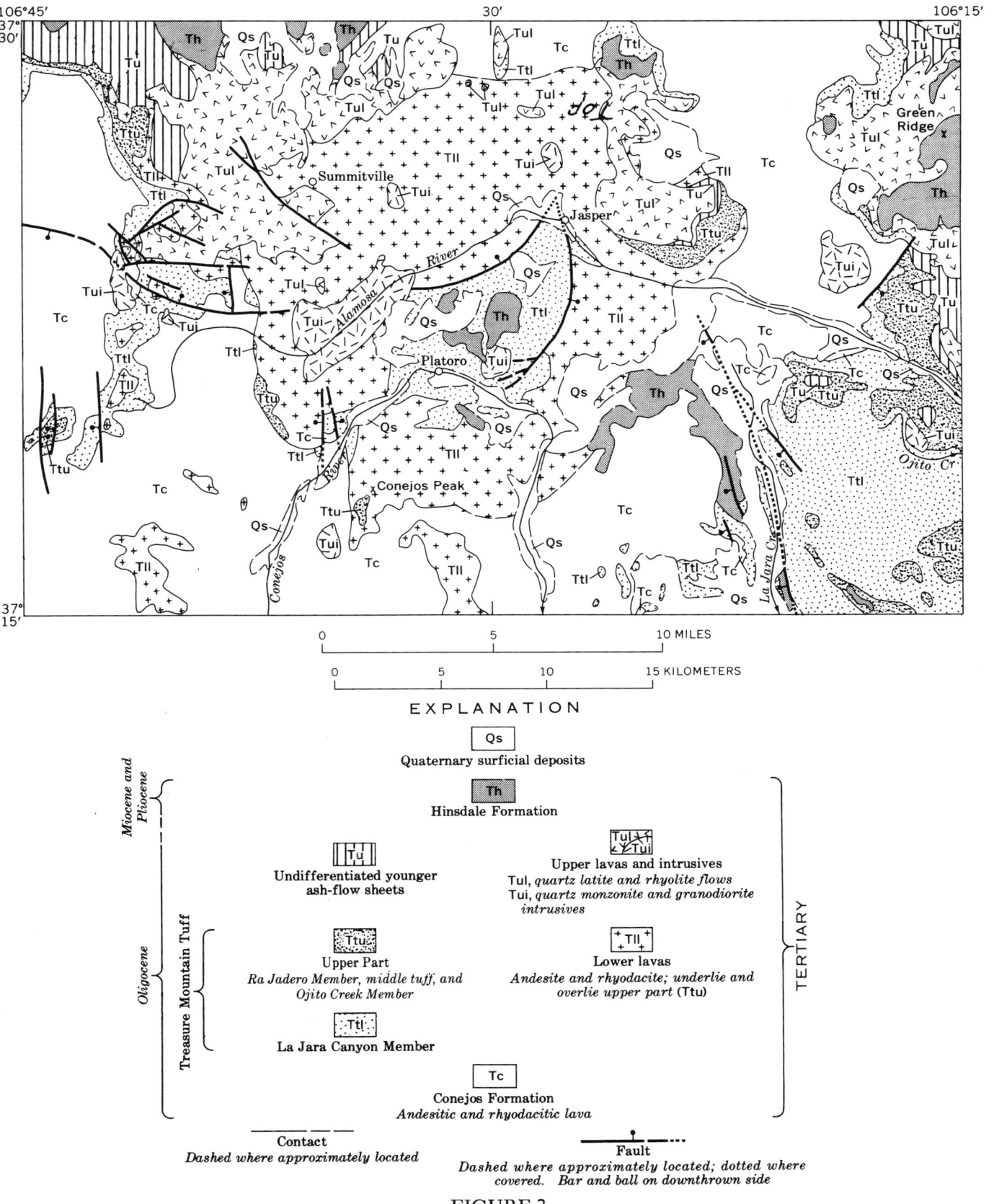

FIGURE 2.
Generalized geologic map of the Platoro caldera area.

makes up the first widespread ash-flow sheet in the eastern and central San Juan Mountains; eruption of these ash-flows resulted in the first major collapse of the Platoro caldera. At its type locality in La Jara Canyon (37°10′ N., 106°20′ W.), about 27 km southeast of Platoro, this sheet is about 100 m thick (fig. 3), and its maximum thickness outside the Platoro caldera is about 300 m. Within the caldera it is much thicker; near Jasper (fig. 2), where its top is eroded and its base is not exposed, it is more than 800 m thick. The original total volume of the La Jara Canyon Member was more than 500 km^3 and possibly more than 1,000 km^3.

Tuff in the La Jara Canyon Member contains 20-40 percent phenocrysts, mostly plagioclase, accompanied by some biotite, augite, and opaque oxides. Silica content is 65-70 percent. La Jara Canyon within the Platoro caldera is somewhat different from the outflow tuffs that occur outside the caldera: it is lower in silica, contains more phenocrysts, and is propylitically altered. The K-Ar radiometric age of the La Jara Canyon Member at Treasure Mountain is 29.8 m.y. (mean of biotite and plagioclase; Lipman and others, 1970, table 3, No. 1). The tuff is everywhere characterized by reversed magnetic polarity, as indicated by about 25 field determinations.

Outside the Platoro caldera the La Jara Canyon Member is generally separated from the Ojito Creek Member by the middle tuff, consisting of 10-70 m of ash-fall and weakly welded ash-flow tuff that is almost everywhere poorly exposed.[1]

The Ojito Creek and Ra Jadero Members are relatively thin widespread ash-flow sheets of similar petrography and megascopic appearance; accordingly, they are described together and combined with the middle tuff in Figure 2. Each is typically 10-20 m thick (fig. 3), dark brown where densely welded, and quartz latitic in composition. The initial volume of the two sheets together was probably about 100 km^3. The Ra Jadero Member is virtually coextensive with the La Jara Canyon Member; the Ojito Creek Member does not extend as far north and is missing from the type section of the formation at Treasure Mountain. Both members are well exposed together in their respective type localities: at the head of Ojito Creek (37°20′ N., 106°17′ W.), about 22 km east of Platoro, and in the Ra Jadero Canyon (37°14′ N., 106°16′ W.), about 26 km miles southeast of Platoro.

The Ojito Creek and Ra Jadero Members contain 10-15 percent phenocrysts, and are distinctly less crystal rich than the La Jara Canyon Member. Plagioclase is the major phenocryst constituent in both, accompanied by augite and opaque oxides. The Ra Jadero Member, unlike other tuffs in the Treasure Mountain, contains fairly abundant sanidine. The Ojito Creek Member has normal magnetic polarity; the Ra Jadero Member is reversed. These rocks have not yet been dated radiometrically, but relations to other dated units in the area suggest that they are no more than about 1 m.y. younger than the La Jara Canyon Member (29.8 m.y.).

LAVAS AND INTRUSIONS OF THE CALDERA

Lavas related to the Platoro caldera are generally divisible into two groups: older nonporphyritic dark-gray to black andesite and rhyodacite (lower lavas, fig. 2), and younger more silicic lavas (upper lavas, fig. 2), mostly light-gray rhyodacite and quartz latite that characteristically contain large feldspar phenocrysts as well as biotite and augite or hornblende.

The dark older lavas flooded the caldera moat to overflowing shortly after the core of the caldera was resurgently domed; they are more than 700 m thick at Conejos Peak in the southern part of the caldera. The obscurity of contacts at caldera walls between these flows and petrographically similar lavas of the Conejos Formation has contributed to the delayed recognition of the Platoro caldera. Although the dark lavas were correctly described as overlying the Treasure Mountain Rhyolite in the Platoro-Summitville area by Patton (1917, p. 36), who designated them the Summitville Andesite, they were mistakenly assigned to the Conejos Formation by Larsen and Cross (1956, p. 36), who also considered the Treasure Mountain Tuff inside the Platoro caldera to represent an older part of the Conejos Formation (p. 101-102). Steven and Ratté (1960)

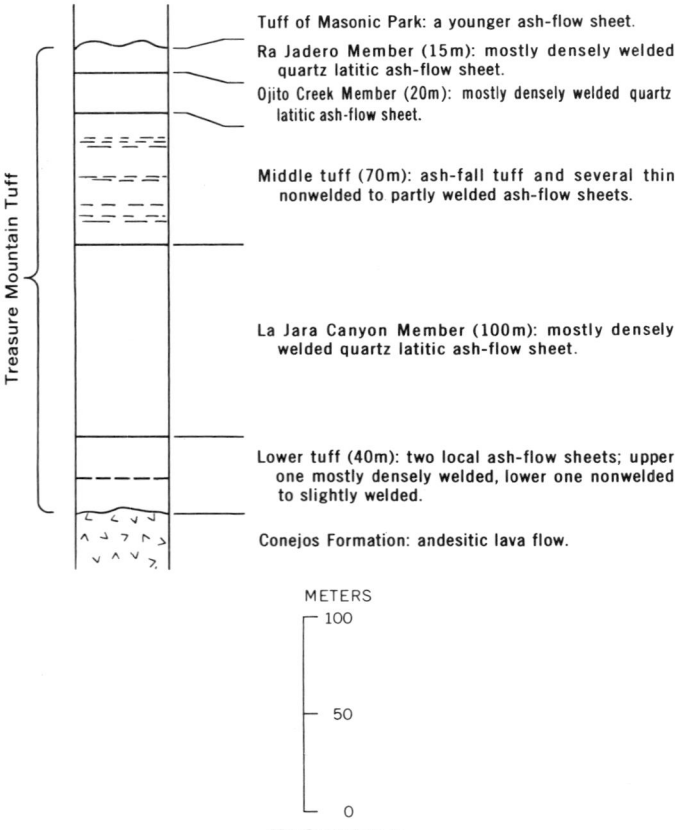

FIGURE 3.
Columnar section of the Treasure Mountain Tuff at La Jara Canyon.

---

[1]The lower and upper tuffs, of similar lithology, are not well developed within the area of Figure 2. Thick lower tuffs are present a few kilometers to the south, at La Jara Canyon (fig. 3).

and Calkin (1967) followed Larsen and Cross in assigning the dark lavas, including those at Conejos Peak, to the Conejos Formation.

The younger porphyritic lavas occur in a broad zone along the north side of the Platoro caldera from Summitville to Green Ridge (fig. 2); they are remnants of a partial ring of caldera-margin lava domes. The lavas at Summitville were, until recently, assigned to the Fisher Quartz Latite (Larsen and Cross, 1956, p. 172; Steven and Ratté, 1960), but Steven and Ratté (1965, p. 43-44) later restricted use of this formational name to late lavas and breccias localized around the Creede caldera. The Summitville-Green Ridge assemblage occupies a similar position with respect to the Platoro caldera, and was erupted independently of the type Fisher Quartz Latite. K-Ar ages of porphyritic lavas of the Summitville-Green Ridge zone range from 27.8 to 20.2 m.y., but the distribution of certain younger ash-flows tuffs suggests that most of these lavas were erupted in a relatively brief interval close to the older date (Lipman and others, 1970), and are largely Oligocene in age.

Several fine- to medium-grained granodioritic to quartz monzonitic stocks within and near the Platoro caldera appear to be genetically related to the lava-flow activity at this center. The largest granitic body, the Alamosa River stock, intrudes the dark lavas that filled the moat of the resurgent Platoro caldera, but relations with its alteration halo indicate that at least some of the upper lavas are younger (Steven and Ratté, 1960, p. 38). Dikes that are petrographically similar to the porphyritic lavas define an incomplete radial pattern around this stock (fig. 4), indicating closely associated activity. The Alamosa River stock has yielded a K-Ar age of 29.1 m.y., in good agreement with the other geologic relations (Lipman and others, 1970).

UNDIVIDED YOUNGER ASH-FLOW SHEETS

Younger ash-flow sheets that were erupted from calderas farther north in the San Juan volcanic field (fig. 1) are present within the mapped area (fig. 2) around the north side of the Platoro caldera and locally within the caldera. Units present but not shown separately include the tuff of Masonic Park (Lipman and others, 1970) erupted from the Mount Hope caldera (fig. 1), Fish Canyon Tuff (Olson and others, 1968) erupted from the La Garita caldera, Carpenter Ridge Tuff (Olson and others, 1968) erupted from the Bachelor caldera, Wason Park Rhyolite (Ratté and Steven, 1967) erupted from the Creede caldera area, and Snowshoe Mountain Quartz Latite (Ratté and Steven, 1967) erupted from the Creede caldera.

HINSDALE FORMATION

The last volcanic activity in the Summitville-Platoro area is represented by the Hinsdale Formation, which consists of alkalic olivine basalt, basaltic andesite, and small scattered plug domes of silicic alkali rhyolite. These rocks probably range widely in age and are not closely related in origin to the Platoro caldera. Basalt and rhyolite from Beaver Creek, just north of the area of Figure 2, have yielded K-Ar ages of 23.4 and 21.9 m.y., respectively, but other Hinsdale basalts in the southeastern San Juan Mountains are as young a 5 m.y. (Lipman and others, 1970).

STRUCTURAL EVOLUTION OF THE PLATORO CALDERA

Before ash-flow eruptions began in the southeastern San Juan Mountains, the central volcanoes of the Conejos Formation had been extensively eroded and the intervening basins filled with the resultant detritus, producing a widespread surface of low relief. As a result, phenocryst-rich quartz latitic ash-flows from sources in the Summitville-Platoro region were able to spread 30-40 km in all directions, depositing the La Jara Canyon Member of the Treasure Mountain Tuff.

Collapse of a subcircular block about 20 km in diameter began before completion of these eruptions, with the result that the later ash-flows of the Jara Canyon Member were ponded and accumulated to a thickness in excess of 800 m within the caldera. These later tuffs were somewhat more mafic and phenocryst rich than the initially erupted tuff of the widespread thin outflow sheet, reflecting differentiation in the source magma chamber similar to that described for other ash-flow deposits in the San Juan Mountains and elsewhere (Ratté and Steven, 1964; Lipman and others, 1966). The concurrent eruption and collapse at the Platoro caldera clearly differ from those of some other carefully studied areas such as the Valles caldera in New Mexico, where the last erupted units are no thicker inside the caldera than outside, demonstrating that eruption was virtually complete before major subsidence occurred (Smith and Bailey, 1968, p. 638). Other calderas in which thick intracaldera accumulations of ash-flow tuff demonstrate collapse contemporaneous with eruption have been recognized in the San Juan Mountains (Steven and Ratté, 1965, p. 59) and in southern Nevada (Christiansen and others, 1965; Byers and others, 1969). Collapse probably occurs concurrently only with ash-flow eruptions of very large volume; in some such eruptions initial collapse appears to have coincided approximately with abrupt compositional changes in the zoned ash-flow sheets (Lipman and others, 1966, p. F24-F25; Byers and others, 1969, p. 86).

The thick tuffs of the La Jara Canyon Member within the Platoro caldera are topographically and structurally high as a result of resurgent doming (Smith and Bailey, 1968) shortly after collapse. Early resurgence is demonstrated by the presence of monolithologic talus breccias of the La Jara Canyon that intertongue with the caldera-filling moat lavas adjacent to the resurgent block. This block dips homoclinally to the southwest and is bounded on its north and east sides by normal faults of large displacement. Prior to disruption by these faults there may have existed a more complete structural dome such as characterizes most resurgent cauldrons (Smith and Bailey, 1968).

The dark andesitic lavas (lower lavas of fig. 2) within the Platoro caldera filled the moat after resurgence was virtually complete, and they lap unconformably onto the uplifted central block. A minimum figure for the amount of collapse

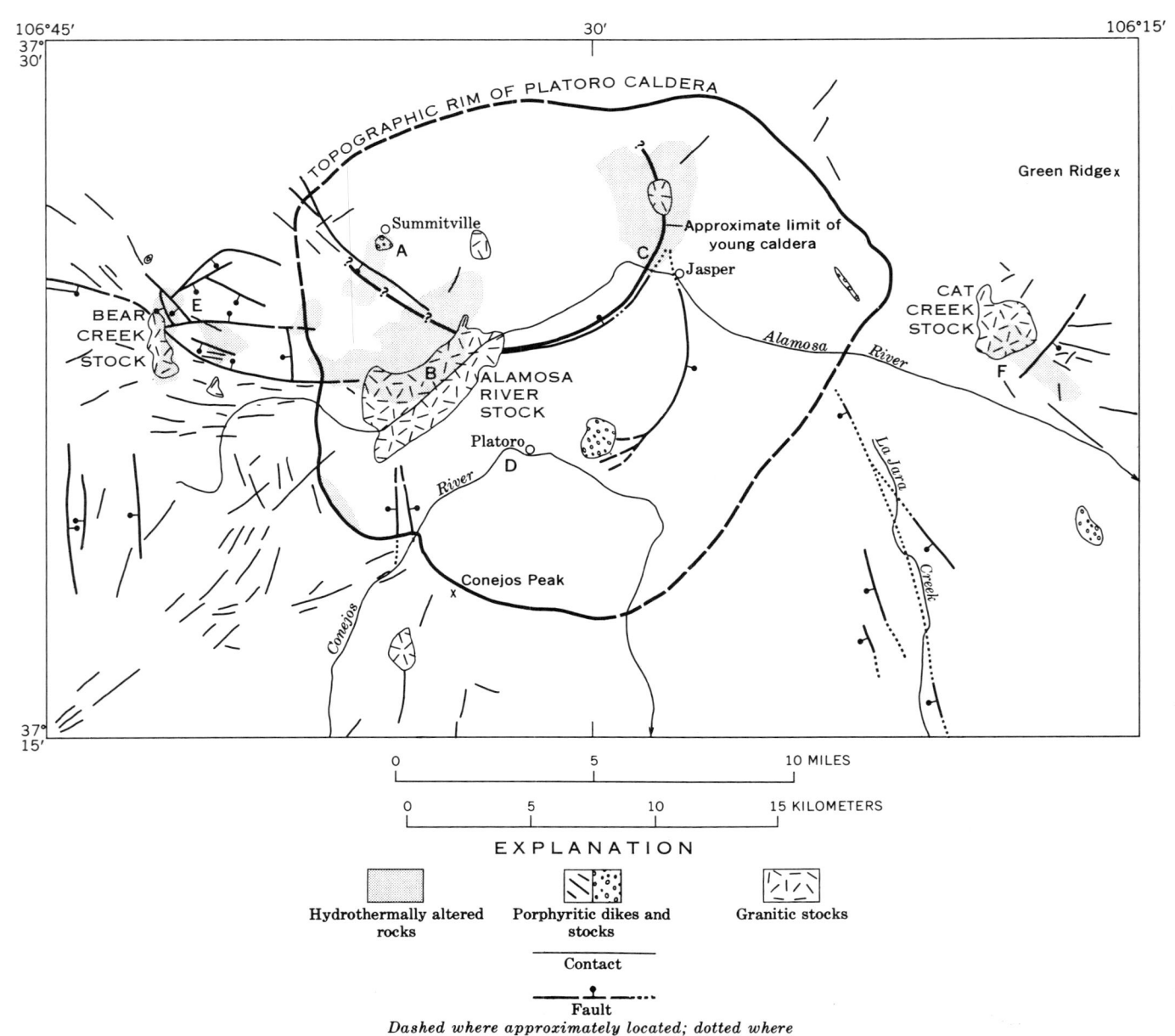

FIGURE 4.

Map showing stocks, dikes, faults, and areas of extensive hydrothermal alteration in the vicinity of the Platoro caldera. A—Summitville district; B—Stunner and Gilmore districts; C—Jasper district; D—Platoro district; E—Crater Creek area; and F—Cat Creek area.

of the Platoro caldera is 1,500 m, as shown by the thickness of these lavas in the caldera moat (about 700 m on Conejos Peak) and the thickness of the La Jara Canyon Member within the caldera (about 800 m with the top eroded and the base not exposed). These andesitic lavas, in essence, represent a continuation of the same type of volcanic activity that characterized the Conejos Formation, with which they are readily confused in the field. Continued andesitic volcanic activity during ash-flow eruptions characterizes other portions of the San Juan volcanic field as well, and this relation is significant in reconstructing the petrologic evolution of the volcanic field (Lipman and Steven, 1969).

Upper tuffs of the Treasure Mountain, including the Ojito Creek and Ra Jadero Members, were erupted after the moat of the early, resurgent part of the Platoro caldera was nearly completely filled by andesitic lavas, as these tuffs are found within the caldera only in a few places above thick accumulations of andesitic lavas (fig. 2). The Ojito Creek and Ra Jadero tuffs are nearly coextensive with the La Jara Canyon Member and must have been erupted from the same general area. Although the volumes of these upper two members are much less than the La Jara Canyon, on the order of 50 km³ each, they are sufficiently large to indicate the likelihood of associated caldera collapse (Smith, 1960, fig. 3). Several features suggest the probability of late collapse related to these tuffs within the northwestern part of the Platoro caldera (fig. 4), although this extensively altered area is not fully understood at the present preliminary stage of study. In this area the arcuate northeast-trending fault that truncates the central resurgent block of La Jara Canyon Tuff (fig. 4) has a displacement of more than 800 m in a direction plausible as a younger caldera-margin fault. The andesitic lavas inside the proposed late caldera differ somewhat from those in other parts of the Platoro caldera: as noted by Steven and Ratté (1960, p. 11), they are exceptionally thick, poorly stratified, and highly brecciated. Although not differentiated on the preliminary map (fig. 2), these flows are probably younger than andesitic lavas in other parts of the Platoro caldera and postdate late collapse related to eruption of the upper two members of the Treasure Mountain Tuff.

Extrusion of the porphyritic (upper) lavas and intrusion of dikes and granitic stocks following collapse and filling of the younger caldera constitute the last phase of igneous activity related to the compound Platoro caldera. The existing area of porphyritic lavas represent remnants of an arc of lava domes around the north side of the Platoro caldera. These lavas may originally have been widely distributed farther to the south as well, having been fed by the numerous dikes and stocks southwest and east of the Platoro caldera (fig. 4), but now completely removed by erosion. Many of the stocks and dikes are petrographically similar to the porphyritic lavas, and they appear to have been emplaced at about the same time. The radiometric age of the Alamosa River stock (29.1 m.y.) is only slightly younger than the La Jara Canyon Member (29.8 m.y), even though this stock is clearly later than the boundary fault of the late caldera. The Bear Creek stock in the western part of the mapped area (fig. 4) is petrographically similar to the Alamosa River stock, but is later than some of the porphyritic lavas, inasmuch as it intrudes a complex graben of several faults which displace these lavas (fig. 2). This structure is clearly a radial graben related to the Platoro caldera.

MINERALIZATION RELATED TO THE PLATORO CALDERA

Recognition of the Platoro caldera, and of the general sequence of igneous events related to its development, has provided at least partial answers to many puzzling questions of long standing concerning the localization of the mineral deposits in the Summitville mining district and nearby mineralized areas. Earlier studies either were done before the concepts of ash-flow tuffs and associated calderas were developed (Patton, 1917) or were too limited in scope for the regional picture to be discerned (Steven and Ratté, 1960; Calkin, 1967). The preliminary summary by Steven (1968, p. 712-713) clearly reflects the uncertainties concerning localization both of the igneous centers and of related hydrothermal activity in the Summitville area.

We now know that the mineralization at Summitville and in certain nearby areas is closely related to intrusive and extrusive centers localized along margin ring structures formed during compound subsidence of the Platoro caldera, and outlying mineralization was controlled mainly by outward-extending fracture zones. The localization is thus closely comparable to that of other highly mineralized areas in the central and western San Juan Mountains (Steven, 1968; Burbank and Luedke, 1968), and it is instructive to consider other possibly analogous features that may bear on the mineral potential of this generally poorly explored area.

SUMMITVILLE AND JASPER DISTRICTS

As described by Steven and Ratté (1969), gold-silver-copper ore in the Summitville district was deposited in a very shallow volcanic environment within a then recently erupted volcanic dome of coarsely porphyritic quartz latite. The ore occurs in intensely altered pipes and irregular tabular masses of quartz-alunite rock that replaced the quartz latite along northwest-trending fracture zones. Metallic minerals, chiefly pyrite and enargite, fill irregular vugs that formed by local intense leaching of the quartz-alunite rock. The quartz-alunite masses are surrounded successively by soft argillically altered envelopes (illite-kaolinite zone) and by pervasively propylitized rock (montmorillonite-chlorite zone). The alteration was interpreted to have resulted from shallow solfataric activity similar to that associated with recent volcanic activity.

The alteration and mineralization at Summitville represents a late stage of a sequence of related igneous and hydrothermal episodes along the southwest margin of the younger collapse structure within the compound Platoro caldera (fig. 4). To the south and southeast, along the Alamosa River, a composite granodioritic to quartz monzonitic stock was intruded somewhat earlier, and much rock adjacent to the north margin of this stock was intensely altered. Calkin (1967, p. 123; 1968) noted that a small intrusive body (which he called the Alum Creek Porphyry) within the northern part of the Alamosa River stock is a focus of intense hydrothermal alteration. The subsidiary body contains locally anomalous quantities of several metals (Calkin, 1967, p. 144-146) and in places is cut by numerous closely spaced quartz veinlets containing abundant pyrite and sparse molybdenite (p. 146-147). As described by Patton (1917, p. 98-101), quartz-pyrite veins with ore shoots containing gold and silver tellurides were deposited locally in the Stunner and Gilmore districts within this mass of altered rock. According to W. N. Sharp of the U.S. Geological Survey (oral commun., 1969), these veins strike generally north-northwest and dip steeply. They are largely limited to the south side of the Alamosa River and do not penetrate the most intensely altered rock north of the river.

Some dikes and plugs of coarse porphyry similar to that in the quartz latite dome at Summitville cut both the intrusive mass and the adjacent altered rock, and these in turn were altered in various degrees (Calkin, 1967, p. 74). Sharp and Gualtieri (1968) described zoned anomalous concentrations of lead, copper, molybdenum, and zinc near one of these porphyry dikes.

The Jasper district, about 12 km east of Summitville, is a comparable area of intensely altered rock associated with a granitic stock. The district is localized along the east margin of the same younger collapse structure within the compound Platoro caldera, as are the Summitville, Stunner, and Gilmore districts. Quartz-pyrite veins with ore shoots containing gold and silver (Patton, 1917, p. 105-108) are localized along the south margin of the highly altered rocks.

The whole area from Summitville south across the Alamosa River and east to Jasper thus marks an area of recurrent intrusion, extrusion, and hydrothermal alteration and mineralization along a cauldron ring fault. The environment is similar to that in the intensely altered and mineralized Red Mountain district along the northwest margin of the Silverton cauldron in the western San Juan Mountains (Burbank, 1941; Burbank and Luedke, 1968). The analogy is even closer when the ores in the Summitville and Red Mountain districts are compared: pyrite and enargite are common in both districts, although numerous other ore minerals, including abundant sulfosalts of copper and silver, are present at Red Mountain. The gangues consist of pipelike masses of strongly leached silicified rock that formed by replacement of preexisting volcanic or shallow intrusive rocks in shallow solfataric environments.

PLATORO DISTRICT

Most veins in the Platoro district are persistent north-northwest-trending quartz-pyrite veins in the thick mass of La Jara Canyon Member within the early, resurgent part of the Platoro caldera. Local ore shoots on these veins containing gold telluride and silver sulfosalt minerals (Patton, 1917, p. 89-96) supplied most of the ore produced in early mining in the district. Most of the La Jara Canyon tuff exposed within the caldera is propylitically altered, apparently unrelated to the later ore deposition. Alteration related to mineralization is restricted to local argillic selvages along the quartz-pyrite veins.

The veins in the Platoro district are about on strike with some of the stronger veins in the Stunner district along the Alamosa River to the north, and the vein mineralogy in the two areas is closely similar. W. N. Sharp (oral commun., 1969) believes that the veins in the two districts are along the same fracture zone. The Platoro veins thus appear to follow radial fractures extending outward from the younger collapse structure in the compound Platoro caldera, and may be only incidentally located within the resurgent dome of the earlier cauldron. Ore deposits are uncommon within resurgent cores of other calderas in the San Juan Mountains, and the closest structural analogy to the Platoro district—the Creede district within the resurgent Bachelor caldera (fig. 1)—is primarily related to radial graben faults of the younger Creede caldera (Steven and Ratté, 1965).

CRATER CREEK AREA

Several conspicuous faults comprising a complex radial graben extend westward from the Platoro caldera (figs. 2, 4) and converge toward the north end of the Bear Creek granodioritic stock. Hydrothermally altered rock is apparent at places along these faults, and some rather extensive areas within the faulted zone and around the stock are pervasively altered. Numerous dikes of coarsely porphyritic quartz latite similar to the rock in the plug dome at Summitville fill subparallel fissures within and near the graben.

Shallow prospect pits are scattered through the faulted and discontinuously altered area, and the Crater Creek drainage area near the north end of the Bear Creek granodioritic stock is currently being explored (1967-70). According to Mr. William Ellithorpe of Monte Vista, Colo. (oral commun., 1969) and Mr. Harry V. Ellithorpe, Pueblo, Colo. (written commun., 1970), by the fall of 1969 this exploration had disclosed several veins ranging in width from less than a foot to more than 10 feet that contain significant quantities of lead, zinc, and silver. Through the courtesy of Mr. William Ellithorpe, we examined several selected high-grade samples of the vein consisting almost wholly of galena and sphalerite. As of October 1969, only a limited lateral extent of the vein had been explored.

A close analogy exists between the environment of the lead-zinc-silver vein along Crater Creek and that of the major producing base-metal veins in radial faults around the margins of the Creede caldera (Steven and Ratté, 1965) and the Lake City and Silverton cauldrons (Burbank and Luedke, 1968).

CAT CREEK AREA

An outlying stock of monzonite (Larsen and Cross, 1956, p. 110) is exposed in the Cat Creek drainage basin about 5 km east of the Platoro caldera (fig. 4). An extensive area including the southeastern part of the stock and adjacent volcanic rocks is pervasively altered. Numerous prospect pits and small shafts were noted during reconnaissance mapping, but the altered rock was not examined closely. We know of no recorded production from this area, but its possible mineral potential is not known.

CONCLUSIONS AND ECONOMIC SIGNIFICANCE

The altered and mineralized areas near Summitville and Platoro in the southeastern San Juan Mountains are localized within and adjacent to a compound cauldron subsidence structure that we have called the Platoro caldera. Foci of hydrothermal alteration and mineralization seem to be along the ring-fracture zone of the younger collapse structure in the northern part of the compound caldera, which was the locus of repeated intrusion of equigranular quartz monzonite and coarsely porphyritic quartz latite in stocks, plugs, dikes, and volcanic necks. Radial fracture zones extending outward from the younger subsidence structure localized numerous coarsely porphyritic dikes, as well as hydrothermal alteration and local ore deposition. The older larger cauldron structure apparently exerted little control on either exposed hypabyssal intrusions or related hydrothermal activity.

The areas of most widespread and intense alteration between Summitville and the Alamosa River show evidence of repeated intrusion and hydrothermal activity. The composite granodioritic-quartz monzonitic Alamosa River stock apparently was intruded first, and a large block of rock along its northern margin was pervasively altered. Alteration was in part localized around a subsidiary intrusion in the northern part of the Alamosa River stock, and anomalous concentrations of metals were introduced locally (Calkin, 1967, p. 144-147). These altered rocks are overlain by unaltered quartz latitic lavas that were erupted from the vicinity of Summitville to the north (Steven and Ratté, 1960, p. 38) and are locally cut by similar coarsely porphyritic quartz latitic dikes and plugs. Some of the quartz latitic lavas at Summitville were in turn altered and mineralized, and ores from this center have provided most of the metals produced from the Platoro caldera area. Related porphyry dikes and plugs to the south also are altered in various degrees, and at least one area containing anomalous metal concentrations is localized near one of these later dikes (Sharp and Gualtieri, 1968).

The whole environment, with repeated hypabyssal intrusion of differentiated granodioritic to quartz monzonitic (quartz latitic) plutons, widespread and intense hydrothermal alteration, and local anomalous concentrations of gold, silver, copper, and molybdenum, is similar to that in which "porphyry-type" disseminated deposits of copper and molybdenum occur throughout western North America. Presently exposed levels are relatively shallow within the volcanic pile (Steven and Ratté, 1960, p. 51-52), whereas porphyry-type deposits appear to have formed in lower volcanic levels, or in the upper part of the basement beneath the volcanic pile. Favorable zones for exploration thus still exist at depth.

The granodioritic and quartz monzonitic compositions of the known intrusive bodies in the Summitville-Alamosa River area are more common for predominantly copper-bearing porphyry deposits (Stringham, 1966) than for the predominantly molybdenum-bearing deposits such as those at Climax, Colo. (Wallace and others, 1968), or Questa, N. Mex. (Carpenter, 1968), where mineralization is related to relatively silica-rich rhyolite and granite porphyry. The abundance of copper and the dearth of molybdenum in the known ores at Summitville further suggest this association. Molybdenum and copper, however, both are present in the areas with anomalous metal content south of Summitville described by Calkin (1967, p. 144-147) and by Sharp and Gualtieri (1968).

Mineral deposits in the outward-extending radial fracture zones range from quartz-pyrite veins with shoots of gold and silver tellurides with associated silver and copper sulfosalt minerals in the Stunner, Gilmore, and Platoro districts to a silver-bearing galena-sphalerite vein in the Crater Creek area. The Crater Creek area is appreciably farther from the apparent focus of intrusion and hydrothermal activity between Summitville and the Alamosa River than are the Stunner, Gilmore, and Platoro areas. Although the data are too sparse to be very significant, this general distribution of gold, silver, and copper relatively near the source and of silver, lead, and zinc more distant is reminiscent of the metal zoning around many western mining districts, as previously suggested by Calkin (1967, p. 154). The outward-extending fracture zones have been poorly explored, and would seemingly deserve more attention.

ACKNOWLEDGMENTS

We express our appreciation to W. N. Sharp, U.S. Geological Survey, for making available unpublished data on the veins and the altered and mineralized rocks in the Alamosa River-Platoro area. Russel Burmester assisted P. W. Lipman in reconnaissance geological mapping in and adjacent to the area covered by this report and helped develop the general geologic history of the region.

REFERENCES

Burbank, W. S., 1941, Structural control of ore deposition in the Red Mountains, Sneffels, and Telluride districts of the San Juan Mountains, Colorado: Colorado Sci. Soc. Proc., v. 14, no. 5, p. 141-261.

Burbank, W. S., and Luedke, R. G., 1968, Geology and ore deposits of the western San Juan Mountains, Colorado, in Ridge, J. D., ed., Ore deposits of the United States, 1933-1967 (Graton-Sales volume), v. 1: Am. Inst. Mining, Metall., and Petroleum Engineers, Rocky Mtn. Fund Ser., p. 714-733.

Byers, F. M., Jr., Carr, W. J., and Orkild, P. P., 1969, Volcano-tectonic history of southwestern Nevada caldera complex, U.S.A. [abs.], p. 84-86 in Symposium on volcanoes and their roots: Oxford, England, Internat. Assoc. Volcanology and Chemistry of the Earth's interior, v. abs., 281 p.

Calkin, W. S., 1967, Geology, alteration, and mineralization of the Alum Creek area, San Juan volcanic field, Colorado: Colorado School of Mines unpub. Ph.D. thesis, 177 p.

——— 1968, Geology and petrology of the Alum Creek area, San Juan Mountains, Colorado, in Abstracts for 1967: Geol. Soc. America Spec. Paper 115, p. 410.

Carpenter, R. H., 1968, Geology and ore deposits of the Questa molybdenum mine area, Taos County, New Mexico, in Ridge, J. D., ed., Ore deposits of the United States, 1933-1967 (Graton-Sales volume), v. 2: Am. Inst. Mining, Metall., and Petroleum Engineers, Rocky Mtn. Fund Ser., p. 1328-1350.

Christiansen, R. I., Lipman, J. W., Orkild, P. P., and Byers, F. M., Jr., 1965, Structure of the Timber Mountain caldera, southern Nevada, and its relation to basin-range structure, in Geological Survey Research 1965: U.S. Geol. Survey Prof. Paper 525-B, p. B43-B48.

Cohee, G. V., chm., and others, 1961, Tectonic map of the United States, exclusive of Alaska and Hawaii: U.S. Geol. Survey and Am. Assoc. Petroleum Geologists, scale 1:2,500,000. [1962]

Larsen, E. S., Jr., and Cross, Whitman, 1956, Geology and petrology of the San Juan region, southwestern Colorado: U.S. Geol. Survey Prof. Paper 258, 303 p.

Lipman, P. W., Christiansen, R. L., and O'Connor, J. T., 1966, A compositionally zoned ash-flow sheet in southern Nevada: U.S. Geol. Survey Prof. Paper 524-F, 47 p.

Lipman, P. W., and Steven, T. A., 1969, Petrologic evolution of the San Juan volcanic field, southwestern Colorado [abs.], p. 254-255 in Symposium on volcanoes and their roots: Oxford, England, Internat. Assoc. Volcanology and Chemistry of the Earth's Interior, 281 p.

Lipman, P. W., Steven, T. A., and Mehnert, H. H., 1970, Volcanic history of the San Juan Mountains, Colorado, as indicated by potassium-argon dating: Geol. Soc. America Bull. [In press]

Luedke, R. G., and Burbank, W. S., 1963, Tertiary volcanic stratigraphy in the western San Juan Mountains, Colorado: Art. 70, in U.S. Geol. Survey Prof. Paper 475-C, p. C39-C44.

———— 1968, Volcanism and cauldron development in the western San Juan Mountains, Colorado, p. 175-208 in Epis, R. C., ed., Cenozoic volcanism in the southern Rocky Mountains: Colorado School Mines Quart., v. 63, no. 3, 287 p.

Olson, J. C., Hedlund, D. C., and Hansen, W. R., 1968, Tertiary volcanic stratigraphy in the Powderhorn-Black Canyon region, Gunnison and Montrose Counties, Colorado: U.S. Geol. Survey Bull. 1251-C, 29 p.

Patton, H. B., 1917, Geology and ore deposits of the Platoro-Summitville mining district, Colorado: Colorado Geol. Survey Bull. 13, 122 p. [1918]

Ratté, J. C., and Steven, T. A., 1964, Magmatic differentiation in a volcanic sequence related to the Creede caldera, Colorado: Art 131 in U.S. Geol. Survey Prof. Paper 475-D, p. D49-D53.

———— 1967, Ash flows and related volcanic rocks associated with the Creede caldera, San Juan Mountains, Colorado: U.S. Geol. Survey Prof. Paper 524-H, 58p.

Sharp, W. N., and Gualtieri, J. L., 1968, Lead, copper, molybdenum, and zinc geochemical anomalies south of the Summitville district, Rio Grande County, Colorado: U.S. Geol. Survey Circ. 557, 7 p.

Smith, R. L., 1960, Ash flows: Geol. Soc. America Bull., v. 71, No. 6, p. 795-842.

Smith, R. L., and Bailey, R. A., 1968, Resurgent cauldrons, p. 613-662 in Coats, R. R., Hay, R. L., and Anderson, C. A., eds., Studies in volcanology—A memoir in honor of Howel Williams: Geol. Soc. America Mem. 116, 678 p.

Steven, T. A., 1968, Ore deposits in the central San Juan Mountains, Colorado, in Ridge, J. D., ed., Ore deposits of the United States, 1933-1967 (Graton-Sales volume), v. 1: Am. Inst. Mining, Metall., and Petroleum Engineers, Rocky Mtn. Fund Ser., p. 706-713.

Steven, T. A., and Epis, R. C., 1968, Oligocene volcanism in south-central Colorado, p. 241-258 in Epis, R. C., ed., Cenozoic volcanism in the southern Rocky Mountains: Colorado School Mines Quart., v. 63, no. 3, 287 p.

Steven, T. A., and Lipman, P. W., 1968, Central San Juan cauldron complex, Colorado [abs.], p. 209 in Epis, R.C., ed., Cenozoic volcanism in the southern Rocky Mountains: Colorado School Mines Quart., v. 63, no. 3, 287 p.

Steven, T. A., and Ratté, J. C., 1960, Geology and ore deposits of the Summitville district, San Juan Mountains, Colorado: U.S. Geol. Survey Prof. Paper 343, 70 p.

———— 1965, Geology and structural control of ore deposition in the Creede district, San Juan Mountains, Colorado: U.S. Geol. Survey Prof. Paper 487, 87 p.

Stringham, Bronson, 1966, Igneous rock types and host rocks associated with porphyry copper deposits, p. 35-40 in Titley, S. R., and Hicks, C. L., eds., Geology of the porphyry copper deposits, southwestern North America: Tucson, Ariz., Arizona Univ. Press, 287 p.

Wallace, S. R., Muncaster, N. K., Jonson, D. C., Mackenzie, W. B., Bookstrom, A. A., and Surface, V. E. 1968, Multiple intrusion and mineralization at Climax, Colorado, in Ridge, J. D., ed., Ore deposits of the United States, 1933-1967 (Graton-Sales volume), v. 1: Am. Inst. Mining, Metall., and Petroleum Engineers, Rocky Mtn. Fund Ser., p. 605-640.

MINERALS OF THE SAN LUIS VALLEY AND ADJACENT AREAS OF COLORADO

by

CHARLES F. BAUER

Adams State College
Alamosa, Colorado

Between the narrow, jagged Sangre de Cristo Mountains on the east and the broad San Juan Mountains on the west lies the vast flat region of the San Luis Valley which contains some 5,000 square miles, an area about the size of Connecticut. The northern half of the San Luis Valley opens south from Poncha Pass like a horseshoe, enlarges to a width of 50 miles and extends 100 miles to the New Mexico border.

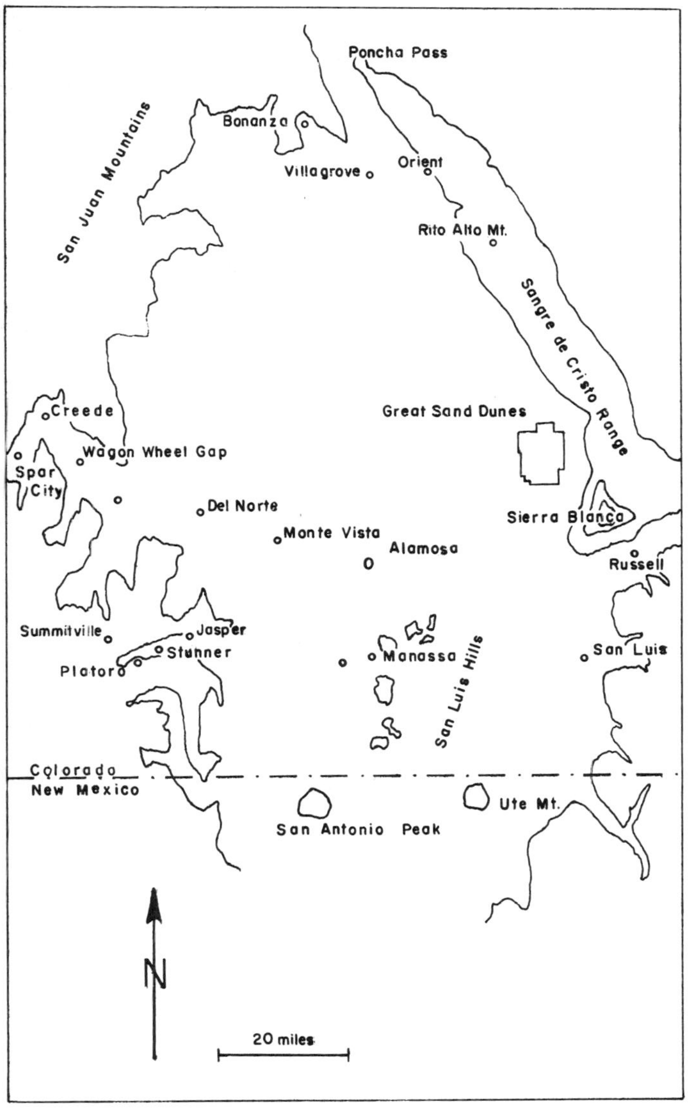

The minerals of this region are found in five major districts (fig. 1). The first district is the San Luis Valley proper. The second district includes minerals of the Sangre de Cristo Mountains. The Bonanza mining area is the third district of mineral wealth. Located northwest of Del Norte, in a narrow gorge of the San Juans is Creede, the center of the fourth mineral district of the area. The fifth and final district discussed is the Platoro-Summitville mining district on the southwest edge of the valley.

SAN LUIS VALLEY DISTRICT

Within the San Luis Hills, a group of volcanic mesas trending northeast across the southern edge of the valley and 9.6 miles east of the town of Manassa is the King Turquoise Mine. It was worked in prehistoric times by Indians, whose crude implements of stone hammers, deer and elk horns, presumably used as picks, have been found on the property (Pearl, 1941, p. 25). Today the mine consists of a pit about 330 feet long, 180 feet wide and 65 feet deep. Turquoise found here ranges from clear blue to green of varying shades, with many combinations of these two colors.

Exploration and some mining work took place in the 1890's northeast of the town of San Luis. The ore found consisted of galena, anglesite, and cerussite associated with some sulfides of copper, silver, gold, and iron (Van Diest, 1894, p. 79).

Along the eastern edge of the San Luis Valley at the base of the Sangre de Cristo Mountains are some 400 square miles of shifting sand. A large portion of the Great Sand Dunes are composed of dark grains giving the dunes a salt and pepper appearance. Feldspar, quartz, hornblende, magnetite, and ilmenite are easily recognized. The dunes also contain hypersthene, sphene, epidote, pyroxene, fluorite, apatite, sanidine, cristobalite, and microcline.

Southeast of Villa Grove is the Orient Iron Mine where hematite, limonite and goethite are found. These workings once furnished ore to the steel mill at Pueblo.

Along Old Woman Creek, northwest of Del Norte in the Summer Coon volcanic area, plume agate, varicolored chalcedony, and opal are found associated with "thunder eggs."

FIGURE 1.
Mineral Districts of the San Luis Valley.

SUMMARY LIST OF MINERALS

Anglesite	Hornblende
Apatite	Hypersthene
Cerussite	Ilmenite
Chalcedony	Iron sulfides
Copper sulfides	Limonite
Cristobalite	Magnetite
Epidote	Opal
Feldspar	Plume agate
Fluorite	Pyroxene
Galena	Quartz
Goethite	Silver sulfides
Gold sulfides	Sphene
Hematite	Turquoise

SANGRE DE CRISTO MOUNTAIN DISTRICT

Starting at Poncha Pass, the Sangre de Cristo Range trends southeast to La Veta Pass then southward to Santa Fe, New Mexico, where its termination marks the southern limits of the Rocky Mountains. Its elevation is culminated in Sierra Blanca which rises to a height of 14,363 feet.

Knowledge of the geology and mineral wealth of this interesting range is somewhat limited, probably because no great mining centers have yet been developed north of the New Mexico border. The major mining area of this district is found around Grayback Mountain north of Russell, Colorado, on La Veta Pass. Here, iron ores occur as replacements of metamorphosed carboniferous limestone in which garnet is usually an abundant constituent. These ores consist mainly of magnetite in somewhat granular masses and show small amounts of calcite, epidote and chlorite. Occasionally particles of gold telluride, and calaverite are found. Sometimes a grain is part metallic gold and the rest telluride, bearing a strong resemblance to some of the particles contained in partially oxidized Cripple Creek ores (Patton, 1910, p. 69). Although occasional pockets yielding good assays for copper and some silver have been found, the amount of the high-grade ore was too small to mine for profit. Lead and zinc have also been found in small amounts throughout the district.

Occurrence of telluride, possibly a variety of nagyagite or petzite, was reported by Richard Pearce (1898, p. 4), on the slopes of Sierra Blanca. Pearce found the ratio of gold to silver to be one to ten. The lode is situated on the northwest slope of Sierra Blanca, 400 feet vertically and 300 feet horizontally from the highest point on the mountain.

The base of Rito Alto, in the northern Sangre de Cristos, has been the site of some development of copper properties. Some of the workings have exposed considerable chalcopyrite and chrysocolla. The ore averaged about 10 per cent copper with a small amount of silver and a trace of gold (Ragg, 1908, p. 745). Rito Alto Mountain ores are primarily due to faulting of the sandstone, permitting passage of copper sulfide bearing solutions which deposited the ore along fractures and adjacent fault planes.

SUMMARY LIST OF MINERALS

Apatite	Gold (placer)
Augite	Hematite (specularite)
Biotite	Hornblende
Calaverite	Kaolinite
Calcite	Limonite
Chalcocite	Magnetite
Chalcopyrite	Malachite
Chlorite	Marcasite
Chrysocolla	Muscovite
Epidote	Pyrite
Feldspar	Quartz
Fluorite	Silver
Galena	Sphalerite
Garnet	Sphene

BONANZA DISTRICT

Bonanza is located within the Bonanza caldera at the northeastern edge of the San Juan volcanic province and the northwestern edge of the San Luis Valley.

The main deposits of the Bonanza mining district are lead, zinc, copper, silver, and gold. Lead and silver, up to the present time, have furnished the greater part of the productive value. W. S. Burbank (1932, p. 60) has stated that the veins contain pyrite, sphalerite, galena, chalcopyrite, bornite, silver bearing temmamtite, and stromeyerite as principle sulfide minerals in a gangue of quartz, manganiferous calcite, rhodochrosite and barite. A number of other sulfides and gangue minerals are found in small amounts.

Considerable bodies of manganiferous ore are found in several mines of the district. This ore is found in the oxidized part of the vein and is only valuable as a flux since no pure deposit of manganese is known to occur in this area (Muilenburg, 1919, p. 32). Fluorspar crystals, both cubes, and octahedra, are found in some mines associated with the crystals of manganiferous calcite.

Also located in the district is the Hall Turquoise Mine. The bright blue color and relative freedom from matrix makes this turquoise some of the best found in Colorado.

SUMMARY LIST OF MINERALS

Adularia	Fluorite
Altaite	Galena
Alunite	Gold (native)
Anatase	Gypsum
Anglesite	Hematite
Apatite	Hessite
Argentite	Jarosite
Azurite	Kaolin
Barite	Limonite
Bornite	Malachite
Calcite	Manganite
Cerargyrite	Manganosiderite
Cerussite	Muscovite
Chalcocite	Orthoclase
Chalcedony	Petzite
Chlorite	Psilomelane
Chrysocolla	Pyrargyrite
Copper (native)	Pyrite
Covellite	Pyrolusite
Diaspore	Quartz
Dolomite	Rhodochrosite
Empressite	Rhodonite
Enargite	Rickardite
Epidote	Rutile

Sericite
Siderite
Silver (native)
Sphalerite
Stromeyerite
Sylvanite
Tellurium (native)
Tennantite
Tetrahedrite
Turquoise
Zunyite

CREEDE DISTRICT

A detailed study of Thomas Steven and James Ratté of the volcanic rocks in the central San Juan Mountains has defined a subcircular caldera about 10 miles in diameter which they have called the Creede caldera after the nearby town and mining district.

The ores of the Creede district are localized along faults in a complex north-south trending graben that extends outward from the major lead, zinc, and silver deposits of the area. Ore near the surface is oxidized, or nearly so, and consists of cerussite, limonite, manganese, small amounts of galena and spalerite, and a great deal of pyrite.

Small quantities of fluorite and rhodochrosite are also present. An apparent hypogene alteration of chlorite has produced some hematite, which also is found as a primary mineral (Steven and Ratté, 1965, p. 74).

Spar City, also located in the Creede district, is a small mineralized area along the south flank of the Creede caldera. Workings have revealed a few small veins containing galena, sphalerite, barite, manganese oxides, and jaspery to amethystine quartz.

South and east of Creede, just outside of Wagon Wheel Gap, Colorado, is a small fluorspar mine. The ore is found to contain two rare fluoride minerals, gearksutite and creedite (Eckel, 1961, p. 26). Gearksutite characterizes the lower levels whereas creedite represents the upper parts of the mine.

SUMMARY LIST OF MINERALS

Alunite
Ankerite
Anglesite
Argentite
Barite
Beidellite
Bromyrite
Carnelian agate
Cerargyrite
Cerussite
Chalcopyrite
Chlorite
Chrysocolla
Creedite
Feldspar
Fluorite
Galena
Gearksutite
Goslarite
Halloysite
Hematite
Jarosite
Kaolinite
Limonite
Manganese dioxide and oxides
Marcasite
Melanterite
Pyrite
Pyromorphite
Quartz
Rhodochrosite
Silver (native)
Sphalerite
Stephanite
Turquoise

PLATORO-SUMMITVILLE DISTRICT

Four mining camps are located within this district. They are: Summitville, Platoro, Stunner, and Jasper. These camps have seen considerable prospecting and development work in years past. A number of mines have been opened but only in the Summitville area have extensive shipments of ore occurred. Mining operations are presently being conducted in this area.

Gold was first discovered in the Summitville area in 1870. The chief values have come from gold, silver, copper, and lead. Gold usually occurs with limonite or with limonite mixed with clay. The ores of the oxidized zone are free from copper and the values are almost entirely from gold with a small amount coming from silver. In the sulfide zone silver remains the same while the amount of gold dwindles to very small values, and copper shows higher values than that of gold and silver combined (Patton, 1917, p. 83).

Copper occurring in the form of enargite, covellite, tetrahedrite, chalcocite, and chalcopyrite is found with pyrite. These copper minerals compose the major ore presently being taken from the ground at Summitville. Sphalerite and galena are found sporadically. Apatite, barite, and magnetite form the abundant accessory minerals. Alunite occurs fairly uniformly and thickly distributed through the rock in well developed crystals.

The Platoro camp came into being some ten years after ore was found in Summitville. Silver, the major value in this area, soon gave out and the boom was over. The gangue was composed of quartz, marcasite and arsenopyrite while the ore was a sulpho-telluride. The tellurium is present in the form of silver telluride and petzite $(Au,Ag)_2Te$. Other minerals of the ore are argentite, pyrargyrite, and proustite (Patton, 1917, p. 92).

Very little ore was actually found in Stunner and Jasper after the discovery of the rich Summitville ore. Vugs were found that contained some sphalerite, galena, and pyrite but the values, if present, have not yet beeen discovered.

As a general rule the gold-silver-copper ores of this district were deposited in very shallow volcanic environments. The metallic minerals, chiefly pyrite and enargite, fill vugs that formed by local intense leaching of the quartz alunite rock (Lipman and Steven, 1970, p. 25).

SUMMARY LIST OF MINERALS

Alunite
Apatite
Argentite
Arsenopyrite
Barite
Chalcocite
Chalcopyrite
Covellite
Diopside
Enargite
Galena
Gold
Hornblende
Huebnerite
Hypersthene
Ilmenite
Limonite
Magnetite
Marcasite
Petzite
Proustite
Pyargyrite
Pyrite
Quartz
Sanidine
Sphalerite
Sphene
Sulfur
Tetrahedrite
Tridymite
Zircon (rare)

REFERENCES

Burbank, W. A., 1932, Geology and Ore Deposits of the Bonanza Mining District, Colorado: U.S. Geological Survey Professional Paper 169.

Eckel, E. B., 1961, Minerals of Colorado: a 100-year Record: U.S. Geological Survey Bulletin 1114.

Lipman, P. W., and Steven, T. A., 1970, Reconnaissance Geology and Economic Significance of the Platoro Caldera, Southeastern San Juan Mountains, Colorado: U.S. Geological Survey Professional Paper 700, p. 19-29.

Muilenburg, G. A., 1919, Manganese Deposits of Colorado: Colorado Geological Survey Bulletin 15, p. 25-53.

Patton, H. B., 1917, Geology and Ore Deposits of the Platoro-Summitville Mining District, Colorado: Colorado Geological Survey Bulletin 13.

Patton, H. B., 1917, Geology and Ore Deposits of the Platoro-Sum- Geology of the Grayback mining district, Costilla County, Colorado: Colorado Geological Survey Bulletin 2.

Pearce R., 1898, Telluride Ore from Sierra Blanca, Colorado: Colorado Scientific Society Bulletin 6, p. 4-6.

Pearl, R. M., 1941, Colorado Turquoise Localities: The Mineralogist, Vol. IX, No. 1, p. 3-4 and 24-27.

Ragg, R. M., 1908, Some Copper Deposits in the Sangre de Cristo Range, Colorado: Economic Geology, Vol. 3, p. 739-749.

Steven, T. A., and Ratte, J. C., 1965, Geology and Structural Control of Ore Deposition in the Creede District, San Juan Mountains, Colorado: U.S. Geological Survey Professional Paper 487, p. 58-86.

van Diest, E. C., and van Diest, P. H., 1894, Notes on the Geology of the Western Slope of the Sangre de Cristo Range in Costillo County, Colorado: Colorado Scientific Society Proceedings 5, p. 76-80.

SOME PETROLOGIC AND ALTERATION ASPECTS OF THE ALUM CREEK AREA, SAN JUAN VOLCANIC FIELD, COLORADO

by

WILLIAM S. CALKIN

Department of Geography
University of Denver
Denver, Colorado

ACKNOWLEDGMENTS

The writer expresses his appreciation to Professors Hutchinson, Epis, and Carpenter of the Colorado School of Mines under whose direction this study was conducted. I gratefully acknowledge the support received by W. S. Moore Company and Earth Sciences, Inc. Helpful discussions with Messrs. Lipman, Steven, Meyer, and Vallet have answered some questions and raised others.

INTRODUCTION

The area of Figure 1 was mapped during the summers of 1964 and 1965. Since then the writer has continued to work within this area that has now been defined to lie within the west central resurgent portion of the Platoro caldera (Lipman and Steven, 1970). The extremely altered rocks located near Alum Creek provide the fundamental basis or foundation for the detailed explanation of the geology including both petrology and alteration.

GEOLOGIC SETTING

TIME-SEQUENCE OF IGNEOUS ROCKS

The igneous rock units in the Alum Creek area consist of extrusive, intrusive and hypabyssal rocks that are spatially associated with the Platoro caldera (fig. 1). The extrusive units consist of the Lower and Upper lavas within the Platoro caldera and vent-dome complexes. The Lower lavas are a complex series of andesite flow breccias, massive andesite flows and tuffaceous andesites that are unconformably overlain by Upper lavas of quartz latite which flowed from local volcanic vents. The unconformity is occasionally marked by well-charred log fragments with preserved woody texture. The vent-dome complexes, which are viscous protrusions of lava that were unconformably deposited upon the altered Upper and Lower lavas, are well-exposed around Lookout Mountain. These vent-dome complexes represent the final phase of volcanic activity.

The intrusive rock units consist of the equigranular augite quartz monzonite Alamosa River stock and the Alum Creek porphyry, which is an augite biotite quartz monzonite porphyry. The Alamosa River stock intrudes the Lower lavas and the Alum Creek porphyry intrudes the Alamosa River stock. No contacts were observed between the Upper lavas or the intrusions.

The hypabyssal rocks consist of sanidine quartz latite and quartz latite dikes. The sanidine quartz latite dikes are well-distributed throughout the area. Many of the quartz latite dikes probably represent chilled facies of the intrusive rocks.

STRUCTURE

The two most prominent faults are the east-west trending Red Mountain fault and the northwest trending South Mountain fault. The structure of the area is characterized by weaknesses along east-west, northwest, and northeast trends (fig. 1). The Red Mountain and South Mountain faults are the major zones of weakness that have permitted (1) local resurgent igneous activity and (2) a complex network of channels for solfataric and hydrothermal solutions.

The faulting is both pre- and post-alteration. The Red Mountain fault has a trend of east-west ± 20 degrees, dips 80 south to 80 north, has an intense fracture zone some 200 feet wide, and breccia zones 1-3 feet wide. Within the mapped area the Red Mountain fault is a high-angle normal fault with a left lateral map separation. The Red Mountain fault cuts the northwest trending South Mountain fault, which is a high-angle normal fault with a right lateral map separation. The Red Mountain and South Mountain faults have many associated subsidiary faults.

PETROLOGY

LOWER LAVAS

The field relations indicate that the Lower lavas are a heterogeneous group of andesite flow breccias, massive andesite flows and tuffaceous andesites. These multiple discontinuous flow units are thin (10 in.) to very thick (greater than 30 ft.). Within some of the thicker units the slower cooling has allowed a weakly porphyritic crystalline phase to develop in the central portion of the more massive flows. These phases resemble the chilled or fine-grained facies of the Alamosa River stock.

The characteristic texture displayed by the Lower lavas is holocrystalline, weakly porphyritic, very fine-grained to aphanitic, pilotaxitic, and weakly glomeroporphyritic. Lithic and crystal fragments attest to the flow breccia nature of this unit. The small plagioclase phenocrysts have a size range of 0.5-1.8 mm and a composition range of An_{36}-An_{48}. Augite is the characteristic mafic mineral and is commonly partially resorbed with clusters of fine-grained magnetite around irregular borders. Biotite generally is not

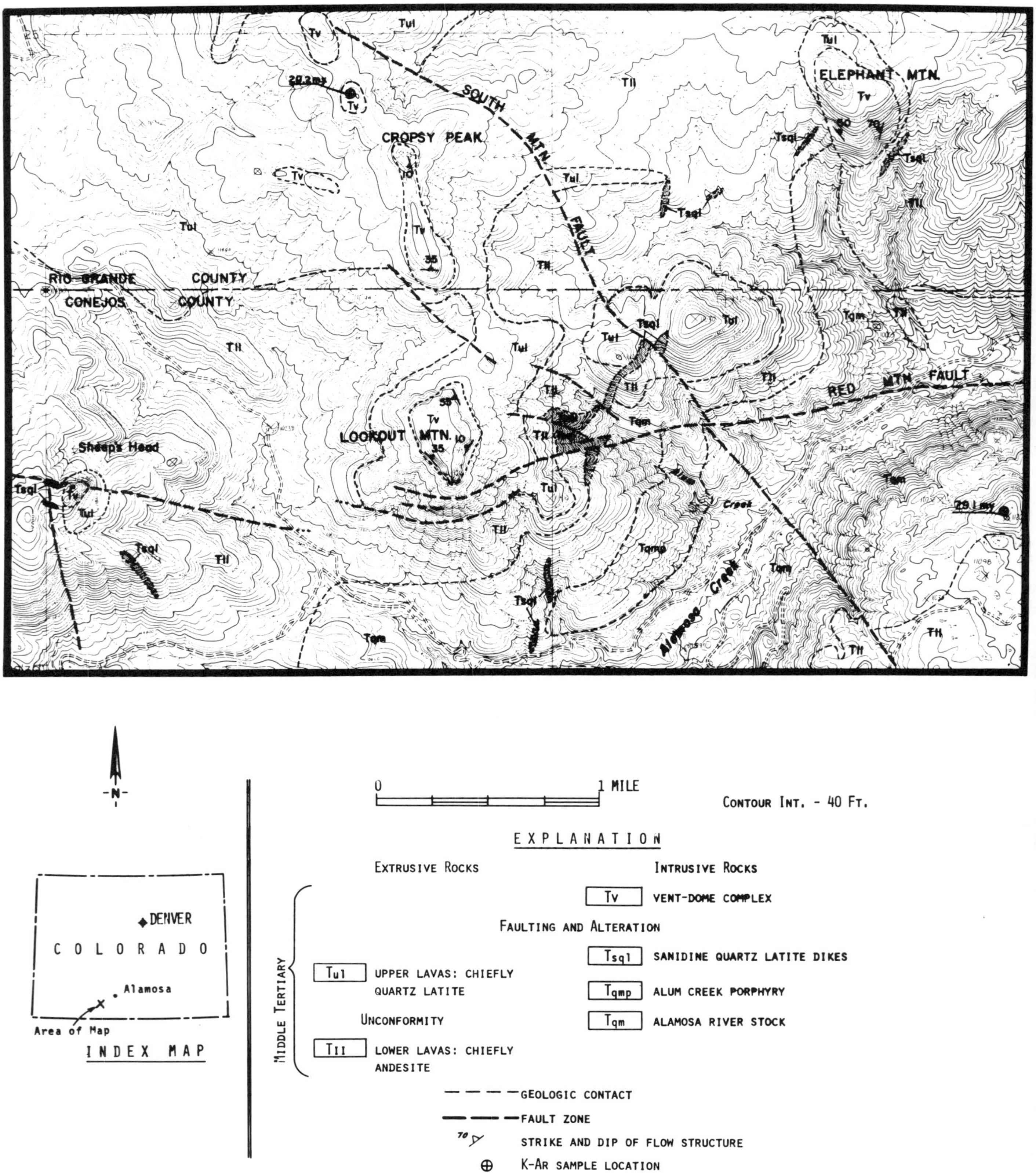

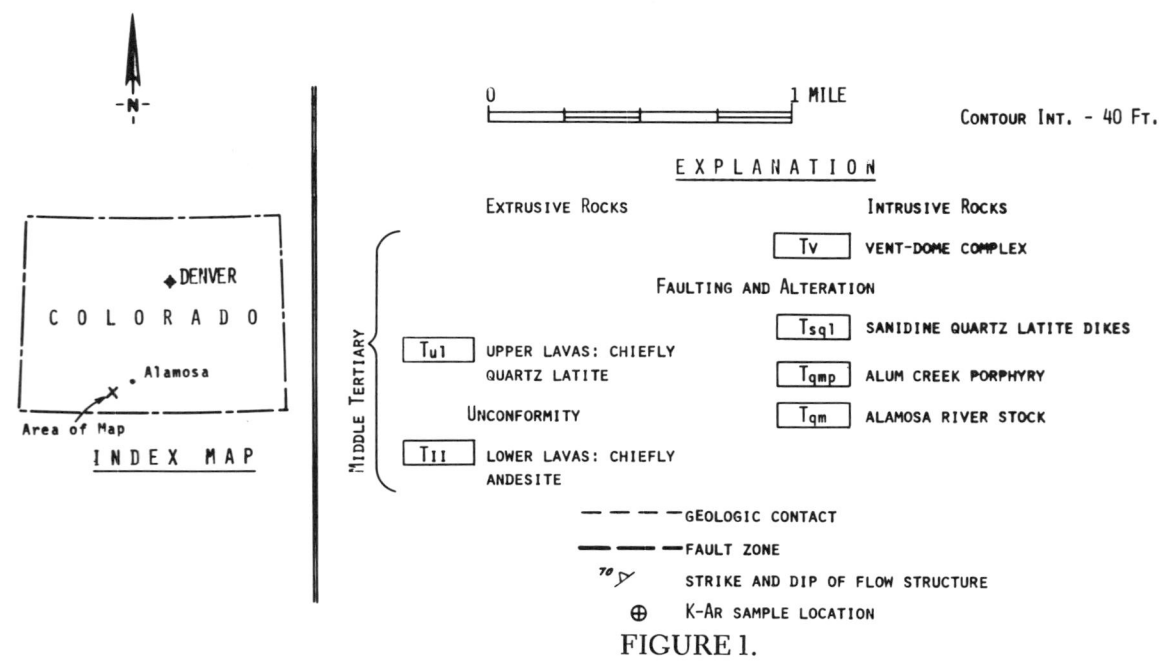

FIGURE 1.
Geologic map of the Alum Creek area, Colorado.

present. Accessory minerals include 1-2 percent magnetite and traces of apatite. The groundmass consists of very fine-grained intergrowths of plagioclase laths and aphanitic crystalline material. Sodium cobaltinitrate staining tests indicate approximately 20-25 percent of the total feldspar content is a potash feldspar. Minor to trace amounts of quartz occur in the groundmass.

The modal composition of 23 thin sections of the Lower lavas is as follows: phenocrysts—30%: plagioclase—25%, augite—5%, biotite—trace; groundmass—70%: plagioclase—50%, K-feldspar—13%, quartz—5%, and magnetite—2%.

The Lower lavas maintain a uniformly aphanitic to weakly porphyritic texture throughout the various stages of increasing intensity of alteration which include prophylitization, argillization, silicification, and alunitizaton. Magnetite is present in the unaltered rock, while 2-3 percent pyrite occurs in the altered rock. The Lower lavas are particularly susceptible to selective alteration.

ALAMOSA RIVER STOCK

The intrusive contacts have associated xenoliths and roof pendants of Lower lavas. The small inclusions rapidly disappear 5-10 feet from the sharp contact. The 100-foot-wide border zone is generally covered by alluvium but indicates a chilled facies of the intrusive stock and no discernible metamorphism of the adjacent volcanic rock. These diagnostic features indicate that the Alamosa River stock is an epizonal pluton. The field evidence indicates that the stock is post-Lower lavas. K-Ar dating gives an age of 29.1 million years (Lipman and others, 1970). The present level of erosion and outcrop distribution illustrates that the Alamosa River stock does not intrude the Upper lavas of quartz latite composition.

The characteristic texture of this stock is holocrystalline, hypidiomorphic-granular, fine-grained to medium-grained with the outer chilled margins having an inequigranular-seriate texture. Poikilitic textures exist with biotite in plagioclase, plagioclase in biotite, and plagioclase in orthoclase. Both normal and weakly discernible oscillatory zoning exist in the plagioclase crystals. Microscopic-sized subgraphic textures frequently occur with the Alamosa River stock and are interpreted to be the result of late magmatic separation and simultaneous crystallization of quartz and potash feldspar. The grain size of the feldspars ranges from 0.1-5 mm, ferromagnesians from 0.1-2.5 mm, and quartz from 0.1-0.5 mm. The andesine plagioclase crystals are euhedral to subhedral, while the orthoclase crystals are anhedral. The mafic minerals, biotite and augite, are partially resorbed with associated clusters of magnetite-ilmenite. The quartz content is seldom recognized in the field due to the marginal content and the small size of the interstitial grains.

A typical composition based on modal compositions of 28 thin sections from this equigranular stock is as follows: plagioclase—38%, orthoclase—36%, quartz—14%, augite—6%, biotite—3%, hypersthene—trace, apatite—trace, and magnetite—3%. The Alamosa River stock is a biotite augite quartz monzonite.

Upon alteration the equigranular monzonite retains its original texture with argillized plagioclase and bleached ferro-magnesian crystals megascopically evident. The Alamosa River stock is generally propylitized with definite areas of selective alteration throughout the northern portion of the stock. However, in the vicinity of Alum Creek, the Alamosa River stock is pervasively altered.

ALUM CREEK PORPHRY

The small Alum Creek stock is a complex quartz monzonite porphyry with related fine-grained and chilled phases. The zone of contact is steep, indicates no contact metamorphism, and exhibits foliation and lineation of the plagioclase phenocrysts only within a few feet of the contact. Small inclusions of the older equigranular stock occur near the contact zone, while small wisps or shoots of porphyry extend outward discontinuously into the older stock. Near the contact a coarser-grained facies of the porphyry predominates, but the phaneritic groundmass gradually becomes fine-grained to microphaneritic toward the core. These phases of the complex Alum Creek porphyry are interrelated, intermingled and generally intensely altered.

The characteristic texture of this small stock is holocrystalline, porphyritic-microphaneritic. The subhedral to euhedral phenocrysts of plagioclase, augite, and biotite range in size from 1-3 mm. The groundmass consists of discrete, identifiable randomly distributed anhedral crystals of quartz and orthoclase which range in size from 0.04-0.25 mm. The texture may also be piokilitic with biotite in plagioclase or plagioclase in biotite and indicates a simultaneous crystallization sequence. The oligoclase-andesine plagioclase phenocrysts exhibit normal and oscillatory zoning (Vance, 1962). The original euhedral-subhedral crystal borders of the phenocrysts have been modified by partial resorption which is developed to a greater degree in augite and biotite than in plagioclase. Within the ferromagnesians the resorption is frequently accompanied by clusters of minute magnetite-ilmentite grains around the border. The quartz and orthoclase content is seldom recognized in the field as these grains occur only in the microphaneritic groundmass. The texture of the groundmass exhibits differences caused by chilling associated with the border zones.

A typical sample of the Alum Creek porphyry based on the modal composition of 31 thin sections is as follows: phenocrysts—40%: plagioclase—30%, biotite—6%, augite—4%, hypersthene—trace; groundmass—60%: orthoclase—32%, quartz—25%, apatite—trace, and magnetite—3%. The rock is an augite biotite quartz monzonite porphyry.

The Alum Creek porphyry ultimately alters to a distinctly porphyritic rock consisting of phenocrysts of light brown bleached biotite and sericitized plagioclase in a groundmass of interstitial quartz and sericite with disseminated pyrite. The rock is commonly highly fractured and veined by an intricate network of quartz stringers with associated pyrite and molybdenite.

UPPER LAVAS

The Upper lavas lie unconformably over the Lower lavas. The Upper lavas are a biotite quartz latite with a gray aphanitic groundmass and exhibit moderate flow structure. The thickness of the Upper lavas varies as its base rests upon a surface of erosion and its top is an erosional surface.

The characteristic texture of the Upper lavas is holocrystalline, porphyritic-aphanitic to porphyritic, very fine-grained, and poikilitic. The phenocrysts consist principally of plagioclase, sanidine and biotite with lesser amounts of quartz, hornblende and augite. No hypersthene was detected in these flows. The oligoclase and particularly the sanidine phenocrysts are well-zoned with both normal and oscillatory zoning present. The phenocrysts of feldspar and ferromagnesians are commonly partially resorbed with the sanidine crystals showing the least amount of resorption. The phenocrysts range in size from 0.8-5 mm, while the groundmass crystals are aphanitic to 0.2 mm in size. Flow structure is generally pronounced as indicated by oriented feldspar phenocrysts and flow banding in the groundmass. The groundmass consists of intergrowths of feldspar laths, interstitial quartz, and aphanitic crystalline material.

Based on the modal analysis of 25 thin sections, an average composition is as follows: phenocrysts—28%: plagioclase—15%, sanidine—5%, quartz—3%, biotite—4%, hornblende—1%, augite—<1%; groundmass—72%; plagioclase—22%, K-feldspar—40%, quartz—9%, and magnetite—1%. The rock is a quartz latite with biotite as the characteristic mafic mineral.

The porphyritic-aphanitic texture of the Upper lavas is preserved throughout propylitic and argillic alteration but is essentially obliterated by the alunite-silica alteration.

Quartz Latite and Sanidine Quartz Latite Dikes

Dikes are ubiquitous within the Alum Creek area and have local concentrations near the border zones of the intrusions and around the vent sources of the local Upper lavas of quartz latite composition. The radial and concentric pattern of dikes around Sheep's Head, and to a lesser extent Elephant Mountain, attest to the volcanic activity around the vents and the associated structural doming. The dike rocks are of two major types, quartz latite and sanidine quartz latite. These dikes are separated into mappable units by the presence of 1 in. x 2 in. sanidine phenocrysts characteristic of the sanidine quartz latite dikes. A major sanidine quartz latite dike crops out periodically along a northeast trend, while others emanate from the vents. These large sanidine crystals occur only within the central portion of these prominent hypabyssal units which have a wide chilled zone that megascopically resembles the quartz latite dikes. The emplacement of the dike units occurred throughout post-Lower lava time in conjunction with the resurgent intrusive activity. The major dike activity is probably post-Upper lava in age as dikes cut the Upper lavas. Most of the dikes in the Alum Creek area were emplaced in cracks or zones of weakness and are believed to be genetically related to the magmatic activity which formed the extrusive Upper lavas and the intrusive porphyry.

The characteristic texture is holocrystalline, porphyritic-aphanitic to porphyritic-microphaneritic. Poikilitic textures are evident with biotite in plagioclase and plagioclase in biotite and indicate simultaneous and overlapping crystallization of the constituents. The phenocrysts range in size from 1-5 mm and are principally oligoclase-andesine plagioclase, sanidine, biotite, with minor occurrences of quartz and hornblende. The feldspar phenocrysts, and particularly the sanidine crystals, exhibit both oscillatory and normal zoning with the outer more alkalic zone more susceptible to alteration. The biotite and quartz phenocrysts are generally partially resorbed. The groundmass consists of intergrowths of quartz and orthoclase.

The modal composition of 16 thin sections from the dike units gives an average composition for the quartz latite dike units as follows: phenocrysts—33%: plagioclase—27%, biotite—5%, and hornblende—1%; groundmass—67%: plagioclase—14%, orthoclase—33%, quartz—18%; and magnetite—2%. An average composition for the sanidine quartz latite dikes is as follows: phenocrysts—39%: sanidine—3%, quartz—2%, plagioclase—28%, biotite—5%, and hornblende—1%; groundmass—61%: plagioclase—10%, orthoclase—30%, quartz—20%; and magnetite—1%.

Upon alteration the dike units retain their characteristic porphyritic-aphanitic texture. The intensity of alteration within the dike units is not consistent and indicates some dikes are intra-alteration. The sanidine quartz latite dikes generally have less pyrite than the quartz latite dikes. The quartz latite dikes are often more altered than the country rock.

Vent-Dome Complexes

The locality of the vent-dome complexes initially served as centers for local eruption of the Upper lavas, later as sources of solfataric alteration, and, finally, as centers for the viscous protrusions of quartz latite to rhyolite.

The vent-dome complexes are symmetrically located with respect to the local vents and the surrounding alteration haloes. Morphologically they are circular to elliptical in plan and mushroomed or bulbous in cross section with quaquaversal dips and contorted fan-like flow structures. The vent-dome complexes consist of three units based on lithology and texture. These distinctions are caused by differences in emplacement, cooling, and welding processes. Good outcrops of all three units generally exist somewhere at each vent-dome complex, and the spatial relationships of the three units are always the same. The lower friable agglomeratic tuff to tuffaceous agglomerate is conspicuous in all vent-domes. Toward the contact of an overlying vitrophyre unit the frequency of the vitrophyre blocks increase. The middle unit consists of a black vitrophyre which varies in thickness from 3-40 feet. Eutaxitic structures exist, and the vitrophyre is intermixed and intercalated with an upper unit of quartz latite. This upper unit of quartz latite occupies the core of all domes except Elephant Mountain, which is filled with white rhyolite containing no ferromagnesian constituents. Within the four principal volcanic domes the prominent flow structures are vertical to S-shaped in cross section and arcuate in plan with quaquaversal dips. K-Ar dating gives an age of 20.2 million years (Lipman and others, 1970).

Distinct textural differences associated with the groundmass exists within the three mappable units of the vent-dome complexes. The characteristic texture of the lower unit is hypocrystalline, porphyritic-aphanitic. The texture of the middle unit is hypocrystalline, vitrophyric. The texture of the upper unit is holocrystalline, porphyritic-aphanitic. Axiolitic structures exist in all three units. The phenocrysts within the three units are similar in size and are principally oligoclase, sanidine, quartz, and biotite with trace amounts of hornblende and augite. The ferromagnesians have a smaller grain size than the essential minerals and are weakly resorbed. The plagioclase and sanidine phenocrysts exhibit strong oscillatory and normal zoning. The groundmass consists of intergrowths of quartz, potash feldspar, and glass with the percentage of the constituents depending upon the dominant texture of the unit. The textures within the groundmass exhibit distinct megascopic and microscopic flow structure.

The modal composition of 15 thin sections from the different units of the vent-dome complexes has an average composition as follows: phenocrysts—28%: plagioclase—16%, sanidine—6%, quartz—2%, biotite—3%, hornblende—1%; groundmass—72%: glass—30%, quartz—15%, potash feldspar—26%; and magnetite—1%.

There has been no solfataric or hydrothermal alteration of the vent-dome complexes. A type of post-emplacement alteration caused by the latent heat of crystallization has produced partial fusion and recrystallization of the plagioclase crystals. Hematite coloration occurs within the flow structures of the groundmass and as rims around the magnetite and ferromagnesian grains. Partial oxidation of the iron-bearing minerals is believed to have occurred both during the emplacement and as a post-crystallization phenomenon.

PETROGENESIS

Feldspar Relations

The composition of the plagioclase within the different rock units was determined on a universal stage utilizing the methods described by Slemmons (1962) and the curves for volcanic plagioclase. Only unaltered crystals were utilized as secondary calcite within the plagioclase was found to significantly lower the anorthite content. Primary plagioclase crystals occur in all rock units. The results of the determinations from unaltered crystals are tabulated here by anorthite content:

ROCK FORMATION	CRYSTALS MEASURED	RANGE OF AN	AVG. AN	
Vent-dome complexes	9	17.4-27.3	22.5	youngest
Sanidine quartz latite dikes	6	26.8-28.7	27.5	
Quartz latite dikes	6	32.7-37.1	34.7	
Upper Lavas	9	19.8-26.7	23.9	
Alum Creek porphyry	9	26.8-32.2	29.2	
Alamosa River stock	9	31.9-41.6	35.9	
Lower Lavas	9	35.7-48.3	41.6	oldest

With the exception of the dike activity that has occurred intermittently throughout post-Lower lava time, the major rock units show a systematic decrease in the plagioclase from An_{42} to An_{22}. This relationship corresponds with the relative ages of the rock units as determined in the field and is believed to represent the sequence of crystallization of the plagioclase feldspars.

Ferromagnesian Relations

The characteristic ferromagnesian minerals include augite and biotite. Less than one percent of hypersthene occurs in the early rocks and minor amounts of hornblende occur in the late rocks. The Ca-Mg pyroxenes were investigated on the universal stage to determine the exact nature of the extinction angles. Within the pyroxenes of the Alamosa River stock seven determinants have an average value of $Z_\wedge C = 56°$ with a range of $Z_\wedge C$ of 47-61°. Four crystals showing both optic axes have an average $2V = 59°$ with a range of 57-61°. Within the pyroxenes of the Alum Creek porphyry six determinations have an average value of $Z_\wedge C = 48°$ with a range of $Z_\wedge C$ of 44-52°. The principal pyroxene in the intrusive rocks is augite. Hornblende is scarce in the rocks of the Alum Creek area.

In a magma under high partial pressure of water hornblende is a stable mineral phase; however, a rapid decrease in pressure will cause a shift in the mineral stability field and hornblende will invert to a pyroxene in conjunction with resorption of biotite (Turner and Verhoogen, 1960, p. 139). Within some of the small intrusive masses of the San Juan region, Larsen (1937, p. 893) states that most of the pyroxenes have developed from the resorption of hornblende. The presence of augite and resorbed biotite within the Alamosa River stock and the Alum Creek porphyry suggest that a rapid decrease in the partial pressure of water occurred during the emplacement of these stocks.

The biotite from unaltered post-Lower lava rock units was investigated by oil immersion media techniques to determine N_z in order that any significant trends in the iron content might be ascertained. The results of the determinations are tabulated below.

	N_z	FE/(FE + MG)
Vent-dome complexes	1.615 ± 0.003	.03
	1.630 ± 0.003	0.4
	1.650 ± 0.003	0.6
Upper Lavas	1.640 ± 0.003	0.5
	1.590 ± 0.003	0.2
Alum Creek porphyry	1.640 ± 0.003	0.5
	1.640 ± 0.003	0.5
Alamosa River stock	1.630 ± 0.003	0.4
	1.630 ± 0.003	0.4

The Fe/(Fe + Mg) values were determined from Wones and Eugster (1965), and a brief summary of their work follows. The composition of biotites lie in the ternary system annite $[KFe_3^{2+}AlSi_3O_{10}(OH)_2]$, phlogopite $[KMg_3^{2+}AlSi_3O_{10}(OH)_2]$, and "oxybiotite" $[KF_3^{3+}AlSi_3O_{12}(H_{-1})]$. Comparing phlogopite with annite, phlogopite has the lower N_z value and lower Fe/(Fe + Mg) ratio. Two biotite trends exist during the crystallization of a magma. Trend I: During the crystallization and cooling of a magma that becomes saturated in water with the fugacity of oxygen remaining constant or increasing slightly, there is a slight decrease or little change in the Fe/(Fe + Mg) ratio of the biotites, and the final products of crystallization include magnesium-rich biotite and magnetite. Trend II: During the crystallization of a magma that has low water content there is a noticeable increase in the Fe/(Fe + Mg) ratio of the biotites and the final products of crystallization include iron-rich biotite and very little magnetite.

The biotites from the rock units of the Alum Creek area indicate a generalized 50-50 relationship in the annite-phlogopite solid solution series with a slight increase in the Mg-rich biotites of the younger rock units. Magnetite occurs continuously throughout the volcanic sequence. This evidence indicates the biotites crystallized according to Trend I of Wones and Eugster (1965).

PETROGENETIC INTERPRETATION

The petrogenetic interpretation of the rocks in the Alum Creek area is based upon rock textures and both feldspar and ferromagnesian relations. The porphyritic, vitrophyric, aphanitic and phaneritic textures that exist in the rock units are related to differences in the cooling environment associated with the mode of emplacement. The porphyritic textures reflect intratelluric crystallization. The oscillatory and normal zoning in the plagioclase phenocrysts and the resorption of augite and biotite phenocrysts indicate changes in the stability relations of mineral phases during emplacement and crystallization.

In the rocks of the Alum Creek area from oldest to youngest there is a systematic change in plagioclase from An_{42} to An_{22}, while the biotite shows little or no change in the Fe/(Fe + Mg) ratio. With decreasing age there is a loss of hypersthene and a gradual loss of augite. Hornblende occurs only in the youngest rock units. Biotite occurs throughout the rock sequence increasing to a maximum content in the Alum Creek porphyry and then decreasing in percentage. The siliceous rhyolite core of the Elephant Mountain vent-dome complex contains only trace amounts of biotite and no other ferromagnesians. Hypersthene, augite, hornblende, and biotite crystals occur in this volcanic sequence and indicate the ferromagnesians form a discontinuous series. Magnetite has continuously crystallized throughout the rock sequence. The combined relations of plagioclase feldspar, augite and biotite ferromagnesians, and magnetite suggest that the rocks of the Alum Creek area crystallized according to Trend I (Bowen trend).

The spatial association of extrusive, hypabyssal, and epizonal plutonic rocks combined with the petrologic conclusions strongly suggest a genetic relationship, or consanguinity, among these rocks. The rocks of the Alum Creek area are believed to substantiate the concept of a volcanic association as defined by Kennedy (1938) and support the concept of the Bowen trend as restated by Osborn (1962).

ALTERATION

Both solfataric and hydrothermal alteration products are found within the Alum Creek area. The areas of intense alteration can be interpreted from knowledge gained in some areas of limited alteration.

As seen in the Alum Creek porphyry the changes caused by alteration are mineralogical, chemical, and in some cases textural. Upon initial examination of the altered rocks, it may erroneously appear that the alteration products bear no resemblance to the original rock. There is, however, a general persistence of the original texture of the rocks. Field observations indicate that the alteration has an intimate association with structural features. On the basis of the extensive fracturing that controlled the alteration patterns and zones, the rocks of the area were well-fractured before the solfataric and hydrothermal alteration activity commenced. Alteration is a multicomponent metamorphic reaction with the consequent development of alteration facies and alteration zones.

ALTERATION FACIES

The concept of hydrothermal alteration facies has been discussed by Burnham (1962) and Creasy (1959 and 1966) through the application of ACF and AFK diagrams and later treated by Lowell and Guilbert (1970). The propylitic facies is characterized by a prominence of lime-bearing minerals such as calcite, epidote, and chlorite. The argillic facies is characterized by the presence of clay minerals of the kaolin and montmorillonite groups in conjunction with strong leaching of CaO. The phyllic facies is characterized by a quartz-sericite assemblage. The potassic facies is characterized by newly formed phases of biotite and K-feldspar. This concept of hydrothermal alteration facies is utilized in the Alum Creek area to describe the different aspects of dominant alteration types. In the field the propylitic facies is readily recognized by the green color of the rocks; the argillic facies is recognized by the white chalky appearance of kaolinite which replaces all phenocrysts, and the phyllic facies is recognized by minute flakes of sericite, "bleached biotite," and associated quartz.

The concepts of solfataric alteration facies has been discussed by Mukaiyama (1959). Solfataric alteration is formed by gaseous sulfurous exhalations from volcanic vents and fissures. Sulfurous gases are of limited abundance in fumarolic activity. The solfataric alteration facies progress through saponitized, kaolinized, alunitized, opalized, pyritized, and sulfurized rock. The saponitized rock is formed by alkaline solutions, the kaolinized rock is formed by weakly acidic solutions, and the alunitized rock is formed by strongly acidic solutions.

ALTERATION ZONES

The pervasive areas of solfataric alteration are best developed around the volcanic vents such as Lookout Mountain. The most intense hydrothermal alteration is best developed in proximity to the Alum Creek porphyry. Zones of decreasing intensity of alteration extend outward from the Lookout Mountain volcanic vent and the Alum Creek porphyry.

Solfataric Alteration: Zones of propylitized rock, with some veinlets of amorphous silica, occur in an outer zone ranging from hundreds to several thousands of feet peripheral to the Lookout Mountain volcanic vent. Argillized rock occurs in an intermediate zone hundreds of feet away from this vent. Quartz-alunite rock occurs in an inner zone adjacent to the volcanic vent. The degree of silicification associated with both the Lower and Upper lavas becomes more intense as one approaches Lookout Mountain from any direction. This evidence indicates that the zones of solfataric alteration become more intense toward the volcanic vents.

Hydrothermal Alteration: Propylitic, argillic, and phyllic hydrothermal alteration facies are areally distributed around the Alum Creek porphyry. The selective alteration near the Alum Creek porphyry is a hood or cap region of propylitic alteration with the more intense and pervasive argillic and phyllic alteration in the deeper exposed portions of the Alum Creek drainage.

Alteration Interpretation: The combined evidence from the volcanic vents and the Alum Creek porphyry indicates that there is a broad zonal pattern of alteration facies increasing in intensity toward the major local centers of solfataric and hydrothermal alteration. The principal centers or sources of solfataric alteration are the volcanic vents, and the principal center of hydrothermal alteration is the Alum Creek porphyry. Local zonal patterns of intense or selective alteration are associated with faults, dikes, and fissures. In the Alum Creek area the solfataric alteration is centered around volcanic vents that are 1,500 to 2,000 feet higher in elevation than the hydrothermal alteration around the Alum Creek porphyry. Spatial relationships of alteration in the Alum Creek area indicate a depth-zone transition of solfataric and hydrothermal environments associated with epithermal, xenothermal, and mesothermal conditions. A vertical transition between solfataric and hydrothermal alteration through a depth-zone concept is suggested within the Alum Creek area.

SUMMARY

Time-Sequence of Igneous Rocks

The rock units in the Alum Creek area consist of extrusive, hypabyssal, and epizonal plutonic rocks that are spatially associated with the Platoro caldera in a region of mid-Tertiary volcanic activity in the San Juan Mountains of southwestern Colorado. From oldest to youngest, the major rock units include Lower lavas, Alamosa River stock, Alum Creek porphyry, Upper lavas, and vent-dome complexes. The Lower lavas are a complex group of andesite flow breccias, massive andesite flows, and tuffaceous andesite that are unconformably overlain by the Upper quartz latite lavas that erupted from local volcanic vents. The equigranular augite quartz monzonite Alamosa River stock intrudes the Lower lavas. The augite biotite quartz monzonite Alum Creek porphyry intrudes the Alamosa River stock. Both the equigranular and porphyritic stock lack planar flow structure or foliation, have narrow chilled border facies, contain small inclusions of the country rock, and show no discernible metamorphism of the adjacent rock. Both stocks are considered to be epizonal plutons. Quartz latite and sanidine quartz latite dike activity occurred intermittently throughout post-Lower lava time. The alteration activity is post-Upper lava in age. The vent-dome complexes are siliceous viscous magmatic protrusions that formed local volcanic domes upon the highly altered Upper and Lower lavas.

Structure

Faults, structural trends of the rock units, and joint sets were utilized for the local tectonic interpretation. The two most prominent faults are the east-west trending Red Mountain fault and the northwest trending South Mountain fault. The predominant trend of the dikes and the Alum Creek porphyry occur in a N30-50E zone. This northeast trending zone is believed to represent a zone of tensional weakness along which igneous activity occurred periodically.

Petrology

From oldest to youngest the major rock units show a systematic change in the plagioclase content from An_{42} to An_{22}. With decreasing age there is a loss of hypersthene and a gradual loss of augite. Biotite occurs throughout the sequence increasing to a maximum content in the Alum Creek porphyry and then decreasing in percentage. The biotite shows little or no change in $Fe/(Fe + Mg)$ ratio. The siliceous rhyolite core of the Elephant Mountain volcanic dome contains only trace amounts of biotite. Magnetite has continuously crystallized throughout the sequence. The trends of the feldspar and ferromagnesian relations indicate a sequence of crystallization comparable to the middle-to-lower portion of Bowen's reaction series.

The spatial association of the rock units combined with the petrologic conclusions strongly suggest a consanguinity or genetic relationship among the rocks. Thus the Alum Creek area represents a volcanic association of extrusive, hypabyssal, and epizonal intrusive rocks.

Alteration

Surface coloration and altered rocks are areally extensive in the Alum Creek area. On the basis of the extensive fracturing that has controlled the selective alteration trends, it is apparent that the rocks of the area were well-fractured before the solfataric and hydrothermal alteration activity commenced. Local zonal patterns of selective alteration are associated with joint sets, faults, and dikes.

Propylitic, argillic, and phyllic facies of hydrothermal alteration exist in a zonal pattern around the Alum Creek porphyry. Propylitic, argillic, and quartz-alunite facies of solfataric alteration exist in a zonal pattern around the volcanic vents. The spatial relationships suggest a vertical transition of solfataric alteration that grades downward into hydrothermal alteration.

Significance of Volcanic Association

Field relations and petrology have indicated a spatial and genetic association of extrusive, hypabyssal, and epizonal plutonic rocks with associated solfataric and hydrothermal alteration in the Alum Creek area. This relationship indicates a volcanic association. These calc-alkaline rocks of a volcanic association have characteristic petrologic features similar to Bowen's reaction series. In the Alum Creek area the associated solfataric alteration is suggested to grade downward into hydrothermal alteration as exposed over a vertical range of some 2,000 feet.

In conclusion, the rocks presently exposed in the Alum Creek area strongly suggest important petrologic and alteration correlations. A lower level of erosion in the earth's crust probably would have removed the geological evidence needed to establish a volcanic association and a vertical transition of solfataric to hydrothermal alteration.

REFERENCES

Barton, P. B., 1959, The chemical environment of ore depositions and the problem of low temperature ore transport: Researches in Geochemistry, ed. Abelson, New York, John Wiley & Sons, Inc.

Buddington, A. F., 1959, Granite emplacement with special reference to North America: Geol. Soc. America Bull., p. 671-748.

Burnham, C. W., 1956, Facies and types of hydrothermal alteration: Econ. Geology, v. 57, p. 768-784.

Creasy, S. C., 1959, Some phase relations in the hydrothermal altered rocks of porphyry copper deposits: Econ. Geology, v. 57, p. 351-373.

——— 1966, Hydrothermal alteration in Geology of the Porphyry Copper Deposits: Tucson, University of Arizona Press, p. 51-74.

Hemley, J. J., and Jones, W. R., 1964, Chemical aspects of hydrothermal alteration with emphasis on hydrogen metasomatism: Econ. Geology, v. 59, p. 538-569.

Kennedy, W. Q., 1938, Crustal layers and the origin of magmas: Bull. Volcanol., series 2, v. 3, p. 23-41.

Larsen, E. S., Jr., Irving, Jr., Gonyer, F. A., and Larsen, E. S. 3d., 1936-1937-1938, Petrologic results of a study of the minerals from the Tertiary volcanic rocks of the San Juan region, Colorado: Am. Mineralogist, v. 21, p. 667-701; v. 22, p. 889-905; v. 23, p. 227-257 and p. 417-429.

Larsen, E. S., Jr., and Cross, Whiteman, 1956, Geology and petrology of the San Juan region, southwestern Colorado: U.S. Geol. Survey Prof. Paper 258, 303 p.

Lipman, P. W., Steven, T. A., and Mehnert, H. H., 1970, Volcanic history of the San Juan Mountains, Colorado, as indicated by potassium-argon dating: Geol. Soc. America Bull., v. 81, p. 2329-2352.

Lipman, P. W., and Steven, T. A., 1970, Reconnaissance geology and economic significance of the Platoro caldera, southeastern San Juan Mountains, Colorado: U.S. Geol. Survey Prof. Paper 700-C, p. C19-C29.

Lowell, J. D., and Guilbert, J. M., 1970, Lateral and vertical alteration-mineralization zoning in porphyry ore deposits: Econ. Geology, v. 65, p. 373-408.

Mukaiyama, H., 1959, Genesis of sulfur deposits in Japan: Jour. of Faculty of Sci., Univ. of Tokyo, v. 2, sec. 2.

Osborne, E. F., 1962, Reaction series for subalkaline igneous rocks based on different oxygen pressure conditions: Am. Mineralogist, v. 47, p. 211-226.

Slemmons, D. B., 1962, Determination of volcanic and plutonic plagioclases using a three- or four-axis universal stage: Geol. Soc. Amer. Spec. Paper 69.

Steven, T. A., and Ratté, J. C., 1960, Geology and ore deposits of the Summitville district, San Juan Mountains, Colorado: U.S. Geol. Survey Prof. Paper 343, 70 p.

Turner, F. J., and Verhoogen, J., 1960, Igneous and metamorphic petrology: New York, McGraw Hill Book Company.

Vance, J. A., 1962, Zoning in igneous plagioclase; normal and oscillatory zoning: Am. Jour. Sci., v. 260, p. 746-760.

White, D. E., 1955, Thermal springs and epithermal ore deposits: Econ. Geology, 50th Volume, Part I, p. 99-154.

Wones, D. R., and Eugster, H. P., 1965, Stability of biotite: Experiment, theory and application: Am. Mineralogist, v. 50, p. 1228-1272.

THE SAN LUIS VALLEY—A LAND OF PARADOX

by

ROBERT H. BUCHANAN

History Department
Adams State College
Alamosa, Colorado

Today it seems that any discussion of the valley history must begin with Alamosa, for its location is near the geographic center of the area and several accidents both happy and unhappy in the history of the valley have contributed to its prominence, the chief being the bankruptcy of the Rio Grande Railroad in 1878 and the founding of Adams State College in 1921. Other towns of the valley have more right to claim historical importance than Alamosa. La Loma, now an archaeological site, was once considered a possible site for the capitol of Colorado. In general it is agreed that San Luis is the oldest town in Colorado, but this claim can be seriously argued by the citizens of Antonito. With due respect for various historical arguments, Alamosa does represent an ideal base point from which to explore the area in all directions.

Alamosa is located in the center of one of the largest mountain basins in the world—a basin some one hundred miles long and sixty miles wide, enclosed on the east by the Sangre de Cristo Range and on the west by the La Garita, the San Juan, and the Conejos-Brazos Mountains. Alamosa is located in the center of miles of sand and chico which cannot be called desert despite appearances because there is so much water standing around. The ecology of the area has been radically changed by man over the last century. Once the land immediately north of Alamosa stretching to Saguache was excellent for the production of wheat. In 1867 when Otto Mears introduced wheat farming near Saguache, his two hundred acres of wheat averaged sixty bushels per acre. In 1890, when the Villa Grove branch of the narrow gauge was extended to Alamosa, several communities based upon wheat immediately blossomed along the route—Garrison, Mosca, and Moffat. Once the valley was a place of grain elevators and flour mills. Now much of the land to the north of Alamosa is wasteland covered with the growth that comes when land is abandoned in the valley. Apparently wheat farming was cut short by seepage from areas to the north and west, but this is a problem to which a final answer has not been given. It points to the fact that the area because of altitude and climate is marginal. Thus, the impact of man upon the area has been much greater than other locales. To date, changes wrought by man on the valley are primarily known through the tales of old timers.

The story is told that one morning in 1878, in an air of excitement, breakfast was served in the hotel at Garland City, some five miles east of present-day Ft. Garland. After breakfast the hotel was loaded on flatcars, moved, reassembled, and to its regular customers served supper that evening in what was to become Alamosa. Yet today when one looks at Alamosa and about the valley there is a feeling of change—a newness in appearances which is in fact paradoxical, for much of the history of the San Luis Valley is lost deep in the shadows of centuries.

In the history of the valley are many broken threads, many mysteries. When the first settlers came into the valley between 1800-1860, here and there across the valley great arrastras were found. Arrastras were devices used by the Spanish for crushing ore. They were a mill-like device of stone; massive in proportions. Some of these arrastras were found close to ore sites such as the one found in the vicinity of Summitville. Others were found far out on the floor of the valley. How they were moved such great distances is an unanswered question. One was found on the stream immediately to the south of the Great Sand Dunes; thus, the stream today is called North Arrastras. This milling device and the placer gold to be found in the creek convinced early settlers that somewhere up the creek must be a mother lode of ore. In search of the old Spanish diggings, the towns of Placer and Uracca were founded. For a time these towns survived on the placer gold of the creek. But the ore sources to supply the arrastras have never been found.

These arrastras apparently date before the Indian uprisings in northern New Mexico in 1680. Among the Spanish-speaking people of northern New Mexico there is no myth or memory of these mining operations. At times it is speculated that they date from the 16th century—the first century of Spanish occupation in the New World. At times they have been connected with the legends revolving about the Seven Cities of Cibola. Although no written records exist, there is the opinion that colonists came into the area shortly after 1600 from the San Gabriel settlement—the predecessor of Santa Fe. Oral history holds that they explored the valley and its mountains, mined gold, and even traded with the Utes.

On the eastern slopes of the Sangre de Cristos there is a series of tunnels high on a mountainside marked by a Visigothic cross which indicates Spanish origin. The cross apparently marks a great mine, but exploration has never uncovered an ounce of ore. Between the time of these ore mills and the settlement of the valley in the 19th century there was a period in which the Ute Indians were masters of the area. Because they had dark complexions, the Utes were referred to by neighboring Indians as being "blue" and their valley as the "Land of The Blue Sky." The valley is often called this by its residents, although now it has come to mean that the sun shines close to 365 days a year.

Perhaps this phase of valley history began in 1641 when

an expedition led by Governor Luis de Rosas captured eighty Utes and returned them to Santa Fe where they were forced to labor in workshops. Indian slavery is part of the valleys' history and records indicate that emancipation did not come to the Indians until some five years after the Emancipation Proclamation was put into effect. From their association with the Spanish the Utes learned horsemanship and by 1670 were ranging widely in all directions. Artifacts indicate that the Utes even traded with Indians of the Great Lakes region. The Moache band of Utes, which centered in the San Luis Valley, made many raids upon the Indian pueblos of northern New Mexico.

For a time the Ute problem was intensified by the fact that the Utes were allied with the Comanches of the Arkansas Valley who were brought into the sphere of French influence. For a time the valley was a kind of "no-man's-land" between New France and Mexico. Not too far from Huerfano, a battle was fought between the French, the Spanish, and their various Indian allies. The alliances of the Comanches with the French were to draw the attention of the Spanish away from the San Luis Valley to the Arkansas Valley; this involvement undoubtedly delayed the settlement of the area by at least a half century.

In the face of the Utes, the Spanish settlements spread north from Santa Fe. They centered about fortified plazas —miniature walled courts containing residences and quite often a chapel. Such a plaza in good repair dating from 1720 can be seen today at Sanctuario, near Chimayo in northern New Mexico.

The first Spanish fort of the valley was built on top of Cerro San Antonito (the round-topped mountain to the south of the valley), in 1768 to defend Ojo Caliente against Comanche raids. This fort was manned only for a summer and then abandoned. The fort is an indication that the Spanish settlements of northern New Mexico were gradually spreading north like the cells of a honeycomb—each cell being a small, self-sufficient, defensible, agricultural community.

With the acquisition of the Louisiana Purchase fur trappers began to follow in the footsteps of the French into the valley. The first to reach Santa Fe did so in 1739-1740. Among those to come from St. Louis was Kit Carson, who arrived at Taos, age 16, in 1826. With the coming of the American trappers the demand for alcoholic beverages prompted Simon Turley to build his famous Taos Lightning Mill on the Arroyo Hondo in 1831.

The turning point in the history of the valley came with the treaty of Guadalupe Hidalgo. With this treaty the United States pledged to grant protection to the Spanish-speaking peoples in the territory acquired by conquest from Mexico. To meet this treaty promise, Ft. Massachusetts was founded in 1852 only to be abandoned and replaced by Ft. Garland in 1858. The United States Cavalry was to provide protection to settlers who flowed into the valley from Taos, Arroyo Hondo, and El Rito in the decade prior to the Civil War.

Ft. Garland was not only to play a role in the Indian wars, but also the Civil War and the Morman wars. Ft. Garland was an important outpost in the Civil War at a time when the South was attempting to transport gold and silver from western mining areas. It played a supporting role in the battle of Glorieta Pass, which has sometimes been called "The Gettysburg of the West."

The attractiveness of the San Luis Valley as a base of supply so enticed those who created the Territory of Colorado that the valley was taken out of the Territory of New Mexico and placed under the jurisdiction of Colorado on February 26, 1861. On a map this transfer of territory was quite easy, but in reality it never occurred. The ties of the valley to Santa Fe were too strong. The settlers who came into the valley after the Civil War were Anglos and made up several unique elements of the population. After World War I a significant number of Japanese settled in the valley. Despite the barriers of mountains which surround it, the valley is in fact quite cosmopolitan. For this reason first assumptions about the character of the valley and its people are often wrong. The San Luis Valley is a land of surprises and a land of paradox that remains little explored by historians, social scientists, and geoscientists.

In recent years the San Luis Valley Historical Society, founded in 1968, has been working to collect materials on the valley and to stimulate research in the area. The bibliography which follows first appeared in the quarterly of the Society in July, 1969.

REFERENCES

Adams, E. B., and Chavez, F. A., ed. 1956, *The Missions of New Mexico, 1776*, University of New Mexico Press, Albuquerque, New Mexico.

Athearn, R. G., 1962, *Rebel of the Rockies*, Yale University Press, New Haven and Lovdou.

Bailey, L. R., 1966, *Indian Slave Trade in the Southwest*, Western Press, Los Angeles.

Bancroft, H. H., 1889, *History of Arizona and New Mexico*, reprint Horn and Wallace, Albuquerque, New Mexico.

Bean, L. E., 1962, *Land of the Blue Sky People*, The Monte Vista Journal, Monte Vista, Colorado.

Beebe, L., and Clegg, C., 1958, *Narrow Gauge in the Rockies*, Howell-North, Berkeley, California.

Beebe, L., and Clegg, C., 1962, *Rio Grande, Mainline of the Rockies*, Howell-North, Berkeley, California.

Bennett, E. L., and Wright, A. S., 1966, *Boom Town Boy*, Sage Books, Swallow Press, Chicago.

Bolton, H. E., 1950, *Pageant in the Wilderness*, Utah State Historical Society, Salt Lake City, Utah.

Brandon, W., 1955, *The Men and the Mountain*, Morrow and Co., New York.

Brayer, H. O., 1948, *William Blackmore: The Spanish-Mexican Land Grants of New Mexico and Colorado, 1863-1878*, and *William Blackmore: Early Financing of the Denver Rio Grande Railway*, Bradford and Robinson, Denver.

Breck, A. D. P., 1963, *The Episcopal Church in Colorado*, Big Mountain Press, Denver.

Brewerton, G. D., Lt., 1930, *Overland with Kit Carson*, Stallo Venton, ed., A. L. Burt Co., New York.

Carter, H. L., 1968, *Dear Old Kit*, University of Oklahoma Press, Norman.

Chapman, A., 1924, *The Story of Colorado*, Rand McNally, New York.

Coffin, M. H., 1965, *The Battle of Sand Creek*, W. M. Morrison, Publisher, Waco, Texas.

Colorado Press Association, 1948, *Who's Who in Colorado*, Boulder.

Colorado State Department of Game, Fish and Park, 1957, *The Fact Finder*, Denver, Colorado.

Colorado Year Book, 1923, 1924, The Bradford-Robinson Printing Co., Denver, Colorado.

Connelly, W. E., 1907, *Doniphan's Expedition*, Bryant and Douglas Book and Stationery Co., Kansas City.

Coues, E., 1898, *The Journal of Jacob Fowler*, ed., Francis P. Harper, New York.

Crofutt, G. A., 1966, *Grip Sack Guide of Colorado*, Vol. II 1885, reprint Cubar Associates (R3), Golden, Colorado.

DAR, Sara Platt Decker Chapter, Durango, Colorado, 1942, 1946, *Pioneers of the San Juan*, vol. I and II, Out West Printing and Stationery Co., Colorado Springs, Colorado.

Darley, A. M., 1968, *The Passionists of the Southwest*, reprint, Rio Grande Press, Glorieta, New Mexico.

Dunning, H. M., 1956, *Over Hill and Vale*, Johnson Publishing Co., Boulder, Colorado.

Dyer, J. L., 1890, *Snow Shoe Itinerant*, Cranston and Stowe, Cincinnati.

Eberhart, P., 1968, *Guide to Colorado Ghost Towns and Mining Camps*, Sage Books, Swallow Press, Chicago.

Espinosa, J. M., 1936, *Governor Vargas in Colorado*, New Mexico Historical Review, University of New Mexico, Albuquerque, New Mexico, Vol. II.

Feitz, L., 1969, Platoro, Golden Bell Press, Denver.

Fossett, F., 1880, *Colorado Tourist Guide*, C. G. Crawford Printer.

Frazer, R. W., 1965, *Forts of the West*, Norman, University of Oklahoma Press.

Gladwin, S., 1947, *Men Out of Asia*, McGraw-Hill Book Co., New York.

Goetzman, W. H., 1959, *Army Exploration in the American West, 1803-1863*, Yale University Press, New Haven.

Hafen, L. R., 1958, *Life in the Far West by George Ruxton*, ed., University of Oklahoma Press, Norman.

————, and Hafen, A. W., 1948, *Colorado and Its People*, 4 vols., Lewis Historical Publishing Co., New York.

————, and Hafen, A. W., 1957, *Central Route to the Pacific by Gwin Harris Heap*, ed., The Arthur H. Clark Co., Glendale, California.

————, and Hafen, A. W., 1954, *The Colorado Story*, The Old West Publishing Co., Denver.

————, and Hafen, A. W., 1954, *The Fremont Disaster 1848-1849*, ed., The Arthur H. Clark Co., Glendale, California.

————, and Hafen, A. W., 1954, *Old Spanish Trail, Santa Fe to Los Angeles*, The Arthur H. Clark Co., Glendale, California.

————, and Hafen, A. W., 1961, *Reports from Colorado, 1858-1865*, ed., The Arthur H. Clark Co., Glendale, California.

————, and Hafen, A. W., 1958, *Mountain Men*, 6 vols., The Arthur H. Clark Co., Glendale, California.

————, and Hafen, A. W., *The Utah Expedition, 1857-1858*, The Arthur H. Clark Co., Glendale, California.

Jackson, C. S., 1947, *Picture Maker of the Old West*, Charles Scribner's Sons, New York.

Jocknick, S., 1968, *Early Days on The Western Slope*, 1913 reprint, The Rio Grande Press, Inc., Glorieta, New Mexico.

La Font, O., 1951, *Rugged Life in the Rockies*, Prairie Publishing Co., Cooper, Wyoming.

Lavender, D., 1968, *The Rockies*, Harper-Row, New York.

Lemassena, R. A., 1965, *Colorado Mountain Railroads*, Vols. II & IV, The Smoking Stack Press, Golden, Colorado.

MacGowan, K., and Hester, J. A., 1962, *Early Man in the New World*, The Natural History Library, Doubleday & Co., Inc., Garden City, New York.

Mansfield, E. D., 1848, *The Mexican War*, A. S. Barnes & Co., New York.

Martin, B., 1956, *The People of the Book*, The Monte Vista Journal, Monte Vista.

McAdow, B., 1961, *From Crested Peaks*, Big Mountain Press, Denver, Colorado.

Mumey, N., 1949, *Creede*, Artcraft Press.

Oehlerts, D. E., 1964, *Guide to Colorado Newspapers, 1859-1963*, Bibliographical Center to Research, Denver, Colorado.

Quaife, M. M., 1925, *The Southwest Expedition of Zebulon Pike*, Lakeside Press, Chicago.

Read, B. M., *Illustrated History of New Mexico*, New Mexican Printing Co., Santa Fe.

Richardson, A. D., 1867, *Beyond The Mississippi*, American Publishing Co., Hartford, Connecticut.

Ritch, W. R., 1968, *New Mexico Blue Book, 1882*, reprint, University of New Mexico Press, Albuquerque, New Mexico.

Rockwell, W., 1956, *The Utes, A Forgotten People*, Sage Books, Denver, Colorado.

Sabin, E. L., 1935, *Kit Carson Days*, 2 vols., The Press of the Pioneers, Inc., New York.

Schroeder, A. H., and Matson, D. S., 1965, *Colony on The Move, Gaspar Gatano de Sosa's Journal 1590-1591*, School of American Research, Alphabet Printing Co., Salt Lake City, Utah.

Sommers, H. M., 1966, *My Story of Early Summitville*, private printing, Penton and Birkbland, Colorado Springs, Colorado.

Spencer, F. C., 1930, *Colorado Story*, The World Press Inc.

————, 1927, *The Story of the San Luis Valley*, Alamosa Journal, Alamosa, Colorado.

Sprague, M., 1964, *The Great Gates*, Little, Brown and Co., Boston, Massachusetts.

Steinel, A. T., and Working, D. W., 1926, *History of Agriculture in Colorado 1858-1926*, State Agriculture College, Fort Collins, Colorado.

Stone, W. F., 1918, *History of Colorado*, The S. J. Clark Publishing Co., Chicago, Illinois.

Taylor, R. C., 1963, *Colorado, South of the Border*, Sage Books, Allan Swallow, Denver, Colorado.

Tate, B., 1966, *The Penitentes of the Sangre de Cristos*, Tate Gallery, Truchas, New Mexico.

Twitchell, R., 1963, *Leading Facts of New Mexico History*, Vol. I, II, 1911-1912, republished Horn and Wallace, Albuquerque, New Mexico.

Twitchell, R. E., 1963, *The History of the Military Occupation of the Territory of New Mexico, 1846-1851*, 1909, reprint, The Rio Grande Press Inc., Glorietta, New Mexico.

Thomas, A. B., 1932, *Forgotten Frontiers, A Study of the Spanish Policy of Don Juan Bautista de Anza, Governor of New Mexico, 1777-1778*, University of Oklahoma Press, Norman, Oklahoma.

Whitford, W. C., 1906, *Colorado Volunteers in The Civil War*, State Historical and National History Society, Denver, Colorado.

Williams, , 1965, *Williams Tourist Guide of Colorado, 1877*, Cubar Associates R3, Golden, Colorado.

Whitmer, R. R., *Documents on Use and Control of the Waters of Interstate and International Streams*, U.S. Department of the Interior, Washington, D.C.

Wolle, M. S., 1949, *Stampede to Timberline*, Arthur Zeuch Printing, Poertner Lithographing Co., Denver, Colorado.

Wood, S., 1906, *Over the Road to the Golden Gate*, Donnelly and Sons, Chicago, Illinois.

Wormington, H. M., 1957, *Ancient Man in North America*, Museum of Natural History, Denver, Colorado.

Wright, C., and Wright, C., 1964, *Tiny Hinsdale of the Silvery San Juans*, Big Mountain Press.

CREEDE SHALE FOSSILS

by

J. ROBERT THOMPSON, JR.

Glendale Community College
Glendale, Arizona

Approximately 50 miles west of Monte Vista, Colorado, is the mining and summer retreat town of Creede. The area around Creede has often been a point of interest to mining geologists. There are, at present, several mines in operation in the Creede district, including Homestake's Bulldog Mountain Project and Emperius' Commodore Mine. Mineralization and related geologic studies of the Creede mining district have been well documented by Bethke, et al. (1960), Emmons and Larsen (1913, 1923), Steven and Ratté (1960, 1965), and others.

As Creede is located in the San Juan Mountains, most of the rock units in the area are volcanic. One exception, however, is the Creede Formation, which was originally named and described by Emmons and Larsen (1923). The Creede Formation was formed primarily of lake and stream deposits and travertine from mineral springs; all of which accumulated around the margin of the Creede caldera in a structural trough. Based upon fossil plant studies the formation is probably Late Miocene to Middle Pliocene in age. After an undetermined amount of erosion the Creede Formation now extends over a vertical range of over 2,400 feet.

Several distinct facies, each of which shows many local variations, have been observed in the Creede Formation. The unit is largely a thin-bedded shale and sandstone with some tuff beds. The shale varies from fine, thin laminations to beds several inches thick. Volcanic ash is a major constituent of the usually soft and clayey shales.

At many locations, along shaley partings, carbonized plant and insect remains may be found. Knowlton (1923) mentioned 19 genera of plants, along with feathers and one possible beetle. Steven and Ratté (1965), along with Estella Leopold of the U.S. Geological Survey and R. W. Brown identified and listed the following 22 plant genera.

Pteridophytes:
  Polytrichium
  Chamaebatiana
  Selaginella
Gymnosperms:
  Picea
  Pinus
  Ephedra
  Abies
  Juniperus
Dicots:
  Salix
  Poplus

Anlus
Carya
Quercus
Acer
Sarcobatus
Planera
Edwinia
Cercocarpus
Crategus
Sheperdia
Berberis
Artemisia

Fossils of the Creede Formation are similar to those from the more famous Florissant lake beds. Knowlton (1922, p. 183), however, claims that the most abundant and best preserved plant remains have been collected from the Creede Formation.

Although there has been adequate description of the plant community, and mention of feathers (Emmons and Larsen, 1923; F. H. Knowlton, 1922; Steven and Ratté, 1965), it is interesting to note the apparent lack of information concerning insects. The author has rarely failed to find insects at most of the shaley exposures of the formation. At many localities there have been inumerable finds of well preserved carbon impressions of what appear to be bees, flies, and mosquitos, as well as abundant plant and feather remains (see Plate I). As insect studies are presently incomplete, further description cannot be presented at this time.

Two of the best areas for collecting plant and insect fossils are (1) next to Seven Mile bridge, and (2) at the intersection of the Creede airport road and Colorado Highway 149, about one-half mile southwest of Creede. Care should be taken when collecting in these areas as they are close to the highway, and it would be undesirable to either destroy the scenery or impede traffic.

REFERENCES

Bethke, P.M., Barton, P. B., Jr., and Bodine, M. W., Jr., 1960, Time-space relationships of the ores at Creede, Colorado (abs.): Geol. Soc. America Bull., v. 71, no. 12, pt. 2, p. 1825-1826.

Emmons, W. H., and Larsen, E. S., 1913, A preliminary report on the geology and ore deposits of Creede, Colorado: U.S. Geol. Survey Bull. 530-E, p. 42-65.

———— 1923, Geology and ore deposits of the Creede district, Colorado: U.S. Geol. Survey Bull. 718, 198 p.

Knowlton, F. H., 1923, Fossil plants from the Tertiary lake beds of south-central Colorado: U.S. Geol. Survey Prof. Paper 131, p. 183-192.

Steven, T. A., and Ratté, J. C., 1960, Relation of mineralization to caldera subsidence in the Creede district, San Juan Mountains, Colorado, in Short papers in the geological sciences: U.S. Geol. Survey Prof. Paper 400-B, p. B14-B17.

———— 1965, Geology and structural control of ore deposits in the Creede district, San Juan Mtns., Colorado: U.S. Geol. Survey Prof. Paper 487, 90 p.

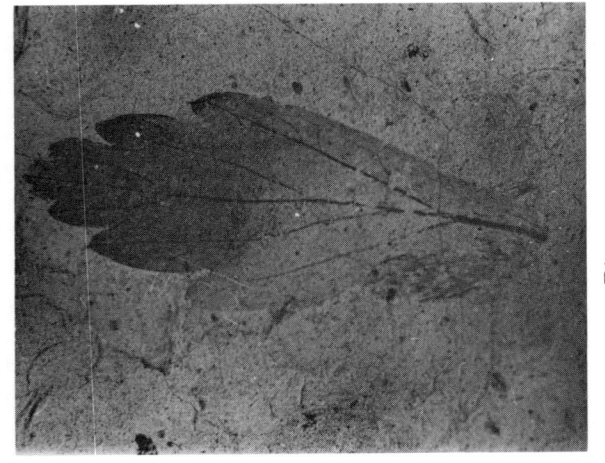

Pinus stem

Insect

Phyllites leaf

Ribes leaf

PLATE I.
Fossils of the Creede Shale Formation.

Feather

Pinus needles

GEOLOGICAL DEVELOPMENT OF THE BONANZA-SAN LUIS VALLEY-SANGRE DE CRISTO RANGE AREA, SOUTH-CENTRAL COLORADO

by

Daniel H. Knepper, Jr.

and

Ronald W. Marrs

Colorado School of Mines
Golden, Colorado

INTRODUCTION

General

Interest in the Cenozoic geologic history of Colorado has intensified in recent years with increasing emphasis on research projects by U.S. Geological Survey geologists and university and industry personnel. The complex volcanic stratigraphy and the history of the geomorphic and structural development are only slowly being pieced together.

This paper summerizes contributions made by previous workers and work presently in progress by the authors in the area of the Bonanza volcanic field and northern San Luis Valley and Sangre de Cristo Range (fig. 1). This area is part of a comprehensive remote sensing test site where personnel of the Bonanza Remote Sensing Project (N.A.S.A. Grant NGL 06-001-015) at the Colorado School of Mines are investigating the application of remote sensing to geologic problem solving. Our work has entailed: (1) detailed and reconnaissance field mapping, (2) remote sensor data interpretation and field checking, and (3) compilation, field checking, and modification of geologic maps covering various portions of the area (fig. 2).

Geographic and Geologic Setting

Several factors influenced the choice of this area for concentrated geologic investigation: (1) It includes representative examples of fold-thrust structures produced during the Laramide orogeny; (2) Details of Cenozoic volcanism in the Bonanza volcanic field are critical to unraveling the history of volcanic activity in central and southwestern Colorado and understanding the relationships among individual volcanic fields (Bonanza, San Juan, Thirtynine Mile, etc); (3) The complex internal portion of the Rio Grande depression emerges from beneath Quaternary alluvial deposits in this area; (4) The structural link between the San Luis Valley and Arkansas River Valley occurs in this area.

Topographically the area consists of a horseshoe-shape of mountains including the northern Sangre de Cristo Range on the east, the high peaks of the Bonanza volcanic field and southern Sawatch Range on the west, and the Poncha Pass area separating the San Luis and Arkansas valleys on the north. The Villa Grove reentrant of the northern San Luis Valley occupies the center of the horseshoe (fig. 3).

Several hot springs emerge in the area (table 1). Mineral Hot Springs, a one-time resort, is at the southern edge of the area in the San Luis Valley. Valley View Hot Springs is several miles northeast of Mineral Hot Springs along the Sangre de Cristo Range front. Poncha Hot Springs, at the northern edge of the area near the town of Poncha Springs, is currently the source of hot water for the Salida municipal swimming pool.

TABLE 1.
TEMPERATURES OF LOCAL HOT SPRINGS

HOT SPRINGS	TEMPERATURES
Poncha Hot Springs	153° F
Mineral Hot Springs	90°-131° F
Valley View Hot Springs	87°-92° F

ACKNOWLEDGMENTS

Over the years numerous persons have studied the geology of various portions of the area. Of particular interest is the work of Burbank (1932), Gableman (1952), Litsey (1958), Van Alstine (1968; 1970), and Van Alstine and Lewis (1960). In addition, unpublished graduate theses by students of the Colorado School of Mines and the University of Colorado have contributed immeasureably to understanding the geology of the region.

We gratefully acknowledge the financial and moral support given us by the Bonanza Project team at the Colorado School of Mines. Pilots and crew aboard N.A.S.A. remote sensing aircraft have done an outstanding job of providing remote sensor data over most of the area.

We are indebted to Dr. Robert J. Weimer, Dr. Rudy C. Epis, and Dr. Keenan Lee of the Colorado School of Mines for critically reading the manuscript.

STRATIGRAPHIC SUMMARY

Precambrian

Precambrian igneous and metamorphic rocks are exposed (1) in the Kerber Creek area, (2) within the Bonanza volcanic field, (3) at the southern end of the Sawatch Range, and (4) in the northern Sangre de Cristo Range. Very

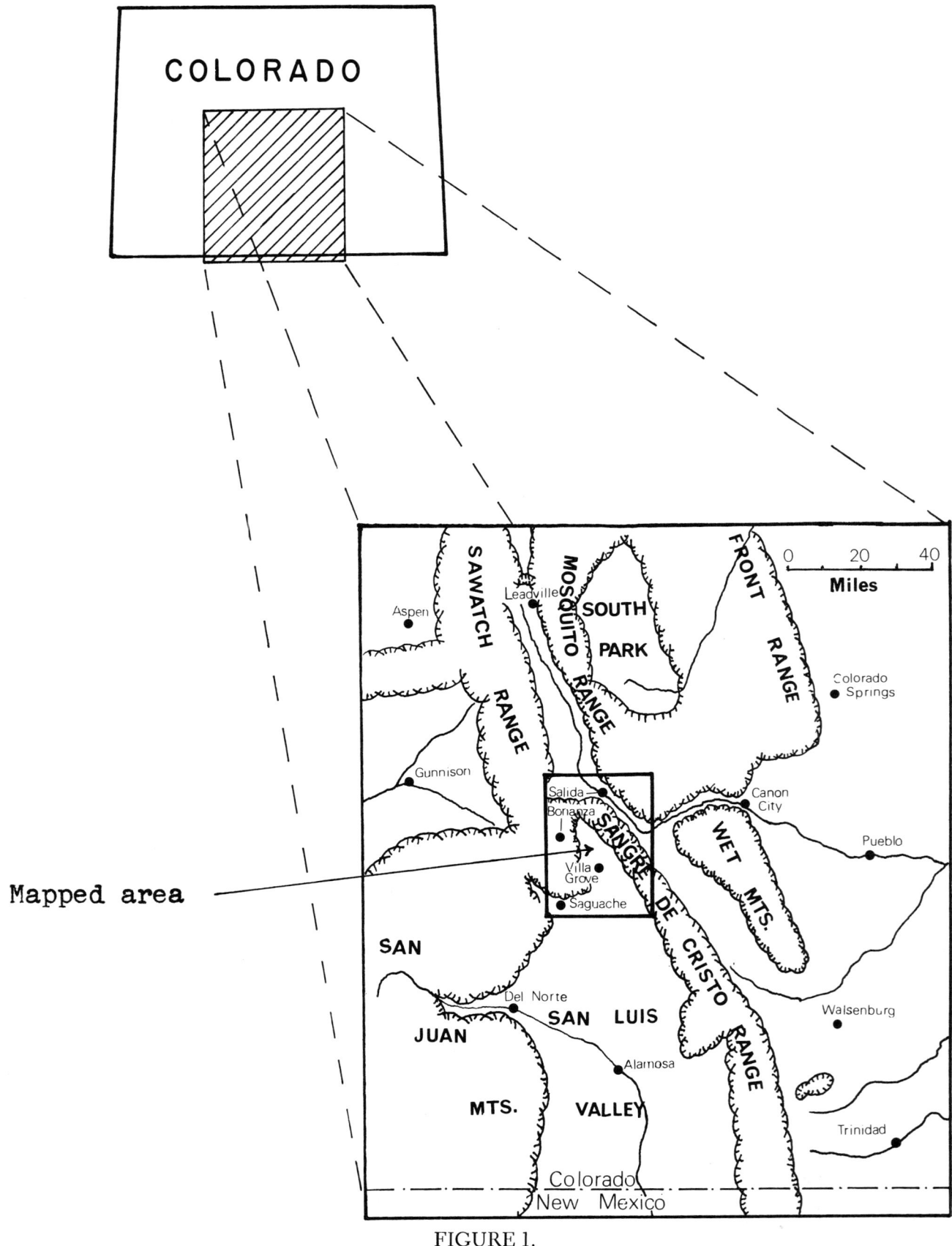

FIGURE 1.
Index map of Bonanza-Northern San Luis Valley-Northern Sangre de Cristo area.

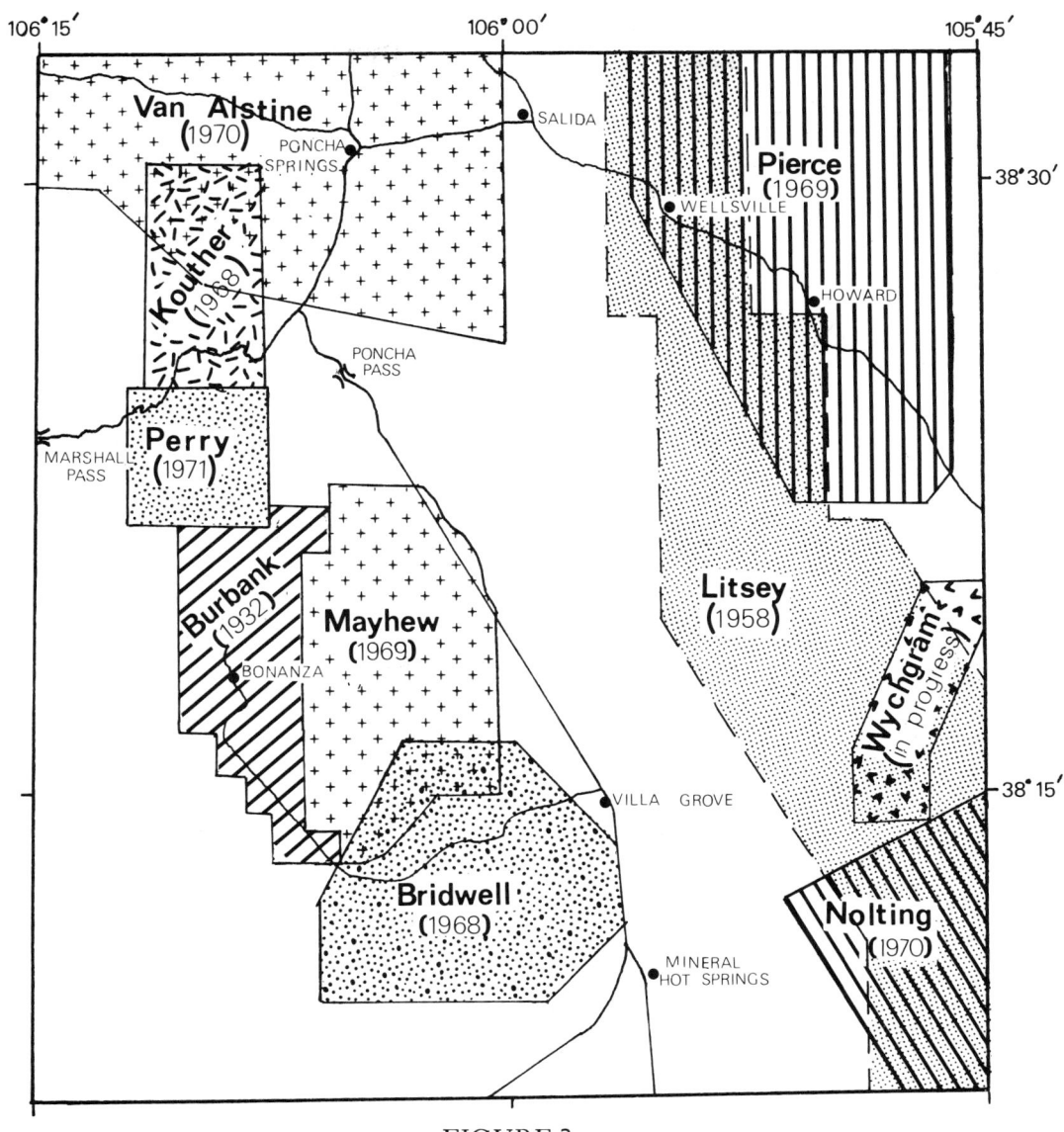

FIGURE 2.
Index of previous investigations in study area.

little detailed work has been done on the Precambrian rocks of the map area, and the summary will be correspondingly brief.

Southern Sawatch Range

Precambrian rocks of the southern Sawatch Range are exposed in the northwest portion of the map area (see plate 1, back pocket). The detailed work of Kouther (1968) and Perry (1971), and observations of the authors in this area are summarized below.

Metamorphic Rocks.—The texture and composition of the metamorphic rocks are variable, but these rocks can be generally grouped into three units: (1) muscovite-quartz schist, (2) amphibolite gneiss, and (3) quartz-feldspar gneiss. Remnant sedimentary structures have not been observed in the metasedimentary layers so the original stratigraphic sequence cannot be determined with certainty. Because of structural relations, the muscovite-quartz schist is believed to be the oldest unit and the quartz-feldspar gneiss the youngest. The older basement upon which the metamorphic rocks lie is not exposed in the map area; the metamorphic rocks are, therefore, the oldest rocks in the area.

Igneous Rocks.—Precambrian igneous rocks in this area consist of granodiorite, graphic granite, diorite, and pegmatite. This igneous sequence has intruded the older metamorphic complex. Occurrences of these rock types are local and represent only a small portion of the Precambrian terrain.

Bonanza Volcanic Field

Rocks of Precambrian age are exposed within the Bonanza volcanic field as a result of faulting and the exhuming of hills once covered by a sequence of Tertiary volcanic

FIGURE 3.
View southwest over extreme north end of San Luis Valley. North end of Sangre de Cristo Range lower left. San Luis Valley directly above. Ring of mountains in upper left is Bonanza volcanic field; note collapsed central portion. Snow-covered peak on extreme right is Ouray Peak. Prominent drainage channel in center of picture is Poncha Creek. Photo taken with panchromatic infrared film by Dr. Keenan Lee aboard N.A.S.A. C-130 remote sensing aircraft in June 1971.

rocks. In the northern part of the field, the Precambrian rocks consist of an older metamorphic complex similar to that of the southern Sawatch Range, which has been intruded by medium-grained aplitic granite (Burbank, 1932, p. 6). South of Kerber Creek, the Precambrian rocks are predominantly coarse-grained, porphyritic granite containing local xenoliths of gneisses and schists.

Kerber Creek Area

Precambrian and Paleozoic rocks are exposed over a wide area at the southeastern edge of the Bonanza volcanic field. The Precambrian rocks occur in the cores of the Central and Eastern anticlines (Burbank, 1932) and on the upper plates of the Kerber and Noland faults. The Precambrian rocks of these two areas are markedly different and distinct.

On the upper plates of the Kerber and Noland faults, coarse-grained, well-foliated, porphyritic granite containing potash feldspar phenocrysts from 10 to 20 mm long is exposed (Bridwell, 1968, p. 9). The granite contains local xenoliths of metamorphic rocks including hornblende-biotite gneiss and biotite-hornblende schist. A tectonic breccia composed primarily of this granite, but also including a few boulders of Paleozoic sedimentary rocks, is exposed at the nose of the ridge between Kerber and Little Kerber creeks. The breccia is probably an outlier of the sole of the Kerber fault.

Fine-grained biotite granite (aplitic granite of Burbank, 1932) occurs in the cores of the Central and Eastern anticlines. Xenoliths of quartz-mica gneiss and biotite schist occur in the granite (Bridwell, 1968, p. 9). Cross-cutting relationships suggest that the coarse-grained granite intruded into the metamorphic complex and was subsequently invaded by the fine-grained granite (Bridwell, 1968, p. 9). These same relationships have been observed just north of Saguache in the Precambrian rocks exposed in windows through the Bonanza volcanics.

Northern Sangre de Cristo Range

Precambrian rocks of the northern Sangre de Cristo Range have not been studied in detail. Gableman (1952) reported the occurrence of schists, fine-grained hornblende and biotite gneisses, quartzites, and granites. The metamorphic rocks have been intruded in varying degrees by dikes of granite and pegmatite, and several small granitic plutons. Foliation in the metamorphic rocks is generally well developed and at a distance is easily mistaken for stratification in the Paleozoic sedimentary sequence. The metamorphic foliation defines distorted north-trending isoclinal folds with steeply dipping limbs (Gableman, 1952, p. 1581).

The unconformity developed on Precambrian rocks below the Paleozoic sedimentary sequence generally displays less than 10 feet of relief. The weathering zone developed at this surface is generally thin, not exceeding 5 feet in most places (Litsey, 1958, p. 1147).

CAMBRIAN

No rocks of Cambrian age have been reported in the northern Sangre de Cristo Range. In the Kerber Creek area the Late Cambrian Sawatch Quartzite (0-20 feet) is sporadically present at the base of the Paleozoic sedimentary sequence. The thickness of the Sawatch is variable, but locally it attains a thickness of 20 feet. Where present, the Sawatch lies on a relatively flat surface cut on Precambrian rocks. The Sawatch is composed of hard, fine- to medium-grained quartz sandstone containing lenses of quartz-pebble conglomerate in the upper portion (Bridwell, 1968, p. 11).

ORDOVICIAN

Manitou Formation (90-225 feet)

Throughout the map area, except where the Sawatch Quartzite is present, the Manitou Formation lies at the base of the Paleozoic sedimentary sequence, nonconformably overlying Precambrian crystalline rocks. Where the Sawatch Quartzite occurs below the Manitou the contact between the two units is gradational. This relationship observed by Bridwell (1968) suggests that the absence of the Sawatch Quartzite in some areas is due to non-deposition rather than erosion. The Manitou is a thinly-bedded, brown to gray dolomite and dolomitic limestone containing lenses and nodules of white to black chert aligned parallel to stratification. In the Kerber Creek area the chert is predominantly in the middle portion of the unit (Bridwell, 1968, p. 15). In the Sangre de Cristo Range chert is most prominent at the base and in a zone near the top (Gableman, 1952, p. 1582).

Faunal evidence from various locals in Colorado indicate an Early Ordovician age for the Manitou (Johnson, 1945, p. 18).

Harding Sandstone (60-116 feet)

The Harding Sandstone disconformably overlies the Manitou throughout the map area. The Harding is a hard, white, fine- to medium-grained quartz sandstone with a silica cement (Bridwell, 1968, p. 16). The quartz grains are generally well-rounded and well-sorted. Iron oxide from the oxidation of magnetite gives the Harding a red to brown coloration (Gableman, 1952, p. 1582). In the northern Sangre de Cristo Range the Harding has a basal zone of grayish-red to green shales with thin interbedded sandstones totaling 15 to 30 feet thick (Litsey, 1958, p. 1152). This shale section has not been reported to the west.

The Harding Sandstone is generally unfossiliferous. Fish plates have been identified by Kouther (1968, p. 34) and Bridwell (1968, p. 16) as belonging to *Eriptychius americanus* Walcott and *Astraspis desiderata* Walcott indicating a Middle Ordovician age for the Harding.

Fremont Formation (229-300 feet)

The Fremont Formation disconformably overlies the Harding Sandstone. The Fremont consists of gray, thick- to massive-bedded dolomite locally interlayered with thin sandy dolomites and cherty dolomites (Bridwell, 1968, p. 17; Gableman, 1952, p. 1583). Rough pit and cusp weathering surfaces are characteristic of most Fremont outcrops.

Although the Fremont is fossiliferous, preservation of fossils is generally poor. Horn corals and the chain coral *Halysites* are common, and fragmental brachiopod shells and straight cephalopod shells have been reported from the Fremont (Litsey, 1958, p. 1154). Remains of *Ephippiorthoceras sp.*, a straight-shelled cephalopod, were identified by Bridwell (1968, p. 18) in the Kerber Creek area, and Kouther (1968, p. 18) to the north along Droz Creek. The faunal remains in the Fremont indicate a Late Ordovician age (Bridwell, 1968, p. 18).

SILURIAN

No rocks of Silurian age have been discovered in the map area. Remnants of Silurian carbonate strata near the Colorado-Wyoming state line suggest that Silurian sedimentary rocks may once have covered the area, but have since been removed by erosion prior to the deposition of the first Devonian rocks.

DEVONIAN

Chaffee Formation

The stratigraphic break represented at the contact between the Chaffee Formation and the underlying Fremont Formation is the largest gap in the pre-Pennsylvanian sedimentary record (Litsey, 1958, p. 1154). The Chaffee Formation consists of two members: the lower Parting Quartzite Member and the upper Dyer Dolomite Member.

Parting Quartzite Member (10-62 feet).—The Parting Quartzite is a lithologically variable unit containing resistant quartzite, varigated siltstones and shales, limestones, conglomerate, and friable sandstone (Bridwell, 1968, p. 19; Litsey, 1958, p. 1154). The unit is everywhere present in the Paleozoic section except in a small area near Bushnell Lakes in the northern Sangre de Cristo Range (Litsey, 1958, p. 1154). It is easily distinguished in the field by its overall red to pink coloration making it an excellent stratigraphic marker (Gableman, 1952, p. 1584). The Parting is thought to be of Late Devonian age based on fish remains (Behre, 1932).

Dyer Dolomite Member (87-123 feet).—The contact between the Dyer Dolomite and the underlying Parting Quartzite is gradational through several feet. The Dyer is composed of yellow- to tan-weathering microcrystalline dolomite, interlayered with thin-bedded cherty limestones (Litsey, 1958, p. 1155; Bridwell, 1968, p. 20). Fragments of fish bones, teeth, and plates in the Dyer suggest a Late Ordovician age (Johnson, 1945, p. 329).

MISSISSIPPIAN

Leadville Limestone (210-336 feet)

The Leadville Limestone disconformably overlies the Dyer Dolomite Member of the Chaffee Formation. The Leadville consists predominantly of blue to gray, fine-grained, massively-bedded limestone and gray to black, medium-bedded dolomite. Intraformational breccias are locally present particularly near the base (Litsey, 1958, p. 1157; Bridwell, 1968, p. 21).

The lower portion of the Leadville is generally chert-free, but thick-bedded irregular black and gray chert nodules are locally present in the upper portion (Gableman, 1952, p. 1586).

The thickness of the Leadville is quite variable due to extensive erosion, including the development of karst topography, prior to deposition of the first Pennsylvanian sediments.

Fossils are relatively rare in the Leadville. Litsey (1958, p. 1157) observed poorly preserved brachiopods and horn corals in the northern Sangre de Cristo Range. Faunal evidence elsewhere in the state indicates an Early Mississippian age (Kinderhookian or Osagian) for the Leadville (Johnson, 1945, p. 52).

PENNSYLVANIAN AND PERMIAN

Pennsylvanian and Permian rock outcrops cover more area than all of the pre-Pennsylvanian Paleozoic units combined. Because the stratigraphy of the Pennsylvanian and Permian rocks will be comprehensively treated elsewhere (see De Voto and Peel, this guidebook) only a few general remarks will be given here.

The older Pennsylvanian rocks consist of fine- to medium-grained clastic rocks and limestones, typically gray or black. The younger Pennsylvanian rocks are primarily fine- to coarse-grained micaceous clastic rocks characterized by red to brown colors. The Pennsylvanian-Permian and Permian units are primarily coarse to very coarse-grained clastic rocks, but they also include finer grained material and nodular limestones (Litsey, 1958, p. 1159-1161).

TERTIARY

Bonanza Volcanic Field

Oligocene volcanic rocks of the Bonanza volcanic field (Steven, Mehnert, and Obradovich, 1967; Epis and Chapin, 1968) cover most of map area west of the Villa Grove re-entrant of the San Luis Valley. The volcanic rocks are primarily lava flows, breccias, tuffs, and ash-flow tuffs. Locally, irregular masses and dikes of rhyolite, latite, and monzonite porphyry occur in the extrusive sequence (fig. 4).

The volcanic sequence was subdivided by Patton (1916) and Burbank (1932) into Rawley Andesite, Hayden Peak Latite, Bonanza Latite, Squirrel Gulch Latite, Porphyry Peak Rhyolite, and Brewer Creek Latite. The lower part of the division (Rawley and Bonanza units) is applicable throughout the Bonanza area with relatively little modification. The units above the Bonanza Latite have rather limited distributions and considerable lithologic variation. Individual investigators have, therefore, divised somewhat different subdivisions for units above the Bonanza Latite (see Bruns, Epis and Weimer, this guidebook).

Rawley Andesite (200-2,600 feet).—The earliest flows, named for an occurrence on the slopes of Rawley Gulch, fluctuate markedly both in thickness and composition. The great variation in thickness is mostly due to the pre-volcanic topography present at the time of extrusion. The earliest flows were concentrated in topographic lows, but the Rawley sequence accumulated until even the hill-tops were buried.

The Rawley flows are predominantly andesites and latites. However, ash beds and lahar breccias are locally present in considerable quantities. The lahar breccias are generally quite thick and consist of blocks and boulders of andesite and latite in an ashy matrix.

Lithologic subdivisions within the Rawley have been made at many locations throughout the area, but correlation of these various units across the area has been impossible due to extreme lateral variation within the lithologic sequence. The Rawley is a conglomeration of units originating from several sources, some within and others outside of the Bonanza area. Correlation of these units is further hindered by complex structure and the erosion locally evident on the upper surface and between units within the Rawley.

Hayden Peak Latite (1,000-1,500 feet).—The Hayden Peak Latite is a series of latite, andesite, and rhyolite flows cropping out in the eastern part of the Bonanza volcanic field. Mayhew (1969, p. 11) observed that the Hayden Peak Latite and Rawley Formation were interstratified in the eastern Bonanza area and thus, are contemporaneous. In addition, flows of the Hayden Peak Latite are lithologically similar to the flows of the Rawley Formation. The authors have, therefore, considered the Hayden Peak Latite as part of the Rawley.

Bonanza Tuff (500-1,000 feet).—The Bonanza Latite of Burbank (1932), recently renamed the Bonanza Tuff (Mayhew, 1969, p. 14-15), overlies the Rawley Formation almost everywhere in the area. It consists of at least five cooling units of red to buff biotite-rich latite ash-flow tuff. Compaction foliation and flattened pumice lapilli are common. Typically the Bonanza Tuff contains abundant purplish andesite fragments. Because the Bonanza Tuff is such a distinctive unit and is present throughout the Bonanza volcanic field, it plays an important role in correlation and mapping of the total volcanic sequence.

In the central Bonanza volcanic pile the Bonanza Tuff is highly welded and only two units can be distinguished. Toward the south, particularly along the prominent ridge west of Findley Gulch, the Bonanza Tuff separates into five distinct cooling units (fig. 5). Northward along this ridge the various units merge together until they appear as one. This southward separation of the Bonanza into several cooling units indicates that the source of the Bonanza Tuff lies to the north where the temperature and thickness of the successive ash-flows was sufficient to weld them together as they cooled.

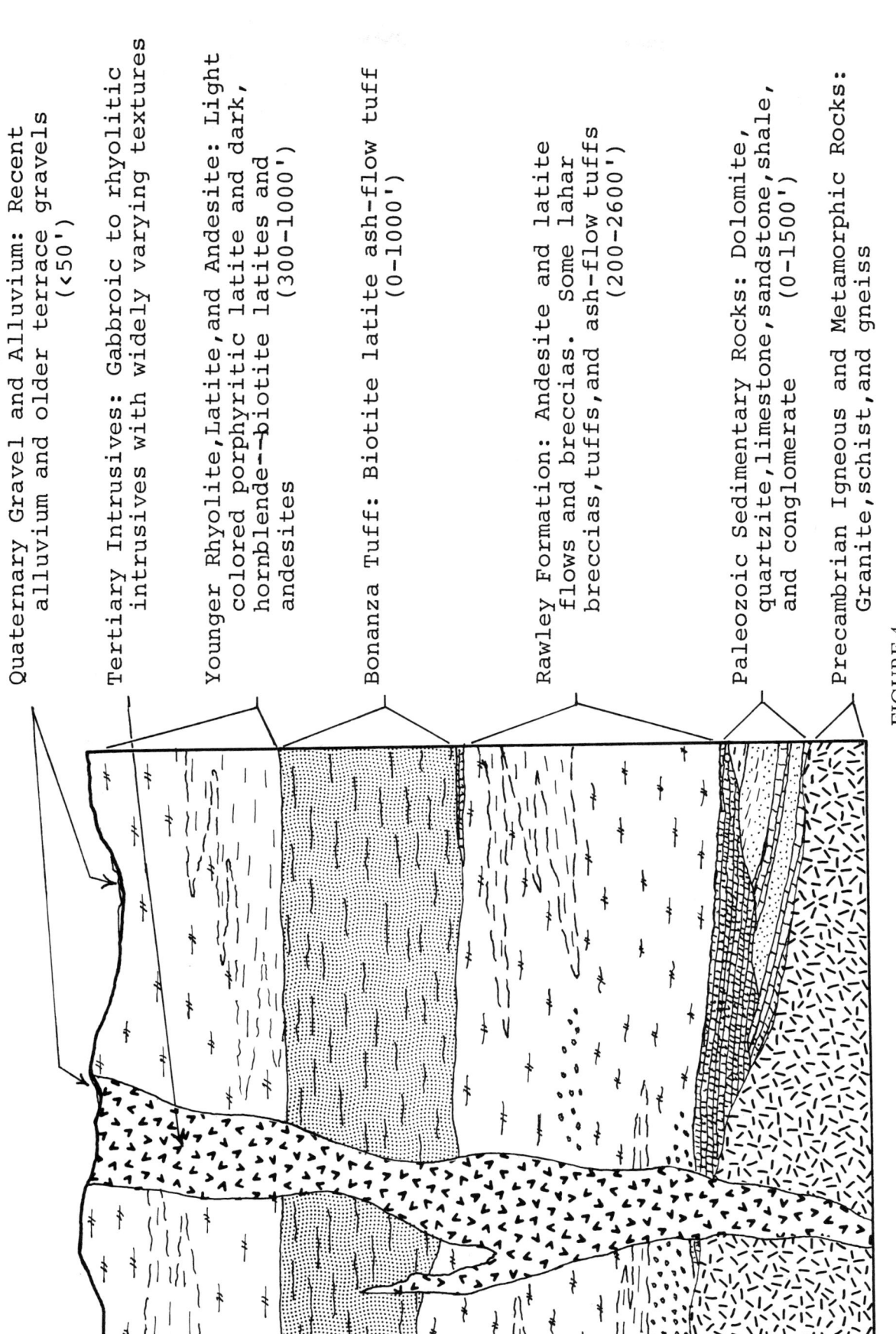

FIGURE 4. Generalized columnar section of Bonanza area.

FIGURE 5.
Photograph showing five separate cooling units of Bonanza Tuff along ridge west of Findley Gulch (near Saguache, Colorado).

The erosion surface on which the Bonanza was deposited has more than 200 feet of relief locally, indicating that the Bonanza Tuff is considerably younger than the underlying Rawley Formation. Pseudo-synclinal structures that normally develop during compaction of an ash-flow in a valley are not present in the Bonanza area to any degree. The earlier ash-flows of the Bonanza Tuff quickly buried the pre-existing topography; the later Bonanza ash-flows spread out from the source in sheet-like masses producing units with broad, uniform distribution.

Younger Rhyolite, Latite, and Andesite Flows (300-1,000 feet).—Burbank (1932) divided the flows overlying the Bonanza Tuff into four units; Squirrel Gulch Latite, Porphyry Peak Rhyolite, Brewer Creek Latite, and Younger Andesite. With the exception of the Porphyry Peak Rhyolite, these are dark, hornblende-biotite latites and andesites. The Porphyry Peak is a light-colored biotite rhyolite which crops out in the vicinity of Porphyry Peak. Burbank (1932, p. 26) describes this unit as a sequence of flows and some intrusive rhyolite, but Perry (1971) believes that the Porphyry Peak Rhyolite is an endogenous dome.

Mayhew (1969) separated the flows above the Bonanza Tuff into three units which he called the Younger Andesite, Younger Ash-Flow Tuff, and Younger Latite. These units were not positively correlated with Burbank's upper units. Mayhew also distinguished a separate quartz latite unit which crops out on the upper slopes and summit of Hayden Peak. Burbank (1932) included this unit in the Hayden Peak Latite, but Mayhew believes it is definitely post-Hayden Peak Latite and may be younger than the Bonanza Tuff. Furthermore, he believes that the Hayden Peak Quartz Latite is an endogenous lava dome (Mayhew, 1969, p. 34).

Current work in the southern Bonanza volcanic field has revealed that a sequence of dark andesite and latite flows overlie the Bonanza Tuff in that region. This sequence has been tentatively called the Dry Gulch Andesite for excellent exposures along Dry Gulch northwest of Saguache. The Dry Gulch Andesite may prove equivalent to Burbank's Squirrel Gulch Latite, Brewer Creek Latite, and Younger Andesite.

OTHER VOLCANICS

Mapping in the Howard area has distinguished at least three volcanic units existing as scattered erosional remnants (Pierce, 1969, p. 71). These include (1) a gray, sanidine-rich, welded, lapilli tuff which may be equivalent to Ash-flows 1 and 2 of the Thirtynine Mile volcanic field to the north (Chapin and Epis, 1964), (2) other tuffaceous units mapped as Undifferentiated Tuff, and (3) a sequence of andesite and basalt lava flows. Pierce believes that the ash-flows are of Oligocene age and correlate with lower flows of the Thirtynine Mile volcanic field which are time equivalents of parts of the Rawley Formation in the Bonanza volcanic field. He correlates the andesite and basalt flows with probable Miocene-age flows mapped by Duhamel (1968) in the Waugh Mountain area of the Thirtynine Mile field (Pierce, 1969, p. 98).

Intrusive Rocks

Intrusive rocks ranging from rhyolite to gabbro are concentrated in the central portion of the Bonanza volcanic field. Emplacement of many of the smaller intrusive bodies was obviously fault controlled. The relative ages of the intrusives is often difficult to establish, but relationships that can be established seem to indicate that the more silicic intrusives represent late stages of the intrusive activity.

Several intrusives have also been mapped in the northeastern part of the map area. These include the Rito Alto stock east of Valley View Hot Springs, the Slide-Rock Mountain stock in the Hayden Pass area, and the Whitehorn stock in the Wellsville area to the north. These intrusives range in composition from rhyolite to monzonite and have intruded into Pennsylvanian-Permian sedimentary rocks (Burbank and Goddard, 1937; Toulmin, 1953; Rold, 1950; Litsey, 1958; Pierce, 1969; Nolting, 1970). According to Litsey (1958, p. 1168) the Rito Alto stock is probably Early to Middle Miocene. Pierce (1969, p. 68) found that the contact between the Whitehorn stock and the Pennsylvanian-Permian sedimentary rocks suggests a very Late-Laramide or post-Laramide emplacement.

Tertiary Sedimentary Units

Sediments deposited in a Tertiary trough between the Arkansas and San Luis valleys include several thousand feet of clays, silts, sands, and gravels with minor amounts of limestone and volcanic ash (Van Alstine, 1968, p. C158). Fossil horse teeth and camel bones (Powers, 1935, p. 189; Van Alstine and Lewis, 1960) found at localities in the Arkansas Valley indicate that these sediments are mainly of Pliocene age although the lower part of this sedimentary sequence is of Late Miocene age. These sediments can be correlated with the Dry Union Formation in the Leadville area (Tweto, 1961).

An equivalent formation was mapped by Pierce (1969) in the Howard area. He called this sequence the Pleasant Valley Conglomerate and postulated that it resulted from fluvitile deposition contemporaneous with the uplift of the Sangre de Cristo Range in Miocene and Pliocene time (Pierce, 1969, p. 98).

QUATERNARY

Quaternary sediments occur in the Arkansas Valley, the Howard area, the Villa Grove reentrant of the San Luis Valley, and along major drainage channels. Of primary interest are the large alluvial fans along both the east and west sides of the Villa Grove reentrant, and gravel-capped pediment surfaces on the west side of the Villa Grove reentrant and in the Howard area. Both alluvial fan deposits and pediment gravels are characterized by locally derived material.

In the Howard area, four pediment levels were mapped by Pierce (1969, p. 76-78). The four pediment surfaces are 265, 200, 110, and 70 feet above modern stream base, respectively. Pierce (1969) tentatively correlates the two highest surfaces with the Rocky Flats and Verdos surfaces developed along the eastern flank of the Front Range. These surfaces are interpreted by Scott (1963, p. 11) to be Nebraskan and Kansan age respectively.

On the west side of the Villa Grove reentrant, Mayhew (1969, p. 41) mapped three surfaces as pediments. Subsequent work indicates that only the highest surfaces are remnants of gravel-capped pediments now largely destroyed by erosion. Later alluvial fan deposits cover much of the area. The exact age of the pediment surfaces has not been determined; nor have these pediments been successfully correlated with the pediments in the Howard area.

Along the eastern side of the Villa Grove reentrant four ages of alluvial fans have been mapped. No pediments have been found. The different fans can be distinguished by their areal extent, degree of dissection, angle of slope, and amount of vegetative cover (table 2). The three older fans are outwash fans developed during Bull Lake and Pinedale (Wisconsinian) glacial stades (Scott, 1970, p. C17).

TABLE 2.
DESCRIPTIONS OF QUATERNARY ALLUVIAL FANS
ALONG THE WEST FLANK OF THE
SANGRE DE CRISTO RANGE

HOLOCENE
   Qaf 1—Small, steepy-sloped cones deposited along pre-existing erosional and fault scarps.
PLEISTOCENE
   Qaf 2—Large, gently-sloped, undissected fans supporting moderate vegetation growth.
   Qaf 3—Large, steeply-sloped, dissected fans with sparse vegetation.
   Qaf 4—Large, steeply-sloped, highly dissected fans with sparse vegetation. Only relatively small remnants preserved.

Two features, one along Carr Gulch and the other along Piney Creek, were identified on air photos as debris or mud flows. It appears that unconsolidated material deposited in the canyons moved in-mass out onto the surface of fan system 3. These features have not yet been studied in the field.

Pleistocene moranial material occurs at high elevations west of the Villa Grove reentrant. East of the reentrant moraines extend to the mouths of some canyons facing the San Luis Valley near the southeast corner of the map area (Nolting, 1970, p. 53). Effects of alpine glaciation have not yet been investigated in detail.

Quaternary sediments in the Bonanza mountains occur mostly along stream valleys. These include narrow strips of alluvium along some streams, a few small terrace remnants, and landslides. The stream terrace remnants are of particular interest because they are displaced along youthful faults.

GEOLOGIC HISTORY

PRECAMBRIAN

Details of the Precambrian geologic history of the map area are sketchy at best, however, a generalized sequence of events can be tentatively outlined.

Record of the Precambrian geological development of the area begins with the deposition of an unknown thickness of silicious clastic sediments, probably in Late Precambrian time. The basement upon which these sediments accumulated is not exposed anywhere in the map area.

The sediments were metamorphosed and intensely deformed. Pods and lenses of mafic magma were syntectonically emplaced in the sediments and subsequently metamorphosed to amphibolites (Pierce, 1969, p. 10). Both sediments and intrusives acquired strong primary foliation during this initial phase of deformation.

The metamorphic rocks were subsequently invaded by silicic to intermediate plutons, sills, and dikes. The oldest intrusive rock is the coarse-grained, porphyritic granite of the Kerber Creek area. Emplacement of this unit was followed by intrusion of aplitic granite of the Kerber Creek area. Foliation in both units suggests that they were emplaced syntectonically. Pegmatites crosscut both rock types (Bridwell, 1968, p. 9). Small local intrusions of granodiorite, diorite, and graphic granite invaded all older Precambrian rocks and post-date major Precambrian deformational episodes.

The Precambrian rocks were uplifted and underwent erosion in Late Precambrian (?) and Cambrian time before being submerged beneath the Late Cambrian sea.

PRE-PENNSYLVANIAN

During Early and Middle Cambrian time Colorado was a highland along the northeast-trending Transcontinental arch. By Late Cambrian the eastern and western seas had merged through a structurally low area on the arch called the Colorado sag (Haun and Kent, 1965, p. 1783). The map area was located in the Colorado sag on the north flank of the Sierra Grande uplift (fig. 6).

Fine-grained sand of the Sawatch Quartzite was deposited in the area during the Late Cambrian. Slight uplift of the Sierra Grande Highland raised the area above the sea and much of the Sawatch was stripped off. The

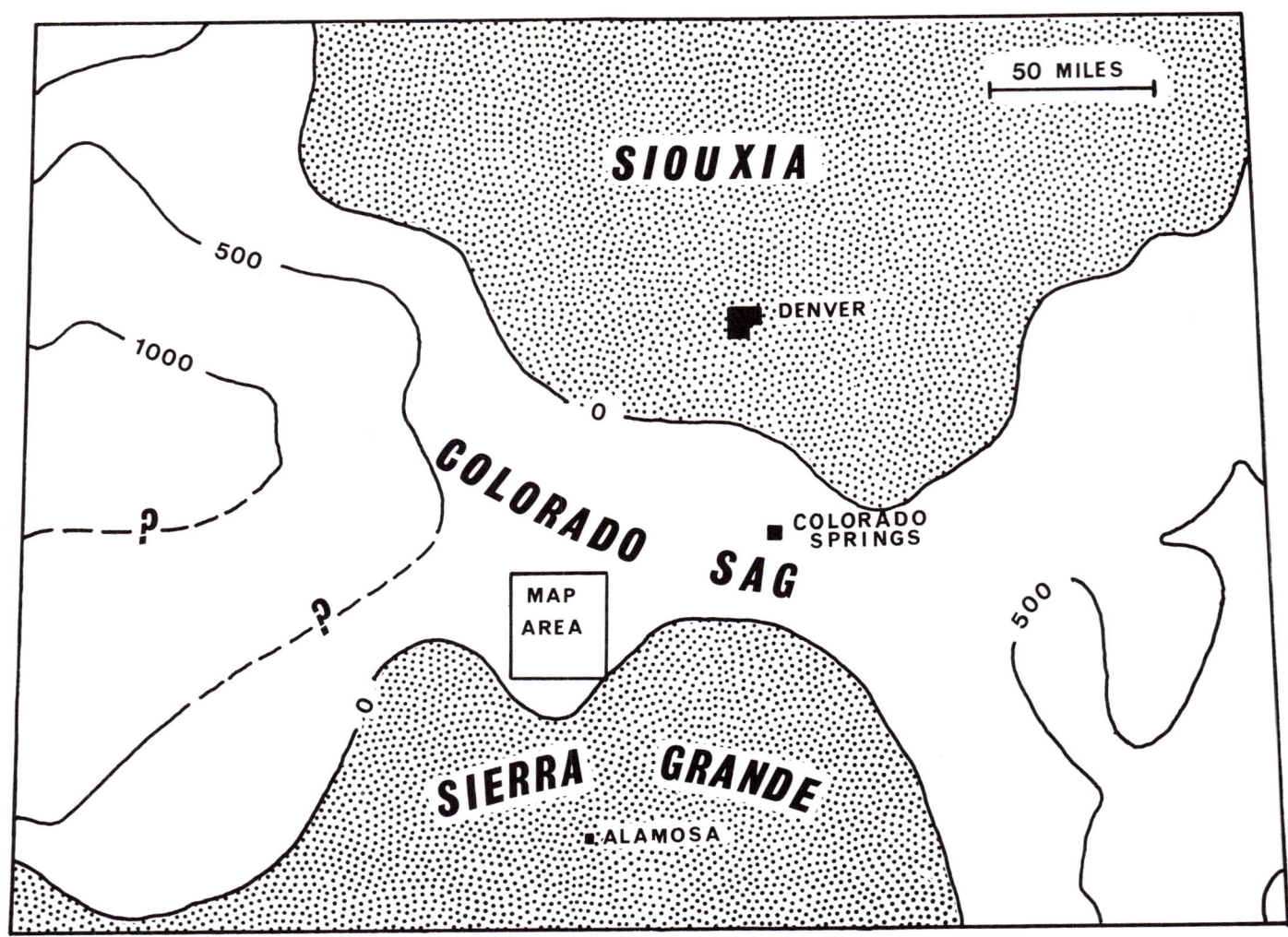

FIGURE 6.
Isopach map of Cambrian and Lower Ordovician rocks in Colorado outlining Early Paleozoic high areas. (Modified from Berg, 1960).

area then subsided and was once again covered by the sea (Gableman, 1952, p. 1582). As the sea returned to the area the Early Ordovician Manitou Formation was deposited over exposed Precambrian crystalline rocks and erosional remnants of the Sawatch Quartzite. The sea briefly retreated from the area before the Harding Sandstone was deposited in Middle Ordovician time. Brief uplift before the deposition of the Late Ordovician Fremont Formation is postulated for the eastern half of the area while continuous deposition took place in the western half.

Although Silurian strata do not occur in central Colorado, regional data suggest continuous marine deposition from Late Ordovician through Silurian time. In Early Devonian time the sea withdrew and a period of extensive erosion ensued lasting until the Late Devonian (Haun and Kent, 1965, p. 1784). In the map area all Silurian strata (if present) were removed and the Fremont Formation extensively eroded, but not entirely removed.

During Late Devonian the sea transgressed eastward from the Cordilleran geosyncline across the map area into eastern Colorado (Haun and Kent, 1965, p. 1785; Litsey, 1958, p. 1172). As the sea advanced over the area it reworked weathered debris on the surface into the Parting Quartzite Member of the Chaffee Formation. Deposition of these basal clastics was followed by carbonate sedimentation forming the Dyer Dolomite Member of the Chaffee.

In Early Mississippian time (Kinderhookian and Osagian) the Leadville Limestone was deposited across the map area. A northwest-southeast trending facies change at the base of the Leadville reveals that the eastern half of the map area was briefly raised above the sea prior to Leadville deposition. The facies change probably reflects an early pulse of the building of the ancestral Rockies which followed in Pennsylvanian and Permian time.

Near the close of Late Mississippian time broad regional uplift raised the area above sea level and widespread erosion lasting into Early Pennsylvanian time removed large quantities of Mississippian rocks (Litsey, 1959, p. 1172).

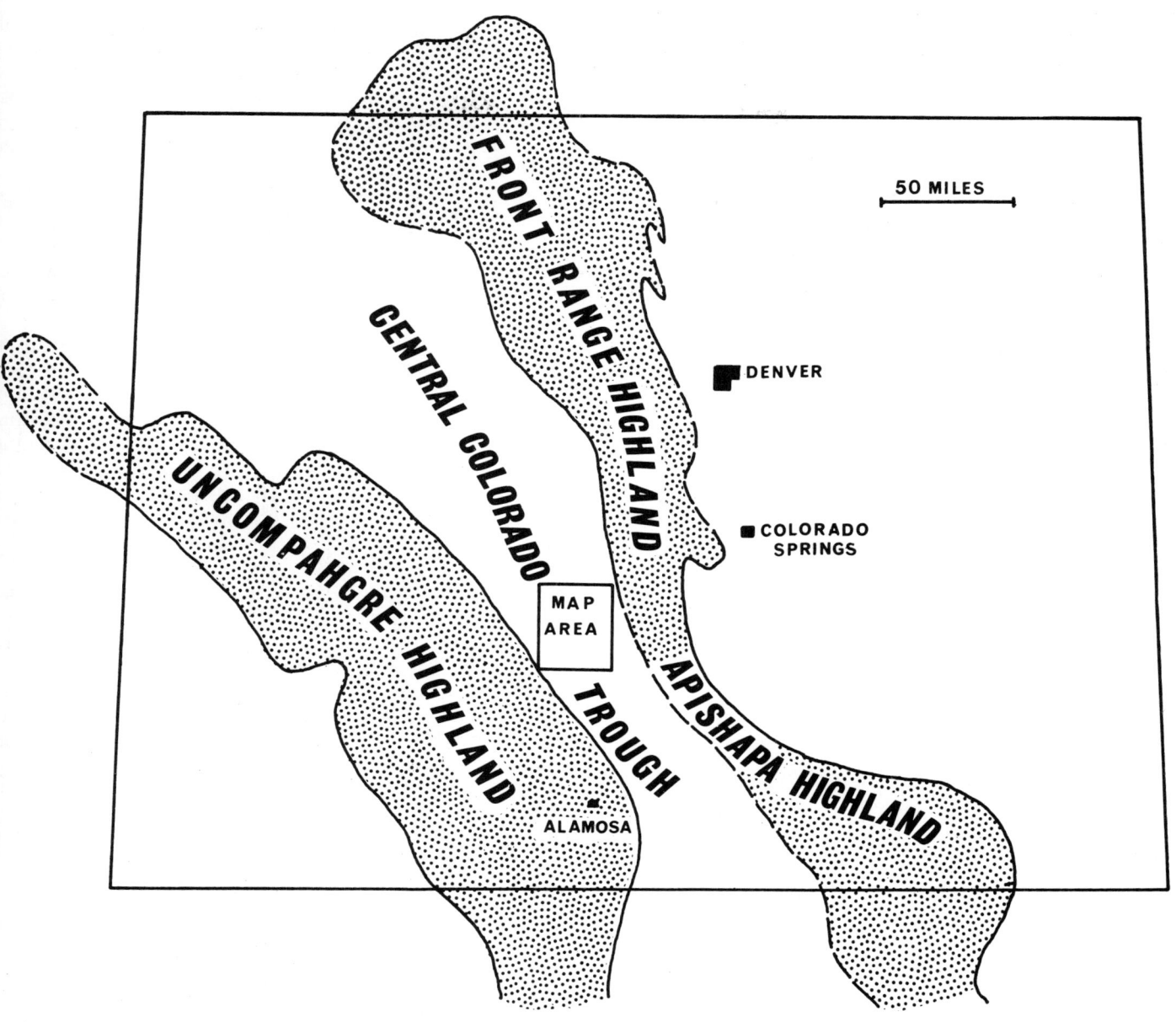

FIGURE 7.
General outline of major Pennsylvanian and Permian highland areas in Colorado. (Modified from Mallory, 1960).

PENNSLVANIAN AND PERMIAN

The Pennsylvanian and Permian geologic history of central and western Colorado was controlled by two northwest-southeast elongate highlands, the Front Range and the Uncompahgre. The map area was located in the relatively narrow structural and depositional trough between the two highlands generally referred to as the Central Colorado trough (fig. 7).

Initially fluvial sediments derived from older Paleozoic rocks on the rising highlands were deposited in the area by northwest-flowing streams (Pierce, 1969, p. 21). Fluvial sedimentation was intermittently interrupted by minor marine transgressions (Pierce, 1969, p. 94). Precambrian rocks were finally exposed and redbed deposition followed, periodically interrupted by carbonate deposition. Because the map area was located in a relatively narrow portion of the Central Colorado trough, minor movements in the nearby highlands frequently influenced depositional patterns.

The most vigorous uplift of the Uncompahgre and Front Range highlands took place during the Permian. In the Howard area at the northeast corner of the map (see plate 1, back pocket) movement along the Pleasant Valley fault displaced basement rocks as much as 10,000 feet and folded the older Paleozoic strata into a series of northwest-trending anticlines and synclines. Erosion beveled the Paleozoic strata and Permian fluvial sediments from the highland east of the Pleasant Valley fault spread over the beveled surface in angular discordance with the older Paleozoic strata (Pierce, 1969, p. 96).

At the same time, extremely coarse clastic sediments of the Crestone Conglomerate were being shed eastward into the Sangre de Cristo Range area from a highland (San Luis Highland) that occupied the present position of the San Luis Valley (Gableman, 1952, p. 1588). The highland was probably an eastward-projecting lobe of the Uncompahgre Highland. The alluvial fan deposits of the Crestone Conglomerate probably represent the upstream facies of the fluvial clastics which accumulated in the Howard area, all of which were shed into a narrow, deep, northwest-trending trough between the Front Range and the Uncompahgre Highland (Pierce, 1969, p. 97).

Aggregate thickness of the Pennsylvanian and Permian sediments that accumulated in the Central Colorado trough was great. In the Howard area between 10,000 and 18,000 feet of dominantly clastic sediments were deposited (Pierce, 1969, p. 3). In the northern Sangre de Cristo Range, south of Hayden Pass, more than 14,500 feet of clastic sediments accumulated (Litsey, 1959, p. 1172).

Mesozoic

Rocks of Mesozoic age are not present in the map area. Regional considerations, however, indicate that Mesozoic strata once covered the area, but have been removed as a result of erosion following strong uplift associated with the Laramide orogeny in Late Cretaceous-Early Tertiary time.

By Early Mesozoic time only remnants of the ancestral Rockies were present in central Colorado. They were so subdued that they contributed little sediment. By Late Jurassic time (Kimmeridgian or Portlandian) the ancestral Rockies in central Colorado were finally buried beneath the continental-fluvial sediments of the Morrison Formation (Oriel and Craig, 1960, p. 43).

During Late Jurassic and Early Cretaceous time a north-south elongated seaway connecting the Arctic Sea and the Gulf of Mexico transgressed over the western interior (Weimer, 1970, p. 173). The map area appears to have been located on a deltaic plain near the western shore of the seaway during Early Cretaceous (Weimer, 1970, fig. 1-a, p. 160). In Late Cretaceous the sea expanded westward and marine sediments were deposited in the map area. Sedimentation ceased with the beginning of the Laramide orogeny in Late Cretaceous time.

Laramide Orogeny

In central Colorado the Laramide orogeny began near the end of Cretaceous time and lasted into Late Eocene (Haun and Kent, 1965, p. 1794; Gableman, 1952, p. 1609-1610). Dating of the deformational episodes is difficult in the map area because erosion has removed any tectonically-derived sediments which may have accumulated as well as all Mesozoic strata.

Structural development during the Laramide took place in three major phases. On a regional scale this deformation was intimately related to the development of the broad anticlinal uplifts of the Front Range-Wet Mountain anticlines and the Sawatch arch.

The map area was on the southeastern flank of the Sawatch arch. As the arch rose, strata on the east flank were tilted. The present outcrop pattern of Paleozoic strata in the northern Sangre de Cristo Range, and in the Mosquito Range to the north, roughly outlines the east flank of the Sawatch arch.

The second major phase of deformation produced northwest-trending asymmetrical anticlines and synclines which, under continuing stresses, failed with westward-directed thrust faults. A similar sequence of events is recorded in the Paleozoic strata of the Kerber Creek area. Gableman (1952, p. 1610) interpreted the westward-directed stresses as related to relative westward movement of the Front Range and Wet Mountain anticlines.

The third phase of Laramide deformation is recognized only in the Kerber Creek area and in the Sangre de Cristo Range south of the Orient Mine (Gableman, 1952, p. 1574). It consisted of eastward and northward thrusting accompanied by folding. Thrusts of this phase, such as the Kerber and Noland thrusts of the Kerber Creek area, truncate the older Laramide structures. Burbank (1932, p. 287) attributed this period of deformation to northward and eastward movement of a highland which occupied the present position of the San Luis Valley. Boundaries of the highland are generally vague, but the eastern margin was probably near the eastern side of the present San Luis Valley from Sierra Blanca northward to the vicinity of Major Canyon, where it turned westward south of the Kerber Creek area.

By Late Eocene time the Laramide highlands were reduced to relatively low relief. However, local relief of up to 2,000 feet is indicated within the Bonanza volcanic field.

Middle and Late Tertiary

The advent of plutonism and volcanism in Oligocene time signaled a major change in the geologic phenomena controlling the tectonic development of the mapped area. Regional tension may have been a primary factor in allowing magma to rise along zones of weakness.

Volcanism accompanied by minor intrusive activity dominated the Oligocene epoch. Voluminous flows of basic to intermediate lavas were erupted from several local centers in and around the Bonanza volcanic field forming the Rawley Formation. Two flows near the base of this sequence have been dated by Van Alstine and Marvin (reported by Lipman and others, 1970, p. 2336) at 34.2 m.y. and 33.4 m.y. and thus, are age equivalents of flows in the Conejos and San Juan formations in the San Juan volcanic field to the southeast. The Rawley Formation also appears to be roughly equivalent in age and composition to the Lower Andesite of the Thirtynine Mile volcanic field (Epis and Chapin, 1968, p. 64-65). Locally, within the Bonanza field, the Rawley is greater than 2,500 feet thick.

In Late Oligocene time the pattern of volcanism in the Bonanza field shifted to explosive ash-flow eruption of the Bonanza Tuff. The switch from basic and intermediate volcanism to explosive ash-flow eruption parallel the trend observed by Lipman and others (1970) throughout south-central Colorado.

Following the extrusion of the Bonanza Tuff and the

younger latites and andesites overlying it, the area centered around the town of Bonanza collapsed within a set of concentric ring fractures forming a caldera. The concentrac faults apparently controlled the emplacement of shallow silicic intrusions and endogenous domes along the rim of the caldera. Other fault patterns that developed include a set of poorly developed high-angle radial faults radiating outward from the central Bonanza area. The radial faults curve around and merge with concentric faults inward toward the central caldera. A set of high-angle shear faults, also formed during tilting, parallel the concentric faults but dip more gently toward the central caldera.

Collapse of the Bonanza center resulted from removal of support from below as the contents of the underlying magma chamber flowed out onto the surface. Normal faults bounding the southwest and northeast sides of the caldera are relatively well-developed and moved in a narrow zone. Displacement on the northwest and southeast portions of the rim is spread over broad zones. The present structural configuration of the Bonanza caldera (see plates 1 and 2, back pocket) may be due either to (1) an initial hinge-like subsidence of the caldera with the western part dropping farther than the eastern part, or (2) subsequent subsidence of the San Luis Valley and eastern rim of the caldera resulting in some degree of structural compensation for an original large displacement along the eastern rim of the caldera.

Sometime after the last Oligocene volcanic activity and before deposition of Late Miocene sediments of the lower Dry Union Formation, a fault-bounded trough extending from the Arkansas Valley southward into the San Luis Valley developed (Van Alstine, 1968; 1970). This trough was part of the Rio Grande depression, a complex series of horsts and grabens extending from southern New Mexico into central Colorado.

Within the trough clastic debris shed from the surrounding highlands accumulated. These sediments comprise the Miocene-Pliocene Dry Union Formation which is equivalent to a portion of the Santa Fe Group deposited in the Rio Grande depression in southern Colorado and New Mexico (Van Alstine, 1970, p. B46). The position of the trough is outlined by the San Luis-Arkansas trough, the Poncha Loop syncline, and the Villa Grove reentrant of the northern San Luis Valley. Contemporaneous with the development of the trough, a small graben, the Pleasant Valley graben, evolved in the Howard area. Coarse clastic sediments of the Pleasant Valley Conglomerate were dumped into the graben and subsquently faulted as the graben further subsided (Pierce, 1969, p. 85).

The eastern boundary fault(s) of the trough lies along the west side of the Sangre de Cristo Range and is largely buried beneath Quaternary sediments. In the northern part of the area, similarly trending steep faults in Precambrian rocks probably are the continuation of the eastern boundary fault system. Movement along this fault system in Miocene and Pliocene time raised the Sangre de Cristo Range to most of its present elevation.

Along the western boundary fault(s) the Dry Union Formation is often faulted, probably reflecting recurrent movement during development of the trough (Van Alstine, 1970, p. B48). The western boundary fault continues southward from the southwest edge of the San Luis-Arkansas trough into the Bonanza volcanic field where it joins the system of normal faults developed during collapse of the Bonanza caldera. Reactivation of these faults in the Quaternary is indicated by displaced gravels along Little Kerber Creek at the southern end of the fault system.

Late in the Pliocene or early in the Pleistocene, the trough connecting the San Luis and Arkansas valleys was fragmented by transverse faults. The largest of these transverse faults is the Salida-Maysville fault at the north end of the area. Movement along the Salida-Maysville fault raised the area south of the fault a minmium of 2,500 feet near Poncha Mountain.

Similar faults truncated the southern end of the San Luis-Arkansas trough. Erosion on the southern block removed much of the Dry Union Formation except for the sediments in the Poncha Loop syncline and in the O'Haver Lake area. South of the Poncha Loop syncline the Dry Union Formation, if present, is covered by Quaternary sediments. Many other minor faults served to further fragment the original structural and depositional trough connecting the San Luis and Arkansas valleys.

QUATERNARY

In Early Pleistocene time, regional climatic fluctuations produced periods of erosion alternating with periods of alluviation in the map area. Pediments were locally cut along the flanks of the mountain ranges during periods of erosion; gravels were deposited on the pediments during periods of alluvation. Each successive period of pedimentation tended to destroy the older gravel-capped surfaces.

During Late Pleistocene (Wisconsinian), alpine glaciers carved the scenic mountain peaks in the Sangre de Cristo Range, the Bonanza volcanic field, and the southern Sawatch Range. Morainal material was deposited in the high cirque basins and in some of the major canyons of the Sangre de Cristo Range. Outwash fans representing several stades of Bull Lake and Pinedale glaciation (Scott, 1970, p. C17) were deposited along the steep western front of the Sangre de Cristo Range and on the eastern side of the Bonanza volcanic field. Periods of erosion between episodes of fan deposition partially removed the earlier fan systems.

After, and probably during, deposition of Pleistoscene outwash fans along the Sangre de Cristo Range, the pre-Quaternary Sangre de Cristo fault system was reactivated displacing Pleistocene gravel as much as 20 to 25 feet. This Quaternary fault system bifurcates in the vicinity of Valley View Hot Springs. One branch continues north-northwest along the front of the Sangre de Cristo Range. The second branch trends more northwestward toward the town of Villa Grove.

Faults along the north-northwest branch displace the heads of nearly every alluvial fan along the range front (fig. 8). Displacement of faults along the northwest

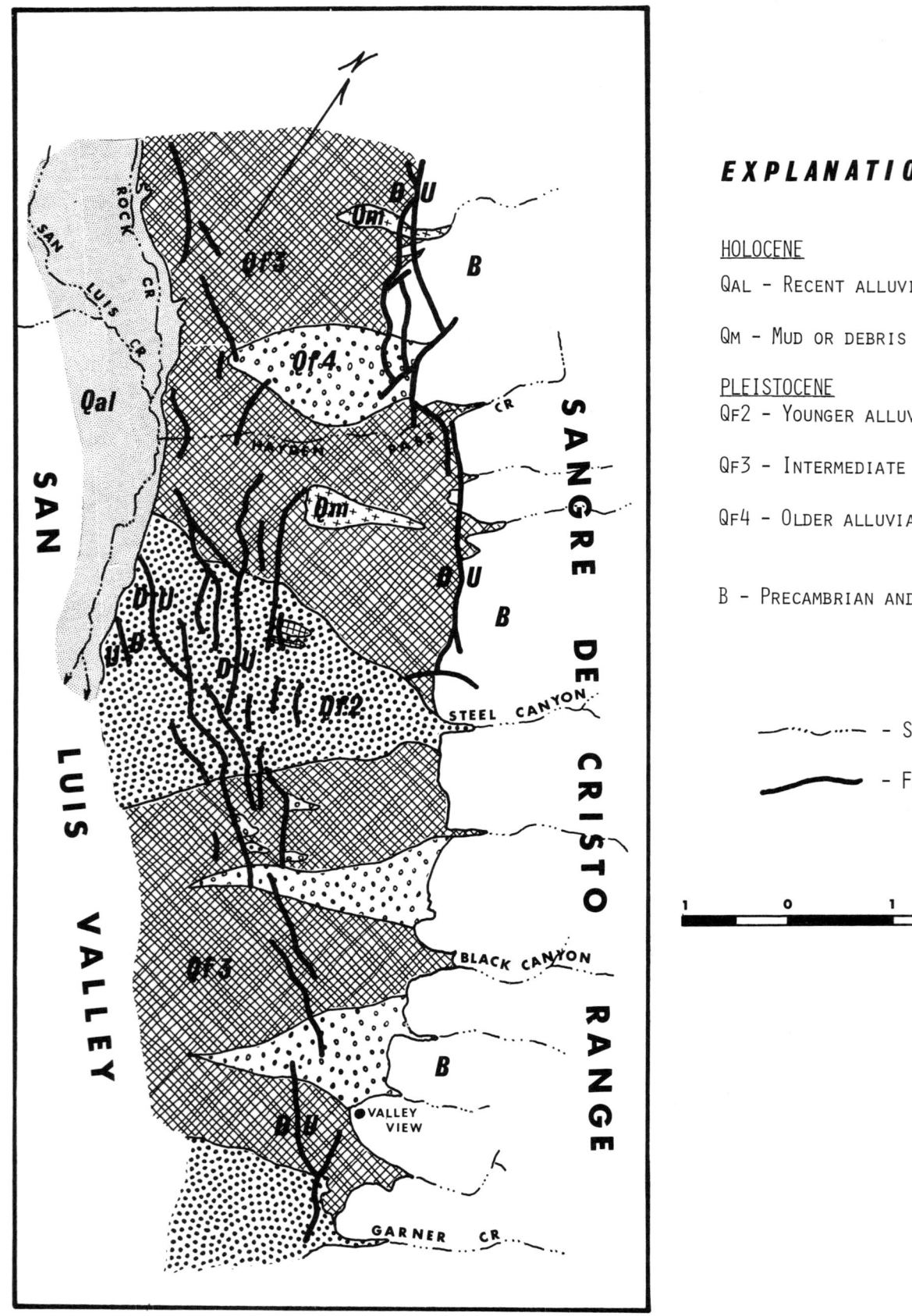

FIGURE 8.
Geologic map of a portion of east side of the San Luis Valley near Villa Grove. Faults displace Pleistocene outwash fans.

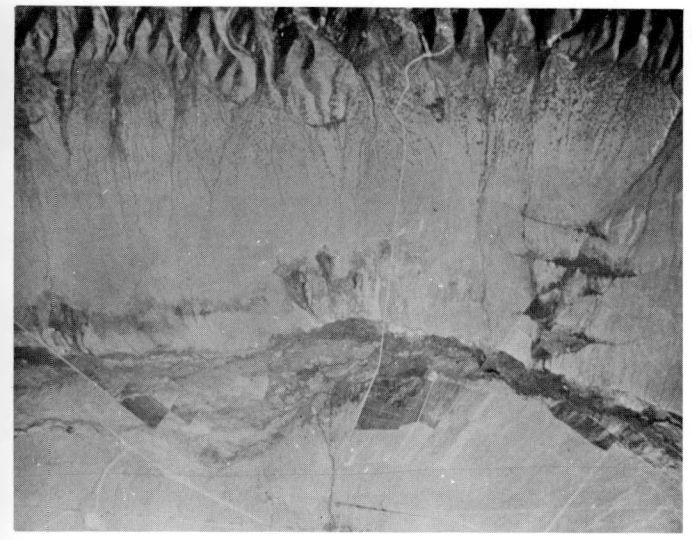

FIGURE 9.
Faults displacing Quaternary deposits and partially damming ground water. (East of Villa Grove).

Aerial photograph courtesy of Colorado School of Mines, Bonanza Project (101).

branch decreases to the northwest finally dying out north of Villa Grove. Along the central portion of this branch the faults have partially dammed groundwater circulation forming marshy and densely vegetated areas on the upslope-side of individual faults (fig. 9). Sense of movement along both fault systems is predominantly up on the east.

The north-northwest fault system apparently reflects recurrent movement along the pre-Quaternary Sangre de Cristo fault system. The northwest fault system roughly outlines a graben within the major part of the Rio Grande depression which may be filled with Miocene-Pliocene sediments. Gravity data (Gaca, 1965) indicates the presence of a narrow graben south and east of Villa Grove. Recurrent movement along the border of this graben has displaced the Quaternary gravels. North of the graben the thickness of the Quaternary deposits decreases rapidly.

In Holocene time small alluvial fans were formed, commonly at the base of pre-existing fault and erosional scarps. Recent erosion, particularly gullying, has greatly modified all older Quaternary features.

ECONOMIC GEOLOGY

Mineral deposits of the area vary widely in type and mode of occurrence. In the northeastern part of the area lime deposits from travertine and the Leadville Limestone have been mined as material for steel processing. Gypsum and bentonite deposits have also been worked from time to time. Other minerals in the northeast sector that might possibly become economically important are emuscovite, which is locally present in considerable quantities within the Precambrian rocks, and copper, which has been found in small quantities in Permian and Pennsylvanian sands interbedded with carbonaceous shales.

Further south, along the Sangre de Cristo Range, iron minerals were mined at the Orient Mine east of Valley View Hot Springs. The ore was mainly siderite from the Leadville Limestone.

In the San Luis Valley and its Villa Grove reentrant many deposits of sand and gravel are found which of excellent commercial grade. Several of these are being actively worked for materials for roads and other structures.

The Marshall Pass district which lies just to the northwest of the area has produced some uranium from quartzite beds in the Ordovician Harding Formation, from Eocene (?) soils lying on Precambrian rocks and from pitchblende and pyrite veins in the Belden and Leadville limestones along the Chester fault. It is possible that some mineralization of this sort extends southeastward into the Precambrian and volcanic terrain of the map area.

The Bonanza center, itself, has been the source of many varieties of base metal ores. The mineralization in the Bonanza district apparently occurred in two phases after major deformation in the area ceased. Silver, lead, gold, and zinc are the primary metals in the ore veins and they usually occur in a gangue of quartz. Burbank (1932, p. 60) divides the ore bearing veins into two classes: (1) quartz veins of relatively high sulfide content, carrying lead, zinc, copper and silver and (2) quartz-rhodochrosite-fluorite veins. The major production of the area was largely from veins of the first class which are mostly located in the northern part of the district. Veins of the second class are more common in the southern area and production in this part of the district was relatively small.

The total production of the Bonanza district is estimated at more than $9,000,000 prior to 1946 (Vanderwilt, 1947, p. 445) and this was mostly the output of the Rawley Mine. Production from the Rawley Mine ceased in 1930 with the sale of the Rawley mill. Subsequent attempts to revive the mine have proven sub-economic.

The major potential of the Bonanza district lies in the chance for the discovery of new, high-grade veins or large, lower grade mineral deposits that might occur at depth where Paleozoic carbonates or other favorable horizons have been buried in the volcanics and might have been subsequently mineralized.

REFERENCES

Behre, C. H., Jr., 1932, The Weston Pass mining district, Lake and Park Counties, Colorado: Colorado Sci. Soc. Proc., v. 13, p. 57-60.

Berg, R. R., 1960, Cambrian and Ordovician history of Colorado *in* Guide to the geology of Colorado: Rocky Mtn. Assoc. Geologists, p. 10-17.

Bridwell, R. J., 1968, Geology of the Kerber Creek area, Saguache County, Colorado: Unpub. Colo. School of Mines M.S. thesis, no. 1177, 104 p.

Bruns, D. L., 1971, Geology of the Lake Mountain northeast quadrangle, Saguache County, Colorado: M.S. thesis, Colo. School of Mines, no. 1367, 79 p.

Burbank, W. S., 1932, Geology and ore deposits of the Bonanza mining district, Colorado: U.S. Geol. Survey Prof. Paper 169, 166 p.

Burbank, W. S., and Goddard, E. N., 1937, Thrusting in Huerfano Park, Colorado, and related problems of orogeny in the Sangre de Cristo Mountains: Geol. Soc. America Bull., v. 48, no. 7, p. 931-976.

Chapin, C. E., and Epis, R. C., 1964, Some stratigraphic and structural features of the Thirtynine Mile volcanic field, central Colorado: Mtn. Geologist, v. 1, no. 3, p. 145-160.

Cook, D. R., 1960, Bonanza Project, Bear Creek Mining Co.: American Inst. Mining, Metall., and Petroleum Engineers, Trans., v. 217, p. 285-295.

Del Rio, S. M., 1960, Mineral Resources of Colorado First Sequel: State of Colo. Mineral Resources Board, 764 p.

DuHamel, J. E., 1968, Volcanic geology of the upper Cottonwood Creek area, Thirtynine Mile volcanic field: M.S. thesis, Colo. School of Mines, 120 p.

Epis, R. C., and Chapin, C. E., 1968, Geologic history of the Thirtynine Mile volcanic field, central Colorado: Colo. School of Mines Quart., v. 63, no. 3, 287 p.

Gableman, J. W., 1952, Structure and origin of northern Sangre de Cristo range, Colorado: Am. Assoc. Petroleum Geol. Bull., v. 36, no. 8, p. 1547-1612.

Gaca, J. R., 1965, Gravity studies in the San Luis Valley area, Colorado: Unpub. M.S. thesis, Colo. School of Mines, no. 1021, 73 p.

Haun, J. D., and Kent, H. C., 1965, Geologic history of Rocky Mountain region: Am. Assoc. Petroleum Geol. Bull., v. 49, no. 11, p. 1781-1800.

Johnson, J. H., 1945, A resume of the Paleozoic stratigraphy of Colorado: Colo. School of Mines Quart., v. 40, p. 1-109.

Karig, D. E., 1965, Geophysical evidence of a caldera at Bonanza, Colorado: U.S. Geol. Survey Prof. Paper 525-B, p. B9-B12.

Kouther, M. J. M., 1968, Geology and mineralization of northwest part of Bonanza Quadrangle, Chaffee and Saguache counties, Colorado: Unpub. M.S. thesis, Colo. School of Mines, no. 1237, 93 p.

Lipman, P. W., Steven, T. A., and Mehnert, H. H., 1970, Volcanic history of the San Juan mountains, Colorado, as indicated by Potassium—argon dating: Bull. Geol. Soc. America, v. 81, no. 8, p. 2329-2352.

Litsey, L. R., 1958, Stratigraphy and structure of the northern Sangre de Cristo mountains, Colorado: Geol. Soc. America Bull., v. 69, no. 9, p. 1143-1178.

Mayhew, J. D., 1969, Geology of the eastern part of the Bonanza volcanic field, Saguache County, Colorado: M.S., thesis, Colo. School of Mines, no. 1226, 94 p.

Nolting, R. M., III, 1970, Pennsylvanian-Permian Stratigraphy and structural geology of the Orient-Cotton Creek area, Sangre de Cristo mountains, Colorado: Unpub. M.S. thesis, Colo. School of Mines, no. 1311, 102 p.

Oriel, S. S., and Craig, L. C., 1960, Lower Mesozoic rocks in Colorado in Guide to the geology of Colorado: Rocky Mtn. Assoc. Geol., p. 43-58.

Patton, H. B., 1915, Geology and ore deposits of the Bonanza district, Saguache County, Colorado: Geol. Survey Bull. 9, 136 p.

Perry, H., 1971, Geology of the northern part of the Bonanza volcanic field, Saguache County: M.S. thesis, Colo. School of Mines, 362 p.

Pierce, W. H., 1969, Geology and Pennsylvanian-Permian stratigraphy of Howard area, Fremont County, Colorado: Unpub. M.S. thesis, Colo. School of Mines, 136 p.

Powers, W. E., 1935, Physiographic history of the upper Arkansas River valley and the Royal Gorge, Colorado: Jour. Geo., v. 43, no. 2, p. 184-199.

Rold, J. W., 1950, The structure and Pre-Pennsylvanian stratigraphy of the Wellsville area, Colorado: M.S. thesis, Univ. of Colo., 49 p.

Scott, G. R., 1963, Quaternary geology and geomorphic history of the Kassler quadrangle, Colorado: U.S. Geol. Survey Prof. Paper 421-A, 67 p.

Scott, G. R., 1970, Quaternary faulting and potential earthquakes in east-central Colorado: U.S. Geol. Survey Prof. Paper 700-C, p. C11-C18.

Steven, T. A., Ratté, J. C., Mehnert, H. H., and Obradovich, J. D., 1967, Age of volcanic activity in the San Juan mountains, Colorado. in Geol. Survey Research: U.S. Geol. Survey Prof. Paper 575-D, p. D47-D55.

Toulmin, P., III, 1953, Petrography and petrology of Rito Alto stock, Custer and Saguache Counties, Colorado: Unpub. M.S. Thesis, Univ. of Colo.

Tweto, O., 1961, Late Cenozoic events of the Leadville district and upper Arkansas valley, Colorado, in Short Papers in the Geol. and Hydrologic Sci.: U.S. Geol. Survey Prof. Paper 424-B, p. B133-B135.

Van Alstine, R. E., 1968, Tertiary trough between the Arkansas and San Luis valleys, Colorado: U.S. Geol. Survey Prof. Paper 600-C, p. C158-C160.

Van Alstine, R. E., 1970, Allochthonous Paleozoic blocks in the tertiary San Luis-upper Arkansas Graben, Colorado: U.S. Geol. Survey Prof. Paper 700-B, p. B43-B51.

Van Alstine, R. E., and Lewis, G. E., 1960, Pliocene sediments near Salida, Chaffee County, Colorado, in Short Papers in the Geol. Sci.: U.S. Geol. Survey Prof. Paper 400-B, p. 245.

Vanderwilt, J. W., 1947, Mineral Resources of Colorado: State of Colo. Mineral Resources Board, 547 p.

Weimer, R. J., 1970, Dakota Group (Cretaceous) Stratigraphy, Southern Front Range, South and Middle Parks, Colorado: Mtn. Geol., v. 7, no. 3, p. 157-184.

THE SUMMER COON VOLCANO, EASTERN SAN JUAN MOUNTAINS, COLORADO

by

Stanley A. Mertzman, Jr.*
Case-Western Reserve University
Cleveland, Ohio

FIGURE 1.
Central core area of Summer Coon volcano.

INTRODUCTION

The San Juan volcanic field extends over approximately 5,000 square miles in the southwestern part of Colorado. The stratigraphic section, which is applicable to the central and eastern segments of the volcanic field, is listed in Table 1. The pioneering work in this area was performed by E. S. Larsen, Jr. and Whitman Cross, spanning nearly forty years and culminated in U.S. Geological Survey Professional Paper 258, which summarized the geology and petrology of the entire region. Since 1960 an extensive program of field mapping has been carried on by the Denver Branch of the U.S. Geological Survey. The data published by the various coworkers of this program, including R. G. Dickinson, W. R. Hansen, P. W. Lipman, R. G. Luedke, J. C. Olsen, J. C. Ratté, and T. A. Steven, are listed in the bibliography.

The specific area of interest is called the Summer Coon volcano. The intrusive rocks that appear to mark the central conduit of the volcano are located 6½ miles north of Del Norte, Colorado (fig. 1). Rocks related to the volcano underlie approximately seventy square miles, which include parts of four 1:24000 quadrangles (Twin Mountains, Twin Mountains S.E., Indian Head, and Del Norte). Previous work in the area involves only two field-based studies; a fast reconnaissance visit to the area by Larsen and Cross (1956) and a detailed reconnaissance project by Lipman (1968), which involved outlining the basic field relationships of the complex, examination of thin sections and several chemical analyses. Subsequently Doe et al. (1969) published lead and strontium isotope data for three samples from the Summer Coon area and Lipman et al. (1970) reported three potassium-argon age dates.

SUMMER COON'S RELATIONSHIP TO REGIONAL GEOLOGY

In a general manner the geologic map of the Summer Coon area (see plate 1, back pocket) shows two relationships which are important to the interpretation of the overall geologic development of the eastern San Juan volcanic field. The first is the nearly perfect pattern of radial dikes about the central intrusive area. No transverse or ring dike

---
* Presently Division of Volcanology, Smithsonian Institute, Washington, D.C.

TABLE 1.
GENERALIZED VOLCANIC STRATIGRAPHY OF THE GENERAL AND EASTERN PARTS OF THE SAN JUAN MOUNTAINS COLORADO
(with mean ages of dated units).
(Modified from Lipman et al., 1970)

Late Basalts and Rhyolites

Servilleta Formation of Montgomery, 1953 (3.6 to 4.5 m.y.) Hinsdale Formation
    Basalt (4.7 to 23.4 m.y.)
    Rhyolite (4.8 to 22.4 m.y.)

Lavas and Related Rocks Erupted Concurrently with the Ash-flow Tuffs
Local andesitic-quartz latitic flows and breccias that intertongue with the ash-flow sequence in and near the central San Juan complex. The Fisher Quartz Latite (26.4 m.y.) overlie the entire ash-flow sequence.
Ash-flow Tuffs
Snowshoe Mountain Quartz Latite (greater than 26.4 m.y.) Rat Creek and Nelson Mountain Quartz Latite Wason Park Rhyolite Mammoth Mountain Rhyolite (26.7 m.y.) Carpenter Ride Tuff-Bachelor Mountain Rhyolite Fish Canyon Tuff-La Garita Quartz Latite (27.8 m.y.) Tuff of Masonic Park (28.2 m.y.) Treasure Mountain Rhyolite (29.8 m.y.)
Early Intermediate Lavas and Breccias
Conejos Formation (31.1 to 34.7 m.y.)

pattern has been discovered, nor any indication that a graben type structure was ever developed in the core area. These characteristics, by analogy with a scale model study of salt dome intrusion by Parker and McDowell (1951) indicate that only the mildest doming took place during the Summer Coon intrusive and extrusive activities. In addition, the regional stress regime must have been isotropic or only mildly anistropic, otherwise one would expect the dike pattern to become more complex, as it did at Spanish Peaks where the regional stress system was at least moderatly anistropic.

The second important relationship is the asymmetrical distribution of dips about a north-northeast line through the center of the complex. To the east and southeast of the core area dips range from 25° to 35°; on the north and west sides the dip vary between 5° and 15°. This demonstrates that the Summer Coon area has been tilted east-southeastward toward the San Luis Valley. This regional warping must have occurred after the cessation of volcanic activity because the original dip of the flows and breccias around the caldera was probably essentially symmetrical. Moreover, if the volcano did form during the tilting process, the dike pattern probably would have reflected an anisotropic stress condition.

These facts demonstrate that the initial development of the Rio Grande depression could not have taken place prior to the extinction of the Summer Coon volcano (Lipman, 1968). Lipman and Mehnert (1969) have shown from other evidence that subsidence of the Rio Grande depression east of the Summer Coon area did not begin until Early Miocene, by which time Summer Coon was extinct.

FIELD GEOLOGY

The initial development of the Summer Coon volcano was upon a terrain of older volcanic rocks of rhyodacitic composition. A window of these rocks outcrops just north of La Garita Creek along the boundary between NE¼ Sec 6, T41N, R6E, and NW¼ Sec 5, T41N, R6E (see Plate 1, back pocket). A rock from this outcrop has been dated at 34.0 ± 1.5 m.y. by Lipman et al. (1970), which provides a maximum age for the complex.

The Summer Coon volcanics are part of the Conejos Formation as outlined in Table 1. This correlation is based on the potassium-argon dates reported in Lipman et al. (1970). The stratigraphic nomenclature that will be used in this paper is outlined in Table 2. This sequence

TABLE 2.
VOLCANIC STRATIGRAPHY OF THE SUMMER COON SHIELD SEQUENCE, COLORADO

Summer Coon Volcanics	Conejos Formation	Late Intermediate Unit	Upper Andesite Member
			Lower Pyroclastic Member
		Middle Silicic Unit	Upper Rhyolite Member
			Lower Rhyodacite Member
		Early Mafic Unit	

is based solely upon field geologic relationships since no radiometric dating was performed.

Rocks derived from the Summer Coon volcano can be divided into two distinct groups: a shield sequence of flows, breccias, and dikes, which can be further subdivided into three units and a central intrusive complex which includes some intra-caldera lava flows. Each of the three units of the shield sequence consists of varying proportions of breccias, flows and dikes. The lower part of this shield sequence is overlain by younger lava flows and breccias of the Conejos Formation to the northwest, by younger ash-flow tuffs to the north and east, by volcaniclastic sediments to the south (some of which is probably detritus eroded from Summer Coon itself), and is intruded and hydrothermally altered by rhyolite plugs and vents to the east.

EARLY MAFIC UNIT

The Early Mafic Unit is 2800-3100 feet thick, of which 85-90% consists of weakly stratified breccia occurring in beds 5 to 75 feet thick and having essentially uniform appearance throughout the entire sequence. In general the breccia is composed of angular blocks 10 to 15 inches across which contain few if any vesicles. A matrix of coarse tuff (Williams and McBirney, 1969) is usually present, although occasionally the intervening space between blocks is empty. The tuff contains the same minerals as those constituting the breccia blocks, as determined by oil immersion methods. Lenses of well stratified tuffaceous sandstone and siltstone occur sporadically in the Early Mafic Unit. These strata are never more than two feet thick and are usually crossbedded, clearly indicating their reworked nature. Also occasionally present are thin beds (2 to 5 feet thick) of scoracious lapilli containing large vesicles. These beds are confined to a circular area approximately one mile in diameter that lies abutted to the inferred caldera rim depicted in Plate 1. These strata infrequently contain spindle-shaped bombs which strongly suggest an origin as an explosion breccia fairly near to the volcanic vent. Lava flows, which are not plentiful in any part of the mafic unit, are petrographically equivalent to the breccia blocks and generally have a thickness of 5 feet or less, except near the margins of the volcano, where some flows reach a thickness of 20 feet. In every location where flows were mapped they grade into breccia both upward and downward. In sections north of La Garita Creek the proportion of flows to breccia increases to approximately 20 to 25%. Outcrops closer to the intrusive area, like those in the N½ Sec 7, T41N, R6E and all of Sec 17, T41N, R6E, contain only 3 to 5% lava flows. The fact that one finds a great proportion of lava flows as well as thicker flows toward the flanks of the volcano would seem to indicate that most of the breccia was formed by flow brecciation of relatively thin flows, as postulated by Lipman (1968). The less viscous part of the lava flow moved rapidly down the slopes leaving the upper part behind as a bed of angular blocks of lava. The distribution of flows and breccias and the relative proportion of one to the other agree with this interpretation.

Dikes constitute a significant part of the Early Mafic Unit and number well over 700, most of which radiate from the central core zone. All the dikes of this unit could not be included in Plate 1 because in several locations large numbers of dikes outcrop over a relatively small area. For example, along the bed of the intermittent stream in N½ SW¼ Sec 29, T41N, R6E, 27 dikes outcrop over a distance of only 1600 feet. These dikes, like many of the dikes of this unit, are 1 to 2 feet thick, have no topographic expression, and are very short (less than 500 feet). However, some mafic dikes, usually olivine bearing reach a thickness of 12 feet and are continuous over a distance of a mile or more. The radial pattern of mafic dikes is so nearly ideal that only 2 intersections between mineralogically distinct mafic dikes have been observed. The locations of these crosscuttings are: E½ SW¼ Sec 12, T41N, R5E, and E½ SW¼ Sec 17, T41N, R6E. In both cases dikes containing numerous large feldspar phenocrysts cut fine grained olivine bearing dikes. Chemical information for an intersecting pair of dikes is listed in Plate 2 in the back pocket (See 69-10 for olivine bearing dike and 69-31 for large feldspar dike).

MIDDLE SILICIC UNIT

The Middle Silicic Unit of the shield stratigraphic sequence can be conveniently subdivided into two parts: a Lower Rhyodacite Member and an Upper Rhyolite Member. The Lower Rhyodacite Member consists of dikes and a sparse number of correlative lava flows, which have an aggregate thickness of 100 feet. An intrusive stock in the core area, which probably is equivalent to the Rhyodacite Member of the shield sequence, would line-up as a likely focal point for this magmatic activity if these dikes could be extended along their strike direction. The major proportion of this member outcrops southeast of the core area in the following locations: SE¼ Sec 30, T41N, R6E; E½ Sec 31, T41N, R6E; W½ Sec 32, T41N, R6E; N½ Sec 5, T40N, R6E; W½ Sec 4, T40N, R6E. Several of these dikes are 50 feet thick and form vertical walls that occasionally rise as high as 150 feet above the surrounding topography. Two other dikes belong to this member, one of which outcrops in N½ NW¼ Sec 26, T41N, R5E; N½ Sec 27, T41N, R5E; E½ Sec 28, T41N, R5E; the second outcrops in NW¼ NE¼ Sec 14, T41N, R5E and continues to the northwest. All dikes and flows of the Rhyodacite Member either cut or rest upon only Early Mafic Unit material.

An unusual dike and lava flow outcrops in S½ Sec 26, T41N, R5E; NE¼ Sec 34, T41N, R5E; E½ Sec 4, T40N, R5E and along the boundary between NW¼ Sec 1 and NE¼ Sec 2, of T40N, R5E. These rocks have been included in the Lower Rhyodacite Member of the Middle Silicic Unit because they are chemically very similar to rocks of this subdivision; however, they are mineralogically distinct and somewhat resemble rocks of the Late Intermediate Union (see 69-12, 70-44, and 70-55 in Plate 2 for analytical data). The dike, besides cutting the mafic unit, also cuts the earliest flows of the Late Intermediate Unit of the shield stratigraphic sequence. The lava overlies mafic unit rocks; no upper contact could be seen. The flow has a minimum thickness of 50 feet.

The second subdivision of the Middle Silicic Unit consists of the Upper Rhyolite Member. This member is composed of both intrusive and extrusive rocks. With the exception of two short dikes one of which outcrops in SE¼ SE¼ Sec 14, T41N, R5E, and N½ NW¼ Sec 24, T41N, R5E; and the other which outcrops in E½ NE¼ Sec 24, T41N, R5E, all rhyolite dikes follow a distinct northeast-southwest trend (see Plate 1, back pocket). One dike is over 5 miles long and outcrops within 25 yards of the intrusive rocks on both sides of the volcanic core. Since the most intense alteration and brecciation of the core rocks occur along a line connecting the two closest rhyolite dike outcrops, it seems likely that the dike cross-cuts the entire core area. Additional credence is lent to this hypothesis by a resistivity map that was constructed by a geophysical company for the owner of the mineral rights in this area. A marked northeast-southwest surface of equipotential resistivity cuts across the core area essentially identical to a line connecting these two closest rhyolite dike outcrops. To the southeast this same rhyolite dike strikes toward a rhyolite plug, but one cannot actually trace one into the other. This plug is located in E½ SE¼ Sec 27, T41N, R5E, and is characterized by well-developed flow lineation which strikes in every conceivable direction and whose dip is vertical. The rhyolite plug can be traced into a rhyolite breccia and, a little further to the southwest, into a rhyolite flow. The flow has a maximum thickness of 330 feet and overlies mafic breccia. It is overlain by a lava flow of the Late Intermediate Unit. Therefore, in this ¼ square mile area, the relative time sequence of the shield stratigraphic units is outlined in graphic detail.

The Twin Mountains Rhyolite outcrops west of the Summer Coon volcano and covers extensive portions of Sec 17 through 20 and Sec 29 through 32, T41N, R5E. This rhyolite is younger than the Upper Rhyolite Member of the Middle Silicic Unit because it intrudes and hydrothermally alters rocks belonging to both Early Mafic and Late Intermediate Units of the Summer Coon shield sequence. Extensive silicification and some mineralization has accompanied the intrusion of parts of the Twin Mountains Rhyolite, and these areas are conspicuously marked by prospector's pits and trenches.

LATE INTERMEDIATE UNIT

The third and last division of the shield stratigraphic sequence consists of the Late Intermediate Unit, which like the Silicic Unit, can also be broken down into two smaller units. The Lower Pyroclastic Member contains mostly breccia and outcrops in the N½ Sec 33, the SW¼ Sec 28, and the SE¼ NE¼ Sec 29, all of T41N, R6E. It also outcrops in the NW¼ SE¼ Sec 14, T40N, R5E. The total thickness of this subdivision is indeterminate because nowhere are both the top and bottom of the Lower Pyroclastic Member exposed. A minimum thickness, however, is 600 feet. The part of the Lower Pyroclastic Member which outcrops in T41N, R6E consists exclusively of breccia and overlies the Early Mafic Unit. It is unconformably overlain by younger ash-flow tuffs from the central San Juan cauldron and is cut by a dike of the Upper Andesite Member of the Late Intermediate Unit. The part of the Lower Pyroclastic Member which outcrops in T40N, R5E also probably overlies the Early Mafic Unit although this contact is not actually seen in the field. It is apparently conformably overlain by 10 to 15 feet of pumiceous quartz latite, the top of which has been eroded and tuffaceous sediments of a very similar composition deposited upon it. These sediments, which are 15 to 25 feet thick, are well stratified, sorted, and cross-bedded; they are probably reworked pumiceous quartz latite. These sediments are overlain by a thick porphyritic hornblende-rich flow of the Upper Andesite Member. The length of time represented by these sediments is open to conjecture, but it does seem to mark a somewhat prolonged period of inactivity during the life of the volcano.

Most individual blocks within the breccia are two feet or less in diameter and are surrounded by a matrix that is identical in composition to the blocks. Some large blocks were noted during the course of mapping; the dimensions of the largest block were 5 feet by 5 feet by 8 feet. Taking into account the lack of air sculptured bombs and the presence of significant quantities of matrix material, it is likely the breccia was originally a lahar and formed contemporaneously with major eruptions at a time when large amounts of unconsolidated fragmental material were erupted onto the slopes of the volcano.

The Upper Andesite Member of the Late Intermediate Unit contains the youngest rocks of the Summer Coon volcano. Dikes and lava flows of this member either cut or overlie rocks belonging to both the Early Mafic and Middle Silicic Units. Dikes of the Upper Andesite Member also cut lava flows which are also part of this member. One fact is missing, however, and pertains to the relationship between the Upper Andesite Member dikes and the anomalous dike that was placed in the Lower Rhyodacite Member of the Middle Silicic Unit. Both cut Upper Andesite Member flows, but no other diagnostic relationship could be found in the field which would give a relative time stratigraphic sequence between the two. Eight of these dikes radiate about the central intrusive area, analogous to the spokes of a wheel. Most of these dikes are 25 to 50 feet wide and two to four miles long. They are usually much more resistant to weathering than the rocks they intrude and, therefore, tower 50 to 200 feet above the surrounding topography. The natural arch, which is located in the NW¼ SE¼ Sec 12, T41N, R5E, is actually a hole that has been eroded in one of these Upper Andesite Member dikes. Indian Head, named for its peculiar outline, is either a dike or a plug and probably was a vent for some of the Upper Andesite lava flows. This topographic landmark is located in the W½ SW¼ Sec 13, T40N, R5E. Upper Andesite Member flows extend about one mile south of Del Norte, Colorado, where they are overlain by volcaniclastic sediments. The best estimate of the total thickness of this member can be made in the southern portion of the complex. The aggregate thickness appears to be on the order of 4000 to 5000 feet, but in several areas the dip of the lava flows becomes indeterminate. The thickness of individual flows varies between 50 and 300 feet. The basal portion of the thicker flows is flow brecciated as is the uppermost portion; the central portion is usually quite massive. The best example of this flow structure can be found on the bluff situated on the east bank of the Rio Grande by the dam in the NW¼ NW¼ Sec 30, T40N, R6E.

Most of the Lava flows of the Upper Andesite Member were probably erupted from local fissures as lava lakes or pools. The subcircular pattern of dips one occasionally finds around some of these thick flows adds credence to this point of view. Even though an intrusive pipe of very similar composition to the Upper Andesite Member dikes is present in the caldera area, its small size (20 feet in diameter) and other characteristics make it a very unlikely source for most of these flows. It is possible, however, that some of the Upper Andesite Member flows were erupted from Indian Head, which could have been a parasitic volcano of the main Summer Coon caldera.

INTRUSIVE COMPLEX OF THE VOLCANIC CORE

The intrusive rocks that appear to mark the conduit of the volcanic outcrop as a series of low hills which are aligned in a north-northwest direction. The core rocks outcrop in the NW¼, the NE¼, and the SE¼, of Sec 24, T41N, R5E; in the NE¼ Sec 25, T41N, R5E; in the E½ Sec 19, T41N, R6E; and in the NW¼ Sec 30, T41N, R6E. The intrusives are surrounded by an ellipsoidal valley which probably marks the location of what once was a caldera rim. The interpretation of this topographic feature is based on several outcrops in the N½ SW¼ Sec 18, T41N, R6E, where a lava flow was found to have a dip which varied from horizontal to slightly southeastward. Moving northward into the NW¼ Sec 18, T41N, R6E, widespread breccia and an occasional flow of the Early Mafic Unit dip to the north at 10° to 15°. This has been interpreted to mean that the essentially horizontal flow was part of an intracaldera sequence of lava flows. Since this is the sole area where any evidence could be found to support the idea of a possible caldera structure, the whole interpretation is open to considerable debate.

The stratigraphic nomenclature that will be used to describe the Summer Coon intrusive rocks is outlined in Table 3. The time relationship between the Middle Intru-

TABLE 3.
VOLCANIC STRATIGRAPHY OF THE
SUMMER COON INSTRUSIVE ROCKS, COLORADO

Summer Coon Volcanics	Conejos Formation		
		Late Intrusive Unit	
	Middle Intrusive Unit	Upper Breccia Member	
		Lower Granodiorite Porphyry Member	
	Early Intrusive Unit		

sive Unit and the Late Intrusive Unit is constructed by analogy with the shield sequence because of the lack of a mutual contact between the corresponding rock units. The Late Intrusive Unit does cross-cut the Early Intrusive Unit which adds some substance to the proposed analogy with the shield sequence.

The Early Intrusive Unit is characterized by various lithologic types which vary predominately in phenocryst size and percentage groundmass, the later of which is indicative of the cooling history of the sample. Mineralogically and chemically these rocks are very similar, as indicated by nine chemical analyses listed in Plate 2 (those up to 58% SiO_2). The spatial distribution of the Early Intrusive Unit is outlined in Plate 1. A very porphyritic facies of this unit forms the southernmost hill in the W½ NW¼ Sec 30, T41N, R6E and the E½ NE¼ Sec 25, T41N, R5E. Phenocrysts are prominently developed in this stock-like body and range up to 6 mm. across. The most plutonic appearing samples are found in the extreme eastern part of the SW¼ NE¼ Sec 24, T41N, R5E. The rock has an equigranular salt and pepper type of appearance. The samples from this small area are the only ones from the entire Summer Coon complex that have completely crystallized. In this case the rate of cooling has been sufficiently slow to permit what is normally called "groundmass" to crystallize, consisting of an interlocking network of potassium feldspar and quartz.

The field relationships between the various lithologic types of the Early Intrusive Unit are obscured by poor exposures in the core region, but apparently small cupolas or chambers existed as offshoots from the main magma source. These cupolas gave rise to the different lithologies as a result of their variation in geometric shape, size, and rate of cooling. The small intrusives are probably separated from one another by intra-caldera lava flows or by masses of the Early Mafic Unit. No reliable interpretation can be made due to the lack of exposures in critical areas.

The Lower Member of the Middle Intrusive Unit consists of granodiorite porphyry and outcrops in the NW¼, NE¼ and the SE¼ Sec 24, T41N, R5E and in the W½ Sec 19, T41N, R6E. This rock type has suffered varying degrees of alteration, the maximum of which lies along a NE-SW trend which is identical to the projected strike of a rhyolite dike which outcrops on both sides of the central complex. The contact between the Lower Granodiorite Porphyry and the Early Intrusive Unit is very sharp, but on the basis of the granodiorite porphyry becoming finer grained toward the contact and the lack of such a characteristic in the Early Intrusive Unit, it is concluded that the Lower Granodiorite Porphyry Member is younger. However, several thin dikes of the Early Mafic Unit do intrude the granodiorite porphyry and indicate the time interval between the two intrusions was not large. The wide-spread alteration of the granodiorite porphyry is in all likelihood the result of the intrusion of a rhyolite dike. The Upper Breccia Member formed during this intrusive activity. The boundary lines between it and the Lower Granodiorite Porphyry Member are arbitrarily drawn on the basis of the presence or absence of significant silica veining and/or pumiceous fragments. The actual rhyolite dike does not outcrop within this strongly brecciated and silicified zone, but several small rhyolite dikes do outcrop in the E½ NE¼ Sec 24, T41N, R5E and cross-cut the Early Intrusive Unit. The actual breccia consists of granodiorite porphyry fragments in a matrix of cryptocrystalline quartz with occasional lumps or balls of pumice.

On the basis of the mineralogy and bulk chemistry (see samples 70-69 and 70-72) the Lower Granodiorite Porphyry Member of the Middle Intrusive Unit is correlated with the Lower Rhyodacite Member of the shield stratigraphic sequence. Due to the lack of a distinct rock-type in the Upper Breccia Member, no bulk chemical analyses are presented. As a result of the alteration, all mineral identification was done by x-ray diffraction because of the smallness of the grain size. Based on the field evidence and the geophysical work outlined in the section on the Middle Silicic Unit. The Upper Breccia Member is correlated with the Upper Rhyolite Member of the shield stratigraphic sequence.

The last intrusive phase of the Summer Coon complex is appropriately termed the Late Intrusive Unit. It consists of a twenty feet diameter pipe or plug which outcrops in the NW¼ NW¼ Sec 30, T41N, R6E. There is a significant amount of brecciation and veining of the Early Intrusive Unit as one approaches this outcrop. The vein material is composed of the same mineralogy as the small intrusion. No field relationship exists between this intrusion and the rocks of the Middle Intrusive Unit. Therefore, the correlation of the intrusion with the Late Intermediate Unit of the shield sequence is based on mineralogy and bulk chemistry (see sample 69-19) and is placed as the latest intrusive phase by analogy.

BULK CHEMICAL ANALYSIS

The chemical analyses reported in this paper were performed by a combination of x-ray fluorescence and atomic absorption methods. SiO_2, Al_2O_3, TiO_2, total iron, CaO, K_2O, MnO, and MgO were analyzed by fluorescence, while Na_2O was analyzed by atomic absorption. The FeO content, which one needs to know to calculate CIPW norms, was determined using the method of Reichen and Fahey (1962). Samples were ground to approximately —200 mesh, fired at 1000°C. to oxidize all the FeO to Fe_2O_3, and then diluted 2:1 with lithium tetraborate. This mixture is fused, reground, and then pressed into a pellet, using boric acid as a backing. All analyses were made under vacuum, using a Chromium target x-ray source. U.S. Geological Survey analyzed rocks were used as standards because a large compilation of data exists concerning their major constituent composition (Fleisher, 1965; Flanagan, 1967; 1969). The data was corrected for absorption and enhancement effects due to differences in sample matrix by an iterative computer program designed by John Hower (Hower et al., 1964). Table 4 provides a listing of the suggested accuracies of each component in a typical analysis. These values were calculated from a series of ten analyses of one sample, 69-21, using W-1 as a standard.

The system outlined by Irvine and Baragar (1971) has been employed to chemically classify this volcanic suite. In general their approach to chemical classification is to use simple graphical plots which permit various volcanic rocks to be distinguished and named in accordance with compositional fields that are rationally consistent with current usage. The chemical analyses, which provide the basis for the following diagrams are listed in Plate 2. The locations of these samples are plotted on Plate 1.

Figure 2 is an alkalies vs silica plot which allows one to differentiate between alkaline and subalkaline volcanics. Subalkaline is a term introduced by Wilkinson (1968) to include both the calc-alkaline and tholeiitic series. The dividing line used in the diagram is the same one constructed by Irvine and Baragar (1971), which is based on 2500 chemical analyses. It is clearly demonstrated that the

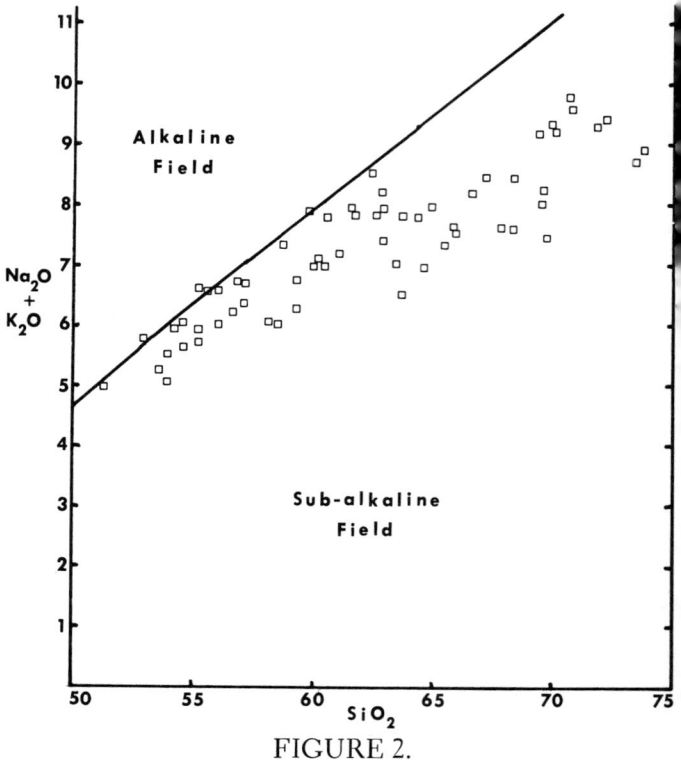

FIGURE 2.
Alkalies vs. silica plot for Summer Coon chemical analyses.

rocks of Summer Coon volcano belong to the subalkaline field.

Figure 3 is an AFM diagram and in this case was used to distinguish between rocks of the calc-alkaline and tholeiitic series. The solid line provides the best separation between chemical data that was taken from areas that are more or less typical of the calc-alkaline and tholeiitic trends. It clearly shows that the Summer Coon volcanics belong to the calc-alkaline trend. Another interesting point that is brought out in this diagram is the total lack of any sign of iron enrichment in the Summer Coon rocks. If there were some tendency toward iron enrichment, the data would plot in an arcuate pattern somewhat like that of the separation line. This characteristic separates Summer Coon from some other calc-alkaline provinces, most not-

TABLE 4.
CALCULATED STANDARD DEVIATION, REPRODUCIBILITY
AND THE SUGGESTED ACCURACY OF EACH REPORTED VALUE CONTAINED IN PLATE 2

	WEIGHT % (MEAN)	STD. DEVIATION	REPRODUCIBILITY	ACCURACY IN REPORTED VALUE
SiO_2	54.20	.05	0.53%	0.27%
Al_2O_3	17.06	.09	1.16%	0.21%
Fe_2O_3*	10.20	.05	0.58%	0.07%
FeO	7.08	.25	2.82%	0.20%
Fe_2O_3	2.41			
TiO_2	1.23	.01	0.77%	0.01%
MgO	3.97	.15	5.60%	0.22%
K_2O	1.88	.03	0.29%	0.01%
Na_2O	4.08	.07	2.21%	0.09%
CaO	7.30	.02	0.53%	0.04%

* Total Fe as Fe_2O_3

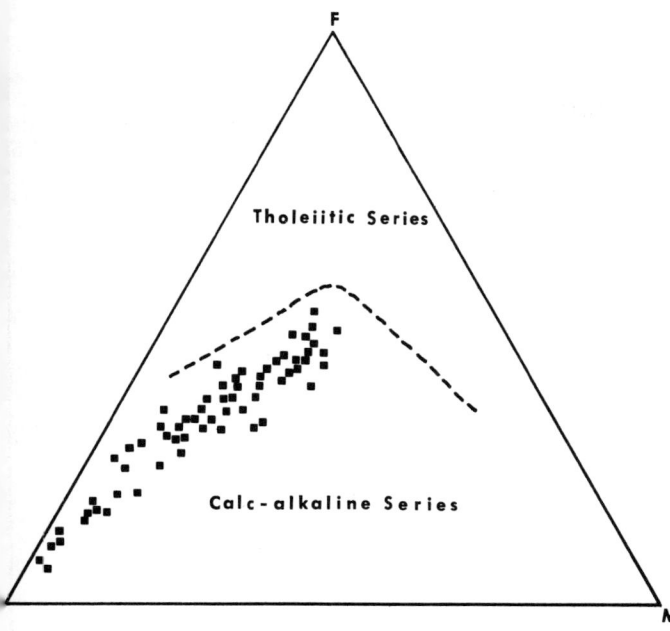

FIGURE 3.
(A = $Na_2O + K_2O$; F = $FeO + 0.8998\ Fe_2O_3$;
M = MgO)

able of which is the Aleutians. On the other hand, the trend outlined by the Summer Coon analyses is very similar to the one determined for the Cascade calc-alkaline province (Smith and Carmichael, 1968).

The third and last diagram (fig. 4) is a plot of normative anorthite(An), albite(Ab), and orthoclase(Or). The purpose of this diagram is to help one decide whether a series of rocks are potassium-poor, average, or potassium-rich and put such a determination on an objective level. The diagram indicates that the Summer Coon rocks are K-rich toward the An-Ab binary, but as the rocks approach the Ab-Or binary they have crossed the boundary into the "Average" field. It is helpful to remember when interpreting this diagram that the Na_2O content of a rock is somewhat sensitive to any alteration or weathering which may have taken place.

SUMMARY

The Summer Coon volcanic complex is part of the Conejos Formation and is divisible into two parts; a shield sequence and a central intrusive area. The shield sequence can be divided into three units, each containing varying proportions of lava flows, breccias, and dikes. The three units from oldest to youngest are the Early Mafic Unit, the Middle Silicic Unit, which is further subdivided into a Rhyodacite Member and an Upper Rhyolite Member, and the Late Intermediate Unit, which is further subdivided into a Lower Pyroclastic Member and an Upper Andesite Member. The subdivision of the units into members was made on the basis of optical mineralogy and bulk chemistry. The intrusive area of the volcano is also divisible into three units which can be correlated with the units of the shield stratigraphic sequence. The three units from oldest to youngest are the Early Intrusive Unit, the Middle Intrusive Unit, which is further subdivided into a Lower Granodiorite Porphyry Member, and an Upper Breccia Member, and a Late Intrusive Unit. On the basis of bulk chemistry it is demonstrated that the best classification of the Summer Coon volcanics is that they are "transitional high potassium calc-alkaline rocks."

REFERENCES

Doe, B. R., 1968, Lead and strontium isotopic studies of Cenozoic volcanic rocks in the Rocky Mountain region—a summary: Quarterly Colorado School of Mines, 63, no., pp. 149-175.

Doe, B. R., et al., 1969, Radiogenic tracers and the source of continental andesites: a beginning at the San Juan volcanic field, Colorado: in Proceedings of the Andesite Conference: Oregon Dept. Geol. Mineral. Industries Bull. 65, pp. 143-149.

Flanagan, F. J., 1967, U.S. Geological Survey silicate rock standards: Geochim. et Cosmochim. Acta, 31, pp. 289-308.

Flanagan, F. J., 1967, U.S. Geological Survey standards-II: Geochim. et Cosmochim. Acta, 33, pp. 81-120.

Fleischer, M., 1969, U.S. Geological Survey standards-I: Geochim. et Cosmochim. Acta, 33, pp. 65-79.

Hower, J., et al., 1964, X-ray spectographic major constituent analysis in undiluted silicate rocks and minerals: Geol. Soc. Amer. Spec. Paper 82, pp. 96-97.

Irvine, T. N., and Baragar, W. R. A., 1971, A guide to the chemical classification of the common volcanic rocks: Cana. Jour. Earth Sci. 8, pp. 523-548.

Johnson, R. B., 1961, Patterns and origin of radial dike swarms associated with west Spanish Peak and Dike Mountain, south-central Colorado: Geol. Soc. Amer. Bull. 72, pp. 579-590.

Larsen, E. S., Jr., and Cross, W., 1956, Geology and petrology of the San Juan region, southwestern Colorado: U.S. Geol. Sur. Prof. Paper 258, 303 pp.

Lipman, P. W., Geology of Summer Coon volcanic center, eastern San Juan Mountains, Colorado: Quarterly Colorado School Mines 63, no. 3, pp. 211-237.

Lipman, P. W., 1969, Alkalic and tholeiitic basaltic volcanism re-

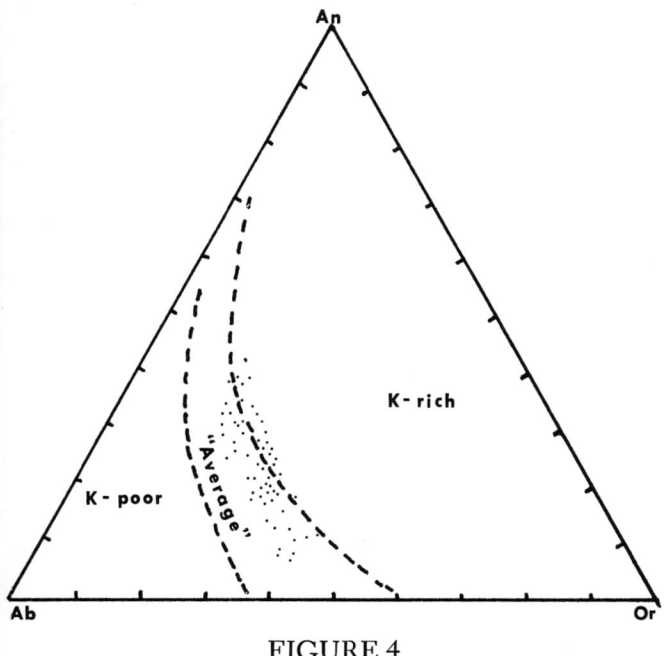

FIGURE 4.
An-Ab-Or diagram of Summer Coon analyses.

lated to the Rio Grande depression: Geol. Soc. Amer. Bull. 80, pp. 1343-1354.

Lipman, P. W., and Mehnert, H. H., 1969, Structural history of the eastern San Juan Mountains and San Luis Valley, Colorado: in Abstracts for 1968: Geol. Soc. Amer. Spec. paper 121, pp. 525-526.

Lipman, P. W., Steven, T. A., and Mehnert, H. H., 1970, Volcanic history of the San Juan mountains, Colorado, as indicated by potassium-argon dating: Geol. Soc. Amer. Bull. 81, no. 8, pp. 2329-2352.

Luedke, R. G., and Burbank, W. S., 1963, Tertiary volcanic stratigraphy in the western San Juan mountains, Colorado: in Short papers in geology and hydrology: U.S. Geol. Sur. Prof. Paper 475-c, pp. c39-c44.

Odé, Helmer, 1957, Mechanical analysis of the dike pattern of the Spanish Peaks area, Colorado: Geol. Soc. Amer. Bull. 68, pp. 567-576.

Parker, T. J., and McDowell, A. N., 1951, Scale models as guide to interpretation of salt dome faulting: Bull. American Asso. Petrol. Geol. 35, pp. 2076-2094.

Ratté, J. C., and Steven, T. A., 1967, Ash flows and related volcanic rocks associated with the Creede caldera, San Juan mountains, Colorado: U.S. Geol. Sur. Prof. Paper 524-H, 58 pp.

Reichen, L. E., and Fahey, J. J., 1962, An improved method for the determination of FeO in rocks and minerals including garnet: U.S. Geol. Sur. Bull. 1144-B, pp. B1-B5.

Smith, A. L., and Carmichael, I. S. E., 1968, Quaternary lavas from the southern Cascades, western U.S.A.: Contr. Mineral. and Petrol. 19, pp. 212-238.

Steven, T. A., Mehnert, H. H., and Obradovich, J. D., 1967, Age of volcanic activity in the San Juan mountains: in Geological Survey research 1967: U.S. Geol. Sur. Prof. Paper 575-D, pp. D47-D55.

Williams, H., and McBirney, A. R., 1969, An investigation of volcanic depressions, Parts I and II: NASA Research Grant Progress Report, pp. 1-92.

A STUDY OF RECENT SEDIMENTATION IN THE SAN LUIS HILLS

by

Robert P. Fling

Adams State College
Alamosa, Colorado

The San Luis Hills of south-central Colorado are located in the southern part of the San Luis Valley. They extend from a point about nine miles east of Sanford and ten miles southwest of Blanca to the Colorado-New Mexico state line. The purpose in studying these partially exhumed hills was to quantify the sedimentary processes presently at work in this area. Originally the author thought that there would be three fairly equal sources of sediments; (1) the Rio Grande, (2) mass wasting from the hills, and (3) aeolian deposits produced by the prevailing southwesterly winds. Gradations in the percentages of each are due to the topography and the nearness to the hills and river.

The criteria used to classify these sediments was sieve analyses according to Folk (1968, p. 3-4). To obtain samples a series of Brunton and tape traverses were made. The main series of samples were in a line from the top of the northwestern corner of the eastern San Luis Hills directly down and out across the floodplain region to the Rio Grande at the eastern edge of the La Sauses Quadrangle (fig. 1). There were two other series of samples taken that ranged from the river to the flanks of the hills. These

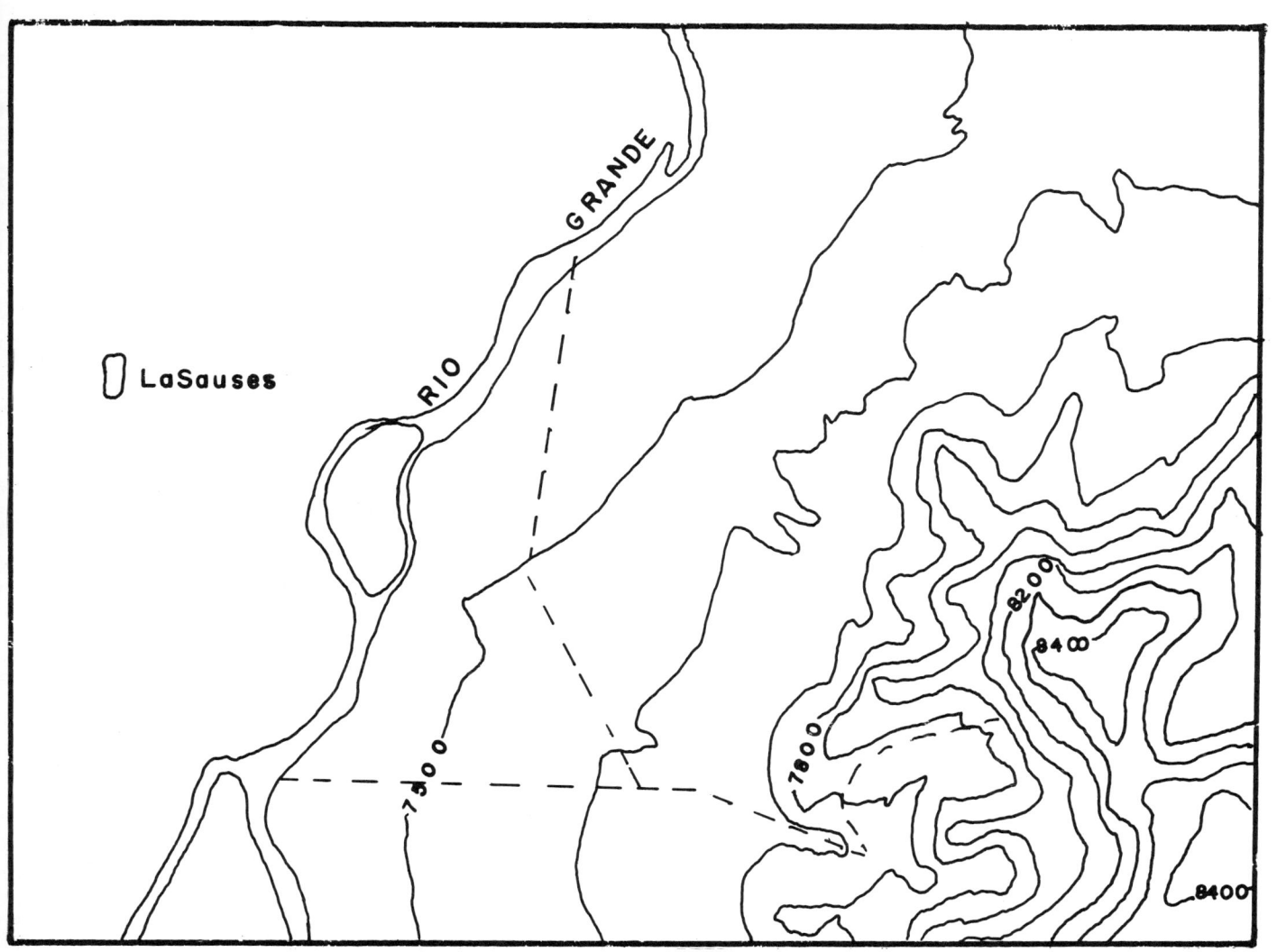

FIGURE 1.
Eastern portion of La Sauses Quadrangle. Scale 1:24000. Contour interval 100 feet. ----- sampled area.

samples were taken at 200 foot intervals at a depth of one foot. The depth was established to eliminate as much of the recent effects as possible, especially organic material.

Samples were split evenly to 100 grams. Each 100 gram sample was run through a set of ten sieves graduated from −4 phi (16mm) to +5 phi (1/32mm) in one phi increments. Each of the phi sizes was weighed and calculated as a percentage of the total sample.

Four statistical tests were made of these samples; mean grain size, a test of the average particle size. Sorting, a measure of the degree of particle similarity in a sample, or the spread of a distribution on either side of an average. Inclusive graphic skewness, a measure of the departure of a frequency curve describing the sediment from a normal curve. A normal curve is unimodal while a skewed curve is usually bimodal. Kurtosis measures the difference in the sorting of the tails of the curve versus the central portion, thus indicating the proportion of the modes. A well sorted sample with one dominant mode is leptokurtic while a bimodal sample with subequal modes is platykurtic.

Histograms of phi size versus percentage were made for each sample. These histograms fell into three basic categories: strongly bimodal sediments with subequal amounts of two modes (playtykurtic, river environment); weakly bimodal with one dominant mode (leptokurtic, composite of mass wasting and dune environment); and well sorted with a mean size of +1 phi to +2 phi (dune environment).

The floodplain deposits had a composite mean size of −1.7 phi. They were strongly bimodal with one mode in the −6 phi to −5 phi range and one in the 0 phi to +2 phi range. According to Folk (1968, p. 44) there is a relative scarcity in nature of very coarse sand so that a mean size in the −1 phi to −2 phi range would indicate a mixture of sand and pebbles. As seen in figure 2, the floodplain samples have kurtosis values of +0.5 to +0.7 indicating a bimodal characteristic which accounts for an extremely platykurtic value.

Samples progressively away from the river channel across the floodplain, show progressively better sorting approaching a value of 0.5 indicating a dune type deposit (fig. 2). The distribution curves for the samples also approach normal nonskewed distributions indicating per-

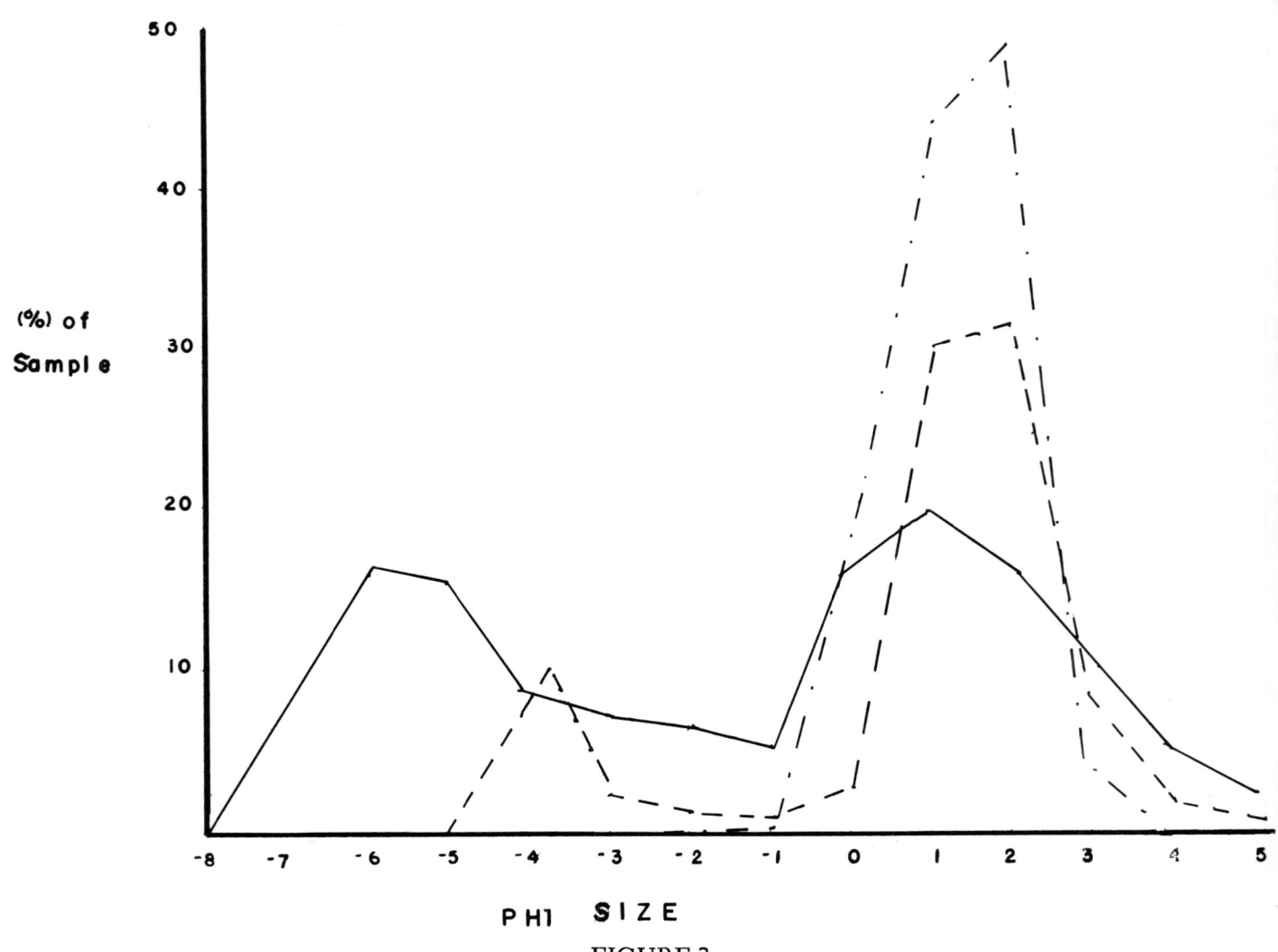

FIGURE 2.

Composite histogram of sedimentary environments in the San Luis Hills. ——— river environment; —·— aeolian environment; — — — mass wasting and aeolian environments.

haps a single origin. A great abundance of particles in the +1 phi to +3 phi range were found in these samples. This range was found to comprise at least 30% of every sample and ranged up to a maximum of 88%. The best sorting was found near the middle of an alluvial fan area with poorer sorting both above and below it.

At the top of the alluvial fan the samples were once more bimodal, but in this case the two modes were extremely unequal. The dominant mode was in the +1 phi to +3 phi range with the secondary in the −4 phi to −3 phi range (fig. 2). This is indicative of a mixing of the mass wasting environment from above and the aeolian deposits being swept up from below.

On the northeast faces of the summits of the lower hills extensive dune deposits were found that had dropped into the wind shadow of the prevailing southwesterly winds. Analysis of these deposits showed 84% to 91% in the +1 phi to +3 phi range for all samples. This gives a sorting value of 0.62 indicating a very well sorted sample.

At this stage of the study it may be concluded that at an elevation of 7,470 feet the river is depositing a highly mixed load in the floodplain region. This is subsequently being reworked by the wind with grains in the +1 phi to +3 phi range being transported across the flat alluvial fan up to the higher reaches where dunes have developed at elevations of about 8,100 feet.

Suggestions for future studies to substantiate the theory might include heavy mineral analysis and mineralogy of the sediments.

REFERENCES

Folk, Robert L., 1968, Petrology of Sedimentary Rocks: Hemphill's, Austin, Texas, 170 p.

GEOLOGY OF THE SAN LUIS HILLS, SOUTH-CENTRAL COLORADO

by

RICHARD L. BURROUGHS

Geology Department
Adams State College
Alamosa, Colorado

INTRODUCTION

The San Luis Hills occupy an area of 428 square miles in the center of the San Luis Basin. They consist of volcanic rocks of the Tertiary Conejos Formation intruded by Late Oligocene stocks dated at 27.4 ± 0.6 and 27.9 ± 0.6 m.y. Three local members of the Conejos Formation are recognized; the Wildhorse, La Sauses, and Manassa Members. The Conejos volcanics are rhyodacites of intermediate composition having a SiO_2 content ranging from 53 to 65 percent. The rock suite has a Peacock alkali-lime index of 55.8, falling on the boundary between the alkali-calcic and calc-alkalic classes.

Beginning with Wildhorse time the eruptions became more silicic through La Sauses time. With the beginning of eruptions in Manassa time the relationship was reversed as volcanism progressed, suggesting differentiation of the magma chamber during an interval of quiescence in which the La Sauses Member was subjected to considerable erosion. The center of this volcanic activity appears to be in the general vicinity of the King Turquoise Mine.

After volcanism a major north-south fault zone developed passing through the center of previous eruptions. This faulting resulted in uplift of the eastern San Luis Hills relative to those west of the fault zone. Large dikes intruded along planes of weakness produced by the faulting. The course of the Rio Grande presently follows the fault zone although it is not controlled by it.

As subsidence and tilting of the San Luis Basin took place, beginning in Miocene time, the hills were further uplifted resulting in those east of the Rio Grande being broken into a series of southeastward tilting fault blocks. The hills were subsequently eroded to a mature topography and surrounded by sediments of the Santa Fe Formation as the basin continued to subside. In Late Pliocene time tholeiitic olivine-tholeiitic basalts of the Servilleta Formation flooded around the south and east margins of the hills and became islands in a sea of lava. After deposition of additional sediments around the hills the area was rejuvenated resulting in the Rio Grande being superposed across the hills and forming the La Sauses Gorge. The hills are presently being exhumed.

Normative classification of rock types is based on a modified Johannsen (1939, p. 144) triangular diagram (fig. 2) in which normative quartz, potassium feldspar and plagioclase feldspar are plotted to determine rock name. The rhyodacite-trachyandesite boundary has been placed at 5 percent normative quartz after recalculation of end members to 100 percent.

The author is greatly indebted to the Adams State College Research Council and to a Penrose Bequest Research Grant provided by the Geological Society of America. He gratefully acknowledges their generous financial support. I would like to thank J. Paul Fitzsimmons for reading the manuscript.

PREVIOUS WORK

Very little previous work has ever been done in the San Luis Hills although the hills have been noted by several authors: Hayden (1869), Stevenson (1875, 1881), Conkling (1876), Endlich (1877), Siebenthal (1910ab), Bryan (1927ab, 1928, 1938), Atwood and Mather (1932), Upson, J. E. (1938ab, 1939, 1941), Pearl (1941ab, 1942, 1957), Larsen and Cross (1956), Powell (1958). Of the above the most extensive notations were by Atwood and Mather (1932), Upson (1938) and by Larsen and Cross (1956) although only two or three paragraphs from each reference apply to the San Luis Hills. Larsen and Cross (1956, p. 87) published six chemical analyses from this area and Upson (1938, p. 48) mentioned seeing a field map of the area by E. S. Larson, Jr. This map, however, has never been published and its whereabouts is not known to the author.

PHYSIOGRAPHIC SETTING

The San Luis Basin, an intermontane structural depression, is made up of the San Luis Valley in south-central Colorado and the Taos Plateau in north-central New Mexico. On the east it is bounded by the Sangre de Cristo Mountains and on the west by the San Juan Volcanic province and the Tusas uplift. The northern portion of the San Luis Basin from Villa Grove to Poncha Pass was referred to as Homan's Peak by Endlich (1877, p. 140). Siebenthal (1910a, p. 9 and 10) described the basin as a great lowland about 150 miles long and 50 miles wide, arbitrarily placing its southern limit about 15 miles south of the Colorado border. Bryan (1938, p. 199) marks the southern end of the basin at the San Luis Hills where a shallow canyon has been developed by the Rio Grande 15 miles north of the New Mexico line. Upson (1939, p. 722) subdivided the basin into five physiographic provinces (see Upson, this guidebook); the Alamosa Basin, the San Luis Hills, the Taos Plateau, the Costilla Plains and the Culebra reentrant, a subdivision generally accepted today.

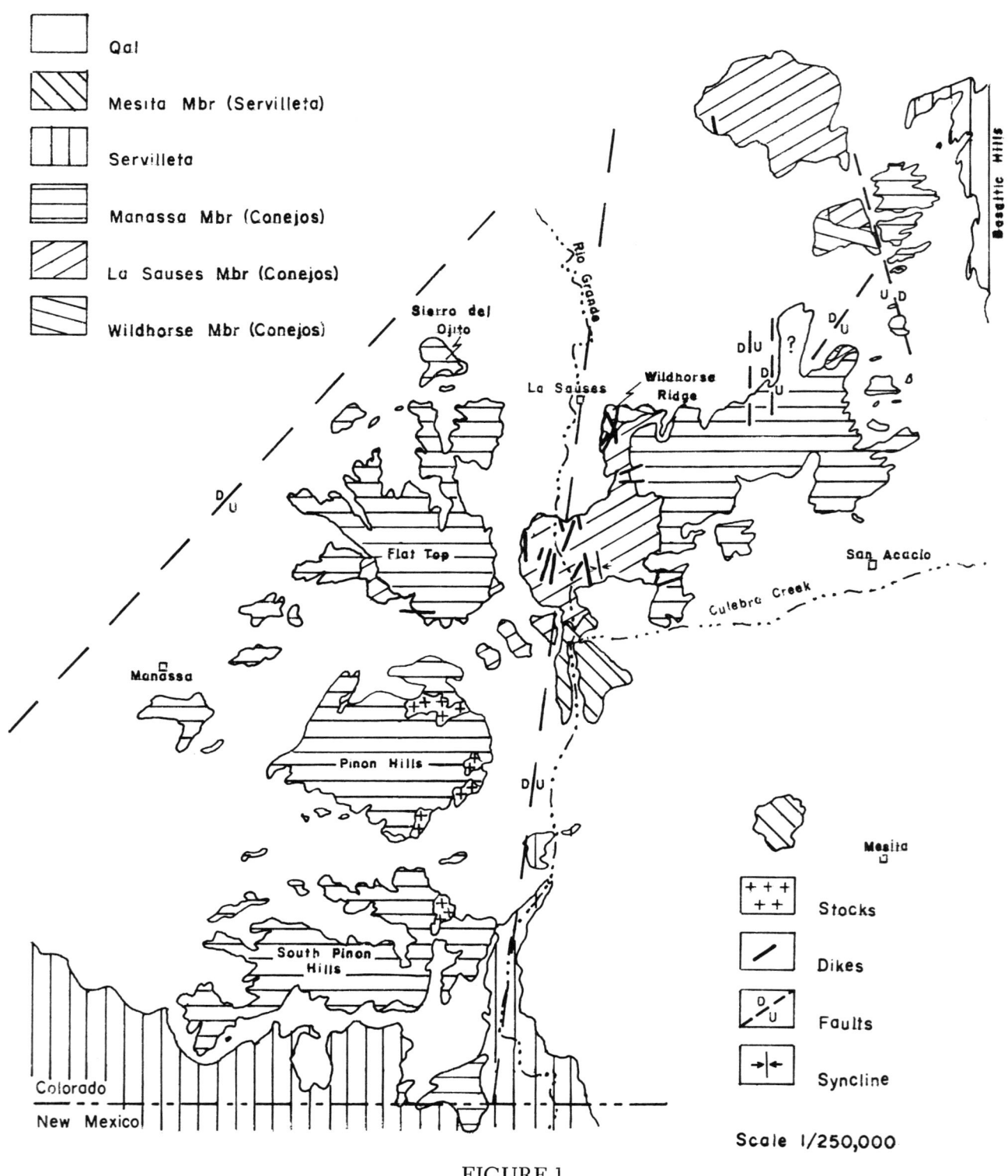

FIGURE 1.
Generalized geologic map of the San Luis Hills, Colorado.

After perhaps a long, hard day in the field Stevenson (1875, p. 422) described the basin along the Colorado-New Mexico state line as he looked eastward from the foothills of the San Juan Mountains: "From these mountains eastward, across San Luis Valley to the Spanish Range, one sees nothing but a dull repulsive plain of lava, from which rise the high basaltic domes known as Ute Peak and Cerro San Antonio." Although I can at times understand Stevenson's feelings, I would tend to agree more with the descriptions of Pearl (1942, 1957) as he pointed out the

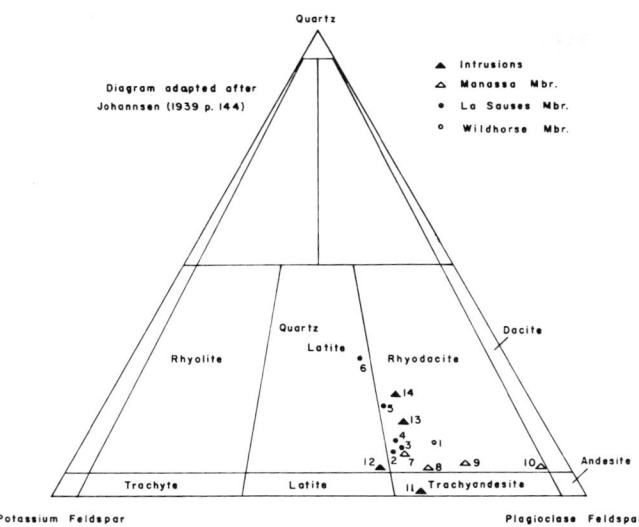

FIGURE 2.
Normative composition of rocks from the Conejos Formation plotted on a Johannsen diagram. Numbers refer to analysis given in Table 1.

remarkable combination of scenic beauty and natural wealth which the valley possesses—a land of many contrasts, both geologically and historically: a land which is the driest and wettest part of Colorado—both at the same time; an area in which one finds shrubs characteristic of arid regions along with alkali flats next to saturated ground, lakes, sand dunes and disappearing streams.

TECTONIC SETTING

The Rio Grande depression, as defined by Bryan (1938, p. 199) extends from Poncha Pass at the head of the San Luis Basin, southward for about 450 miles through New Mexico to about El Paso, Texas. It is not a single graben structure but consists of a series of en echelon grabens with a northerly trend; the grabens being arranged northeasterly along the course of the Rio Grande (Kelley, 1952, p. 93). Until recently it was believed that the San Luis Basin was the most northerly of this series of en echelon basins, with its northern end being bounded by a complex fault zone within Precambrian rocks in the vicinity of Poncha Pass. However, Van Alstine (1968, p. C158) has shown that a north-trending structural trough 3 to 4 miles wide in the vicinity of Poncha Pass connects the San Luis Basin and the upper Arkansas River Valley. Along the western flank of this trough Van Alstine has postulated that a fill of about 10,000 feet may be present. Kelley (1970, p. 157) has continued with this idea of extending the Rio Grande depression northward. He said, "the Rio Grande depression is an integral part of the Eastern Rockies tectonic belt which, from a regional point of view, extends from southern Wyoming through Colorado and most of New Mexico. In this belt the Rio Grande depression, Colorado 'Parks,' and possibly the Laramie Basin form a grand linked right-echeloned system of intermontane troughs."

The San Luis Basin includes all the physiographic provinces of Upson (1939, p. 722) with its northern boundary at Poncha Pass and its southern boundary being defined by Kelley (1956, p. 109) as that of the Embudo constriction. On the east the basin is bounded by the Sangre de Cristo uplift along the high-angle Sangre de Cristo fault zone. On the west the boundary is that of the San Juan volcanic province in Colorado and the Tusas uplift in New Mexico.

The basin, a complex hinged graben having an eastward tilt, began subsiding in Miocene time and has continued to subside to the present. Siebenthal (1910a, p. 51), and Bryan (1938, p. 204) noted that wide-scale volcanic activity and uplift of the adjacent mountains along with corresponding sedimentation began in Miocene time. This was also suggested by Kelley (1956, p. 113) who attributed the initial development of the Rio Grande depression to the Late Miocene. From studies of the upper Arkansas River Valley, Chapin and others (1970, p. 159) found a series of paleovalleys trending at right angles to the present day major structural and topographic features. Studies of these valleys along with studies of the Thirtynine Mile volcanic field to the east show that Ash-Flow 1 of that area, dated at 36 m.y. (Early Oligocene), erupted west of the Salida-Buena Vista region prior to the development of the upper Arkansas River Valley. On the basis of vertebrate fossils the graben-filled sediments of that area have been dated as Late Miocene and Early Pliocene. Lipman and Mehnert (1969) suggested that subsidence of the San Juan Basin began in Early Miocene time. They point out that ash-flows from the San Juans dated at 27 m.y. thin toward the basin indicating that no depression existed in that area during Late Oligocene time and that an angular unconformity exists between flows dated at 21 m.y. indicating an eastward tilting of the basin beginning with the Early Miocene. The continual development of the basin into the Holocene has long been recognized: Bryan (1938, p. 204); Upson, J. E. (1938b, p. 316-317); Upson, R. H. (1940, p. 72); Knepper (1970, p. 158); Scott (1970, p. C16-C17).

Baltz (1965, p. 2068) suggested that the deepest part of the basin was adjacent to the Sangre de Cristo Mountains and within the physiographic Alamosa Basin. Kleinkopf and others (1970, p. B79) show a large gravity minimum of about 30 mgal centering 10 miles northwest of the Great Sand Dunes National Monument. On the basis of gravity data Gaca and Karig (1966) concluded that within this area the graben contained a maximum of 30,000 feet of sediment. At the north end of the basin the structural trough linking the upper Arkansas River Valley with the San Luis Valley can be traced only a few miles south of Poncha Pass (Van Alstine, 1968, p. C158). According to Knepper (1970, p. 158), the area between Poncha Pass and Mineral Hot Springs has 0 to 300 feet of Tertiary volcanics, pediment gravels and alluvial fan material overlying Precambrian rocks. South of the Mineral Hot Springs fault the basement is 1,800 to 2,200 feet below the surface becoming progressively deeper to the area of the 30 mgal minimum. South of here the trough becomes structurally shallower. About 10 miles northwest of Alamosa the sedimentary material is about 8,000 feet thick and along the Colorado-New Mexico border, just east of the Rio Grande, about 6,000 feet of buried sedimentary and volcanic material is present (Kleinkopf and others, 1970, p. B79). Between these later two areas is located the up-faulted blocks of the San Luis Hills volcanics.

ROCK UNITS

GENERAL

The volcanic and plutonic rocks of the San Luis Hills are of Oligocene age, representing a local accumulation equivalent to that of the Conejos Formation of the San Juan Mountains. On the State Geologic Map of Colorado (1935) the hills are mapped as Conejos and other Potosi rocks undifferentiated. Upson (1938, p. 40) states that the hills belong to the Potosi volcanics of the San Juans. He gained this information from a field map of the area and by personal communication with E. S. Larsen, Jr. Sometime between 1938 and 1956 Larsen apparently changed his mind as to the age of these volcanics as Larsen and Cross (1956, p. 81, 86) indicated that these rocks along with those of the Beidell, Tracy Creek and Bonanza centers are of pre-Potosi age. On the basis of more recent field work and isotopic data Lipman and others (1970, p. 2332) stated that the Beidell, Tracy Creek and Bonanza centers represent local accumulations within the Conejos Formation. Potassium-Argon dates of 27.4 ± 0.6 and 27.9 ± 0.6 m.y. (uppermost Oligocene) have been obtained from the South Piñon Hills stock, which intrudes flows of the Manassa Member (later) of the Conejos Formation. The author believes that the times of the intrusions in the San Luis Hills are closely related to the volcanic events.

Within the San Luis Hills five volcanic units have been recognized. The three lowermost units are hereby named the Wildhorse, La Sauses and Manassa Members of the Conejos Formation. This subdivision is proposd as local usage and should probably be confined to the San Luis Hills. The contact of each member is marked by an unconformity in which alluvial deposits are locally present. Overlying these units is the Servilleta Formation of Butler (1946) and a younger member of that formation hereby named the Mesita. The Mesita Member is probably equivalent to the Upper Series of Aoki (1967, p. 191) of the Taos Plateau.

WILDHORSE MEMBER

The Wildhorse Member of the Conejos Formation is named for exposures at the north end of Wildhorse Ridge, a cuesta, 1 7/10 miles east of La Sauses, Colorado. Exposures are limited and found only along the lower portion of the scarp (fig. 1). The maximum thickness noted for the unit is about 650 feet. The lower boundary is covered by alluvium, however, the lower part of the section is composed of mudflows and basaltic-appearing flow breccia grading upward into an autobreccia and overlying lava flows, which are dominant in the upper half of the unit.

Within the section moderately sorted to well-sorted, cross-bedded, tuffaceous sediments of fluvial origin are present, the material being derived from adjacent volcanic rocks. Breccia fragments making up the lower half of the section are homogeneous in composition, subangular- to angular, dense to somewhat vesicular and are generally poorly sorted. Fragments up to 1½ feet in size are common. Petrographically the rock is porphyritic andesite with a felty groundmass. Phenocryst (augite and andesine) content ranges from 10 to 40 percent, averaging about 0.3 mm in long dimension in the breccias and about 1 mm in the overlying flows. The upper flows are generally glomeroporphyritic, contain minor hypersthene and biotite and are characterized by an intense alteration of some augite to fibrous actinolite (?). Chemically the rocks are mafic rhyodacites (fig. 2).

LA SAUSES MEMBER

The Las Sauses Member of the Conejos Formation is named for the major cliff-forming exposures along the entire length of Wildhorse cuesta east of the town of La Sauses. Exposures continue southward and are present on both sides of the La Sauses Gorge 3 miles south of La Sauses. It makes up the hills east of the gorge and is locally found in buried hills beneath the Manassa Member west of the river (fig. 1). The highly variable thickness of the unit, about 50 to 800 feet, is due principally to pronounced erosion of the upper surface that took place before deposition of pyroclastic breccias, flow breccias, mudflows and lava flows of the Manassa Member. Relief of this surface may amount to several hundred feet. Unconformities within the unit, normal thinning of volcanic rocks and their often small lateral extent account for further thickness variability. With detailed mapping the member can be locally subdivided into two or more units.

East of the Rio Grande the section is composed of fresh to highly-oxidized, grayish-pink, dark-reddish-brown and light- to dark-gray interbedded tuff-breccias, mudflows, lava flows and dense crystal tuffs, along with thick local epiclastic deposits. The crystal tuffs are generally massive, while lava flows often show well-developed flow structure (fig. 3). Vitrophyres up to 5 feet thick at the base of some flows have served as local marker horizons; unfortunately they do not have great lateral extent. Exposures east of Wildhorse cuesta often consist of pumiceous tuffs interbedded with cross-bedded sediments of fluvial origin. West of the river exposures are locally present beneath the Manassa volcanic rocks. Near Pikes Stockade soft, light-colored, crystal tuffs are present along the south side of Sierro del Ojito. On the southwest side of Mesa de La Sauses (Flattop) are tuff-breccias, lava flows and dense crystal tuffs. South of here on the northwest side of the Piñon Hills are soft crystal tuffs. Crudely stratified, light gray ash and tuff-breccias of pyroclastic origin are present along the south side of the hills. Along the southern edge of the South Piñon Hills adjacent to Punche Valley about 200 feet of soft, homogeneous, light tan ash is present. In each case these isolated deposits in the western San Luis Hills are beneath basaltic-appearing volcanic rocks of the

FIGURE 3.
Typical flow structure of lava flows of La Sauses Member. "Most geologists use picks as scale indicators."—Ed.

Manassa Member and are thus believed to be roughly stratigraphically equivalent representing isolated buried erosional remnants of this unit.

Petrographically, rocks of the La Sauses member are typically glomeroporhyritic, augite-biotite-sanidine latites with a felty groundmass. The sanidine is generally resorbed and is characteristic of the formation although it is not always present. Magnetite and biotite, partly to completely altered to hematite are also typical, with fresh magnetite being very scarce. Some pigeonite is present in the upper two-thirds of the section. Plagioclase crystals have commonly been subject to resorption; some being deeply embayed. The crystals are commonly zoned and broken, with broken ones serving as centers for precipitation of additional zoned plagioclase suggesting a complex history in the magma chamber. Apatite and sphene have also been noted and secondary calcite is abundant adjacent to fault zones. Chemically the rocks are rhyodacites (fig. 2).

MANASSA MEMBER

The Manassa Member of the Conejos Formation is named for exposures throughout the western San Luis Hills east of Manassa, Colorado. Maximum thickness of the unit is about 1,500 feet. Explosive breccias, flow breccia and lava flows, all of basaltic appearance, make up the section. About 800 feet of highly oxidized dark-red scoria with fine tuffaceous binding material is present along the southeast side of Mesa de La Sauses. It grades both laterally and vertically into flow breccias and lava flows along the north side of the mesa. This is the most extensive pile of scoriaceous material in the San Luis Hills. Basaltic-appearing lava flows cap the mesas throughout the western San Luis Hills. At Sierro del Ojito the lava flows lie unconformably on crystal tuffs of the La Sauses Member. In the Piñon Hills and South Piñon Hills flows are dominant throughout the section, with scoria similar to that at Mesa de La Sauses being generally absent. In the eastern San Luis Hills basaltic-appearing flows of the Manassa Membei cap the Wildhorse cuesta and represent the dominant unit throughout the hills east of the cuesta. Locally minor ash deposits are found between flows and volcaniclastic sediments are often present at the base of the unit filling in topographic lows before eruption of the lava flows.

Petrographically the upper and lower parts of the Manassa section are basaltic-appearing andesites. The upper flows capping the mesas west of the Rio Grande are characterized by the presence of olivine altering to iddingsite and by the notable absence of abundant plagioclase phenocrysts. These are the only rocks within the San Luis Hills in which plagioclase phenocrysts are not abundant. The matrix texture of the upper flows is generally pilotaxitic. Beneath the upper flows the pyroclastic breccias, flow breccias and lava flows are characterized by plagioclase phenocrysts of 1-5 mm long; a general absence of olivine and a presence of biotite. Texturally the rocks are commonly glomeroporphyritic with a felty groundmass. All parts of the section are characterized by fresh magnetite in contrast to highly oxidized magnetite of the underlying units. Augite and orthopyroxene are present throughout the section. Apatite and quartz have been locally recognized. Chemically the rocks are mafic rhyodacites (fig. 2). They are slightly more basic than the basaltic-appearing rocks of the Wildhorse Member.

SERVILLETA FORMATION

The Servilleta Formation was named by Butler (1946, p. 133) for Late Tertiary basalts flooding the Taos Plateau in the southern half of the San Luis Basin. This usage was continued by Montgomery (1956, p. 53) and by Lipman (1969, p. 1347). The rocks are informally termed "Taos basalts" of Aoki (1967, p. 195). The Servilleta basalts of the Rio Grande gorge were dated by Ozima and others (1967, p. 2618) as 3.6 to 4.5 m.y. (Upper Pliocene).

After the San Luis Hills were eroded to a mature topography, the Servilleta basalts flooded the southern and eastern margins of the hills; the hills thus becoming islands in a sea of lava. Within the San Luis Hills the Servilleta basalts are present throughout Punche Valley lapping upon the southern margin of the South Piñon Hills and completely isolating Cerrito del Poncho, which straddles the Colorado-New Mexico state line. Good exposures make up the cliffs along the Rio Grande at the Old State Bridge 5½ miles north of the border. Exposures are also present on the northeast side of the San Luis Hills along Trinchera Creek 4 miles south of Blanca,, Colorado. The Servilleta basalts are those found throughout the Basaltic Hills south of Smith Reservoir. They continue south of San Luis, Colorado, forming the caprock of San Pedro Mesa. They are also present as the caprock of Garland cuesta southeast of Fort Garland.

The lava flows of the Servilleta Formation are predominantly olivine-tholeiite basalts in which the olivine is altered to iddingsite. The olivine, along with plagioclase and clinopyroxene, is relatively coarse-grained and closely spaced, but with angular cavities present between feldspar laths of random orientation; a typical diktytaxitic texture is produced. Rock texture and presence of olivine generally make the Servilleta basalts easy to recognize in the field.

Rocks of the youngest volcanic unit in the San Luis Hills are locally referred to as the Mesita Member of the Servilleta Formation; named for exposures in Mesita Crater near Mesita, Colorado. These rocks represent local eruptions forming small hills above the plateau basalts. In the San Luis Hills area two such volcanic centers are recognized: the Mesita Crater and Volcano de La Culebra at the mouth of Culebra Creek. The Mesita Crater is a small volcanic center composed predominantly of loose, highly oxidized scoria. Mr. George M. Oringdulph of the Colorado Aggregate Co., Inc. has graciously furnished a chemical analysis of the scoria. The analysis indicates that the rock is a trachyandesite. No quartz is present in the norm. No analysis is presently available for rocks from Volcano de La Culebra; however, rocks from the upper part of that structure appear andesitic. Those from cliffs adjacent to the Rio Grande appear more like typical Servilleta basalts. The two small volcanic centers of Mesita age are probably equivalent to the Upper Series andesites of Aoki (1967, p. 192).

INTRUSIVE ROCKS

Several stocks and dikes intrude the Conejos volcanics of the San Luis Hills. The stocks are located west of the Rio Grande being concentrated in the Piñon Hills and South Piñon Hills. Within the Piñon Hills four major intrusions have been mapped; one is present in the South Piñon Hills (fig. 1). The possible edge of a small intrusion has been noted at the northeast corner of Cerrito del Poncho along the Colorado-New Mexico state line. In the field rock exposed in the intrusions is very similar and it is presently believed that all the stocks were intruded at about the same time and that they have a common source. The rock making up the stocks is generally medium-crystalline, white to light tan, weathering to a light rust color. Detailed studies of the stocks would probably reveal significant variation in rock type with granodiorites and quartz monzonites being most abundant. Some rocks contain abundant quartz, while in others it is completely lacking. Three different analyses indicate that the stocks are chemically granodiorites, quartz monzonites and syenodiorites (table 1).

Dikes are concentrated in a zone adjacent to the La Sauses Gorge and have a general northerly trend (fig. 4). A small number of dikes have a general easterly orientation, the largest being the Manassa dike (fig. 5) along the south slope of Mesa de La Sauses. Some of the dikes are quite large, as much as 80 ft. thick and a mile long. Dike rocks are generally light gray, coarsely porphyritic, biotite-rich granodiorites. Large, green hornblende phenocrysts up to 5 mm in length have been recognized, but they do not occur in all the dikes. A few very small basic dikes are present but no chemical data are presently available for these dikes. Future petrographic and chemical studies of

FIGURE 4.
Looking south into La Sauses Gorge. North trending dikes intruding volcanics of La Sauses Member of Conejos Formation. Volcano de La Culebra of Mesita age (upper trachyandesite of Servilleta Formation) upper left. Rio Grande superposed across San Luis Hills at this point.

FIGURE 5.
East-west striking Manassa dike intruding Manassa Member of Conejos Formation. South side of Mesa de La Sauses (Flattop).

the dikes may show a relationship between rock type and dike orientation as well as a relationship to stocks mentioned above and to enclosing volcanic rocks.

STRUCTURE

The San Luis Hills are a series of upthrown rocks in the central part of the San Luis Valley. A major north-south fault zone structurally divides the hills into eastern and western components. Although not controlled by it, the Rio Grande follows this fault zone through the hills and separates them physiographically.

Strata of the western hills are essentially horizontal while those of the eastern hills have a general southeasterly dip of 10 to 15 degrees. Local variations from the norm are

TABLE 1.
Chemical analyses and normative compositions of rocks of Conejos age, San Luis Hills.

	CONEJOS FORMATION														SERVILLETA FORMATION		
	Wildhorse Mbr.	La Sauses Member					Manassa Member				Intrusions				Mesita Mbr.		
	1	2	3	4	5	6	7	8	9	10	11	12	13	14	15	16	17
Field Spl. No.	LS-80	SLH 3	SLH 36	LS 170	PS 2	M 144	LS 175	SLH 26	SLH 68	M 150	SLH 61	SLH 134	KH 6	M 18	KH 4	---	---

CHEMICAL ANALYSES

	1	2	3	4	5	6	7	8	9	10	11	12	13	14	15	16	17
SiO_2	57.53	59.91	60.68	60.69	65.51	64.65	58.38	56.34	55.48	53.83	59.68	58.45	60.75	64.79	49.71	50.60	54.34
TiO_2	1.01	1.54	0.93	0.80	0.44	0.72	0.99	1.08	1.58	1.29	1.28	1.38	0.65	0.51	1.04	1.30	1.56
Al_2O_3	18.50	16.92	17.14	17.75	16.36	19.32	16.86	16.34	15.04	15.08	18.40	16.61	16.37	15.42	16.73	16.30	17.42
Fe_2O_3	4.85	4.06	4.63	5.15	3.62	2.02	5.13	3.76	3.68	3.60	2.54	2.74	4.05	3.79	2.83	2.80	5.04
FeO	1.87	0.98	0.58	0.51	0.54	0.14	1.96	3.68	4.77	6.28	1.05	3.44	2.31	1.30	8.75	8.30	4.43
MnO	0.05	0.07	0.04	0.05	0.07	tr	0.14	0.06	0.07	0.15	tr	0.08	0.11	0.08	0.17	0.20	0.10
MgO	1.10	1.83	1.82	1.18	1.33	0.14	1.67	3.81	5.92	6.17	1.14	2.58	2.65	1.58	7.09	7.00	3.70
CaO	5.73	4.02	4.00	3.72	3.23	0.52	4.70	5.96	6.72	8.57	4.24	4.66	4.02	3.24	9.52	8.60	6.33
Na_2O	3.72	4.26	4.27	3.98	3.81	3.93	4.07	3.70	3.62	2.87	6.40	4.16	3.65	3.74	2.88	3.00	5.21
K_2O	3.49	4.66	4.37	4.48	4.31	3.83	4.28	3.56	2.14	1.04	4.42	4.66	3.75	3.69	0.20	0.80	2.28
P_2O_5	0.50	0.33	0.41	0.45	0.25	0.20	0.48	0.51	0.52	0.44	0.45	0.51	0.40	0.45	0.35	0.20	---
H_2O^+	1.26	0.73	0.85	0.80	0.22	2.68	0.79	0.75	0.65	0.74	0.36	0.46	0.90	0.87	0.58	0.80	---
H_2O^-	0.76	---	---	0.36	0.14	1.58	0.37	---	---	0.06	tr	0.14	0.12	0.22	0.18	0.20	---
Total	100.37	99.31	99.72	100.18	99.83	99.73	99.82	99.55	100.19	100.12	99.96	99.87	99.73	99.68	100.03	100.10	100.41

NORMATIVE COMPOSITIONS

	1	2	3	4	5	6	7	8	9	10	11	12	13	14	15	16	17
Quartz	9.89	8.21	9.17	11.04	17.37	25.61	7.83	4.94	4.91	6.63	---	4.45	13.00	19.72	---	---	---
Orthoclase	21.15	27.95	26.10	26.85	25.60	23.70	25.80	21.30	12.65	6.25	25.75	27.70	22.60	22.30	1.20	4.80	13.35
Albite	34.30	38.80	38.75	36.25	34.50	36.95	37.25	33.65	32.55	26.20	53.30	37.60	33.35	34.35	26.20	27.30	46.35
Anorthite	24.10	13.48	14.88	16.95	14.55	1.37	15.43	17.73	19.50	25.60	7.25	12.97	17.53	13.45	32.55	29.05	17.30
Nepheline	---	---	---	---	---	---	---	---	---	---	2.04	---	---	---	---	---	---
Corundum	---	---	---	0.27	0.18	9.43	---	---	---	---	---	---	---	---	---	---	---
Diopside	1.40	0.40	1.12	---	---	---	4.08	7.08	8.40	11.80	6.20	5.36	0.08	---	10.36	10.28	11.08
Wollastonite	---	---	---	---	---	---	---	---	---	---	0.98	---	---	---	---	---	---
Hypersthene	2.42	4.92	4.52	3.30	3.98	0.40	2.66	8.72	14.90	16.92	---	5.98	7.42	4.46	23.16	22.34	0.86
Olivine	---	---	---	---	---	---	---	---	---	---	---	---	---	---	1.32	0.99	3.69
Magnetite	2.31	---	---	---	0.33	---	2.55	3.98	3.80	3.83	---	2.88	4.17	2.10	3.00	2.97	5.19
Hematite	1.93	2.87	3.26	3.62	2.33	1.47	1.95	---	---	---	1.75	---	0.10	1.30	---	---	---
Ilmenite	1.44	1.54	0.90	0.80	0.62	0.22	1.40	1.52	2.20	1.82	1.60	1.94	0.86	0.72	1.46	1.82	2.16
Titanite	---	0.64	0.40	---	---	---	---	---	---	---	0.16	---	---	---	---	---	---
Rutile	---	---	---	0.16	---	0.42	---	---	---	---	---	---	---	---	---	---	---
Apatite	1.07	0.69	0.88	0.96	0.53	0.43	1.01	1.07	1.09	0.93	0.93	1.07	0.85	0.96	0.75	0.43	---
Total	100.01	99.50	99.98	100.02	99.99	99.98	99.96	99.99	100.00	99.98	99.96	99.95	99.96	99.36	100.00	99.98	99.98

No. 1, 4, 5, 6, 7, 10, 13, 14, 15 --- New analyses.
No. 6 --- Kaolinized and sericitized rock of King Turquoise Mine.
No. 11, 12 --- Stock north side of Pinon Hills.
No. 13 --- South Pinon Hills stock.
No. 14 --- La Sauses Dike.
No. 2, 3, 8, 9, 11, 12 --- After Larsen and Cross (1956, p. 87).
No. 16 --- Average of 17 analyses from Taos Plateau. After Aoki (1967, p. 197).
No. 17 --- Furnished by Mr. George M. Oringdulph, Colorado Aggregate Co., Inc., Mesita, Colorado.

FIGURE 6.
Looking east toward eastern San Luis Hills from Mesa de La Sauses. Note irregular nature of topography in contrast to flat surfaces of western San Luis Hills (fig. 9). North trending La Sauses dike (arrows) west of La Sauses Gorge (fig. 4). Cerrito de La Culebra is first large hill east of most extensive dike exposure.

present in both areas; being most common east of the Rio Grande (fig. 6). Along their western margin the western hills have been upthrown in respect to the San Luis Valley. The eastern hills are upthrown in respect to the western hills forming a southeasterly tilted fault block. Within the eastern hills this relationship is repeated forming a series of west-facing scarps. Scarps throughout the area are not always controlled by faulting but it is evident that major topographic features of the eastern San Luis Hills have been greatly influenced by structure.

East of La Sauses Gorge and Cerrito de La Culebra a small north striking syncline is present. Its eastern limb is also the western limb of an adjacent monoclinal flexure. Within this same general area several deviations of attitude from the norm are present; accounted for by minor folds, faults and by the movement of flows within the La Sauses Member over irregular topography.

Dikes of the La Sauses Gorge formed after the faulting, having intruded along planes of weakness produced by a north striking fault zone dividing the eastern and western hills. East of here one dike is offset about 20 feet and to the north two adjacent dikes have been offset by faulting along Wildhorse Ridge. The faulting that offset these dikes probably occurred very late in the tectonic history, not developing during the initial uplift of the hills. Two small northeast trending faults are present near the southern end of Wildhorse Ridge. These faults offset the upper part of the La Sauses Member and flows of the overlying lower Manassa Member. About four miles east of Wildhorse Ridge two north striking faults are present. The block between these two faults has dropped down and tilted eastward into the scarp formed by the eastern fault. This relationship is rather typical of the eastern San Luis Hills.

The eastern margin of the San Luis Hills is represented by flows of the Manassa Member dipping under Servilleta basalts. In the Basaltic Hills the contact relationship is depositional; however, as one goes southward displacement of the basalts is noted along San Pedro Mesa. According to Upson (1938, p. 149) displacement along this fault is minimal at Rio Culebra and gradually increases southward to the Colorado-New Mexico state line. Upson suggests a stratigraphic throw of 2,100 feet from the top of the mesa to the basalt underlying the Costilla Plains west of the fault.

On the basis of gravity and magnetic data, Kleinkopf and others (1970, p. B82-84) indicate the presence of possible northeasterly trending faults or shear zones in the crystalline basement. One of these flanks the northern side of the San Luis Hills and another, parallel to this, the south side of the eastern San Luis Hills. The latter extends in a southwesterly direction beneath the Piñon Hills to Lobatos, Colorado. Renewed movement along these deep-seated fractures may have played a role in the general uplift of the San Luis Hills.

PETROLOGY

Petrologic studies of the San Luis Hills are still in progress, and therefore will be considered only briefly at this time. The available chemical data (table 1) for the rock units and related intrusions are incomplete. Of the dikes only one, the La Sauses dike, has been chemically analyzed. More chemical data of the La Sauses Member, the lower half of the Manassa Member and of the dikes are desirable.

In spite of the above limitations it is evident that, when considered together, a close genetic relationship is present between the Conejos volcanics and associated intrusive rocks. This is evident in the field, but the chemical relationships are probably best illustrated by a series of Larsen (1938) type variation diagrams (fig. 7).

The chemical class of the rock suite, according to the Peacock alkali-lime index (Peacock, 1931) is 55.8. This is only 0.2 from the dividing line of the alkali-calcic and calc-alkalic classes at 56.

A triangular variation diagram plot of the Na_2O, K_2O and CaO shows the chemical variations within the rock suite (fig. 8). In this case it also shows the unconformable relationship between the La Sauses Member and the overlying Manassa Member. Beginning with Wildhorse time the nature of the eruptions became more silicic through La Sauses time. With the beginning of Manassa eruptions the relationship was reversed as volcanism progressed, suggesting differentiation of the magma chamber during erosion of the La Sauses Member.

GEOMORPHOLOGY

After uplift and erosion to a mature topography, the hills were surrounded by Servilleta basalts along their southern and eastern margins. This was followed by continuous burial of the hills with sedimentary debris from the adjacent mountains. It is doubtful that the hills were ever completely buried but they have been buried to a greater extent than presently observed and are now being exhumed.

The topography of the San Luis Hills has been greatly influenced by underlying rock type and structure. The

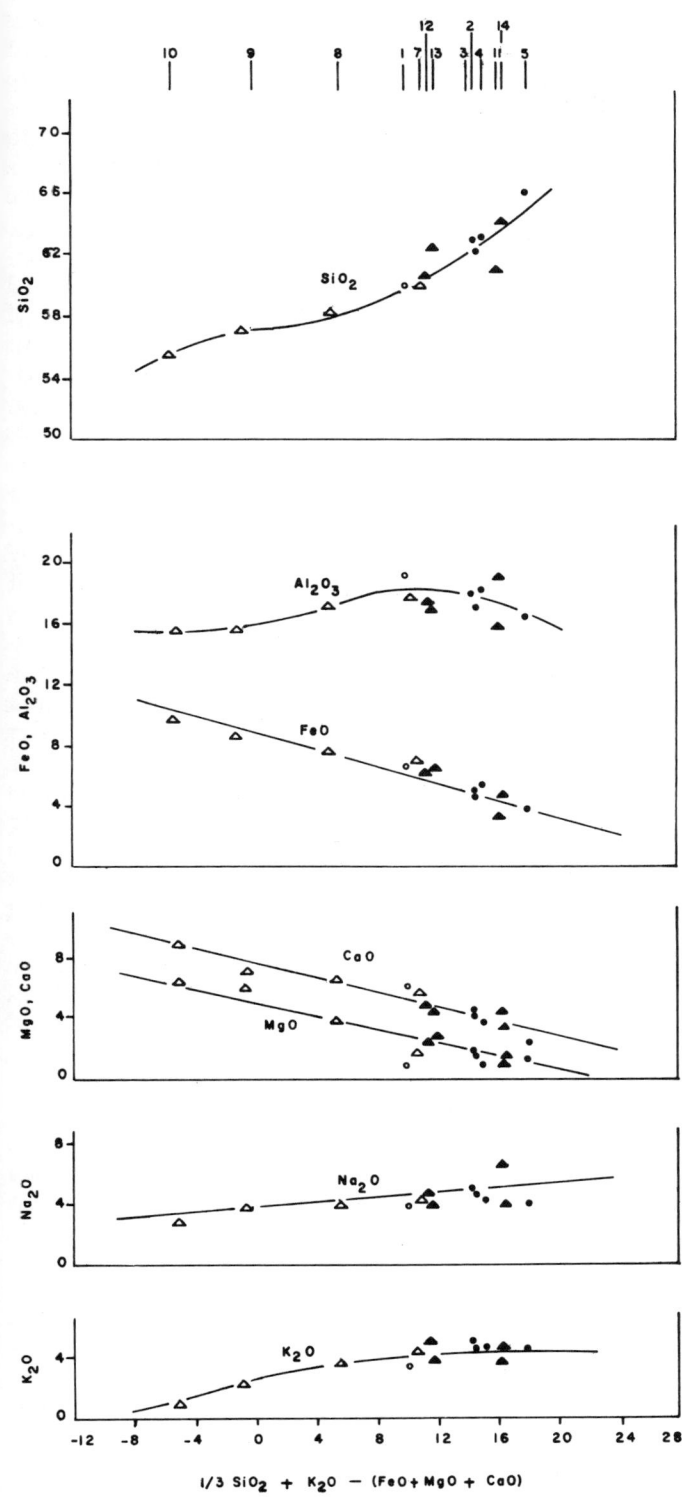

FIGURE 7.

Larsen (1938) type variation diagram of rocks of Conejos age, San Luis Hills. Numbers refer to analysis given in Table 1. For symbols see Figure 2.

western hills are characterized by flat-topped buttes: Sierro del Ojito, Mesa de La Sauses (fig. 9), the eastern Piñon Hills and the southern half of the South Piñon Hills. In

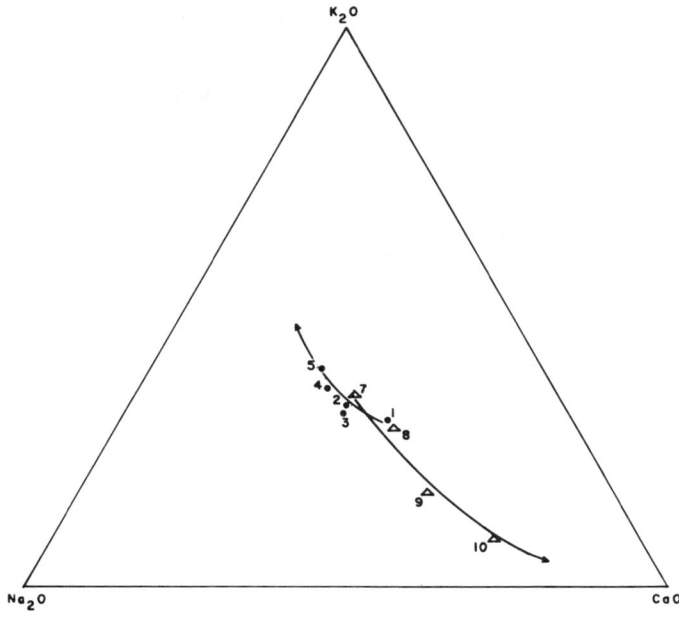

FIGURE 8.

Variation diagram of K_2O, Na_2O and CaO for rocks of Conejos age, San Luis Hills. Numbers refer to analysis given in Table 1. For symbols see Figure 2.

FIGURE 9.

Looking west across top of Mesa de La Sauses (Flattop). Surface is made up of lava flows of Manassa Member of Conejos Formation.

each case the caprock is composed of horizontal cliff-forming lava flows of the Manassa Member. The eastern hills with their steep west-facing scarps and low eastward sloping gradients are a reflection of the tilted fault blocks. As seen from a distance these hills have a more irregular topography in contrast to the sharp angular topography of the western hills (fig. 5, 6). This is produced as the crests of the west-facing scarps are subjected to erosion and where flows of the Manassa Member are stripped away exposing crystal tuffs and tuff-breccias of the underlying La Sauses Member. In the vicinity of Cerrito de La Culebra the effect is also produced by minor folding and faulting and by flows within the La Sauses Member moving over an irregular surface.

Only a few dikes, namely the Manassa and La Sauses dikes, are more resistant to erosion than the surrounding volcanic rock which they intrude (figs. 5, 6). Most dikes are very difficult to recognize from a distance and often show no major change in topographic relief because of the enclosing rocks. Some dikes have proven very difficult to follow on the ground, although they have been recognized from the air and from aerial photographs.

The San Luis Hills have been buried to a greater extent than is presently observed and are now being exhumed. That this relationship is true is best illustrated in the area extending from the north end of Wildhorse Ridge southward to Culebra Creek. In the Wildhorse Ridge area small superposed intermittent creeks have cut across ridges of volcanic rock forming shallow canyons (fig. 10). A study

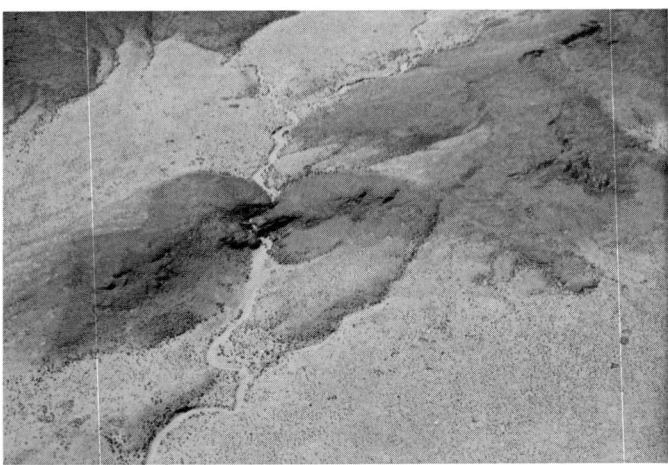

FIGURE 10.
Small superposed creek across breccias of Wildhorse Member of Conejos Formation. Just north of Wildhorse Ridge.

by Fling (1970, this guidebook) of recent sediments in this area shows present-day river deposits along the Rio Grande at an elevation of 7,470 feet and in the adjacent higher reaches along Wildhorse Ridge sand dunes developed at elevations as high as 8,100 feet. When one considers the Rio Grande terrace levels north of La Sauses Gorge it is apparent that a correlation of surfaces can be made with levels near the mouth of Culebra Creek. Upson (1938, p. 195) believed that his 55- and 100-foot benches near the mouth of the Culebra were cut by the Rio Grande.

The Rio Grande has been superposed across the San Luis Hills and with rejuvenation has cut the La Sauses Gorge (fig. 4). Evidence of stream piracy is present throughout the area as west and south-flowing creeks erode headward into the eastern San Luis Hills. Eastward-flowing creeks, controlled by the dip slope of tilted fault blocks, are being captured by west and south-flowing creeks, diverting the drainage toward the Rio Grande and Culebra. Canyons 200 feet deep have been produced in this manner, although these creeks are dry most of the time and contain water only when it rains.

SUMMARY AND CONCLUSIONS

The San Luis Hills are composed predominantly of Oligocene volcanic rocks of the Conejos Formation. Beginning in Wildhorse time and continuing through La Sauses time the eruptions became progressively more silicic. Following a period of erosion in which a surface of considerable relief was developed (locally several hundred feet) eruption of volcanic material of the Manassa Member took place. During these eruptions the volcanic material became progressively more basic, the reverse of the earlier eruptions. From field data all evidence seems to point to the general area of the King Turquois Mine as the center of this volcanic activity. In close association with the volcanic activity Late Oligocene stocks intruded the Piñon Hills and South Piñon Hills. Some dikes of the area may be related to these intrusions, but the main dike swarm of La Sauses Gorge was intruded along planes of weakness produced by north-south faulting parallel to the present-day Rio Grande. The displacement along this fault resulted in uplift of the eastern San Luis Hills relative to the western hills. The fault passes through the probable center of the previous volcanic activity. With subsidence and eastward tilting of the San Luis Basin, beginning in Early Miocene time, the San Luis Hills were uplifted. This may have been the time of formation of the tilted fault blocks east of the Rio Grande. In conjunction with this uplift the area was eroded to a mature topography as it was being surrounded by sediments of the Santa Fe Formation accumulating in the subsiding basin. With eruption of the Late Pliocene Servilleta basalts from deep-seated fractures in the Rio Grande rift zone the hills were flooded around their southern and eastern margins. During the eruption of these plateau basalts the San Luis Hills acted as islands in a sea of lava. Following these eruptions the hills were further buried by sedimentary debris. With rejuvenation of the area the Rio Grande was superposed across the San Luis Hills gradually cutting down to form the La Sauses Gorge. The hills are presently being exhumed.

REFERENCES

Aoki, Ken-ichiro, 1967, Petrography and petrochemistry of latest Pliocene olivine-tholeiites of Taos area, northern New Mexico, U.S.A.: Mineralogy and Petrology Contr., v. 14, no. 3, p. 191-203.

Atwood, W. W. and Mather, K. F., 1932, Physiography and Quaternary geology of the San Juan Mountains, Colorado: U.S. Geol. Survey Prof. Paper 166, 176 p.

Baltz, E. H., 1965, Stratigraphy and history of Raton Basin and notes on San Luis Basin, Colorado-New Mexico: Am. Assoc. Petroleum Geologists Bull., v. 49, no. 11, p. 2041-2075.

Bryan, Kirk, 1927a, Geology of the state line dam site: New Mexico State Eng. 8th Bienn. Rept., p. 253-258.

─────── 1927b, Geology of the state line dam site: New Mexico State Eng. 9th Bienn. Rept., p. 101-106.

─────── 1928, Preliminary report on the geology of the Rio Grande canyon as affecting the increase in flow of the Rio Grande south of the New Mexico-Colorado boundary: New Mexico State Eng. 9th Bienn. Rept., p. 106-120.

─────── 1938, Geology and ground-water conditions of the Rio Grande depression in Colorado and New Mexico: in Regional

Planning, pt. VI—the Rio Grande joint investigation in the upper Rio Grande Basin in Colo., N.M., and Texas 1936-1937, Washington, D.C., Nat'l. Res. Comm., v. 1, pt. 2, sec. 1, p. 197-225.

Butler, A. P., Jr., 1946, Tertiary and Quaternary geology of the Tusas-Tres Piedras area, New Mexico: Unpublished Ph.D. dissertation, Harvard Univ., Cambridge, Mass., 188 p.

Chapin, C. E., Epis, R. C., Lowell, G. R., 1970, Late Eocene paleovalleys and Oligocene volcanic rocks along the upper Arkansas Valley segment of the Rio Grande rift zone in Colorado (abs.), New Mexico Geol. Soc. 21st. Field Confs. p. 159.

Conkling, A. R., 1876, Physical features of San Luis Valley: in Wheeler, G. M., Ann. Rept. for 1876, U.S. Geog. and Geol. Surveys W. 100th Mer., p. 86-88.

Endlich, F. M., 1877, Geological report on the southeastern district: in Hayden, F. V., 9th Ann. Rept., Geol. and Geog. Survey of the Territories for 1875, p. 103-235.

Fling, R. P., 1970, A study of recent sedimentation in the San Luis Hills: in New Mexico Geol. Soc. Guidebook, 22d Field Conf.

Gaca, J. R., and Karig, D. E., 1966, Gravity survey in the San Luis Valley area, Colorado: U.S. Geol. Survey open-file rept., 21 p.

Hayden, F. V., 1869, Preliminary field report of the United States Geological Survey of Colorado and New Mexico: Wash. Govt. Printing Office, 155 p.

Johannsen, A., 1939, A descriptive petrography of the igneous rocks: 2d ed., Chicago Univ. Press, v. 1, 318 p.

Kelley, V. C., 1952, Tectonics of the Rio Grande depression of central New Mexico: in New Mexico Geol. Soc. Guidebook, 3d Field Conf., p. 93-105.

———— 1956, The Rio Grande depression from Taos to Santa Fe: in New Mexico Geol. Soc. Guidebook, 7th Field Conf., p. 109-114.

———— 1970, The Rio Grande depression, New Mexico and Colorado (abs.): in New Mexico Geol. Soc. 21st Field Conf., p. 157.

Kleinkopf, M. D., Peterson, D. L. and Johnson, R. B., 1970, Reconnaissance geophysical studies of the Trinidad quadrangle, south-central Colorado: U.S. Geol. Survey Prof. Paper 700-B, p. B78-B85.

Knepper, D. H., Jr., 1970, Structural framework of the Rio Grande rift zone—Poncha Springs to Mineral Hot Springs, Colorado (abs.): New Mexico Geol. Soc. 21st Field Conf., p. 158.

Larsen, E. S. and Cross, W., 1956, Geology and petrology of the San Juan region, southwestern Colorado: U.S. Geol. Survey Prof. Paper 258, 303 p.

Lipman, P. W., 1969, Alkalic and tholeiitic basaltic volcanism related to the Rio Grande depression, southern Colorado and northern New Mexico: Geol. Soc. America Bull., v. 80, no. 7, p. 1343-1354.

———— and Mehnert, H. H., 1969, Structural history of the eastern San Juan Mountains and the San Luis Valley, Colorado (abs.): Geol. Soc. America Spec. Paper 121.

———— Steven, T. A. and Mehnert, H. H., 1970, Volcanic history of the San Juan Mountains, Colorado, as indicated by potassium-argon dating: Geol. Soc. America Bull., v. 81, no. 8, p. 2329-2352.

Montgomery, A., 1953, Pre-Cambrian geology of the Picuris Range, north-central New Mexico: New Mexico Bur. Mines and Mineral Resources Bull. 30, 89 p.

Ozima, M., Kono, M., Kaneoka, I., Kinoshita, Hazimu, Kobayashi, Kazuo, Nagata, Takesi, Larson, E. E., and Strangway, D. W., 1967, Paleomagnetism and potassium argon ages of some volcanic rocks from the Rio Grande gorge, New Mexico: Jour. Geophys. Research, v. 72, no. 10, p. 2615-2621.

Pearl, R. M. 1941a, Colorado turquoise localities: Mineralogist, v. 9, no. 1, p. 3-4 and 24-27.

———— 1941b, Turquoise deposits of Colorado: Econ. Geology, v. 36, no. 3, p. 335-344.

———— 1942, Minerals of San Luis Valley, Colorado: Mineralogist, v. 10, no. 8, p. 237-238 and 249-253.

———— 1957, San Luis Valley, land of contrasts (Colorado): Earth Science, v. 10, no. 1, p. 9-11.

Powell, W. J., 1958, Ground-water resources of the San Luis Valley, Colorado: U.S. Geol. Survey Water Supply Paper 1379, 284 p.

Scott, G. R., 1970, Quaternary faulting and potential earthquakes in east-central Colorado: U.S. Geol. Survey Prof. Paper 700-C, p. C11-C18.

Siebenthal, C. E., 1910a, Geology and water resources of the San Luis Valley, Colorado: U.S. Geol. Survey Water Supply Paper 240, 128 p.

———— 1910b, The San Luis Valley, Colorado: Science, n. s. 31, p. 744-746.

Steven, T. A., 1968, Critical review of the San Juan peneplain, southwestern Colorado: U.S. Geol. Survey Prof. Paper 594-I, p. I1-I19.

Stevenson, J. J., 1875, Report on the geology of a portion of Colorado examined in 1873: in Wheeler, U.S. Geog. and Geol. Surveys W. 100th Mer., Final Reports or Monographs, v. III, Geology, Part IV, p. 303-501.

———— 1881, Report upon geological examinations in southern Colorado and northern New Mexico during the years 1878 and 1879: in Wheeler, U.S. Geog. and Geol. Surveys W. 100th Mer., Final Reports or Monographs, v. III, Supplement-Geology, 420 p.

Upson, J. E., 1938a, Tertiary geology and geomorphology of the Culebra reentrant, southern Colorado: Unpublished Ph.D. dissertation, Harvard Univ., Cambridge, Mass.

———— 1938b, Late Tertiary and Quaternary faulting in the San Luis Valley, Colorado (abs.): Geol. Soc. America Proc. 1937, p. 316-317.

———— 1939, Physiographic subdivisions of the San Luis Valley, southern Colorado: Journ. Geol., v. 47, no. 7, p. 721-736.

———— 1941, The Vallejo formation; new early Tertiary red-beds in southern Colorado: Am. Jour. Sci., v. 239, no. 8, p. 577-589.

Upson, R. H., 1940, Pleistocene and recent normal faulting in southern Colorado (abs.): Northwest Sci., v. 14, no. 3, p. 72.

U.S. Geological Survey, 1935, Geologic Map of Colorado.

Van Alstine, R. E., 1968, Tertiary trough between the Arkansas and San Luis Valleys, Colorado: U.S. Geol. Survey Prof. Paper 600-C, p. C158-C160.

TERTIARY VOLCANIC STRATIGRAPHY OF THE EASTERN TUSAS MOUNTAINS, SOUTHWEST OF THE SAN LUIS VALLEY, COLORADO-NEW MEXICO*

by

ARTHUR P. BUTLER, JR.

U.S. Geological Survey
Denver, Colorado

INTRODUCTION

Tertiary rocks in the upland of the southeast part of the San Juan Mountains, Colorado, and the Tusas Mountains, New Mexico (fig. 1), southwest of the San Luis Valley, consist of effusive and pyroclastic volcanic rocks that alternate and interfinger with fluvially transported debris eroded from them. Locally, some fluvial beds consist entirely of material derived from Precambrian crystalline rocks. Volcanic rocks predominate near the large centers of eruption in southern Colorado (Lipman and Steven, 1970, fig. 1) but are generally subordinate to fluviatile sedimentary rocks in eastern Rio Arriba County, New Mexico. Along the eastern margin of the upland south of the San Luis Valley in New Mexico the top of the sequence is represented by widespread flows of basaltic lavas.

Many major units of the sequence were first delineated during extensive investigations of the San Juan volcanic field by Larsen and Cross (1956). Subsequent study by T. A. Steven and P. W. Lipman and their associates have resulted in better definition of the relations among interfingering volcanic units erupted from different centers, in establishing a chronology of events based on radiometric determinations of age that fits well with observed stratigraphic relations (Lipman and others, 1970) and in an improved understanding of the petrologic evolution of the rocks.

The units of the volcanic sequence established by Larsen and Cross in the southeastern San Juan Mountains in Colorado were traced southward by the author (Butler, 1946) and mapped in the eastern part of the Tusas Mountains, New Mexico, and along the western margin of the Taos Plateau.

This mapping resulted in an interpretation of the relation between the volcanic sequence and the Santa Fe Formation, as used by Bryan (1938), that differed from earlier interpretations by Atwood and Mather (1932) and Smith (1938) and forms the basis for the description of the Tertiary stratigraphy presented herein. The descriptions presented here are modified, however, to conform with the stratigraphy, nomenclature, and chronology as revised by P. W. Lipman and T. A. Steven and their associates (Lipman and Steven, 1970; Lipman and others, 1970), and with some results of work in New Mexico by Barker (1958), Bingler (1968), and Muehlberger (1968).

OLDER ROCKS AND SURFACE BENEATH THE TERTIARY VOLCANIC SEQUENCE

The Tertiary rocks west of the southern part of the San Luis Valley rest with marked unconformity on older rocks. In Colorado, the older rocks are exposed only at the present southwest limit of the Tertiary volcanic sequence, but in New Mexico some parts of the basement were never completely covered by the Tertiary rocks, and other parts have been exhumed by subsequent erosion. In most of the area described in this report (fig. 2) the exposed basement consists of metamorphic and igneous rocks of Precambrian age. Near their present western limit in southern Colorado and in New Mexico the Tertiary rocks overlie unconformably the beveled edges of Mesozoic sedimentary rocks, which dip southwestward into the San Juan Basin (Larsen and Cross, 1956; Muehlberger, 1968).

The Precambrian terrane beneath the volcanic sequence in New Mexico represents the southeastern continuation of the Uncompaghre-Needle Mountain highlands of Colorado and, like them, was uplifted during Laramide orogeny. Prior to deposition of the Tertiary volcanic rocks erosion had removed any Paleozoic and Mesozoic rocks that may have once covered the older rocks and had sculptured a fairly rugged topography on them. The maximum relief of this topography approached 2,000 feet in the vicinity of T. 28 N., R. 8 E., and was 1,500 feet near the Rio de Los Pinos in the northwest part of the mapped area.

TERTIARY ROCKS

INTRODUCTION

The Tertiary rocks within the area shown on the accompanying geologic map (fig. 2) comprise seven formations (table 1) and several local bodies of volcanic rock that accumulated around individual vents. Some of the formations are composed largely of effusive and pyroclastic volcanic rocks and subordinately of interbedded clastic sedimentary rocks; some largely of clastic sedimentary

---

*Publication authorized by the Director, U.S. Geological Survey.

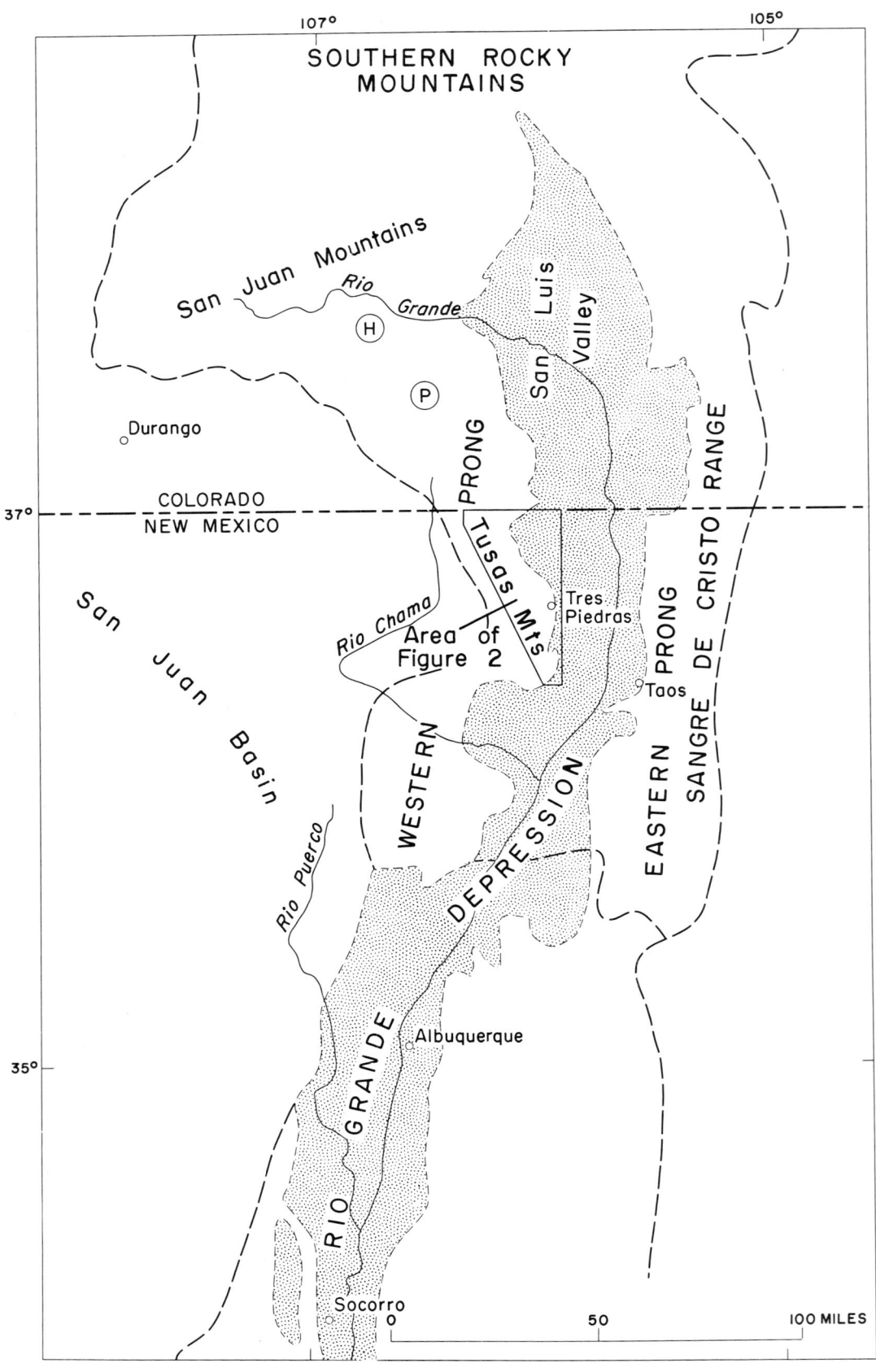

FIGURE 1.

Index map of south-central Colorado and north-central New Mexico showing locations of accompanying geologic maps Figure 2 and of calderas mentioned in text; H, Mt. Hope; P, Platoro.

TABLE 1. TERTIARY ROCKS OF THE EASTERN PART OF THE TUSAS MOUNTAINS AND ADJOINING PART OF THE TAOS PLATEAU, NEW MEXICO

AGE	FORMATION AND MEMBER	DESCRIPTION	THICKNESS (FEET)[1]
Pliocene	Servilleta Formation	Flows of coarse-grained, porous, tholeiitic basalt and interbedded gravel	10-100
	Unconformity		
Pliocene and Miocene	Hinsdale Formation		
	Upper Basalt Member, (Dorado Basalt of Barker, 1958)	Flows of xenocrystic, quartz-bearing alkalic basalt and basaltic andesite in disconnected bodies	10-150
	Lower basalt member, (Cisneros Basalt of Barker, 1958)	Flows of fine-grained, slightly porphyritic, alkalic basalt in disconnected bodies	10-50
	Hypersthene Quartz Latite	Flows form San Antonio Peak and some other domes; relation to basalts uncertain	0-2000
	Rhyolite of No Agua Mountain	Dissected local mass of perlitic and spherulitic rhyolite	undetermined
	Unconformity		
Pliocene (?) and Miocene (?)	Santa Fe Formation as used by Smith (1938)	Fluvial and eolian sandstone in southeast part of area	0-900
Pliocene to Oligocene	Los Pinos Formation		
	Rhyolite Member	Sandstone, conglomerate, tuff, and flows or ash flows in which rhyolitic rock predominates	0-700
	Jarita Basalt Member of Barker (1958)	Flows of basalt of locally different characteristics in many disconnected bodies	10-100
	Undivided in northern part of area	Tuffaceous sandstone, conglomerate, and tuff, largely equivalent to two lower members in southern part of area	0-700
	Coarsely porphyritic Quartz Latite Member	Tuffaceous sandstone, conglomerate containing abundant clasts of coarsely porphyritic quartz latite, and tuff	0-600
	Quartz Latite-Andesite member	Breccia and conglomerate in which clasts of dark quartz latite or andesite predominate, tuff, and intrusive breccia	0-700
Uncertain	Ritito Conglomerate of Barker (1958)	Conglomerate of angular fragments of Precambrian rock. Present only in southwest part of area. Underlies rhyolite member of Los Pinos Formation, correlation otherwise uncertain	0-400
Oligocene	Tuff of Masonic Park	Ash-flow tuff of quartz latite, mostly welded	0-275
Oligocene	Treasure Mountain Tuff	Tuff, sandstone, conglomerate, and discontinuous welded ash-flow tuff near base. Absent south of center of T. 28 N., R. 8 E.	
	Unconformity		
Oligocene and older (?)	Conejos Formation	Breccia, flows, agglomerate, of varicolored andesite and quartz latite, tuff, tuffaceous sandstone, and conglomerate, crudely and irregularly bedded	0-1000

[1]The maximum thickness of different units are not superposed. Thus the total aggregate thickness at any one place is much less than the sum of individual maximums and may not be much in excess of 2,000 feet.

rocks and subordinately of effusive and pyroclastic material; and two composed mostly of basaltic lava. Their general relations are shown diagrammatically on Figure 3. As a group, these formations dip gently east-northeastward from the headwaters of the Rio de Los Pinos in Colorado and from the Tusas Mountains in New Mexico toward the San Luis Valley and Taos Plateau. In consequence of this dip and dissection by streams, the lower units are more widely present at the surface in the western part of the general upland, and successive younger units are more widely present in the eastern part.

Three other formations of Tertiary age are present mostly west and southwest of the area of the map and are only briefly mentioned here. Two of them—The Blanco Basin Formation (Larsen and Cross, 1956) and the El Rito Formation of Smith (1938)—are older than the volcanic sequence and consist of sandstone, arkose, and conglomerate composed largely of debris eroded from Precambrian rocks. The Blanco Basin Formation underlies the volcanic rocks discontinuously at their western margin in Colorado (Larsen and Cross 1956, p. 60-61) and northern New Mexico (Muehlberger, 1968, p. 3). The El Rito occupies a generally similar position from about latitude 36°49′ N. southward to the Chama River (Smith, 1938, p. 940). These formations are thought to be of Eocene age (Lipman and others, 1970; Bingler, 1968). The third of the three units—the Ritito Conglomerate of Barker (1958) —is a "conglomerate of gravel-size fragments of Precambrian rocks" that rests directly on the source rocks. Near its type locality in secs. 11 and 14, T. 27 N., R. 7 E., it underlies the topmost rhyolite member of the Los Pinos Formation and may be correlative either with rocks questionably equivalent to the Conejos Formation or with beds in the lowermost quartz latite-andesite member of the Los Pinos Formation (Barker, 1958, p. 43). Southwest of the area of the map with this report (fig. 3) beds of Ritito lithology are partly gradational to the underlying El Rito (Bingler, 1968, p. 33), but beds of generally similar lithology are also present locally in several formations of the volcanic sequence (Butler, 1946). Thus, away from the type locality all beds of Ritito lithology are not stratigraphic equivalents.

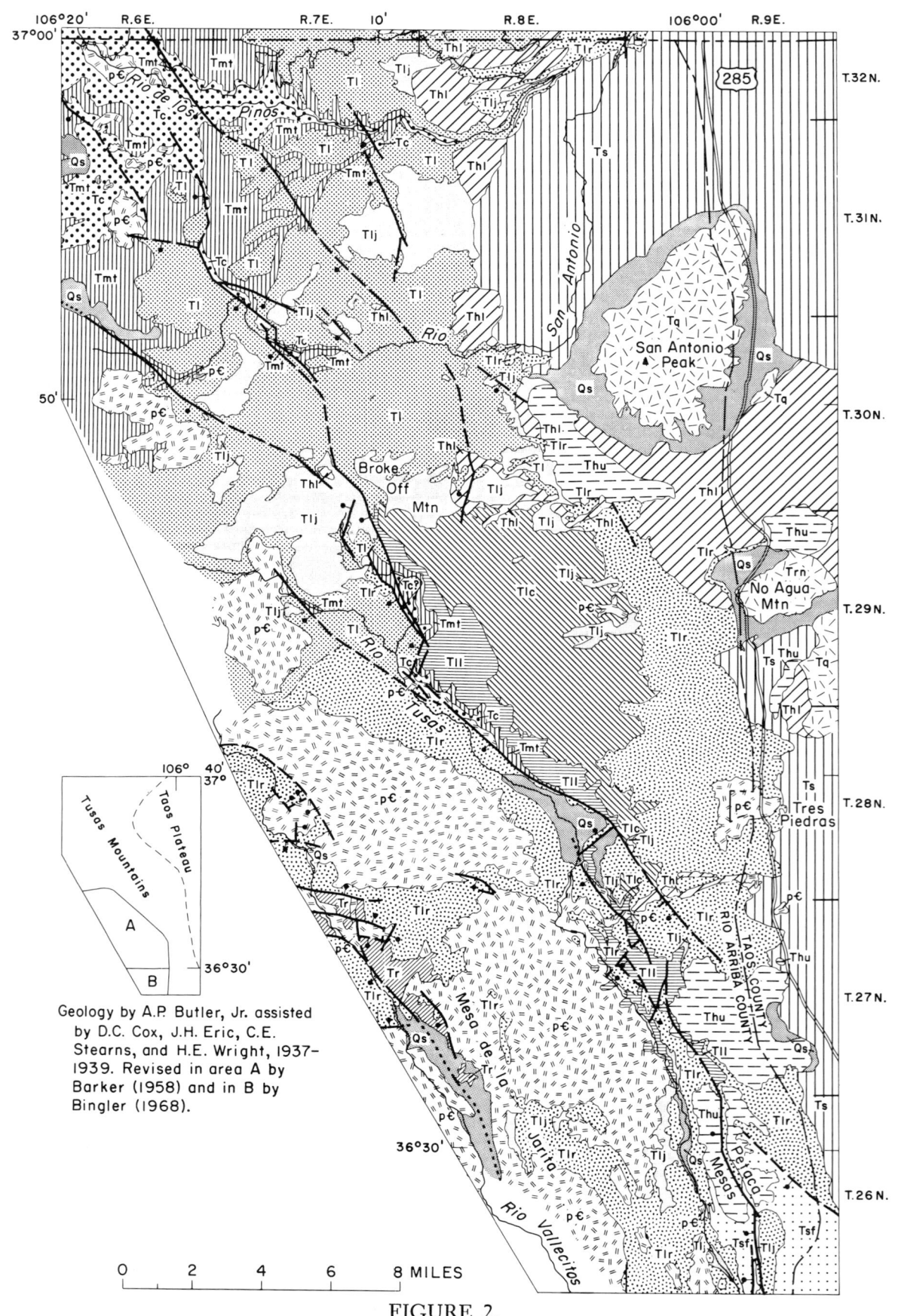

FIGURE 2.

Geologic map of the eastern part of the Tusas Mountains and western part of the Taos Plateau, Rio Arriba and Taos Counties, New Mexico.

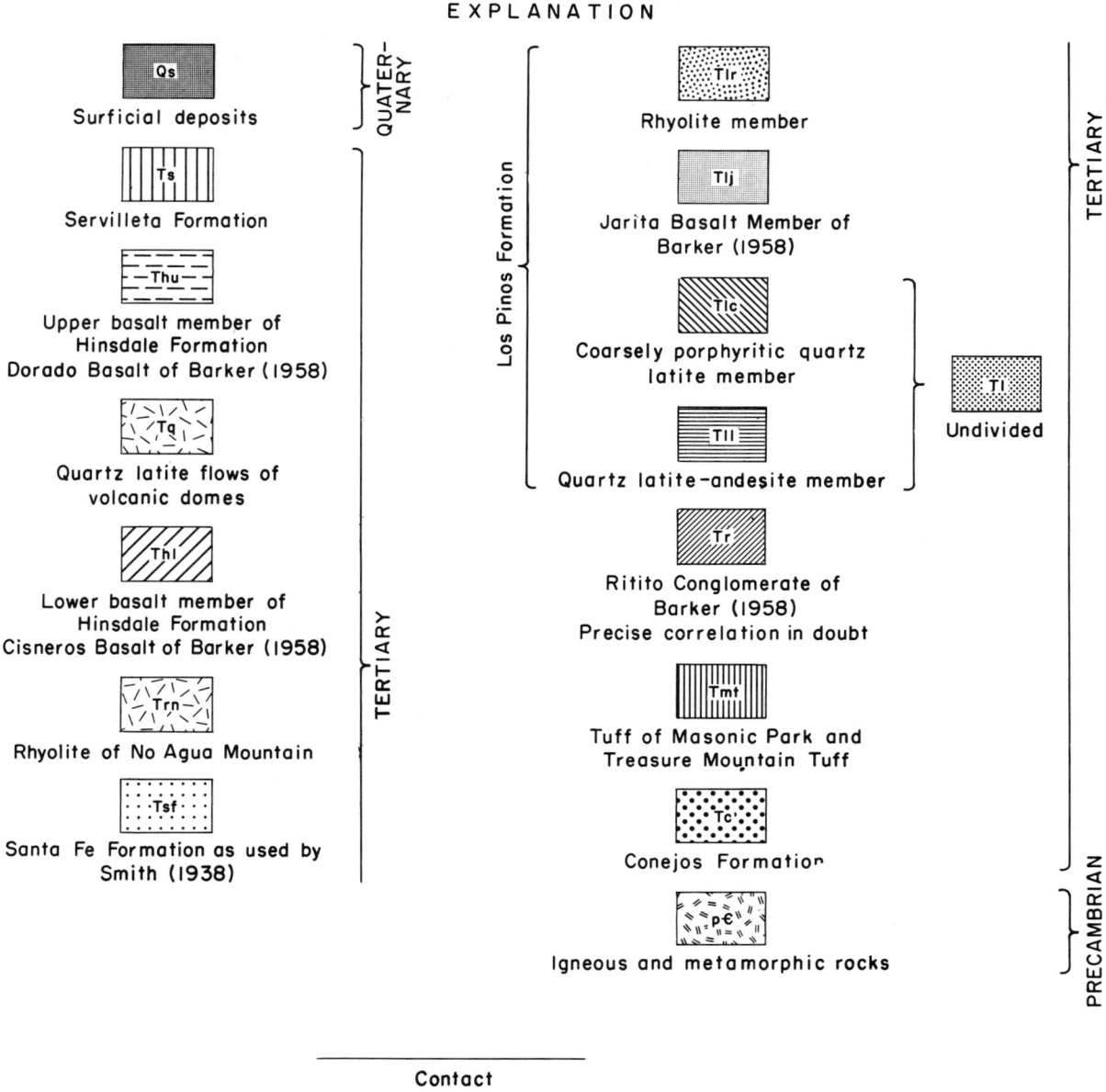

CONEJOS FORMATION

The Conejos Formation, Conejos Quartz Latite of Larsen and Cross (1956), is the oldest unit of the volcanic sequence in the southern part of the San Juan Mountains, Colorado. It was named for its outcrops in the valley of the Conejos River, Colorado (Cross and Larsen, 1935), and comprises most of the "early intermediate lavas and breccias" (Lipman and others, 1970) in the southeast part of the volcanic field.

Within the map area (fig. 2) the Conejos Formation crops out mainly in the valley of the Rio de Los Pinos and its immediate tributaries and locally in the valley of the Rio San Antonio. Farthur south, in the northern part of the Rio Tusas Valley, rocks in scattered outcrops underneath the Treasure Mountain Tuff may be a distal facies of the Conejos Formation although their volcanic constituents are not typical. The formation underlies much of the upland west of the map area south to the canyon of the Rio Brazos (Muehlberger, 1968) and is well exposed at places along the narrow gauge railway north of the Rio de Los Pinos Valley.

The Conejos Formation within the map area is a rather chaotic assemblage of varicolored effusive and volcaniclastic rocks in which breccia predominates over flows, tuff-

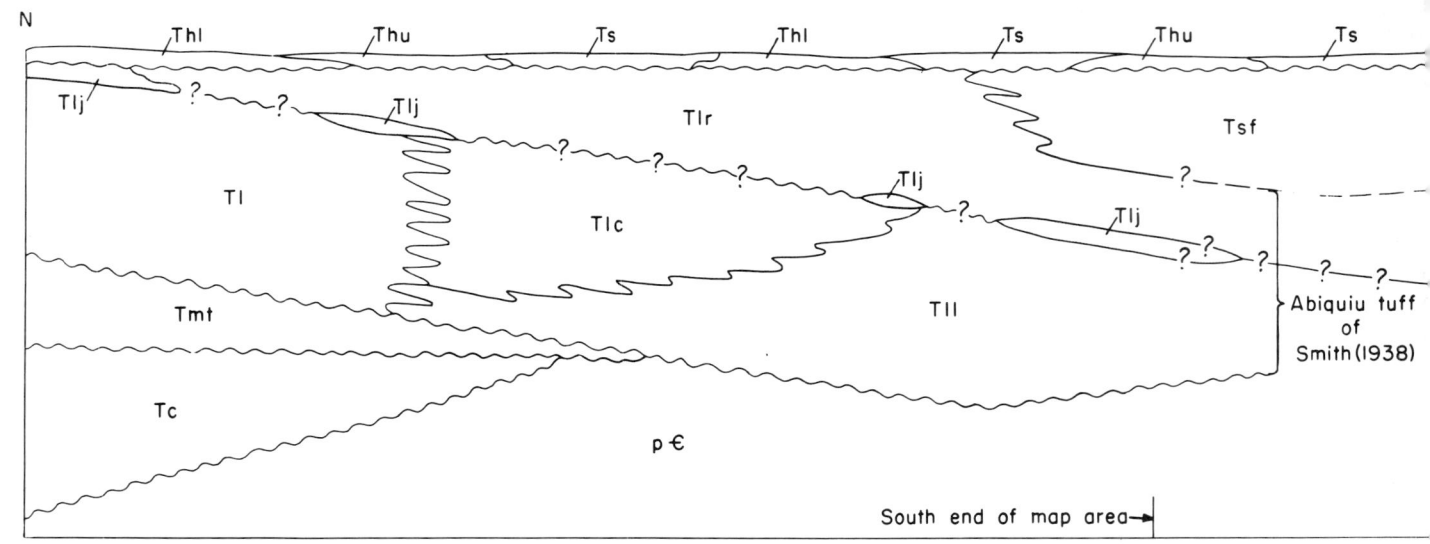

FIGURE 3.
Diagrammatic correlation chart showing the general stratigraphic relation of the Tertiary rocks from north to south along the east side of the Tusas Mountains, New Mexico. Ritito Conglomerate of Barker is omitted. See Figure 2 for explanation of symbols. Chart is not to scale.

breccia, agglomerate, tuff, tuffaceous arenite and conglomerate. Breccia and flows are generally more abundant in the upper part of the formation and other kinds of rock in the lower part. All lithologic types are interbedded in crude, irregular lenses of mostly local extent. Beds are generally massive, and those of one type pass laterally into or end abruptly against another type. Individual flows, which range from less than 10 to 50 feet in thickness, are traceable only from 1 to 2 miles. The coarsely clastic tuffaceous rocks weather to conspicuous pinnacles that can be observed from the railway line on the north side of the Rio de Los Pinos.

The rock of breccia, agglomerate, and flows is mainly dark-colored and is andesite to quartz latite in chemical composition (Lipman and others, 1970, p. 2331), but was considered to be petrographically mainly quartz latite by Larsen and Cross (1956, p. 97). Some of the rock is more felsic, and that of some flows is basaltic andesite. Most of the rocks are somewhat porphyritic and contain megascopically recognizable phenocrysts set in an aphanitic groundmass, but some dark rocks are fine grained and nonporphyritic. Plagioclase, dark-green pyroxene, and altered olivine are the commonly recognizable phenocrysts in gray and dark-green rocks; plagioclase and biotite are those in other lighter colored rocks.

Colors range from black to various shades of gray in mafic andesite and from gray or grayish green to grayish and reddish purple in more felsic rocks. Tuff is various pastel shades of pink and gray. It is more indurated than similar appearing tuff in the younger Los Pinos Formation.

The Conejos Formation is about 1,000 feet thick from the bottom of the Rio de Los Pinos Valley in the east center of R. 6 E., but the maximum thickness is not known because the base is not exposed and its top is an irregular surface. At places it wedges out against hills of Precambrian rock.

No vents for Conejos rocks are known in northern New Mexico and the rocks were probably erupted from volcanic centers in southern Colorado (see Lipman and others, 1970, fig. 1).

The age of the formation as determined by the potassium argon method is between 31 and 35 m.y. (Lipman and others, 1970, tables 1 and 2), or largely Early and Middle Oligocene, rather than Miocene as once thought (Larsen and Cross, 1956, table 18).

TREASURE MOUNTAIN TUFF

Both the unit now called Treasure Mountain Tuff and the overlying unit now referred to as tuff of Masonic Park (Lipman and Steven, 1970) were included in the Treasure Mountain Rhyolite by Larsen and Cross (1956). The extension of their units into New Mexico was traced in the field by the writer (Butler, 1946) and they were distinguished in mapping, although they are combined on figure 2.

The Treasure Mountain Tuff crops out in a thin interval on the sides of valleys in part of the basin of the Rio de Los Pinos, in Rs. 6 and 7 E. in the basin of the Rio San Antonio, and east of the Rio Tusas south to the center of T. 28 N., R. 9 E. It also crops out more broadly in the upland in the northwest part and west of the map area.

The Treasure Mountain Tuff was deposited on an irregular surface of the Conejos Formation, which has a relief of as much as 300 feet in a few places, and also abuts against hills of Precambrian rocks, which rise above it.

In Colorado, three welded ash-flow sheets are recognized as formal members and some underlying and intervening welded and nonwelded ash flows and air-fall tuffs as informal members of the Treasure Mountain Tuff (Lipman and Steven, 1970). All were erupted from the site of the Platoro caldera. At the state line and in New Mexico, however, only one welded ash-flow sheet is irregularly present at or close to the base. Its distribution is incompletely known, either because it is absent as a result of the relief of the underlying surface, or because it is concealed by colluvium. This ash flow consists of two parts where it is most complete: (1) a lower interval that grades vertically and horizontally from black vitrophyre into gray unwelded tuff, and (2) a more persistent upper dull-brown, aphanitic, porphyritic, firmly welded interval. Phenocrysts of plagioclase and biotite are more abundant in the upper part. The combined thickness of the two parts is at least 50 feet in some places. Its stratigraphic position relative to the units recognized in Colorado is not known.

The rest of the Treasure Mountain Tuff consists of interbedded nonwelded ash-flow and air-fall tuff, tuffaceous sandstone, and conglomerate. In the northern part of the area, tuff generally predominates in the lower part of the formation; fluviatile deposits in the upper part. Much of the tuff is buff, but some is pink and some is dark gray. It consists of crystal fragments, mainly plagioclase and biotite, in a matrix of devitrified glass shards. Fragments of pumice are common in some beds.

The fluviatile rocks consist of buff to gray tuffaceous sandstone and lenticular beds of conglomerate. Some boulders in the conglomerate are as much as 3.5 feet in diameter, and large boulders fill some channels cut into fine-grained beds, as can be seen in railway cuts near the east side of sec. 29, T. 32 N., R. 7 E. Dark-colored rocks predominate among clasts in the conglomerate beds and may have been derived from the lower lavas related to the Platoro caldera (Lipman and Steven, 1970, p. C23) and less distant high-standing parts of the Conejos Formation.

The Treasure Mountain Tuff is about 250 feet thick on the north side of the Rio de Los Pinos and about 60 feet near the southern limit of its outcrop in T. 28 N., R. 8 E.

Tuff of Masonic Park

The tuff of Masonic Park is an ash-flow sheet that is mostly welded. It rests with apparent conformity on and is essentially coextensive with the underlying Treasure Mountain Tuff southward as far as the most northerly large tributary of the Rio Tusas in sec. 24, T. 29 N., R. 7 E. The main welded part of the sheet is the most distinctive of the Tertiary rocks in the map area. It is a gray to purple-gray and locally reddish rock that tends to weather into platy tablets which are recognizable in hillside float even where the tuff is not exposed. In places it stands as a cliff. The welded tuff is fine-grained fragmental to aphanitic and generally porphyritic rock. Plagioclase and biotite are the common phenocrysts and sparse green pyroxene is generally present. At many places the lowest part of the sheet is pink to buff nonwelded tuff about 10 feet thick.

The tuff of Masonic Park is about 100 feet thick in the southeast corner of T. 32 N., R. 7 E. It thins westward and southward from there and is only about 15 feet thick in the western part of the map area and in the northern part of the Rio Tusas Valley.

The tuff was erupted from the Mount Hope caldera and has an age of 28.2 m.y. (Lipman and others, 1970).

Los Pinos Formation

The Los Pinos Formation, formerly Los Pinos Gravel (Atwood and Mather, 1932), was named for exposures in the canyon of the Rio de Los Pinos. It is the most continuous and widespread of the Tertiary formations within the map area. It is present north of the Rio de Los Pinos eastward from the west part of R. 7 E. and underlies much of the broad belt that extends southeast from the southeast part of T. 31 N., R. 6 E. beyond the south edge of the map. Along part of the west side of the belt, the formation pinches out against the highland of Precambrian rocks, but it extends west of the map area to the rim of the Brazos Canyon (Muehlberger, 1968) and into much of the upper drainage area of the Rio Vallecitos (Barker, 1958, pl. 1). It declines eastward with the general dip of the rocks and is covered by flows of younger basalt everywhere in about the eastern third of the area. The formation extends northward many miles along the eastern flank of the San Juan Mountains in Colorado (Larsen and Cross, 1956). South of the map area, rocks that are equivalent to parts of the Los Pinos Formation constitute much of the Abiquiu Tuff of Smith (1938, p. 944).

The Los Pinos Formation rests with apparent conformity on the tuff of Masonic Park in the north half of the area and unconformably on Precambrian rocks or nearly conformably on the Ritito Conglomerate of Barker (1958) in much of the south half, except in Tps. 28 and 29 N., R. 8 E., where it rests on Treasure Mountain Tuff.

The Los Pinos Formation comprises a varied assortment of lithologies that includes widespread beds of fluvial, partly tuffaceous sandstone and conglomerate, air-fall and fluvially reworked tuff, welded ash-flow tuffs several square miles in extent, small masses of intrusive rock, and an interval of discontinuous but widespread basalt flows, which may belong in the Hinsdale Formation, but for convenience are here described as a unit of the Los Pinos.

South of Broke Off Mountain, mostly in and east of the valley of the Rio Tusas, the predominantly clastic part of the Los Pinos Formation is divisible into three local members. These are distinguished by the kinds of rock that occur as clasts in conglomerate and fragments in pyroclastic breccia and as flows. North of Broke Off Mountain, the kinds of rock in conglomerate are mixed and the two lower members recognized farther south cannot be distinguished. The bulk of the formation that underlies the basalt unit in this part of the area is undivided but corresponds generally to the lower two clastic members farther south.

From near the middle of the Petaca Mesas southward, the upper part of the top clastic member partly underlies and partly interfingers with arkosic sandstone and sandstone that are continuous with the Santa Fe Formation as used by Smith (1938).

Undivided part of the formation

The undivided part of the Los Pinos Formation consists of sandstone, tuffaceous sandstone, conglomerate, and some pyroclastic tuff. Tuff is more common near the bottom than near the top and a relatively persistent zone of conglomerate occurs about 100 feet below the top.

The tuffs are felsic, buff, light gray, and creamy white. They are composed of angular mineral grains in a fragmental matrix of partly devitrified glass. Some contain uniformly distributed angular pebbles.

Conglomerate, in beds 1-10 feet thick, forms only a small portion of the formation, but cobbles and boulders litter most of the slopes underlain by it. Pebbles and cobbles less than 4 inches in diameter are most common, but some boulders are as much as 4 feet in diameter. They are mostly volcanic rocks of felsitic to intermediate composition. Dark-colored andesite-like rocks are distributed throughout but are particularly abundant in angular conglomerate near the base, which in this respect resembles that in the lowest member farther south. Other conspicuous clasts are gray to maroon coarsely porphyritic felsite containing phenocrysts of feldspar as much as 1.5 centimeters long. Many other less distinctive types are also present.

Quartz Latite-Andesite Member

The lowest clastic member of the formation, the Biscara Member of Barker (1958), is characterized by the abundance of fragments of generally dark-colored quartz latite or andesite in beds of conglomerate and breccia. In general, the member is present mainly on lower valley slopes east of the Rio Tusas, and only locally west of the river in T. 27 N. Within the area, it disappears under younger units south of that township, but Smith's (1938) description of the Abiquiu Tuff suggests that part of that formation may correspond to this member.

The combination of lithologies in the Quartz Latite-Andesite Member is much like that in the undivided part of the Los Pinos Formation, but tuff is more abundant. The member also includes bedded breccia of volcanic rocks, conglomerate composed of fragments of Precambrian rocks, and dikes and small pipes of volcanic breccia that are too small to show at the scale of the map.

Breccia of dark-colored quartz latite locally cliff-forming in Tps. 28 and 29 N., R. 8 E., and conglomerate of similar rock form much of the upper part of the member. Gray to blue-gray aphanitic rhyolite occurs as local bodies of breccia and as pebbles in conglomerate near the middle of the member.

Fragments of Precambrian rocks form masses of rubble and beds of conglomerate close to and locally some distance above the base.

The quartz latite or andesite of the breccia and conglomerate is light gray-green to maroonish gray and black, generally finely crystalline to aphanitic, and porphyritic. Plagioclase and shiny black hornblende are the common phenocrysts. Rusty iddingsite and biotite occur in some of the rock, and pyroxene is a phenocryst in some bodies of intrusive rock.

Coarsely Porphyritic Quartz Latite Member

The coarsely porphyritic Quartz Latite Member, Esquibel Member of Barker (1958), is characterized by the kind of rock most abundant in the conglomerate beds in it. Otherwise it is much like the undivided part of the Los Pinos Formation, with which it may be in large part correlative.

The member is confined largely to the highland east of the Rio Tusas from Broke Off Mountain southward to the northwest corner of T. 27 N., R. 8 E., where it pinches out between the underlying and overlying clastic members. It is also present, but not mapped separately, west of the Rio Tusas in T. 29 N., R. 7 E. (Barker, 1958, pl. 1). To the east it dips under the overlying Rhyolite Member.

The rock of the most abundant clasts in the conglomerate beds is coarsely porphyritic quartz latite in which phenocrysts of feldspar as much as 8 mm long, and subordinate biotite and hornblende are set in a gray to purple-pink groundmass. Unusually large boulders of this rock 4-9 feet in diameter, near the top of the member in sec. 30, T. 28 N., R. 9 E., suggest the proximity of a bedrock source that is not exposed. The lower part of the member is transitional to the underlying Quartz Latite-Andesite Member, and at places clasts of Precambrian rocks and arkosic sandstone predominate in the top 25 feet.

Jarita Basalt Member of Barker (1958)

Widespread but discontinuous flows of basalt that rest mainly on older parts of the Los Pinos Formation, and locally on Precambrian rock, constitute the Jarita Basalt Member of Barker (1958), a name adopted from Butler (1946). For convenience herein, these flows are included with the Los Pinos Formation because of their stratigraphic position in New Mexico, but they may be equivalent to older parts of the Hinsdale Formation in Colorado, where some basalt in that formation intertongues with the Los Pinos Formation as mapped by Larsen and Cross (1956, pl. 1) and by P. W. Lipman (oral commun., 1971).

In the northern part of the area, basalt of this member caps Broke Off Mountain and other inclined mesas on the divides between the Rio San Antonio and the Rio Tusas and between the Rio San Antonio and Rio de Los Pinos. To the south, disconnected bodies of the basalt are present on the east slope of the mountains, in the valley of the Rio Tusas and locally on its eastern slopes, and on part of the west rim of the Mesa de La Jarita. At different places the flows rest on Precambrian rocks or conglomerate of fragments derived therefrom, on the two older clastic members, and, north of Broke Off Mountain, on the undivided part of the Los Pinos Formation. On the lower slopes east of Broke Off Mountain and in much of the valley of the Rio Tusas, the Jarita Basalt Member is overlain by the Rhyolite Member.

The basalt on mesas in the north part of the area consists of two megascopically slightly different varieties. The more widespread, and upper one where both are present, is fine grained and only slightly porphyritic, has considerable intergranular pore space and phenocrysts of rusty iddingsite after olivine, and locally contains amygdules of chalcedony. The other variety contains phenocrysts of only slightly altered olivine, phenocrysts of pyroxene in some flows, and veinlets and amygdules of calcite, and lacks intergranular pores.

Basalt in and near the valley of the Rio Tusas in the southern part of the area differs from that of the northern mesas in various megascopic details. Some flows are characterized by moldy-appearing pale-green or yellow-green spots, possibly a superficial alteration of plagioclase. Many have intergranular pores and sparse inconspicuous phenocrysts of hypersthene but lack the rusty altered olivine of the northern porous basalt. Non-porous rock in other flows has phenocrysts of rusty, altered olivine and, generally, of plagioclase. In a few flows, a dark-green pyroxene is the principal phenocryst and olivine is inconspicuous.

The Jarita Basalt Member is 100 feet thick on the north side of the Rio de Los Pinos and east of the Rio Trusas south of the Petaca Mesas. Elsewhere it is thinner.

Rhyolite Member

The top member of the Los Pinos Formation, the Cordito Member of Barker (1958), is characterized by rhyolitic rock that makes up the predominant fragments in the conglomerate and occurs as local flows or welded ash flows and a few small intrusive bodies.

The Rhyolite Member is most continuous on the eastern slope of the highland area south from Broke Off Mountain beyond the limit of mapping but extends west, as mapped by Barker (1958, pl. 1), into the basin of the Rio Vallecitos. On the sides of the canyon of the Rio de Los Pinos, sandy tuff above the Jarita Basalt Member and under the Hinsdale and Servilleta formations is also included in it.

The member consists predominantly of fluvially deposited beds that range from mudstone to conglomerate and subordinately of beds of tuff and lava or ash flows. Much of the member is poorly consolidated and exposures are generally confined to some indurated beds of conglomerate and to parts of some lava or ash flows.

North of the Petaca mesas the common clasts in the conglomerate consist of white, brownish-red, blue, and gray porphyritic rhyolite, and a blue slightly porphyritic variety. Quartz is an abundant phenocryst in all but the blue variety. Sanadine and sodic plagioclase phenocrysts are present in all varieties. The more phenocryst-rich rock occurs as a 70-foot thick flow, possibly an ash-flow tuff, and as tuff in the north-central part of T. 27 N., R. 8 E., and as a flow in the Rio Tusas Valley.

In the vicinity of and southward from the Petaca mesas, the predominant clasts in the conglomerate beds consist of coarsely porphyritic rock in which abundant phenocrysts of feldspar are accompanied by some biotite and hornblende and sparse quartz. Rock of this type occurs as a flow east of the Petaca mesas.

A third variety of somewhat glassy purple-pink porphyritic rhyolite, which lacks sanadine phenocrysts, forms a massive to brecciated flow in the Tusas Valley and in the valley east of the Petaca mesas, where it is 150 feet stratigraphically below the coarsely porphyritic flow. It also occurs in a few small dikes and plugs in the west-central part of T. 26 N., R. 9 E.

Southward from the middle of the Petaca mesas conglomerate beds are less abundant than farther north, and interbedded friable tuffaceous arkose and sandstone are more abundant. Upward in the section east of the Rio Tusas, volcanic components diminish to disappearance, and the rocks are arkose and sandstone like those of the Santa Fe Formation as used by Smith (1938).

Thickness

From the south side of Broke Off Mountain northward to the Rio de Los Pinos, the Los Pinos Formation is between 600 and 700 feet thick to the top of the Jarita Basalt Member. In the northern part of T. 28 N., R. 9 E., the formation is between 1,300 and 1,400 feet thick below the eroded top of the Rhyolite Member. It thins out completely against hills of Precambrian rock, especially those west of the Rio Tusas.

Origin and age

The fluvially deposited rocks that make up the larger part of the Los Pinos Formation consist largely of material of volcanic origin and very subordinately of materials eroded from Precambrian rocks. A large part of the fluviatile beds probably represents a clastic facies spread as an apron around centers of nearly contemporaneous volcanic eruption. The components of the undivided part of the formation may have come from varied sources including the younger lavas erupted from vents east of the Platoro caldera (Lipman and Steven, 1970). South from the northern part of the Tusas Valley, the coarser components in the fluviatile beds change in type systematically upward through the different members. The clasts in conglomerate beds of the Lower Quartz Latite-Andesite Member and the Upper Rhyolite Member have counterparts in associated eruptive and intrusive rocks. The largest boulders in the coarsely porphyritic member are near the center of the map area. These features suggest that the components of these members came from local centers of eruption rather than from those that supplied the undivided part of the formation farther north. Such centers may be largely concealed, for the known bodies of intrusive rocks appear too small to represent vents that supplied all the volcanic material of these units.

The Los Pinos Formation was deposited subsequent to emplacement of the tuff of Masonic Park, which has an age of 28.2 m.y. Bingler, (1968, p. 36) reported that a sample of welded ash-flow tuff from the Rhyolite Member west of the Rio Tusas in T. 26 N., R. 9 E. yielded a potassium argon age of 25.9 ± 1.8 m.y. The part of the formation bracketed by these ages is mostly Late Oligocene. Some beds in the southeast part of the area which are in the Rhyolite Member but which appear to be transitional into the Santa Fe Formation, may be considerably younger.

SANTA FE FORMATION

Rocks that are continuous with the Santa Fe Formation as used by Smith (1938) are confined to the southeastern corner of the map area. The lower boundary of the formation is gradational with the top of the Rhyolite Member of the Los Pinos Formation, and the lower beds interfinger with and appear to overlap northward onto that member.

This same kind of transition zone also marks the boundary between the Abiquiu Tuff and the Santa Fe Formation immediately south of the area of the map (Smith, 1938).

The Santa Fe Formation consists chiefly of light-buff, thin- to thick-bedded, clean to silty sandstone. Some beds near the base are brownish red. High-angle, possibly eolian, crossbedding that extends across layers 10-20 feet thick is a characteristic of some beds.

The position of the rocks of the Santa Fe Formation in this area relative to the stratigraphy in its main area of outcrop farther south in the Rio Grande Valley has not been clearly determined. However, the interval with large-scale crossbedding may correspond to similar strata in a member near the top of the Tesuque Formation as used by Galusha and Blick (1971), to which they assign an Early Pliocene age.

RHYOLITE OF NO AGUA MOUNTAIN

No Agua Mountain is the eroded remnant of a local mass of rhyolite that was extruded after all, or nearly all, of the uppermost member of the Los Pinos Formation had been deposited and before eruption of the Lower Basalt Member of the Hinsdale Formation, which is younger than all of the Los Pinos Formation and is described below. The rhyolite consists mostly of finely flow layered spherulitic pitchstone and granules of obsidian set in a webwork mesh of glass. It has a fission track age of 4.8 m.y. (Lipman and others, 1970, p. 2346). Sand and gravel derived from the mountain are exposed under the Lower Basalt of the Hinsdale Formation in a cut on U.S. Highway 285 about 1 mile north of the base of the mountains.

HINSDALE FORMATION

The Hinsdale Formation (Lipman and others, 1970), formerly a part of the Hinsdale Volcanic Series (Larsen and Cross, 1956), is a bimodal association of rather local bodies of rhyolite and more extensive sheets of alkali olivine basalt. On the east flank of the Tusas Mountains and near the west edge of the Taos Plateau the formation comprises two basaltic members.

Lower Basalt Member, Cisneros Basalt of Barker (1958)

The Lower Basalt Member, the Cisneros Basalt of Barker (1958), of the Hinsdale Formation in the area of the map, consists of disconnected bodies in the northeast part of the area and some isolated bodies in the south part of T. 28 N., R. 9 E. and north part of T. 27 N., R. 9 E. It rests with a slight but distinct angular unconformity on all members of the Los Pinos Formation except the lowest. It partly fills shallow valleys eroded in the Jarita Member east of Broke Off Mountain and in the Upper Rhyolite Member south of Tres Piedras.

On the lower east slope of Broke Off Mountain, the basalt is dark gray, maroon streaked, very fine grained, nonporous, and carries sparse phenocrysts of relatively fresh irridescent olivine. Other flows, particularly some in the southern part of the area and at places north of the Rio de Los Pinos, are more porphyritic and contain phenocrysts of plagioclase, as well as olivine, and some are slightly porous. The plagioclase in the groundmass is generally finer grained than that in most flows of the Jarita Member of the Los Pinos Formation and Servilleta Formation.

Upper Basalt Member, Dorado Basalt of Barker (1958)

The Upper Basalt Member, the Dorado Basalt of Barker (1958), includes the flows that cap the Petaca Mesas and a mesa north of them and several other separated bodies of quartz-bearing basalt southwest of San Antonio Peak and north and south of No Agua Mountain. In some areas north of No Agua Mountain, this basalt member is included with the Lower Basalt Member on the map.

The southern bodies of the Upper Basalt Member (Dorado Basalt) are unconformable on the Quartz Latite-Andesite and Rhyolite members of the Los Pinos Formation and the Santa Fe Formation. They were erupted after erosion had obliterated the topographic effect of post-Los Pinos movement on a fault that bisects the Petaca mesas. Some of the northern bodies of quartz-bearing basalt rest on the slightly eroded Lower Basalt Member (Cisneros Basalt). All bodies of the Upper Basalt Member (Dorado Basalt) contain quartz xenocrysts, and some in the northern part of the area also contain xenocrysts of sodic plagioclase. Rock in the southern bodies is fine grained, nonporphyritic to porphyritic, finely to coarsely vesicular; that of the northern bodies is conspicuously porphyritic. Plagioclase and sparse olivine are phenocrysts in porphyritic rock.

In T. 27 N., R. 9 E., the Upper Basalt Member (Dorado Basalt) is at least 150 feet thick; elsewhere its maximum thickness is not known, and at the edge of individual flows it thins to about 10 feet.

Source vents of the Dorado and related quartz basalts are more numerous than those of any other volcanic rock in the area. They include remnants of cinder cones southwest and south of San Antonio Peak, on the south rim of a depression about 6 miles southeast of the peak, and a cone on the east side of Petaca Mesa.

Age

In the San Juan Mountains, Colorado, basalts of the Hinsdale Formation have ages that range from about 23 m.y. for a body north of Summitville, Colorado, to about 5 m.y. for the average of a dike and flow high on Los Mogotes (Lipman and others, 1970, table 5), about 5 miles north of the map (fig. 2) with this report. The ages of the basalt members of the Hinsdale Formation within the area of the geologic map probably are close to the younger limit of the range. Some of the Lower Member (Cisneros Basalt) north of the Rio de Los Pinos may have come from Los Mogotes, and another body of this basalt, as mentioned above, overlies gravel derived from rhyolite of No Agua Mountain which has a fission track age of 4.8 m.y. (Lipman and others, 1970, p. 2346). The volcanic rocks of the Hinsdale Formation near the east margin of the mountains and west edge of the Taos Plateau in New Mexico appear to have been erupted in a brief time span near the close of Hinsdale volcanism, but radiometric ages of some bodies of basalt are still undetermined.

Quartz Latite Flows of Volcanic Domes

San Antonio Peak and several other domal mountains of the Taos Plateau are constructed largely of two varieties of hypersthene-bearing quartz latite. The more abundant rock on San Antonio Peak is various shades of gray, aphanitic, sparsely porphyritic, and partly vesicular. The other is black, glassy, and breaks with a good conchoidal fracture.

The age of the rock of San Antonio Peak relative to that of basalts of the Hinsdale Formation is unclear, as the contact is obscured by alluvium or slope wash. On rather tenuous evidence it is thought to be younger than the Lower Basalt Member of the Hinsdale (Cisneros Basalt).

SERVILLETA FORMATION

The Servilleta Formation is the youngest unit of the Tertiary sequence in the map area. It is part of the fill of the Rio Grande depression as described by Bryan (1938) rather than a part of the mountain sequence. The western edge of the formation coincides with much of the boundary between the depression and the upland to the west. The contact between the Servilleta Formation and underlying rocks is a slight but distinct unconformity that is suggested largely by the way the basalt flows in it lap on various older rocks at different places. The unconformity can be seen on the southeast rim of the canyon of the Rio de Los Pinos in T. 32 N., R. 8 E. and in a shallow valley west of U.S. Highway 285 about 5.5 miles south of Tres Piedras (fig. 4). The formation is inferred to be younger than the rock of San Antonio Peak, but that relation is not clear.

Flows of basalt that extend from the vicinity of Antonito, Colorado, 5 miles north of the state line, southward 20 miles beyond the limit of the map and underlie much of the Taos Plateau (see Upson, this guidebook, fig. 5) are the most distinctive feature of the formation. Lenticular beds of sand and gravel intertongue with the basalt, but are mostly poorly exposed except in excavations and in the canyon of the Rio Grande, 15 miles east of the area. The fluvial beds, like the basalt, are unconformable on the Los Pinos Formation and on the Santa Fe Formation as used by Smith (1938) and Bryan (1938) and are younger than rocks included in the Santa Fe Group as used by Galusha and Blick (1971). They accumulated in response to relatively late downwarping of the Rio Grande depression and are related in time and position but not in provenance to the basalt.

Basalt of the Servilleta Formation is at least 100 feet thick along part of the course of the Rio San Antonio and about 40 feet thick at places on its west margin in T. 26 N., R. 9 E. Elsewhere within the area its thickness is less than 40 feet or mostly indeterminate. The formation thickens eastward to at least 500 feet along the canyon of the Rio Grande.

Most of the basalt is medium to dark gray, medium to coarse rather even grained, mostly nonporphyritic, and has abundant intergranular pore space, or as Lipman (1969) has mentioned, a diktytaxitic texture. Plagioclase, and olivine, and in some specimens pyroxene, are distinguishable megascopically. The relatively coarse, even grain and porosity of the groundmass are the features by which this basalt generally can be distinguished from the older basalts.

The basalt of the Servilleta Formation is an olivine theoleiite (Aoki, 1967*, and Lipman, 1969) and differs somewhat in chemical composition as well as megascopically from basalt in the Hinsdale Formation. It contains considerably less K_2O, P_2O_5, Sr, Rb, Pb, V, and Th; slightly less Na_2O and TiO_2; and little more Al_2O_3, MgO, and total Fe than alkali olivine basalt of the Hinsdale Formation (Lipman, 1969, p. 1349).

Basalt flows of the Servilleta Formation exposed in the canyon of the Rio Grande northwest of Taos have ages of 3.6 to 4.5 m.y. (Ozima and others, 1967). These are compatible with the stratigraphic position of the formation.

Unlike the effusive and volcaniclastic rocks of the older Tertiary formations, which were spread as vent and clastic apron facies around various volcanic centers, the Servilleta Formation accumulated in an asymmetric, subsiding basin of the Rio Grande depression. The subsidence was induced or accompanied by rifting. Lipman (1969) postulated that the difference in tectonic setting and difference in composition between the tholeiitic basalt of the depression and alkali basalt of the bordering highlands are

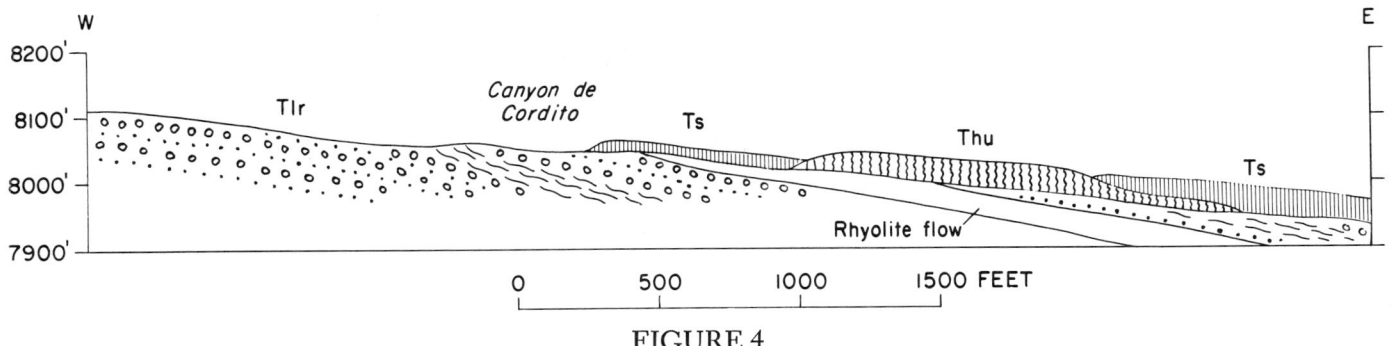

FIGURE 4.

Cross section in the southern part of secs. 10 and 11, T. 27 N., R. 9 E. showing Upper Basalt Member of the Hinsdale Formation (Thu), Dorado Basalt of Barker (1958) resting unconformably on the Rhyolite Member of the Los Pinos Formation (Tlr) and basalt of the Servilleta Formation (Ts) unconformable on both older units.

* Aoki refers to the basalt as "Taos basalts."

STRUCTURE OF THE TERTIARY ROCKS

The Tertiary rocks of the area are mildly deformed by gentle eastward tilting, and most of the units are displaced by normal faults. The Los Pinos Formation and underlying formations commonly dip from 4° to 6°, younger formations mostly less than 3°. North of the latitude of Tres Piedras the strike of the beds is mostly between N. 15° W. and N. 30° W., but at places is east of north. South from there the strike is more northerly.

Several normal faults divide the rocks of the area into tilted blocks that are elongated in a north-northwesterly direction and have relatively steep west slopes and gentle east slopes. North of the Rio San Antonio there are five principal blocks, but south of it, owing to dying out of some faults and merging of others, there are only three.

The principal faults strike north-northwesterly, are downthrown mostly on their southwest sides, and are arranged partly en echelon or connected by northerly to northeasterly striking subsidiary faults in such a way that a more southerly fault is southwest of a more northerly one.

The maximum displacement on a single fault is about 1,200 feet in T. 28 N., R. 6 E., but elsewhere it is mostly less than 500 feet and diminishes to 0 at points where the faults die out.

CONCLUDING REMARKS

Study of the stratigraphy of the Tertiary rocks in the area of the Tusas Mountains reported on here has resulted in showing: (1) that the Los Pinos Formation is largely a product of waning phases of mid-Tertiary volcanism in the southeast extension of the San Juan Mountains; (2) that much of the Los Pinos Formation and the Abiquiu Tuff of Smith are equivalents, a relation further substantiated by Bingler (1968); and (3) that the Los Pinos Formation is mostly older than but also partly contemporaneous with the Santa Fe Formation as used by Smith (1938) rather than younger as once thought (Atwood and Mather, 1932). In addition the Servilleta Formation was recognized as a separate unit more closely related to events that affected the Rio Grande depression than to volcanism in the San Juan field.

ACKNOWLEDGMENTS

The author is particularly indebted to the late Kirk Bryan and Esper S. Larsen, Jr., under whose inspiring guidance the original work was done. He also greatly appreciates the opportunity provided by the New Mexico Geological Society to present a long-dormant account, which has never been formally published; the gracious acknowledgment accorded him by other workers in northern New Mexico, especially Fred Barker (1958), E. C. Bingler (1968), Arthur Montgomery (1953), and W. H. Muehlberger (1968), who have had access to his thesis; and constructive suggestions by P. W. Lipman.

REFERENCES

Aoki, Ken-ichiro, 1967, Petrography and petrochemistry of latest Pliocene olivine-tholeiites of Taos area, northern New Mexico U.S.A.: Contr. Mineralogy and Petrology, v. 14, no. 3, p. 191-203.

Atwood, W. W., and Mather, K. F., 1932, Physiography and Quaternary geology of the San Juan Mountains, Colorado: U.S. Geol. Survey Prof. Paper 166, 176 p.

Barker, Fred, 1958, Precambrian and Tertiary geology of Los Tablas quadrangle, New Mexico: New Mex. State Bur. Mines and Mineral Resources Bull. 45, 104 p.

Bingler, E. C., 1968, Geology and mineral resources of Rio Arriba County, New Mexico: New Mex. State Bur. Mines and Mineral Resources Bull. 91, 158 p.

Bryan, Kirk, 1938, Geology and ground-water conditions of the Rio Grande depression in Colorado and New Mexico, p. 197-225 in Regional planning, pt. 6, Upper Rio Grande: Washington, Natl. Resources Comm., v. 1, pt. 2, sec. 1.

Butler, A. P., Jr., 1946, Tertiary and Quaternary geology of the Tusas-Tres Piedras area, New Mexico: Harvard Univ., Cambridge, Mass., Ph.D. dissert., 188 p.

Cross, Whitman, and Larsen, E. S., 1935, A brief review of the geology of the San Juan region of southwestern Colorado: U.S. Geol. Survey Bull. 843, 138 p.

Galusha, Ted, and Black, John C., 1971, Stratigraphy of the Santa Fe Group, New Mexico: Am. Mus. Nat. History Bull., v. 144, Art. 1, 127 p.

Larsen, E. S., Jr., and Cross, Whitman, 1956, Geology and petrology of the San Juan region, southwestern Colorado: U.S. Geol. Survey Prof. Paper 258, 303 p.

Lipman, P. W., 1969, Alkalic and tholeiitic basaltic volcanism related to the Rio Grande depression, southern Colorado and northern New Mexico: Geol. Soc. America Bull., v. 80, no. 7, p. 1343-1354.

Lipman, P. W., and Steven, T. A., 1970, Reconnaissance geology and economic significance of the Platoro caldera, southeastern San Juan Mountains, Colorado, in Geological Survey Research 1970: U.S. Geol. Survey Prof. Paper 700-C, p. C19-C29.

Lipman, P. W., Steven, T. A., and Mehnert, H. H., 1970, Volcanic history of the San Juan Mountains, Colorado, as indicated by potassium-argon dating: Geol. Soc. America Bull., v. 81, no. 8, p. 2329-2352.

Montgomery, Arthur, 1953, Pre-Cambrian geology of the Picuris Range, north-central New Mexico: New Mex. State Bur. Mines and Mineral Resources Bull. 30, 89 p.

Muehlberger, W. R., 1968, Geology of Brazos Peak quadrangle, New Mexico: New Mex. State Bur. Mines and Mineral Resources Geol. Map. 22.

Ozima, Minoru, Kono, M., Kaneoka, I., Kinoshita, H., Kobayashi, K., Nagata, T., Larsen, E. E., and Strangway, D. W., 1967, Paleomagnatism and potassium-argon ages of some volcanic rocks from the Rio Grande gorge, New Mexico: Jour. Geophys. Research, v. 72, no. 10, p. 2615-2621.

Smith, H. T. U., 1938, Tertiary geology of the Abiquiu quadrangle, New Mexico: Jour. Geology, v. 46, no. 7, p. 933-965.

HISTORICAL SKETCH OF FORT GARLAND

by

WILLIAM HOAGLAND

State Historical Society of Colorado
Fort Garland, Colorado

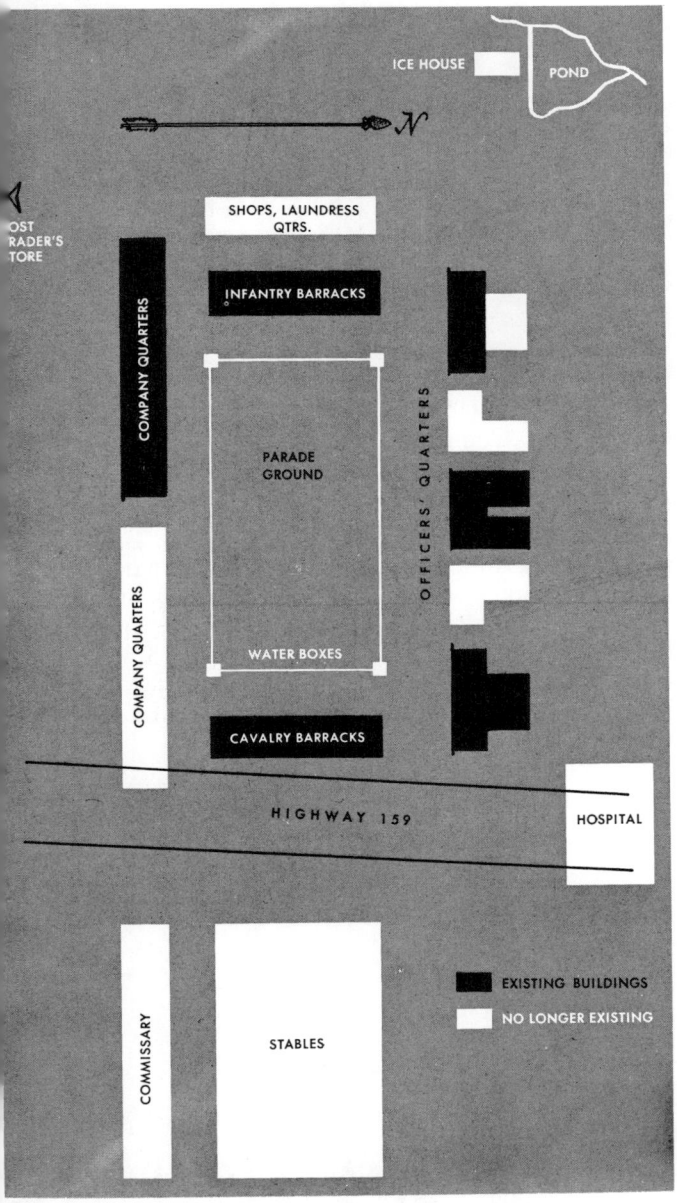

Fort Garland about the time Kit Carson commanded.

An early view of the fort looking northwest from the hill east of the fort. The commissary and stables, no longer existing, are in the foreground.

Fort Garland was established by the War Department in 1858, in what was then the Territory of New Mexico and is now Costilla County, Colorado. It is 25 miles east of Alamosa and 33 miles from the northern boundary of New Mexico.

Fort Garland replaced Fort Massachusetts, which had been built in 1852 six miles north. Fort Massachusetts was abandoned because it was found vulnerable to Indian attack, being so situated that hostiles could fire from the hills down into the fort.

The new fort was named after the commander of the Department of New Mexico, Colonel Brevet Brigadier General John Garland. For 25 years it was a garrison for troops protecting settlers.

The buildings were made of adobe, their interiors plastered with mud and whitewashed with lime. Roofs were of sod. There were board floors, and open fireplaces, with stoves for additional heat. Water was obtained from Ute Creek, by means of an *acequia* (Spanish for canal or

At one time the flagpole was on the south side of the parade ground, near the sally port. Vestibules can be seen on several doors.

trench) flowing around the parade ground. Sanitary provisions, even at the post hospital, were primitive. When the fort was built, the nearest railroad was 950 miles away and six weeks were required for mail to go from Fort Garland to Washington.

The post buildings formed a parallelogram around the parade ground. On the north side were the officers' quarters, on the east the cavalry barracks, on the west the infantry barracks, and on the south were two long buildings which served as offices and store rooms and housed the guard room and adjutant's headquarters.

Fort Garland was built by the men of Company E, U.S. Mounted Riflemen, and Company A, 3rd U.S. Infantry, under Captain Thomas Duncan of the Mounted Riflemen. It was planned for two companies of about 100 men and seven officers.

The two units that constructed the buildings remained at Fort Garland until July, 1860, when they were relieved by Companies A, F and H of the 10th U.S. Infantry, under Major E. R. S. Canby. The 10th Infantry had formed part of the expedition to Utah under Colonel A. S. Johnston during the "Mormon War," and Canby's detachment marched the 640 miles to Fort Garland from Camp Floyd, Utah Territory, near Salt Lake City.

In August, 1860, Company A of the 10th U.S. Infantry left the post to take part in an expedition against the Navajo Indians of New Mexico. In 1861, after the Civil War began, the other units of the 10th were sent to New Mexico, under Canby, except for a small detachment left at Fort Garland.

Two companies of Colorado Volunteers arrived in December, 1861, and were mustered into Federal Service at Fort Garland as Companies A and B, 2nd Colorado Infantry Volunteers. They departed in 1862 to join Canby's forces in New Mexico. During the rest of the Civil War, the Fort Garland garrison consisted largely of volunteers, the regulars all being on duty with the Union forces in the main theaters of the war.

Heads rolled on the ground in front of the Commandant's quarters one day in 1863. During that year a band of desperadoes known as the Espinosas blazed a trail of crime through the San Luis Valley. Military efforts to capture the bandits failed and Lieutenant Colonel Samuel F. Tappan, 1st Colorado Cavalry, then in command at Fort Garland, summoned Tom Tobin and told him to get the Espinosas. Tobin, an old scout, set out with a detachment of one officer and fifteen soldiers. The fourth day out, Tobin found the two bandits, slew them, cut off their heads and placed them in a sack. Riding back to Fort Garland, he called Colonel Tappan from his quarters, and threw the heads out of the sack on the ground at the officer's feet. Thus ended the bloody trail of the Espinosas who had killed at least thirty men. Tom Tobin lived on a ranch in the San Luis Valley many years, and was a member of the Costilla County School Board in 1896.

At war's end, some of the volunteer units were retained in Federal Service pending return of the regular troops to man the western frontier outposts. One of these units was a regiment of New Mexico Volunteers commanded by Kit

Life-size diorama of Kit Carson conferring with Chief Ouray in the Commandant's quarters.

Carson, a colonel and brevet brigadier general. Carson had rendered notable service in action against the Navajos and in 1866 he was ordered to Fort Garland with a detachment of his regiment.

The Ute Indians were warlike, and settlers in the San Luis Valley were justifiably apprehensive. Kit Carson knew the Utes, and had their confidence. His understanding of Indian psychology averted open war and saved the settlements.

Lieutenant General William Tecumseh Sherman made an inspection trip to Fort Garland in 1866. While there he held a conference with Ouray, the chief of the Utes, and

Company D, 15th Infantry camped at Fort Garland, Colorado Territory, March 11, 1872.

ther Indian leaders. General Sherman later paid tribute to Carson's influence for peace.

In the summer of 1867 the Volunteers were mustered out, and Kit Carson with his wife and six children moved to Boggsville, near present Las Animas, Colorado. There, in 1868, Kit Carson became ill and was taken to near-by Fort Lyons, where he died at the age of 58.

Fort Garland was again garrisoned by regulars, sometimes infantry units, sometimes cavalry, and at times, both. War Department records show that detachments of the following regiments served at the fort at various times: 2nd, 3rd, 4th, 7th, 8th and 9th Cavalry, 5th, 10th, 14th, 15th, 19th, 22nd and 37th Infantry.

During the critical period following the Meeker Massacre at White River Agency in 1879, and the subsequent removal of the Uncompahgre Utes to Utah in 1881, the garrison was considerably increased. At one time during this period 1,500 men were at Fort Garland, camping in the fort area.

With the Utes on reservations, and other Indians peaceful, Fort Garland was no longer needed and on November 30, 1883, Fort Garland was abandoned as an active post of the United States Army. Its last garrison was Company A, 22nd Infantry, Captain Javan B. Irvine commanding.

In 1928 a group of public-spirited citizens of the San Luis Valley bought the property to preserve the fort and in 1945 they presented it to the State Historical Society of Colorado for restoration and preservation.

NARROW GAUGE OVER CUMBRES

by

Gordon Chappell

Santa Fe, New Mexico

Shortly after 8:00 a.m. on Wednesday, September 2, 1970, the engineer on locomotive 483 pulled the whistle cord, notched the throttle back an inch or two, and a string of narrow gauge freight cars rolled westbound out of Antonito for the first time in nearly twenty-one months. In the month and a half that followed, train after train of historic rolling stock polished the rusty rails of what had been the Denver And Rio Grande Western narrow gauge main line, and wore down the weeds along a right-of-way, now ninety years old.

It was an historic reversal of a half-century old trend of discontinuance and abandonment which had robbed most Rocky Mountain towns of the railroads which had once served them. Indeed, the *Cumbres And Toltec Scenic Railroad*, a name adopted for the 64 miles of trackage from Antonito, Colorado to Chama, New Mexico, operated more trains over the historic line in two months than the D&RGW had run in two years. Once again the pungent aroma of coal smoke wafted through the lonely rooms of the abandoned section house at Cumbres, and the mournful wail of a steam whistle echoed down the cañons of the River of the Pines.

Cumbres! To say Cumbres Pass is redundant, for "Cumbres" is Spanish and translates as "summits"; Los Cumbres —The Summits. But the name of this 10,015 foot mountain pass is really a word of many meanings. To the tough old soldiers who campaigned out west before the Civil War, Cumbres recalled the site of a bitter battle with Indians fought on its western slope. To an old retired section hand living at Juanita, it meant years spent spiking down rails and maintaining a steep mountain railroad. To hardy engineers such as Ben Greathouse and Bill Holt it recalled bitter winter cold with deep drifts of snow and the danger of winter avalanches which could sweep whole trains into the cañons below. Cumbres connotes days of diamond stacks on locomotives and diamond tiepins on gamblers and mineowners and the beauty of a summer thunder shower on the heights of the Conejos Range.

The story of rails over Cumbres began on October 24, 1879, when Construction Engineer Robert F. Weitbrec huddled with Denver & Rio Grande Chief Engineer J. A. McMurtrie in the latter's South Pueblo office, and drew up a "Plan of Campaign" for the San Juan Extension—also sometimes called the Silverton Extension—in a little notebook bound in red leather. That year the railroad stretched all the way from Denver to Alamosa, and had already been graded from the end of track at Alamosa southward down the San Luis Park to the Conejos River.

Early in November, Weitbrec ran advertisements for bids in local newspapers: "Proposals will be received at the office of the undersigned until noon Nov. 20th, 1879, for the grading of the San Juan Extension of the Denver & Rio Grande Railway . . ." One day after the closing date, the San Juan Extension Company, which was in charge of construction for the railroad, signed contracts for grading and bridging from the Conejos westward to the Rio de Las Animas Perdidas, and the various subcontractors soon had their men at work in the wild hills west of the San Luis Park (later to be called the San Luis Valley).

On February 20, 1880, construction crews commenced laying track south from the railhead at Alamosa on the roadbed which had been built to the Conejos in 1879. From the railroad's new town of Antonito, a short distance south of the Conejos, the company planned simultaneously to build two lines: one southward toward El Paso, the other westward toward Silverton.

Labor was extremely scarce that winter, and the company had to search far and wide. In April, 125 men were shipped from Hayes City, Kansas, and others came from St. Louis and even Chicago. That same month the company advertised in Montreal newspapers for tie cutters:

> De BONS BUCHERONS disposes a aller au Colorado gagner de $3 a $5 par jour, en coupant des ties en bois de pin blanc . . . peuvent obtenir un engagement signe par la "*Denver and Rio Grande Railway Company*" . . .

"Good wood cutters disposed to go to Colorado to earn from $3 to $5 a day cutting white pine ties . . . can obtain a contract signed by the Denver and Rio Grande . . ." Despite labor shortages that required recruiting as far away as Canada, the line was steadily if slowly driven westward, through winter snows and spring rains which turned the Conejos Range into mounds of mud.

The extension company, once rails were being laid, used a "boarding train" of about eight sleeping cars, three dining cars, one cook car, one commissary car, and one store room car. By stretching a point, one might consider this the first "passenger" train on the rails to cross Cumbres.

The line over Cumbres lay in extremely rough country, and construction took more than a year just to reach the Chama River. While most narrow gauge railroads in the Rockies followed streams and their canyons, this particular extension cut across from one watershed to another. From the Conejos it cut across to the Rio de Los Pinos, which it followed awhile, and then over to the watershed of the Rio Chamita, or Little Chama River, by way of Cumbres—which Weitbrec initially referred to as the "Pinos-Chama Summit."

The eastern approach to Cumbres was on a gentle 1.42 per cent grade, but to the west the approach from the Chama River comprised fourteen miles of 4 per cent. Here, in the vicinity of Cumbres, were the two largest bridges on the line, each crossing an insignificant stream: Cascade Creek, eleven miles east of Cumbres, and Wolf Creek (Lobato, in Spanish), nine miles to the west. These deep ravines were temporarily bridged by spindly wooden trestles which were replaced with iron bridges within a year.

The railhead reached the Little Chama River on New Year's Eve, 1880. Here the railroad began a five-stall brick roundhouse, a frame station, and other permanent facilities, for Chama was to become a substantial lumber town, a railroad division point, and the base for helper locomotives needed for the steep grade eastward up to the pass. Track crews meanwhile worked to upgrade the newly completed track from Antonito and prepare it for operations.

On February 1, 1880, a month after the first wobbly rails had reached Chama, the track to that point was transferred from the Extension Company to the railroad, which began running passenger and freight trains over the new line. From Chama, passengers could take J. L. Sanderson & Company stage coaches on to Animas City, Parrott City, Silverton, Rico, and other mining camps in the San Juan Country. Heavy freight wagons, their teams struggling through the axle-deep mud, carried on a brisk commerce between the railhead and the mines.

The El Paso Extension had also been progressing south from the Conejos River towards Santa Fe, though it was destined to be halted temporarily at Espanola by agreement with the AT&SF Railway, and never to extend any further south than Santa Fe. From Chamita on that line, where the Rio Chama emptied into the Rio Grande, the construction engineers began laying out and grading another line to Chama, thus to form a triangle from Antonito to Chama to Chamita. But after forty miles of grading was completed, the project was dropped without rail ever having been laid.

Construction continued westward from Chama. In May the head of track had reached Amargo, 23 miles further west, and was quickly turned over to the railroad so it could get the business west of Chama that otherwise would benefit the Sanderson stages and the numerous wagon freighters.

Over on the Animas River, forty-four miles south of Silverton, the town of Animas City had sprung up in 1876 as a smelter and shipping town supplying the mining camps north and west. But true to its exploitive character, the Denver & Rio Grande had its own plans, and in September, 1880, surveyed a townsite a mile to the south of Animas City which it called Durango after the city of the same name in Mexico. Protest as they might, the citizens of Animas City could do nothing, and Durango took its place, ultimately to absorb completely the pioneer town on the River of Lost Souls. Durango was born in the form of coin jingling in the Rio Grande's pockets.

Telegraph construction was proceeding apace with the railhead, and as the rails reached Arboles, the new wire were flashing news that President James Garfield had been shot by an assassin. Despite optimistic early reports on his condition, the President died. In September, members of the National Association of General Passenger and Ticket Agents held a memorial service alongside the new track in Toltec Gorge just east of Cumbres, and subsequently erected a stone monument which still stands near the west portal of Toltec Tunnel.

In June, Arboles, 37 miles west of Amargo, became the new operating terminus where passengers transferred from the little narrow gauge coaches to the stages. The schedule of the passenger train to this point, according to a time table published on June 12, 1881, called for departure from Denver at 8 a.m. and arrival in Alamosa at 10:25 that night after more than fourteen hours in the rocking little coaches. The train continued right on through the night the little narrow gauge Pullman Palace sleepers swaying through the dark, past La Jara at 11 p.m., Antonito at 11:47, Big Horn at 4:55, Los Pinos at 7 a.m., Cumbres a full day after departure from Denver, and Chama an hour after that. The train reached Amargo, where passenger interchanged for Pagosa Springs, at twenty minutes before noon, and finally halted at the temporary operating terminus at Arboles at 2:35 p.m. It was a long, hard trip even by rail.

The track reached the Florida River early in July, and the grading camp at that site was the scene of a violent gunfight over the ownership of a revolver, resulting in one dead, three badly wounded, and one slightly nicked. Sheriff Hunter from Durango arrested three of the participants—the wounded ones—but the others got away.

Rails finally reached Durango at 5 p.m. on Wednesday July 27, 1881. That afternoon the assayist, F. A. Foin, had made a silver spike from ore from the Junction Creek Mines, and when the track reached G and Railroad Streets, the spike was driven in a little ceremony presided over by Mayor Taylor. But the big celebration was scheduled for August 5, with a special excursion train due to arrive from Alamosa and points east. The town madly threw itself into planning a program including a parade, races, a dance, speeches, a shooting match, and a baseball game between Durango and Silverton teams. Meanwhile, in the next few days a freight and pay train arrived, but there was still no passenger service over the new and still wobbly rails.

On the day of the great celebration, the parade marched up one street and down another, but still no train appeared. Finally, J. L. Pennington announced to the crowd that the train had been delayed by washouts, and the people had to go ahead without the excursionists.

Weather had seemed to conspire against the Denver & Rio Grande all during those two years of construction. It was not the snowstorms themselves that caused most of the trouble, but the melting snows of spring, coupled with spring and summer rains. On the line over Cumbres, fills

Famous William H. Jackson view taken during the eighties typifies early day operation over the Cumbres Pass line. The location is Big Horn, 17 miles west of Antonito, in the foothills. Here the track passes up the near side of the valley (foreground), loops around to the left and climbs the opposite side where the train is standing. After making another loop behind the hill, the track can be seen behind the train, still higher, on a third level. The train would appear to be a regular passenger during the period when Pullmans were not run beyond Alamosa; baggage-mail, coach and chair car are drawn by one of the three small 1883 eightwheelers of Class 42½. (State Historical Society of Colo.)

Big Horn

settled and cuts sloughed in over the rails. Swollen streams attacked new and untried bridges. A new railroad track undergoes a process of appreciation over a considerable period; the fills solidify and wild grasses cover bare earth and fight erosion. The track becomes more solid over a period of months before the counter process of depreciation sets in. The Cumbres line was still new and raw and unduly susceptible to the elements. The day before the great celebration in Durango rain fell heavily from noon 'till four southeast of Durango, and the Rio Navajo tore out one bent of the railroad bridge. Even then a train might have been run out of Durango to pick up passengers who could have crossed the stream on foot where the train could not, but four miles to the west, the same rains washed out a large fill, leaving a gap trains could not cover which was too great for passengers to walk. Durango's initial experience with the railroad was not exactly auspicious.

Durango was not the end of the line anyway; it was merely a stop on the extension to Silverton. Engineer Thomas Wigglesworth and a survey and grading party were already at work in the canyon above Rockwood, where his men were lowered over the cliff with ropes and scaling ladders to locate the line and drill and blast the rocks. Track-laying ceased temporarily at Durango and some workmen were transferred to the Gunnison Extension, but on October 3, 1881, crews began laying rails northward to Rockwood, which they reached December 11, before stopping for the worst of the winter.

Near the end of the following March the company resumed laying track north from Rockwood, but three miles into the canyon ran out of rail, and had to discharge the construction crews until more arrived. The Colorado Coal and Iron Company of South Pueblo had failed to deliver rails on schedule. These rails, first to be rolled in Colorado, were made on April 28 and 29, 1882, and finally reached the Silverton Extension late in May, when tracklaying resumed and reached Silverton on July 8.

Surveyors continued running their lines over canyon and pass, from Silverton to Howardsville and Red Mountain, from Hermosa to Rico, from Durango to Dolores and Rico, and wherever there seemed business for the tentacles of steel. But the Denver and Rio Grande had overextended itself, and it would be left to other companies to build further into the San Juan Mountains.

Now the railroad could run the passenger trains over the whole line from Denver to the silver camps on the Rio de Las Animas Perdidas—the River of Lost Souls.

On April 22, 1883, the railway issued its twenty-second employees' timetable. The new Alamosa-Silverton line was a part of the Second Division, administered by Superintendent Cole Lydon from Alamosa. The passenger train over Cumbres was Number 5 westbound and Number 6 in the other direction. Leaving Denver at 2:35 in the afternoon, it struggled over Veta Pass and reached Alamosa at 3:55 a.m. Continuing on down the valley, at 5:15 it was heading westward from Antonito, and by dawn it was climbing through the sagebrush toward the forested slopes of the Conejos Range. At 6:35 a.m., the little 4-4-0 locomotive pulled into Big Horn, where the railroad operated a small eating house and the passengers had twenty minutes in which to step down and eat breakfast. At 6:55 the engineer whistled off and headed his train for Tolte Gorge and the pass. At 8:20 the engine was passing Osier at 8:40 Los Pinos. At 9:20 it was at the summit, where there was a water tank, a station, and a snowshed-covered wye. Besides water, coal was available at Sublette, Osier Los Pinos and Cumbres. Ahead lay Coxo, Siding No. 9 Lobato, and Chama. Chama had a roundhouse and shops and the railroad's boarding and eating house, where the train paused for another twenty-minute meal stop, though it was yet only the middle of the morning.

Leaving Chama at 10:55, the passenger train went on through Willow Creek and Azotea and Monero, the coal mining town. Three minutes after noon it was in Amargo here was the connection with Pagosa Springs. At the Springs in those years was an army camp, soon to be moved to the new Fort Lewis west of Durango. The military operated its own stage service with the customary use of army ambulances as passenger vehicles. On specified days when Indians from the nearby Jicarilla Apache agency were to be issued their annuities, Amargo was a busy little camp with an ample supply of soldiers on hand, the yellow trouser strips of cavalry mixing with the light blue of infantry, and the Eugenie bonnets of curious officers' wives and daughters bobbing among the spectators. Old Christopher Carson, the famous "Kit" Carson, dead since '68, had whipped these Indians two decades earlier, and they were a pretty tame lot by the time the railroad came through.

But that could *look* menacing enough, and one engineer recalled the ominous crowd which had gathered around his work-train engine near Ignacio one day. Despite a spell of hot weather, he had locked himself in the cab, acutely aware of the Winchester which hung from the cab roof. But those dusky faces, so solemn and strange to him, signified curiosity more than hostility, and Indian troubles were about the only kind the railroad didn't face.

Westward lay Dulce, Navajo, Juanita, and Carracas, where at 1:25 the eastbound and westbound trains met and passed. The little train was now nearing the end of its run as it steamed into Durango at 4:25 p.m.

At Durango the passengers had a brief ten minute layover before continuing on toward Silverton. At Hermosa, eleven miles north of Durango, the passenger northbound passed a side-tracked southbound freight at 5:25. It took another half hour to climb through the pine-studded hills to Rockwood, a full hour to run from Rockwood through the canyon of the River of Lost Souls to Cascade siding. At 7:10 the little train was at Needleton, under the brooding spires of the aptly named Needle Mountains; forty minutes later coal smoke from the train was drifting through Elk Park and around Garfield Peak. Finally, at 8:20 p.m., the weary passengers could step down onto the wooden station platform in Silverton and board a horse-drawn hack for one of the hotels uptown. The engine would be put away in the little two-stall roundhouse which stood a couple of hundred feet south of the station, on the other side of the tracks.

Silverton, which had been a thriving mining camp since

the early 1870's, lay in a particularly beautiful setting. Baker's Park—"park" was frontier terminology for a high mountain valley surrounded by peaks—was a small flat meadow only a mile or so in diameter, ringed by towering peaks separated by four canyons. Two on the north and one on the west fed mountain streams into the park, and in the southwestern corner the precipitous canyon of the River of Lost Souls drained the glacial waters toward the San Juan. In the center of the park, amid alpine grasses, lay the dirt streets and the log, frame, brick and stone buildings of Silverton, containing a variety of Victorian hotels, saloons, druggists, assayists, wagon freighters, brothels, and all of the typical establishments of a frontier mining town. The arrival of the railroad was stimulating an already booming economy, and within two decades each of the four canyons which met in Baker's Park would boast its own individual narrow gauge. But in 1883 the newly completed Denver & Rio Grande Railway alone spit its fiery cinders of coal into the rare mountain air.

The passenger returning from Silverton to Denver had to be on the cars by six in the morning for the run down the canyon to Durango. Reaching the latter town at 9:35, the train paused but ten minutes, and then headed east to Arboles, where at 12:32 the passengers were given an 18-minute lunch stop. The train reached Cumbres at 5:48 in the evening and Alamosa not until 11 p.m. Then Denver-bound passengers would not reach their destination until a quarter after noon the next day. The Victorian opulence of the cars, both inside and out, hardly compensated for the fatigue of the thirty hour trip from Silverton to Denver.

The regular through passenger trains would operate under varied names down through the years. At first the westbound was called the *Durango Mail*, and the eastbound, logically, the *Denver Mail*, attesting to the importance of the federal postal contracts which played an important part in supporting the trains. At one time the westbound was known as the *Colorado, New Mexico and San Juan Express*, while in the other direction it was the *San Juan, New Mexico and Colorado Express*—the sequence merely reversed with direction. Around the turn of the century the passenger trains were called the *Colorado and New Mexico Express*, and then a couple of decades later, as the *San Juan and New Mexico Express*. In its last years, the passenger route was known as the *San Juan Express*.

The engines with their Russia-iron boiler jackets and gold lettering, and the little Tuscan red passenger coaches, varnished to a mirror-finish with gold-leaf striping and gold lettering above the windows, hauled a steady flow of tourists and travelers over the heights of Cumbres. In the earliest years little 4-4-0 locomotives hauled the "varnish," but they were soon replaced with heavier 4-6-0 passenger engines of the 160-174 series. Diamond stacks remained on most of the freight engines until about 1910, but the passenger engines lost theirs before the turn of the century.

In the later '80s, under the direction of its General Passenger and Ticket Agent, "Major" Shadrack K. Hopper, the Denver & Rio Grande began to advertise "Around the Circle" tours, and coaches were especially lettered for that service. There was at that date no complete narrow gauge circle, but the gap, between Silverton and Ouray, was a small one. Out of Denver the traveler road to Pueblo, Walsenburg, over Veta Pass to Alamosa, over Cumbres to Durango, and north to Silverton. There he boarded one of the Watson stages for the jolting ride over spectacular Sheridan Pass (later to be called Red Mountain Pass) to Ouray. At Ouray, after 1887 he could again board the railroad to ride north to Montrose and then east over the main line from Salt Lake City via Gunnison, Salida and the Royal Gorge to Pueblo.

In succeeding years, the narrow gauge circle was modified by railroad growth in the San Juan country and in the San Luis Park. In 1887 toll-road builder Otto Mears began his Silverton Railroad which was in the 1890's to connect Silverton over Red Mountain Pass with Ironton, leaving but a nine mile gap between the latter camp and Ouray for Watson's stages to complete. In 1890, Mears began laying the rails of the Rio Grande Southern Rail road from Ridgeway (on the D&RG's Ouray Branch) to tap the mining camps of Ophir and Telluride. In the next two years, he completed the new line all the way south and east over Lizard Head Pass, through Rico and Dolores and Mancos and over Cima Summit to Durango. In 1892 the circle of narrow gauge rails was complete!

But of course the western end of the circle constituted 160 miles of railroad not owned by the Denver & Rio Grande, and the latter preferred not to give business to the new RGS if it could avoid doing so. Consequently Major Hooper's advertising pamphlets, while they did include the RGS, continued to feature the route via Silverton and the short Silverton Railroad with the connecting nine-mile stage trip from Ironton to Ouray.

A more important modification to the narrow gauge circle occurred to the east in 1890. From Mears Junction, on the main line from Salida over Marshall Pass to Salt Lake City, southward over Poncha Pass to Villa Grove in the San Luis Valley and on to the iron mines at Orient on its eastern edge, the railroad had in 1881 built a branch line to carry ore. Spurred by the possibilities of a great farming boom in the northern end of the broad valley, in 1890 the Rio Grande connected Villa Grove with Alamosa. The 53 miles of narrow gauge track was entirely straight between the two points, unique on the Rio Grande system. Upon its completion, this connection bisected the existing narrow gauge circle, creating for a brief period two narrow gauge circles, the one westward via the Rio Grande Southern and another to the east via Walsenburg and Pueblo.

The company meanwhile had been experimenting with standard gauge since 1888. By 1890 third rail (forming a dual gauge utilizing one rail in common) had been laid from Denver to Trinidad, and the company had already begun removing the middle rail which formed the narrow gauge on selected segments, leaving a standard gauge to replace the dual gauge. In 1891 the middle rail was lifted from the dual gauge between Pueblo and the town of La Veta (not Veta Pass), thus converting the eastern end of the old narrow gauge circle to standard gauge. And so after 1891, the narrow gauge circle was a smaller one connected from Alamosa to Salida on the eastern edge, rather

Two photos: State Historical Society of Colo.

Toltec Gorge

As the rails climb higher towards Cumbres, the valley below grows ever deeper, and the terrain more spectacular. Nearing Toltec, the line circles around raw volcanic rock outcroppings such as those at right—being smokily negotiated by diamond-stacked 2-8-0s nos. 43 and 202. A few miles beyond, after passing through the second of the only two tunnels on the entire D&RG narrow gauge, the line bursts out over the breath-taking precipice of Toltec Gorge. The two views here (one taken from a rock promontory only part way down into the Gorge) are probably of the same train, apparently a construction special at the time the line was being built. The precarious wooden trestle-work was later replaced by a substantial rock wall and fill.

than from Alamosa to Walsenburg, Pueblo, and Salida.

The immediate consequence of this change was the necessity of rerouting both the narrow gauge freight traffic and the passenger trains from Denver and Pueblo to the San Juan country, to go through the Royal Gorge to Salida and over Poncha Pass to Alamosa, rather than by way of Walsenburg and Veta Pass.

A timetable for January, 1896, showed the *Colorado & New Mexico Express* leaving Denver at 7:45 p.m. and arriving at Salida at 4:30 a.m., while the passengers were still asleep in their coaches or, in the case of the more affluent ones, in the Pullman Palace Car sleepers. After a fifteen minute layover in Salida, the *Express* headed up the grade to Mears Junction, where it turned south to cross Poncha Pass. The long, monotonous stretch of straight track in the semi-desert northern end of the San Luis Valley was crossed as dawn broke over the heights of the Sangre de Cristo Range, and indeed the red alpenglow of the first rays of the morning sun on the snows of Mount Blanca seemed to resemble the blood of Christ for which the Spanish conquistadors of a past century had named the peaks. At 8:15 the little train reached Alamosa, and its yawning occupants stepped down for breakfast. They had a brief 25 minutes in which to eat. From there westward the schedule was typical of earlier years to Durango, which the *Express* reached, if on time, at 6:45 p.m. These were years when the Durango-Silverton line was handled as a branch, and it was necessary for the passenger to stay overnight in one of the hotels before boarding the Silverton "accommodation" train at 7:30 the next morning.

That was not a good decade for the railroad. In 1892 the price of silver began a decline from which it never recovered; and the flood of mining ventures, which had impelled the railroad to throw out its octopus-like tentacles in every direction, suddenly evaporated, leaving the Denver and the Rio Grande high and dry. The financial crisis reached its zenith in the summer of 1893. The "Panic of 1893," as it came to be called, was in some respects the worst depression of the century, and lasted nearly four years. About eight thousand American businesses collapsed, and dozens of railroads went into receivership. The Sherman Silver Purchase Act of 1890 was, oddly enough, permitting a disastrous drain of gold from the treasury, and a reluctant President Cleveland was forced to call for its repeal. Although friends of silver in Congress announced that "Hell would freeze over" before they repealed the act, Cleveland nevertheless forced the measure through, and in November the government placed a ban on the purchase of silver for coinage purposes. It was a blow from which many mining camps never recovered. Coming as it did a mere decade after the Denver and Rio Grande had reached most of the camps, its effect on the railroad was not much less disastrous. Visions of future earnings disappeared before the directors' eyes.

A new timetable of November 12, 1899, introduced yet another major change in the operation of the *Colorado and New Mexico Express*. An entirely new standard gauge line had been built over La Veta Pass, by-passing by many miles the old narrow gauge Veta Pass route. Now a standard gauge train made the trip from Denver and Pueblo to Alamosa overnight, providing coach and Pullman sleeper service; the narrow gauge train for Durango made an early morning connection. Initially Pullman sleepers continued to be provided on the narrow gauge portion of the journey, but as it was a daylight trip of reasonable length the sleepers were soon dispensed with—for all time. Actually, Pullman sleeper service on the narrow gauge had been rather flexible for the entire two decades. There is evidence that sleepers were run right through to Silverton for a few months after service was begun, but thereafter sleeper service seems to have been terminated at Durango. During the '80s Pullmans were in short supply on the narrow gauge, and for a great deal of this time no sleeper service was offered west of Alamosa, although "chair cars" were provided in such cases in addition to coaches. After the main line was standard gauged in 1890, Pullmans were available and were then operated through from Denver to Durango via Salida a great deal of the time. Even then—in 1894, for example—there were times when sleeper service was offered on a Denver-Salida and Salida-Durango basis, which certainly must have been inconvenient.

After dropping of the through train via Salida, the Valley Line north of Alamosa remained a part of the Third Division operated from Salida, and was served by a little mixed train. (The lines west of Alamosa were by this time known as the Fourth Division.)

By 1905 it seemed necessary to build a branch south from Durango to Farmington to preempt the grade, primarily in order to keep the Southern Pacific's subsidiary, the Arizona & Colorado Railroad, from building into S.P. coal holdings near Durango, as well as to capture the agricultural traffic of the Farmington basin. The Farmington branch was built standard gauge using equipment shipped dismantled over the narrow gauge main line across Cumbres and assembled in Durango. This was done in anticipation of building a standard gauge line into Durango; after all, the rest of the system was being progressively standard gauged, and inevitably, the management thought, this would happen west of Alamosa. Further steps in that direction were taken in 1909 when the bridges at Cascade and Wolf Creeks were replaced with steel bridges of standard gauge dimensions. About the same time, section crews began using standard gauge ties in the tie replacement program.

Another plan developed around 1915 contemplated by-passing Cumbres and building an entirely new standard gauge line from South Fork, west of Alamosa, over the mountains to Juanita, and standard gauging the line from Juanita into Durango. Including an estimated $300,000 for improving shop facilities in Alamosa and Durango, the anticipated cost of the proposed line was $4,800,000. Still another step recommended by the D&RG engineering department was the building of a standard gauge from Arboles down the San Juan River to Farmington, thence up the La Plata Valley through Mancos into the Montezuma Valley. But the railroad was beset with financial ills, due in part to the Western Pacific burden, and its management became preoccupied with economizing. The

Farmington branch remained an orphan standard gauge segment isolated by narrow gauge on all sides, until 1923. Following a petition from Farmington citizens to change the gauge in order to eliminate the interchange problem in Durango, the railroad management resigned itself to the fact there was no immediate prospect of building standard gauge from Alamosa to Durango, and one weekend had the Farmington line narrowed to conform with the rest.

These same decades witnessed continual modernization of equipment. Due to an interstate commerce law, the Rio Grande was required to have automatic couplers on its equipment by September, 1903; the railroad had neglected to do this, and was forced into a crash program to apply knuckle couplers to the freight cars. The passenger equipment had been built with Miller Hook Couplers, which qualified as automatic; however, it was necessary gradually to change the Miller to knuckle in order to standardize couplings on locomotives and to permit mixed train service.

The same economy drive that doomed extensions and relocations in the San Juan country resulted in changes to passenger color schemes. On October 22, 1912, the Superintendent of Motive Power and the Car Department, J. F. Enright, wrote from Burnham that due to the expense, the railroad had decided to discontinue striping the passenger equipment with gold paint. At the same time, he decided to phase out the use of imitation gold paint for the remaining lettering and to go back to the use of genuine gold leaf, as the additional expense for the real article was more than compensated for by the fact it lasted considerably longer.

Six years later the whole paint scheme was changed. On September 6, 1918, Enright's successor, W. W. Leman, wrote the division superintendents:

> We have in the past, painted our narrow gauge equipment a Tuscan red, but as economy will result from the use of the Pullman [green] color, as we figure about 3 months longer service and $1.25 per car less cost for material, wish you would arrange hereafter as narrow gauge equipment passes through the shop, to adopt the Pullman color as our standard.

Since this was to be done only as cars came in for other repairs, the *San Juan & New Mexico Express* soon assumed a mixed color scheme, with shiny, freshly painted Pullman green cars among faded and weathered Tuscan red coaches. Gold remained the color used for lettering.

What was it like to travel over Cumbres on the *San Juan & New Mexico Express* of say, 1919? Let's travel back in time and see.

The eight little passenger cars, same red, some green, await their customers at the Alamosa depot in the early rays of the morning sun. At 7 a.m., the engineer on No. 172 pulls twice on the whistle cord, eases back the throttle, and they are off and running. Ahead lies the 29 miles of nearly straight and level track down the valley, through the little towns of Henry, Estrella, La Jara, Bountiful, and Romeo. Arriving at Antonito at 8:20, the passengers spy another little 4-6-0 locomotive waiting outside the single-track, two-locomotive capacity engine house, waiting for passenger coaches to be added to its freight cars so it can go about its business as the *Denver and Santa Fe Mixed*. A baggage-mail car and two coaches are cut out of the *San Juan* for the trip to Santa Fe, and will reach the New Mexican capital at 4:25 that afternoon.

The remaining five cars of the *San Juan & New Mexico Express* depart Antonito westward for the heights of Cumbres, where clouds are already beginning to gather for afternoon thundershowers. Ahead lies wild mountain country, with nothing along the railroad but a few section houses until the top of the pass is reached. Oddly, the Conejos Range is almost entirely devoid of mining ventures; timber remains its primary resource. The little engine puffs steadily up the moderate grade, spewing diamond-hard cinders of coal everywhere—into eyes, pockets, purses, carpetbags. The railroad climbs in and out of side canyons which pour their streams into the Los Pinos, not even pausing at the double loop at Big Horn, once the breakfast stop for passengers in the 1880's. A little further is the "Mud Tunnel," its insubstantial earthen walls reinforced with timbers, and the spectacular conglomerate needles of Phantom Curve towering above the little train. Finally the rock tunnel at Toltec looms ahead, and just out of the west portal the *San Juan* makes a five minute stop to enable passengers to gape at the thousand-foot depths and read the inscription on the Garfield Monument. Just out of the west portal of the tunnel the track originally crossed a short wooden trestle built on stonework foundations against the cliff wall; by 1905 the railroad had replaced this with a solid fill and safer, impressive rock wall.

Rolling down the track again, the train soon passes Osier, now nothing more than a section house and tank, but in construction days a roaring log-cabin town. The country ahead is green with wild grasses, but the hills are sparsely forested, never having recovered their growth after the disastrous fire which swept the Los Pinos area in 1879. The canyon has become a shallow valley, and soon the train is just a few feet above the River of the Pines. After crossing the little stream, the rails curve back in a huge horseshoe and begin the final climb up Cumbres Creek. Through another double horseshoe, a much sharper one called Tanglefoot Curve, the *San Juan* gains final altitude and is at the top. Here is a station, section house, a water tank, and a snowshed-covered wye. Members of the crew make an inspection of the airbrakes which will be sorely needed on the steep descent to Chama, and again the train is off and running. This afternoon on the return eastbound trip the *Express* will require a helper engine, probably a 2-8-0 locomotive of the 200 or 400 series, to climb this steep grade to the top.

On schedule, the train slows to a stop in Chama at one minute to noon, and the conductor announces a twenty-one minute lunch stop. The Chama yard is full of engines and cars, some locomotives switching, others waiting to make hill turns—hauling a small number of freight cars up the steep grade to the summit, where the cars will be set out on a siding and the double or triple-headed engines

West of Toltec Gorge, lies the lonely, windswept station of Osier. Here 478 has just made its station stop.

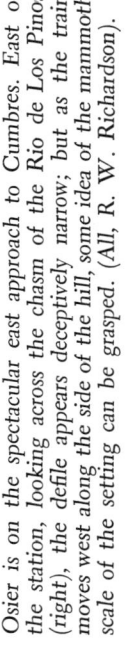

Osier

Osier is on the spectacular east approach to Cumbres. East of the station, looking across the chasm of the Rio de Los Pinos (right), the defile appears deceptively narrow; but as the train moves west along the side of the hill, some idea of the mammoth scale of the setting can be grasped. (All, R. W. Richardson).

will repeat the process until there are enough cars at the top to make up a train for the downhill run east to Alamosa. Chama in 1919 is a busy railroad and lumbering town, permeated by the pungent aroma of coal smoke, the hiss of steam, and the scream of whistles.

Westward from Chama the little train puffs over the Continental Divide near Willow Creek. Contrary to popular assumption, Cumbres, the highest point on the railroad, is *not* the divide, which is actually crossed in unimpressive foothill country that hardly seems to be the "crest of the continent."

Onward the train runs, through Azotea, past Biggs Spur, and into the coal-mining town of Monero. Monero is where the eastbound and westbound passenger trains meet and pass. Westward from Monero is Amargo, of little importance since the days when it was end of track, and Lumberton and Dulce.

At Lumberton, two other railroads joined the Rio Grande. In 1895, E. M. Biggs (who had operated a lumber railroad built three miles south of Chama in 1888, and extended another eleven and a half miles in 1896 to Ensenada) formed the New Mexico Lumber Company and incorporated the Rio Grande and Pagosa Springs Railroad to build north from Lumberton. The company had established its shops in a new town called Edith, after Biggs' little daughter, six miles north of Lumberton. The RG&PS was a typical lumber line whose branches wandered around the canyons of the Navajo River and its tributaries. Eventually its rails reached within five miles of Pagosa Springs, but by 1901 another railroad had already connected the resort town with the D&RG. Later, in 1903, the Chama lumber spur was torn up and the rail relaid south of Lumberton to El Vado for the Rio Grande & Southwestern, another new firm owned by Biggs, though it was built with D&RG assistance and the latter planned to absorb it as a part of a connection between Lumberton and Chamita. The RG&PS, meanwhile, had been washed out by the great floods of 1911 and never rebuilt, and its equipment transferred to the Rio Grande & Southwestern. A spur to Gallinas Mountain, another seven miles, was added to the RG&SW's original 33 miles in 1918. A short distance westward, another lumber line ran south, this one from Dulce, operated by both Biggs' New Mexico Lumber and the Sullenbergers' Pagosa Lumber Company.

The *San Juan Express* might pick up a casual passenger or two from any of these connecting lines, but there are no scheduled trains waiting to meet it.

At Pagosa Junction, however, it is a different matter. The Rio Grande, Pagosa & Northern Railroad, incorporated by the Pagosa Lumber Company, had built north from this point in 1901, using D&RG rails and ties and their own labor. Later operations were taken over by the D&RG, and a mixed train connects with the *Express*—although the number company still operates lumber spurs stretching many miles into the woods. The *San Juan & New Mexico Express* is scheduled to arrive at Pagosa Junction, located on Cat Creek (Gato, in Spanish), at 2:35 p.m. Five minutes later the *Denver & Pagosa Springs Mixed* pulls out for the resort springs.

Westward lay the small farming and ranching towns of the San Juan River Valley, and the Ute Indian Reservation town of Ignacio, named for a famous chief. At 5:2? p.m. the *San Juan* pulls into Durango. Here the passenge could stay overnight and take the mixed train to Farming ton on the standard gauge segment, known locally as the *Red Apple Flyer*. Here also the D&RG connects with the Rio Grande Southern, whose passenger train goes on to Mancos, Dolores, Rico, Ophir, Telluride, and Ridgway to complete the west end of the narrow gauge circle.

Just after pulling into the Durango station a baggage mail car and a coach are uncoupled, and the remnant of the train—a baggage car, a coach, and the parlor car, still constituting the *San Juan Express*—departs for Silverton arriving at 8:35 p.m., and our trip of half a century ago is completed.

While the line from Durango to Silverton was considered a branch and had a daytime mixed train which would long outlast the *San Juan*, still the *San Juan & New Mexico Express* of 1919 was a through train from Denver to Silverton, and Durango was merely a 15 minute stop enroute, not the terminus.

The returning eastbound *San Juan* had to leave Silverton at 6:20 in the morning in order to arrive in Alamosa at 8:10 p.m. Trains frequently were late, delayed by weather or man, and even when on time it was a long, hard trip.

These were years of great variety in equipment used over Cumbres. The heaviest of the narrow gauge engines, the K-27 "Mudhens" built in 1903, provided helper service from Chama to the pass, after heavier second-hand 65-pound (weighing 65 lbs. per yard) rail had been laid on that fourteen and a half miles of the route in 1913. But they were outlawed east and west of that short segment of track by the 40- and 45-pound rail which remained. They had to be hauled to Chama dead, at the rear of freight trains, as the rails from Alamosa to Cumbres were too light to carry a K-27 loaded with coal and water. Most frequently used on the steep grade up Cumbres were some of the C-16 and C-19 2-8-0 "Consolidation" type freight locomotives, one of which, No. 406, a Baldwin product of 1881, was named "Cumbres."

In 1923 a passenger on the *San Juan* could observe even more widely varied styles of locomotive in helper service on Cumbres. A shop strike left the Rio Grande increasingly short of power as it was unable to effect necessary repairs, and consequently had to borrow engines from neighboring narrow gauge lines. On August 21, for instance, RGS 12 was to be seen struggling over Lobato Trestle with a haul of merchandise; in September and October Silverton Northern 34 was noted working on the west slope of the pass.

That same year the company completed relaying the whole line from Antonito to Durango with 70 pound rail. This permitted "Mudhen" locomotives of the 450-464 series to be used over the whole line, along with new 470-series "Sports Model" engines then being built by the American Locomotive Company. The "Mudhens" and the new 470-series engines were all of the 2-8-2 "Mikado" pattern and were of outside frame construction, offering quite a contrast to the earlier and much lighter inside-frame 2-8-0's.

Similar relaying of rail on the Santa Fe Branch began at that time, but was carried out sporadically and in haphazard fashion, resulting in a mixture of 45, 52, 57, 65, and 70 pound rail installed in the late 1920's. Nevertheless, by 1934 the line had rail of sufficient weight to carry the relatively new 470-class engines. The two-stall engine house which protected Chili line engines at Antonito was torn down, and common practice from then until the line was abandoned in 1941 was to run the *San Juan Express* double-headed down the San Luis Valley from Alamosa, the train then splitting at Antonito to go in different directions.

The depression years were to be the beginning of a long decline in railroad service in the San Juan country. All over the Rio Grande system branch lines were pared away and service cut back. But this was not essentially a product of the depression, although the crash of 1929 undoubtedly aggravated the situation. As early as 1915 the automobile began making substantial inroads on railroad passenger traffic across the nation, and the rapid development of motor stages—as busses were initially called—as well as trucking firms, all cut into railroad revenues.

One of the Rio Grande's first answers to truck competition was to begin hauling "less-than-carload" freight—"l.c.l." in railroad parlance—in extra baggage cars on the *San Juan Express* in 1925. Hauling such freight on a passenger schedule permitted the railroad to compete more effectively with truck lines. An answer to bus competition was the modernization of passenger equipment. In 1937 the railroad rebuilt some of the original open-platform coaches into closed vestibule coaches, with electric lights replacing the original coal-oil lamps and with more modern sanitary arrangements. A stainless-steel kitchen and a dinette section were added to the parlor cars, and for the first time in its history, passengers could eat on the train. They could even make advance arrangements for special menus, steak for instance, and the steward would then purchase the necessary items for the specified day's trip. The *San Juan* steward also served as an ice cream vendor to children on the Indian reservations and in the little settlements along the line; the parlor car carried ice cream and a stock of cones on board, a very popular service along the border. The steward normally delivered newspapers all along the route. He could also be persuaded to buy small items, such as thread, for families living in remote country served by the railroad; local residents would give him money and a shopping list one day, and he would return with the merchandise on the next.

The vestibuled equipment was used only on the *San Juan Express*, however, and open platform coaches, little changed from the 80's, still rolled to Silverton and Santa Fe.

But at the same time the railroad was taking such constructive measures as hauling l.c.l. freight in baggage cars to compete with trucking schedules on the dirt road over Wolf Creek Pass and modernizing the passenger equipment to retain and attract business, the management was adopting other policies which worked toward the reduction of the railroad's revenues in the San Juan country.

These policies were referred to as the philosophy of "total transportation." If the railroad could not compete with trucks and busses, so some executives reasoned, then it would go into the trucking and bus business also, and compete with the opposition on its own terms. What management overlooked was the fact that the company was undercutting its own rail lines by so doing.

It was in the late 1920's that the railroad began buying into trucking lines, and in April, 1930, several such firms were consolidated as the Rio Grande Motorway, Inc. Increasingly the new company scheduled truck and bus traffic in direct competition with the rail lines; indeed, during the early 1940's, Motorways President T. L. James admitted that one of the justifications for railroad ownership of truck and bus lines was "to substitute highway service on branch lines operating at substantial losses . . ." Branch lines could not be torn up without Interstate Commerce Commission approval, but by operating competing highway service the railroad could sap revenues from parallel rail lines, thus showing increasing losses as justification for abandonment. Freight intended to go by rail ended up traveling by truck, and the revenue went to fatten the Motorways' annual reports while the railroad line starved. A stockman would order a specified number of narrow gauge cars to haul his sheep to market; on the appointed day an equivalent number of Motorways trucks would appear instead. The Durango Chamber of Commerce protested such practices as early as 1941, and said that it felt the D&RGW was following "a well-organized scheme to abandon all narrow gauge railroad operations in southwestern Colorado."

The negative attitude of the Denver & Rio Grande Western toward narrow gauge passenger service in later years was often obvious. Some agents, particularly those in Denver, would even deny the existence of any such train as the *San Juan Express*, and would sell tickets on Motorways busses instead. Nor was the practice restricted to Denver. In 1941 one passenger had to argue with the Alamosa agent for a rail ticket to Durango. The agent insisted on selling him a Motorways bus ticket that he didn't want; finally the exasperated customer had to threaten to come around behind the counter and make out his own rail ticket before the agent would do it for him.

But the railroad was not alone in undermining the *Express*; equally disastrous for the passenger train from Alamosa to Durango was a 1938 action by the railroad labor unions. The brotherhoods at that time challenged the practice of handling l.c.l. freight in baggage cars, demanding extra pay for the switching involved. In 1939 the Railroad Labor Board awarded the train crews *ninety thousand dollars* in back claims from the railroad, and prohibited further l.c.l. shipment on the passenger train unless the railroad paid the crews freight handling salaries *in addition* to their regular passenger wages. That killed the l.c.l. business and made it impossible for the railroad to compete with truckers in l.c.l. handling. It was a blow from which the *San Juan Express* never financially recovered. The railroad brotherhoods got their tribute, but in the long run they helped kill off the train and put many of their own members out of jobs, a scathing indictment of the shortsightedness of brotherhood leadership.

Meanwhile, the management had indeed drawn up plans for eventual abandonment of its narrow gauge lines. The ultimate goal of the railroad was to exist as a "bridge railroad," a railroad with no branches and no local traffic, hauling freight in carload lots from one end of the system to the other.

The first to go was the Pagosa Springs branch, abandoned and the track removed in 1936. Next was the "Chili Line" from Antonito to Santa Fe. Trucking, adverse freight rates, and the disastrous decision prohibiting handling of l.c.l. freight in baggage cars had taken their toll, and the railroad was able to prove a substantial loss. Despite bitter opposition, including a United States Senate hearing, the branch was abandoned and the track torn up in 1941. (Other connecting railroads had already disappeared; the Silverton Railway was discontinued in the middle 1920's; the Rio Grande & Southwestern was torn up in 1928 and 1929; the Silverton, Gladstone & Northerly had long since been absorbed by the Silverton Northern and eventually scrapped.)

World War II was the occasion for the shipment of seven of the ten large 470-series passenger engines to Alaska for service on the strategic White Pass & Yukon Route, where Army crews and severe Alaskan weather managed to ruin in three brief years locomotives whose sisters were still gallantly serving the Colorado Rockies more than two decades later. On some occasions after that, the Rio Grande would find it necessary to assign 480- or 490-series freight engines to haul the *San Juan* passenger train, if more than one of the three 470s was in the shop.

Despite often precarious track, the passenger trains suffered few wrecks through the years. The last was the most spectacular. Bill Holt was at the throttle of the *San Juan Express* eastbound between the two tunnels near Toltec on the afternoon of February 11, 1948. It was a cold day and, with the cab curtains drawn, noisy aboard the engine. Suddenly the airbrakes set up on emergency; a trainman riding the engine climbed down and went back to see what the trouble was. A moment later he came running back to the engine and shouted, "We got no train!" A snowslide had come down the mountain near Phantom Curve right behind the engine, carrying two coaches 300 feet down the mountainside and knocking over the parlor car, without even touching the engine. Suprisingly, no one was killed, and only a handful injured.

The twilight of the *San Juan Express* was at hand by the late 1940's. At the same time, the first break in the narrow gauge circle appeared when on August 29, 1949, the railroad filed an application with the I.C.C. to abandon the track from Mears Junction to Hooper in the San Luis Valley north of Alamosa.

The last act for the passenger train began on Wednesday, September 28, 1949, when the Denver & Rio Grande Western filed an application with the Colorado Public Utilities Commission for authority to discontinue the *San Juan*. A few weeks earlier the railroad had filed for discontinuance on Sundays only, but changed its mind and decided to attempt complete discontinuance, claiming a loss of $80,000 in 1948.

But the railroad did not wait for hearings to begin before it stopped running the train. Due to a nationwide coal strike, the I.C.C. had granted the nation's railroads permission to curtail service where necessary to save coal. With this excuse, the D&RGW discontinued the *San Juan Express* on January 9, 1950. But the paradox was that the mines serving the narrow gauge, such as those at Monero, were nonunion mines unaffected by the strike. Thus there was actually no shortage of coal in the San Juan country.

A week later hearings on the abandonment and on the subsidiary question of the "coal strike" discontinuance began in the La Plata County court room. It was brought out that the U. S. Post Office Department had offered the railroad an additional $20,000 for handling mail on the *San Juan*, which would have cut the railroads' losses by a quarter. One Durango businessman described the railroad as "an arrogant . . . monopoly bent on self-destruction."

On February 6, the P.U.C. approved discontinuance due to the coal strike, however the question of final discontinuance was still undecided, and with the end of the strike, the D&RGW resumed running the *San Juan* on March 11. The State of New Mexico was holding similar hearings in Tierra Amarilla, and one of its members, disturbed at the apparent willingness of the Colorado commission to do the railroad's bidding, was bitterly outspoken in criticism of the Colorado P.U.C.

The situation remained in abeyance all summer and fall, but on November 30, 1950, the axe fell when the Colorado Public Utilities Commission authorized permanent discontinuance of the *San Juan Express*. Subsequent appeals failed to alter the decision.

On January 31, 1951, at 11:20 p.m., narrow gauge engine 488, its pilot plow covered with snow, pulled eight Pullman-green cars into the Alamosa station, completing the last run over Cumbres. The train had left Durango that morning behind Engine 484, which served as the helper engine from Chama to Cumbres, with 488 as the road engine for the final miles to Alamosa. Blizzards in the Conejos Range and the coldest weather in several years had delayed trains in both directions; it ended as it began, in the winter cold.

The New Mexico Corporation Commission, however, had refused permission to discontinue in that state, requiring the D&RGW to operate a stub local remnant of the *San Juan* from Chama to Dulce and return each day. Engine 473 and combination baggage-passenger car 212 commonly made the brief run. However, in light of the Colorado commission's permission for discontinuance, the New Mexico commission could see no further purpose in fighting the railroad, and even the abbreviated *San Juan* ceased to run after May 22, 1951.

In later years, the railroad also applied to abandon the Silverton Mixed, but a 1958 law had placed authority in the hands of the Federal Interstate Commerce Commis-

Cumbres Pass

High, beautiful, desolate, windy, Cumbres was a fitting climax to a ride on the San Juan. Here the little train, powered by the familiar 473, pauses for the station stop before beginning the 4% descent to Chama. Brakes were always carefully checked (right), and passengers could stretch their legs briefly. The drumhead sign on the rear of the parlor car lent a dignified touch—and on occasion the railfans were perplexed by the appearance of the drumhead from the long-discontinued Shavano (Salida-Gunnison) instead. During final days of operation (below), when snow and extra cars required two engines, the loneliness of Cumbres became even more marked because the familiar two-floor passenger depot had already been torn down in a fit of management cost-cutting. (All R. W. Richardson.)

Chama and On

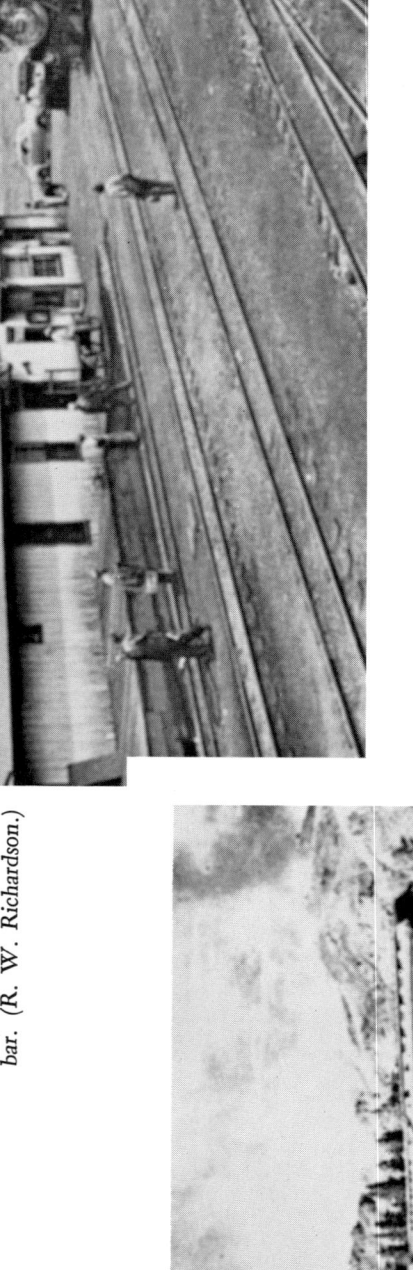

Arrival of the train in Chama inevitably caused a brief flurry of activity; change of engine crew; roundhouse force to service the locomotive; a passenger, someone to meet the train, or just an idle trainwatcher drifted down from Kelly's Shamrock bar. (R. W. Richardson.)

Late on a summer's afternoon the San Juan presented a picture of relaxed, restful travel as it neared Coxo and the top of Cumbres Pass. Earlier it had been charging up the side of the valley near Cresco.

The little 470-series 2-8-2 barking defiance to the surrounding mountain ridges. (All, R. W. Richardson.)

ion, which would not accede to the railroad's wishes. Most important, the Silverton Branch had by that time attracted so much tourist traffic that the railroad had to admit it was making a profit. Permission was refused, and the Silverton Mixed Train today brings in increasing revenue each year.

In addition, each year there were one or more special excursions from Alamosa to Silverton, reminiscent of the old *San Juan Express*, so Cumbres was not entirely devoid of passenger service. These were usually run either in the spring, before summer service on the Silverton Branch commenced, or in the fall about the time the Silverton train was suspended for the winter. In 1951 the railroad had begun experimenting with a bright yellow paint scheme on the Silverton train, and within several years all the passenger cars were that color. Business Car B-2 was last to lose its Pullman green color, in 1963; it, too, appeared in the bright yellow which the railroad called "Rio Grande Gold." The gaudy color had originally been used on Combine 212 for the filming of "Ticket to Tomahawk" in 1950, and was a far cry from the varnished Tuscan red color of the original passenger equipment in the San Juan country. Motion pictures also suggested the use of fake diamond-stacks on the relatively modern 470-series engines, about as effective a disguise as converting a Ford Mustang to a Model T by adding brass-rimmed headlights.

The early 1960's witnessed an increasing schedule of special excursions over Cumbres using the yellow Silverton Train equipment, including the old closed-vestibule cars from the latter-day *San Juan Express*. When in 1962 the Rio Grande began to promote the Silverton Train as a tourist attraction and a Denver newspaperman was brought in to head the project, he considered resuming operation of a train from Durango to Chama and perhaps eventually Alamosa, but nothing came of it.

Then on January 6, 1967, the Silverton *Standard* carried a headline announcing that the Rio Grande would run no more excursions over Cumbres, because the track had become unsafe for passenger traffic. In the autumn of 1966, excursions had been so popular that they were run three weekends in a row, the last being the ESA trip to Cumbres on October 9, powered, ironically, by engine 484, which had hauled the last *San Juan Express* from Durango to Chama and had helped it to the summit at Cumbres. Now, it had hauled the last excursion special to the crest of the Conejos Range.

Declining freight traffic had led to economies in track maintenance, in turn leading to inevitable deterioration in the line's condition. The D&RGW management had harbored thoughts of abandonment since the early 1940's, and by now the staff of the company's main offices in Denver was drawing up exhibits to be filed with the Interstate Commerce Commission supporting an application to abandon the Alamosa-Durango-Farmington lines. On September 18, 1967, the railroad filed the application for a "certificate of public convenience and necessity" so long feared by the communities along the line. Interstate Commerce Commission Examiner Robert N. Burchmore conducted hearings on the application in Farmington, New Mexico during the last week of April, 1968, and in Durango and Alamosa during the first three days in May. Four months later, Burchmore recommended in his completed report to the Commissioners that the ICC grant permission for the D&RGW to scrap its lines through the San Juan Country.

But already citizens who recognized the historic and recreational values of the old narrow gauge line were taking steps to forestall the scrapping. On November 23 and 24, a Santa Fe group sponsored the operation of a two-day inspection run from Durango to Antonito for the benefit, among others, of National Park Service Regional Director Frank Kowski. But the National Park Service proved unable to move with sufficient speed to forestall demolition of the railroad in question, so that a remarkable show of cooperation the state legislatures of Colorado and New Mexico voted funds to preserve at least the most scenic portion of the historic railroad—the 64 track miles from Antonito to Chama which pass through Toltec Gorge and over the heights of Cumbres.

The Denver & Rio Grande Western operated its last freight westbound from Alamosa to Durango on December 5, 1968. Thereafter the tracks lay dormant until in the summer of 1970 the states of Colorado and New Mexico completed purchase of the line over the Conejos Range. Thus it came to pass that in the fall of 1970 steam locomotives again climbed the heights of Cumbres, and through the efforts of railroad enthusiasts and citizens aware of the importance of preserving this part of our frontier heritage, the diminutive narrow gauge line was prepared to begin its second ninety years of service in the mountains of Colorado and New Mexico.

HISTORY, LOCATION AND DEVELOPMENT OF THE JOHNS-MANVILLE PERLITE DEPOSITS, NO AGUA, NEW MEXICO

by

M. B. MICKELSEN

Antonito, Colorado

Perlite is a mineral of comparatively recent interest. It has only been in the last twenty-five years that commercial uses have been found. Perlite was first described as a glassy rhyolite, but actually it has a very unique composition when compared with other lava flows. Most present day volcanic flows are basaltic in composition, whereas perlite is actually closer to granite in chemical composition with the exception of the additional combined water. There has been considerable controversy involving the presence of water. The conventional theory has been that the water was dissolved in the volcanic liquid and upon eruption was quenched within the mass. A more recent theory is that the volcanic liquid was erupted as an obsidian and that the water occurred later through a hydration mechanism. The rock is actually an acid volcanic derivation containing 2 to 5 percent water. Upon being heated rapidly to the point where the glass softens, the combined water having reached the point of volatilization, expands rapidly and explodes.

The perlite deposits at No Agua are located in Township 29 N., Range 9 E., in Sections 11, 12, 13, 14, 23, and 24 (fig. 1). The total area covered by these claims is in excess of 2,000 acres. The deposits were located by the author in the fall of 1948. In the summer of 1950 the deposits were sold to F. E. Schundler and Company, of Joliet, Illinois. Erection of the mill was started in November, 1950. Preliminary stripping operations were begun a short time later. By early September of 1951 the plant was placed in operation. The mill crushes, screens and grades into particle sizes desired by various clients. The material is then conveyed into storage bins. The different products in these storage bins are in turn trucked to the railhead at Antonito, Colorado, some 22 miles away.

In the fall of 1959 Johns-Manville purchased the operation from the F. E. Schundler Company and are presently mining, crushing, screening and blending with mostly all new equipment at the mine. New improvements have also been added at the Antonito loading site.

FIGURE 1.
Johns-Manville operations at No Agua, New Mexico.

ABSTRACTS OF TECHNICAL PAPERS, NEW MEXICO GEOLOGICAL SOCIETY

Presented at the 25th Annual
Meeting, Roswell, New Mexico
May 14, 1971

PENNSYLVANIAN SEDIMENTS DERIVED FROM THE PEDERNAL UPLIFT

by

FRANK KOTTLOWSKI
New Mexico Institute of Mining & Technology,
Socorro, New Mexico

and

WALDEMERE BEJNAR
Dept. of Earth Sciences, New Mexico Highlands Univ.,
Las Vegas, New Mexico

ABSTRACT

The Pedernal uplift, elongated northward from southern Otero County, New Mexico, to the present-day position of Pedernal Hills, was a late Paleozoic positive feature 40 to 75 miles wide and about 225 miles long. The southern Pedernal area was beneath pre-Pennsylvanian seas, which derived their minor detritus from Peñasco dome of northern New Mexico and southern Colorado. The Pedernal uplift emerged during Early Pennsylvanian time. Clastic sediments were deposited westward in Orogrande and Estancia basins and eastward in Delaware basin.

Beginning in late Missourian time, the uplift took on the aspect of a tilted fault block, with the western edge higher and providing more detritus westward, whereas only minor amounts of fine-grained materials swept eastward. These conditions culminated during the late Virgilian and early Wolfcampian with westward dumping of a thick sequence of subgraywacke, arkose, and red to dark-gray shale. This late detritus derived from west side of Pedernal uplift ranged from quartzite and granite-cobble conglomerate to red shale.

By late Wolfcampian time, most of the Pedernal uplift was buried beneath redbeds. Only locally, as at the present-day Pedernal Hills and Pajarita Mountain, did remnant Precambrian-rock monadnocks rise above the red clastic flood.

THE PENNSYLVANIAN SYSTEM AT SILVER CITY, GRANT COUNTY, NEW MEXICO

by

DAVID V. LE MONE
University of Texas at El Paso, El Paso, Texas

and

WILLIAM E. KING
New Mexico State University, Las Cruces, New Mexico

and

J. CUNNINGHAM
Western New Mexico University, Silver City, New Mexico

ABSTRACT

The Pennsylvanian (Morrow-Missouri) Oswaldo Formation is exposed in faulted eroded remnants of a maximum thickness of 186 feet immediately north of Silver City, New Mexico. The Oswaldo Formation unconformably overlies the Mississippian (Osage) Lake Valley Formation. The Upper Cretaceous (?) Beartooth Quartzite unconformably overlies the Oswaldo Formation. The eroded upper portion of the Oswaldo Formation, the Missouri-Virgil Syrena Formation, and the Lower Permian Abo Formation are missing because of probable post-Leonard to pre-Gulfian uplift and erosion.

The fauna of the Oswaldo Formation consists primarily of foraminifera, rugosan and tabulate corals, crinoids, brachiopods, bryozoa, gastropods, ostracods, some sponge spicules, and trilobite fragments. The fusulinids are represented in three well defined zones; they are (in ascending order): Morrowan *Millerella-Paramillerella* zone, Atokan *Profusulinella* zone, and Atokan *Fusulinella* zone. Three biohermal to biostromal zones of *Chaetetes milleporaceous* were observed in the Profusulinella zone. The algal flora is most notably represented by dasycladacean any phylloid algae.

Petrographic analysis of the Oswaldo carbonate sequence indicates a shallow water, normal marine, low to moderate energy, open shelf environment. Silicification, apparently confined to the surface, is recorded. The upper surface of the Oswaldo Formation has a zone of limonite weathering. Patchy recrystallization is noted throughout the sequence.

The presence of this Morrow-Atokan sequence of carbonates develops two interesting paleogeographic speculations. The Oswaldo Formation at Silver City could represent a sag in the positive Florida Islands-Zuni Arch axis. This Silver City Sag could be an interconnecting link between the marine sediments of the Florida Shelf of the Pedregosa Basin and the Robledo Shelf of the Orogrande Basin. It could also represent the westernmost known Robledo Shelf Lower Pennsylvanian sequence.

LATE PALEOZOIC PLATY ALGAE LIME MUD MOUNDS IN NEW MEXICO

by

JAMES LEE WILSON
Department of Geology, Rice University
Houston, Texas

ABSTRACT

In the vast and largely subsurface area of Late Paleozoic strata underlying the southwestern U.S.A. from Kansas and Oklahoma through Texas to Utah and Arizona and south to Chihuahua, a common oil reservoir facies is known to consist of lime mud mounds with abundant phylloid algae. Pennsylvanian and Wolfcampian mountain outcrops in New Mexico offer an excellent opportunity to study this and associated facies formed on the edges of Late Paleozoic basins. Lime mud mounds occur on the eastern flank of the Oro Grande basin (Hueco and Sacramento Mountains) and at a shelf margin transected by the San Andres Range on the western side of the basin. They are known in the Big Hatchet Mountains on the northeastern flank of the Pedregosa basin and farther south in Chihuahua at Mina Plomosas. Extensive study of these features permits the following conclusions about their stratigraphy, depositional environments, and diagenesis: (1) In a typical sedimentary cycle the facies develops in a clear-water shoaling phase at the beginning of marine regression in an environment where no fine clastics are introduced. (2) The mounds consist of brecciated lime mudstone with abundant phylloid algal plates and may contain the problematical organism *Tubiphytes* and tubular encrusting foraminifera as a capping boundstone; an associated facies is thin and wavy-bedded packstone of organic detritus derived from the mound. (3) The mounds form in individual bread-loaf shapes elongate parallel to the margins of paleotectonic highs. (4) They represent accumulations which originated slightly below wave base and which commonly grew upward into the zone of wave action. When this happened they off-lapped each other and grew downflank of anticlinal structures and faults; on shelf margins of rapid subsidence mounds may be superimposed. (5) Subaerial exposure was common during development of mound complexes and following mound formation; this resulted in collapse, brecciation, leaching, and to some extent filling with internal sediment and cement. Although fabrics observed in outcrops are generally tight, the same fabric disarrangement is commonly seen in the less cemented reservoir rock and petrographic study of outcrops may be a valuable tool for understanding diagenesis of producing horizons in the subsurface.

A small Virgilian mound, one-half mile north of the Alamogordo-Cloudcroft highway on the western edge of the Sacramento Mountains, is cut through to a depth of 80 feet by a small arroyo. Petrographic study of closely-spaced samples from traverses across this mound permits understanding of its facies and a reconstruction of its development. The mound is complex. The oldest beds exposed (masses of foraminiferal boundstone with detritus of dasycladacean algae) formed within wave base on the crest of an early mound and constitute a type of organic reef. The top of this mound was subaerially exposed and leached while a thick accumulation of lime mud replete with the platy algae *Ivanovia* began forming against its western and seaward flank. As sea level rose over the early mound, the algal lime mud accumulation kept pace with the rise and, despite two or three apparently brief interruptions, eventually buried the older mound. When the mound grew into wave base, a different biofacies developed toward the top of the later algal plate accumulation through concentration of sandsized bioclastic debris. The mound top rocks contain abundant foraminifera, both cornuspirid and chambered forms such as paleotextularids *Bradyina*, *Globivalvulina*, and fusulinids. Fish remains and conodonts also occur. A detrital wackestone facies of broken algal plates and concentrated remains of the foraminifera inhabiting the upper mound exists on the shelfward (lee) side of the mound, level with or slightly below its top. Mound growth ceased, sea level dropped, and subsequently smaller boundstone growths were formed down the offshore flank of the main mound. The complex history of this small mound and related bodies demonstrates how much opportunity existed for subaerial and littoral sedimentary and diagenetic processes to act on the various original facies of the Late Paleozoic carbonate bodies. Recognition of the geographic position of the various facies themselves can be a useful tool for determining proximity to such sedimentary bodies in the subsurface.

A THEORETICAL EXPLANATION OF THE FLUID DISTRIBUTION AND PRODUCTION CHARACTERISTICS OF THE BOUGH "C" FORMATION

by

L. D. SIPES, JR.
Baily, Sipes, Williamson & Runyan, Inc., Consulting Engineers
Midland & Houston, Texas

ABSTRACT

The Bough "C" Formation in southeastern New Mexico is a biostromal reef of Pennsylvanian age found at depths of between 9,000 and 10,000 feet on the edge of the Tatum Basin. For more than a decade it was an enigma to oil men. Conventional oil accumulations were found on some structural closures. The production mechanism appeared to be water drive which yielded high recovery of the calculated oil in place.

Below the apparent oil-water contact of the structural closures sufficient oil saturation was calculated from the well logs to entice oil operators to run a large number of drill stem tests on wildcat wells. A few operators completed wells in the Bough "C" below the oil-water contact and began to produce large volumes of water. As the reservoir pressure declined oil production increased.

The unusual fluid distribution and producing characteristics of the Bough "C" Formation can be explained on a microscopic scale by the evolution and configuration of the pore spaces and subsequent migration of oil into the reservoir. Umbrella shaped voids were formed by the leaf-like algae during deposition. As oil migrated into the reef it filled these voids to the spill point. There was not enough oil to fill the entire pore volume and the interconnecting pores remained water filled. Upon a decrease in pressure tiny gas caps formed in the umbrella shaped voids pushing oil out to be produced. High recovery efficiencies resulted from this mechanism.

PENNSYLVANIAN TRENDS OF NORTHERN CHAVES COUNTY, NEW MEXICO

by

PATRICK J.F. GRATTON
Consultant
Dallas, Texas

ABSTRACT

Pennsylvanian gas has been found in several widely separated locales 20 to 50 miles north of Roswell, New Mexico under a variety of shallow (5,000 to 7,500 feet) trapping conditions. Potentials up to 150,000,000 cubic feet per day have been calculated from limestone reservoirs of Cisco age and excellent gas shows have been tested from Atoka and/or Morrow sandstones.

Pennsylvanian stratigraphy outlines a basin (sometimes called the Olive Basin) of shallow water marine and continental deposits east of the Pedernal-Sacramento land mass and southwest of the poorly defined Matador uplift. This prospecting area covers over 1,000,000 acres and extends in a northwesterly direction through northern Chaves County and into adjoining portions of De Baca and Roosevelt Counties.

Within this large area, hydrocarbons have been discovered at Lone (Cisco ls., oil) Lightcap (Cisco ls., gas-condensate), Hystack (Cisco ls., gas) and Newmill (Atoka [?] sd., gas) fields in anticlines, structural noses with updip porosity pinchouts and strickly stratigraphic traps on homoclinal dip.

To date, pre-Permian exploration has been guided by geophysics in what is very difficult seismic country. Rapid lateral changes in near-surface velocities, high local relief on the pre-Pennsylvanian unconformity and areas of difficult correlation (buried faults?) all contribute to the seismic problem. As a result, less than one pre-San Andres test per township has been drilled. Careful review, analysis, interpolation and projection of the several Pennsylvanian trends in the area should allow concentration of exploratory effort in the most probably rewarding portions of the Olive Basin.

The demonstrated gas-prone nature of the area, presence of a large gas transmission line through the heart of the prospective portions, immediate markets with rising gas prices, shallow depth, satisfactory reserves and deliverability, multiple objectives (San Andres and pre-Pennsylvanian in addition to Cisco and Atoka/Morrow) and good land conditions all work toward making northern Chaves County a good area for profitable prospecting.

PROFESSIONAL DIRECTORY

GEOLOGY IN A NUT SHELL

by

Anonymous*

Geology is the thing that tells you all about stones and rocks before they're dug out of their native haunts. It also tells us about fossils which are supposed to be the remains of big fierce animals that were supposed to be turned into stone in the Stone Age. The biggest of these animals is called the Dinnasour and there is one in the park in Calgary that was turned into concrete and remained there to this day along with other fearsome beasts of the time. This is no lie for I seen them with my own eyes. The dinnasour is as long as from here to goodness knows where and about three times as high as our sealing. There was no people in those distant times except a few bible characters. One of them was called Mrs. Lot and she was turned into salt.

People who study geology are called geologists. Much of their time is spent searching for samples to put in museums for to encourage others to study geology and keep the business going. A lot of their time is also spent in looking for better jobs and for oil, and going to conventions and things like that. My pop says they're just like doctors. They put a lot of letters after their name and look wise and tell you nuthin and charge you plenty for it. All the mines are found by a kind of geology labourer called prospectors. These poor prospectors have no book learning, but make use of their thumb in a secret way called the rule of thumb. When they discover a good thing the geologists and their pals called promoters swindle him out of it. This kind of swindling is supposed to be fair game and it is called litigation or something like that. My pop wasn't sure.

* * *

* Canadian Elementary School Student
  From *Western Miner And Oil Review*

View of Ball Mill Section of Concentrator for Processing Copper Ore at Tyrone Branch

GOOD LUCK and BEST WISHES

to

THE NEW MEXICO GEOLOGICAL SOCIETY

and the

22nd ANNUAL FIELD CONFERENCE

from

PHELPS DODGE CORPORATION

Tyrone, New Mexico

and

Ajo, Bisbee, Douglas, Morenci, Arizona

ENERGY is our business!

Born in the oil fields of Oklahoma, Kerr-McGee has grown steadily through the years and is now internationally recognized for its success in finding and producing natural resources, including the four basic sources of energy — oil, gas, uranium and coal.

KERR-McGEE CORPORATION
Developers of FUELS FOR THE FUTURE

Prepared by
LOWE RUNKLE CO.
Advertising-Marketing-Public Relations
Oklahoma City • Tulsa

EL PASO CHEMICAL LABORATORIES

2315 Myrtle Ave. Ph. 915-532-3831
P.O. Box 1565, El Paso, Texas 79948

ASSAYING—GEOCHEM—SAMPLING
SPECTOGRAPHIC & ATOMIC ABSORPTION

BOKUM CORPORATION

Exploration—Mining

Box 1833   Santa Fe, N.M. 87501

PHILLIPS PETROLEUM COMPANY

1300 Security Life Building
Denver, Colorado 80202

Exploration and Production Department
Western District

UNITED NUCLEAR Corporation

AN EQUAL OPPORTUNITY EMPLOYER

AMERICAN EXPLORATION & MINING CO.

Suite 2500, One California Building
San Francisco, California 94111

A Subsidiary of Placer Development Limited of Vancouver, B.C., Amex is the managing partner of Cortez Gold Mines and is currently involved in exploration work throughout the Western States and Alaska.

Mr. Art Tipton
5214 East Pima Street
Tucson, Arizona 85716

Mr. R. G. Garwood
N. 1023 Monroe
Spokane, Wash. 99201

Mr. Roger Banghart
P.O. Box 769
Ely, Nevada 89301

Mr. Benno Patsch
P.O. Box 619
Anchorage, Ak. 99501

REGIONAL OFFICES

Core Laboratories, Inc.
WORLDWIDE

LIMBAUGH ENGINEERS, INC.

Civil Engineering—Photogrammetry

3125 Carlisle, N.E., Albuq.　　　　　344-3577

MINERAL ABSTRACT SERVICE, INC.

Mineral Reports, Federal & State

CONFIDENTIAL...
- Land Status
- Abstracts
- Filing Service

VOLA HORST
505 982-2316

528 Don Gaspar
P.O. Box 1057
Santa Fe, N.M. 87501

CLYDE L. JONES DRILLING CO.

P.O. Box 3405

Phone 299-4426

Albuquerque, New Mexico 87110

Phone 287-4273

Grants, New Mexico

Stewart Brothers DRILLING CO.
- EXPLORATION
- DRILLING

- P.O. BOX 2067, MILAN STATION
- GRANTS, NEW MEXICO
- A/C 505 287-2986

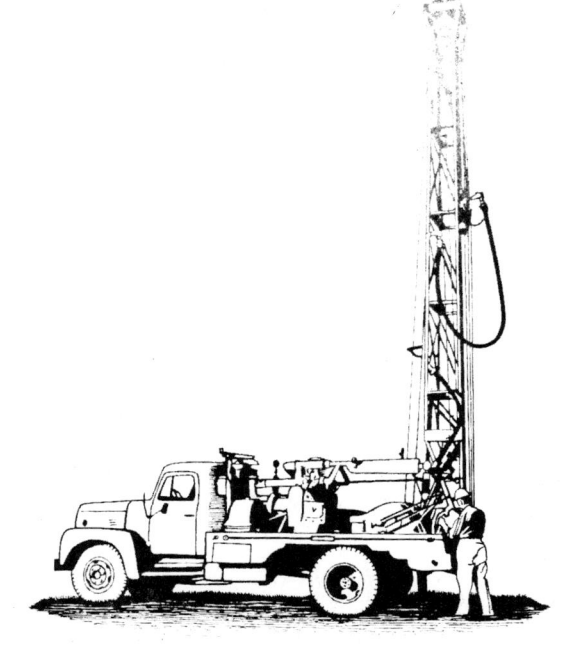

Operating in the Permian Basin,
Four Corners, Rocky Mountains,
Gulf Coast and Canada

Field Offices in
Farmington and Hobbs,
New Mexico
and
Calgary, Alberta, Canada

AZTEC
OIL & GAS COMPANY

2000 First National Bank Building   Dallas, Texas 75202

JOHN C. KEPHART & CO.
GRAND JUNCTION LABORATORIES
CHEMISTS AND ASSAYERS

PHONE 242-7618   439 NORTH AVENUE
GRAND JUNCTION, COLO. 81501

HOLMAN'S INC.
401 Wyoming Blvd, N.E.
Albuquerque, New Mexico 87123
Phone (505) 265-7981

ENGINEERING & DRAFTING SUPPLIES
TECHNICAL BOOKS—MAPS

Established 1880      1435 South 10th Ave.

JACOBS ASSAY OFFICE
REGISTERED ASSAYERS

Phone 622-0813   P. O. Box 1889

TUCSON, ARIZONA 85702

5 ROTARY DRILLING RIGS
SERVING THE
ROCKY MOUNTAIN AREA

MANAGEMENT & BIDDING

John E. Schalk
915 Midland Savings Building
444—17th Street
Denver, Colorado 80202
Telephone 534-0836

ACCOUNTING AND BOOKKEEPING

P. O. Box 2078
Farmington, New Mexico 87401
Telephone 325-5018

William H. Hallcroft   Joe D. Christesson
Office Manager   Drilling Superintendent

Office Phone 325-7685	Home Phone 325-3351

E. L. POTEET
POTEET ENGINEERING COMPANY
Box 27—Farmington, New Mexico
Engineering & Surveying

Arizona • Colorado • New Mexico • Nevada • Texas • Utah

LONG ENGINEERING CO.
MUD LOGGING—WELL SITTING
CASPER, WYOMING

Ed Pallansch
Geologist   Phone 307-237-2256

SHOP PHONE
852-2391
MONTE VISTA, COLORADO

M & G DRILLING & SUPPLY CO.
WATER WELL DRILLING
WELL CASING—PUMPS—PIPE FITTINGS
STEEL AND PLASTIC PIPE

C. E. "PETE" MERRIFIELD   J. A. "JACK" JENNINGS
852-2445   852-3784

DUGAN
PRODUCTION CORP.

OIL AND GAS PROPERTY MANAGEMENT

GEOLOGICAL AND ENGINEERING
CONSULTANTS

709 Bloomfield Road
P.O. Box 234
Farmington, New Mexico 87401
Telephone: 505-325-0238

Thomas A. Dugan—Petroleum Engineer
Jim L. Jacobs—Production Superintendent
Don W. Mitchell—Chief Geologist

GEOPHYSICAL SURVEYS & INTERPRETATIONS

geoterrex ltd.

AIRBORNE: MAGNETIC · ELECTROMAGNETIC · RADIOACTIVITY
GROUND: RESISTIVITY · INDUCED POLARIZATION · MAGNETIC
RADIOACTIVITY · GRAVITY · SEISMIC · ELECTROMAGNETIC

HOUSTON: 8120 WESTGLEN 713·781·9830 **OTTAWA:** 1312 BANK STREET 613·731·9571

American Stratigraphic Company

- LITHOLOGY FOR COMPUTER INPUT
- STRATIGRAPHIC STUDIES
- SAMPLE LIBRARIES
- WELL-SITE CONSULTING

CASPER, WYOMING
524 EAST YELLOWSTONE

BILLINGS, MONTANA
17 NORTH 31ST STREET

DENVER, COLORADO
6280 E. 39TH AVE.

ANCHORAGE, ALASKA
BOX 2127

CANADIAN STRATIGRAPHIC SERVICE, LTD.
3613 33RD STREET NW
CALGARY 44, ALBERTA

CANADIAN STRATIGRAPHIC SERVICE, LTD.
2166 BROAD ST.
REGINA, SASKATCHEWAN

GRANTS RADIOTELEPHONE SERVICE
* RADIO DISPATCH SERVICE   * WE GIVE AND TAKE MESSAGES
* FLAT MONTHLY RATE   * 24 HOUR SERVICE
* NO EQUIPMENT TO BUY OR MAINTENANCE EXPENSE
Radio Room 247-9482 Albuquerque—Radio Room 722-3016 Gallup—Radio Room 287-2923 Grants—Office 287-4100 Grants

1005 Uranium Avenue, P.O. Box 2127 Milan, New Mexico 87020
Vernon H. Johnson

505/255-2351

SHERMAN A. WENGERD, A.I.P.G.

Certified Professional Geologist

1040 Stanford Drive, Northeast

Albuquerque, New Mexico 87106

CHARLES A. MARDIROSIAN

Consulting Geologist

Regional Mineral Evaluation Studies

Mineral Property Examinations

Geochemical Exploration

1945 South 13th East   Salt Lake City, Utah 84105

801/486-7737

Keeping Watch In All Directions

As We Look To Future Needs For Energy And Minerals

Humble Oil & Refining Company

An equal opportunity employer

CHAPMAN, WOOD & GRISWOLD, INC.
Mining Engineers & Geologists
4011 Silver Avenue, S.E., Albuquerque, N.M.
Tel. (505) 265-5794, Telex 66-0416

CHAPMAN, WOOD & GRISWOLD, LTD.
145 E. 15th Street, No. Vancouver, B.C.
Tel. (604) 985-9191, Telx 04-50690
Cable Address both offices: CHAPWOLD

WILLIAM J. LEMAY

CONSULTING GEOLOGIST

AC 505 982-3211　　　　　　　　　　Box 2244
214 College St.　　　　　　　　Santa Fe, New Mexico

RONALD E. TYREE

REGISTERED PROFESSIONAL
LAND SURVEYOR

NEW MEXICO—COLORADO
ARIZONA

U.S. MINERAL SURVEYOR

Phone 298-0660　　　　2329-A Wisconsin N.E.
　　　　　　　　　　　Albuquerque, N. Mex.

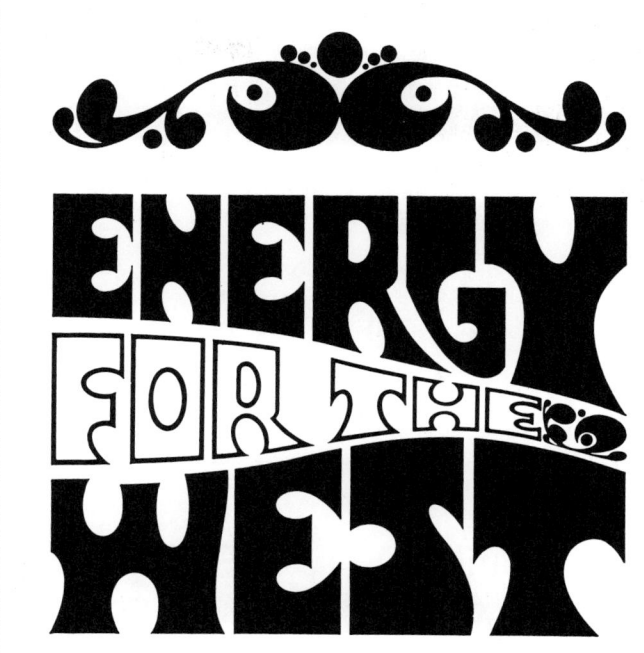

El Paso Natural Gas Company

SSC is where YOUR action is.

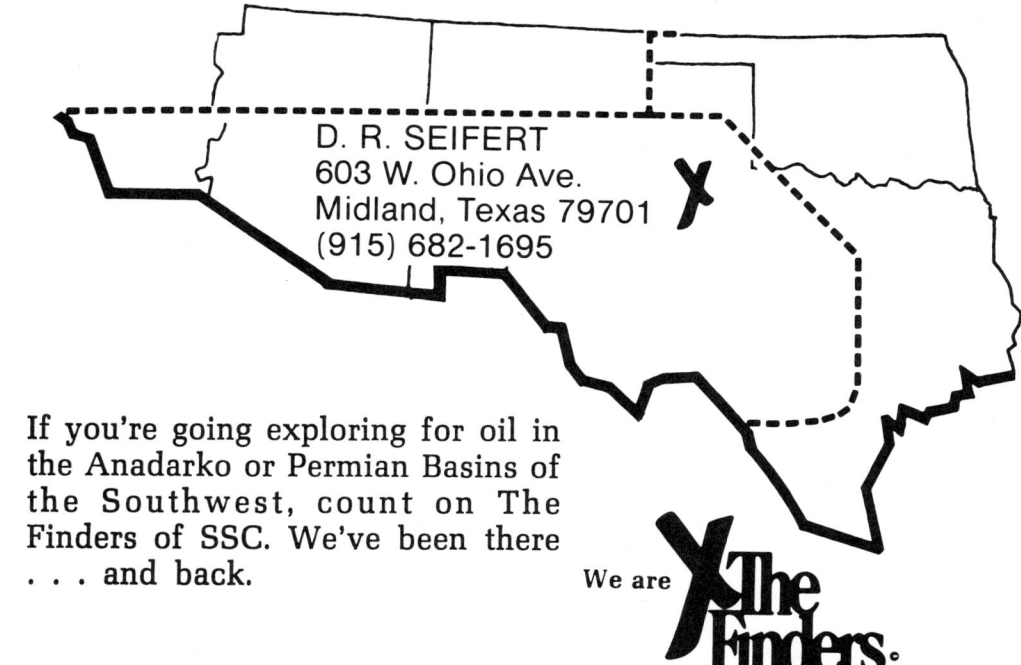

D. R. SEIFERT
603 W. Ohio Ave.
Midland, Texas 79701
(915) 682-1695

If you're going exploring for oil in the Anadarko or Permian Basins of the Southwest, count on The Finders of SSC. We've been there . . . and back.

We are **The Finders**

 *Seismograph Service Corporation*
A SUBSIDIARY OF RAYTHEON COMPANY

CRANE DRILLING CO.
FARMINGTON, NEW MEXICO
P. O. BOX 1774

Water Wells • Core Drilling • Surface Holes
Shallow Production • Cathodic Ground Bed Holes

BOB CRANE, JR.   PH. 325-7360

Serving our friends in the
Exploration, Mining, and Water Well Drilling
Business.

O'TOOL BIT CO. INC.

Box 245

Cortez, Colo. 81321

UNITED NUCLEAR-HOMESTAKE PARTNERS

Grants, New Mexico

An Equal Opportunity Employer

WOODWARD-CLEVENGER & ASSOCIATES, INC.

Consulting Engineers and Geologists

W. A. Clevenger   S. T. Thorfinnson

Subsoil investigations; Design criteria for earth dams, utilities, and structure foundations, Tailing Dam engineering; Engineering Geology; Ground and surface water development; Drainage; Water rights and hydrology

2909 WEST 7th AVENUE
DENVER, COLORADO 80204
(303) 222-9434
An Affiliate of Woodward-Clyde Consultants

⟵ JET↔VAC ⟶

West Texas Division Locations

Midland, Texas 915/682-2418
Abilene, Texas 915/692-5430
Farmington, N. M. ... 505/325-3544
Snyder, Texas 915/573-7131
Roswell, N. M. 505/622-3152
Hobbs, N. M. 505/393-9166
Monahans, Texas 915/943-4713
Odessa, Texas 915/563-1100
San Angelo, Texas ... 915/653-2640
Wichita Falls, Texas . 817/767-1431

A **Halliburton** Company

Yes,...

...Scintrex was here.

For further information and case histories, please write:

 **SCINTREX**

Mineral Surveys, Inc.

180 W. 2950 SOUTH

SALT LAKE CITY, UTAH 84115

CLARK SYSTEMS, INC.
E. M. CLARK & ASSOCIATES

4362 East Evans, Denver, Colorado 80222
Phone: 303/756-7773

REMOTE SENSING
RESOURCE SURVEYS
AERIAL PHOTOGRAPHY
PHOTO INTERPRETATION
OPTICAL SYSTEMS DESIGN
PHOTOGRAMMETRIC ENGINEERING

The Imaginative Advertisers in Our
Professional Directory Contribute Heavily to
the Cost of Printing Our Guidebook.
Patronize Them!

Four Corners Exploration Co.

Exploratory Drilling

Contract Mining

Uranium Development Is Our Forte

Box 116   Grants, N.M.   287-4722

VAL R. REESE, C.P.G.

Geological Consultant

900 Bank of New Mexico Building

Albuquerque, New Mexico 87101

Oil/Gas/Mining

Office: Phone 243-0665
Home: Phone 255-9749

Petroleum Information.
CORPORATION
A Subsidiary of A.C. Nielsen Company

serves the industry with
Oil Reports • Production Data
Completion Records • Maps

Area Office: 835 Second Avenue,
Durango, Colorado 81301
Home Office: Denver, Colorado
Other offices throughout the United States & Canada

West Texas Electrical Log Service

Complete File of Reproduced Well Logs in the
Permian Basin of West Texas and New Mexico

105 WEST WALL

MIDLAND, TEXAS

MUtual 2 9796

Determine formation productivity with Baroid's
- *ppm Log*
- *Show Evaluation Report*

Mud Logging Service

INDUSTRIES

BAROID DIVISION N L INDUSTRIES, INC.,
P.O. BOX 1675, HOUSTON, TEXAS 77001

DEALERS FOR: FREDERICK POST CO.
FILM ENLARGEMENTS & REDUCTIONS

BLUEPRINTS PHOTOCOPIES XEROX COPIES
BLUEPRINTING
COMPLETE LINE OF ARCHITECTURAL & ENGINEERING SUPPLIES

PICK-UP & DELIVERY
247-1578

Reliable REPRODUCTIONS INC.
1100 2 N.W.

Field Conference Notes:
First Day

Field Conference Notes:
Second Day

Field Conference Notes:
Third Day